1/10: Thru chap. 6
456

Advertising theory
and practice

Advertising theory and practice

C. H. SANDAGE Ph.D.

Professor Emeritus
University of Illinois
President, Farm Research Institute

and

VERNON FRYBURGER Ph.D.

Professor of Advertising and Marketing
Chairman, Department of Advertising
Northwestern University

Ninth Edition 1975

RICHARD D. IRWIN, INC. Homewood, Illinois 60430

Irwin-Dorsey Limited Georgetown, Ontario L7G 4B3

© BUSINESS PUBLICATIONS, INC., 1935 and 1939
© RICHARD D. IRWIN, INC., 1948, 1953, 1958,
    1963, 1967, 1971, and 1975

Ninth Edition

First Printing, January 1975
Second Printing, November 1975
Third Printing, March 1976
Fourth Printing, August 1976
Fifth Printing, January 1977
Sixth Printing, May 1977

ISBN 0-256-01655-0
Library of Congress Catalog Card No. 74–18705

Printed in the United States of America

Preface

This book is intended to give the student a broad perspective and penetrating understanding of advertising—its social and economic functions, its role in business, how it works, how it is planned and created, its challenges and opportunities.

Advertising is dynamic. It changes with changing markets, changing life styles, changing methods of distribution, and changing techniques of communication. Significant developments during the past few years include a growing awareness that advertising is an institution performing essential social and economic functions, a recognition that advertising must be planned in the context of total marketing strategy, a more sophisticated use of research to better understand consumer motivation and behavior, a more concerted effort to build favorable brand and corporate identities, a greater use of information bearing on media audiences, and a burgeoning concern about consumer welfare.

In this ninth edition of *Advertising Theory and Practice* recognition has been given to the substantial changes of the past few years in such areas as government and self-regulation, political advertising, ecology, product scarcities, and consumerism. Statistical data have been brought up to date. New illustrations have been added.

While this edition provides a thorough revision it retains the social consciousness of previous editions and continues to emphasize the importance of professional standards of performance. It holds that there should be no basic conflict between the interests of consumers and the practice of advertising professionals. The authors believe that if the principles developed in this book are followed benefits will accrue both to consumers and to business.

Part One identifies advertising as a subsystem within an economic system which in turn is part of a larger system of social values. As a form of communication, advertising is viewed as being neither good nor bad. It can, however, be used for purposes that may be regarded as good or bad, depending on the value system by which it is judged. Generalizations about advertising should distinguish between process and practice. The great diversity of practices and the uniqueness of each advertising situation make any generalizing tenuous at best. Therefore, emphasis is placed on acquiring a disciplined approach to solving advertising problems, whatever the set of circumstances, instead of setting forth a standard formula for success.

Part Two engages the student in planning advertising campaign strategy. Here is set forth the basic philosophy that advertising should interpret want-satisfying qualities of products in terms of consumer wants. This becomes the unifying theme for a logical progression through all stages of advertising planning and execution.

Research is emphasized to highlight the importance of building an advertising program on a foundation of facts, to indicate the kinds of facts that should be sought, and to demonstrate how such information can be used in solving the full range of advertising problems. With a research viewpoint the student is more apt to think analytically, to probe for deeper understanding, and to develop a healthy respect for the uncertainties in the present state of the art. New material on positioning and product concept testing, along with currently accepted approaches to market segmentation, such as psychographics, life style, and buyer behavior patterns are included in Part Two.

Recognizing that the quality of an advertisement largely depends on the quality of the thinking that precedes the writing and designing, Part Three concentrates on creative strategy. Chapters 12, 13, and 14 seek to explain how advertising works in the context of prevailing concepts of communication and consumer behavior. Chapters 15, 16, and 17 relate theory to the development of advertising ideas, ideas that can be extended to a continuing campaign as well as executed in a single advertisement. Chapter 18 describes modern graphic arts processes and television production.

Significant among recent trends is the top priority that management is assigning to measures of advertising effectiveness. With larger budgets, keener competition, greater plant capacity, and greater dependence on new products, the need for more efficient advertising is apparent. Part Five evaluates current methods of measurement and indicates techniques that hold promise for the future.

The general organization of previous editions is retained. It is based on the idea that a sound theoretical approach is the most practical way to tackle any problem, that one should have a clear concept of advertising before he begins constructing an advertisement. Such a treatment appeals to the student's desire to learn the "whys" as well as the "hows."

To the many educators, former students, and practitioners who gave counsel and advice, a note of deep gratitude. Their number is legion. Failure to enumerate names here does not indicate lack of appreciation, but rather failure in keeping a catalog of all who have influenced our thinking.

December 1974   C. H. SANDAGE
                                             VERNON FRYBURGER

Contents

Physical standards for consumer goods. **Information on product labels:** Hidden psychological qualities. The road map concept. Who should initiate communication? The protection of competition. Consumer education. The factor of persuasion.

part two
**Background for planning
advertising strategy**

Single-factor indexes. Multiple-factor indexes. Problem of the new company.

part three
The advertising message

part six
The advertising organization

part one

Basic values and functions

1

Introduction

Perhaps no student will approach the reading of this book without already having formed some ideas about advertising. Nearly everybody encounters advertising every day. Nearly everybody, therefore, has some thoughts on the subject. The tendency is to judge advertising as good or bad, to single out ads that one likes or dislikes, to wonder if advertising is worth the large sums of money spent on it, to question the contribution advertising makes to social welfare. Public opinion on these matters warrants consideration. However, exposure to advertising does not reveal the thinking behind it. Hopefully, the reader of this book will discover "there is more to it than meets the eye."

Several views

Advertising is multidimensional. It can be viewed as a form of communication, as a component of an economic system, and as a means of financing the mass media.

As a *form of communication* the advertising message, or advertisement, is delivered to its intended audience through the various media including newspapers, television, magazines, radio, billboards, and direct mail. Advertising is distinguished from other forms of communication in that the advertiser pays the medium to deliver the message. For this payment the advertiser receives the opportunity to control the message.

3

Within legal constraints designed to prevent deception and assure fair competition, and within standards of practice enforced by the media, the advertiser is free to say what he wants to say the way he wants to say it. He can select the particular issue of a newspaper or magazine in which the message will run. He can select the hour and even the minute when the television or radio message will be broadcast. The style of presentation usually identifies the message as an advertisement. If it is not readily distinguishable from a medium's editorial or program content, the notation "this is an advertisement" and the name of the advertiser or sponsoring organization are included. As a form of communication advertising is used to promote the sale of a product or service, to influence public opinion, to gain political support, to advance a particular cause, or to elicit some other response desired by the advertiser.

As a form of communication, advertising is neither good nor bad. It can be used for good or bad, but in itself it is neither. Like atomic energy, advertising can be used to advance or to subvert the welfare of mankind. Judgments of good and bad, therefore, are more appropriate when confined to specific uses of advertising.

As a *component of an economic system* advertising has been most highly developed in countries having a free-market system. In a free market system consumer choices determine what goods and services will be produced. A consumer's decision to buy this item instead of that in effect is telling the economic system to make more of this and less of that. The many suppliers competing for consumer favor use advertising to influence those decisions by informing consumers that a given product exists, that it is available at certain retail outlets, that it is priced at a certain amount, and that it offers certain want-satisfying qualities. The "middleman" nature of advertising should be highlighted. It serves as a specialized intermediary between business firms with goods and services to sell and individuals who might benefit from the purchase of those goods and services. Advertising thus performs the function of *interpreting the want-satisfying qualities of goods and services in terms of consumer needs and wants.*

Advertising functions quickly and efficiently. A manufacturer can reach 60 to 70 percent of the nation's population in a week's time, and he can do so at a cost as low as $3 per thousand people reached. There is no alternative for reaching so many people so quickly at so low a cost. Personal selling is appropriate for reaching relatively small, well-defined, highly concentrated markets such as industrial buyers, but advertising is the only feasible means for communicating with the millions of ultimate consumers. Advertising hastens the trial and acceptance of new products. It also hastens the rejection of those items that fail to live up to expectations. Advertising, therefore, helps make the economic system more sensitive to consumer needs and wants.

Advertising's contribution to economic growth derives primarily from its role in expanding consumer needs and wants. In a modern industrial society the basic wants of food, clothing, and shelter are reasonably well met for most people. For them to spend more they must want more. As Professor Frank H. Knight wrote, "The chief thing that the common-sense individual actually wants is not satisfaction for the wants which he has, but more and better wants."[1] Professor David Potter, who referred to advertising as "the institution of abundance," stated that "the only institution we have for instilling new needs, for training people to act as consumers, for altering men's values, and thus for hastening their adjustment to potential abundance is advertising."[2] Economist O. J. Firestone, in a paper on advertising's role in economic growth, concluded:

> To the extent that advertising affects want creation and want change, it can have a fundamental effect on the will of society to devote its efforts to material pursuits. It is an essential function of advertising to persuade consumers to buy, and businessmen do not deny that persuasion, and not information, is the main reason they employ advertising. Once growing consumer wants are translated into effective demand, markets expand, businessmen profit, the economy prospers, and continuing economic growth and development take place.[3]

Changes in our economic system that will be reflected in advertising may occur in the latter part of the 1970s (indeed, many such changes are already taking place). The character of goods and services is likely to be in line with consumer demand. Accordingly, there may be somewhat less focus on personal consumption items, with a correspondingly greater emphasis on broader societal needs such as pollution control, medical care, safer driving, and the like.

As a *means of financing the mass media* advertising provides 60 to 70 percent of the total revenue of newspapers and magazines. Commercial television and radio broadcasting are financed entirely by advertising. The notion that "he who pays the fiddler calls the tunes" underlies the suspicion that advertisers influence news coverage by suppressing and distorting the news to their own advantage. The only formal study of the matter, *A Free and Responsible Press*, which was undertaken by the Commission on Freedom of the Press, reported that "the evidence of dictation of policy by advertisers is not impressive. Such dictation seems to occur among the weaker units. As a newspaper becomes financially stable it becomes more independent and tends to resist pressure from advertisers."[4] As we shall

---

[1] Frank H. Knight, *The Ethics of Competition* (New York: Harper & Bros., 1935), p. 22.

[2] David Potter, *People of Plenty* (Chicago: University of Chicago Press, 1954), p. 175.

[3] O. J. Firestone, "An Economist Looks at Advertising," *Frontiers of Advertising Theory and Research,* ed. Hugh W. Sargent (Palo Alto, Calif.: Pacific Books, 1972), pp. 63–64.

[4] Commission on Freedom of the Press, *A Free and Responsible Press* (Chicago: University of Chicago Press, 1947), p. 62.

see, perhaps the strongest deterrent to intrusion on press freedom is the advertiser's dependence on the press. He needs their circulation and audiences to advertise effectively. If advertisers influenced news coverage, the press would risk losing public confidence, which in turn would reduce circulation and jeopardize the effectiveness of the press as an advertising medium. CBS newsman Walter Cronkite recently provided his views on this matter when he said:

> Myths die hard, and one of the myths that persists about our business is that advertisers attempt to control or influence what we say and how we say it. Or that we are responsive to sponsor eyebrow-raising and censor ourselves in order to attract or keep advertisers.
>
> The remarkable thing is that in a short time, relatively, the best broadcast news organizations have established a total independence from advertisers. The wall between sales and evening news content, at least in our shop, is quite impregnable. Advertisers have no rights of approval, no rights of review. Our journalistic independence of advertisers is a good deal greater than exists in many magazines and most newspapers.
>
> But the *truly* remarkable thing is not our own insistence on independence—but that advertisers have come to *accept* this independence in broadcast journalism. Whatever difficulties we might have with others in maintaining our integrity and independence, it is an immense tribute to advertisers in general that they have come to accept, and even embrace, this fundamental character of journalism.
>
> I cannot recall in recent years a single example of even the most subtle attempt by an advertiser, or a prospective advertiser, to breach the wall of our journalistic independence and integrity on the evening news.[5]

Advertising may also be viewed as a *social institution,* as an *art form,* as an *instrument of business management,* as a *field of employment,* and as a *profession.* Therefore, this book offers no single definition. Instead, it seeks to widen the reader's scope of observation and deepen his understanding by approaching the study of advertising from several points of view.

Classification of advertising

The layman is inclined to view all advertising as being much the same. Yet, no two advertising situations are exactly alike. Different kinds of businesses use advertising to motivate different kinds of markets toward different kinds of responses.

The following classification outlines the broad scope of these differences. Each class is described in terms of *who* advertises *what* to *whom* and *where* to bring about what *response.*

---

[5] Walter Cronkite, Speech before the Washington Advertising Club, September 15, 1970.

1. National Advertising:
    Who: Producers of consumer goods and services.
    What: Branded products or services closely identified with firm's name. (Examples: Plymouth automobile, Campbell's Soup, Ivory Soap, Allstate Insurance.)
    To whom: Ultimate consumers.
    Where: Nationwide.
    Response: "Buy my brand."

2. Retail Advertising:
    Who: Retail stores, such as department stores, grocery stores, drugstores, and clothing stores. Service institutions such as dry cleaners, laundries, and banks.
    What: The items and services available at the particular retail establishment.
    To whom: Ultimate consumers.
    Where: Within a local market area.
    Response: "Buy at my store."

3. Industrial Advertising:
    Who: Producers of industrial goods such as steel, machinery, lubricants, packaging, and office equipment.
    What: Items and services that are used in manufacturing or that facilitate operation of the business.
    To whom: Industrial buyers.
    Where: Nationwide or regionally, depending on the degree of geographic concentration of the industry involved. Practically every industrial buyer can be reached through one or more specialized business publications.
    Response: "Use my product or service in your business operation."

4. Trade Advertising:
    Who: Producers and distributors of branded and nonbranded consumer goods.
    What: Products ready for consumption that are bought by merchants for resale.
    To whom: Retailers and wholesalers of consumer goods.
    Where: Nationwide.
    Response: "Stock and promote the sale of my product."

5. Professional Advertising:
    Who: Producers and distributors who depend on professional men to recommend, prescribe, or specify their products to buyers.

> *What:*   Items the purchase of which is strongly influenced by
>   a professional person. (Examples: baby foods, ethical
>   drugs, building materials, textbooks.)
> *To whom:* Doctors, dentists, architects, engineers, educators.
> *Where:*   Nationwide.
> *Response:* "Recommend, prescribe, or specify my product."

6. Nonproduct or "Idea" Advertising:
   > *Who:*   Churches; political parties; fraternal, trade, and social
   >   groups; and individuals.
   > *What:*   Institutions, ideologies, and social betterment. (Exam-
   >   ples: religion, political candidates, Red Cross, United
   >   Way, safety, education.)
   > *To whom:* Lay citizens, voters, community leaders.
   > *Where:*   Nationally and locally.
   > *Response:* "Accept my idea, vote for my candidate, or contribute
   >   to my cause."

This classification is not intended to be all-inclusive. However, it does demonstrate that the scope of advertising is wider than the small fraction one sees in his newspaper, in the few magazines he reads, and on his favorite television programs. This classification also demonstrates that each advertising situation is a unique set of circumstances. Therefore, any generalization is tenuous. Perhaps the only appropriate generalization is that one should not generalize.

The advertising process

The advertisements we see and hear are end products of a series of investigations, strategic plans, tactical decisions, and executions that all together comprise the total advertising process. The field is much broader than the construction of advertisements. It includes (1) researching consumers, the product or service to be advertised, and the market to be cultivated; (2) strategic planning in terms of objectives, market delineation, setting the appropriation, developing creative strategy and media plans; (3) tactical decisions in regard to budgeting expenditures, buying media and scheduling insertions and broadcasts; and (4) advertisement construction including copywriting, layout, art, and production. Figure 1–1 diagrams these various components of advertising and indicates the sequence of events.

Money spent for advertising

Something of the importance of advertising in our economic life can be seen from an analysis of the money spent for it. The total amount spent

FIGURE 1–1
Components of advertising

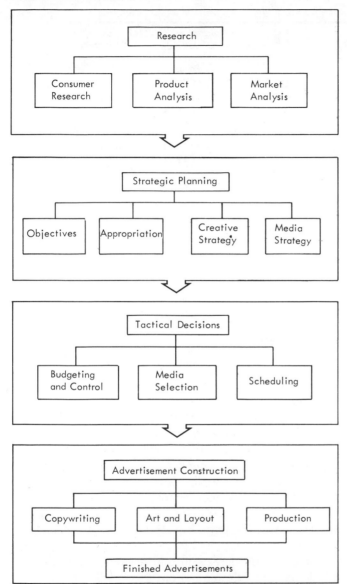

for advertising in 1973 was more than $25 billion. This was double the amount spent in 1960 and four times what was spent in 1950.

Some of the increase in dollar expenditures has been the result of cheaper dollars, but the ratio of advertising expenditures to the gross

TABLE 1-1

Total U.S. advertising expenditures and personal consumption expenditures, 1950–72

Year	For advertising	Expenditures (in millions of dollars) For personal consumption	Advertising expenditure as percent of consumption expenditure
1950	$ 5,710.0	$194,026	2.94
1951	6,426.1	208,342	3.08
1952	7,156.2	218,328	3.27
1953	7,755.3	230,542	3.36
1954	8,164.1	236,557	3.45
1955	9,194.4	254,421	3.61
1956	9,904.7	267,160	3.71
1957	10,310.6	285,200	3.62
1958	10.301.8	293,200	3.51
1959	11,254.8	315,500	3.57
1960	11,931.7	328,500	3.63
1961	11,845.0	338,000	3.51
1962	12,380.8	355,057	3.48
1963	13,107.4	374,982	3.49
1964	14,155.0	401,356	3.52
1965	15,255.0	431,465	3.53
1966	16,545.0	465,000	3.56
1967	16,866.0	492,200	3.43
1968	18,127.0	536,600	3.38
1969	19,482.0	579,500	3.36
1970	19,600.0	616,800	3.18
1971	20,840.0	664.900	3.13
1972	23,060.0	721,000	3.20

Sources: *Advertising Age,* February 19, 1973; *Survey of Current Business,* May 1973.

national product and to total consumption expenditures also increased markedly during the 1950s. The ratio of advertising dollars to personal consumption expenditures remained fairly constant during the first half of the 1960s. However, it would appear that advertising expenditures did not keep pace with the inflation that accompanied the South Vietnam war from 1967 to 1972. A comparison of expenditures for advertising and personal consumption items for a period of 23 years is shown in Table 1–1.

The implications of this steady increase in total investment in advertising are substantial. It is, in part, an indication of our expanding economy, but more particularly a product of the changing character of the economy. We have moved rapidly from a need to a need-want economy, where an increasing amount of personal consumption expenditures are for products and services that persons do not need to meet the physical *needs* of living (food, shelter, clothing) but choose to purchase to satisfy psychological *wants*. It requires more information and stimulation to bring consumers into the marketplace to purchase *want* goods than it does to get them to buy *need* goods. Advertising is ideally suited to provide this information and stimulation.

There also has been increased usage of advertising in the nonproduct, or idea, classification. Churches, politicians, labor unions, and a host of institutions and individuals increasingly use advertising as a means to efficiently and effectively communicate a particular message. The U.S. government, for example, spent over $16 million advertising in major media in 1972 and thus joined the ranks of the 100 leading national advertisers for the first time ever (ranking 79th).[6] This advertising effort on the part of the government was mostly for armed services recruiting.

Advertising is also assuming an increasingly important role in the total marketing mix. Supermarkets, self-service shopping, and discount houses tend to place more responsibility on the manufacturer of consumer goods to educate and sell consumers concerning the want-satisfying qualities of his brands than was true when retail merchants had more personal contact with their customers. Advertising is thus being called on to do some of the work previously performed by personal salesmen.

The addition of a relatively new advertising medium—television—to other media has also helped to increase the role of advertising in the marketing mix and invite the investment of additional advertising dollars. Television permits product demonstration and personal selling on a mass basis. This has resulted in some diminution of direct selling and some increase in total advertising expenditures.

Media other than television have also played their part in making investments in advertising productive, thus attracting additional advertising dollars. Table 1–2 lists each of the major media and also provides a breakdown of advertising expenditures in each for 1972.

TABLE 1–2
U.S. advertising expenditures in 1972, by media

	Amount spent	
Medium	Dollars in millions	Percent of total
Newspapers	$ 6,960	30.2
Magazines (including national farm papers)	1,480	6.4
Farm publications (regional)	29	0.1
Business papers	770	3.3
Television	4,110	17.9
Radio	1,530	6.6
Direct mail	3,350	14.5
Outdoor	290	1.3
All other	4,541	19.7
Total	$23,060	100.0

Source: *Advertising Age,* February 19, 1973, p. 64.

[6] *Advertising Age,* June 25, 1973, p. 1.

The people who perform the advertising function

There are more than 4.5 million business firms and service establishments in the United States. Each does some advertising at one time or another. The very small firm can seldom afford to operate with any significant departmentalization of functions or do much in the way of specialization of labor. In the case of such firms any advertising that is done must usually be handled by the manager or proprietor.

Larger firms may establish a department of advertising with one or more employees whose sole responsiblity is to plan and execute the advertising program for the firm. Common examples of such firms are department stores, large men's and women's specialty stores, furniture stores, mail-order houses, book publishers, and other large retail and service organizations.

Business firms and institutions that do not wish to do their own advertising work can secure help from outside sources. Retailers especially get much assistance from the various advertising media such as newspapers, radio and television stations, outdoor poster companies, car-card operators, and specialized direct-mail organizations. These media usually have men and women who devote their entire time to helping business firms plan their advertising operations.

The most highly specialized and perhaps most competent personnel in the field of advertising are to be found in the general advertising agencies. There were 5,700 advertising agencies in the United States in 1973. About two thirds of these were equipped to render a complete advertising service for business firms and institutions.

Personnel needs

The total number of persons engaged full time in some aspect of advertising work is not known. Estimates range all the way from 200,000 to 500,000. The 1967 Census of Business listed 212,000 employees and proprietors of firms whose principal occupation was that of rendering specialized advertising service to other business enterprises.

This number would probably more than double if we added to it those persons employed by manufacturers, retailers, mail-order houses, and media who devote most or all of their time to company advertising. It is perhaps reasonable to estimate the total number of persons devoting full time to advertising practice as being somewhere between 450,000 and 500,000 in 1974. Future manpower needs will be large. The need will be for both quantity and quality. Leaders in the field estimate that approximately 20,000 to 25,000 newcomers are attracted each year to advertising positions. In terms of the quality of people needed Martin Mayer says, "Few occupations are as dependent as advertising on the quality of the incoming talent, and nowhere does the absence of talent show so plainly."[7] With such need it is important that an increasing number of young men and women undertake to prepare themselves for effective careers in advertising.

A career booklet available from the American Association of Advertising Agencies, 200 Park Avenue, New York, New York 10017, provides information on advertising as a career, with special emphasis given to advertising agencies.

Advertising policy

Of course, the men and women who devote their full time to the practice of advertising exert a great deal of influence in the determination of advertising policy at the executive level. Final responsibility for policy, however, must rest with the owner or executive head of the firm or department. There has been a growing tendency among large national advertisers to have a vice president in charge of advertising. This person is usually not concerned with the details of advertisement construction or media selection but is vitally interested in the overall advertising program and how it dovetails with the overall marketing activities of the company. It is important that this person understands something of advertising techniques, too, in order that he can properly appraise the work of the advertising practitioners.

Advertising policy should be correlated with overall business objectives. Since such objectives must be concerned with the products, services, or ideas that are to be promoted, policy makers must consider not only the seller's wares but also the buyer's interests. Here, again, the importance of research as a guide to sound policy is evident.

With this brief look at what advertising is, its functions, scope, and personnel, we are ready to examine various aspects of advertising in detail. First consideration might properly be given to reviewing the long history of advertising.

QUESTIONS AND PROBLEMS

1   In the light of what you have read in this chapter and your attitudes toward advertising before that, what do you now believe the function or functions of advertising to be?

2   Do you think it is logical to make a distinction between the words "advertising" and "advertisement"? What distinction do you make between these words?

3   Even though you are probably just beginning your study of advertising, you no doubt have some rather definite ideas about it. Prepare a 200-word state-

[7] Martin Mayer, *Madison Avenue, U.S.A.* (New York: Harper & Bros., 1958), pp. 322–23.

ment of your ideas about advertising. Include in that statement any ideas you might have as to whether it is good or bad for (1) the nation as a whole; (2) individual consumers; (3) individual business firms; (4) organizations such as schools, churches, or political parties; and (5) yourself. You might also point out why you believe as you do.

4 Many people think of advertising only in terms of the promotion of goods and services. Bring to class recent magazine or newspaper ads (or descriptions of broadcast commercials or other types of advertisements) that deal with other subject matter. What is your assessment of such advertising?

History of advertising

Advertising is only one of several selling tools which businessmen have used for centuries to assist them in getting their wares into the hands of consumers. Its early use was distinctly a minor supplement to other forms of selling. Storekeepers erected signs on or in front of buildings or placed posters in public places, merely to draw the attention of prospective customers to their places of business. After customers were thus attracted, personal selling and display of merchandise were depended upon to make the sale.

Today advertising has become a major form of selling. It not only supports other forms of selling but also frequently serves as the only selling tool used to move merchandise. Whereas early advertising might have been referred to as written or printed publicity, serving wholly as an adjunct to personal selling, today it takes a position on a par with personal selling. This does not mean that the two are competitive; instead, one complements, rather than supplants, the other.

Modern advertising is closely associated with the development of mass selling. The manufacturer who sells his merchandise throughout an entire nation or in many nations finds advertising a valuable ambassador. Messages dealing with new or old products, their qualities and want-satisfying characteristics, can be sent to millions of people at low cost through newspapers, magazines, television, radio, direct mail, billboards, car cards, and motion pictures. Dealers in every market, stocked with such merchandise, find it relatively easy to meet the needs and desires of people. Thus, automobiles, refrigerators, radios, electrical equipment, and many other items can be manufactured and sold on a basis to obtain the advantages of mass production and distribution.

Modern advertising has demonstrated its power as an independent and complementary selling tool. So important has it become, that careful attention has been given to its scientific application to modern business. Thus, modern advertising covers a broad field. Its effective application requires a thorough understanding of the importance of its various component parts. An approach to such an understanding can be gained by looking backward for a brief moment to trace the evolution of advertising. This remigration will provide a contrast with the character of our present-day forms of advertising. It will also furnish a picture of the general direction toward which advertising is traveling and thus give a possible insight into its immediate future.

Broadly speaking, the history of advertising might be divided into six periods or stages, as follows:

1. Pre-printing period, prior to the 15th century.
2. Early printing period, from the 15th century to about 1840.
3. Period of expansion, from 1840 to 1900.
4. Period of consolidation, from 1900 to 1925.
5. Period of scientific development, from 1925 to 1945.
6. Period of business and social integration, from 1945 to the present.

PRE-PRINTING PERIOD

Signs

Perhaps some form of advertising has existed as long as we have had buying and selling. The nature of such advertising has depended upon the media available for carrying the message of the seller to the prospective buyer. Before the days of the newspaper and magazine, almost the only media available were signboards and town criers.

Sampson, in his *History of Advertising,* published in 1874, points out that "signs over shops and stalls seem naturally to have been the first efforts in the direction of advertisements and they go back to the remotest portions of the world's history."[1] These early signs were, for the most part, made of stone or terra cotta "and set into the pilasters at the sides of the open shop fronts."[2] Later, signs were hung over the walks and above shop entrances. Some extended entirely across the street.

[1] Henry Sampson, *History of Advertising* (London: Chatto & Windus, 1930), p. 19.
[2] Ibid., p. 22.

The principal function of these early signs was to identify a merchant's place of business. A valuable by-product, however, was that of providing a landmark for the citizens of a town. House numbers were unknown; and directions, such as "three doors down from the sign of the Three Crowns," provided a real service.

In addition to being the first major form of advertising, signs have continued to serve as an important advertising medium. The relative importance, rather than the absolute position, of this means of advertising has been reduced by the increase in literacy, development of the printing press, growth of electronic media, and other marks of progress.

The town crier

The town crier was the first means of supplementing sign advertising. The criers had charters from the government and were often organized in a sort of union. Their numbers were usually restricted. In the province of Berry, France, in the year 1141, twelve criers organized a company and obtained a charter from Louis VII giving them the exclusive privileges of town crying in the province.[3]

The power of commercial criers grew until they were able in some instances to obtain an edict from the ruler of the land forcing shopkeepers to employ a crier. Typical of such orders was the decree issued in France by Philip Augustus in 1258:

> Whosoever is a crier in Paris may go to any tavern he likes and cry its wine, provided they sell wine from the wood and that there is no other crier employed for that tavern; and the tavern keeper cannot prohibit him.
>
> If a crier finds people drinking in a tavern, he may ask what they pay for the wine they drink; and he may go out and cry the wine at the prices they pay, whether the tavern keeper wishes it or not, provided always that there be no other crier employed for that tavern.
>
> If a tavern keeper sells wine in Paris and employs no crier, and closes his door against the criers, the crier may proclaim that tavern keeper's wine at the same price as the king's wine (the current price) that is to say, if it be a good wine year, at seven dinarii, and if it be a bad wine year, at twelve dinarii.
>
> Each crier to receive daily from the tavern for which he cries at least four dinarii and he is bound on his oath not to claim more.[4]

Some of our modern "criers" of merchants' wares would no doubt like to have a government order similar to that issued by Philip Augustus. And such an order might be of benefit to some merchants.

[3] Frank Presbrey, *The History and Development of Advertising* (Garden City, N.Y.: Doubleday & Co., Inc., 1929), pp. 10–11.

[4] Ibid., pp. 11–12.

EARLY PRINTING PERIOD

The invention of the printing press and the revival of learning meant much to business. It, of course, made possible the production of advertisements in large quantities for wide distribution. The first printed English advertisement was a handbill or "poster" announcement written by William Caxton in 1472. That advertisement is reproduced in Figure 2–1. Translated into modern English the advertisement would read as follows:

> If anyone, cleric or layman, wants to buy some copies of two or three service books arranged according to the usage of Salisbury Cathedral, and printed in the same desirable type in which this advertisement is set, let him come to the place in the precincts of Westminster Abbey where alms are distributed, which can be recognized by a shield with a red central stripe (from top to bottom), and he shall have these books cheap.
>
> *Please don't tear down this notice.*[5]

In addition to handbills, the printing press gave rise to mass media in the form of newspapers, magazines, and books. These agencies served as media to carry messages of sellers to potential buyers. Authors of pamphlets, servants seeking positions, people wanting servants, announcements of runaway slaves, slaves listed for sale, publication of articles of association of public companies, and the formation of deeds of partnership illustrate the type of advertising material run in the early newspapers.

According to Blanche B. Elliott, probably the first English Press advertisement appeared in 1622 and was by an author of a series of pamphlets who inserted a note in *The Times Handlist* to inform buyers and prospective buyers that the pamphlets would be continued and available for purchase. The text of that early advertisement follows:

> If any Gentleman or other accustomed to buy the Weekely Relations of Newes, be desirous to continue the same, let them know that the Writer or Transcriber rather of this Newes hath published two former Newes, the one dated the second and the other the thirteenth of August, all of which doe carrie a like title, with the Armes of the King of *Bohemia* on the other side of the title page, and have dependance one upon another: which manner of writing and printing he doth propose to continue weekly by God's assistance, from the best and most certain intelligence.
>
> Farewell; this twenty-third of August 1622.[6]

This "first press advertisement" was a soft, dignified announcement of a pure informative nature. Unfortunately, it did not set the tone for later advertising of the period. Instead, this early period saw the use of exaggeration in its boldest form. Beverages, cosmetics, and patent medicines held a prominent place in the early media. The famous coffee advertisement

---

[5] This translation was made by Dr. Edward Pousland of Worcester Junior College.

[6] Blanche B. Elliott, *A History of English Advertising* (London: Business Publications Ltd., 1962), p. 22.

FIGURE 2–1
First printed English advertisement

If it plese ony man spirituel or temporel to bye ony
pyes of two and thre commemoracios of Salisburi vse
enprynted after the forme of this preset lettre whiche
ben wiel and truly correct, late hym come to westmo;
nester in to the almonestye at the reed pale and he shal
have them good chepe. ⋰

Supplico stet cedula

**Translation of First
Printed English Advertisement**

If it please any man spiritual or temporal to buy any
piece of two and three commemorations of salisbury use
emprinted after the form of this present letter which
been well and truly correct, let him come to westmin-
nster into the almonestry at the reed pale and he shall
have them good cheap ⋰

Supplico stet cedula

-William Caxton, 1472

printed as a handbill in 1652 is illustrative of the early beverage advertisements. It might be interesting to compare this more than three-century-old selling appeal with some of the advertising of today. The 1652 advertisement is here reprinted:

THE VIRTUE OF THE COFFEE DRINK
First made and publicly sold in England by
PASQUA ROSEE

The grain or berry called coffee groweth upon little trees only in the deserts of Arabia. It is brought from thence and drunk generally throughout all the Grand Seignour's dominions. It is a simple, innocent thing, composed into a drink, by being dried in an oven, and ground to powder, and boiled up with spring water, and about half a pint of it to be drunk fasting an hour before, and not eating an hour after, and to be taken as hot as can possibly be endured; the which will never fetch the skin of the mouth, or raise any blisters by reason of that heat.

The Turk's drink at meals and other times is usually water, and their diet consists of much fruit; the acidities whereof are very much corrected by this drink.

The quality of this drink is cold and dry; and though it be a drier; yet it neither heats nor inflames more than hot posset. It so incloseth the orifice of the stomach, and fortifies the heat within, that it is very good to help digestion; and therefore of great use to be taken about three or four o'clock afternoon, as well as in the morning. It much quickens the spirits, and makes the heart lightsome, it is good against sore eyes, and the better if you hold your head over it and take in the steam that way. It suppresseth fumes exceedingly, and therefore is good against the headache, and will very much stop any defluxion of rheums that distil from the head upon the stomach, and so prevent and help consumptions and cough of the lungs.

It is excellent to prevent and cure the dropsy, gout, and scurvy. It is known by experience to be better than any other drying drink for people in years, or children that have any running humours upon them, as the king's evil, etc. It is a most excellent remedy against the spleen, hypochondriac winds and the like. It will prevent drowsiness, and make one fit for business, if one have occasion to watch, and therefore you are not to drink of it after supper, unless you intend to be watchful, for it will hinder sleep for three or four hours.

It is observed that in Turkey, where this is generally drunk, that they are not troubled with the stone, gout, dropsy, or scurvy, and that their skins are exceedingly clear and white. It is neither laxative nor restringent.

Made and Sold in St. Michael's Alley, in Cornhill, by
Pasque Rosee, at the sign of his own Head.[7]

The quest for beauty provided a fertile field for quackery in the sale of cosmetics in the 18th century, as in the 20th century. Note the following advertisement, which appeared in the *Spectator* in 1712:

The Gentlewoman who lived 20 years in Raquet-Court, and 7 years in

[7] Sampson, *History of Advertising,* pp. 68–69.

Crane-Court, Fleet-street, and has served most of the Quality in England, Scotland and Ireland, also the East and West Indies, with the most excellent Curiosoties for preserving the Face, Hands, and Teeth, in present Beauty; for colouring red or grey Hair to a lovely brown or black, a Cosmatick that certainly takes away the Spots and Marks remaining after the Small-Pox with many other rare Secrets in Physick, is now removed to her own House the upper End of Wine-Office-Court in Gough-Square next Door to the Sun-dial on the Left hand, where you may be furnished with all things as formerly, and all prepared with her own hand. She is to be spoken with every Day from 9 to 12, and from 2 till 8 at night. . . .[8]

Or here is a "modern" one, printed in 1711:

A most incomparable Paste for the Hands, far exceeding anything ever yet in Print: It makes them delicately white, sleeke and plump; fortifies them against the scorching Heat of the Fire or Sun, and Sharpness of the Wind. A Hand cannot be so spoil'd but the Use of it will recover them. Sold only at Mr. Allcraft's Toy-shop, over-against the Royal-Exchange, at 1 s. 6 d. a Pot, with Directions: Where is sold the excellent German Powder for the Scurvy in the Gums and Teeth, which by only scouring them every Morning, whitens and fastens the Teeth to A Miracle, at 1 s. a Seale.[9]

A few examples of patent medicine advertising will serve to illustrate the dependence of the early vendors upon the credulity of afflicted persons. The following example, published in the *Spectator* in 1711, introduces the testimonial feature:

This is to certify, That my Child being almost reduced to the very Grave from the extream Agony he underwent by violent Breeding of Teeth, was thro'-God's Goodness restored to perfect Ease and Safety, upon the use of that truly Noble Medicine, prepared for those Cases, by Mr. Perronet Surgeon in Dyot-Street near Bloomsbury, Witness my Hand, S. Warburton, Raisor-maker in Grays-Inn-Passage, by Red Lyon-Square. This medicine is sold at 2 s. 7 d. the Vial, by the Author aforesaid, Mr. Alcraft at the Blew-Coat Boy Against the Royal Exchange, Cornhill, and by Mr. Watkins Tobaconist against the Market, in King-street Westminster.[10]

It is difficult to determine from the advertisement whether it was "God's Goodness" or the medicine which restored the youngster to "perfect ease and safety." The same dilemma is presented in the following example. In both cases, however, the makers of the "medicine" are willing to attribute credit to their concoction and ask a price for it.

R. Stoughton, Apothecary, in Southwak, having some Time since, by Order of a Merchant, sent 50 Dozen of his Cordial Elixir to Sweden, has lately receiv'd Advice, that Numbers of People finding it a great Preserver

[8] Lawrence Lewis, *The Advertisements of the Spectator* (New York: Houghton Mifflin Co., 1909), pp. 116–17.

[9] Ibid., pp. 117–18.

[10] Ibid., p. 113.

of Health, drink it every Morning: And further to assure it is so, hath a Certificate from thence, That (to the Person's best Knowledge and Observation) not one who took it hath had the Disease; and many are of the Opinion it hath been of great Use in stopping the Progress of it. He hath also a certificate from on board a Ship at Jamaica, That after 6 or 7 of the men died in 24 hours of a malignant Distemper, the Captain himself (fearing he should lose all his Men) gave the rest, who were seiz'd plentifully of this Elixir (which for many Years he took with him) and by God's Blessing on it saved every Man after. He is not only willing, but desirous this may be publish'd for the Good of others. Few now will go to Sea or travel without it. The certificates themselves any Gentleman may see if they please. Another large box is just now ordered again for Sweden.[11]

The center of advertising growth during the first half of the early printing period was England. It began to develop in America in significant amounts in the 1700s. Early American advertising, however, was largely devoid of the exaggeration found in English ads. James Young, in comparing patent medicine advertising in these two countries up to 1750, said, "While the English proprietor sharpened up his adjectives and reached for his vitriol, in America, with rare exceptions, advertisers were content merely to list by name their supplies of imported English remedies."[12]

An example of the mild form of American advertising in this period is the following that appeared in Benjamin Franklin's newspaper in 1735.

TO BE SOLD

A Plantation containing 300 Acres of good Land, 30 cleared, 10 or 12 Meadow and in good English Grass, a house and barn &c. lying in Nantmel Township, upon French-Creek, about 30 Miles from Philadelphia. Enquire of Simon Meredith now living on the said place.

ALL Persons indebted to the Estate of Joseph Harrison, Carpenter, late of Philadelphia, deceased, are hereby required to make speedy Payment to John Harrison, or John Leech, Executors. And those that have any Accounts to settle, are desired to bring them in.

These examples give some idea of the character of the advertising of the early printing period. In general, the growth of advertising during this period in both Europe and the United States paralleled the increase in population, learning, and number of periodicals and newspapers. However, in 1712 England levied a tax on newspapers and advertising which retarded the growth of both newspapers and advertising. It caused the death of such a leading publication as Addison's *Spectator*. The first tax amounted to a halfpenny, then increased to fourpence (eight cents), and reduced to a penny a paper in 1837. The tax on each advertisement,

---

[11] Ibid., p. 114.

[12] James H. Young, *The Toadstool Millionaires* (Princeton, N.J.: Princeton University Press, 1961), p. 10.

regardless of size, amounted to 84 cents at its peak. Taxes on both newspapers and advertisements were abolished in 1853.

The circulation of newspapers in the United States, where no tax was imposed, was much greater than in England during this period. Presbrey compares the two countries for 1850 as follows:[13]

	Population	Number of papers	Annual circulation
United Kingdom	27,368,736	500	91,000,000
United States	23,191,876	2,302	422,600,000*

* Estimated.

PERIOD OF EXPANSION

This period includes, roughly, the 60 years between 1840 and 1900. It was during these six decades that great changes were witnessed in the United States—changes which had a vital influence on the business of advertising.

Transportation

By 1840, railroads in the United States were recognized as an efficient means of transportation. They were rapidly piercing the West and causing businessmen to look beyond their own small communities for trade. This broadening of markets encouraged the use of advertising in magazines which served large territories, and the growth of magazines was likewise encouraged and made possible by the development of rapid and long-distance transportation.

Figures 2–2 and 2–3 give a graphic presentation of the growth of newspapers and magazines during this period. Figure 2–2 shows the parallel growth of the number of publications and railway mileage from 1840 to 1890. This parallel movement is rather striking. While it does not prove a causal relationship between the growth of long-distance transportation and advertising media, it is logical to believe that the increase of transportation facilities did have a definite influence on the rapid rise in the number of publications. Certainly a wide distribution of magazines was absolutely dependent upon an efficient method of long-distance transportation. Of course, increased revenue from the sale of advertising space encouraged a growth in the number of publications, and the wider circulation, in part made possible by improved transportation facilities, attracted more advertisers.

Figure 2–3 is even more striking. It is adapted from a study made by

[13] Presbrey, *History and Development of Advertising,* p. 75.

FIGURE 2–2

Relative changes in number of publications, railway mileage, and illiteracy in the United States from 1840 to 1890

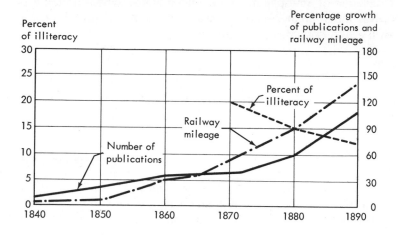

FIGURE 2–3

Growth of advertising space in the *Century Magazine* and in two newspapers from 1860 to 1890

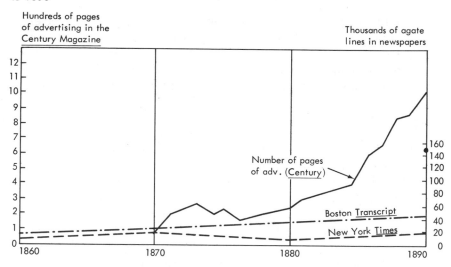

Daniel Starch.[14] Here we see a comparison of the volume of advertising in a typical magazine and two newspapers. The volume of advertising in the *Century Magazine* increased more than elevenfold between 1860 and 1890. The best that the *Boston Transcript* could do in the same period

[14] Daniel Starch, *Principles of Advertising* (New York: McGraw-Hill Book Co., 1923), p. 34.

was to double its advertising volume, while the *New York Times* had only a small percentage increase.

Since the markets opened up by railway transportation were perhaps best reached by magazines, the increase in the advertising volume of the *Century Magazine* would seem to be due, in large part, to the increase in railway mileage. It is evident that the railroad did have a tremendous influence on broadening markets and thus gave encouragement to an increase in the volume and scope of advertising.

Education

Until the advent of radio, most forms of advertising required an ability to read on the part of the prospective buyer. Today the literacy of the American people is high, but such was not the case at the beginning of the period of advertising expansion. It was during this period, however, that tremendous advances were made in educational facilities for the masses. It was during this period that free schools were provided for workers' children. Some compulsory school-attendance legislation was enacted. These forces reduced the amount of illiteracy in the United States. Twenty percent of the population ten years of age and over could not read in 1870. By 1890, this had been reduced to 13 percent. An interesting comparison can be made between the decline in illiteracy and the growth in the number of magazines and newspapers by referring to Figure 2–2.

The advertising agency

The growth of advertising during this period encouraged individuals to set themselves up as specialists in the sale of advertising space. Those who made this work their major occupation established themselves as a general advertising agency in that they would represent a number of media in the sale of space to advertisers. While there were agencies in England as early as 1800, the first agency in the United States was organized by Volney B. Palmer in 1840 or 1841. Palmer's organization served as salesman of space in magazines and newspapers, as did all subsequent agencies for many years. They received "inside" prices from publishers and made their money by selling space to advertisers at a higher rate. There was no standardization of prices, and no services were rendered by the agent such as writing copy, making layouts, or doing research work. The agent was strictly a seller of space.

Nevertheless, the growth in the number of men devoting their time to promoting the sale of space in publications tended to focus attention upon themselves, and later led to the recognition of the advertising agency as a vital factor to both the publisher and the advertiser. This specialized group of salesmen helped to increase the volume of advertising.

PERIOD OF CONSOLIDATION

By 1900 the area of the United States had been rather completely explored and settled. No longer was there a frontier to conquer. The territorial expansion of domestic markets had been halted. The job of the businessman was to cultivate the territories already existing.

New functions assumed by agency

In like fashion the business of advertising as exemplified by the agency had reached a point where continued growth depended upon changing the methods of operation. By 1890, as one writer put it, "the woods were full" of advertising agents. To consolidate their gains, new functions were assumed. These included the writing of copy, selection of media, and occasionally some analysis of the market. It was also during this period that a fairly stable method of paying the agency was developed.

Truth crusade

In 1911 a crusade against the ranker types of untruthfulness in advertising was launched. Printers' Ink, Inc., the Curtis Publishing Company, and other organizations led the fight to reduce or eliminate the use of gross exaggeration, false testimonials, and other forms of misleading and untruthful advertising. Although the motive for this crusade was perhaps an attempt to benefit the publisher rather than the consumer, the progress made reacted to the mutual benefit of all parties concerned.

The establishment of the Audit Bureau of Circulations in 1914 was another move for less untruth in the field. This Bureau served to validate the circulation statements made by publishers. The guaranteed circulation figures of members of the Bureau thus carried conviction. Again, this was a measure for self-preservation, but it served to consolidate the gains made in the heyday of publication and advertising growth.

Advertising organizations

Various advertising organizations were formed or became active during this period. A list of some of the leading groups would include the Advertising Federation of America, American Association of Advertising Agencies, Association of National Advertisers, Audit Bureau of Circulations, Direct Mail Advertising Association, Outdoor Advertising Association, and various publishers' associations.

These groups tended to give a semiprofessional character to the advertising business. They have had some influence in solidifying the business and in raising the ethics somewhat above the level of previous periods.

PERIOD OF SCIENTIFIC DEVELOPMENT

The designation of this period may be questioned by those who object to associating the word "science" with advertising. Few will deny, however, that this period saw the application of the scientific method to problems of advertising. Knowledge was systematized to a much greater degree than before; and facts were observed, recorded, and classified.

Decline of blind faith in advertising

For years advertising grew upon the success of those firms spending great sums in printed forms of sales promotion. If the question, "Are we big because we advertise, or do we advertise because we are big?" were ever asked, it was always answered in favor of advertising. The advertising agency, with its income depending upon the size of the advertising appropriation, helped to foster and perpetuate a blind faith in the efficacy of advertising. Did not St. Jacob's Oil and Pear's Soap lose out when they stopped advertising? Was not the success of Campbell's Soup due to advertising? Such questions, by inference, contained their own answer. It was absurd to be a disbeliever in the face of such "conclusive" evidence. No one stopped to ask how Hershey's Chocolate continued to be a success in the face of little or no advertising. The answer might have been found in Hershey's fine dealer organization, its early start, and its use of other sales promotional methods; but these were kept out of the discussion.

There were a few "radical" advertising men before 1920 who were so bold as to suggest that advertising be subjected to tests to prove or disprove its ability to work the wonder claimed for it. Not until the depression, starting in 1929, did these men get much of a hearing. But with advertising appropriations receiving liberal cuts, both professional advertising men and advertisers set out to test the effectiveness of advertising as a selling tool.

Market research and consumer analysis

This period witnessed a revision of advertising philosophy. It saw advertising men come to the realization that their business was only a part of the great field of selling, and that to be successful in their work a close harmony of effort with all other factors in the problem of selling must be obtained. Not merely was a consideration of the former "all-important" factors of art, copy, layout, and typography necessary; but thought must be given to the product to be advertised, the character of the prospective buyers, their purchasing power, their place of abode, etc.

Some of these factors were emphasized by the American Association of Advertising Agencies as early as 1918. In a report issued in that year, the Association laid down the following program as vital to an advertising campaign:

1. A study of the product or service in order to determine the advantages and disadvantages inherent in the product itself, and in its relation to competition
2. An analysis of the present and potential market for which the product or service is adapted:
   As to location
   As to the extent of possible sale
   As to season
   As to trade and economic conditions
   As to nature and amount of competition
3. A knowledge of the factors of distribution and sales and their methods of operation
4. A knowledge of all the available media and means which can profitably be used to carry the interpretation of the product or service to consumer, wholesaler, dealer, contractor, or other factor
   This knowledge covers:
   Character
   Influence
   Circulation.................. $\left\{\begin{array}{l} \text{Quantity} \\ \text{Quality} \\ \text{Location} \end{array}\right.$
   Physical Requirements
   Costs

Acting on the study, analysis and knowledge as explained in the preceding paragraphs, recommendations are made and the following procedure ensues:

5. Formulation of a definite plan
6. Execution of this plan:
   a. Writing, designing, illustrating of advertisements or other appropriate forms of the message
   b. Contracting for the space or other means of advertising
   c. The proper incorporation of the message in mechanical form and forwarding it with proper instructions for the fulfillment of the contract
   d. Checking and verifying of insertions, display or other means used
   e. The auditing, billing and paying for the service, space and preparation
7. Cooperation with the sales work, to insure the greatest effect from advertising.[15]

It is interesting to note that the A.A.A.A. in 1918 placed little or no emphasis on the importance of studying the consumer, his buying habits, needs, and desires. This factor emerged as a vital element in advertising later.

By the end of this period many advertisers had established their own

[15] *Report of American Association of Advertising Agencies* (New York, 1918).

market- and consumer-research departments, and specialized research firms had been organized to make independent and unbiased investigations for advertisers and media. This increased the quality of advertising strategy and performance as well as the benefits rendered consumers.

Testing results

During the period of scientific development serious attention was given by many agencies and organizations to methods for testing the sales effectiveness of advertising strategy, media, and copy. This was a new philosophy in that it meant subjecting the work of the creative man—the artist, the person who depended upon his own insights and intuition—to some kind of performance yardstick.

PERIOD OF BUSINESS AND SOCIAL INTEGRATION

During the decade following World War II advertising was recognized and accepted as an essential part of total business in the plentiful economy of free America. Production techniques and facilities were greatly increased during the war years, and these facilities were released after the end of armed conflict for use in producing consumer goods. There was purchasing power in the pockets of consumers to pay for all that industry could produce. However, there was not always the will to buy.

Economists both inside and outside of business pointed to advertising as a necessary ingredient in the total business mix to stimulate consumption to a point where it would balance production. Economists pointed out that high-level production and full employment could be sustained only by high-level consumption. Emphasis was placed on the fact that consumers needed to learn to live better in the future in order to absorb all of the goods and services that industry could supply. Under such circumstances advertising became an integral part of the total economy, taking its place alongside production, finance, distribution, and entrepreneurship as a part of the whole.

Social integration, too

During the past two decades the institution of advertising has also been accepted as a part of the total fabric of society. It has become a common medium whereby churches, political parties, labor groups, trade associations, and lay citizens communicate their ideologies, platforms, ideas, and concepts to the many publics making up total society. Advertising has become an institution of persuasion to promote such social and economic values as safety, health, education, benevolence, liberty, democracy, free enterprise, and tolerance.

This trend has been enhanced by the Advertising Council, an outgrowth of the War Advertising Council of World War II, which donates its time to develop complete advertising campaigns to promote ideas and projects that are recognized as being in the public interest.

Along with social integration has come a deeper appreciation of social responsibilities that rest upon the institution of advertising.

New emphasis has been given to the problem of untruthful advertising. The old organizations developed to foster truth in advertising have attacked the problem with new vigor, and new agencies have supplemented the work of the old. Legislation, both state and national, has been sought and obtained to promote a greater degree of truthfulness in advertising. Machinery for self-regulation of advertising has been set up. There seems to have been a growth in the belief that advertising effectiveness will be increased by making it more truthful.

Strong leadership in the renewal of the truth crusade was again taken by various publishers and leading practitioners.

The character of modern advertising is such that it must be accorded a vital position in our total economic and social life. Its power is substantial; its responsibility even greater.

Summary

The foregoing brief history of advertising is intended to give a bird's-eye view of the evolution of this selling tool from its simple beginning to its present position. It is in no way intended as a complete history.

The important features of modern advertising will be treated at length in the chapters that follow. Emphasis will be placed upon those qualities peculiar to its modern development. Consideration will be given to the place which advertising might properly and profitably hold in our social and economic order. The problems and techniques of consumer, product, and market analysis will form an important part of our further study. Attention will be given to the preparation of advertising messages that will be effective and to the selection of media to carry such messages.

The organization of modern advertising, including the general advertising agency, special agencies, and the advertising departments of the manufacturer and retailer, will be treated in detail. Finally, attention will be given to the philosophy and techniques of testing advertising effectiveness.

Thus, the features of modern advertising which we have viewed but briefly here will be amplified in the material which follows.

QUESTIONS AND PROBLEMS

1   Contrast the advertising of the "early printing period" with that of today, and account for the factors that influenced the change.

2   "Advances in educational facilities in the period of expansion resulted in increasing not only the use but also the quality of advertising." Do you agree? Why?

3   What influence do you think World War II might have had on advertising during the war period?

4   What might have been some of the reasons for a slower expansion of advertising in England than in the United States in the early printing period?

5   Wherein do the modern beverage advertisements differ from those exemplified by the early coffee advertisement reproduced in this chapter?

6   How did the development of our transportation industry after 1840 affect advertising? Why was it that the advertising in some media was influenced more by the growth of transportation than that in other media?

7   In view of the trend of the changing character of advertising in the past, what forecast would you make as to the character of the advertising business for the future?

8   Would a law which forced present-day businessmen to employ a "town crier" or modern advertising expert be particularly detrimental to business? Explain.

9   If you can secure copies of newspapers or magazines that are ten or more years old, compare the advertisements of that period with those in current media to see if you can detect any fundamental differences in the advertisements of the two periods.

10   Do you see any evidence to suggest that we might now be entering a seventh period in the history of advertising—the period of social responsibility?

3

Social and economic aspects of advertising

Advertising is a subsystem of an economic system which, in turn, is a subsystem of a larger system of social values and beliefs. To understand how advertising works, one must first understand how the total system works.

Reflecting different values and beliefs, different political philosophies, and different stages of industrial development, different nations have devised different economic systems. Whatever the system, be it a primitive barter system or a modern price system, it is called upon to do certain things: (1) to determine what goods and services will be produced and in what quantities, (2) to allocate scarce resources (land, labor, and capital) among alternative uses, and (3) to distribute goods and services among individuals and occupational groupings. Inasmuch as advertising has developed most rapidly and has reached its highest level of sophistication in one particular kind of economic system, let us consider how that system works.

A FREE MARKET SYSTEM

In a free market system consumers tell the system what to produce. Their decisions to purchase this item and not that, say in effect, "make more of this, less of that." Millions of these "dollar votes" are registered every hour of every day. Relayed from retailers to wholesalers to manufacturers to farmers, miners, lumbermen, oil drillers, fishermen, etc., consumer choices guide the allocation of resources. It is assumed that each consumer acting in his own self-interest not only advances his own welfare, but all consumers collectively advance the welfare of society.

In a free market system there are many suppliers competing for consumer favor. Just as each consumer is free to choose, each supplier is free to enter. Competition among suppliers is counted on to provide the incentive for innovation and greater efficiency. As each supplier seeks to offer a better value—that is, a better product at the same price or the same product at a lower price—the total supply of products increases, quality improves, and costs decrease. Prices represent a balancing of consumer satisfactions and supplier production costs. Prices are free to fluctuate in accordance with fluctuations in supplies and demands. Thus, consumers ultimately control the system, not only through the choices they make but also through the prices they pay.

This, of course, is an oversimplified version. Among other omissions it leaves out the intricate and automatic adjustments that distribute the gross national product in the form of wages, rents, interest payments, and dividends, thus providing consumers with purchasing power to complete the cycle. Concentrating on the marketplace, the purpose here is simply to spotlight the pivotal role of the consumer. The system assumes that the consumer is competent not only to maximize his own satisfactions but, in so doing, also to advance the interests of society at large.

How competent is the consumer? Does he choose wisely and well? Does he function as a rational "economic man" weighing carefully the pros and cons? How independent, how reasonable, how well informed is he? Proponents of a free market system have faith in the ability of large numbers of consumers to choose well. Opponents are skeptical. They assume the consumer needs to be protected against himself. They place their faith in some form of centralized government authority. In their view, economic control should rest with the few at the top instead of the many at the bottom. However, even the proponents recognize that a free market system cannot be left entirely free. Some laws have to be passed and some regulatory agencies established to assure safety in the use of foods, drugs, cosmetics, automobiles, etc. Other laws are needed to protect the consumer against fraudulent and deceptive practices. Still others are required to foster competition. Because the system fails to directly provide schools, roads, social welfare programs, and national defense, a considerable amount of consumer spending is diverted in the form of taxes to government spending. As a result, what we have in the United States is a "mixed economic system," both free and regulated. However, in the consumer goods market, in the supermarkets, department stores, discount stores, and in the field of consumer services, where a wide assortment of competing

mixed Economy

goods and services are available, it can be assumed that the forces of consumer choice are relatively free.

There have, on occasion, been major, but temporary, restraints placed on the operation of the free-market system in the United States. In time of war, particularly, government leaders have depended on government order rather than price and consumer demand in the allocation of resources. Such an approach has also been used in peacetime when the health of the economy seemed threatened. A notable example of this was in 1973 when prices on commodities were frozen as of a given date. The results of this tampering with the free market system, with its dependence on price to adjust supply to demand, were almost disastrous. For example, it reduced the number of beef-breeding herds and thus worsened the future supply of beef. It caused a number of producers of poultry and pork to destroy baby chicks and sell pregnant sows because the "frozen" price for broilers and hogs was too low to cover costs of production. The freedom of consumers to encourage producers to increase supply, through their willingness to pay higher prices for meat, was curtailed.

How well has the system worked? This can only be answered in terms of a nation's larger system of values and beliefs. If a relatively high standard of living, an abundance of material goods, widely distributed purchasing power, and personal freedom are highly valued—the system in those countries where it exists has performed reasonably well. If, on the other hand, the national interest as perceived by government leaders is more highly valued than individual preferences and material well-being, then some other system probably would be adopted.

ADVERTISING'S ROLE IN THE SYSTEM

An economic system that depends on the choices of millions of consumers in many widely scattered markets requires a highly developed communication system. Every buyer cannot transact business directly with every seller nor can every buyer examine every product offered for sale. Both buyers and sellers depend on advertising to carry the news of available products and services, to establish them in consumers' minds, to interpret their want-satisfying qualities. Through advertising, consumers are able to anticipate satisfactions, to compare values, and to do much of their shopping before they ever leave home. Consumers tend to choose products they know and trust. Advertising creates awareness and builds confidence. Consumers forget. Advertising reminds.

These communication functions are performed quickly and efficiently. The vast network of newspapers, magazines, television and radio stations, direct mail, etc. makes it possible for a single manufacturer to reach millions of consumers throughout the country in a week's time, or for a retailer to reach the hundreds or thousands of his customers every day. Such efficient communication hastens the trial and acceptance of new products. It also hastens the rejection of those items that fail to live up to their claims. In this way advertising helps make the economic system more responsive to consumer preferences. Ultimately it speeds up the process of resource allocation.

Advertising contributes to a dynamic, expanding economy. In fact, Professor Neil H. Borden in his exhaustive study of the economic effects of advertising concluded that this was the outstanding contribution.

> Advertising's outstanding contribution to consumer welfare comes from its part in promoting a dynamic, expanding economy. Advertising's chief task from a social standpoint is that of encouraging the development of new products. It offers a means whereby the enterpriser may hope to build a profitable demand for his new and differentiated merchandise which will justify investment. From growing investment has come the increasing flow of income which has raised man's material welfare to a level unknown in previous centuries.[1]

Knowing they have a quick and efficient means to introduce a new or improved product to a large market, manufacturers are willing to make substantial investments in new product research and development. The faster they can get millions of consumers to try and accept a new product, the faster they can build a profitable volume of sales and the faster they can recover their investment in research and development.

Having the means to tell the consuming public about a new product is, in itself, an incentive to invention and innovation. Having the means to proclaim a product's superiority is an incentive to making it live up to its claim. Having the means to compete in advertising stimulates competitive rivalry in the laboratories and factories. Advertising enhances the opportunity to succeed. It also enhances the opportunity to fail. Even though it may not be the cause of a successful or an unsuccessful product introduction, advertising accelerates both outcomes.

Expanding consumption is essential to an expanding economy. Expanding consumption involves more people spending more money for more goods and services to satisfy more wants. In a modern industrial society the basic wants of food, clothing, and shelter are reasonably well met for most people. For them to spend more they must want more. As Professor Frank H. Knight wrote, "The chief thing that the common-sense individual actually wants is not satisfactions for the wants which he has, but more and better wants."[2] It might be assumed that consumer wants are automatically and infinitely expansible. Such is not the case. Once the appetite for food and drink as nourishment becomes satiated, the satisfactions

---

[1] Neil H. Borden, *The Economic Effect of Advertising* (Homewood, Ill.: Richard D. Irwin, Inc., 1942), p. 881.

[2] Frank H. Knight, *The Ethics of Competition* (New York: Harper & Bros., 1935), p. 22.

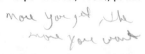

to be derived from menu planning from more exotic foods and serving rituals must be learned. Similarly, once the need for clothing and shelter as means of protection against the elements is met, the uses of these items for self adornment, social approval, and hedonistic pleasures must be recognized. In our affluent society a multiplicity of services accounts for a large portion of the nation's economic activity. These have to be sold.

The view expressed in The Twentieth Century Fund study of American needs and resources highlights the importance of advertising in a luxury economy:

> In a scarcity economy the consumer needs no conditioning to make him want enough food to keep alive, sufficient clothing and shelter to keep warm. But in an economy of luxury and plenty, the consumer has to be persuaded to want, for example, an electric blanket with a separate thermostatic control for each side of the bed, or an air-conditioned automobile with power steering and a hydramatic drive. This constant "education" of consumers to desire products never heard of before is just as essential to the smooth functioning of an economy which is geared to turn out a steady flood of new and different products as are an adequate supply of electric energy and plentiful raw materials. The American standard of living is thus the cause no less than the result of American creativeness and productivity.[3]

In the decade of the 70s the term "quality of life" was conjoined with the term "standard of living" when considering national goals and evaluating the economy. The emphasis placed by The Twentieth Century Fund on the need to constantly educate "consumers to desire products never heard of before . . ." is equally applicable to elements associated with the quality of life. Such "education" would apply to acceptance of higher prices to pay for reducing various kinds of pollution, higher taxes to pay for more parks and recreation areas, smaller automobiles to reduce consumption of gasoline, power-saving appliances to replace power-wasting ones, and how to enjoy increased leisure time.

Alfred J. Seaman, in a presentation before the Federal Trade Commission, emphasized the importance of advertising in these terms:

> Advertising is both the spark plug and the lubricant of the economic machinery which creates consumer wealth. As such, its job is to inform, as all critics and practitioners agree. But its job is not just to inform. Its function is to *sell*. Sell products. Sell ideas. Sell styles of living. . . .[4]

In a sense all marketing activity, which includes advertising, is designed to sell a higher standard of living and to improve the quality of life.

As an individual's wants are expanded and intensified his motivation

---

[3] J. Frederic Dewhurst and Associates, *America's Needs and Resources* (New York: The Twentieth Century Fund, 1955).

[4] J. Robert Moskin, ed., *The Case for Advertising* (New York: American Association of Advertising Agencies, 1973), p. 15.

to work increases. Basically, one does not work for money but rather for the satisfactions that money can buy. His anticipation of satisfactions to be derived from additional products, services, and financial security stimulates his incentive to work and increase his earnings. Thus, we see the circularity of the free market system. Consumer wants not only support production—they also provide the incentive to produce. In a primitive economy where only the essentials for survival are available, there is much leisure time. There is little or no incentive to do more work because there is little or nothing more to have. This suggests that economic progress in the so-called underdeveloped nations rests largely on the concurrent growth of their wants, productivity, and production. Advertising can make only a modest contribution in the early stages of development. However, as discretionary spending power increases, as the distribution of income widens, and as the supply of goods and services grows, advertising becomes a more important part of the system.

Some observers suggest that the power of advertising is so great that it deprives consumers of their discretion in the marketplace and makes it possible for suppliers to "manage demand." John Kenneth Galbraith, one of the more articulate of these observers, notes:

> The control or management of demand is, in fact, a vast and rapidly growing industry in itself. It embraces a huge network of communications, a great array of merchandising and selling organizations, nearly the entire advertising industry, numerous ancillary research, training and other related services, and much more. In everyday parlance this great machine and the demanding and varied talents that it employs, are said to be engaged in selling goods. In less ambiguous language it means that it is engaged in the management of those who buy goods.[5]

Mr. Galbraith overrates the power of advertising and underrates the power of consumers. As we shall see in subsequent chapters the consumer controls his own behavior. He is highly selective, accepting that which serves his purpose, rejecting the rest.

VALUE ADDED

Value, in an economic sense, is not easily defined. Various terms have been used to describe it. Various models have been devised to measure it. The fact that different people operate from different standards of value complicates the matter still further. Our purpose here is not to embark on an exhaustive examination of the subject but rather to illuminate the relationship of value and advertising.

[5] John Kenneth Galbraith, *The New Industrial State* (Boston: Houghton Mifflin Company, 1967), p. 200.

Early explanations of value used the word utility (usefulness), and various kinds of economic activity have been explained in terms of the kind of utility they added. Thus, manufacturing adds *form utility* by converting raw materials to a more useful form. Transportation adds *place utility* by moving goods from places where they are abundant to places where they are scarce. Storage adds *time utility* by holding goods for future use. These kinds of utilities are tangible and readily understood. Any activity that increased these utilities was recognized as productive activity. The productivity of any activity that didn't fit into one of these categories was open to question.

The term "value added" has been used to denote increases in value of raw materials as they move through the manufacturing process. The value of lumber is increased when it is cured, cut, and shaped into a piece of furniture. The amount of value added at each stage is the difference in market prices before and after that stage of processing.

A more sophisticated view treats value as an intangible psychological phenomenon. Value exists in the mind or within the person, not in the thing. Value is what it is perceived to be. It is the sum total of all the perceived utilities, satisfactions, and rewards—either in the realm of expectations before purchase or in experiences during and after use. The image of the brand is as much a part of value as the product's utilitarian functions. Obviously, a steel razor blade has greater value than a chunk of iron ore. Also, a Gillette Trac II blade is perceived by some people as having greater value than any other brand of blade. The known and familiar brand has more value than the unknown brand. Confidence in a product or service is worth paying for. Among competing brands in some product categories, such as aspirin, there may be no discernible physical differences. However, the consumer who perceives one brand as being superior will attach greater value to it. For him it is more valuable.

Advertising modifies the consumer's perceptions of goods and services. It might be said that advertising adds *perceptual utility.* Insofar as these changes in perceptions make the product more desirable, advertising adds value. Martin Mayer, in his book *Madison Avenue, U.S.A.,* stated this concept succinctly: "Whenever a benefit is promised from the use of a product, and the promise is believed, the use of the product carries with it a value not inherent in the product itself."[6] The fact that a consumer will pay more for an advertised brand than an unadvertised brand clearly demonstrates that advertising has added value. For example, all aspirin tablets are required by the U.S. Pharmacopoeia to contain the same quantity and purity of active ingredients, yet millions of consumers pay two to three times more for Bayer than for unadvertised brands. Even though all brands of aspirin are technically identical they are perceived as being

[6] Martin Mayer, *Madison Avenue, U.S.A.* (New York: Harper & Row, 1958).

different, and for the perceiver they are different. As Professor George J. Stigler has observed:

> "Reputation" is a word which denotes the persistence of quality and reputation commands a price (or extracts a penalty) because it economizes on search. When economists deplore the reliance of the consumer on reputation . . . they implicitly assume that the consumer has a large laboratory, ready to deliver current information quickly and gratuitously.[7]

Reputation of the brand is largely the result of product performance and advertising.

Consumer surplus In assessing value the final measure must be the satisfaction of human needs and wants. From an accounting standpoint, business firms can add to goods the dollar cost of all phases of production and distribution in arriving at a "book" or inventory value. Such dollar figures, however, must be tested in the marketplace where buyers will make the final decision. Such decisions will be based, to a significant degree, on *perceptual utility*.

Advertising can often increase the perceptual utility of a product over and above the dollar price. When that occurs the result might be called *consumers' surplus*. For example, the maximum price consumers are willing to pay for a product before it is supported by advertising might be $1. If, after informative and persuasive advertising, the appreciation for the product is increased sufficiently so that consumers would be willing to pay $1.50 rather than do without the product, then the surplus in satisfaction has been increased 50 percent. This is as productive as an increase in the quantity of goods. The satisfaction of human wants is the measure of productivity.

Consumer deficit It would also appear that advertising can and does at times reduce the perceptual utility of a product, thus producing a deficit in consumer satisfaction. False or misleading advertising may lead consumers to expect solutions to needs that cannot be met by using the product. In monetary terms advertising may have persuaded consumers to expect at least $1 of satisfaction from use of the product. If, after use, consumers equate their satisfaction to be less than $1, the discount provides a measure of the deficit.

In respect to the sum total of all products and services there is an element of countervailing power operating in the marketplace. The advertising slogan, "It is a matter of life and breath," is designed to create a deficit of satisfaction from smoking cigarettes. The same was true in the energy conscious mid-1970s with the advertising of small automobiles. Some of that advertising was designed to create a deficit in the satisfaction received by those who drove large, gasoline-hungry automobiles. This

[7] George J. Stigler, "The Economics of Information," *The Journal of Political Economy,* June 1961, p. 224.

countervailing element is a significant factor in an economic system where competition and consumer freedom of choice are present.

ADVERTISING, COMPETITION, AND MONOPOLY

Underlying the classic theory of pure competition are two assumptions: (1) a large number of sellers each operating independently so that no single seller can control supply, and therefore, price; (2) a standardized product so that any seller's product is substitutable for anothers', thereby depriving every seller the opportunity to distinguish his product and command a higher price than his competitor's. Under these conditions prices move freely, reflecting the counter forces of supply and demand. Such a situation is approximated in the commodity markets but otherwise does not exist in the real world. At the other extreme is monopoly, a single seller who controls the supply, and therefore, the price. Except for so-called natural monopolies in the field of government-regulated public utilities, monopolies do not exist in the real world either. What we have in most industries are relatively few competitors, each differentiating his product in an attempt to attain some degree of monopoly power. Professor Edward H. Chamberlin labelled this kind of activity "monopolistic competition."[8]

Product differentiation may be based on certain characteristics of the product itself, such as exclusive patented features, trademark, and brand name; or on the uniqueness of the package; or on any singularity in quality, design, color, or style. Patents and copyrights confer a monopoly granting "for limited times to authors and inventors, exclusive rights to their respective writings and discoveries." The inventor has the sole right to manufacture and sell his invention for a given number of years. Thus, even though a patent confers a monopoly, it also stimulates competition by encouraging initiative, invention, innovation, and enterprise. Similarly, the exclusive right to use a particular trademark or brand name stimulates competitive rivalry among brands. The advertiser seeks to differentiate his brand, to embellish it with attractions so that a large number of consumers will prefer it over all others. Whatever reputation he is able to build for the brand accrues solely to that brand. A brand monopoly depends on consumers *thinking* that the brand will give greater satisfaction per dollar spent than some other brand. Such a monopoly is dependent on a control of human attitudes rather than a control of supply.

What kind of monopoly power does a successful brand-name advertiser achieve? In theoretical terms, the demand schedule shifts so that more units will be bought at the same price. Demand also becomes more inelastic, which means he can raise his price while experiencing a less-than-

[8] Edward Hastings Chamberlin, *The Theory of Monopolistic Competition* (Cambridge, Mass.: Harvard University Press, 1947).

proportionate decrease in unit sales. With greater stability in sales he can program production more efficiently. Instead of competing on a price basis alone, he has the option of competing on the basis of advertising and promotion. In effect, he gains some power to maximize revenue and profit by controlling volume and/or price, and/or advertising and promotion. Whatever control he gains is based on the loyalty of his customers to the brand. If the price differential becomes too great, he risks losing customers to competing brands. Brand monopolies, therefore, are subject to the whims of consumers and the counter moves of competitors.

Some observers contend that advertising enhances the monopoly power already enjoyed by large corporations. While Professor Jules Backman does not agree with this contention, he states their case as follows:

1. The large company has the power of the large purse, which enables it to spend substantial sums on advertising, particularly to implement varying degrees of product differentiation which enables a company to preempt part of a market.
2. Advertising thus creates a barrier to new firms entering an industry or a product market.
3. The result is high economic concentration.
4. Because of their protected position and because of product differentiation these firms can charge monopolistic prices which are too high. Moreover, they must recover the cost of the advertising by charging higher prices.
5. High prices in turn result in excessively large profits.[9]

The high cost of using national media such as network television on a large scale restricts the use of such media to the few advertisers who can afford them. This supports the charge that advertising gives an unfair competitive advantage to the large firms. Their ability to bear the high cost of introducing new products nationally and to outspend small competitors is assumed to discourage would-be entrants and also make it difficult for others to survive. It is further assumed that large firms gain a larger share of the market because they can afford to gain a larger share of the public mind. Undoubtedly, large firms with great financial resources can do many things that small firms cannot do—including large-scale advertising. However, the opportunity to advertise gives the small firm a chance to get started. If he has a good product or service fairly priced he can advertise and build a market. He obviously can't match the giant firms on a national scale, but he might be able to outspend them in his local market area. As his business grows he can use advertising to enter new markets and expand his own competitive capabilities. Many local and regional advertisers compete successfully against large national advertisers.

[9] Jules Backman, *Advertising and Competition* (New York: New York University Press, 1967), p. 4.

Ultimately, consumers pay for the cost of all advertising in the prices they pay for goods and services. This leads to the belief that large advertisers must charge higher prices, or that prices would be lower without advertising. Such a belief overlooks the lower unit manufacturing and marketing costs that result from large-scale production. To the extent that advertising builds a mass market, it can be assumed that advertising facilitates mass production with its concomitant lower unit costs. A free market system counts on competition, even competition among a few giant firms referred to as an oligopoly, to pass along the benefit of such cost reductions in the form of lower prices.

In his study of the effects of advertising on competition, Professor Backman concluded:

> Practically all markets are an amalgam of elements of monopoly and of competition. The possession of the monopoly of a brand is not the totality of the market situation. National brands must meet the competition of other national brands, substitute products, private brands, local or regional brands, and products sold solely on a price basis. The dynamic, competitive nature of these markets is underlined by the marked changes in brand shares, the successes achieved by many new national brands and private brands against so-called entrenched brands, and the inability of well-known and financially strong companies successfully to establish new brands at will. These developments indicate that the degree of market power, which supposedly accompanies product differentiation identified by brand names and implemented by large-scale advertising, is much weaker than claimed and is usually outweighed by competitive pressures.[10]

Professor Yale Brozen points out that competitive advertising is generally employed to attract customers the firm does not now have—either nonusers or customers of competitors. Thus, he says, such "advertising is aimed at destroying loyalty"[11] and, as such, cannot be a decisive force in building a monopoly.

In respect to the high cost of advertising providing a barrier to new firms entering the market, Professor Brozen places this in the same category as other start-up costs of a new firm. He says "advertising is an *investment* and a *cost* of entry. It is not, then, a barrier to entry anymore than any other cost of entry."[12] Professor Phillip Nelson, in a careful analysis of the economic aspects of advertising, observed that "advertising probably reduces barriers to entry."[13]

---

[10] Ibid., pp. 155–56.

[11] Yale Brozen, "New FTC Policy From Obsolete Economic Doctrine," *Antitrust Law Journal,* Issue 3 (1973), p. 481.

[12] Ibid., p. 485.

[13] Phillip Nelson, "The Economic Value of Advertising" (Manuscript, University of Chicago, 1973).

ADVERTISING AND THE PRESS

The fact that the press, including television and radio, is supported financially by advertising raises some questions about the freedom of the press from advertiser control. Newspapers and magazines get 60 to 70 percent of their revenue from advertising. Commercial television and radio broadcasting are financed entirely by advertising. The underlying notion that "money is power" may give rise to the suspicion that advertisers influence news coverage by suppressing and distorting the news to their own advantage.

In the case of labor difficulties in some industrial plants, it has been maintained that the press has built up public opinion against the demands of labor, and that only news items favorable to the employer and unfavorable to the employees have been offered to the public.

Some years ago the Federal Trade Commission, in its inquiry into the publicity and propaganda activities of the electric power and gas industries of the country, presented evidence bearing on the question of the influence of advertisers on the character of news printed. The commission pointed out that, "when it is understood that 'the newspaper or magazine is practically a by-product of advertising,' and that advertising expenditures therefore frequently carry a certain element of goodwill response from the recipients, the large total spent by utilities for advertising is relevant. . . ."[14]

The extent to which advertisers do or do not exercise control over the press has been studied and reported on at various times by objective scholars of the subject. As was noted in a previous chapter, the Commission on Freedom of the Press reported that "the evidence of dictation of policy by advertisers is not impressive. Such dictation seems to occur among the weaker units. As a newspaper becomes financially stable it becomes more independent and tends to resist pressure from advertisers."[15] Theodore Peterson, in commenting on the pressures of advertisers on magazine editorial content in the first half of the 20th century, stated, "A safe generalization perhaps is that direct advertising pressure—especially successful pressure—was much less than the average reader may guess; that most advertising pressure was subtle and just part of a greater pressure, the economic struggle for survival."[16]

Consolation is registered by some from the fact that advertisers make possible low-priced magazines and newspapers and free radio and television entertainment. It is pointed out that the education of the masses is

[14] Federal Trade Commission, "Propaganda Activities of Utility Interests," *Public Utilities Release No. 240,* p. 1.

[15] Commission on Freedom of the Press, *A Free and Responsible Press* (Chicago: University of Chicago Press, 1947), p. 62.

[16] Theodore Peterson, *Magazines in the Twentieth Century,* 2d ed. (Urbana, Ill.: University of Illinois Press, 1964), p. 38.

greatly increased by low-priced newspapers and magazines. The tremendous circulation of newspapers and magazines is made possible by the subsidy rendered by advertisers. If this subsidy were eliminated, either some other means of financing the press would be necessary or a great drop in circulation would result, with many publications going out of existence entirely.

Alternative methods of financing the press perhaps hold many more dangers than the present method of major financial dependence upon advertisers. Early newspapers, both in England and America, were dependent upon the government or political parties for their economic life. With the development of advertising as an important source of revenue for newspapers, the press was able to free itself from political control. Steven Shaw, in reviewing the history of newspapers in colonial America, says, "It was during this period (1690–1750) that freedom of the press was fought for and won, and newspaper advertising was built up to the point where editors could begin to divorce themselves from dependence on political subsidy, postmasterships, job printing, and other revenues except copy sales."[17]

This point is emphasized even more strongly in the history of the *Times* (London) in this statement: "The commercial interest lies at the root of Press independence in daily journalism. . . . In the main, the commercial body is essential in journalism, and such freedom as the Press enjoys is dependent on commercial advertising."[18]

In some countries the press is financed by political parties. If that were true in America freedom in editorial and news policy would be in great danger. In general, the advertiser is not interested in news and editorial policy except as such policy tends to select the kind of audience which he wishes to reach with paid sales messages. This audience selection is left to the medium in the case of newspapers and magazines. The advertiser often influences the program content of radio and television as a means of selecting a desired audience, but such programs are primarily of an entertainment character and are recognized by the audience as sponsored by the advertiser.

There is safety, too, in the large number of advertisers. The influence that one advertiser might like to exert is directly opposite to what another would want. The large number of advertisers also means that a publisher can "afford" to lose some of them without particular financial harm. The most vital factor, however, is the fact that advertisers need the press as much as the owners and managers of the press need advertisers. Advertisers need the press's circulations and audiences to advertise effectively. If

[17] Steven Shaw, "Colonial Newspaper Advertising: A Step Toward Freedom of the Press," *The Business History Review,* Vol. 33, No. 3 (1959), p. 410.

[18] Blanche B. Elliott, *A History of English Advertising* (London: Business Publications, Ltd., 1962), p. xiv.

they succeeded in influencing the news the press would risk losing public confidence which, in turn, would reduce circulation and jeopardize the effectiveness of the press as an advertising medium.

A word should also be said about the control which the press might exercise over advertisers. Since advertisers need the press as much as the press needs advertisers, it would seem that the latter should not be denied access to the various media of communications. This has not always been true. There have been times when publishers have refused to carry the advertisements of legitimate business firms. Refusal has been not on grounds of false or exaggerated claims but rather for purposes of influencing the private business policy of the advertiser.

This control or pressure is illustrated by the case of a Loraine, Ohio, publisher who refused to accept the advertisements of any local business firms that also advertised over the local radio station. The purpose of such action was to injure a competitor of the publisher, but it also injured the advertiser. Both aspects of such action were condemned by the Federal Trade Commission.

ADVERTISING AND FREEDOM OF SPEECH

Freedom of speech has always been a cardinal principle of American life. Freedom to speak one's mind to influence others would generally not be questioned. Ability to speak freely to the masses, however, has usually been limited to those with large financial resources. Editors, columnists, and public speakers whose comments get into news reports have made up the bulk of those able to reach a mass audience. The "layman" without great wealth has been obliged to speak only to the few who can hear his voice.

Very recent developments in advertising have changed this. Today there is a rapidly growing use of the advertising pages of our newspapers and magazines to sell ideas. This development means that our mass media are becoming available as an open forum which can be used by almost any person or group wishing to speak to the masses. Large audiences can thus be reached with a very small financial outlay. For a few thousand dollars one can speak to millions. This use of advertising is expanding the meaning of free speech in a manner never before conceived as being possible.

A slightly different emphasis on advertising's contribution to free speech is given by John Dollard. He says:

> Advertising is one form of free speech in a business society. As such, I see no serious threat in it. So long as we rely on persuasion, in the loose and relatively free situation of the democratic society, advertising cannot be a menace to individual integrity. Totalitarian coercion is indeed something to be feared. Only when there is a monopoly of power over life and death as

FIGURE 3–1

The advertisement that led to the Supreme Court decision affirming the freedom to speak through advertising

> "*The growing movement of peaceful mass demonstrations by Negroes is something new in the South, something understandable....*
> *Let Congress heed their rising voices, for they will be heard.*"
>
> —*New York Times* editorial
> *Saturday, March 19, 1960*

Heed Their Rising Voices

As the whole world knows by now, thousands of Southern Negro students are engaged in widespread non-violent demonstrations in positive affirmation of the right to live in human dignity as guaranteed by the U. S. Constitution and the Bill of Rights. In their efforts to uphold these guarantees, they are being met by an unprecedented wave of terror by those who would deny and negate that document which the whole world looks upon as setting the pattern for modern freedom....

In Orangeburg, South Carolina, when 400 students peacefully sought to buy doughnuts and coffee at lunch counters in the business district, they were forcibly ejected, tear-gassed, soaked to the skin in freezing weather with fire hoses, arrested en masse and herded into an open barbed-wire stockade to stand for hours in the bitter cold.

In Montgomery, Alabama, after students sang "My Country, 'Tis of Thee" on the State Capitol steps, their leaders were expelled from school, and truck-loads of police armed with shotguns and tear-gas ringed the Alabama State College Campus. When the entire student body protested to state authorities by refusing to re-register, their dining hall was padlocked in an attempt to starve them into submission.

In Tallahassee, Atlanta, Nashville, Savannah, Greensboro, Memphis, Richmond, Charlotte, and a host of other cities in the South, young American teen-agers, in face of the entire weight of official state apparatus and police power, have boldly stepped forth as protagonists of democracy. Their courage and amazing restraint have inspired millions and given a new dignity to the cause of freedom.

Small wonder that the Southern violators of the Constitution fear this new, non-violent brand of freedom fighter . . . even as they fear the upwelling right-to-vote movement. Small wonder that they are determined to destroy the one man who, more than any other, symbolizes the new spirit now sweeping the South—the Rev. Dr. Martin Luther King, Jr., world-famous leader of the Montgomery Bus Protest. For it is his doctrine of non-violence which has inspired and guided the students in their widening wave of sit-ins; and it this same Dr. King who founded and is president of the Southern Christian Leadership Conference—the organization which is spearheading the surging right-to-vote movement. Under Dr. King's direction the Leadership Conference conducts Student Workshops and Seminars in the philosophy and technique of non-violent resistance.

Again and again the Southern violators have answered Dr. King's peaceful protests with intimidation and violence. They have bombed his home almost killing his wife and child. They have assaulted his person. They have arrested him seven times—for "speeding," "loitering" and similar "offenses." And now they have charged him with "perjury"—a felony under which they could imprison him for ten years. Obviously, their real purpose is to remove him physically as the leader to whom the students and millions of others—look for guidance and support, and thereby to intimidate all leaders who may rise in the South. Their strategy is to behead this affirmative movement, and thus to demoralize Negro Americans and weaken their will to struggle. The defense of Martin Luther King, spiritual leader of the student sit-in movement, clearly, therefore, is an integral part of the total struggle for freedom in the South.

Decent-minded Americans cannot help but applaud the creative daring of the students and the quiet heroism of Dr. King. But this is one of those moments in the stormy history of Freedom when men and women of good will must do more than applaud the rising-to-glory of others. The America whose good name hangs in the balance before a watchful world, the America whose heritage of Liberty these Southern Upholders of the Constitution are defending, is our America as well as theirs . . .

We must heed their rising voices—yes—but we must add our own.

We must extend ourselves above and beyond moral support and render the material help so urgently needed by those who are taking the risks, facing jail, and even death in a glorious re-affirmation of our Constitution and its Bill of Rights.

We urge you to join hands with our fellow Americans in the South by supporting, with your dollars, this Combined Appeal for all three needs—the defense of Martin Luther King—the support of the embattled students—and the struggle for the right-to-vote.

Your Help Is Urgently Needed . . . NOW!!

Stella Adler
Raymond Pace Alexander
Harry Van Arsdale
Harry Belafonte
Julie Belafonte
Dr. Algernon Black
Marc Blitzstein
William Branch
Marlon Brando
Mrs. Ralph Bunche
Diahann Carroll

Dr. Alan Knight Chalmers
Richard Coe
Nat King Cole
Cheryl Crawford
Dorothy Dandridge
Ossie Davis
Sammy Davis, Jr.
Ruby Dee
Dr. Philip Elliott
Dr. Harry Emerson Fosdick

Anthony Franciosa
Lorraine Hansbury
Rev. Donald Harrington
Nat Hentoff
James Hicks
Mary Hinkson
Van Heflin
Langston Hughes
Morris Iushewitz
Mahalia Jackson
Mordecai Johnson

John Killens
Eartha Kitt
Rabbi Edward Klein
Hope Lange
John Lewis
Viveca Lindfors
Carl Murphy
Don Murray
John Murray
A. J. Muste
Frederick O'Neal

L. Joseph Overton
Clarence Pickett
Shad Polier
Sidney Poitier
A. Philip Randolph
John Raitt
Elmer Rice
Jackie Robinson
Mrs. Eleanor Roosevelt
Bayard Rustin
Robert Ryan

Maureen Stapleton
Frank Silvera
Hope Stevens
George Tabori
Rev. Gardner C. Taylor
Norman Thomas
Kenneth Tynan
Charles White
Shelley Winters
Max Youngstein

We in the south who are struggling daily for dignity and freedom warmly endorse this appeal

Rev. Ralph D. Abernathy
(Montgomery, Ala.)

Rev. Fred L. Shuttlesworth
(Birmingham, Ala.)

Rev. Kelley Miller Smith
(Nashville, Tenn.)

Rev. W. A. Dennis
(Chattanooga, Tenn.)

Rev. C. K. Steele
(Tallahassee, Fla.)

Rev. Matthew D. McCollum
(Orangeburg, S. C.)

Rev. William Holmes Borders
(Atlanta, Ga.)

Rev. Douglas Moore
(Durham, N. C.)

Rev. Wyatt Tee Walker
(Petersburg, Va.)

Rev. Walter L. Hamilton
(Norfolk, Va.)

I. S. Levy
(Columbia, S. C.)

Rev. Martin Luther King, Sr.
(Atlanta, Ga.)

Rev. Henry C. Bunton
(Memphis, Tenn.)

Rev. S. S. Seay, Sr.
(Montgomery, Ala.)

Rev. Samuel W. Williams
(Atlanta, Ga.)

Rev. A. L. Davis
(New Orleans, La.)

Mrs. Katie E. Whickham
(New Orleans, La.)

Rev. W. H. Hall
(Hattiesburg, Miss.)

Rev. J. E. Lowery
(Mobile, Ala.)

Rev. T. J. Jemison
(Baton Rouge, La.)

COMMITTEE TO DEFEND MARTIN LUTHER KING AND THE STRUGGLE FOR FREEDOM IN THE SOUTH

312 West 125th Street, New York 27, N. Y. UNiversity 6-1700

Chairmen: A. Philip Randolph, Dr. Gardner C. Taylor; *Chairmen of Cultural Division:* Harry Belafonte, Sidney Poitier; *Treasurer:* Nat King Cole; *Executive Director:* Bayard Rustin; *Chairmen of Church Division:* Father George B. Ford, Rev. Harry Emerson Fosdick, Rev. Thomas Kilgore, Jr., Rabbi Edward E. Klein; *Chairmen of Labor Division:* Morris Iushewitz

Please mail this coupon TODAY!

Committee To Defend Martin Luther King
and
The Struggle For Freedom In The South

312 West 125th Street, New York 27, N. Y.
UNiversity 6-1700

I am enclosing my contribution of $ _____
for the work of the Committee.

(PLEASE PRINT)

_____

_____

☐ I want to help   ☐ Please send further information

Please make checks payable to:
Committee To Defend Martin Luther King

well as a monopoly of influence is there a real possibility of the robotized public. In a democratic society with its freedom of thought and speech advertising may be at times a blessing and at others a nuisance but it can never be a menace to the free man.[19]

Mr. Dollard was referring primarily to the freedom to speak about one's products and commercial services. Perhaps even more basic from a social viewpoint in a democracy is the availability of advertising as a medium for distributing the thoughts and ideas of individuals and groups who wish to "speak" to the multitudes—ideas that have no direct commercial implications.

The famous "Heed Their Rising Voices" advertisement (Figure 3–1) that ran in the *New York Times,* March 29, 1960, illustrates this point. Here a group of serious people wanted to get a message before a large audience and chose an advertisement as the method to do so. The message criticized public officials and brought violent reaction from some officials who sued the *Times* and the advertisers for libel.

Had this same message been delivered by a speaker from a public platform or presented as an editorial by the newspaper, it is likely that no action would have been taken. The plaintiff, however, argued that because the message appeared as a paid advertisement, it did not have the protection of the guarantee of freedom of speech and press in the Constitution.

The U.S. Supreme Court in the *New York Times Co.* v. *Sullivan* decision (March 10, 1964) denied the plaintiff's claim. It held that "any other conclusion would discourage newspapers from carrying 'editorial advertisements' of this type, and so might shut off an important outlet for the promulgation of information and ideas by persons who do not themselves have access to publishing facilities—who wish to exercise their freedom of speech even though they are not members of the press."[20]

Additional attention to this aspect of advertising is given in Chapter 6. Certainly the development of editorial advertising has great social significance.

SOCIAL INFLUENCE

Historian David Potter, in his book *People of Plenty,* observed that "advertising now compares with such long-standing institutions as the school and the church in the magnitude of its social influence." He says "it dominates the media, has vast power in the shaping of popular standards, and is really one of the very limited group of institutions which

---

[19] John Dollard, "Fear of Advertising," in C. H. Sandage and Vernon Fryburger, *The Role of Advertising,* (Homewood, Ill.: Richard D. Irwin, 1960), p. 317.

[20] *New York Times Co.* v. *Sullivan* 376 U.S. 254 (1964).

exercise social control."[21] Mr. Potter concludes that advertising, unlike the school and the church, makes people like what they get, diminishes the range and variety of choices, and "exalts the materialistic virtues of consumption." Other observers subscribing to this "powerful force" theory claim that advertising distorts human values, that it makes people want the wrong things (too much beer, liquor, and cigarettes; not enough schools, antipollution controls, and urban renewals), that it promotes private luxuries at the expense of public squalor, that it creates discontent by making people dissatisfied with what they have or by making them wish for things beyond their reach, and that it contributes to waste by encouraging people to discard clothing, appliances, automobiles, and the like before they are worn out.

Observers holding these views of social influence are making various assumptions about the power of advertising, about the wisdom of people, and about the importance of the individual. They assume that the power of advertising is so great it can get people to do what they don't want to do—that people are not capable of making choices in their own self-interest. They assume that individual free choice should be superseded by authoritarian control.

The power of advertising is not that great. The audience's predispositions, their attitudes, beliefs, motives, and values largely determine the media they select, the advertisements they see, the messages they accept, and the products they buy. Instead of forcing a response, advertising elicits responses the audience was predisposed to make. Advertising succeeds when it gives people what they want. Consumer responses in the marketplace are free and voluntary. *Caveat emptor* (let the buyer beware) has given way to *caveat venditor* (let the seller beware).

Evidence that consumers are competent to advance social welfare while functioning as consumers is abundant. Individual efforts to advance one's standard of living helps expand the economy which, in turn, provides the financial support for government programs. As voters in a democratic society, consumers voluntarily support social welfare legislation and foreign-aid programs. As taxpayers they pay the society's bills. Advertising communicates a wide range of choices and facilitates the selection process. Much as a democratic society depends on an informed electorate, a free market system depends on informed consumers.

If consumers are not competent to choose wisely, who is? Can any one person decide better than consumers themselves what best serves their interest? In view of the great diversity of tastes, preferences, life styles, means of self-expression, and measures of success, should anyone be empowered to impose his choices on others? A free market system assumes that everybody allocates resources better than anybody.

---

[21] David Potter, *People of Plenty* (Chicago: University of Chicago Press, 1954), Chap. 8.

Advertising does educe dissatisfaction, but ordinarily it does so by holding forth the benefits of superior products. Changing from less satisfying to more satisfying products should result in a net gain. Again, it should be noted that expanding consumption is essential to an expanding economy. Insofar as advertising stimulates greater consumption, sells a higher standard of living, or promotes an improved quality of life, it contributes to social progress.

Advertising is now being used more frequently to meet social problems head-on, as evidenced by the Advertising Council's campaigns dealing with drug abuse, crime prevention, rehabilitation of the handicapped, continuing education, and traffic safety. The advertisers, agencies, and media who finance these campaigns recognize the potential of advertising for influencing the conscience of society as well as the spending of consumers.

QUESTIONS AND PROBLEMS

1 Review the advertising of oil companies and electric utilities in the middle 70s. Do you believe that such advertising had an influence on the allocation of more resources to the exploration for oil and the installation of more nuclear generating plants? Explain.

2 Discuss the part advertising might play in stimulating the development of power-saving appliances and hastening their acceptance by consumers.

3 Assume that changes in the "way of life" in the United States significantly reduces dependence on the private passenger automobile for long-distance vacation travel. How do you think this should influence the character of advertising by motels?

4 Advertising in an affluent society is desirable because it encourages people to want products and services they do not really need. Do you agree? Why?

5 Advertising makes people choose the wrong things—too much beer, liquor, and cigarettes; not enough schools, urban renewals, and foreign aid. Do you agree or disagree? Why?

6 "Since manufacturers that advertise could sell their products for less if they did not spend so much on advertising, the consumer will usually get better value for his money in unadvertised brands of products than in advertised brands." Do you agree? Why?

7 Advertising gives a competitive advantage to "big business" because big advertisers can win a larger share of the public mind than smaller advertisers. Do you agree or disagree? Explain.

8 Borden says: "Advertising's outstanding contribution to consumer welfare comes from its part in promoting a dynamic, expanding economy." Explain.

9 In a free market system the producers of goods and services allocate the nation's economic resources. Do you agree or disagree? Why?

10 Assuming that a product has qualities that will meet consumer needs, how does advertising enhance its value?

11 A young business firm has developed a product that it thinks is superior to a heavily advertised product already well established in the market. To what extent is advertising a barrier to the young firm attempting to enter the market with its new product?

12 Comment on the following statement: "Freedom of speech in modern America is largely a hollow freedom unless those who wish to speak have available modern facilities for distributing their speech to the masses." Is advertising one of the "modern distribution facilities" for free speech?

13 To what extent might a manufacturing firm be able to use advertising to build a monopoly for its product?

14 Democracies point with pride to their freedom of the press. Do advertisers threaten this freedom? Explain.

4

Advertising as communication

In a complex economy such as that in the United States, it is essential to have some system of mass communication between producers and consumers. This was not so essential before our great industrial development with its concentration of production facilities and wide dispersion of consumers. It was not too many years ago that production was highly localized, and producers depended largely on consumers who lived close by to take their products. Under such circumstances face-to-face and word-of-mouth communication was generally sufficient to inform consumers of what goods were available to them. Furthermore, there was a relative scarcity of production, and it was largely confined to meeting the basic physiological needs of people. The variety of choices available to consumers was minimal. With need as a motivating force consumers would exert extra effort to seek out sources of supply, thus diminishing the necessity for producer-originated information about their commodities.

Today, consumers are highly mobile. They move from one to another part of the country with significant frequency. Producers do not limit their market to people living in the immediate vicinity of their farms or factories but consider the entire nation and much of the world as their market. Also in the United States, and to an increasing degree in other countries, production is plentiful, and the variety of choices available to consumers is great.

With specialization and centralization in production, with dispersion of consumers, and with great abundance of supply, it is imperative that some kind of formalized machinery be available to provide effective mass communication between producers and consumers. Advertising performs this role in modern society in both capitalist and communist countries. In speaking of advertising in Russia, D. Kurnin said, "Thanks to well-organized advertising, the consumer can more rapidly find the goods needed by him, purchase them with a smaller expenditure of time, and select the goods according to his particular taste."[1]

What to communicate

In general, the communication function of advertising should serve to assist consumers in their search for goods and services and to satisfy their needs and wants. In short, it should be a guide to buying. Communication, to be helpful to consumers in guiding them in their search for satisfaction, should be informative, educational, and persuasive. It should tell consumers of (1) the existence of want-satisfying products and services; (2) where they can be obtained; and (3) the qualities possessed, expressed in terms that will enable the consumer to make an intelligent choice. It should be educational in the sense that it not only increases consumer knowledge but also enhances judgment in the process of reaching a buying decision. It should be sufficiently persuasive to move people to try the new and to test their inherent skepticism.

Notice of existence and where available

When we consider products in a generic sense, advertising in America has served and is now serving many of the functions of a buyer's guide. Such advertising has acquainted consumers with the existence and general utility of electric refrigerators, radios, telephones, television sets, and so on through practically every item of human consumption.

It lets people know of the existence of organizations that render service to people who need or want family counseling, help with alcohol or drug problems, protection of civil rights, or aid for dependent children. It tells people of the existence of art galleries, music festivals, symphony concerts, havens of rest and relaxation, physical fitness centers, and religious services.

The need for informing consumers of the existence of new products and services is especially acute in an affluent society where discretionary purchasing power is high. In such a society consumers have the leisure and money to provide themselves with things that will satisfy wants as well as needs if such things are available.

[1] D. Kurnin, "Iz Opyta Sovetskoi Torgovloi Reklamy," *Sovetskaia Torgovlia,* February 1958, p.46.

Consumers cannot be expected to seek out luxury and semiluxury items that manufacturers have just made available. Each year sees the introduction of many new consumer items in the American and international markets. Out of the several hundred consumer products currently made by one of America's large manufacturers, 50 percent of them were not even in existence in 1960.

Consumers may leaf through the advertising pages of almost any magazine and learn something about more products (new and old) than would generally be possible from visits to scores of manufacturing plants. Figure 4–1 is an example of one of the many ads that could be found in general magazines.

Advertisements in specialized business and professional publications are regularly checked by purchasing agents and others to note announcements of new products and pertinent information about old ones. An example of such a guiding help to prospective buyers is shown in Figure 4–2.

Advertisements in local newspapers serve consumers as guides to retail outlets, cultural facilities, service establishments, and professional offices where new as well as familiar products and services can be obtained. Another type of advertising that provides a guide to consumers in this respect is the familiar classified section of the telephone book. Figure 4–3 shows this type of guide provided through advertising.

The need for some kind of guide to bring buyers and sellers together was recognized by Montaigne more than three centuries ago. He wrote:

> In every town I would like to see established an official with a great register. On one side would be inscribed all those things which their owners desired to sell: a pearl necklace, a horse, a house; on the other side of the register a list of all those things sought by those desiring to purchase: this burgher, it may be, needing a horse, that one a house. And it would be the duty of this official to make known the existence of the two parties, the one to the other. Too often it happens that the man wanting the horse does not know of the horse for sale, or vice versa, and both are the losers by this ignorance.

The nearest approach today to such a register is the want-advertisement sections of our modern newspapers. Here we do have the seller listing his wares and the buyer listing his wants.

During the time of Montaigne, the supply of goods for consumers was quite meager, and buyers often found it necessary to seek out suppliers rather than to wait until sellers came to them. The "register" or "want-ad" kind of advertising was then, as now, initiated by the buyer as well as by the seller (see Figure 4–4).

The general supply of goods today is such that sellers initiate most of the advertising and do so for purposes of guiding consumers toward their

FIGURE 4–1
Consumers are informed of the new through ads like this

The SX-70:
why and when.

Perhaps once or twice in a lifetime, there comes an invention so radically new, it actually changes the way we live our lives.

Television was one.

We at Polaroid believe the SX-70 is another.

The virtual cascade of revolutions, mechanical, chemical, optical and electronic, that made the SX-70 possible had only one purpose: to free you from everything cumbersome and tedious about picture-taking, so that it could become at last, the simple creative act it should be.

Now that all you need to do is frame your picture, bring it into perfect focus and push a button, now that the picture is automatically delivered into your hand in less than two seconds, to time itself and develop into a photograph of a depth and brilliance unparalleled in amateur photography, what might once have seemed like a family duty or even just an interesting hobby, can become a spontaneous and constant pleasure in your daily life.

The SX-70, with a suggested list price of $180, is available now in limited quantity at your Polaroid Land camera dealer. We are increasing the supply as quickly as possible. Meanwhile, visit your dealer now to see a demonstration and to place an order for your own SX-70.

The SX-70 camera with optional leather carrying case.

Polaroid ®

Keep paper rolls round and presses rolling
with new Clark vacuum clamps

When your customer has to shut down a high-speed press because of creasing or ovality of newsprint rolls, you're in trouble. Clark paper handling experience keeps you out of trouble.

"Our new Clarklift® with Vacuum Newsprint Roll Handler substantially reduces paper damage and roll distortion—major causes of web tearing," says Ken Daniels, Pressroom Foreman of one of the nation's newest, most modern printing plants, the Binghamton, N.Y., Evening Press.

Here's how the Clark vacuum clamp works. Vacuum power forces the paper roll against gripper pads. Shear reducing strips, plus a vacuum seal on the outer edges of the pad, provide a secure, fast pick-up. Fail-safe indicator lights and a reserve tank provide a hold period in case of vehicle power failure.

The Vacuum Roll Handler permits rapid breakout of rolls for unloading, eliminating gouging by completely eliminating manhandling of key rolls. And since you don't have to leave room for hydraulic clamp arms, you save 15% floor space by touch stacking.

To help make sure your newsprint rolls arrive in top condition, start them on their way with a Clark Vacuum Roll Handler. For a demonstration, call your local Clark dealer listed in the Yellow Pages under "Trucks, Industrial."

Clark *is* material handling

Battle Creek, Michigan 49016

FIGURE 4–2. Information helpful to industrial buyers

FIGURE 4–3
A familiar guide for buyers

Air Conditioning Equipment & Systems
(Continued)

CARRIER AIR CONDITIONING

From Room & Whole House Air Conditioning To The Largest Units Required For Commercial And Industrial Application. Specify CARRIER — The World's Largest Manufacturer Of Air Conditioning Equipment.

Carrier
NUMBER 1
AIR CONDITIONING MAKER

"FOR INFORMATION CALL"
DEALERS

Air Comfort Corp 1845 W 37th Av
  Gary Ind -------ChgoTelNo 768-6060
Chicagoland Heating & Air Condtg
  146 E 154th Harvy---------333-2217
Hoekstra Heating Company
  17853 Dixie Hwy Hornewd----798-3444
R M C Inc 321 E Grand Chgo-----321-1333
Service Town Refrigeration Corp
  Factory Authorized Sales & Service
  1911 S Halstd Chgo Hts-----747-4600
Suburban Heating Co
  3017 Jacksn S Chgo Hts-----755-5650
DISTRIBUTOR
Temperature Equipment Corp
  2000 Ruby Melros Pk--------681-6220

COMFORT-AIRE CENTRAL AIR CONDITIONING SYSTEMS—
DISTRIBUTOR
TEECO
  169th & VanDam Rd S Holnd-596-1212
DEALER
J & J REFRIGERATION
  14927 Lincln Doltn-------841-1749

Consolidated Refrigeration Inc
  1226 Halstd Chgo Hts---------SK 4-0290
  (See Advertisement This Classification)
COOL-RITE 17025 Crane Hzl Crst----335-3400
  (See Advertisement This Classification)
DE NOVI A REFRIGERATION HEATING & AIR CONDTG
  14611 Waverly Midlthn--------388-4000
DOC'S TIN SHOP 15032 Page Harvy--331-6484
DUANE HEATING & COOLING
  9806 SWHwy Oak Lwn-------424-6663
DUNHAM-BUSH RESIDENTIAL AND UNITARY AIR CONDITIONING—
DEALER
AIR-RITE HEATING & COOLING INC
  13443 S Cicero
  Crstwd - -----RivrdlTelNo 849-4848

FEDDERS CENTRAL AIR CONDITIONING & HEATING—
ALLEN'S HEATING & COOLING
  10050 S Ewing Chgo------ES 5-9843
LANSING HOME MAINTENANCE & HEATING SERVICE
  17839 Torrence Lansng-----474-2243
CONTINUED NEXT COLUMN

Air Conditioning Equipment & Systems
(Continued)

FEDDERS CENTRAL AIR CONDITIONING & HEATING—
CONTINUED FROM PRECEDING COLUMN
VAN DRUNEN HEATING & AIR CONDTG
  168th & VanDam Rd
  S Holnd ----------------339-6444
SERVICE
SERVICE TOWN REFRIGERATION CORP
  1911 S Halstd Chgo Hts---747-4600

FRIGIDAIRE ROOM AIR CONDITIONERS—
AUTHORIZED SALES & SERVICE
SERVICE TOWN REFRIGERATION CORP
  Factory Auth Sales Service & Parts
  1911 S Halstd Chgo Hts---747-4600

GEORGE'S FURNACE & SHEET METAL SHOP
  85 E 154th St Harvy-----------331-7543
  (See Advertisement This Classification)
GENERAL ELECTRIC CENTRAL AIR CONDITIONING

Air Conditioning for new homes or to add to present heating system, including Weathertron® Heat Pumps & Electronic Air Cleaners. Also industrial units.

"WHERE TO CALL"
DEALER
Spiekhout Heating
  536 E 162 S Holnd---------331-7305
Suburban Electric
  18717 Dixie Hwy Homewd----798-0909

GIBSON AIR CONDITIONERS—
SERVICE
CROSS TOWN REFRIGERATION CORP
  800 DesPlaines For Pk-----771-4800

GREAT LAKES COOLING & HEATING INC
  7345 Calumet Av Hamnd Ind 219 932-8800
  616 W 11th Gary Ind-ChgoTelNo 374-2382
  (See Advertisement This Classification)
GUARANTEE HEATING & SHT METAL

| 24 HOUR SERV | AIR CONDITIONING
Fedders - Bryant - Bard |

International-Air-Ease-Mueller Climatrol
Roof Top Heating & Cooling
Custom Fabricated Ducts
Repairs - Parts - Conversions - Installations
Electronic Air Cleaners
Repairs On All Makes & Models
TO 2-8040
591 Burnham Ave   Calumet City

FIGURE 4–4
A modern Montaigne register that brings buyers and sellers together

wares. There are still, however, many consumers who place their own ads when they want to buy a piece of furniture, an automobile, or an appliance. The same is often true for people who are seeking employment or a place to live.

Guides to want-satisfying qualities

Another element in communication to guide consumers in their search for satisfaction of their needs and wants is that of telling them the qualities possessed by products and services in terms that will help them make an intelligent choice. The problem of decision making is not an easy one to solve in our highly competitive economy that offers a great variety of brands within any given generic classification of products. If only one supplier existed for each generic product, decision making would be relatively easy; but if such were the case, consumer freedom of choice would be greatly reduced.

The concept of freedom to choose from among the many brands of commodities available is a freedom that consumers generally wish to preserve—even though it involves making comparisons among vast numbers of brands. That there are vast numbers is well illustrated by data presented annually by the *Milwaukee Journal* for the greater Milwaukee market. In its 1973 report[2] the *Journal* included only those brands that were purchased by 2 percent or more of all buyers of the product in a 30-day period. A partial list of products and the number of brands reported include: pipe tobacco, 15; regular coffee, 13; canned tuna fish, 7; fresh milk, 12; laundry soap, 19; shampoo, 16; deodorant, 15; low-calorie soft drinks, 12; butter, 12; margarine, 20; and white bread, 15.

The consumer is generally benefited by having a number of producers competing for his (her) business. But when the number of brands available becomes great, the consumer is often bewildered and confused. It is here that the advertiser needs to give maximum attention to detailed description and meaningful exposition of the want-satisfying qualities of his particular brand. The consumer wants intelligent guidance. To receive intelligent guidance through advertising, individual ads must be abundantly informative.

Complete presentation

Unless an advertisement contains statements that are true, it cannot serve as a real guide to consumer purchases. Untruthful advertisements would establish false direction posts to lead the consumer astray. Truth is necessary not only for the individual advertiser but for the great bulk

[2] *Consumer Analysis* (Milwaukee, Wis.: *Milwaukee Journal,* 1973).

of advertising. Consumers wish to compare one brand with another; hence, it is quite vital that each producer be honest in presenting the merits of his particular brand. The presence of only a few false prophets makes it practically impossible for the consumer to distinguish the true from the false.

To be an effective guide, truth must be interpreted to mean the inclusion of all quality factors that would have a bearing on the ability of the product to meet the needs and wants of consumers. This means that some characteristics of the product which might appear to be negative in character should be mentioned. If a particular brand of canned peas is grade C in quality, that might be a factor of importance to the consumer, and if so, it should be mentioned in the advertisement. That brand would undoubtedly have a lower price, too, than a brand that was grade A quality. If the consumer is told both the grade and the price, a more intelligent decision can be made than if only one factor is presented.

In considering the element of complete presentation, one must recognize that completeness usually cannot be achieved in one advertisement or commercial announcement. The concept of completeness must encompass a series of advertisements, including not only those in the mass media but also direct mail, package inserts, and dealer-distributed brochures. The significant point is that through the institution of advertising, consumers can be helped in their understanding of products and services and the benefits to be derived from them.

While advertising can help to increase consumer understanding, it can also mislead or develop confusion if information is inaccurate or incomplete in matters of product quality. Government agencies have recognized this, as noted earlier, requiring a "warning" statement on cigarette packages and "corrective" advertising by those who have made incomplete or inaccurate presentations of product qualities.

Adequate information

The information in advertisements must be adequate to meet the needs of those who seek guidance in their purchasing problems. Contrast the two advertisements reproduced in Figures 4–5 and 4–6. Both are truthful, but one is full of information that should help the consumer evaluate the product and make a choice while the other tells the consumer very little that would contribute to decision making.

It is easier to provide adequate information in advertisements for consumer guidance if there is a "language" or vocabulary of terms having precise meaning applicable to the field or product being advertised. There are many areas where words do have precise meaning and aid the process of communication. Analyze, for example, the copy in the ad reproduced in Figure 4–7 to evaluate the extent to which a prospective buyer of a

FIGURE 4–5
An inadequate guide to buying

ONE PAINT FOR *5* EXTERIOR SURFACES

PENTAFLEX
FLAT EXTERIOR PAINT

- For shakes—wood shingles—
clapboard and trim—
—asbestos shingles—
stucco, brick, cement.

SEE YOUR BENJAMIN MOORE PAINT DEALER
FOR THE BEST IN PRODUCTS AND SERVICE

FIGURE 4–6
A helpful guide for the consumer

FIGURE 4–7
Effective use of terms to provide measure of hidden qualities

roll-paper color printer might judge its quality and capacity on a rather exact basis. Various types of controls can be compared on the basis of power—in terms of watts—and resistance—in terms of ohms. Should the prospective buyer wish to compare the Allen-Bradley printer with another make, there would be no difficulty in making exact comparisons in respect to power and resistance.

In the industrial-goods field, terms having exact qualitative meaning are commonly used in advertisements to describe the product and guide the buyer. A milling machine may be described as being capable of machining a bearing with a tolerance of 0.0005 inches. The noise level of a ballast for a fluorescent light may be rated in terms of so many decibels. The pressure capacity of a compressed air tank can be given in pounds per square inch.

Such terms are not the creation of advertising persons, but their existence helps the advertiser in performing his function of interpreting the qualities of want or need satisfaction embodied in the product to be advertised. Their use helps the buyer to evaluate the product and compare it with other makes before a purchase is consummated.

Physical standards for consumer goods

In the field of consumer goods many terms with precise meaning also exist and can be used by advertisers for providing qualitative information. Many weights and measures have standard meanings. A foot is 12 inches long, and a gallon is equivalent to four quarts. A size 16 dress, however, is not always the same for all manufacturers of garments.

An advertisement for a dress manufacturer which says that his brand of dresses are cut "extra" full would not provide a particularly helpful guide to buyers. Would a size 16 dress in that brand be equivalent to a size 18 of a competing brand? Such confusion and difficulty in making qualitative comparisons make for confusion and difficulty in buying.

Terms such as "colossal" to designate size and "super quality" to describe grade do not contribute to ease of understanding or of comparison among brands. Such use complicates the problems of free exchange. That is why our commodity exchanges have established quality standards with precise meaning for such commodities as wheat, corn, lard, butter, cotton, and coffee.

Perhaps manufacturers themselves could make their communication task easier by giving somewhat greater attention in the future than they have in the past to the development of terminology having easily defined meaning when applied to certain characteristics of their products. Such terminology or standardization of terms would be limited to physical qualities of a product, and they should be applicable to all units within a given industry. Considerable progress has been made in this direction. Examples would include the "approved" stamps or labels on gas and electrical appliances and precise meanings attached to "mahogany" furniture and "Sanforized" garments.

INFORMATION ON PRODUCT LABELS

In respect to food products, consumers are increasingly concerned with calories, vitamins, minerals, polyunsaturated and saturated fats, protein,

FIGURE 4–8
Detailed information can be persuasive, too

Borden cuts cheese calories in half

New LiteLine slices give you half the calories, yet more protein.

LiteLine is our new Pasteurized Process Cheese Product that tastes like the best Process American Cheese, <u>provides good sensible nutrition,</u> but has only half the calories.

LiteLine is made from Skim Milk and American Cheeses, so you get that good cheese taste the whole family loves. Yet you get substantially less fat. And an <u>extra</u> supply of protein.

The nutritional chart below compares LiteLine to other cheese slices. Note the low calorie count and higher protein content of LiteLine.

Per Slice (Average wt. 21 grms)	LiteLine (12 oz., 16 slice size)	Process American Cheese	Process Cheese Food
Calories	39	78	66
Milk Fat %	8	30	23
Protein %	26	23	20
Carbohydrates %	2	2	7
Ash %	6	5	6
Moisture %	58	40	44

LiteLine slices cost a little more, but isn't this kind of modern nutrition worth it?

carbohydrates, and other nutritional factors. The number of food processors that include nutritional information on their product labels is significant, but the U.S. Food and Drug Administration exerts pressure and persuasion to increase the number. Following is a summary of significant parts of a nutritional labeling program instituted by the FDA in the mid-70s:

> Whenever a food is labeled with nutrition information, the label must follow this standard format:
> 1. Serving size
> 2. Servings per container
> 3. Caloric content or calories
> 4. Protein content or protein
> 5. Carbohydrate content or carbohydrates
> 6. Fat content or fat
> 7. Percentage of U.S. Recommended Daily Allowances (of vital nutrients)[3]

The FDA explains in its information directed to food processors that "nutrition labeling is voluntary for most foods. However, if a nutrient is added to any product, even to replace those lost in processing, or if a nutritional claim is made for the food in the labeling or in an advertisement, that product's label must have full nutritional labeling."[4]

Regardless of whether there is government pressure or regulation in respect to providing more information to consumers, it is good business and advertising practice to give the kind and amount of information that will aid consumers in their buying. This can often be the most persuasive element in a company's advertising. Note the use of detailed information, combined with an appropriate illustration, in Figure 4–8.

Hidden psychological qualities

Not all communication about products should be devoted to giving information about their physical or chemical properties. Many items are purchased or sought to provide psychological values. It was noted in an earlier chapter that advertising can add value or utility to a product in a number of ways. One way is to extract from the product hidden psychological values that are not apparent from a consideration of its physical properties. The satisfaction many men get from wearing a Hathaway shirt is the feeling of being well dressed. They could "get by" with a brand having less prestige. They could even buy one that would wear longer and cost considerably less, but would not receive from it the psychological lift afforded by a Hathaway. This factor is emphasized in the Sears advertisement reproduced in Figure 4–9. Truly, some of the satisfaction received from many products is the feeling of self-confidence they impart.

Perfume for the lady could be advertised in terms of its chemical com-

[3] Publication No. (FDA) 73–2036 (Washington, D.C. 1973), p.1.
[4] Ibid.

FIGURE 4–9
Satisfaction comes from both feeling and being well dressed

FIGURE 4–10
Beauty is in the eye of the beholder

Sea Horse and bowl—both by Steuben

STEUBEN piques your decorative urge with this unusual centerpiece. Use it to create arrangements to your heart's content. The crystal Sea Horse can frolic in a foam of flowers, an ocean of fruit, or a sea of mints.

Or you can free the Sea Horse to go elsewhere while you use the bowl alone. Bowl, diameter 12 inches, $80. Sea Horse, 9 inches tall, $100.

Made at the Corning Glass Center, Corning, New York.

STEUBEN GLASS

FIFTH AVENUE AT 56th STREET · NEW YORK 22, N.Y.

position, its evaporation factor, and its low price, but these are not the basic elements for which women choose their perfume. Instead, they are seeking some hidden factor that will make them feel accepted and permit them to live on "cloud nine" even if only for a short time.

Study carefully the advertisement for Steuben Glass reproduced in Figure 4–10. Physical properties of glass are, of course, important to the buyer, but the buyer of glass for decorative purposes is more concerned with what the product will do for her "frame of mind" than with such elements as durability, specific gravity, weight, or fusion point. Primary values sought are psychological, and the advertiser has a responsibility to help guide the consumer in her search for psychological satisfaction.

Many more examples could be presented to emphasize the nonphysical qualities of a product that contribute to human satisfaction. If advertising is to serve as a guide to buying, it cannot ignore this aspect of consumer desire. It is therefore not only proper but also vital in a consumer-oriented economy to use advertising to communicate the psychological as well as the physical properties of products to prospective buyers.

The road map concept

Advertising as a communication aid to buying is somewhat like a road map, supplemented with a tour book with perhaps minimum, but significant, information about places or items of interest. In the case of the traveler seeking a vacation spot, he may not know exactly where he wants to go or what specific places he would like to see. He can, however, spread his map before him and note the great variety of opportunities available to him. He will find the names and locations of cities, mountains, resort areas, lakes, deserts, and national monuments. He will find detailed guides as to roads to take and the cost in time and miles to get to the various places available to him.

Our traveler may have little interest in certain kinds of places and will quickly reject them. For those places that remain on his list, more detailed information may be needed before a choice is made. For this he may turn to his tour books to learn what each of several places has to offer. He eventually makes a specific decision and sets forth on his journey confident that his map will guide him to the place of his choice.

Advertising provides service of much the same kind to persons seeking goods or services to satisfy a need or want. Newspapers and magazines, television and radio, direct mail, and outdoor posters carry the road maps that list the products that are available for purchase, give some information about each product, and directions as to where to go to get them. "Tour guides" in the form of booklets, folders, and package inserts are available from product manufacturers to those who wish more detailed information about specific products.

Who should initiate communication?

In capitalist, free enterprise countries the major responsibility for preparing product "road maps" and "tour guides" has been assumed by the manufacturer or seller. In other countries the state performs this service.

Some have questioned the wisdom of depending largely on sellers to provide consumers with product information. Sellers are obviously biased. They wish always to present their products in the best possible light. They cannot be wholly objective or impartial.

Professor Nicholas Kaldor, an English economist, has stated that "impartial and unbiased information could only be provided if the writers of 'advertisements' were financially independent of the products advertised."[5]

As yet no independent source of product information is available on a broad scale. There are organizations such as Consumers Union and Consumer Research that provide independent information infrequently on a minimum of products. These organizations are financed by consumers and hence should be impartial. Some product information is also provided by the press, but this is relatively meager.

There is, however, a growing recognition that the professional advertising man is more and more assuming the role of impartial and unbiased communicator of product information. As will be seen in a later chapter, the advertising agency is now at least partially financially independent of the seller in that much of its compensation comes from the media. But even if this were not true, the truly professional advertising man will not falsify product qualities or knowingly mislead the consumer. He is more and more recognizing his responsibility to serve as a helpful guide to consumers in their quest for products and services to satisfy needs and wants.

The protection of competition

The force of competition provides consumers with significant protection against false guides. In an economy of abundance the power of the consumer becomes extremely evident and meaningful. Manufacturers vie with each other to produce goods with a maximum of want-satisfying qualities per dollar of cost. In many respects they become self-appointed employees of consumers. As such they recognize the necessity of keeping their master informed of what is available and the various qualities possessed by such products. They also feel obliged to point out directly or indirectly how their products compare with or differ from those of competitors. The famous "We Are Number Two" campaign of the Avis au-

[5] Nicholas Kaldor, "The Economic Aspects of Advertising," *The Review of Economic Studies,* Vol. 18 (1), No. 45 (1949–50), p. 6.

tomobile rental company forced a mental comparison with Hertz, the number one company in that field.

There are times, too, when a given company has competing products offered under different brand names or the same brand with different quality and price classes. Qualitative information supplied through advertisements of such competitive items can be helpful to consumers in making their buying decisions.

Consumer education

In many respects the communication function of advertising contributes substantially to education in consumption. This is vital in a society where consumers enjoy great freedom in choosing what to buy and where the level of discretionary buying power is high.

We have already seen how such communication provides consumers with knowledge of the existence and qualities of goods and services. Education, however, must go deeper than that—it must be concerned with the development of judgment on the part of consumers. Advertising should not be called upon to assume the full responsibility for educating consumers at the judgment level, but this is one of its significant roles.

In a free society high emphasis is placed on human dignity and the right of the individual to make his own decisions. There are, of course, people who suffer through making wrong decisions in their buying. The philosophy underlying freedom, however, is not to take freedom away from those who make errors in judgment but rather to educate them in the effective exercise of their freedom.

Perhaps this concept of the educational function of advertising can be clarified with an illustration and a comparison. There are many advertisers of many kinds of products and services competing for the patronage of consumers. Each advertiser presents his case with conviction and hopes it will be accepted. Descriptive materials and persuasive literature are made available to consumers for review and analysis. One group of advertisers provides material that extolls the merits of investing in stocks, bonds, savings and loan associations, or insurance companies. These messages emphasize the values of postponing consumption in order to have greater consumption rewards in the future.

Opposed to the idea of current saving are advertisements that present the merits of spending now for such things as a trip to Europe, a new home, a second automobile, a pleasure boat, or a new lawn mower. These opposing views will create conflicts in the minds of consumers. It is through such conflicts that consumers are forced to examine the pros and cons of alternative choices and weigh them against their individual goals. This is, in itself, an educational process and is enhanced by the supply of advertisements made available to consumers.

Compare this with the process of education in our schools where we insist on presenting students with conflicting ideologies, hypotheses, theories, and descriptive matter, with the knowledge that this will help to develop discrimination, enhance judgment, and sharpen the intellect. Uni-

FIGURE 4–11
Smoking encouraged

Come to where the flavor is.
Come to Marlboro Country.   Marlboro

You get a lot to like with a Marlboro—filter, flavor, pack or box.

versities purposely include on their staffs professors with differing beliefs
so that students can become acquainted with the existence of such differences and thus strengthen their own independence of thought.

An interesting challenge to consumers in respect to their freedom to

FIGURE 4–12
Smoking discouraged

No, he's not a free-fall parachutist. Or an X-15 test pilot. Or a stock car racer. With a wife and kids to think about, he can't afford to take chances.

But he goes on taking the *big* risk...clinging to a habit which *every day* causes 100 deaths from lung cancer and contributes to many more from coronary artery and respiratory diseases. Studies show that the death rate from lung cancer alone for cigarette smokers (one-pack-a-day or more) is 10 times higher than for nonsmokers.

Nobody says it's easy to stop. But living *that* dangerously often winds up in not living at all.

american cancer society

choose is illustrated in Figures 4–11 and 4–12. To smoke or not to smoke is a proposition many consumers are facing. Each of the two advertisements shown presents a strong case for its viewpoint; and though neither begins to supply all the information the consumer might desire, it may influence his final decision to buy or not to buy.

The factor of persuasion

Advertising, in any form, contains within itself an element of persuasion. Advertising that is purely informative is often all that is needed to persuade a reader or listener to buy the product. In periods when some consumer goods have been very scarce, bare announcement by any local merchant that a shipment has been received is enough to produce a rush for the store. There is much persuasion in the one word "fire" when shouted with sincerity and truth to persons in a burning building.

Persuasion is not the result merely of using strong words and phrases to urge people to buy a product or accept an idea. Persuasion is a two-way process. In the case of advertising, it involves a recognition or belief on the part of the reader or listener that the advertised product will satisfy a need or desire. When a person is already clearly conscious of some need or want, and a product exists which will satisfy that need or want, it requires very little in the way of advertising to persuade the person to buy. Under such conditions, about all an advertisement needs is an announcement of the product's existence, its price, and where it can be bought. Such advertising, however, will be highly persuasive. When consumers are not conscious of specific needs or wants or when the qualities of a product are not clearly observable, it then becomes the task of advertising to interpret the hidden qualities of the product in terms of basic human desires. Such was the situation and such the task of advertising when new products such as the bathtub, toothbrushes, mechanical refrigerators, television receivers, and garden tractors were first available. Each such product was capable of meeting some fundamental human desire, but this fact was not appreciated by the consumer. The desire for cleanliness may have been recognized, but not the desire for a bathtub. Good advertising would explain the qualities of the bathtub in terms of the human desire for cleanliness and, through such explanation, would exercise persuasive powers.

Certainly there is nothing about buyer's guide advertising that would rule out the element of persuasion. In fact, persuasion is necessary to get people to enrich the range of their wants and, therefore, their lives.

QUESTIONS AND PROBLEMS

1   What comparisons would you make between a road map which directs or guides travelers to a desired destination and the advertisements in a mail-

order catalog, a newspaper, or a magazine which may guide consumers in their quest for goods or services?

2 From a recent issue of a newspaper, select three advertisements which you believe are good and three which you believe are poor guides for the consumer.

3 Is the use of advertising to build psychological values into a product socially justified? Explain.

4 Discuss the merits and shortcomings of having some agency other than the seller be responsible for communicating the characteristics and qualities of a product to potential consumers.

5 "The only real justification for advertising is to give product information; advertising should not seek to persuade people to buy products or services." Do you agree with that statement? Why or why not?

6 Compare the buyer's guide character of advertisements in the following types of media: newspapers, radio and television, mail-order catalogs, general magazines, and specialized trade or business magazines.

7 Do you agree or disagree with the position of the Food and Drug Administration on labeling, as presented on page 65 of this chapter? Support your stand.

8 Engage yourself for a moment in introspection and answer as honestly as possible whether you have been influenced by antismoking advertisements either to (1) not start smoking, (2) stop smoking, or (3) advise any of your friends to avoid smoking.

9 Will buyer's guide advertising generally be less or more effective as a sales force than advertising that does not meet the requirements of buyer's guide advertising?

10 How might advertisers function to educate consumers to a higher level of buying sophistication?

5

Ethics and truth
in advertising

Advertising is a powerful economic and social force. Consumers look
to it for information in respect to products and services that might
help to meet their material needs and wants. Consumer actions are influenced by the character of advertisements that are distributed by our
mass media.

Because of the power and influence of advertising, it is vital to the
welfare of society that high ethical standards guide the actions of advertising practitioners.

High ethical standards are also vital to the long-run economic health
of advertising itself. If advertising does not have the confidence of most
consumers, it will lose its influence and surely die. If people grow to
disbelieve a substantial percentage of the advertising messages that come
to them, they will soon tend to reject most or all advertising.

Ethics and morality should be considered primarily at the personal level.
Unethical practices are the result of unethical practitioners. If the individual is guided by high ethical and moral standards, his business or
professional practice will most likely be on the same high plane.

Individual leaders of thought in the field of advertising have been striving to establish standards of practice that will, hopefully, be followed by
all practitioners. Fairfax Cone, a leading advertising agency man, expresses
his own credo as follows:

I believe that advertising should be done *by* us precisely as we would like it done *to* us: clearly as to its promises, honestly as to its intentions, and with sufficient substance to allow each reader or listener or viewer to make up his or her own mind with regard to the proposition that is presented. Its single appeal, whether large or small, should be to *reasonable* self-interest.[1]

Paul Foley, another of the leaders in the advertising agency field, in making reference to the impact of the consumer movement on advertising, spoke to much the same theme when he said:

The purpose of the advertising agency is to persuade people to buy goods and services of our clients.

Assume a developing, consumer-based economy.

Assume that our present world of well-educated, younger, well-heeled, skeptical, largely urbanized consumers will become even more so.

Who will communicate with them persuasively?

Only those who speak to them honestly in their own best interest.

Advertising, therefore, must speak in the honest voice of the consumer. Advertising must speak the truth as the consumer sees the truth—not simply in the narrow, legal or protective sense—but a whole truth.[2]

Unfortunately, not all advertising follows these recommendations. There is too much that is untruthful, exaggerated, misleading, in poor taste, disparaging of competitors, and inconsiderate of the reader, listener, or viewer.

Perhaps attention here to some of the practices that are to be condemned will help reduce such practices in the future. If you are planning to enter the field of advertising practice, you can exercise direct leadership in increasing the ratio of good to bad advertising. If you are to be a "consumer" of advertising, perhaps you can learn not to be misled by the bad and to inform the unethical advertiser of your disapproval.

Untruthful advertising

Untruthfulness is practically undefinable. It is easy to pick out statements in advertisements that are definitely untrue and others that are definitely true; but the dividing line between truth and untruth is difficult, if not impossible, to determine.

From an advertising viewpoint, how far can the advertiser legitimately go in using superlatives or in exaggerating the merits of his product? The Federal Trade Commission and other government regulatory agencies have sanctioned the use of some exaggeration. This has been allowed under the phrase "trade puffing." A case prosecuted by the Bureau of

[1] Fairfax Cone, "The Case against Advertising" (Speech before the Regent Advertising Club, London, England, April 28, 1961).

[2] Paul Foley, "Sweet Talk" (Speech before the American Association of Advertising Agencies, White Sulphur Springs, West Virginia, May 15, 1971).

Animal Husbandry of the United States Department of Agriculture illustrates the attitude of one government agency. Action was brought against the Jones Dairy Farm, Inc., for the use of false advertising. Dr. John R. Mohler, chief of the bureau, explained the position of the government in the following words:

> Our only desire is to see that the Jones advertising, or any other, does not overstep that indefinite boundary which suggests to the reader a fact which cannot be proved, even with the addition of considerable poetic license. There is no objection to reasonable trade puffing. We are concerned only with what may be called extreme assertions giving definite suggestions of fact which cannot be literally proven.

The problem of defining untruthfulness in a legal sense has been of concern to both legislators and judges. During the early 1930s, when much social legislation was enacted by the federal government, legislators debated the question of what constituted untruthful advertising. There were many who held that an advertisement should be labeled as false if it were untrue in any particular sense or if, by ambiguity or inference, it created a misleading impression in the minds of consumers.

Others held that legislation that defined false advertising in terms of erroneous impressions created in the minds of consumers would make enforcement extremely difficult, if not impossible. It was argued that if enforcement were to be effective, advertisements should be judged in terms of *material facts* rather than in terms of the *attitude of mind* of consumers.

As a result of the many debates in Congress the Wheeler-Lea Amendment to the Federal Trade Commission Act was enacted in 1938. It defined false advertisement as follows:

> The term "false advertisement" means an advertisement, other than labeling, which is misleading in a material respect; and in determining whether any advertisement is misleading, there shall be taken into account (among other things) not only representations made or suggested by statement, word, design, device, sound, or any combination thereof, but also the extent to which the advertisement fails to reveal facts material in the light of such representations or material with respect to consequences which may result from the use of the commodity to which the advertisement relates under the conditions prescribed in said advertisement or under such conditions as are customary or usual [sec. 15].

More recently, in discussing the Federal Trade Commission's "substantiation program" (to be discussed more fully further on in this chapter), Robert A. Skitol, assistant to the director of the Bureau of Consumer Protection in the FTC stated,

> It's clear that permissible puffing covers less territory today than it did a few years ago. In reviewing new campaigns and preparing substantiation before

dissemination, advertisers and agencies would be well advised to take a narrow view of the puffing concept, to resolve all doubts in favor of insisting that adequate substantiation exists to support a new representation.[3]

Thus, the Wheeler-Lea Act focused attention on the *material* aspects of a statement to determine whether it is true or false. This approach is tangible and makes administration easier than would be true if dependence were placed on consumer attitude. However, the Federal Trade Commission (which administers the Wheeler-Lea Act) has progressively "liberalized" its interpretation of the law by placing increasing emphasis on impressions which advertisements create in the minds of consumers. This is illustrated by the following excerpt from a Federal Trade Commission ruling: "The buying public does not weigh each word in an advertisement or a representation. It is important to ascertain the impression that is likely to be created upon the prospective purchaser."[4]

The advertiser, however, must be interested in more than the law when he is preparing his message to the consumer. He must be interested in the *attitude of mind* created by his advertisement. He must give thought to the degree to which the message offered the public is accepted as truthful. Much of the power of the advertisement is lost if it creates in the mind of the potential buyer an impression which is not supported by results obtained from use of the product.

To test the reaction of consumers on this point, the copy in ten advertisements of well-known products was taken recently from reputable magazines. This copy was submitted to 46 potential buyers of the advertised products. They were asked to mark whether the copy *impressed* them as being true or untrue. Of the ten advertisements, only three received a majority vote for giving a truthful impression. One piece of copy had a 100 percent vote for an untruthful impression. Regardless of the nature of legislation or the attitude of the courts concerning untruthful advertising, the advertiser cannot afford to ignore the effect which his message will have on consumer attitudes. He cannot afford to write advertising that will meet the legal requirements alone; but, in addition, he must consider whether consumers will believe his message.

Testimonials

The use of testimonial advertising is based upon a fundamental human quality—namely, that people like to read about other people. It is to satisfy this human quality that a goodly portion of the small-town newspapers

[3] Robert A. Skitol, "What is an Adequate Substantiation?" (Speech before the Eastern Annual Conference, American Association of Advertising Agencies, New York City, June 5, 1972).

[4] *Aronberg et al.* v. *Federal Trade Commission,* 7 Cir., 132 F. 2d 165, 167 (65 F.T.C. 979; 3 S & D-647).

are devoted to news items about persons. The success of the tabloid newspapers and picture magazines is no doubt due in part to the fact that news is presented in terms of people and that photographs intensify the reality and intimacy of the personal approach. Confession magazines utilize this same human trait in their presentation of intimate gossip about ostensibly real people. The use of the first person magnifies the appeal of such magazines.

The spirit of emulation is, in part, the basis of this desire of people to read about other people. Human beings want to copy those whom they deem superior in taste or knowledge or experience. In large part this spirit of emulation gives the advertising testimonial its strength. Psychologists claim that people have an ability to excite their imagination with external objects. This enables women to become princesses, movie queens, sweethearts, or brides by using the cold cream or toilet soap recommended by their "superior."

Advertisers have recognized the value of getting the testimonials of persons acknowledged as leaders and authorities—persons whom prospective purchasers would wish to emulate or to use as their guides in consumption. Figure 5–1 illustrates a dignified, honest, and effective use of testimonials.

There are times, however, when some advertisers use unethical methods in obtaining the "proper" testimonials. The term "testimonial racket" has been aptly applied to the techniques used by such advertisers. The payment of large sums of money for the testimonials of particular persons has been very common. Baseball and football players, movie stars, dentists, physicians, lawyers, the socially elite, and others with a large popular following have been richly rewarded for allowing their names to be attached to a testimonial for a given product or products.

Too often the testimonial has not been written by the person whose signature is attached; and the cases are not uncommon in which the signatory is not even a user of the product praised. There are also instances in which a testimonial of the same person has appeared on competing brands. In the case of movie stars and others under contract, the manager of the individual often has the right to endorse any product in the name of the celebrity. This leads to insincerity and misrepresentation.

In 1930 the Federal Trade Commission attempted to check the practice of buying testimonials. In a decision handed down on this subject, the commission stated that when a company paid for and used a testimonial in its advertising, it must also print in the same advertisement, and in equally conspicuous type, a statement that the testimonial had been paid for. This decision of the commission was overruled in 1933 by the United States Circuit Court of Appeals. The court held that paid testimonials need not be labeled as such so long as they were truthful.

Patent medicine manufacturers have less difficulty in obtaining free

"I've got 300 feeder pigs on Aureo S·P 250 right now, with no trouble from scours," says Harley Doyle, Wymore, Nebraska.

"I produce 1,500 feeder pigs a year free of scours thanks to AUREO S·P® 250"

"I put my pigs on feeds with Aureo S·P® 250 as soon as they start eating ...about four to five days old. And I keep them on it, until I sell them as feeders at 40 to 45 pounds. That's usually seven to eight weeks of age," says Mr. Doyle.

"Freedom from disease is the main thing with Aureo S·P 250. But I also find pigs grow faster on less feed, and they reach selling

weights earlier on Aureo S·P 250. There was some atrophic rhinitis in the area last year, but with this feed additive I've run into no losses from the disease."

Whether you're raising feeder pigs or finishing them out, don't take chances. Start them on formula feeds with Aureo S·P 250 and finish them on Aureomycin. *Aureo S·P is the trademark for a premix of Aureomycin® chlortetracycline, Sulmet® sulfamethazine and penicillin.*

CYANAMID > SERVES THE MAN WHO MAKES A BUSINESS OF AGRICULTURE

AMERICAN CYANAMID COMPANY
PRINCETON, NEW JERSEY

FIGURE 5–1. An honest and effective use of testimonials

testimonials than almost any other kind of company. Nature will cure most common human ailments if allowed to do so. If the medicine taken does no harm, the patient will usually get well in spite of it. But credit is almost always given to the medicine rather than to nature. Many such users are willing and anxious to sing the praises of the curative.

But producers of patent medicines offered as a cure for serious diseases such as tuberculosis, cancer, and diabetes often pay for testimonials. The United States Food and Drug Administration has uncovered many cases of fraudulent practice in this respect. One example offered by them concerns a product sold to the public as a cure for diabetes. Curative claims were made in the advertising, and testimonials from sufferers praising the product's curative value were included. In checking over these testimonials, government investigators were able, in many instances, to obtain the death certificates of the writers. In most cases the certificate listed diabetes as the cause of death. Yet the producers continued to use the testimonials and to deal with relatives of the deceased in paying for their use.

Misleading names and labels

The practice of using names on products and in advertising which tend to give a wrong impression as to quality or origin is to be condemned. The following cases of such use were recorded in reports of the Federal Trade Commission. The word "Havana" or "Habana" was used for a cigar made of tobacco not grown in Cuba. "Dirigold" was used to designate and describe flatware and hollow ware made from an alloy of base metals and containing no gold.

One company used the names "France" and "Paris" in cosmetic advertising when such products were not imported from or manufactured in France. Implication of foreign origin of another company's product was provided by the use of such statements as "Les Parfums des Jardines de Fioret." In all these cases the commission issued complaints or cease-and-desist orders.

Names and labels are used by some companies to confuse the consumer as to the real manufacturer. This is done in an attempt to capitalize on the goodwill enjoyed by the company being imitated. Thus, the name "Uneeda" brought imitators with "Iwanta," "Ulika," "Uwanta," and "Abetta." The name "Zu Zu" was imitated with "Hoo, Hoo." The similarity of "Sparkle" and "Twinkle" causes confusion.

These practices make it difficult, if not impossible, for the consumer always to duplicate previous purchases by depending on remembering a name. The deception is of such character that consumers and dealers have at times ordered company A's product from company B. This is obviously not in the best interests of the consumer or the legitimate businessman.

Exaggeration and misrepresentation

This element in advertising has been an ever-present one. From a consumer's point of view, much of advertising exaggeration is perhaps ignored. Why sellers of merchandise will continue to use such methods when it should be evident that such exaggeration does not carry conviction to most readers is hard to understand. There seems to be less use of superlatives and exaggerated statements in current advertising than was true a few years ago; and yet there can be found plenty of the exaggerated type of copy today.

For example, in a recent issue of a metropolitan newspaper the following statements were found: "Buy now! . . . The quality and beauty of the fur trimmings, the fine fabric values, the variety of styles, and the careful making cannot be matched later on at anywhere near these August prices." It is difficult to see how the writer of this copy could accurately forecast the future. Another advertisement stated: "More lavishly furred models, more beautifully styled, more dollar-for-dollar value than we've ever offered before." And this one: "We are just as certain that the quality could not be better as we are that prices could not be lower." While this last statement may be true, the impression is left that quality could not be better or the price lower, whereas the writer of the copy may have been uncertain about both.

Among advertisements appearing in a well-known magazine was one for a food product which promises to curb nervousness in growing children and add weight at the rate of a pound a week. Another offers the skinny adult a "new discovery which adds solid flesh quick" by using a new double tonic. The following testimonial from a reputed user formed a part of the copy: "I was so skinny and weak that everybody laughed at me and called me a scarecrow. Finally I tried ————. In 5 weeks I gained 14 pounds. Now I go out regularly and enjoy life."

A case involving misrepresentation through outright false statements and inferences is illustrated by a New York firm that made a fire extinguisher and sold it under the name "Kill Flame." In its advertising the company stated that its product was "safe" and "nontoxic." It stated that "Kill Flame positively does not contain carbon tetrachloride, chlorobromomethane (CB), or any other hazardous, toxic, or possibly injurious ingredient."

A complaint against the company was brought before the Federal Trade Commission. The false and misleading character of claims made in advertisements was emphasized in the following excerpt from the commission's findings:

> Said statements and representations were and are false, misleading and deceptive. In truth and in fact, said product is not safe and nontoxic when used to extinguish a fire. The chemical components of "Kill Flame" are Freon

11 and Freon 12. These chemicals tend to and do decompose in a flame and on hot surfaces yielding highly toxic substances such as chlorine, phosgene, carbon monoxide, hydrochloric acid and hydroflouric acid. In a closed room or when no ventilation is provided, these decomposition products may form harmful or lethal mixtures.[5]

Exaggeration and misrepresentation are most frequently encountered at the local level. One of the forms most often used is the "lowest price" claim. Better Business Bureaus challenge these claims as a matter of course. In speaking to this, Douglas Head, chairman of the Minnesota Advertising Review Board, suggests that people in advertising should be more creative. "Making the lowest price claim is an easy solution, but one that should be avoided at all costs."[6]

Creating erroneous impressions

There are also examples of advertising which make no actually false statements but which create a definitely false impression. Thus, one company advertised three yards of pure silk in any one of six colors for $0.25. This carried a guarantee that the advertised merchandise was pure silk of the best quality. Those who sent in their quarter received a spool containing three yards of silk *thread.* The answering of an advertisement offering for $0.25 a picture of George Washington made from a steel engraving brought a postage stamp.

Poor taste

There are also advertisements and advertising practices that are in poor taste or are inconsiderate of the reader, listener, or viewer. The blatant use of sex symbols, unrestrained references to the most personal of body functions, and excessive repetition are all too common.

In the case of radio and television commercials, advertisers are too often insensitive to what the listener or viewer might be doing at the time of the commercial. For example, a manufacturer of a laxative sponsored a radio program of dinner music broadcast from 6:00 to 6:30 P.M. The program was excellent and provided an enjoyable background for gracious family dining, but the commercial messages of the most personal and biological nature broke in on the program two or three times during the half hour. A personal salesman for this company would hardly choose the dinner table as a place to sell his pills. It is equally in poor taste to broadcast commercials of this type at dinnertime.

[5] Federal Trade Commission Decisions, 56 (Washington, D.C.: U.S. Government Printing Office, 1962), pp. 480–82.

[6] "Ad Review Board Alive and Well," *Format,* Vol. 19, No. 1 (August–September 1973), p. 14.

It is true that taste is a personal thing, and what is bad taste in one time may not be in another. What was objectionable to our grandparents may not be objectionable today. And products that were not advertised on television five years ago are advertised today, as witness the advertisements for feminine hygiene products. Still, standards of good taste can be determined at any point in time and should not be violated.

Other examples of inconsiderateness would include the multiple spotting of commercials and increasing the sound volume of commercials over that employed for the program. These practices would probably not be employed if advertisers followed the recommendation of Mr. Cone to advertise to others as we would like others to advertise to us. Advertisements and practices that are in poor taste will, in the long run, be detrimental to the total field of advertising.

Agencies aimed at improving advertising ethics

Much progress has been made in bringing about a decline in the amount of untruthful and fraudulent advertising. It is difficult to find advertisements today in any of the reputable magazines or newspapers that begin to match the exaggeration or misrepresentation found in many advertisements of 20 to 30 years ago. This should not be interpreted to mean that advertising is all above criticism today, but rather that it has been going in the right direction and should continue to improve.

A number of forces have contributed to this improvement in advertising ethics. A list of the more important agencies would include the following:

1. Printers' Ink Statute
2. Better Business Bureaus
3. Publishers
4. Advertising organizations
5. Federal government
6. Self-regulation

Printers' Ink Statute

The truth-in-advertising crusade took root in 1911 when the Printers' Ink Publishing Company prepared a model statute regulating untruthful advertising. In its feature articles and in its editorials, *Printers' Ink* magazine urged the inclusion of its model statute as a part of the law of every state in the United States. The provisions of the statute were as follows:

> Any person, firm, corporation, or association, who with intent to sell or in any wise dispose of merchandise, securities, service, or anything offered by such person, firm, corporation or association, directly or indirectly, to the public for sale or distribution, or with intent to increase the consumption thereof or to induce the public in any manner to enter into any obligation relating thereto, or to acquire title thereto or an interest therein, makes, publishes, disseminates, circulates, or places before the public, or causes, directly or indirectly, to be made, published, disseminated, circulated or

placed before the public, in this State, in a newspaper or other publication, or in the form of a book, notice, handbill, poster, bill, circular, pamphlet, or letter, or in any other way, an advertisement of any sort regarding merchandise, securities, service, or anything so offered to the public, which advertisement contains assertions, representation, or statement of fact which is untrue, deceptive or misleading shall be guilty of a misdemeanor.

Two years after this model statute was suggested by *Printers' Ink,* it was adopted by Ohio, followed closely by Minnesota, Washington, and Nebraska. It is now a law in the District of Columbia and the following 27 states:

Alabama	Louisiana	Ohio
Colorado	Michigan	Oklahoma
Hawaii	Minnesota	Oregon
Idaho	Missouri	Rhode Island
Illinois	Nebraska	Virginia
Indiana	Nevada	Washington
Iowa	New Jersey	West Virginia
Kansas	New York	Wisconsin
Kentucky	North Dakota	Wyoming

Seventeen other states have passed laws similar to that suggested by *Printers' Ink.* In general, such laws are not so effective as those which legalized the model statute in its entirety. The Printers' Ink Statute starts off: "Any person, firm, corporation, or association who. . . ." Many of the substitute laws insert the word "knowingly" or its equivalent. Enforcement of the law is much more difficult when it must be proved that the offender *knew* he was offending.

Many cases involving violations of the model statute have been brought before the courts. The law has been upheld and violators punished. It has been helpful in checking certain types of untruthful retail advertising, particularly in those states where adequate enforcement machinery has been set up. It naturally does not touch advertising classified as interstate in character.

Suggestions are frequently made to strengthen and broaden state laws relating to the regulation of advertising practice. Typical of such suggestions is that offered by Mr. Paul Rand Dixon, chairman of the Federal Trade Commission (1966). He urged states to adopt a general statute that:

. . . is sufficiently broad to reach practices such as bait advertising; deceptive guarantees; fictitious pricing; referral selling, oral misrepresentation by house-to-house salesmen; misbranding; sale of used products as new; false claims as to performance of products; price fixing conspiracies; and boycotts to eliminate competition.[7]

[7] As quoted in *Advertising Age,* July 11, 1966, p. 8.

Such a general statute would encompass more than advertising practices, but much of it would relate to advertising.

Better Business Bureaus

Printers' Ink was instrumental not only in getting legislation adopted making certain types of advertising illegal but also in promoting the establishment of agencies to watch out for infractions of the law, collect evidence, and see that the violators were brought to trial. The development of Better Business Bureaus resulted from the agitation by *Printers' Ink.* These agencies are not confined to the states having laws pertaining to false advertising.

Most large cities in the United States now have their own local Better Business Bureaus. In addition to the local organizations, there is the Council of Better Business Bureaus, which operates on a broader scale, giving assistance to national as well as local advertisers. Both the national and the locals serve to curb unethical advertising and selling practices of the unscrupulous and assist the honest to stay within the bounds of law and accepted ethical practices. False comparisons, misleading statements, false claims as to quality, and "not on sale" and bait advertising are among the factors checked on by both the national and local agencies.

The support of these bureaus comes from business firms desirous of eliminating the unfair practices of unscrupulous competitors. Complaints concerning such practices are made to a bureau which, in turn, investigates the charge and, if it is found to be true, tries to persuade the offender to stop such methods. If this procedure does not bring results, the facts are often published. If this does not work, legal action may be instituted.

The Council of Better Business Bureaus carries on research into the changing tenor of public reaction to different types of advertising, as well as into state and federal legislation affecting advertising and selling methods. It also handles cases of unfair trade practices that are regional or national in scope.

This organization gives further assistance to individual business houses by furnishing suggestions of the types of advertising and selling procedure that should not be used. Its suggestions cover specific trade practices as they might apply to many different kinds of merchandise. Thus, in the case of furniture, specific rules dealing with the use of words or terms such as "veneer," "solid," "finish," and "solid walnut top" are set forth for the guidance of merchants. A *solid walnut top,* according to the Better Business Bureau, should mean a top constructed of walnut throughout and not veneered, while a *walnut top* should mean a solid walnut top or a top constructed of walnut veneer on walnut.

The work of the Better Business Bureaus has been built upon the philosophy that progressive advertisers believe in the policy of fair and truthful advertising. Bureaus generally cooperate with advertisers and advertising media "in the interest of truthful advertising by serving as a consultant to copy acceptance personnel, by providing factual information for determining the accuracy of questioned advertising claims, and by giving objective views concerning the reader effects of particular language usage."[8]

The basic principles that guide Better Business Bureaus are well stated as follows by the New York Metropolitan Bureau:

BASIC PRINCIPLES

1. The primary responsibility for truthful and nondeceptive advertising copy rests with the advertiser. Advertisers shall present substantiation for any claims or offers made, before or after publication, if requested to do so by the advertising medium or by the Better Business Bureau.
2. Advertisements which are untrue, misleading, deceptive, fraudulent, disparaging of competitors, insincere offers to sell, or unprovable as to material claims, shall not be used.
3. Advertisements are to be considered in their entirety and as they would be read by the consuming public.
4. Advertisements are not intended to be carefully dissected and analyzed by the general public, but rather to produce an impression upon prospective purchasers. They must therefore not only be truthful in all particulars but also in the general impression which they convey.
5. Advertisements as a whole may be completely misleading although every sentence separately considered is literally true. This may be because things are omitted that should be said, or because advertisements are purposely composed or printed in such a way as to mislead.
6. Advertisements which are ambiguous and capable of being understood to have two meanings, one true and the second false or misleading, will be interpreted to have the capacity to create the latter effect and, therefore, shall not be used.[9]

The Council of Better Business Bureaus' various publications can provide helpful guides to the advertiser. Particular mention should be made of the *Do's and Don't's of Advertising Copy* and *A Guide for Retail Advertising and Selling*.

In 1971, the Council of Better Business Bureaus joined with the American Association of Advertising Agencies, the American Advertising Federation, and the Association of National Advertisers to establish the National Advertising Review Board, in an effort to achieve a more effective level of self-regulation within the advertising industry. This will be discussed more fully later in this chapter.

[8] Better Business Bureau of Metropolitan New York, *Retail Advertising Copy Standards* (New York, 1961), p. 1.

[9] Ibid., p. 2.

Media

Advertising media have helped materially to bring about better standards in advertising practice. Magazines and newspapers have led the way, but in recent years the broadcast industry has considerably expanded its effort. The owners of those media for which a large volume of advertising and a long life are desired appreciate the wisdom of eliminating from their pages and air waves the worst type of advertising. The position is rightly taken that one rotten apple in a basket can easily pollute the entire basket. Thus, it is felt that sound advertising will be received and continued if the rotten is kept out. One "rotten" advertisement in a medium might easily injure the selling ability of good advertisements.

Most reputable media reserve the right to refuse any advertisement offered for publication if it does not come up to certain ethical standards. Some publishers refuse to accept advertisements for certain drugs, patent medicines, stock-selling schemes, and hidden advertisements.

A number of publishers have set up "advertising acceptability standards" and distributed them to current and prospective advertisers. A good example of this is the set of standards established by *The Detroit News*. Some publishers go even further and provide a consumer protection guarantee as to the basic accuracy of claims made in advertisements appearing in their publications. The number of such publications is, however, limited.

Notable leadership has been given to the fight for high advertising ethics by such trade publications as *Advertising Age* and *Printers' Ink* (until it ceased publication). The former has waged a forthright fight not only for a reduction in untruthful and misleading advertising but also for the practice of good taste in all advertising. In both its editorials and in articles carried in the magazine, standards of practice have been suggested and plans for implementing them offered.

Federal government

Many look to the federal government as the only source capable of policing advertising. Yet it is perhaps no more possible for the government, acting alone, to police advertising than it was for the same agency to bring reform in the use of alcoholic beverages. The federal government, however, must be included in any thoroughgoing system of reform. Through the work of the Federal Trade Commission and the Food and Drug Administration a great deal of reform has been accomplished.

The Federal Trade Commission was established in 1914 "to prevent persons, partnerships, or corporations, except banks, and common carriers subject to the Act to Regulate Commerce, from using unfair methods of competition in commerce."[10] The commission considered false and misleading advertising an unfair method of competition, and it brought action against a number of companies on such grounds. The position of the commission was materially weakened in 1931 by the Supreme Court decision in the *Raladam* case, which held that the commission must establish that questioned advertisements must substantially injure or tend to injure the business of any competitor or competitors in general. This, of course, ignored completely the influence such advertising might have on the public.

A great advance was accomplished in 1938 with the Wheeler-Lea amendments to the Federal Trade Commission Act. These amendments eliminated the difficulties emphasized in the *Raladam* case by amplifying the phrase "unfair methods of competition in commerce" with the addition of "and unfair or deceptive acts or practices in commerce."[11]

This addition makes it no longer necessary for the commission to prove injury to a competitor. If the act of advertising is proved unfair or deceptive, it is unlawful.

A new section dealing specifically with advertising was added by the 1938 amendments. This section labeled false advertising as a definite "unfair or deceptive act or practice in commerce." The new section reads in part:

a. It shall be unlawful for any person, partnership, or corporation to disseminate, or cause to be disseminated, any false advertisement—
  1. By United States mails, or in commerce by any means, for the purpose of inducing, or which is likely to induce, directly or indirectly, the purchase of foods, drugs, devices, or cosmetics or
  2. By any means for the purpose of inducing, or which is likely to induce, directly or indirectly the purchase in commerce of food, drugs, devices, or cosmetics.[12]

It should be noted that these provisions apply only to the advertising of food, drugs, devices, or cosmetics. The definition of false advertising as set forth in the Wheeler-Lea amendment is reproduced in an earlier part of this chapter.

This legislation strengthened the hand of the commission by placing the burden of proof on the offender rather than on the commission. If a cease-and-desist order is issued, the alleged defender has 60 days in which to initiate action in the appropriate United States Circuit Court of Appeals.

[10] Federal Trade Commission Act, Sec. 5 (Washington, D.C.: U.S. Government Printing Office, 1914).

[11] Ibid., as amended, 1938.

[12] Ibid., Sec. 12.

If such action is not taken, the order becomes final, and the offender is liable for monetary penalties in case of future violations.

In 1972, the U.S. Supreme Court made more explicit the role of the commission in protecting the consumer. The Court held that the commission's power reached beyond violations of the letter or spirit of the antitrust laws, and that the commission had broad powers to prevent practices that were unfair to the consumer, as well as those which constitute unfair methods of competition.[13] This was in keeping with the rapidly mounting interest in consumerism throughout the nation and the commission's growing concern for its role as a consumer protection agency, a concern that had its beginnings with the reorganization of the commission in 1970.

Need for this reorganization and revitalization of the commission had first been expressed in 1968 in a report by Ralph Nader and his associates. While it overstated the case, the Nader report did lead to a study by the American Bar Association which found substantial fault with the commission. The author of the ABA report was Miles Kirkpatrick, who in 1970 was persuaded to accept an appointment as chairman of the commission. Bringing to the commission a group of bright and aggressive young lawyers, Kirkpatrick instituted major changes. He established a new Bureau of Consumer Protection and let it be known that the bureau's aim was to seek more effective ways in which to deal with false advertising and to explore the limits of the commission's power.

Basically, the procedures in bringing action against an advertiser were not changed under the Kirkpatrick commission. Complaints may be made by a competitor, by a consumer, or by the commission staff itself. If, on investigation of the complaint, there appears to be sufficient evidence to justify an action, a complaint is issued together with a proposed "cease-and-desist" order. In most instances the advertiser agrees to the cease-and-desist order, which then has the same force as an injunctive decree. Any subsequent violation of the order subjects the offender to the possibility of a fine of up to $5,000 a day or $5,000 for each offense.

If the defendant refuses to agree to the cease-and-desist order, a hearing is held before an FTC hearing examiner. If the defendant or the commission disagrees with the findings of the hearing examiner, the case is reviewed by the full commission. Ultimately it may be appealed through the federal courts.

All of this consumes a great amount of time, a fact that has led many to question the effectiveness of commission procedures. A case in point is that of the *FTC* v. *the J. B. Williams Co.,* manufacturer of Geritol. Investigation of the advertising claims for Geritol was begun in 1959. It was not until 1967 that the cease-and-desist order was agreed to. In December of 1969, the FTC filed a complaint with the Justice Department,

---

[13] *Federal Trade Commission* v. *The Sperry & Hutchinson Co.,* 405 U.S. 233 (1972).

charging that 11 commercials for Geritol and a companion product, Fem-Iron, broadcast between June 2 and October 1, were in violation of the cease-and-desist order. The Justice Department filed suit against the company in the U.S. District Court in New York City, asking fines totaling $1 million—$5,000 against the company and $5,000 against its advertising agency for each of the 100 occasions on which the commercials were aired. The court imposed fines of $456,000 against the company and $356,000 against the agency. In January of 1973, the company and the advertising agency filed an appeal of the judgment in the Second Circuit Court of Appeals. It is not possible to know when all appeals will have been exhausted, but at this point more than 14 years have elapsed since the FTC began its investigations. And meanwhile, the commercials which the FTC charged were in violation of the cease-and-desist order have long since been abandoned by the advertiser, and whatever harm may have been done to consumers is past recall.

All of this has led the "revitalized" commission to seek more effective deterrents, including; complaints seeking affirmative disclosure of important qualifying attributes of a product, asking restitution of monies allegedly appropriated from deceived customers, substantiation of claims, and corrective advertising.

Corrective advertising was introduced in 1972 when the commission brought action against the Continental Baking Co., questioning the advertising claims made for Profile Bread. In accepting the cease-and-desist order, the company agreed to engage in "corrective" advertising. It agreed that 25 percent of the expenditures for advertising in each medium in each market for a period of one year would be used for advertisements stating that Profile was not effective for weight reduction.

Subsequently the commission ordered corrective advertising in complaints brought against Hi-C, a product of the Coca-Cola Co.; Wonder Bread and Hostess Cakes, products of Continental Baking Co.; and Chevron gasoline. In each instance the company refused to sign a consent decree, and the cases were brought before hearing commissioners. In each case the hearing commissioner ruled against the commission. Decisions of the hearing commissioners will be reviewed by the full commission. Findings of the full commission will in turn be subject to appeal in the courts, and so it may be some time before it is finally determined whether corrective advertising is an appropriate instrument.

Another of the commission's efforts to improve the effectiveness of its procedures is the advertising substantiation program. In 1971, the commission requested manufacturers in six product categories to provide data to substantiate claims made in their advertising. The product categories were automobiles, air conditioners, electric shavers, television sets, cough and cold remedies, and tires. Subsequently, the commission asked for similar data from manufacturers of toothpaste and denture products, soaps and detergents, hearing aids, antiperspirants and deodorants, and shampoos. The data were to be available to the commission in determining the validity of advertising claims, and to the consumer to assist in making rational choices between competing claims. A further use for the data, as seen by the commission, was to provide advertisers opportunities to challenge competitors whose advertising claims have no basis in fact.

Commission staff attorneys, evaluating the documentation received in the substantiation program, found serious questions with respect to the adequacy of the data in 30 percent of the claims involved. Another 30 percent were so technical that they were unable to evaluate them. These were referred to experts for analysis.

According to Robert Skitol, assistant to the director of the Bureau of Consumer Protection of the FTC,

> The major disappointment, thus far, has been the apparent failure of consumers, competitors, public interest groups, and others to take full advantage of the availability of the documentation submitted for study and analysis. Unless these groups come in and scrutinize the material and convey the results to the public, the stated twin objectives of education and deterrents simply will not materialize.[14]

Mr. Skitol went on to say, in support of the program:

> The commission's new concern with ad substantiation will be effectively complemented by its vigorous efforts, increasingly in the future, to ensure that advertising performs its intended function in the marketplace, the function of conveying product information in a way that promotes competition among sellers and rational purchasing patterns by the consuming public.[15]

In a further effort to increase its effectiveness, the Federal Trade Commission in 1971 held hearings designed to provide the commission with information that would enable it to function more knowledgeably in its activities relating to the advertising industry. While the hearings were designed to range broadly, several areas were selected for special attention:

1. The impact of advertising directed to children;
2. Whether certain kinds of advertising may unfairly exploit desires, fears, and anxieties of consumers;
3. What kinds of physical, emotional, and psychological responses various kinds of advertising elicit from consumers;
4. Whether modern techniques of design and production—for example, sound effects, cutting, splicing, and color—facilitate unfair or deceptive effects in TV commercials.

[14] Skitol, "Adequate Substantiation?"
[15] Ibid.

In 14 days of hearings extending over a 3-week period, the commissioners heard from more than 90 advertisers, advertising agency executives, members of Congress, academicians, representatives from the major advertising associations, critics of advertising, and representatives from the media. While hardly definitive, the hearings, in the words of Robert Pitofsky, then director of the Bureau of Consumer Protection of the FTC, ". . . turned out to be exceptionally useful, given the original goals of the project."[16] According to Mr. Pitofsky:

> First, they educated the commission and its staff on various questions of modern advertising techniques, where, incidentally, there was relatively little prior reliable scholarship. Second, the record of the hearings and this report have already begun to be used internally at the commission as a planning document. . . . In the long run, the advertising industry as well as consumers will profit from an active program of commission challenges to that portion of advertising that is deceptive or unfair, and exchanges like these can help insure that the commission plays its regulating role in an informed and constructive manner.[17]

A recurrent theme in the FTC hearings and in subsequent discussions has been the need for more precise information as to what constitutes deception in the eyes of the consumer. Gary G. Gerlach, a communications attorney from Washington, D.C., underlined this in a working paper developed for the Marketing Science Institute of Cambridge, Massachusetts.

Mr. Gerlach, in his paper, points out that

> Not until very recently did it begin to dawn on some in the legal community that it might be more important to define what constitutes illegal advertising practices *in terms of the dynamics of consumer behavior,* and, once the dynamics have been defined, to develop more effective remedies for dealing with deception based on those behavioral dynamics.[18]

Arguing that present advertising law relies heavily on hypothetical, rather than actual, evidence of the consumer's state of mind, he suggests that expanded use in legal proceedings of scientific surveys and acceptable standards for such surveys offer the best current hope for sampling the consumer's mind and for basing new remedies on actual evidence of consumer attitudes and behavior.

Within the FTC itself, Commissioner Mary Gardiner Jones has, on more

---

[16] John A. Howard and James Hulbert, *Advertising and the Public Interest* (Chicago: Crain Communications Inc., 1973), Foreword.

[17] Ibid.

[18] Gary G. Gerlach, "The Consumer's Mind: A Preliminary Inquiry into the Emerging Problems of Consumer Evidence and the Law" (Cambridge, Mass.: Marketing Science Institute, November 1972).

than one occasion, addressed herself to the need to adopt a behavioral perspective in the regulation of advertising.[19]

Support for such research was envisioned in legislation introduced in the United States Senate in 1973 by Senator Frank E. Moss of Utah.[20] The bill would establish a National Institute of Marketing and Health within the Federal Trade Commission. Among the responsibilities of the institute would be to undertake research concerning the impact of advertising and marketing on particularly the psychological and social effects of advertising and marketing techniques, and to collect, analyze, and disseminate to the public relevant information on behavior research relating to advertising and marketing.

Other legislation of importance to the advertiser and consumer included the Federal Food, Drug, and Cosmetic Act. This act became operative June 25, 1939. It, like the Wheeler-Lea Act, deals with foods, drugs, devices, and cosmetics but applies primarily to the *labeling* of such products.

The following quotation from the act defines the term "label" and sets forth the elements to be considered in a determination of whether a given label is misleading:

k. The term "label" means a display of written, printed, or graphic matter upon the immediate container of any article; and a requirement made by or under authority of this Act that any word, statement, or other information appearing on the label shall not be considered to be complied with unless such word, statement, or other information also appears on the outside container or wrapper, if any there be, of the retail package of such article, or is easily legible through the outside container or wrapper.

l. The term "immediate container" does not include package liners.

m. The term "labeling" means all labels and other written, printed, or graphic matter (1) upon any article or any of its containers or wrappers, or (2) accompanying such article.

n. If an article is alleged to be misbranded because the labeling is misleading, then in determining whether the labeling is misleading there shall be taken into account (among other things) not only representations made or suggested by statement, word, design, device, or any combination thereof, but also the extent to which the labeling fails to reveal facts material in the light of such representations or material with respect to consequences which may result from the use of the article to which the labeling relates under the conditions of use prescribed in the labeling thereof or under such conditions of use as are customary or usual.[21]

[19] Mary Gardiner Jones, "The FTC's need for Social Science Research" (Address before the Second Annual Conference of the Association for Consumer Research, College Park, Md., September 1, 1971).

[20] S. 805, 93d Cong., 1st sess.

[21] Federal Food, Drug, and Cosmetic Act, Sec. 201 (Washington, D.C.: U.S. Government Printing Office, 1938).

The Federal Trade Commission and the Food and Drug Administration were given additional powers to regulate advertising under the Truth in Labeling and Packaging Law enacted in 1966. Under that law, designated federal agencies were given the charge to promulgate regulations in respect to product labels and packages to insure adequate identification of the product, its producer, and the net quantity of contents. Such agencies were also authorized to develop rules to prevent consumer deception and to facilitate value comparisons.

It is significant that the 1966 legislation made a substantial move from a "thou shalt not" to a "thou shalt" approach. The new law says that government will still be concerned with preventing advertisers from deceiving the consumer but will also take more positive action to see that product labels and packages contain information that will aid consumers in making significant comparisons of product values. This law should enhance the further development of advertising as a helpful consumer's guide to buying.

In addition to the above, the Federal Trade Commission exercises control over the advertising and labeling of products under laws affecting specific industries, including: Wool Products Labeling Act of 1939, Fur Products Labeling Act, Flammable Fabrics Act, Textile Fiber Products Act, and Consumer Credit Protection Act. The latter is also known as the Truth in Lending Act.

Consumerism

Consumer interest groups are not new to the American scene; but it is doubtful whether there has been a time when the impact of consumer movements on society has been as great as in the latter part of the 1960s and in the 1970s. While not all of the efforts of consumer interest leaders are directed toward advertising, advertisers and their advertisements have become prime targets.

As was noted earlier, it was Ralph Nader's report on the Federal Trade Commission in 1968 that gave impetus to the study of the FTC by the American Bar Association and led to the subsequent reorganization of the commission. In 1970 Nader and his associates wrote to 60 leading national advertisers and requested data that would substantiate their advertising claims. It is more than coincidence that in 1971 the FTC introduced its advertising substantiation program, and in 1971 Sen. Frank E. Moss of Utah introduced his Truth in Advertising Act, "a bill to require the furnishing of documentation of claims concerning safety, performance, efficiency, characteristics, and comparative price of advertised products and services."[22] This bill, while it was not passed, does reflect clearly the

[22] S. 1461, 92d Cong., 1st sess.

concerns of the consumer subcommittee of the Senate Committee on Commerce, of which Senator Moss is chairman—concerns that undoubtedly will continue to be expressed in legislation affecting advertisers and advertising.

One of the most controversial proposals being supported by consumer interest groups is that of "counter advertising." As proposed to the Federal Communications Commission by the FTC, the policy would require radio and television broadcasting stations to provide access to counter-advertising messages in amounts up to 100 percent of commercial time for anyone willing to pay the specified rates, and a substantial amount of time at no charge for persons and groups who wish to respond but cannot purchase the time. The FCC has not responded to these proposals. Despite this, consumer interest groups have proceeded to develop counter-advertising messages which they have made available to broadcast and print media.

One of these groups, Concern Firm, developed two television commercials featuring Burt Lancaster, screen star. In one he urges viewers to use "the least expensive plain aspirin you can find." In the other he warns viewers of dangers in driving Chevrolet models of particular years because they were built with faulty engine mounts. Earlier the group had developed a series of counter ads for the print media on topics ranging from advice to 18-year-olds, with respect to the draft, to refutation of claims for analgesic drugs. There is no evidence of any substantial use of these materials by the media.

Another of the major concerns of consumer interest groups has been television advertising addressed to children. Action for Children's Television (ACT), a Boston based group, has urged the elimination of all television commercials directed toward children. The Association of National Advertisers, the National Association of Broadcasters, and the Toy Manufacturers of America responded to these pressures by adopting self-regulatory codes. Three of the leading manufacturers of children's vitamins agreed not to advertise their products on programs directed to children. But pressure from the groups opposing advertising to children has continued. As was noted earlier, this was one of the most important issues covered by the FTC hearings. It is reasonable to assume that the critics will continue their attacks until a satisfactory solution to the problem is found.

At federal, state, and local levels, efforts to provide increased protection for consumers multiplied rapidly in the first years of the 1970s. President Nixon appointed Mrs. Virginia Knauer as his special assistant for consumer affairs. At one point, more than 150 bills relating to consumers and consumerism were reported to be under consideration by Congress. Efforts to establish a Consumer Protection agency failed in Congress in 1972.

Establishment of consumer affairs offices at state, and in some instances local, levels heightened activity on the part of state's attorneys general, and the enactment of state statutes aimed at protecting consumers have given further dimension to consumer protection concerns. While not all of these efforts were directed toward advertising alone, substantial portions were. The Council of State Governments and the National Conference of Commissioners of Uniform State Laws, together with the Federal Trade Commission, prepared model protection acts for adoption at the state level in an effort to promote uniform and public enforcement. The acts grant many remedial devices against deceptive practices of the kind covered by Section 5 of the Trade Commission Act, relating to false and misleading advertising. At the close of 1972, four states had enacted the law. Another six states had adopted the Uniform Deceptive Trade Practices Act, prohibiting bad business practices, including bait and generally deceptive advertising. Eventually these statutes can be expected to achieve more effectively what was sought through the Printers' Ink Statute.

Self-regulation

There is a recognition on the part of most businessmen that truthful advertising is distinctly beneficial if the great majority of members of a trade can be forced or encouraged to eliminate false and misleading advertising. Because of this viewpoint, many industries are glad to accept the presence of government regulations. Some industries go a step further and set up a program of self-regulation which accepts the work of government agencies, but supplements that with a program for checking the advertising of its members against government standards and its own industry standards, which may go beyond those established by law. Such a philosophy is distinctly laudable, as well as good business practice. It will increase the public faith in advertising and make further legislation unnecessary.

The editor of a leading advertising journal, in commenting on this point, said, "Some regulation (of advertising) is necessary and useful. The best and most sensible regulation is self-regulation, imposed by advertisers and media themselves, in an effort to eliminate poor practices and bad taste. The more effective and the more sensible such self-regulation is, the less is the need for government regulation of any kind."[23]

Self-regulation has taken many forms. The work of the Better Business Bureaus is essentially self-regulatory in nature in that these bureaus are financed by advertising and business institutions. Trade associations, media, and individual firms all engage to a degree in regulating their own or their members' advertising practices.

The method followed by one national advertiser is to present "the basic facts about the performance of each product to both its advertising copy section and its legal section. The copy section works with the advertising

[23] Editorial, *Advertising Age,* March 11, 1957, p. 12.

FIGURE 5–2
An example of an industry code of ethics

THE
ADVERTISING CODE
OF AMERICAN BUSINESS

1. **Truth** ... Advertising shall tell the truth, and shall reveal significant facts, the concealment of which would mislead the public.

2. **Responsibility** ... Advertising agencies and advertisers shall be willing to provide substantiation of claims made.

3. **Taste and Decency** ... Advertising shall be free of statements, illustrations or implications which are offensive to good taste or public decency.

4. **Disparagement** ... Advertising shall offer merchandise or service on its merits, and refrain from attacking competitors unfairly or disparaging their products, services or methods of doing business.

5. **Bait Advertising** ... Advertising shall offer only merchandise or services which are readily available for purchase at the advertised price.

6. **Guarantees and Warranties** ... Advertising of guarantees and warranties shall be explicit. Advertising of any guarantee or warranty shall clearly and conspicuously disclose its nature and extent, the manner in which the guarantor or warrantor will perform and the identity of the guarantor or warrantor.

7. **Price Claims** ... Advertising shall avoid price or savings claims which are false or misleading, or which do not offer provable bargains or savings.

8. **Unprovable Claims** ... Advertising shall avoid the use of exaggerated or unprovable claims.

9. **Testimonials** ... Advertising containing testimonials shall be limited to those of competent witnesses who are reflecting a real and honest choice.

*Developed and initially distributed by: Advertising Federation of America;
the Advertising Association of the West; the Association of Better Business Bureaus, Inc.
and adopted by International Newspaper Advertising Executives, 1965.*

agency in the production of the copy. The advertising is then submitted to the legal section, a department completely divorced from advertising, which checks it against the known facts, using policies and rules developed over a period of time from within and without the company."[24] Other individual companies have a practice of submitting all advertising copy to a research or testing division to have claims matched against the results of product tests before approving for release to media.

Trade associations have not been too active in the field of regulation, partly because of their fear that such activity might be construed as a violation of antitrust laws. Many associations do, however, prepare and issue codes of ethics that members are supposed to follow in their advertising practices. One example of such a code is reproduced in Figure 5–2.

On the matter of self-regulation and antitrust, an editorial in *Advertising Age* had this to say:

> Viewed narrowly from an antitrust position, there undoubtedly are aspects of self regulation which could be construed as, in some sense, collusive and involving restraint. But this is not a good reason for abandoning these efforts. In most instances programs of self regulation have come into existence to deal with demonstrated needs. One example consists of the efforts of the tobacco industry, through its code authority, to withdraw from the sponsorship of television programs which appeal to young people. Self regulation developed because efforts of this kind, concerned essentially with matters of "taste," are largely beyond the reach of government—and should be. It is hard to see how "public interest" can be advanced if the concerted efforts of the antitrusters are used to inhibit the development of such programs.[25]

In 1946 the American Association of Advertising Agencies inaugurated a program to reduce to a minimum the amount of objectionable advertising. The Association of National Advertisers joined the endeavor in 1960. The plan was known as the A.N.A.-A.A.A.A. Interchange of Opinion on Objectionable Advertising. "Any agency, member or nonmember, may forward to the Interchange its criticism of any advertisement which, in its opinion, is in any way objectionable. The criticism is reviewed individually by each member of the Interchange's Committee of the Board on Improvement of Advertising Content, and the result is then forwarded to the agency originating the advertisement, along with a report of the Committee vote and remarks, if any. The Interchange promotes this system by periodically distributing brochures to remind all agencies of their affirmative duties to the industry and to the public."[26]

[24] "The Regulation of Advertising," *Columbia Law Review,* Vol. 56 (November 1956), p. 1079.

[25] *Advertising Age,* July 11, 1966, p. 20.

[26] "The Regulation of Advertising," p. 1085.

Figure 5–3 is a reproduction of the cover of a folder designed to urge members to help implement the Interchange. Included in the folder was the following copy code that served as a statement of principles to guide the reporting of objectionable advertising.

COPY CODE OF A.A.A.A., A.N.A., AND A.F.A.

The advertising agency should not recommend, and should discourage any advertiser from using, any advertising of an untruthful, indecent or otherwise objectionable character, as exemplified by the following copy practices disapproved in a code jointly adopted by the American Association of Advertising Agencies and the Association of National Advertisers, and also by the Advertising Federation of America:

a.   False statements or misleading exaggerations.
b.   Indirect misrepresentation of a product, or service, through distortion of details, or of their true perspective, either editorially or pictorially.
c.   Statements or suggestions offensive to public decency.
d.   Statements which tend to undermine an industry by attributing to its products, generally, faults and weaknesses true only of a few.
e.   Price claims that are misleading.
f.   Pseudoscientific advertising, including claims insufficiently supported by accepted authority, or that distort the true meaning or practicable application of a statement made by professional or scientific authority.
g.   Testimonials which do not reflect the real choice of a competent witness.[27]

Figure 5–4 illustrates a poster, mailing piece, or advertisement that could be distributed by an advertiser or agency to encourage professionals and laymen to report questionable advertisements.

The Interchange program had limited success, and in 1971, acknowledging the need for more effective self-regulation if they were to escape more rigorous governmental regulation, representatives of the American Association of Advertising Agencies, American Advertising Federation, Association of National Advertisers, and Council of Better Business Bureaus met to establish a National Advertising Review Council. The council, in turn, formulated by-laws and operating procedures for a National Advertising Review Board (NARB). The board, consisting of 30 advertiser members, 10 advertising agency members, and 10 "public" members, was established in November of 1971.

To initiate review and evaluation of complaints directed to the NARB, a National Advertising Division (NAD) was established within the Council of Better Business Bureaus. In addition to review and evaluation of complaints, the NAD has responsibility for internal monitoring of print and broadcast advertising.

[27] American Association of Advertising Agencies, Inc., New York, December 1959.

FIGURE 5–3
An invitation to assist in self-regulation

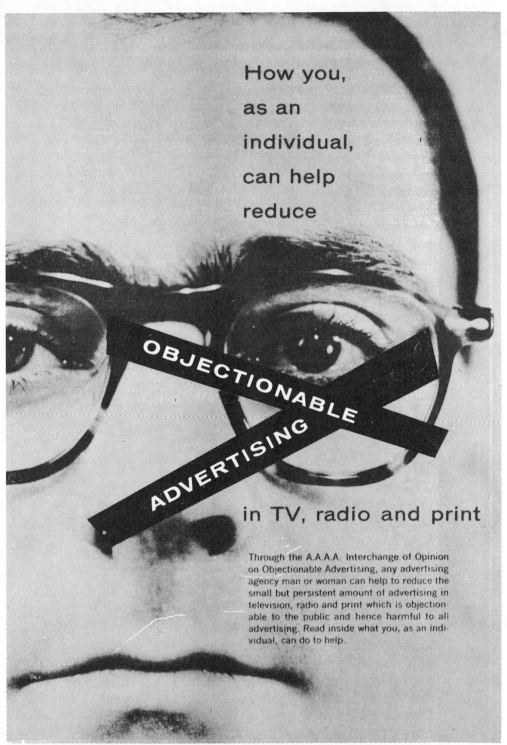

FIGURE 5–4
Brochure encouraging use of Interchange

Don't just get in a stew over objectionable Advertising

Do something about it!

We are cooperating with the ANA-AAAA Interchange to reduce the small but persistent amount of advertising that embodies disparagement or is in questionable taste. Such material offends the public, and hence harms all advertising. You, personally, need only find examples, but that first step is up to *you*.

Here's what do do:

Printed Media. Give tear sheets of objectionable advertisements, with place and date of publication.

Radio and TV. Give name of advertiser, and as exact an account as you can of what was said or shown. If possible give date, time, and station or network. (Report objectionable material, though even if you don't get complete information.)

Outdoor or Car Cards. Give any description that will help to identify the copy in question.

Report examples seen or heard to:

....

(Agency Coordinator)

In evaluating a complaint, the NAD requests substantiation of claims from the advertiser. Following its investigations, the NAD may dismiss the complaint or find it to be justified. If the advertiser disagrees with the findings of the NAD, he may appeal to the NARB where a five-member panel of board members may be appointed to review the case. If the panel members find against the advertiser and the advertiser refuses to change or discontinue the challenged advertisement, the case is referred to an appropriate government agency. In its first full year in existence, the NAD received or initiated 444 complaints against national advertising. Of the total, 131 were dismissed and 84 were upheld. The remaining 227 cases were still under investigation at the end of the year.

From the time of their first meeting in November 1971, NARB members voiced support for the convening of NARB panels to review matters other than truth and accuracy in advertising—specifically, the broader questions of taste and social responsibility. This procedure was approved, with the stipulation that these panel studies were to lead to the development of reports which would ultimately be published as "white papers" to provide guidelines for advertisers.

Parallel self-regulatory agencies have been established at state and local levels. The first of these was in Phoenix, Arizona, where the local advertising club joined with the local Better Business Bureau to establish a review board. Among the first statewide efforts was Minnesota, where, in 1972, the Better Business Bureau of Greater Minneapolis, the Better Business Bureau of St. Paul, and the Minnesota Ad Club joined to create the Minnesota Advertising Review Council. The council, in turn, created the Minnesota Advertising Review Board, with 50 percent of its members being public members, 25 percent advertisers, and 25 percent advertising agency people. The board functions in much the same manner as does the National Advertising Review Board. The two Better Business Bureaus serve as investigative arms. A first effort is made to achieve agreement between the advertiser and the BBB to eliminate the advertising claims in question. If not successful, the BBB refers the matter to the Review Board, where a panel of board members hears the case. If the panel finds against the advertiser and the advertiser refuses to accept this opinion, the matter is referred to the state's attorney general.

A type of partial self-regulation is found in the *trade practice conferences* encouraged by the Federal Trade Commission but entered into voluntarily by members of a trade. These conferences may result in the establishment of rules of fair conduct for an entire industry. Misbranding and misrepresentation in various forms, including deceptive packaging or advertising of industry products, are often covered by the rules promulgated. During recent years, trade rules have been established in the following fields: in the manufacturing of popular-priced dresses, toilet brushes, cotton textiles, luggage and related products, and sunglasses, and in the rayon, fur, wholesale jewelry, and confectionery industries.

Many of the leading newspapers in the country have established their own advertising regulations, censorship, or acceptance committees. In the spring and summer of 1951, when there were exceedingly heavy inventories of television sets throughout the country, a number of manufacturers and dealers forgot their standards of truthfulness. Through the self-regulatory action of many newspapers much of the untruthful and exaggerated copy was eventually eradicated. The *Milwaukee Journal* action illustrates what was done. The paper announced to all television, appliance, and radio advertisers that advertising copy would have to "conform to a single code—clear truth." In announcing this specific regulation the advertising manager of the *Journal* said:

> In the interests of honest advertising, promotional advertising copy which in any way stretches the truth and goes beyond the bounds of reasonableness and fair play, or which may mislead or confuse the reader is to be carefully censored by the *Journal* and omitted if not properly revised. We believe in imaginative, compelling, hard-selling copy. We like attractive, dramatic illustrations. We have faith in the power of words to make people want something, to convince them to buy it from the advertiser who gives him good reason. We know that advertising can sell wanted, good-brand merchandise at profitable, reasonable prices. We know, too, that there is no substitute for truth.[28]

In the words of the Federal Trade Commission "antideceptive work protects consumers and honest sellers of goods and services from the unfair competition of those few who distort truth for profit." It is important to remember that most business firms today operate on an honest basis and see to it that their advertising is honest. False advertising is usually the product of persons inclined toward falsehood. The institution of advertising is, in itself, not false, not untruthful, not misleading. Individual advertisements may, however, be any one or all of these things if the persons behind the ads choose to make them so.

Improvement in personal practice has come about partly through government regulation and partly through industry or self-imposed regulation. That such improvement has occurred is obvious from the following statement of a Federal Trade Commission official as reported by *Advertising Age:* "In recent years," he said, "lots of companies and advertising agencies have come to recognize they have a sacred trust to protect the believeability of advertising. In the recognized media, advertising as a whole is good. And considering the great increase in volume, an amazingly small percentage is questionable."[29]

Lasting improvement, however, can come only through the acceptance

[28] "Milwaukee Journal's Appliance Ad Censorship Called Success," *Advertising Age,* October 1, 1951, p. 60.
[29] "FTC Finds Ad Ethics Better," *Advertising Age,* September 10, 1956, p. 3.

on the part of individuals of the efficacy and profitability of high ethical operations. For the weak and shortsighted, the pressure of external regulation of one type or another will continue to be essential. For the leader in society—be it in religion, philosophy, government, education, science, or advertising—emphasis must be placed on raising the ethical standards of all. As one of the great pioneers in the fight for truth in advertising said, "Advertising . . . by and large reflects the morals, manners, customs, habits, desires, and economic conditions of the community and generation which it serves."[30] Of course, advertising practice should be on a high ethical plane, but one should not expect it to rise too high above its source.

But let not advertising men and women hide behind this concept to justify their failure to assume leadership in building and keeping advertising to a high ethical level. Advertisers would do well to heed the admonition of Earl W. Kintner, former chairman of the Federal Trade Commission, in a statement addressed to them. "Advertising men and women," he said, "must find within themselves a belief in their capacities to meet responsibilities and the will to discharge those responsibilities. It was John Stuart Mill who said that 'one person with a belief is equal to a force of 99 who have only interest.' Now is the time to demonstrate that you have beliefs. Now is the time to demonstrate that you are determined to be responsible citizens in a free society."[31]

Colston Warne has offered, at the policy level, a recommendation that all advertising men could well afford to consider and strive to implement. His recommendation follows:

> Specifically, a policy is proposed of *caveat venditor*—let the seller beware—a policy to be enforced by our social and legal institutions. An advertisement should be a warranty to the purchaser of the price and quality of an article. Thus, the burden of proof as to an advertising claim will lie squarely upon the seller of a branded good. A claim should be accurate and complete as to all essential details, and should constitute full disclosure of both the merits and demerits of the good in its intended use. Advertising should not be poised on the slippery edge of irrelevance, misrepresentation, or deception. The obsolescent and socially destructive idea of *caveat emptor* should be appropriately buried as a relic of the days of simple markets and well-understood commodities.[32]

Willard L. Thompson voices the same view when he says, "What is needed is some means of providing all persons within advertising with a renewed sense of their obligation, not to themselves but to the consumer. This is a seemingly impossible task, considering the breadth of the advertis-

[30] H. J. Kenner, *The Fight for Truth in Advertising* (New York: Round Table Press, 1936), p. xiv.

[31] Earl W. Kintner, "1961—Armageddon for Advertising?" *Printers' Ink,* June 16, 1961,

[32] Colston E. Warne, "Advertising—A Critic's View," *Journal of Marketing,* Vol. 26 (October 1962), p. 14.

ing world. And yet, it must be undertaken if advertising is to approach its fullest success in our society, and if it is to serve society as it must."[33]

QUESTIONS AND PROBLEMS

1   Is "comparative" advertising in the best interest of consumers? Explain.

2   Discuss in some detail the concept of permitting "counter" advertising as a counter force against false advertising.

3   What do you think of the policy of the FTC to require a user of false advertising to devote a percentage of the money spent on such advertising to "corrective" advertising?

4   The previous three questions deal with what has been referred to as the three Cs of controversial policies in respect to advertising regulation—comparative, counter, and corrective advertising. Would you be in favor of modifying or adding to any of these policies?

5   By referring to the library files of popular periodicals, compare three soap advertisements published before 1960 with three of those currently published. Do you note any change toward a greater degree of truthfulness?

6   Why does the advertiser lose when his advertisement creates a *false* impression in the mind of the buyer? Is a deliberate untruth necessary?

7   Discuss in some detail the implications of Mr. Warne's recommendation that *caveat venditor*—let the seller beware—guide the practice of all advertising people.

8   Do you believe that testimonial advertising is convincing? What arguments can be advanced against it? For it?

9   What is to be gained by advertisers and publishers from efforts at self-regulation of advertising?

10   Do you think there is any basic conflict between consumers and most advertisers?

[33] Willard L. Thompson, "Self-Regulation in Advertising" (Ph.D. diss., University of Illinois, Urbana, 1958), p. 382.

6

Nonproduct advertising

The term "nonproduct advertising" is used to cover the vast new field of idea advertising not related directly to products or commercial services. It would include individual company and trade association advertising of a public relations character as well as individual and group efforts to secure action on matters of public interest. It would also include the use of advertising to sell religion, political ideas, social change, and economic ideologies.

Advertorials

Advertising space and time in our mass media can provide a forum for the presentation of information and ideas related to social, economic, political, and personal issues as well as a marketplace for information about products available for purchase. Such space can be used to present ideas and information to readers that might not be presented if complete dependence were placed upon newspaper and magazine publishers and editors to do so on their own initiative. Furthermore, by using advertising space, the sponsoring organization or individual can present information and ideas in the form and manner desired, subject only to the general restrictions of the press.

An interesting example of this use of advertising space is the "advertorial" which was first introduced by *The Atlantic Magazine* in its December 1951 issue. The publisher of *The Atlantic* had this to say in explanation of the first advertorial carried by the magazine:

> The *Atlantic* believes that there is a need for an entirely new kind of advertising, designed to transmit those compelling and often complex facts about American business which are in the public interest—and too little understood . . .
>
> This calls for a new technique in advertising. For generations, *product advertisements* have been based upon the constant repetition of a theme, expressed in a slogan, a picture, a piece of short copy, or a jingle. Such skillful simplification will remain the most effective way to *advertise products.* But business cannot compress its problems and aspirations into a slogan or singing commercial. It cannot depend upon a reflex action; it must appeal to the reader's intelligence and let him draw his own conclusions.
>
> The need creates the opportunity, the opportunity for a new and explicit kind of advertising. Watch the magazines and newspapers and you will see the pioneers are already reaching out for the *intelligence* of readers. These advertisers are beginning to realize that the success of these new advertisements depends upon *trading information for the reader's time.* . . .
>
> To provide the facility for advertising to convey information, the *Atlantic* has developed a new form for the expression of business ideas. We call them advertorials. They will be paid advertisements, of course. . . . They are predicated upon the belief that the free competition of ideas has made this country great.[1]

Figure 6–1 is a reproduction of the first page of a four-page advertorial that illustrates the concept emphasized by Mr. Snyder. This use of advertising can, in fact, make anyone his own editor without the risk and cost of operating his own publishing enterprise.

Figures 6–2 and 6–3 illustrate advertisements of an advertorial nature that deal with subjects more often treated by public speakers, editors, or newspaper columnists.

Advertisements may also be used to bring before the large audiences assembled by newspapers a point of view held by the signers of the advertisement. This view may be different from that of the publishers or editors of the media used but can be presented in advertisement form without being edited by some outside or unfriendly party.

This kind of advertising can provide a forum for the presentation of opposing ideas to the public or ideas that may not be effectively presented in news or orthodox editorial material. Some may fear this use of advertising since it could lead to the presentation of highly unpopular material. For example, Russia purchased advertising space in a number of American newspapers in July 1962 and ran the full text of then Premier Khrushchev's 13,000-word speech before the Communist-organized World Peace Con-

[1] Donald B. Snyder, "Business *Is* the Public Interest," *The Atlantic,* December 1951, p. 19.

FIGURE 6–1
The first page of a four-page "advertorial"

 An Atlantic *Public Interest* Advertisement

There is tumult in transportation circles today arising out of proposals by a Cabinet Advisory Committee recommending major changes in national transportation policy. Only the railroads, among all forms of transport, are actively campaigning for these recommendations which are the outcome of a request made by them. Here is the viewpoint on competition in transport held by a leader in one of the newer forms of transportation.

COMPETITION IN TRANSPORTATION

by NEIL J. CURRY

Chairman, American Trucking Associations, Inc.

As early as 1904 railroads had established a speed record of 115.2 miles per hour. There it remained until 1934, thirty years later, when the Union Pacific achieved the current accepted record of 120 miles per hour for passenger trains. Between 1928 and 1936 the speed of freight trains, not as a record but on the whole, increased 22 per cent.

The significance of these figures is obvious. Not until the auto and airplane became factors in passenger transportation and motor trucks became significant in freight hauling, did the rails have the spur to compel improved performance.

One of the twin gods to which, figuratively, American business builds altars is competition. The other is maximum freedom of action, a notable national credo in all fields of activity, interpreted in business to mean dislike of all but the most essential governmental restraints.

The ideal climate in agriculture, industry and commerce, from the standpoint of the entrepreneur, would be one in which ownership operating through management would have maximum power and discretion to solve any and all problems which arise. Such, at least, would be the impulsive reaction of the entrepreneur, suddenly confronted with an opportunity to state the terms under which he would prefer to function.

Historically, the invasion of the field of management discretion by local, state and federal agencies has seldom been achieved without resistance of varying intensity, whether in the areas of health, insurance and welfare, marketing and trade prac-

tices or labor relations. Each such overlay of ordinances, rules, regulations or statutes has seemed to some segments of management a handicap which was unwarranted or costly or an impediment to full development of potential.

Transportation is "Public" Business

What I have been saying is particularly, but not exclusively, applicable to so-called "private" business. Economists recognize the essential difference between a private business, which is one whose activities reflect impact on a relatively limited number of people or a limited area of the economy and a "public" business, if I may use that term, whose operations cut across the whole economy.

An example of a "private" business might be a television manufacturer. However excellent his product, its purchase by anyone is optional, both as to his particular brand of television and as to television as a whole. An example of a "public" business would be an electric light and power company since it would be difficult if not impossible to operate our economy without that facility.

Despite the "private" nature of the great bulk of American agricultural, industrial and commercial activity there has been a steady trend toward intervention in its operation by government, based on the theory that the public interest can be and is affected by the cumulative or total result of certain practices in business or agriculture, indulged in by otherwise "private" business or farming.

In spite of the vigorous devotion which our people as citizens and as entrepreneurs pay to the

FIGURE 6–2
An editorial type ad

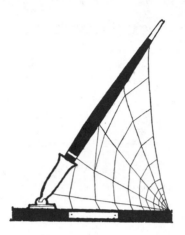

How to retire at 35

It's easy.

Thousands of men do it every year. In all walks of life.

And it sets our economy, our country, and the world back thousands of years in terms of wasted human resources. But worst of all is the personal tragedy that almost always results from "early retirement."

It usually begins with a tinge of boredom. Gradually a man's work begins to seem endlessly repetitious. The rat race hardly seems worth it any more.

It's at this point that many a 35-year-old boy-wonder retires. There are no testimonial dinners or gold watches. He still goes to work every day, puts in his forty hours, and even draws a paycheck. He's retired, but nobody knows it. Not at first, anyhow.

The lucky ones get fired in time to make a fresh start. Those less fortunate hang on for awhile—even decades —waiting and wondering. Waiting for a raise or promotion that never comes, and wondering why.

There are ways to fight back, though, and most men do. They counteract the urge to coast by running as they've never run before. They run until they get the second wind that is now known as "self-renewal."

Self-renewal is nothing more or less than doing for yourself what your parents, teachers, coaches, and bosses did for you when you seemed young enough to need it. It's the highest form of self-discipline. And it can be one of the most satisfying experiences a man can enjoy.

Self-renewal is the adult's ability to motivate himself; to reawaken his self-pride in the face of spiritual fatigue. Self-renewal is the device by which the boy-wonders become men. Leaders. Creators. Thinkers.

Self-renewal is probably the greatest test a businessman must face. It's worth the effort, though. With the life expectancy approaching the century mark, 65 years is a long time to spend in a rocking chair.

MARSTELLER INC.

ADVERTISING · PUBLIC RELATIONS · MARKETING RESEARCH
NEW YORK · CHICAGO · PITTSBURGH · TORONTO · GENEVA · BRUSSELS

FIGURE 6–3
Use of advertising to present an idea

Can a good businessman be a good American?

If your biggest single interest is your company's profit, and if you have to spend eight, ten, twelve hours a day to make it, how can you call yourself a good citizen?

Look at it this way:

Good profits enable your company to offer more jobs. And more secure jobs.

Good profits make your company an attractive investment which gives you more capital to expand to offer still more jobs. And even more secure jobs.

Good profits enable your company to design and manufacture better products. And provide better service to your customers. And make your company a better place to work.

Good profits enable your company to make meaningful bequests to community projects such as new hospitals, new schools, new recreational facilities.

And, of course, good profits make it possible for your company to pay your full share of the cost of government—at all levels. The bigger your profit, the bigger your tax contribution.

Come to think of it, maybe one type of ugly American is the businessman who constantly loses money.

MARSTELLER INC.

ADVERTISING • PUBLIC RELATIONS • MARKETING RESEARCH

NEW YORK • CHICAGO • PITTSBURGH • TORONTO • GENEVA • BRUSSELS • LONDON • PARIS • SÃO PAULO • STUTTGART

gress in Moscow. One newspaper, *The Washington Post,* did not accept the Russian advertisement but wrote the Soviet Embassy that "it would publish the Khrushchev text in its news columns if one of the official Russian newspapers, *Pravda* or *Izvestia,* would do the same with the text of President Kennedy's disarmament speech before the United Nations General Assembly"[2] in September 1961.

One of the most dramatic advertorials of recent years was a two-page advertisement placed in the *New York Times,* May 23, 1966. This was an ad by Morihiro Matsuda, a citizen of Japan and operator of a small business in Tokyo. The headline and theme of the advertisement was "Idea for Peace in Vietnam."

Mr. Matsuda paid $11,184 to have this advertisement carried in the *Times.* This is a large sum for a relatively poor man to pay to have a nonbusiness message distributed to the multitudes. He was motivated by a "burning desire to share his thoughts with the rest of mankind." Such sharing is possible through the medium of advertising.

Public relations

The past few decades have witnessed a substantial increase in attention given by business, government, and social institutions to their relations with various publics. There are many facets to public relations, and these make it difficult to develop a concise and all-encompassing definition. Perhaps the definition given by Cutlip and Center will suffice. They say "public relations is the planned effort to influence opinion through socially responsible performance based on mutually satisfactory two-way communication."[3] They go on to say that "gaining the support and cooperation of others through persuasion is part of the day-by-day work of every organization—government agencies, business firms, labor unions, universities, and welfare agencies."[4] Thus, advertising provides a valuable and efficient instrument of communication in furthering the public relations programs of various institutions.

Business institutions have many groups of people to consider. Among such groups are stockholders, employees, customers, prospective customers, professional educators, legislators, and citizen voters. All these and others have some interest in and association with specific business houses. The attitudes which individuals and groups of people have toward the policies and practices of specific business institutions can have an impor-

---

[2] From UPI wire story, July 27, 1962.

[3] Scott M. Cutlip and Allen H. Center, *Effective Public Relations,* 4th ed. (Prentice-Hall, Inc., 1971), p. 2.

[4] Ibid.

FIGURE 6–4
An effective public relations advertisement

He's the reason we at FS invested several million dollars in additional petroleum product inventories and storage facilities last year.

He's the reason we improved our transportation and distribution systems in the face of continuing agricultural product shortages.

He's the reason we expanded our fertilizer production facilities, but refused to take advantage of the highly profitable export market for these products.

And he's the reason we are spending more time and effort on product research, consumer education and specialized field training than ever before.

Whatever we do and however we serve is for the sole benefit of our farmer patrons in the Midwest.

And these days, that's more important than ever.

THE MIDWESTERN FARMER.

FS
®
...a farmer-owned service

200,000 farmers pulling together.

tant bearing on strikes, slowdowns, consumer patronage, education of youth, and business legislation.

Business firms should, of course, operate in the public interest, but that alone is not enough to develop favorable public opinion. Relations with various publics can be left to develop without a plan, or they can be planned. The producer of a better mousetrap can wait to have customers find out through their own desires about the better trap, or he can plan a program of education or advertising to carry the story of the better trap to would-be buyers. Planned interpretation of the merits of the institution in all its social and economic aspects is equally vital. Advertising is being used in increasing amounts to help in this interpretation.

Figure 6–4 illustrates how one company addressed itself to its customers and would-be customers. The advertisement was run at a time when farmers were experiencing difficulty in obtaining adequate supplies of petroleum products and fertilizer. It explained what the company was

FIGURE 6–5
Questionnaire designed to measure public attitude toward certain business situations

---

1. Just as a rough guess, what percent profit would you say the average manufacturer makes in peacetime?_____
2. After a factory or plant has paid for overhead and materials, which would you say gets the bigger share of what's left—stockholders and top management or workers?
    a._____ Stockholders and top management
    b._____ Workers
3. Out of every dollar paid in dividends, salaries to top management, and wages to workers, how much do you think the worker gets?_____
4. In general, do you think our large corporations are paying too big a share, too small, or about the right share of what they make to their (a) stockholders, (b) top executives, (c) office workers, (d) labor?

	Pay is—		
Worker Classification	Too big	Too small	About right
a. Stockholders			
b. Top executives			
c. Office workers			
d. Labor			

5. Suppose the cost of living went up 15 percent in the next few months. Would you say that most companies could afford a 15 percent increase in wages without raising prices?____ yes;____ no.
6. Does your company make a practice of giving you information about profits? ____ yes;____ no.

FIGURE 6–6
A good use of advertising to increase public understanding

350 days in which to meet our payroll, pay our bills and taxes...

...and 16 days in which to earn a profit

Our net income in 1972 amounted to 4.3 per cent of our total revenues. Stating this in terms of the calendar, we worked 350 days of the year to meet our payroll, pay for materials and services, taxes, depreciation, and interest. In the remaining 16 days we earned a profit.

Our earnings are showing some improvement in 1973. Perhaps we will have a few more profit days than we had last year.

Our revenues in 1973 may be about $4 billion. That's a lot of money. But our operating costs also add up to a whopping total.

We must spend millions of dollars annually to replace worn-out or obsolete facilities. We must keep pace with new technology if we are to remain competitive. At mid-1973 the estimated cost of completing authorized capital expenditures totalled $740 million.

So don't believe it if you hear that

steel corporations are making fantastic profits. In 1972 Bethlehem's net income as a per cent of stockholders' equity was 6.5 per cent. By comparison, the return for all manufacturing industries was almost double, or 12.1 per cent.

We'd be happy to send you our 1972 annual report if you would like to have more details. Write Public Affairs Dept. Bethlehem Steel Corp., Bethlehem, PA 18016.

Bethlehem

FIGURE 6–7
Use of advertising to present a "lesson" in economics

America's farmers and ranchers urge you to consider the whole issue of food prices.

Instead of looking for someone to blame in the present food price controversy, let's look for ways to understand it.

The way things are now, nobody's happy. Some people blame the processors for higher prices. But the facts are that processors' profits are held in line by competition, as well as price controls. Meat packers average less than 1¢ profit per dollar of sales. Some others blame the retailers, yet food retailers average less than three-tenths of a cent profit on each dollar of sales. And some consumers blame them all, including the farmer. Nobody's happy. Is one group **all** to blame? Let's look at all parts of the problem.

Food prices ARE up, no question about it—but the whole cost of living is up. So are wages and salaries. Over the last 20 years, industrial workers have enjoyed a 129% pay hike. Even with food prices moving up 46% during that period, farmers' income has increased only 11% gross.

The cost of PRODUCING food is up, too. Farmers' total costs of producing food have increased 109% over the last 20 years. Taxes are up 297%; labor up 141% and machinery up 100%. On top of all of that, farmers and ranchers are faced daily with the very same cost of living pressures (food, clothing, housing, medical, etc.) we are all feeling.

Are farmers and ranchers entitled to a fair income? Answer quickly. Yes or no? Of course they are—just as we **all** feel we have earned the right to a decent living. But, did you know, for example, that the average farm family's annual income last year was only about two-thirds of the average industrial worker's?

Yet, the fact is—farmers have increased their productivity more than any other industry. (In just the last

13 years, they've increased productivity over 20%—on 7% fewer acres!) If it weren't for that increased productivity, beef prices might have gone up to match hourly pay increases in industry and cattle would be selling at market for $80 per hundredweight, instead of the recent $45!

So WHO is to 'blame'? Well, it's really not possible to point fingers at middlemen or farmers or truck drivers or anybody—and blame them for food price levels. Food prices are a reflection of our whole booming, inflating economy. And what inevitably follows that economy—a rising demand. Food producers, of course, will increase production as long as they can make a decent living at it. Import controls, price controls and boycotting **can** affect demand, but in the main, consumer demand is the one factor that sets the price of food at retail. Just as demand and production costs set the price of clothing, housing and everything else.

What's the ANSWER, then? Farmers and ranchers need your support. They're in this squeeze, too. They need time to increase production. They need a stable situation. They need assurance of fair prices for their present livestock. They need reasonable assurance of a market.

Either an extended, one-sided price freeze or unduly continued boycotts can work against production increases.

Thousands of farmers each make their independent business decisions. If, because of uncertainty about the future, each one decides to raise a few less hogs or cattle, instead of more, the result will be an even smaller supply of meat a year from now. And **that** means even higher prices, perhaps a black market, and truly serious meat shortages. Uncertainty has the same depressing effect on decisions to plant grain or other crops.

Understanding and working together does it. It's not easy, but be patient. It takes 27 months to produce a market-ready steer: 9 months to produce a market-ready hog. But farmers are already working on the problem. At the beginning of this year, cattle and calves on hand were up 4 million head, as compared with a year ago. And this year's calf crop will be 5% to 7% over last year's. In addition, farmers now are expected to return to production more than 40 million acres of farmland.

So, with disposable income rising faster than food costs, the consumers' share of income being spent for food will drop again—to an estimated 15.5%. (Compared to 20% in 1960.) And that's good news.

America's farmers and ranchers are, in the main, dedicated to increased production and efficiency. If thoughtful Americans, and the men they send to Washington, will help, farmers can get the job done.

Farmland Industries
sponsors this message on behalf of America's farmers and ranchers.

doing to meet the vital needs of farmers. The advertisement was not designed to sell specific products but rather to build a favorable image of the company.

Some companies seek to determine the attitude of the public toward them and their business policies and practices as a means of guiding them in their efforts to explain and interpret company action properly. This approach was used recently by a large oil company to find out what people thought about the size of business profits and other aspects of the economics of business. A copy of the questionnaire used in this study is shown in Figure 6–5.

In answer to the first question, one third of all persons withheld an answer, but two fifths guessed that profits ranged anywhere from 25 to over 50 percent. Only six out of a hundred gave the correct answer— something under 10 percent. In harmony with the same attitude, a great majority of people canvassed believed that total payments to stockholders and management exceeded total payments to workers. Only 13 percent thought workers' wages constituted half or more of the total paid out in the form of dividends, top-management salaries, and workers' wages. The great majority of respondents, 79 percent, stated that company heads failed to give information to employees about profits. This survey provided the basis for an informative advertising program to raise the level of general public understanding concerning that particular company.

Quite a number of companies have used advertising to inform the public that their net profit constitutes a relatively small piece of the gross sales or income pie. The advertisement of Bethlehem Steel, reproduced in Figure 6–6, is a good representation of that kind of advertising.

In a similar educational effort Farmland Industries used advertising to give consumers a "lesson in economics." The advertisement reproduced in Figure 6–7 appeared as a full-page ad in April 1974 in a number of city newspapers in America. The personal message from the president of Farmland Industries appearing in the box in the bottom right corner gave additional strength to the message. The ad appeared at a time when consumers were disturbed by sharp increases in food prices and critical of farmers.

Association and group advertising

A significant number of professional, trade, labor, and civic associations make use of idea advertising. During periods of labor strife, both business and labor groups often purchase advertising space or time to present their side of the problem to various publics. In the early 1960s the American Medical Association used advertising extensively to present the case against socialized medicine. Various business groups regularly use advertising to inform and influence readers as to the merits of their "way of life." Others employ advertising in an attempt to influence legislation.

FIGURE 6–8
Use of advertising to influence legislation

It's not right, Senator!

It's not right for the Congress of the United States to deprive countless thousands of housewives all over the country of the benefits of a Washing Machine by imposing an excise tax that would add $25 to $35 to the retail price

Don't Tax Washing Machines!

Washing clothes by hand is probably the ugliest household job a woman has to perform. It is hard, back-breaking work.

In families where every penny counts, women look forward to the day when they'll be able to own a Washing Machine. These women deserve the highest consideration from the Senate of the United States.

Tax money has to be raised. The people know it . . . and the people will pay it. But . . . is it right to tax a woman's health and well-being by making it harder for her to replace the washboard and tub with a labor-saving Washing Machine. An excise tax on Washing Machines would do just that.

By the time this tax is pyramided from the manufacturer—to the distributor—to the retailer . . . it would add a burdensome $25 to $35 to the consumer's cost.

Actually, Congress doesn't like the idea of taxing Washing Machines. It refused to do so during World War II. In the current bill, the House expressly exempted Washing Machines from the excise tax. It accepted the fact that a Washer is an essential household machine tool. Congress has never imposed an excise tax on a machine tool for a factory. Congress should ·not now tax the most essential machine tool in the American home.

A Washing Machine is not a luxury—it is a necessity. It is a labor-saving machine that relieves women of untold drudgery and fatigue—especially among the modest income groups. In all fairness to these women, the Senate, like the House, ought to refuse to impose an excise tax on Washing Machines.

AMERICA DOESN'T WANT THIS, SENATOR

*A consumer tax on Washing Machines would
delay the time when every American housewife
could afford to free herself from the back-
breaking toil of the washboard and tub . . .*

DON'T TAX WASHING MACHINES

AMERICAN HOME LAUNDRY MANUFACTURERS' ASSOCIATION, CHICAGO, ILLINOIS

The American Home Laundry Manufacturers' Association ran, in the *Washington Post,* the advertisement which is reproduced in Figure 6–8. At the time this was run Congress was debating a new tax bill which was designed to increase taxes on many consumer goods. By using the public press to reach senators, the stand of the association was dramatized much more effectively than would have resulted had dependence been placed on direct mail only.

"Never underestimate the power of a woman" is a slogan used in the past to encourage sellers of products to advertise in a magazine edited for women. That slogan took a new twist in the 1970s when women's groups started using advertising to present some of the tenets held by women's liberationists. One such advertisement is reproduced in Figure 6–9.

Some associations or groups use advertising as a means of dispelling erroneous impressions held by different segments of the population. It was for this purpose that various farm cooperatives ran a series of advertisements to emphasize the democratic character of cooperatives. Preceding these advertisements a study was made among business and professional leaders in a midwestern state to determine their attitudes toward farm retail cooperatives. In that study respondents were asked whether they believed the farm retail cooperative with which they were familiar was an asset to *their community.* Of the total answering, 51 percent said yes. When attention was focused on farm cooperatives in general and when respondents were asked whether they believed that "farm cooperatives were an asset to *a* community," only 42 percent answered yes. At best, then, only one half of the business and professional leaders thought farm retail cooperatives were worthwhile.

Even more negative was the attitude on specific aspects of cooperatives. Only 29 percent of the respondents in this study believed that cooperatives stood for or promoted the free enterprise system. Almost one third (32 percent) believed farm cooperatives stood for communism or socialism. Thus, the ad in Figure 6–10 was run to say, in effect, "Cooperatives are democratic."

In the case of a new type of business service or operation, the job of informing or educating the public as to the characteristics and merits of the new is often great. This job of education may be undertaken by individual leaders in the field or by an association of most or all of the members. Such group action is familiar procedure in the product field. Examples include group promotion of oranges, nuts, vegetables, flowers, cement, candy, and silver.

In the nonproduct field such group action to present a business message is less extensive but is increasing in importance. In the early 1970s, for example, associations and individual companies used advertising to promote travel within the United States. "See America First" was a common theme. Government agencies encouraged such advertising as a way of

FIGURE 6–9.
A powerful ad dealing with a social issue

This healthy, normal baby has a handicap. She was born female.

WEINER

When she grows up, her job opportunities will be limited, and her pay low. As a sales clerk, for instance, she'll earn half of what a man does. If she goes to college, she'll still earn less than many men with a 9th grade education. Maybe you don't care—but it's a fact—job discrimination based on sex is against the law. And it's a waste. Think about your own daughter—she's handicapped too.

Womanpower. It's much too good to waste.

For information: NOW Legal Defense and Education Fund Inc., 127 East 59th Street, Dept. K, New York, N.Y. 10022

FIGURE 6–10.
"Cooperatives are democratic," says this advertising message

"OF THE PEOPLE"

*—BY THE PEOPLE—AND FOR THE PEOPLE—*are the standards given a great nation — by a great man. Every school child in America learns this fundamental truth about the government of his United States.

Every American takes simple pride in being part of a government "of the people." It means freedom in the pursuit of life, liberty and happiness for our 140,000,000 citizens. It has given America the mantle of leadership for millions seeking freedom throughout a war-torn world. Democracy is the American way →

Farm cooperatives are founded on the basic principles of American democracy. They too are "of the people." And they contribute to the security and prosperity of thousands of rural communities throughout America —

In Auglaize and Shelby Counties several thousand farm families work together in a pattern of friendly and purposeful cooperation. The more than twenty cooperative enterprises have — by increasing farm purchasing power — helped farmers become the most important customers in the rural community. Cooperatives — of the people — by the people — and for the people — are helping build sound and prosperous American communities.

Cooperatives of Auglaize and Shelby Counties

AUGLAIZE COUNTY FARM BUREAU CO-OP.	WAPAKONETA PRODUCERS LIVESTOCK CO-OP.	THE BUCKLAND COOPERATIVE CO.
AUGLAIZE COUNTY FARM BUREAU, INC.	JACKSON CENTER FARM BUREAU CO-OP.	MIDWEST ELECTRIC INC.
FARMERS EQUITY UNION CREAMERY CO.	SIDNEY FARMER EXCHANGE	MINSTER FOOD STORAGE CO-OP.
MINSTER FARMERS CO-OP. EXCHANGE	MIAMI-DARKE-SHELBY-NAT'L FARM LOAN ASS'N.	POULTRY PRODUCERS ASS'N.
WAPAKONETA NATIONAL FARM LOAN ASS'N.	PIONEER ELECTRIC CO-OP.	WAPAKONETA FARMERS GRAIN
WAPAKONETA PRODUCTION CREDIT ASS'N.	AUGLAIZE COUNTY POMONA GRANGE	SHELBY COUNTY FARM BUREAU

keeping more travel dollars at home and sending fewer abroad. Thus, such advertising, it was thought, could have a beneficial effect on our balance of trade.

Use in politics

Advertising is being used more and more by political parties and candidates as a means of getting their messages before vast numbers of people. In major campaigns professional advertising counselors and practitioners are employed to plan and execute advertising strategy.

The late Senator Richard L. Neuberger, in commenting on political advertising, said, "I consider the trend toward wider use of (advertising) techniques in politics significant. In fact, it is so significant that it may well revolutionize politicking in this country and could definitely turn out to be the most decisive single factor governing American politics during our generation."[5]

Martin Mayer is somewhat skeptical about the value or appropriateness of advertising in political campaigns. The following comment of Mayer is worthy of serious thought:

> The most common objection to the use of advertising to magnify political issues is that advertising oversimplifies. A good part of the technique of advertising has the single purpose of simplification, of finding from the welter of causes which make people buy a product the one or two or three which can be refined down to a "reason" and then blown up to a slogan. Applied to branded products, the technique at its worst can do little harm to society as a whole, because product purchases are trivial matters and because people do not buy even the most heavily advertised product a second time unless it has given satisfaction. Applied to political issues, however, the technique must partially misinform, create undesirable emotions, and distort the realities which, in theory, underlie the decision of the electorate.[6]

The skepticism of Mr. Mayer was substantiated to a significant degree in the 1972 political campaigns. No exact figures are available for the amount spent for political advertising by the two parties in the 1972 presidential election, but it is estimated that at least $80 million was spent. Estimates for political advertising at all levels in the 1972 campaigns amount to more than $400 million.

Such expenditures included not only sums spent in broadcast and print media but also amounts allocated to direct-mail and telephone appeals. In both direct-mail and telephone usage, computer-written letters and tape-recorded telephone messages were employed extensively. This led

---

[5] Richard L. Neuberger, "Madison Avenue in Politics, *Esquire,* August 1957, p. 79.

[6] Martin Mayer, *Madison Avenue, U.S.A.* (New York: Harper & Row, 1958), pp. 300–301.

one analyst to conclude that "the unprecedented use of direct mail and the telephone *demolished* the right of privacy."[7]

A general assessment of advertising used in the 1972 political campaigns must conclude that it was often in bad taste, dealt more with personalities than with issues, often misinformed, and much would hardly pass a Federal Trade Commission examination. It dropped far below the standards advertising professionals strive to maintain for product advertising. Mr. Weiss, in writing about the campaigns, said:

> I strongly believe that 1972 political advertising sowed the seed of its own destruction, and that we may see some degree of improvement by 1976 and, perhaps, major change by 1980. For the sake of our democratic institutions, for the sake of advertising's future, I devoutly hope that this horrible social pollutant will be brought under at least (some) degree of control.[8]

By historical standards the use of advertising in political campaigns is still quite new. Experimentation with different methods of use is still in order. Some strict guidelines for use are also in order. It may be that such advertising will be used more in the "advertorial" sense in the future rather than as a means for merely saturating the media with slogans and some surface issue. In any event, it is perhaps good that political parties and candidates for public office have this means for "direct" communication with the electorate in an age where face-to-face communication is possible to only a limited degree. It is not that advertising can, in itself, determine the course of an election but rather that it can provide another and an important dimension in the process of informing, educating, and persuading the electorate on basic, as well as surface, issues.

The Advertising Council

Organized and systematic group action for idea advertising was developed during World War II. Such organized efforts were centered in the War Advertising Council. The council was established in 1942 as a nonprofit voluntary organization financed by both business and individual sponsors. Its purpose was to marshal the talents of the advertising profession to prepare advertising campaigns which would "induce people to take desperately needed actions" in the interest of national welfare.

The War Advertising Council would select, in cooperation with government agencies, the areas needing strong public support. After selection was made, some agency in the profession would volunteer to develop strategy and prepare advertisements for use in "selling" the public on the

[7] E. B. Weiss, "Political Advertising Blackens the Other Eye," *Advertising Age,* February 12, 1973, p. 35.

[8] Ibid.

need for action. Completed advertisements would be made available to press, radio, and other media for voluntary use.

Accomplishments   During the war period, voluntary contributions of time and space resulting from council action approximated $300 million annually. The organized power of advertising was behind the job of telling American people what needed to be done to speed victory. A partial list of the fields covered by such cooperative support follows:

1. War bond drives.
2. Developing victory gardens.
3. Recruiting women for military service.
4. Urging early mailing for overseas Christmas gifts (95 percent of all such gifts were mailed before the deadline).
5. Reduction of absenteeism in factories.
6. Conservation of food.
7. Salvage of waste fats, paper, tin.
8. Support of Red Cross.

There was no attempt to measure the exact influence of advertising in securing public action on things advertised. However, the tremendous response that paralleled advertising effort indicated that advertising was a powerful stimulus to action. Strong advertising support, work of civic groups, and efforts of other agencies combined to produce outstanding results in many fields. In the field of conservation and salvage, such efforts induced the American people to salvage 538 million pounds of waste fat, 800 million pounds of tin, and 23 million tons of paper. Equally impressive response was accorded other drives, such as those to sell bonds, plant victory gardens, donate blood, and recruit nurses' aides.

Change from war to peace   Group action during a war crisis is a relatively easy thing to accomplish, but it is more difficult to achieve such cooperation when a crisis is less evident. However, the War Advertising Council chose to attempt such cooperation on a regular and continuing basis. It therefore changed its name immediately after the war to the Advertising Council. It has grown apace with the times and has helped to meet some of the increased social responsibilities accepted by the advertising profession.

The council also broadened its function beyond that of its predecessor. It operates as a "nonprofit organization which marshals the forces of advertising in helping to conserve our human resources, to conserve our natural resources, to strengthen our democracy and our national economy, to build our national defense, and to strengthen freedom overseas."[9]

Advertisers and media give free advertising time and space in support of campaigns developed by the council, and agencies prepare materials

[9] Advertising Council, *Fifteenth Annual Report* (New York, 1957), p. 1.

without charge. It is governed by a Board of Directors of 70 businessmen who meet monthly to plan and supervise the various projects accepted for promotion.

Projects are selected by the board and a Public Policy Committee of 20 members. This latter group is recruited from leading citizens represent-

FIGURE 6–11
How the Advertising Council functions

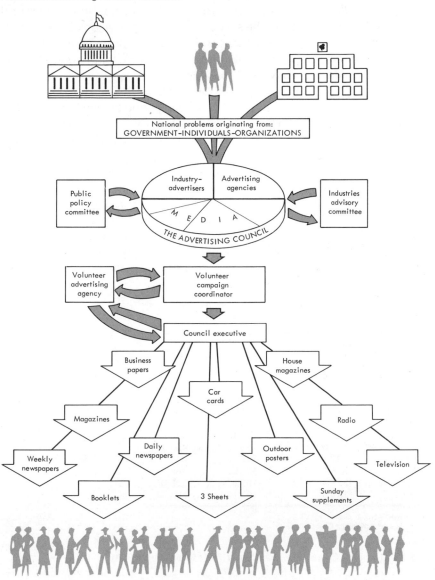

ing all phases of American life. Included on the Policy Committee are representatives from philanthropy, religion, education, labor, business, and foreign affairs. A chart showing the facilities and operations of the council is presented in Figure 6–11.

An average of about 150 requests are received for advertising help each year, but only a fraction of these are accepted by the council for promotion. During a recent 12-month period the council conducted major campaigns for 16 public service projects. These included the promotion of ideologies, alleviation of human distress, and conservation of natural resources. Names of some of the specific projects were: people's capitalism, drug abuse, better schools, American Red Cross, improvement of neighborhoods, traffic safety, accident prevention, crusade for freedom, religion in American life, U.S. Savings Bonds, and prevention of forest fires. The amount of space and time donated by media to the promotion of these and other council campaigns in the 12-month period ending June 30, 1971 amounted to more than $468 million.[10] The value of traceable annual advertising media support donated to council campaigns is shown in Table 6–1.

It is difficult to measure the effect of council campaigns on the attitudes and actions of consumers, but results have been clocked for some campaigns. A few years ago the council developed a campaign on "Help the College of Your Choice" to emphasize the need for financial aid to colleges (see Figure 6–12). After the campaign had been in operation for four years the president of the council reported that "voluntary financing of colleges had stepped up sharply." He said that figures indicated "nonalumni contri-

TABLE 6–1
Dollar value of media time and space donated to support council campaigns

Year	Value in millions	Year	Value in millions
1952	$101.8	1963	$234.0
1953	106.9	1964	264.8
1954	107.7	1965	236.0
1955	118.4	1966	304.6
1956	146.5	1967	352.8
1957	164.7	1968	338.6
1958	171.8	1969	463.2
1959	181.7	1970	451.0
1960	226.7	1971	468.7
1961	225.4	1972	525.0
1962	187.2	1973	N.A.

N.A. = Not available.
Source: Advertising Council.

[10] Advertising Council, *Annual Report 1971* (New York, 1973), p. 1.

FIGURE 6–12
An ad from the council campaign on higher education

WILL I WEAR ONE OF THOSE WHEN I GROW UP?

Will you?

Of course you want to grow up and be like your big brother—go to college, become an electronics engineer, an architect, a doctor. And we hope you do, because our country is growing and we'll need many more highly trained men and women to keep America strong and free.

Of course you want to go to college!

But, will you? Well, that depends.

It depends on you, of course. You've got to be bright, ambitious, hard-working. But it depends on something else, too. For you to go to college, there has to be a college for you to go to—or room for you in the college you select. Because in ten years—maybe less—applications to colleges and universities from bright boys and girls like you are ex-

pected to double. If you and your friends are to receive a really good education, it will mean more classrooms, libraries, up-to-date laboratories—above all, thousands more top-quality professors. And all that will mean money—a great deal of money.

If grown-ups will realize the problem and do something about it, your chances of going to college will improve. Let's hope they start now to give you the gift of knowledge—by helping to support the college of your choice.

If they want to know more about what the college crisis means to you—and to them—tell them to write for a free booklet to Higher Education, Box 36, Times Square Station, New York 36, N. Y.

Good luck, son!

Sponsored in cooperation with The Advertising Council and the Council for Financial Aid to Education.

FIGURE 6–13
A council ad dealing with a social problem

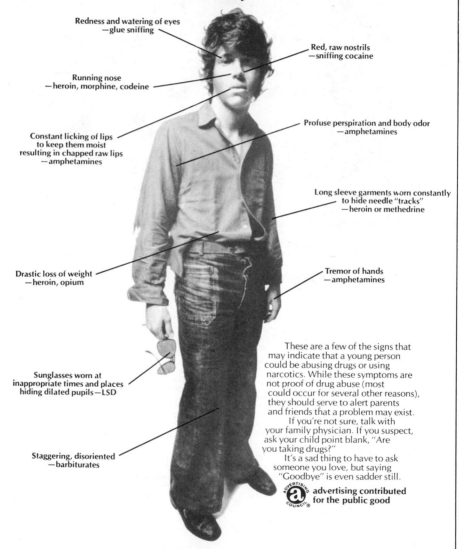

Diagram of a drug abuser

Redness and watering of eyes
—glue sniffing

Red, raw nostrils
—sniffing cocaine

Running nose
—heroin, morphine, codeine

Constant licking of lips
to keep them moist
resulting in chapped raw lips
—amphetamines

Profuse perspiration and body odor
—amphetamines

Long sleeve garments worn constantly
to hide needle "tracks"
—heroin or methedrine

Drastic loss of weight
—heroin, opium

Tremor of hands
—amphetamines

Sunglasses worn at
inappropriate times and places
hiding dilated pupils—LSD

Staggering, disoriented
—barbiturates

These are a few of the signs that
may indicate that a young person
could be abusing drugs or using
narcotics. While these symptoms are
not proof of drug abuse (most
could occur for several other reasons),
they should serve to alert parents
and friends that a problem may exist.
If you're not sure, talk with
your family physician. If you suspect,
ask your child point blank, "Are
you taking drugs?"
It's a sad thing to have to ask
someone you love, but saying
"Goodbye" is even sadder still.

**advertising contributed
for the public good**

DRUG ABUSE INFORMATION CAMPAIGN
MAGAZINE AD NO. DA-1464-70——7″ x 10″ (110 Screen)
ALSO AVAILABLE: AD NO. DA-1465-70——9⅜″ x 12⅛″
Volunteer Agency: Compton Advertising Inc., Volunteer Coordinator: Thomas B. McCabe, Jr., Scott Paper Company

FIGURE 6–14
A positive appeal for better nutrition

This is what little girls are made of.

Every minute, three billion cells in a little girls' body are being replaced by new ones.

The material for each new cell comes from the nutrients in the food she eats. What these nutrients do once they reach her body, and what they do with each other will make her different from every other little girl.

Her life depends on nutrition. She'll grow to live life well or ill because of it. We study nutrition. And we've learned that although poverty is the chief cause of malnutrition, it isn't the only cause.

Almost half of us are under-nourished. And through nothing more than a lack of knowledge about the food we eat.

Every day we're learning more. You should learn more too.

To give you some basic information and valuable guides to preparing meals and diets, we've put together a book entitled "Food Is More Than Just Something to Eat."

Write for it. Nutrition, Pueblo, Colorado 81009. And we'll send it to you.

Free.

 A Public Service of
This Magazine &
The Advertising Council

U S Departments of Agriculture and Health. Education. & Welfare Grocery Manufacturers of America

butions had increased 25 percent; corporate contributions, 41 percent; and annual alumni contributions, 101 percent."[11]

Not all of this, of course, was the result of council advertising, but it is reasonable to assume that such advertising hastened the acceptance of an idea that had basic public values and stimulated action on the part of individuals and corporations.

The drug problem is not an easy one for society to solve. The Advertising Council, however, accepted the challenge in the 1970s to help in doing something about it. The advertisement reproduced in Figure 6–13 was directed to parents to help them detect actual or potential drug problems. The fact that it was directed to parents probably had a greater influence on young people who read it than would have been true if it had been a direct "preaching" message.

Figure 6–14 shows another Ad Council ad with emphasis on the positive rather than the negative. It is an educational and persuasive message designed to raise the nutritional level of home food selection and preparation.

Religious organizations

Various religious groups have been consistent users of idea advertising for some time. Several million dollars are spent annually for radio and television time and publication space by churches to sell a particular creed or a way of life. A number of church users of advertising solicit inquiries and follow up with additional literature in good orthodox selling fashion. Some employ advertising agencies or public relations counsel to direct their advertising efforts.[12]

One of the outstanding examples of this type of advertising is that done by the Knights of Columbus, a society of Catholic laymen. This group started some local advertising in 1944 with the avowed purpose of answering gently but effectively some of the unfavorable ideas some had about Catholicism. The advertising program was expanded to a national and Canadian campaign as early as 1948.

Advertisements generally carry a compelling headline, a very small illustration, and full unbroken copy. The following are some of the headlines used in past advertisements: "Infallible? Yes! Always? No!"; "Is the Catholic Church a Menace to Democracy?"; "Learn the Truth about the Catholic Church by Mail . . . at No Cost!"; "The Real Secret of Successful Marriage"; "But How Can Educated People Be Catholics?" See Figure 6–15 for a reproduction of one of the advertisements.

[11] Theodore Repplier, Speech delivered before Association of National Advertisers, New York, May 1962.

[12] Detailed information on church advertising may be found in James W. Carty, Jr., *Advertising the Local Church* (Minneapolis: Augsburg Publishing House, 1965).

FIGURE 6–15
Use of advertising by religious groups

Jesus Christ Super What?

In the Fourth Century, fringe Christians had a field day with theories about Christ. The pendulum swung first one way and then the other. He was God, yes, but only the shadow of a man—that was one opinion. He was man, yes, but no more God than any other man—that was another view. Scholars, Church Councils and Popes worked their way through the confusion and gave careful, final expression to the truth about Jesus Christ.

But errors die hard and in the ensuing centuries the balance of the human and divine in Christ has been upset more than once. Good people in their zeal to imitate Christ and live by his principles often get carried away in private theories. The intention is good, but the effect is a distorted portrait of the Lord.

Recent developments suggest that distortion is again abroad in the land. It is time to listen again to the authentic Christian teaching on Christ. He is neither superman nor superstar. He is in a category all his own. Read about Him as traditional Catholic teaching sees Him. Write today for our free pamphlet, "Jesus Christ is True Man." No one will call on you.

┌─ **FREE** — Mail Coupon Today! ─────────────┐

Please send Free Pamphlet entitled
"Jesus Christ Is True Man"
This offer is limited to **one** free pamphlet.   58

Name_____

Address_____

City_____ State_____ Zip_____

CATHOLIC INFORMATION SERVICE
KNIGHTS OF COLUMBUS
P. O. Box 1971, New Haven, Conn. 06509

└─────────────────────────────────────┘

Kelly, Zahrndt & Kelly, Inc., of St. Louis, has served as the advertising agency for the Knights of Columbus campaign for many years. Mr. Virgil A. Kelly, president of the agency, comments as follows on the campaign:

> One of the most important things to be kept in mind in appraising this program is its positive character. It aims to present the Catholic doctrine, philosophy and history on their own merits and not by comparison with other creeds. In this respect we conform to the best product advertising by describing what we believe, without trying to point out how much better this may be than some conflicting beliefs. We realize, of course, that conflicting beliefs are inherently and necessarily controversial, whether explained from the pulpit or in paid space; but we are most careful to avoid injecting this inherent controversy into our advertisements. We tell our own story and let our readers judge it and accept or reject it on the basis of its truth and its appeal to their thinking.[13]

The results of this campaign have been substantial. The agency handling this project reported that the average number of requests for copies of the various pamphlets offered in the advertisements averaged better than one thousand per day.[14]

Another example of the use of regular advertising space to sell a religious message is illustrated by the experience of Christ Church in Cincinnati, Ohio. That church was located in the downtown section of the city and was faced with many of its members moving to the suburbs. It chose to remain in its old location and attempt to serve a downtown population. Such a population generally had a high turnover and many belonged to no church.

An advertising agency, whose president was a member of Christ Church, headed a committee to plan and execute an advertising campaign to explain the services offered by Christ Church and to encourage persons to make use of such services. An example of the kind of advertising run in the Cincinnati newspapers is shown in Figure 6–16.

Advertising Age reported on this use of advertising as follows:

> Mr. Sive and his committee embarked on a "fascinating adventure"—to try to reach the populace with modern consumer-appeal advertising, in place of the conventional "religious page" sermon announcements.
>
> He began putting 200-line ads into Cincinnati papers, generally avoiding the Saturday church-listing pages and making it a point to hit readers where they live. "Is it proper to join a church to meet people?" asked one of the most potent ads.
>
> Its answer: "One of the most elementary needs of human beings is to 'belong.' We were never intended to live all alone for ourselves. If you are

[13] From letter in file of author.
[14] Ibid.

FIGURE 6–16
A newspaper ad by a Cincinnati church

Are you all alone in the city?

Everyone needs to "belong." The biggest crowds can be the loneliest places. No one needs to be alone; we were meant not to be. Some try to escape loneliness on a superficial level—at bars, taverns, in clubs. This can never satisfy the deepest longings. If you want to find the secret of escaping loneliness, the Church can show you the most satisfying way never to be lonely again.

There are many organizations, activities, and services of worship at Christ Church to which you would be welcomed. Phone GArfield 1-1266, or come in any time for a talk with one of our clergy.

CHRIST CHURCH
EPISCOPAL
318 East 4th Street   Phone GA 1-1266

Every Monday Evening, 7 to 9 p. m., in the parish house, the Rev. Milton Saville is available for personal counseling or to give information about the Episcopal Church. No appointment is necessary, but you may make one if you wish.

FIGURE 6-17
An example of an unusual religious ad

Father Emerson Moore.
And the miracles
on 134th Street.

Harlem's Joseph P. Kennedy Center
is where over 700 people go when there's
no place else to turn.

There's day-care if you're very small.
Sports and social activities if you're bigger.
Counseling if you're troubled. Company if you're
old and lonely.

There's also never enough money,
too few staff workers, a shortage of equipment,
and not enough time.

And there's Emerson Moore.
He's the Catholic priest who runs the Center,
concentrating on your average, everyday kind of
miracles. Nothing spectacular.

Instead of parting the waters, he may try
to keep a family together. Instead of raising
the dead, he may help teach a kid a new life.

As if that weren't enough, he also works
in a nearby Catholic Charities office and
performs other priestly duties at the
parish house where he lives.

In other words, after celebrating daily
Mass, he starts work at nine in the
morning and finishes up at ten at night.
Six hard-to-believe days a week.

And just to keep in shape, he plans to start
work soon on a degree in psychology to back up
his master's in public administration.

How does he do it?
Easy. Besides having the constitution and
serenity of a rock, he has his own personal
miracle going for him. His priesthood.

And that's what makes Emerson Moore do for love
what he could never do for money.

But there's so much more work to do in the New York
Archdiocese—and too few priests. Could you do
what Emerson Moore is doing? Have you ever
thought about it? There's a phone number where
you can reach him. Just dial P-R-I-E-S-T-S
(774-3787). Or write: PRIESTS, 555 West End
Avenue, New York, N.Y. 10024.

He'll be happy to talk
to you about his vocation.
And yours too.

THE
NEW YORK
PRIEST.
GOD KNOWS
WHAT HE DOES
FOR A LIVING.

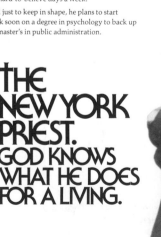

interested in meeting or belonging to a group of people who have learned how to overcome loneliness through a sharing of something worth while . . . you are invited to attend any of our services of worship and to join in the many activities and organizations of Christ Church."[15]

After a few months of advertising Mr. Sive estimated that the campaign had increased regular attendance at Christ Church by 40 or 50 persons and the number of confirmed members by 20.[16]

In the winter of 1973–74, New York's Terence Cardinal Cooke launched a $100,000 ad campaign to present a realistic image of how Catholic priests serve their community. The campaign consisted of five different advertisements run in New York metropolitan newspapers and regional editions of national magazines. One of the ads used in that campaign is reproduced in Figure 6–17.

Government advertising

In recent years federal and state governments have increased substantially their use of advertising as a means of informing, educating, and persuading citizens in respect to various programs. In terms of paid space in major media the U.S. government spent $16,508,800 in 1972.[17] This ranked the government 79th among the leading national advertisers in the country.

The federal government spends much more than the figure listed above in various forms of promotion, much of which would be classified as advertising in business. It is estimated that the total for advertising type promotion in 1973 approximated $100 million.

Major expenditures were made by the Department of Defense, primarily to promote enlistments. For fiscal year 1973 "advertising" expenditures by the various services were as follows: Army, $26.7 million; Navy, $24.6 million; Air Force, $10.9 million, and Marine Corps, $6.2 million. Requests for fiscal year 1974 were for $87.2 million.[18] A partial list of other government agencies using advertising on a national or international basis include the Department of Agriculture, the Agency for International Development, Federal Crop Insurance, U.S. Postal Service, Smithsonian Institute Press, the National Park Service, and the Department of Transportation. The 1973 Federal Aid Highway Act authorized $4 million to promote highway safety via the mass media. Expenditures by these agencies are exclusive of advertising time and space donated through the efforts of the Advertising Council to promote various government programs.

[15] *Advertising Age,* "Consumer-Appeal Ads Attract Members to Downtown Church Deserted by Suburbanites," December 17, 1956, p. 82.

[16] Ibid.

[17] *Advertising Age,* June 15, 1973, p. 1.

[18] Letter in file of author.

At the state level, government advertising is used extensively to bring new industry to the state and to attract tourists. State and local Chambers of Commerce and various trade associations often contribute to the total state industry location and travel budgets, but major amounts are provided by state governments. The U.S. Travel Data Center estimated that $46 million would be spent in fiscal year 1974 by states to promote tourism.[19]

Tourism is of concern to the federal government, too. After a two-year study the presidentially appointed National Tourism Resources Commission issued a report in 1973. In that report the commission recommended the U.S. Travel Service be funded at a $30 million level. It urged aggressive promotion abroad and within this country to attract foreigners to the United States and to encourage Americans to increase their knowledge of their country.

Idea advertising and national welfare

The social and economic welfare of a nation can be greatly enhanced when concerted and harmonious effort is exerted to educate citizens to an understanding of what is beneficial and to urge them to act to secure such benefits. Such efforts can reduce traffic accidents, improve health, conserve natural resources, reduce forest fires, and, in general, serve basic social and economic needs. Stuart Chase and F. J. Schlink emphasized this possibility many years ago when they wrote as follows:

> The technique of advertising is a magnificent technique. Sanely applied, it could remake the world. Think of what might be done with applied psychology in a great publicity drive for public health, for better housing, for cleaning up the slums, for honest and timely information about goods, for genuine education in a hundred fields! Many advertisers see this; a few of them try to practice it, but their hands are tied. Between the interest of the whole community in more abundant life, and the individual in his profit and loss account, there yawns a chasm which no optimism, no sophistries about "service," no pretty little talks by Dr. Frank Crane and his friends may cross.[20]

The vision expressed by Messrs. Chase and Schlink some 40 years ago is being implemented today through the work of the Advertising Council, government agencies, nonprofit corporations, and individual advertisers. A council or a corporate advertising campaign on each of the areas mentioned in the above quotation could be cited. Figure 6–18 is illustrative of ads that could be selected from these areas.

It may well be that the apparent trend toward worldwide depletion of many natural resources will require drastic changes in consumption pat-

---

[19] *Advertising Age,* October 1, 1973, p. 2.

[20] Stuart Chase and F. J. Schlink, *Your Money's Worth* (New York: Macmillan Co., 1935), p. 42.

FIGURE 6–18
Use of advertising to improve our environment

Next time you see someone polluting, point it out.

It's litter in the streets. It's air that smells. It's a river where fish can't breathe.

You know what pollution is.

But not everyone does.

So the next time you see pollution, don't close your eyes to it.

Write a letter. Make a call. Point it out to someone who can do something about it.

People start pollution. People can stop it.

Keep America Beautiful
99 Park Avenue, New York, New York 10016

Ad Council

A Public Service of
This Magazine &
The Advertising Council

terns. It may be that possession of "things" will be downgraded and more emphasis placed on the "quality of life."

Attention to the reduction of pollution of all kinds and the scarcity of energy to meet a growing demand may require a revision of long-standing attitudes in respect to what constitutes healthy economic growth. The U.S. government has long had a policy favoring full employment. To achieve full employment, high-level consumption is essential. In working to achieve such goals emphasis has been placed on the consumption of material goods such as houses, automobiles, appliances, clothing, furniture, boats, sporting equipment, power tools, air conditioning, airplanes, and swimming pools, and on services to keep such "things" in operation. Less emphasis has been placed on so-called social and cultural areas such as public parks, art galleries, recreational areas, libraries, and drama centers.

It was not until 1973 that there was national recognition of the dwindling supplies of energy-producing fuels and that an energy crisis was near at hand. This gave rise to sobering thoughts as to what changes in attitudes and actions on the part of government and consumers should take place. It caused Senator Henry Jackson to comment: "We need to ask whether we must despoil the hills in Appalachia to air-condition sealed-glass towers in New York. We need to ask whether we must put ourselves in hock to Middle East sheikdoms to keep roads clogged with gas-hungry cars."[21]

Senator Jackson suggests some change in our way of life—energy conservation rather than unbridled expansion of demand. E. B. Weiss suggests "a $1 billion paid advertising drive, financed by the federal government, (and) another coordinated $1 billion donated by industry, media, state governments, etc." to promote conservation of energy.[22]

It was estimated that $200 million was spent in 1973 by oil producers, public utilities, and other business firms to promote energy conservation. Small-car manufacturers emphasized the point and increased their share of the market. An ad by Volkswagen was headlined "A rational alternative to rationing gas" and went on to say that if all cars were VWs, 28.56 billion gallons of gasoline would be saved each year. The Texaco ad (Figure 6–19) illustrates another approach.

But Mr. Weiss observed that

> there is not a solitary reason to justify the conclusion that the required degree of conservation will be even remotely approached unless industry and the public have been persuaded to conserve energy by the most powerful, the most dramatic, the most unified communication program ever launched in

[21] *Time*, June 11, 1973, p. 31.

[22] E. B. Weiss, "Wanted: One billion dollar ad budget to sell Energy conservation to public, industry," *Advertising Age*, October 8, 1973, p. 31.

FIGURE 6–19
A gasoline conservation advertisement

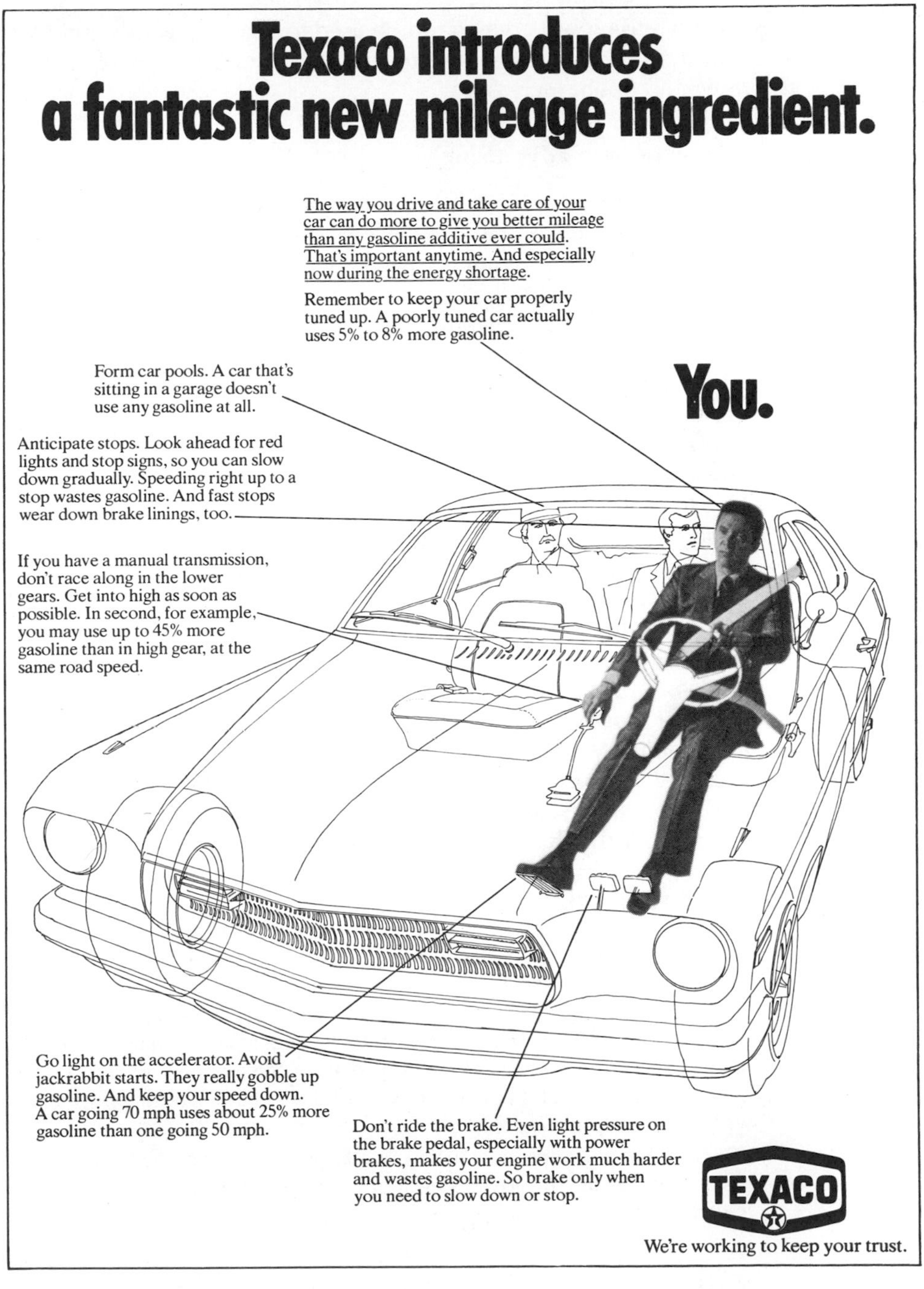

Texaco introduces a fantastic new mileage ingredient.

The way you drive and take care of your car can do more to give you better mileage than any gasoline additive ever could. That's important anytime. And especially now during the energy shortage.

Remember to keep your car properly tuned up. A poorly tuned car actually uses 5% to 8% more gasoline.

You.

Form car pools. A car that's sitting in a garage doesn't use any gasoline at all.

Anticipate stops. Look ahead for red lights and stop signs, so you can slow down gradually. Speeding right up to a stop wastes gasoline. And fast stops wear down brake linings, too.

If you have a manual transmission, don't race along in the lower gears. Get into high as soon as possible. In second, for example, you may use up to 45% more gasoline than in high gear, at the same road speed.

Go light on the accelerator. Avoid jackrabbit starts. They really gobble up gasoline. And keep your speed down. A car going 70 mph uses about 25% more gasoline than one going 50 mph.

Don't ride the brake. Even light pressure on the brake pedal, especially with power brakes, makes your engine work much harder and wastes gasoline. So brake only when you need to slow down or stop.

TEXACO

We're working to keep your trust.

this nation. . . . Add $1 billion for advertising, and energy conservation could become a way of life—as it must."[23]

Most advertising will continue to be used to promote goods and services, but the percentage devoted to the promotion of ideas of a social nature will no doubt increase.

Reversing the flow of idea advertising

The great majority of advertising, regardless of its type, is initiated by the few to influence the many. One retail firm will communicate with thousands of potential customers by means of advertising. One manufacturer, church organization, political party, government agency, or professional association will use advertising to reach millions. Only in the classified or want-ad sections of the press do we find any appreciable use of advertising space by the individual consumer to communicate his needs or wants to potential sellers of goods, jobs, or services.

There are numerous examples of individual citizens and groups who have used advertising to influence the attitudes and actions of political bodies. Mr. Matsuda's ad on Peace in Vietnam was one.

Is it not, however, reasonable to think that at some future time, consumer groups will use significant amounts of paid advertising in business media to influence business attitudes and actions? Such advertising might interpret consumer and general public attitudes and desires to management on such matters as use of quality labels on merchandise, inclusion of complete price and quality information in product advertising, public interest in labor-management peace, wage rates, price levels, high-volume operations and low margins versus low-volume operations and high margins, competitive business practices, and business ethics. It is doubtful whether such a reverse flow of advertising will materialize to any significant degree, but the thought is perhaps worth suggesting.

QUESTIONS AND PROBLEMS

1   Examine several recent issues of some newspaper or magazine to see if you can find any examples of advertorials.

2   Donald Snyder says that the new pioneers of idea advertising "realize that the success of these new advertisements depends upon trading information for the reader's time." What do you think of this concept of the relation between advertiser and consumer? Would the same concept apply equally well to product advertising?

3   "Good public relations cannot be bought, but must be earned." Does this mean that the use of advertising to help build favorable public attitudes toward a company is useless? Explain.

[23] Ibid, pp. 40–42.

4 Would you classify the advertising of NOW (National Organization of Women) as "reverse flow" advertising? Explain.

5 Does public relations concern itself with one large public or with several "publics"?

6 Do you think that advertising could properly be used by an individual or by a group of people to transmit to the management of business firms the individual or group attitudes and wishes toward important business practices and policies? Explain.

7 To what extent might groups of lay citizens use advertising to get their ideas before other citizens or legislative officers at local, state, or national levels?

8 There is strong evidence that the Advertising Council has been highly effective in persuading countless American citizens to act affirmatively on many matters having social, public, and humanitarian values. In recounting some of the successes of such persuasion, Mr. Repplier, former president of the council, said:

"Results are not the real point of the story. The point is that America, alone among the democracies of the world, has a well-tested system, initiated and powered by business rather than by government, for inducing her citizens to take action to correct a crisis. . . . The point is that it relies on the lump of sugar instead of the lash . . . solves the national problem, yet preserves the dignity, decency and self-determination of the individual. I believe this is why word of this American invention has gone almost around the world, and why five of the countries in the free world are now trying to form Advertising Councils of their own."

Comment on the above statement of Mr. Repplier.

9 Someone has said that "the dignity and public service aspects of advertising have been enhanced by the fact that many religious organizations are using it to present their ideas to the millions." What is your attitude toward this use of advertising?

10 Much criticism was leveled at the advertising used in recent political campaigns. Prepare a statement setting forth your evaluation of such advertising, with suggestions for change or control for future political advertising.

11 Would you favor or oppose a mutual agreement among United States and Russian newspapers to accept paid advertising of an ideological nature? Would not such an agreement tend to foster the concept of democracy?

part two

Background for planning advertising strategy

The role
of research

The student of advertising is often overanxious to start writing and designing advertisements. However, in building advertisements, as in building any substantial structure, much attention must first be given to establishing a solid foundation upon which the final edifice is to be erected. In the next several chapters, therefore, major attention shall be given to the foundation work involved in the development of a complete advertising program. The success of other aspects of advertising depends a great deal upon the thoroughness with which this is done.

In Chapter 1, we noted that advertising is essentially a process involving a series of decisions and that the advertisements we encounter as consumers are end products of this process. The advertiser must decide on such matters as what he seeks to accomplish through advertising, what markets to cultivate, how to frame his messages, what media to use, when and how often to advertise, and how much to spend. He must decide which among countless alternatives will most likely lead to business success. He must make these decisions while constantly faced with the risk of making wrong decisions that could lead to business failure.

Each decision maker, whether he is deciding on matters of broad campaign strategy or the content of a specific advertisement is confronted with circumstances that increase the risk of making wrong decisions. He has no direct contact with the thousands or millions of consumers he hopes to influence with his advertising messages. He cannot converse with them as the personal salesman does to gain firsthand knowledge of their wants, their buying behavior, their opinions, their language. He isn't present to answer their questions or see their reactions when his messages arrive. He is called upon to interpret want-satisfying qualities of products to consumers whose wants and satisfactions are different from his own. The temptation to assume that "what I like everybody likes" is always present. His desire to win praise from the boss and his colleagues frequently interferes with his quest for a more substantial reward, that is, purchase by consumers.

He must adapt advertising strategy and tactics to markets that are ever changing and to competition that is ever threatening. A campaign that succeeded last year may fail this year. He must select media to carry his messages to vast audiences he never sees. Therefore, he has no direct way of knowing how many and what kinds of people he is reaching or missing. Superimposed on all these complicating circumstances is the fact that he cannot readily determine the effects of specific decisions. His right decisions as well as his wrong ones are concealed in a maze of multiple causes and effects.

In an environment such as this, the way one makes decisions is of vital importance.

Methods of making decisions

Decisions are made in many different ways, most of them unconsciously geared to substituting something else for logical reasoning. Some people are content to follow whatever is considered standard practice in the trade. What is good for Adam is good for Eve. Others are willing to flip the coin or play the odds. The lucky few among these make out occasionally. A stopped clock is right twice every 24 hours. The so-called "self-made man" is willing to let his feelings dictate the answer. He relies on a sort of sixth sense to do his decision making. Some people in decision-making positions shift this job to the advice of experts—advice which often is given without all the necessary facts, and certainly without the necessary responsibility. Authority without responsibility is not hard to take.

The logical reasoning method involves: (1) a clear understanding of the problem to be solved; (2) recognition of various alternative solutions; (3) collection of all facts that would help in selecting a particular alternative; (4) weighing these facts and applying human judgment to them in the final selection of a course of action. The logical reasoning method is a systematic, factual approach to problem solving and therefore holds the most promise for reducing the risk of wrong decisions.

Logical reasoning is admirably illustrated by a letter that Benjamin Franklin wrote to a young man in response to a request for advice on how to solve a difficult problem. The following is a quotation from Franklin's letter:

> In the affair of so much importance to you, wherein you ask my advice I can not, for want of sufficient premises, counsel you *what* to determine; but if you please, I will tell you *how*. When those difficult cases occur, they are difficult chiefly because while we have them under consideration, all the reasons *pro* and *con* are not present to the mind at the same time; but sometimes one set present themselves, and at other times another, the first being out of sight. Hence the various purposes or inclinations that alternately prevail, and the uncertainty that perplexes us.
>
> To get over this, my way is to divide a half sheet of paper by a line into two columns; writing over the one *pro* and over the other *con;* then, during three or four days' consideration, I put down, under the different heads, short hints of the different motives that at different times occur to me *for* or *against* the measure. When I have thus got them all together in one view, I endeavor to estimate their respective weights; and when I find two (one on each side) that seem equal, I strike them both out. If I find a reason *pro* equal to *two* reasons *con,* I strike out the *three*. If I judge some two reasons *con* equal to *three* reasons *pro,* I strike out the *five;* and thus proceeding, I find where the balance lies; and if, after a day or two of further consideration, nothing new that is of importance occurs on either side I come to a determination accordingly. And though the weight of reason can not be taken with the precision of algebraic quantities, yet when each is thus considered separately and comparatively, and the whole lies before me, I think I can judge better and am less liable to take a false step. And in fact I found great advantage from this kind of equation, in what may be termed *moral* or *prudential* algebra.

Franklin's system, as demonstrated in this letter, depends a great deal on one's own powers of observation, which may be entirely adequate when the decision maker is primarily the person affected. However, when thousands or millions of people are involved, the decision maker needs some means of extending his scope of observation far beyond the range of his own experience. This, in brief, indicates the role of research in advertising. Through research the advertiser projects his scope of observation so that he can see more clearly the characteristics of his widely scattered consuming publics and predict more accurately the effects of his decisions upon them.

The logic of using research in solving advertising problems is now widely acclaimed. Yet, many frontiers remain unexplored and much of the work done under the guise of research is not sound research. Research is often used as a drunk uses a lamp post—for support instead of illumination. To more fully appreciate the role of this vital element in advertising, one must first recognize the characteristics of sound research.

Characteristics of sound research

Research has long been the accepted tool of science. Its association with science has been so close that the term "scientific method" is often used in referring to the use of research in any field. Research in advertising, then, is basically the use of scientific method in solving advertising problems. Soundness of the research depends on the extent to which the precepts of scientific inquiry are followed.

Although there is no single, generally accepted definition of scientific method, there are several standards by which one may judge whether or not a piece of research has been conducted in a scientific way. These standards concern the researcher's attitude toward his work and the procedure he follows from inception of the project to its completion.

The researcher strives for objectivity   He recognizes that as a human being he cannot set himself apart from his own attitudes and preconceived ideas. However, as a researcher he strives to be impartial and takes every precaution to prevent his personal predispositions from coloring his findings. He is dedicated to seeking and reporting facts as he finds them, not as he or someone else would like them to be. He is ever mindful that other researchers confronted with the same evidence should come up with findings the same as his.

The researcher qualifies his measurements   While attempting to obtain the most accurate measurements possible, he is constantly aware of the lack of precision inherent in the measuring devices he uses. All studies in which he surveys samples of the population are subject to error—error stemming from the kinds of questions asked and the way the questions are asked, error in sampling procedures, and error in data processing. However, the researcher can measure the error due to sampling, and he is continuously improving his techniques for controlling other sources of error. He tests his data and qualifies his findings by indicating the probable error present in them, thereby minimizing the chance of reaching erroneous conclusions.

The researcher is creative   Noting that he subordinates intuition to objectivity and that he relies heavily on statistical concepts, many people look upon the researcher as a mechanically inclined, fact-gathering robot. Nothing could be further from the truth. The researcher is primarily creative in his work. He explores the unknown. He charts new areas for investigation. He formulates new theories. He designs new techniques and experimental models. He sees relationships between seemingly isolated phenomena. He is a good researcher only to the extent that he is creative.

Too often research is thought to begin and end with the data-collection operation which actually is only part of a much broader process. Perhaps the tangibility of procedures used in gathering and recording data leads to this misconception. Less apparent, but more important, is the researcher's creative imagination that precedes, governs, and follows the data-collection operation.

Research is continuous   The only aspect of research that is constant is the element of change. New findings generate other new findings. The phenomena under investigation change. For example, in the environment of advertising, markets change, products change, distribution methods change, competition changes, communication techniques change. To keep abreast of these changes research must be continuous.

There are other criteria of sound research, but they pertain more specifically to techniques which are adequately treated in books and journal articles dealing with research methodology.

Research in marketing

The productivity of research has been dramatically demonstrated in the development of new products, new manufacturing processes, new machinery, new equipment, and new management systems. However, many firms that invest great sums in research and development (R & D) consider it a great achievement to develop a new product and then turn the product over to the marketing department with orders to sell it. The use of research to increase the efficiency of marketing is often overlooked. This oversight is due to many factors. The components of selling and advertising are intangible. The processes are not mechanized. The scene of action ranges far and wide. Many forces, such as competitive activity and general economic conditions, are outside of management's control. The value of marketing research cannot be readily translated into dollars and cents. Research techniques that work well in the laboratory cannot be readily applied in the marketplace.

The incentive to use research in marketing has not been as great as in production. In the past the capacity to consume has generally run ahead of the capacity to produce. Under such conditions major attention has been directed to producing goods. Any production-machinery improvements that would increase the amount of goods for sale and reduce manufacturing costs have been immediately beneficial and recognized as such. Selling goods has been comparatively easy; hence, less attention has been given to improving marketing practices.

Now we have an economy of abundance. Manufacturers are finding that their operations and growth are no longer limited by their productive capacity, for they can now produce as much as the market will absorb. The limiting factor now is the physiological and psychological capacity of consumers to assimilate the tremendous outpouring of goods and services. Under these conditions business firms must direct more attention to the psychological needs and wants of consumers, to cultivating new sales opportunities, and to increasing the efficiency of marketing practices. Having used research effectively in production, they are now turning more and more to the same approach as an aid in solving marketing problems.

Along with an increasing use of research as a means of gathering "marketing intelligence" is a greater tendency to use research in the decision-making process itself, to use research as a means of testing alternative actions before the decision is made. Insofar as the decision maker is better able to predict the probable consequences of alternative actions, the more likely he is to choose the best course. A survey by the National Industrial Conference Board reports:

> The changing role of marketing research in recent years is to no small degree attributable to its increased acceptance by management, or to what one sales executive describes as "the change in the nature of managing." In his company, as in so many others, "problem-solving is more clearly organized than ever before. Alternative strategies to reach an objective are being more carefully weighted in advance." And he adds: "Many sectors of management now embrace marketing research information as an aid to the management process, whereas they might previously have been inclined to view it as a threat to management prerogatives."[1]

Research in advertising

To successfully *interpret the want-satisfying qualities of products and services in terms of consumer needs and wants,* the advertiser must have a thorough knowledge of the consumer, the product, and the structure of the market. Three fields of advertising research, therefore, are (1) consumer research, (2) product analysis, and (3) market analysis. Figure 7–1 illustrates how these three fields of research support an effective advertising program.

Consumer research helps the advertiser identify those groups which are most likely to buy. It helps him see through their eyes how they perceive his products and those of his competitors. It helps him understand the satisfactions consumers are seeking in their buying decisions. Product analysis helps him design the kind of product that will deliver those satisfactions and helps him single out the most compelling benefits to communicate. Then he will be able to interpret the qualities of his product to consumers in the language they understand best—the language of their own needs and wants. Market analysis helps him determine where his prospective customers are located so that he can concentrate his advertising where it will be most productive. The chapters immediately following will develop in detail the philosophy and strategic contributions of this research triad.

[1] Lewis W. Forman and Earl L. Bailey, *The Role and Organization of Marketing Research* (New York: National Industrial Conference Board, 1969), pp. 23, 24.

FIGURE 7–1
An effective advertising program must be supported by product analysis, market analysis, and consumer research

No matter how well constructed, the advertising message cannot accomplish its mission until it is delivered to those consumers for whom it is intended. To select media that will deliver his message most efficiently to the right people, the advertiser needs factual evidence concerning the size and character of the audience that each medium reaches. Therefore, a fourth field of research in advertising is media research.

Decisions are based on predictions. When the advertiser decides to present his message in a certain way, he is predicting that among the alternative methods of presentation available, the one he selects will be most effective. Although he cannot predict with certainty, he can reduce the degree of his uncertainty. Consumer research, product analysis, market analysis, and media research all contribute to reducing uncertainty. However, a fifth field of research more directly concerned with predicting the relative effectiveness of alternative strategies and tactics is testing. The value of testing and the experimental procedures used in this field will be covered in Chapters 24 through 27.

We see that research plays a major supporting role in the structure of effective advertising. Yet, it is well to remember that research supplements; it does not replace the artistic skill and experienced judgment required of the executives, writers, and designers who create successful advertising campaigns.

QUESTIONS AND PROBLEMS

1   Advertising decisions are especially vulnerable to one's egocentric predicament. Do you agree or disagree? Explain.

2   Research, in itself, cannot be relied upon to make decisions. It can only help the decision maker predict the consequences of alternative courses of action. Explain.

3   Research extends the decision maker's scope of observation. Why is this important in advertising management?

4   Research can be a useful tool for predicting trends in the marketplace. How might research have been used to predict the switch in demand from large to small automobiles in 1974?

5   What circumstances tend to increase the risk of making wrong decisions in advertising?

6   Would you expect research to play a more important role in retail advertising or national advertising? Explain.

7   Research alone does not assure effective advertising. Why not?

8

Consumer research

In a free market system consumers direct production. Through their
choices voluntarily registered whenever they make a purchase, consumers, in effect, are telling manufacturers what to produce. Recognition
of such sovereignty leads to the expression, "The consumer is king." The
producer who provides products that effectively satisfy consumer needs
and wants will be richly rewarded; and, conversely, the producer who fails
to do so will be penalized by a lack of buyers.

Can the producer create wants?

Some writers question the concept of consumer sovereignty. They assume that human wants can be created or molded to fit the objectives
of producers. Professor John Kenneth Galbraith holds that large corporations have the power to "manage demand" and their "key to the management of demand is effective management of the purchases of final consumers."[1] This notion is not of recent origin. Forty years ago A. S. J. Baster
wrote that "resources are being used to serve not the needs of the people
as they are, but the needs of the people as they are distorted by the uneven
pressure of skillful forcing tactics in selling . . . ."[2] If this is true, then the

[1] John Kenneth Galbraith, *The New Industrial State* (Boston: Houghton Mifflin Company,
1967), p. 200.
[2] A. S. J. Baster, *Advertising Reconsidered* (London: P. S. King & Son, 1935), pp. 99–100.

manufacturer can "distort" consumer needs and make consumers want whatever he wants to sell.

Professor Galbraith elaborates on his point as follows:

> It is true that the consumer may still imagine that his actions respond to his own view of his satisfactions. But this is superficial and proximate, the result of illusions created in connection with the management of his wants. Only those wishing to evade the reality will be satisfied with such a simplistic explanation. All others will notice that if an individual's satisfaction is less from an additional expenditure on automobiles than from one on housing, this can as well be corrected by a change in the selling strategy of General Motors as by an increased expenditure on his house.[3]

Thus, Galbraith assumes that the consumer who thinks he is freely expressing his wants in the marketplace is suffering from illusions, from "illusions created" by General Motors and other large corporations who are "managing his wants."

Those who accept Galbraith's views attribute too great a power to advertising and too little power to the consumer. They overlook the power of basic wants that motivate all human behavior. All mankind seeks to satisfy his needs for self-expression, social approval, love, belongingness, a longer life span, and security for his loved ones. Each consumer may employ somewhat different means toward satisfying these needs, but the means should not be confused with the ends. Differences among consumer preferences for products and brands simply demonstrate that different people find different ways of satisfying the same basic needs.

In testimony before the Federal Trade Commission Alvin A. Achenbaum observed:

> Close scrutiny of the marketing process shows that consumers are not passive participants in their purchasing behavior. They are active, knowledgeable, experienced buyers—particularly for those products which are most likely to be advertised nationally. They seek information given in a persuasive context, and they freely supply information to those advertisers who seek it. There is nothing underhanded or hidden in the process. Moreover, the competition of communications reduces the possibility that market manipulation will occur.[4]

Advertising succeeds when it goes with the tide of consumer demand, but it is doomed to fail in opposition. This point of view was clearly expressed by Walter Weir, a veteran copywriter, when he wrote:

> During the first five years in advertising, I developed the feeling that I was in a sort of superior profession—superior as it dealt in ways and means

[3] Galbraith, *New Industrial State,* pp. 214, 215.

[4] Alvin A. Achenbaum, "Statement in behalf of the Joint A.N.A./A.A.A.A. Committee" (Before the Federal Trade Commission, October 28, 1971).

by which one could influence people he would never see to perform actions they had never thought of performing.

I spent the next 15 years unlearning this misconception. I found that, despite my technical proficiency in the art of persuasion, I was not half so shrewd or wise as those millions I was being paid to address. I had to unlearn the reasons for which I thought they would buy—to learn the reasons for which they actually bought. Actually, *they* were exerting *their* influence on *me*.

I found the great contribution advertising makes is in reverse to what is generally thought. Instead of forcing upon people what advertising wants, it forces upon advertising *what people want.*"[5]

It seems quite apparent that basic human wants cannot be created and that even surface wants can be molded only slightly and gradually by advertising. It would, therefore, seem to be the part of wisdom for businessmen to harmonize their products to basic consumer needs and wants rather than to attempt to mold basic wants to fit their products.

Philosophy of consumer research

Consumer research is built upon the general theory that the consumer is king—that his wants form the foundation of economic endeavor and should direct production. This viewpoint is particularly important in an economy where consumers' freedom of choice is emphasized. The value producers can obtain from information concerning consumer wants is pointed out by Dr. Harry R. Tosdal in the following quotation:

The need on the part of the producers for useful information as to consumer wants exists at every stage of industrial development; but that need is most pressing in the society which aims to give its members freedom of choice as consumers and high standards of living through the utilization of advanced techniques of large-scale production and distribution. Today a large proportion of the products which form the basis of industrial and commercial enterprise in modern states is produced or distributed by large-scale enterprises. Large-scale production requires prior judgments upon direct consumer demand or upon derived demand based upon ultimate consumption. Large-scale distribution likewise compels manufacture and purchase in advance of express demand. Administrators and executives of both large- and small-scale business enterprise must, therefore, make decisions as to the quantity, type, quality, design, style, and other characteristics of products to be offered for sale or allotted to customers. To translate these decisions into working plans for the enterprise requires knowledge not only of the general characteristics of consumer choice but of a vast amount of detail concerning the goods the consumer wishes to buy.[6]

[5] Walter Weir, "After Hours," *Printers' Ink,* October 7, 1949, p. 144.

[6] Harry R. Tosdal, chapter on "Consumer Demand" in *Business and Modern Society* (Cambridge, Mass.: Harvard University Press, 1938), p. 314.

The problems of the modern manufacturer are thus quite different from those confronting the producer under our earlier handicraft system, where the contact between producer and consumer was direct. Under the handicraft system, it was possible for the consumer to inform the producer in detail concerning the type and character of the product desired before the product was made. With the development of a high degree of specialization and division of labor, production took place in advance of specific demand. So long as we operated in a sellers' market, this reversed procedure was not fraught with the dangers of business loss that is true today in a buyers' market. With this shift to a buyers' market, manufacturers are placing increased emphasis on methods of measuring consumer demand before goods are produced. Consumer research is thus devoted to the task of approximating the old and, in many respects, highly desirable direct contact of producer and consumer. The manner in which consumer research serves as a substitute for the old direct-contact method is graphically shown in Figure 8–1.

A determination of consumer demand before goods are produced reduces the risk of making goods that are hard to sell. Under such a philosophy, "low-pressure buying" takes the place of "high-pressure selling." The difference between these two methods is made visual in a demonstration provided by General Motors Corporation. This company has a large, heavy metal ball hanging from a beam. Visitors are asked to

FIGURE 8–1
Consumer research, the link between the manufacturer and consumer

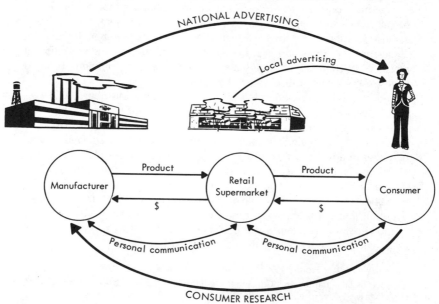

take a 12-pound sledge hammer and to see how far they can move the ball by striking it with the hammer. The usual visitor strikes the ball with a mighty blow only to find that it hardly moves. Instead, the hammer rebounds with such force that the visitor is almost thrown from his feet. This is high-pressure selling.

The visitor is then instructed to drop the hammer and press his finger against the ball. The ball "gives" a little and then swings back. Instructions are given to pull back with the backswing of the ball and then to push again as the ball starts forward. If the visitor will work *with* the laws of nature as demonstrated by the action of the ball, he can get the ball to swing with such power that it would crash through the wall were it to break loose from its mooring. This is low-pressure buying. Advertising is most effective when it works *with* the laws of inertia as they apply to consumer behavior.

H. G. Weaver, pioneer of customer research at General Motors Corporation, recognized the strategic implications of knowing what the customer wants when he said:

> If a company can ascertain concretely and in detail just what its buyers would like to have if it can build its products in conformity with those desires and design its sales and advertising messages so that they will definitely answer the questions that are uppermost in the minds of the motorist, obviously there will be continued improvement in the merchandising processes and a broadening of the service tendered. Merchandising has been aptly defined as a problem of getting the *right product,* at the *right place,* at the *right time,* and at the *right price.* Consumer research contributes to this end.[7]

Mr. Weaver holds that service should be the basic philosophy underlying business activity, and he would use consumer research extensively and intensively to equip the manufacturer with the facts necessary to become an effective servant of the consumer. Weaver says that "the major objective of all business should be that of serving the customer in the way that the customer wants to be served,"[8] and he adopts this philosophy on a purely selfish basis. He seems to agree with that well-known philosopher who said: "He who would be greatest among you must be the servant of all." For, in explanation of General Motors' work with consumer research, Weaver says:

> There is nothing altruistic about General Motors Customer Research. We expect it to broaden our good will. We expect it to sell more automobiles, and we expect these benefits to be permanently assured instead of short lived because having the facilities, the talent, and the desire to serve, coupled with the knowledge of how you want to be served, there seems no reason

---

[7] General Motors Corporation, *The Proving Ground of Public Opinion* (Detroit), p. 9.
[8] Ibid., p. 6.

why we cannot serve you in line with your desires—*serve you in a manner that will merit your continued and increasing patronage.*[9]

The consumer-king philosophy does not mean that consumers are to write their own specifications for commodities. Nor does consumer research insist that this be done. The consumer is not an engineer. He cannot be expected to tell the manufacturer the length of the stroke or the cubic-inch piston displacement of an automobile engine. He can tell the manufacturer that economy of operation is more desirable than excessive speed, and then engineers can attempt to design a product which will give this result. When the manufacturer gets this broad but fundamental picture of human wants, the direction of his manufacturing efforts will be more clearly mapped out for him. His reward will be in proportion to his ability to follow this lead in manufacturing and to present his finished product convincingly to the public.

Advertising and consumer research

By placing emphasis upon the consumer and his wants, advertising will have its most glorious opportunity. Under such a philosophy, the production department of an industry will provide the sales and advertising departments with a product of real merit, a product around which an honest, straightforward, convincing selling appeal can be built.

The function of selling and advertising will thus reduce itself to the problem of *interpreting the utility of the product in terms of the customer's needs and wants.* It will necessitate a clear understanding of consumer tastes and consumer psychology. Selling will really become a teaching, rather than a forcing process. It will point out that XYZ air-conditioning equipment will provide cooler rooms, that it will provide the proper humidity and thus reduce the number of colds contracted in the winter, and that it will increase one's working efficiency.

Glenn Frank expressed this point of view when he stated that "the advertising man is a liaison officer between the materials of business and the mind of the nation. He must know both well before he can serve either wisely."[10] The validity of the social viewpoint is further expressed by Frank:

> The business order and the social order are too intimately related to the advertising man who aspires to be more than a tricky tradester to tear them apart in his thinking. . . . The really great advertising man must be as much interested in increasing the sanity of consumption as in increasing the size of consumption, for great businesses are not built upon fads that are worthless and passing, but upon appetites that are worthy and permanent.[11]

[9] Ibid., p. 6.

[10] Glenn Frank, "The Dignity and Duties of the Advertising Profession," *Printers' Ink,* April 14, 1927, p. 81.

[11] Ibid.

Finding out what consumers want is a far more complex process than simply asking, "What do you want?" Their knowledge of, or experience in, using any of the many brands in many different product categories is different from time to time, from place to place, and from one group of consumers to another. Their perceptions differ, their standards of perform-ance differ, their judgments differ. To illustrate the scope of information required to understand consumer wants, consider the following list of question areas in one study:

QUESTION AREAS COVERED IN MAJOR MARKET STUDY OF AFTER-SHAVE LOTIONS AND COLOGNES

a. Who Uses After Shaves and Colognes?
How many men used these products in the past six months?
What types of products do they use?
How much of an overlap is there in use of after shaves, colognes, and all-purpose lotions?
How often do men use these products?
What are the user's demographic profiles?

b. What Types and Brands Do They Use?
How do people classify brands?
What are the main types?
What types do they use?
What brands do they use?
How often do men use each type?
Where do they apply each type?

c. Who Buys These Products?
Do people buy these products as gifts or for regular use?
How much of the total volume do gift brands account for?
Who buys the regular brands?
Who selects the regular brands?
Where are the regular brands bought?
Who buys the gifts?
What types are bought as gifts?
What brands are bought as gifts?
What product combinations are bought as gifts?
Do women select gifts in the store?
How often are gift brands used?
How often are gift types used?
Are users likely to start buying brands they've received as gift?

d. What Are People Looking For in After Shaves and Colognes?
What dimensions of the product are people concerned with?
Which after shave dimensions are most important?
Which cologne dimensions are most important?
How do the dimensions compare in importance?
Are men and women looking for the same things?
How different are after shaves and colognes?[12]

---

[12] Achenbaum, "Statement," pp. 56–57.

Consumer motivation

Advertisers in recent years are turning more attention to the complex and subtle aspects of human behavior referred to as motivation. The following explanation of motivation by Frederick H. Lund gives some idea of its nature:

> To define motivation is difficult for the reason that there is no one condition with which it can be identified. In the main, however, behavior is said to be motivated when it shows fairly definite directional trends. The motive, in such instances, may be thought of (1) in terms of the external objective of behavior, (2) in terms of the inner condition activating the individual, or (3) in terms of the activities themselves. Popularly, the emphasis is usually placed upon the first of these—the external objective. Psychologically, the emphasis has more frequently been placed upon the second—the source of motivation. Thus, the older psychologists were inclined to trace most behavior to the *will*, an inner agency or power which, while in the body, was assumed to be independent of its structures. As this concept began to lose favor, emphasis tended to shift to the *instincts*. These were conceived as special mechanisms, hidden away within the organism and waiting only to be released through the action of appropriate stimuli.
>
> Today, with our better understanding of body function, we are more inclined to identify motives either with the activities themselves or with the tissue needs which prompt their action. Of these, the tissue conditions may be considered a matter of constitution, while the behavior forms in which they are expressed may be considered a matter of learning.[13]

As the most compelling inner determinants of human behavior, motives are also called drives, urges, impulses, needs, wants, tensions, and willful cravings. Whatever they are called, the assumption is that people consistently seek to satisfy these inner motivating conditions. Psychologist George Horsley Smith says:

> Motivating conditions are varied. Thus we seek sensory gratification, pleasant feelings, emotional variety, and at times even enjoy tension and turmoil rather than the quiescence of a fulfilled appetite. We look for meaning in the environment. We work hard for economic security and acceptance by our fellows and look for ways to express our individuality, satisfy our curiosity, and experience new value qualities. Sometimes we are torn by conflicting needs; for example, we want to be both masterful and submissive, to have fun and to "purge" ourselves through hard work.[14]

Psychologists tend to agree that some human motives are primary and others secondary. They generally include in any list of primary motives those that are or have a strong tendency toward being innate, biogenic, or unlearned and in a secondary list those motives that tend toward being

---

[13] Frederick H. Lund, *Psychology* (New York: Ronald Press Co., 1933), p. 231.

[14] George Horsley Smith, *Motivation Research in Advertising and Marketing* (New York: McGraw-Hill Book Co., 1954), p. 10.

acquired, sociogenic, or learned. There is not much agreement among students of human behavior on any detailed listing of either primary or secondary motives or desires.

The lack of agreement on primary and secondary motives has not deterred persons from providing us with ample lists. C. N. Allen[15] included the following ten motives in a list of primary wants: appetizing food, thirst-quenching drinks, comfortable surroundings, escape from pain and danger, sex companionship, welfare of loved ones, social approval, superiority over others, mastery over obstacles, and play. Allen's secondary list[16] included beauty and style, cleanliness, convenience, curiosity, dependability and quality, economy and profit, education and information, efficiency, health, and universality.

It is claimed by many that advertising appeals directed to primary desires or motives will be more effective than appeals directed to secondary motives. This point of view stems from the belief that primary motives are largely biogenic in nature, and thus closely associated with body needs, while secondary motives are sociogenic and related to learned desires.

This point of view, however, is not necessarily true. It might be true if most human consumption consisted of goods and services to meet these biogenic needs. But in an economic society where many are above the subsistence level of consumption, appeal to other motives may be more powerful in the advertising of certain products. Lund states: ". . . but the satisfaction of organic and bodily needs is surely not the only condition motivating human behavior. In addition to this there are a number of other motives, usually called *social,* which exercise an important and determining influence."[17]

Most psychologists, today, refrain from arranging any list of motives in an order of strength or potency in moving people to act. Dewey and Humber say, "When asked which motive is strongest, the answer must always be in terms of the value systems of particular persons and particular cultures. Universally, there is no strongest motive."[18]

Motivation is always multiple and complex. There is seldom just one reason for doing anything. When a person buys an automobile he may do so because he needs transportation *and* wants to extend his horizons *and* wants to keep up with the Joneses *and* surpass the Smiths *and* proclaim his solvency and status to the world *and* experience the mastery of controlling a powerful new engine, etc. While these motives are apt to have different degrees of importance to different people, they are all likely to be involved to some extent in a purchase of a new car.

[15] C. N. Allen, "A Psychology of Motivation for Advertisers," *Journal of Applied Psychology,* Vol. 25, No. 4 (1941), p. 386.

[16] Ibid., p. 388.

[17] Lund, *Psychology,* p. 243.

[18] Richard Dewey and W. J. Humber, *The Development of Human Behavior* (New York: Macmillan Co., 1951), p. 193.

Motivation patterns change. Motives that are strong today might be weak tomorrow since individual values change as circumstances are altered. The motives which caused a person to buy his first television set will not generally be effective in moving him to purchase a second or third set.

Studies to determine and measure the relative strength of motives underlying the purchase of specific products and services have become an important part of consumer research.

Other motivational variables

In addition to motives there are other variables in the psychological makeup of consumers that predispose them to buy some products and reject others, to respond to some advertisements and ignore others. These variables are attitudes, beliefs, habits, and customs.

Attitudes are states of readiness to make value judgments in support of or against certain stimuli. Consumers are more inclined to buy products or brands toward which they hold positive attitudes. They are less inclined to buy things toward which they hold negative attitudes. Thus, an important function of research is to reveal the direction and intensity of consumer attitudes. If research shows that negative attitudes are hindering a product's sales, then it would behoove the advertiser to change his product and/or his advertising to overcome this handicap.

In a study of consumer attitudes toward tea, the National Tea Council found that tea drinking in the United States was inhibited because many people felt that tea was a weak beverage associated with effeminacy, old age, and sickness. To combat these negative attitudes the Tea Council switched advertising themes from "Nervous? Try tea" to "Make mine hefty, hot, and hearty." A declining sales trend turned sharply upward.

Beliefs are subjective concepts of truth. What people believe is not always true, and what is true is not always believed. Beliefs are based more on feelings and emotion than on reason. People believe what they want to believe. These statements about the nature of belief suggest that of all the claims and counterclaims made in competitive advertising, what consumers believe is a matter of personal interpretation instead of a mere acceptance of facts. Such personal interpretations of advertising claims and product performance can only be made available to advertisers through consumer research.

Habits and customs are closely related. One is individual, the other social. Nystrom says: "Habit is a term that applies to practices of individuals. Customs are habits followed by masses of people."[19] Habits, both

[19] Paul H. Nystrom, *Economic Principles of Consumption* (New York: Ronald Press Co., 1929), p. 61.

individual and social, are of great importance in human life. It has been estimated that three out of every four human acts are habitual.

Motives, attitudes, and beliefs lead to and reinforce habits. However, once they are firmly established, habits themselves become motivating forces for buying activity. Individuals get in the habit of calling for a particular brand of cigarettes. Or custom may dictate that certain members of society should not call for cigarettes at all.

Not only are habits ascertainable, but their relative strength is measurable. Such measurements serve to indicate the advisability of using advertising to break an old habit and establish a new one or to establish the old habit more firmly.

How these motivational variables fit in to the development of advertising strategy will be treated in more detail later.

Sampling

Obviously, an advertiser whose market may number in the millions would not find it feasible to interview each and every consumer. The cost and time required for such an undertaking would be prohibitive. However, by studying a relatively small cross section he can estimate characteristics of his entire market with reasonable accuracy. This process of selecting a representative cross section is called sampling, and its widespread use in consumer research is based on the premise that information obtained from a carefully selected sample closely resembles the information that would be obtained if all consumers were questioned. Thus, sampling makes it possible for the advertiser to study wants, desires, attitudes, beliefs, and buying behavior of his vast consumer market.

Sample surveys do not yield exact measurements. They do provide approximations of what is true in an entire population; and when the laws of chance are given free play in selecting sample members, the researcher can measure the range of error arising from the sampling operation. In effect, he is able to predict the probability, or what the chances are, that sampling estimates approximate the true conditions in the total population from which the sample was drawn.

A question frequently asked is: "How can such a small fraction of people be counted upon to represent accurately the wants and desires of so many other people when we know that each person is different from another?" We can count on relatively small fractions because we can make two valid assumptions about large numbers of people. The first assumption is that sufficient similarity exists among large numbers of people to permit us to accurately predict behavior of the large group even though we can't predict the behavior of any one individual. The second assumption is that errors tend to balance out when a large enough number of people are included in the sample—some sample members who err in one direction are balanced by other sample members who err in the opposite direction.

The predictability of occurrences among large numbers of people is clearly demonstrated in insurance. To insure the life of only one person would be the rankest sort of gambling. But to insure the lives of 10,000 or 100,000 persons widely scattered and engaged in a diversity of occupations is a safe business proposition. Although they cannot predict who will die, life insurance companies can predict that fewer than ten persons in any average thousand will die within any given year. With almost the same certainty, the probability of deaths from automobile accidents, train wrecks, drownings, injuries on the Fourth of July, marriages in June, births in 1980, and suicides in 1985 can be predicted.

Another question frequently asked is: "How large should a sample be?" There is no easy answer to that one. For our purposes here it should be recognized that determining the appropriate size of a sample is a matter of judgment and requires consideration of several factors such as: How homogeneous is the population to be studied? How much error can be tolerated? How much should be spent on the study or what is the information worth? How much time can be allowed for the study? The more homogeneous the population, the smaller the sample required. Theoretically, if all members of a group of consumers were identical and would respond the same way, one member of that group would be an adequate sample. The larger the error that can be tolerated, the smaller the sample required. To obtain a given amount of information from a small sample is less costly and time consuming than from a large sample. Therefore, when deciding on sample size the researcher has to weigh the precision and value of the information needed against the cost and time required for the study.

Structure of consumer research

The structure of a typical consumer research project is graphically illustrated in Figure 8–2. This chart and the following brief outline indicate the major steps involved in research procedure.

The statement of objectives sets forth the specific purposes of the study and defines the scope of the investigation. To do this, a thorough understanding of the advertising problem and how the study will contribute to its solution is essential.

1. *Analysis of internal conditions.* The researcher seeks to obtain all pertinent information concerning the company's product, its marketing and advertising strategy, its competitive strengths and weaknesses, its past experience, and its future goals from company records and executive personnel.

FIGURE 8–2
Organization chart of consumer research

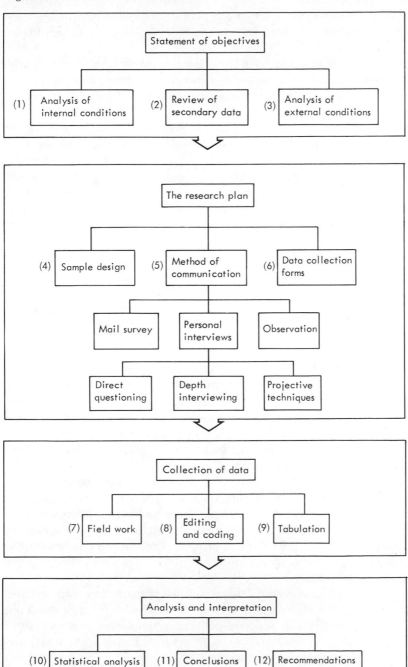

2. *Review of secondary data.* To take advantage of readily available information bearing on the problem and to avoid unnecessary duplication, the researcher reviews data that are published by government agencies, trade associations, universities, business publications, and advertising mediums.

3. *Analysis of external conditions.* The researcher talks informally with consumers, dealers, and company salesmen to appraise the competitive environment and to develop ideas or hunches about the direction the study should take.

4. *Sample design.* The researcher determines the type and size of sample that will yield the desired information within allowable limits of error at minimum cost.

5. *Method of communication.* The researcher decides whether he will gather the desired information by mail, by personal interviews, or by observing consumers' overt behavior. If he decides to use personal interviews, he selects and plans the interviewing procedure most appropriate for his study.

Direct questioning involves the use of a predetermined list of questions that usually anticipates or allows for all alternative answers. Every consumer interviewed is asked the same questions in the same sequence, and his answers are recorded in the same way. This procedure is appropriate when consumers are willing and able to provide the desired information and when quantitative evidence is necessary.

Depth interviewing is the technique of probing beneath the consumer's surface answers to get at underlying motives, attitudes, or beliefs. Instead of using a fixed list of questions, the interviewer improvises and asks leading questions to stimulate free discussion of the subject at hand. This procedure is appropriate for seeking ideas or hypotheses about consumer behavior that may eventually be tested through experimentation.

Projective techniques are borrowed from clinical psychiatry. These techniques include word association, sentence completion, story completion, thematic apperception tests, and others. Their purpose is to get the consumer to project his personality, through a process that is not apparent to him, into the answer that he gives. These techniques are appropriate when seeking information about motives and attitudes that consumers are unwilling to reveal or are unable to provide. These techniques enable the researcher to get at strong motivating forces that consumers are not aware of and cannot verbalize.

6. *Data collection forms.* The researcher prepares forms for eliciting and recording the desired information. A standardized list of questions enhances consistent and accurate collection, tabulation, and analysis of data. The structured questionnaire for direct questioning in personal interviews is the most widely used form.

7. *Field work.* This is the interviewing or data-collecting operation which includes selection, training, and supervision of interviewers.

8. *Editing and coding.* The questionnaires are edited to eliminate errors and coded to facilitate tabulation.

9. *Tabulation.* The data are tabulated to summarize and quantify the responses.

10. *Statistical analysis.* Statistical techniques are used to test the significance of relationships and to determine what the relationships mean.

11. *Conclusions.* The researcher interprets the results with direct reference to the objectives of the study.

12. *Recommendations.* On the basis of his findings the researcher predicts the consequences of alternative solutions to the problem and recommends the course of action that he thinks should be taken.

The student of advertising should seek a more detailed understanding of research techniques through individual reading or in specialized courses in research.

Summary

The importance of the consumer in our economic society has long been recognized. Economic theorists for more than a century have emphasized the fundamental proposition that economic endeavor is built around the production of goods and services for the satisfaction of human wants. A mutuality of interest has been recognized between consumers and producers. One cannot exist without the other. Many business concerns have, therefore, been giving greater thought to the study of consumer needs and wants preliminary to their production of goods.

The study of the consumer has taken the form of analyzing all those forces that tend naturally to influence his buying. Motives, attitudes, beliefs, habits, and custom are fundamental factors. The sampling process makes it possible to study how these factors influence the buying behavior of vast numbers of people.

Consumer research has been accepted as a valuable approach to the preparation of an advertising program. It is recognized that such a program will be more effective if it harmonizes with human desires than if it attempts to alter them.

Consumer research is one answer to the perplexing problem of how to arrive at sound business decisions. It is one link in a fact-finding chain which can be used by the businessman to furnish that foundation of facts upon which a substantial business can be built. Consumer research, properly used, will link the consumer with the manufacturer in a manner which will be beneficial to both parties. It will touch the manufacturer's organization at several points. The engineering department, the production depart-

ment, the sales department, and the advertising department—all will benefit by a use of data obtained through consumer research.

QUESTIONS AND PROBLEMS

1 Motivation is multiple and complex. Seldom, if ever, is there just one reason
for doing anything. How does this complicate the advertising process? How
can research reduce the complications?

2 List all the motives you can think of that might lead to purchase of the
following products:
   a. Mini-pocket hand calculator
   b. Polaroid camera
   c. Mouthwash
   d. Dog food
   e. Guitar

3 Consumers don't really know what they want. Therefore, the job of the
advertiser is to tell them what to want. Do you agree or disagree? Explain.

4 Asking consumers *why* they buy or don't buy a particular product will probably fail to bring out all significant buying motives. Explain.

5 Research is a tool for problem solving. The logical starting point for a research
proposal, therefore, is to define the problem. Explain.

6 Under what circumstances do you think it would be most appropriate to use:
   a. mail survey?
   b. direct questioning?
   c. depth interviewing?
   d. projective techniques?

7 What research plan would you recommend if the immediate problem is to
find out what dissatisfactions, if any, consumers are experiencing with room
airconditioners?

8 For many products the person who buys the product is not the person who
uses it. Which group should be researched, the buyers or the users?

9 With psychological *wants* becoming more significant than physiological
needs, the importance of consumer research becomes more vital than ever.
Explain.

10 The XYZ wallpaper manufacturing company developed a machine which
trims wallpaper to size, evenly pasted, and ready for hanging, called the "Trim
'n Paster." It is small, portable, and sells for about $50.

In the past, the XYZ company had manufactured only wallpaper, which
they sold to retailers through swatch books and catalogs. The company had
done no advertising in the past and employed only three salesmen.

The Trim 'n Paster was placed in a few selected stores in the East, but few
sales resulted. Dealers reported that although homeowners were interested
in this device, they did not feel that they could afford it. Professional paper-
hangers were not interested in it at all—many, because of union rules.

Over $150,000 had been put into the manufacture of the machines, but
the inventory had increased and the machines were simply not moving.

The company's president decided that advertising might move these machines and appropriated $20,000 for advertising expenditures.

Do you believe this product will meet the needs or wants of large numbers of people? What kind of research, if any, would you recommend before undertaking specific consumer advertising?

9

Consumer groups

A dvertising is often characterized as a means of selling to the masses. This leads to the popular misconception that advertising is directed to everyone. But obviously, people of all ages, of all income levels, of all occupations, of all places, and from all walks of life do not want the same thing, do not have the same tastes, do not think the same way, and do not live by the same scale of values. Therefore, no product is consumed by everyone at the same rate, and no advertisement is equally appealing to everyone. Some products have a more universal appeal than others, and some advertisers have wider markets than others; but each advertisement succeeds best when it is directed to a group of consumers who can be reached on a common meeting ground.

MARKET SEGMENTATION

Instead of appealing to one big heterogeneous mass, the advertiser singles out those groups of consumers who are his most promising prospects and concentrates his effort on them. He researches these groups more intensively, designs his messages to fit their way of life, and places his ads in media that reach them efficiently. The process of subdividing a market to isolate the best targets is referred to as *market segmentation.*

A market may be segmented on the basis of any relevant classification factor. Most widely used are *demographic factors,* including age, income,

sex, education, race, nationality, religion, and location. Demographic factors are widely used because they have been found to account for many
differences in consumer behavior. Also, these kinds of data are more
readily available, thereby offering a course of least resistance. However,
demographic factors pertain to characteristics that are interrelated, such
as education and occupation, occupation and income, education and
income, etc. Also, their use does not assure the kind of homogeneity that
may be required. Thus, one person might be in a medium-income group,
have a higher education, and be a member of the legal profession. This
does not mean, however, that his tastes will be the same as others who
are included in any one of these groups. As a lawyer, his tastes probably
will be different from those of a skilled mechanic receiving the same
income.

To delineate more homogeneous market segments, composite classification systems such as *family life cycle* and *social class* have been brought
into play. Family life cycle combines marital status, age, presence of children, and age of children. Social class combines family background, occupation, education, neighborhood, and the source, as well as the amount,
of income. More subtle differences in consumer behavior can only be
explained in psychological terms. Therefore, more attention in recent years
has turned to *psychographics* and *life style* which include classifications
based on personality traits, attitudes, motivations, and self-image. Recognizing that buying behavior in itself can be a meaningful basis for segmenting a market, various *buyer behavior factors* such as product usage, brand
loyalty, and responsiveness to innovations are also used.

The strategic importance of market segmentation can be readily ascertained by examining the structure of our total population and by noting
the differences in buying behavior among different consumer groups.

Age

The number of people within each age group is significant as a guide
to the volume of certain kinds of products that will be consumed currently
and in the future. Estimated sizes of age groups at specified intervals from
the year 1980 to the year 2000 appear in Table 9–1. Changes in the
birthrate and a decline in the death rate bring about marked changes in
the size of each group from year to year; hence, it is good business practice
to keep abreast of these changes. An increase in the birthrate in 1980
would increase the number of children in the "under-5" group that year;
in the 5-to-9 group five years later; and the 10-to-14 group in 1990. This
would influence the sales of toys in 1982 and the sale of bicycles in 1990.

Changes in the age makeup of our population from 1972 to 2000 are
graphed in Figure 9–1. Assuming a fertility ratio of 2.8 births per woman,
the distribution by age groups would not change greatly at the end of the

TABLE 9–1
U.S. population projections 1980–2000 (in thousands)

Age	1980	1990	1995	2000
All ages	230,955	266,238	282,766	300,406
Under 5 years	23,449	27,149	26,748	28,458
5 to 9 years	18,847	26,893	27,275	26,879
10 to 14 years	17,497	23,745	27,058	27,440
15 to 19 years	20,221	19,194	23,903	27,209
20 to 24 years	21,067	17,823	19,346	24,038
25 to 29 years	19,544	20,501	17,990	19,510
30 to 34 years	17,418	21,290	20,599	18,110
35 to 39 years	13,822	19,615	21,259	20,580
40 to 44 years	11,548	17,287	19,471	21,102
45 to 49 years	10,956	13,540	17,023	19,173
50 to 54 years	11,450	11,077	13,171	16,557
55 to 59 years	11,229	10,182	10,599	12,607
60 to 64 years	9,854	10,175	9,494	9,901
65 to 69 years	8,228	9,332	9,122	8,532
70 to 74 years	6,452	7,437	7,913	7,759
75 years and over	9,371	10,999	11,794	12,551

Source: U.S. Bureau of the Census, *Population Estimates and Projections,* Series P–25, No. 493, December 1972.

28-year period. However, assuming 1.8 births per woman, which approximates zero population growth, the proportion in the younger age groups would decrease significantly. This would reduce the need for new school construction, college enrollments probably would decline, and the market would shrink for all the many goods and services uniquely required by young people. With a decrease in the number of women in childbearing ages, the decline in the under-14 age group would continue. With more people in the older age groups the markets for tourism, leisure-time activities, continuing education, and medical care would grow in importance.

Of course, changes in the relative numerical importance of different age groups will not change the problems of determining the desires and habits of those within a given group. Parents will continue to have less influence on the choice of goods to be used by the child as he progresses to a higher age group. Beginning at about age 12, the youth comes into his own as a semiindependent consumer. From this age on, businessmen should direct primary attention to the needs and wants of the individual for whom production is planned.

Desires of young people are more plastic than those of older persons. It is easier to establish new habits of consumption among these groups. This is illustrated by the quicker acceptance of new modes of dress by young people than by older persons.

The other age groups listed above will have their own peculiar needs and wants. Any study of consumer tastes must be made with a thought

FIGURE 9–1
Percent distribution of population by age: 1972 and 2000

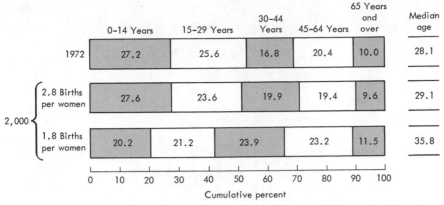

Source: U.S. Bureau of the Census, *Population Estimates and Projections,* Series P–25, No. 493, December 1972.

of measuring tastes—not of people in general, but of people in homogeneous groups. Age provides one important classification to be considered.

Income

People with money to spend make markets, and in most cases money income is the most significant factor influencing what and how much a consumer buys. The number of consumers at various levels of income is an index of potential sales. The unique tastes and desires of different income groups serve as a useful guide when selecting advertising appeals and media.

Personal income in the United States has persistently displayed two marked tendencies: the tendency to rise and the tendency to be more evenly distributed. Great numbers of consumers have been moving up into higher income groups. This fact is illustrated in Figure 9–2. In 1965, 27 percent of the spending units (families) had incomes of $10,000 and over; while in 1970, 44 percent had incomes of $10,000 and over. On the other hand, in 1965, 19 percent of the spending units received an income of less than $3,000. In 1970, only 11 percent of the spending units were in this lower income group. This movement upward in purchasing power by millions of people has been a fundamental factor in our expanding economy.

As consumers move up from one income group to the next, they represent substantially increased markets for goods and services. However, they do not automatically take on the same desires and standard of living of the income group into which they have moved. Habit and inertia tend to perpetuate the earlier way of life. Stimulating their wants and

FIGURE 9–2
The proportion of consumers in higher income groups continues to increase

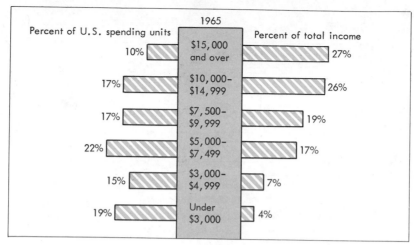

1965

Percent of U.S. spending units

		Percent of total income
10%	$15,000 and over	27%
17%	$10,000–$14,999	26%
17%	$7,500–$9,999	19%
22%	$5,000–$7,499	17%
15%	$3,000–$4,999	7%
19%	Under $3,000	4%

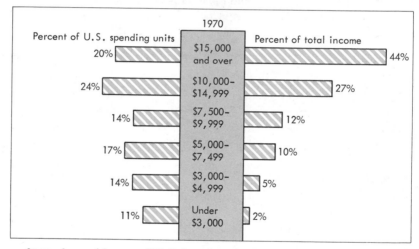

1970

Percent of U.S. spending units

		Percent of total income
20%	$15,000 and over	44%
24%	$10,000–$14,999	27%
14%	$7,500–$9,999	12%
17%	$5,000–$7,499	10%
14%	$3,000–$4,999	5%
11%	Under $3,000	2%

Sources: *Surveys of Consumers, 1971–72,* Survey Research Center, University of Michigan, 1973; *Statistical Abstract of the United States, 1972;* and U.S. Department of Commerce.

spending in line with their increased income is the task and opportunity of advertising.

Even though the concentration of income in the hands of a few has been reduced, it should be noted that in 1970 about 44 percent of the income was received by the top 20 percent of the spending units. Thus, about 84 percent of the new car purchases in 1972 were in the upper-half income groups.

Studies of buying habits of families in different income groups have disclosed facts that proved the fallacy of certain business practices. At one time it was generally believed that yard goods were usually purchased as a means of saving money and, hence, that advertising of such goods should be directed to families with relatively low incomes. However, a study made by R. H. Macy & Co. disclosed the fact that the best users of yard goods were women between the ages of 40 and 50 and were in the top income brackets.

Sex

The question of whether the male or female is more important in the purchase of consumption goods has been debated often and long. The evidence seems to give the female of the species first place as a buyer. This place is established by reason of two facts: (1) the position of women as controllers of income and wealth, and (2) their influence as purchasers for the family.

More than 40 percent of all individual wealth in the United States is owned by women. LIfe insurance companies each year pay to women between one half and three fourths of a billion dollars. Sixty percent of all estates go entirely to women, only 25 percent entirely to men, the remainder being divided.

From this wealth and from their own labor, women rank high as receivers of income. Well over 18 million women earn part or all of their own living in other than family household duties. In a recent year, 54 percent of all Americans reporting incomes over $100,000 were women.

Not only is this purchasing power available to women for spending, but also much of the earnings of men are available to them. As housewives, the influence of women in determining what will be purchased is great. The woman has often been referred to as the purchasing agent for the family. The United States Department of Commerce estimates that 85 percent of all retail purchases are made by women.

There is no doubt about women doing most of the buying of consumption goods. The more important problem of the advertiser, however, deals with the relative importance of the man and the woman in influencing the purchase. Some advertisers have admitted that women do the buying but have insisted that men really "direct" the buying. This point of view has been held by *Time* magazine and popularized in its advertising with the statement, "He who pays the fiddler calls the tune," meaning, of course, that when the man pays the bills he determines in large part what will be purchased. *Redbook* magazine has held the same philosophy and has used in its advertising the slogan, "The shadow of a man stands behind every woman who buys." But the *Ladies' Home Journal* counters with the slogan, "Never underestimate the power of a woman." (See Figure 9–3.)

FIGURE 9–3
Who determines what will be purchased?

Never Underestimate the Power of a Woman!

The power of a woman—and the power of Ladies' Home Journal with women:
together they are the greatest force in advertising today.

LADIES' HOME **JOURNAL**   THE MAGAZINE WOMEN BELIEVE IN

Education

As a classification factor, education is interrelated with age, income, and occupation. Relatively few people in the older age groups went to college. A higher proportion of the younger men and women completed this level of education, and the percentage of high school students going on to college is steadily increasing. College educated people are more apt to be found in the higher income groups, reflecting both the higher family income of their earlier years and the increased productivity made possible by their higher level of education. A college degree has long been recognized as a prerequisite for entering the professions of medicine, law, and engineering. It is becoming an almost universal requirement for top management positions in business and government. The relationship between education and income is dramatically illustrated in Figure 9–4.

Education probably has less effect on what people buy than on how they buy and how they are influenced by advertising. Perhaps better educated people are more discerning, more discriminating, and more rational buyers. Perhaps they are less suggestible, less susceptible to nonrational appeals, and less responsive to persuasion. If so, it would seem that advertising addressed to better educated groups should be more factual, more informative, and more reasonable. These specifications certainly should be considered, but they overlook the fact that man is a bundle of emotions regardless of the kind or degree of his education. A blending of

FIGURE 9–4
College education boosts income

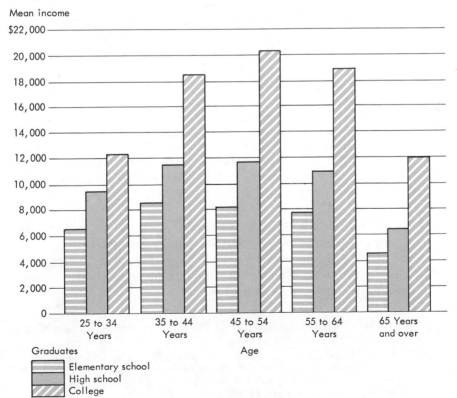

Source: U.S. Bureau of the Census, *Current Population Reports,* Series P–60, No. 92, March 1974.

reason and emotion can be effectively used in all persuasion. Talking the consumer's language is axiomatic. As the consuming public becomes better educated the advertiser should avoid talking beneath their notice.

Race

Eleven percent of the U.S. population are blacks. However, in the ten largest cities blacks account for 31 percent of the population; in the 78 largest cities they account for 25 percent. Black family income in 1970 was reported to be $8,530 in Detroit, $8,517 in Chicago, $7,140 in New York, and $8,410 in Washington, D.C.[1] This urban, growing, middle-class market has demonstrated some distinctive buying patterns.

The black household consumes 8 percent more meat of all kinds by weight than the white family, 6 percent more poultry, and 34 percent more pork. The black family consumes less coffee and tea than the white family; but consumption of soft drinks is 9 percent more. Since a greater percentage of blacks wives work, convenience foods are important. Black families with income above $4,000 buy 26 percent more frozen vegetables than white families. In the under-$2,000 income group they spend 19 percent more on canned vegetables than white families.[2]

Controversy over whether the United States is an integrated society or a dual society has extended to advertising strategy. Alternative approaches to blacks were categorized by D. Parke Gibson as follows:

> We have white-oriented advertising that appears in primarily white-oriented media; we have white-oriented advertising that appears in primarily black-oriented media; we have integrated advertising that appears in white-oriented and black-oriented media; we have some black-oriented advertising that appears in white-oriented media; and, of course, we have black-oriented advertising in black-oriented media.
>
> In this confusion we have reflections of social responsibility, misunderstood public relations objectives, mis-directed marketing considerations, some do-goodism and, last but certainly not least, some clear-cut marketing objectives with on-target advertising directed to specific markets.[3]

Black-oriented media include radio stations, magazines, and newspapers. Negroes listen to radio considerably more than the average white person and are slightly less interested in TV and much less interested in print media. When the black person does tune in the radio, he is inclined to listen to black-programmed stations.[4]

---

[1] Raymond O. Oladipupo, *How Distinct Is The Negro Market?* (New York: Ogilvy & Mather, Inc., 1970), p. 23.

[2] Ibid., pp. 30, 31.

[3] D. Parke Gibson, *Negro-Oriented Advertising—the Other Side of the 1970s* (New York: American Association of Advertising Agencies, 1969), p. 1.

[4] Oladipupo, *Negro Market,* pp. 48, 49.

Different attitudes, different product preferences, and different media usage clearly indicate that there is a specific market among blacks for which specific advertising strategies should be designed.

Nationality

The melting pot is supposed to have erased much of the variation normally existing between different nationalities. As yet, the melting process has not been completed in the United States; some 24 million people living in the continental United States are foreign born or had foreign-born parentage. This represents approximately one eighth of the entire population. In many ways, however, the buying habits and motives of these groups are similar to those of the native born. This is true where the melting pot has resulted in merging the culture patterns of the foreign-born and the native population. There do exist, however, sufficient differences in product preferences and buying behavior to warrant careful analysis by the advertiser.

The advertiser desiring to reach these groups in their entirety must use the newspapers and periodicals read by them. There are many foreign-language publications, about 720 being listed by the 1974 *Ayer Directory of Publications*.[5] There are 95 Spanish, 44 German, 32 Italian, 28 Czechoslovak, 23 Polish, 30 French, and 11 Yiddish publications listed among the total. Also, there are 253 radio stations regularly scheduling Spanish language programs. This would indicate the existence of rather large ethnic groups which still maintain a considerable part of their native culture.

Religion

Our present age has been referred to as the "age of religious decay." Perhaps religion does not play the part in human lives that it did at an earlier date. Yet it holds a stronger grip and a deeper significance on human actions than surface observations would indicate. Even an adult may feel that the religious forces which helped to direct his childhood actions have been discarded. But nothing which has grooved itself into our life at any time can be entirely erased. To a degree, it still, consciously or unconsciously, influences our daily actions.

The things we eat and wear, the recreation in which we indulge, the character of our reading material, our marriage relationships, and our personal habits in regard to smoking and drinking have in many cases been influenced by religion. In certain parts of the United States it would be suicidal for a meat merchant to stock up with pork and beef on a Friday and fail to have plenty of fish on hand, while in some spots much Kosher

[5] *1974 Ayer Directory of Publications* (Philadelphia: Ayer Press, 1974), pp. 1032–39.

meat is sold. In other sections, the druggist that kept open on Sunday would sell few products during the week, the restaurant that sold beer on Sunday would find few customers, and the promoter of a dance hall would probably be ushered out of town. There are exceptions; but to a greater degree than many advertisers realize, religious elements provide almost fixed grooves for the purchase of many products.

The seller of coffee would find returns from his advertising in Salt Lake City much less than returns from similar advertising in Cincinnati. A few years ago when Lucky Strikes made their first appeal to women, an indirect and subtle approach was used. Eventually, however, the company became bold enough to make the appeal direct and to picture a girl actually smoking a cigarette. Such illustrations were made a part of a national outdoor poster campaign. The company found it necessary, however, to paint out the cigarette in the girl's mouth in certain sections of the country.

It would be absurd for advertisers to play the part of the crusader in attempting to break down buying habits and motives founded on a religious background. Give the religious element what it wants. If Salt Lake City people do not want coffee, then sell them postum or cocoa. The cost of selling them coffee, even though it were possible, would be prohibitive.

Location

The needs of people are materially altered by the differences in climate, topography, and general character of the section of the country in which they reside. The influence of location is distinctly heterogeneous in many respects, in that so many factors are associated with a given territory. Social customs, dress, type of recreation, racial elements, type of homes, and general energy are all factors that might be associated with location. The very heterogeneity occasioned by location increases the importance of study of this factor. An attempt should be made to divide these unlike elements and give each its proper weight as a factor influencing needs and wants.

Some of the obvious influences of location might be noted. Certainly the demand for lightweight suits will be much greater south of the Mason-Dixon Line than north of it. The same will be true for ice, lawn furniture, and electric fans. The demand will be less for fur coats, ice skates, sleds, furnace equipment, and skis. Only by a study of individual needs, shaped and altered by location, will the true significance of this factor to a particular producer be ascertained.

The family life cycle

The family life cycle refers to the progression of important stages in adult life. It breaks through the arbitrary classification of people in terms of calendar age and groups them according to more meaningful periods of their life. For example, if we assume that in family A there are two children under 6 and the parents are age 42; in family B there are two children under 6 and the parents are age 28; in family C there are no children and the married couple are age 42; we will find that for many products the buying behavior of families A and B will be more nearly alike than the buying behavior of families A and C. The presence of young children can be a more significant classification factor than calendar age.

The life cycle of a family begins with the marriage of two people and continues throughout the remaining span of their lives. It can be subdivided into stages marked by the birth of children, age level of the youngest child, the departure of children to set up their own homes, and the death of one of the spouses.

John B. Lansing and James N. Morgan, in their study "Consumer Finances Over the Life Cycle," used these stages:

1. *The bachelor stage.* Single individuals living alone. They have left the home in which they were reared, but they have not founded a new home.
2. *The newly married couple* with no children.
3. *Young married with children,* youngest under 6.
4. *Young married with children,* youngest over 6.
5. *Older married (over 45)* with children.
6. *The empty nest,* the married couple after the children have left home.
7. *The solitary survivor.* In the natural course of events one of the couple dies before the other.[6]

Some comparisons of buying behavior at different stages in the life cycle are indicated in Table 9–2. For reasons obvious to parents the most washing machines are bought by young married families with children under six years of age. These families with young children also appear to be the best prospects for houses, used cars, and television sets. Purchases of furniture, refrigerators, and stoves are frequent among all married people under 45 years old, but less common in the older groups.

Families with young children are the most frequent purchasers of chest rubs, cough syrups, and packaged detergents. Newly married housewives are prime prospects for cake mixes, precooked foods, new recipes, and new labor-saving devices.

Inasmuch as the family is the important consuming unit for appliances, furniture, home furnishings, and most grocery items, the life cycle is a promising classification system for structuring consumer markets.

[6] John B. Lansing and James N. Morgan, "Consumer Finances Over the Life Cycle," *Consumer Behavior,* Vol. 2 (New York: New York University Press, 1955), pp. 36–37.

TABLE 9–2
Proportion of spending units at different stages in the life cycle purchasing houses, cars, and other selected durables (by percent)

Item purchased	All spending units*	Young, single	Stage					
			Young married			Older married		Older, single
			Childless	Youngest child under 6	Youngest child 6 or over	Over 45, with children	No children under 18	
House	4	†	6	9	7	4	3	†
New car	9	5	11	11	20	11	9	2
Used car	14	11	22	23	18	14	11	4
Furniture	16	10	26	23	27	16	11	5
Refrigerator	9	1	14	12	12	8	7	5
Stove	7	3	13	10	7	5	7	4
Washing machine	6	1	10	13	9	8	4	1
Television set	14	5	14	22	19	16	12	7

* A spending unit is defined as all persons living in the same dwelling and related by blood, marriage, or adoption, who pool their incomes to meet their major expenses. However, any individual who earns $15 a week or more and keeps more than half of it for his own use is treated as a separate unit. Thus, an employed bachelor son living with his parents appears as separate spending unit.
† Less than 0.5 percent.
Source: John B. Lansing and James N. Morgan, "Consumer Finances Over the Life Cycle," Consumer Behavior, Vol. 2 (New York: New York University Press, 1955), p. 43.

Social class

The concept of social class is especially useful in studies of consumer motivation. One's goals, attitudes, value systems, standards of taste, and behavior patterns are largely influenced by the social world in which he lives.

Social classes are determined by combining such factors as occupation, family background, education, neighborhood, and the source as well as the amount of income.

Social Research, Inc., an organization that specializes in motivation studies, uses these six social classes:

1. Upper upper— The "aristocracy" of a community, the old-line families with inherited wealth who can live comfortably on income derived from investments.
2. Lower upper— Families with newly gained economic and social power.
3. Upper middle— Families in which husbands are likely to be successful business executives, or be occupied in one of the professions. Their incomes average somewhat less than the people in the upper classes and are predominantly salary and current earnings, rather than income from invested wealth.
4. Lower middle— White collar workers, tradesmen, a few skilled workers, and their families. They have accumulated little property, but are frequently homeowners.
5. Upper lower— Skilled and semiskilled workers who participate relatively little in educational and other advantages of our society.
6. Lower lower— Unskilled laborers, people on relief, unassimilated foreign groups. Many of them are poor and lack the ambition or opportunity to improve their lot.

The general distribution of our population among these groups is about 3 percent or less for the entire upper class and around 12 percent for the upper-middle class, with about 65 percent clustered in the lower-middle and upper-lower classes, and about 20 percent in the lower-lower classes. There is considerable psychological and social distance between the three top classes and the mass of people immediately below them. Although few people are able to move up the social ladder, it is likely that our rising level of incomes will produce greater similarities among all classes.

Both conformity to the standards of one's class and emulation of the classes above can be seen in consumer behavior. Where people live, their houses, furniture, home furnishings, food preferences, and entertainment tend to be the same as those of other people in their class. On the other hand, their automobiles and clothing may reflect a desire to emulate the classes above.

> As middle-majority people become more prosperous, they may try to translate their money into higher status by the education given their children, by moving to a new neighborhood, by buying products they think suited to a higher social level. But not all will want to do this; many who feel stable and not motivated to be mobile will continue to live much as before, perhaps saving more money, enjoying inconspicuous luxuries, or spending more on recreation.[7]

PSYCHOGRAPHICS

Many differences in what consumers buy can only be explained in terms of their psychological makeup. We see older men driving flashy sports cars instead of more conservative models, thereby demonstrating that they are young in heart, if not in years. Perhaps all men who prefer to smoke a pipe instead of cigarettes have similar personality traits regardless of their socioeconomic status. People whose taste in houses and furniture runs toward contemporary instead of traditional design may be near each other psychologically even though they are far apart economically. Sophisticated urbanites who enjoy listening to country music may have much in common with farm and ranch people who also like that kind of music. Such similarities of taste and preferences among people from different walks of life suggest that in many instances psychological groups are more pertinent than sociological groups.

Classifying consumers according to psychological characteristics is not easily done. A person's attitudes and personality traits are not so readily ascertained as his age and occupation. His psychological characteristics can only be inferred from how he scores on appropriately designed tests such as the more familiar I.Q. tests, aptitude tests, and attitude scales.

In a study of *Better Homes and Gardens* readers, Alfred Politz tested and classified respondents according to their venturesomeness, a characteristic which he describes as follows:

> In the course of studying the reaction of consumers to products which have been introduced, it was observed that individuals do differ with respect to venturesomeness. There are some individuals who are of the adventurous type. They are the people who are the first to buy new products and try innovations. On the other end of the scale there are people who tend to be cautious. These are the people who will buy a new product only after they have been convinced that the new product is worthwhile. While a venturesome person will tend to shift from one new product to another; a

---

[7] Harper W. Boyd, Jr. and Sidney J. Levy, *Promotion: A Behavioral View* (Englewood Cliffs, N.J.: Prentice-Hall, Inc., 1967), p. 44.

cautious person, once he has been persuaded to try a new product, will tend to be loyal to that product.[8]

As one would expect, Politz found that deep-fat fryers, electric skillets, electric rotisseries, and window air conditioners were more prevalent in households inhabited by venturesome people than in those where cautious people lived. Young people tend to be more venturesome than old. However, a large number of old people are venturesome and a large number of young people are cautious. Venturesomeness is not concentrated in any particular income group. People on the lower rungs of the income ladder are about as likely to be venturesome as those on the higher rungs.

One study of the relationship between personality traits and cigarette smoking showed that the average U.S. male smoker scored significantly higher than the average U.S. male in his expressed needs for sex, aggression, achievement, and dominance, and significantly below average in compliance, order, self-depreciation, and association.[9]

The trend toward psychological groupings is evidenced in the way some magazines are now characterizing their readers. *Sports Illustrated* describes their readers as the "enthusiastic ones." *Holiday* refers to their readers as the "spirited leaders of this more-fun-and-fine-living age."

Life style

To identify more meaningful segments in the market, consumers are grouped according to clusters of attitudes, values, and behavior patterns they hold in common. Such descriptions are referred to as *life style*. As Boyd and Levy observed: "Everyone's life has a style of some kind, and his wishes to develop it, sustain it, and show it make it a coherent and visible thing that other people can recognize. Because of the coherence and visibility of life styles, those who share them are likely to react similarly to marketing communication, to buy the same or similar products."[10]

In one study, for example, 214 attitude statements were presented to a sample of housewives who were asked to indicate the degree to which each statement fit their self-concept.[11] Typical attitude statements were:

1.   When it comes to a choice between nutrition and taste in my family meal planning, I put nutrition first.
2.   I wouldn't let animals come into the house because of the dirt.

---

[8] *A 12-Month's Study of Better Homes & Gardens Readers* (Des Moines, Iowa: Meredith Publishing Company, 1956), p. 147.

[9] Arthur Koponen, "Personality Characteristics of Purchasers," *Journal of Advertising Research,* September 1960 (New York: Advertising Research Foundation), pp. 6–12.

[10] Boyd and Levy, *Promotion,* pp. 37–38.

[11] Ruth Ziff, "Psychographics for Market Segmentation," *Journal of Advertising Research,* April 1971 (New York: Advertising Research Foundation), pp. 3–9.

3. I get upset when things are out of their place in my house.
4. If there's a flu bug going around, I'm sure to catch it.
5. Once you've got a cold, there is very little you can do about it.

Respondents to the 214 attitude statements were then classified into 6 groups described as:

1. *Outgoing Optimists* are outgoing, innovative, community oriented, positive toward grooming, not bothered by delicate health or digestive problems or especially concerned about germs or cleanliness.

2. *Conscientious Vigilants* are conscientious, rigid, meticulous, germ-fighting, with a high cleanliness orientation and sensible attitudes about food. They have high cooking pride, a careful shopping orientation, tend not to be convenience oriented.

3. *Apathetic Indifferents* are not outgoing, are uninvolved with family, irritable, have a negative grooming orientation, are lazy—especially in terms of cooking pride.

4. *Self-Indulgents* are relaxed, permissive, unconcerned with health problems, interested in convenience items but with relatively high cooking pride, self-indulgent towards themselves and their families.

5. *Contented Cows* are relaxed, not worried, relatively unconcerned about germs and cleanliness, not innovative or outgoing, strongly economy oriented, not self-indulgent.

6. *Worriers* are irritable, concerned about health, germs, and cleanliness, negative about grooming and breakfast, but self-indulgent with a low economy and high convenience orientation.

Various other designations such as bargain hunter, swinger, child oriented, and fashion conscious are used to describe different life styles. Demonstrating the opportunity for imaginative thinking in this kind of segmentation Alvin Toffler, author of *Future Shock,* suggests:

> If we were to survey consumers we would find significant differences be-
> tween various cultural and economic groups with respect to time, to their
> durational relationships. Some people hold on to things longer than other
> people. If we made a similar analysis of the *duration* of place relationships,
> the *duration* of friendships, the *duration* of the individual's affiliations, and
> the *duration* of key values, we would find fascinating and useful patterns.
> This "transience index" could be invaluable to the advertiser because dura-
> tional patterns are likely to correlate with consumer patterns.[12]

Heavy users

A more direct approach to pinpointing market targets is to find out who are the heavy users of the product. For many product categories we find that a small proportion of the population consumes a large proportion of

[12] "An Interview With Alvin Toffler," *Advertising Age,* November 21, 1973, p. 201.

the product. Note in Table 9–3, that only 3.6 percent of the male population accounts for 89.6 percent of all car rentals, that only 11.3 percent of the women use 88.1 percent of all hair colorings, that 20 percent of total households use 99 percent of prepared dog food, etc. Even in the case of popular products such as soft drinks, tomato sauce, facial tissues, and frozen vegetables we find that less than one half of the population accounts for 80 to 90 percent of the usage.

TABLE 9–3
Percent of total product usage accounted for by the heavy users of specific products

	Heavy users	
	Percent of population group	*Percent of total usage*
Car rentals in past year (men)	3.6	89.6
Liquid dietary products	4.1	98.0
Air trips in past year (men)	7.8	87.3
Automatic dishwasher detergents	9.0	100.0
Hair coloring rinse or tint (women)	11.3	88.1
Scotch whiskey	12.6	98.6
Cigar smoking (men)	17.1	98.6
Rye or blended whiskey	18.4	98.5
Bourbon	18.8	98.7
Canned type dog food	19.3	99.2
Dry dog food	20.7	99.2
Canned ham	22.8	83.0
Instant coffee	26.1	80.6
Cold or allergy tablets	27.0	84.3
Cigarettes (all adults)	27.2	84.1
Hair tonic (men)	27.8	76.8
Laxatives	28.2	92.8
Rice	28.8	82.7
Peanut butter	29.6	82.4
Cake mix	34.1	84.4
R.T.E. cereal	37.2	80.2
Upset stomach remedies	37.3	89.2
Shaving cream in pressurized cans (men)	38.7	98.0
Frozen orange juice	41.0	92.1
Soft drinks	41.8	84.9
Paper napkins	42.9	83.2
Bleach	43.7	81.6
Tomato sauce	44.9	90.7
Cleansing or facial tissues	45.2	82.9
Frozen vegetables	49.9	92.1
Regular ground coffee	50.5	92.7
H. H. laundry detergents	50.8	81.4
Headache remedies	52.6	93.1

Note: The total population group is based on total households except for those products specifically designated otherwise.
Source: Norton Garfinkle, "The Marketing Value of Media Audiences—How To Pinpoint Your Prime Prospects" (Paper presented at A.N.A. workshop, January 19, 1965).

Once the heavy-user group is identified, their demographic characteristics can be described. Then advertising appeals most appropriate for that group and media most efficiently reaching that group can be employed. For example, heavy users of automatic dishwasher detergents are concentrated in the upper and upper-middle social class households, heavy users of laxatives are concentrated in lower-income households, and heavy users of hair tonic are concentrated among men 18 to 35 years of age. Heavy users of facial tissues tend to be in upper middle income, larger family, and suburban households.

Even though the heavy-user group is well identified, important strategy questions remain to be answered. Should all advertisers concentrate on the heavy users? Or, should some concentrate on other segments of the total market? Commercial success can sometimes be achieved by building a strong brand preference among light or moderate users. Perhaps gaining 80 percent of the moderate users can be more profitable than 10 percent of the heavy users. Chances are usually greater, however, that those people who are responsive to a particular product category, as indicated by their higher rate of purchase, will be the most profitable market to cultivate.

A cross-tabulation of consumer purchases is likely to show that heavy users of one product are also heavy users of other products. For example, heavy users of ready-to-eat cereals are also heavy users of peanut butter, laundry detergent, toothpaste, shampoo, gelatin desserts, and canned soups.

A further classification of consumers, based on their willingness to accept new products, identifies five adopter categories: *innovators, early adopters, early majority, late majority,* and *laggards.* The *innovators,* representing 2.5 percent, of the product's eventual users, are the most venturesome and are the first to try a new product, even at some risk. The *early adopters,* representing the next 13.5 percent, adopt new ideas early, but with discretion. They are likely to be opinion leaders in their community. The *early majority,* representing 34 percent, adopt before the average, but do so only after considerable deliberation. The *late majority,* representing another 34 percent, wait until the weight of public opinion establishes the product as the thing to buy. The *laggards,* representing the last 16 percent, stubbornly resist change. They adopt so late that the product may already have been replaced by a new and superior product.[13]

Summary

The study of people by groups is not valuable for its own sake, but rather as a means of ascertaining more clearly the real needs and wants of people

---

[13] See Everett M. Rogers, *Diffusion of Innovation* (New York: The Free Press, 1964).

as influenced by membership in given groups. It is an attempt to determine the culture patterns of people so that advertising may be harmonized with these patterns. It is necessary at all times to recognize that people are members of more than one group. The advertiser must attempt to correlate these various influences into a composite picture of needs and wants.

John Cover has stated the problem as follows:

> The concept of an "average consumer" is fallacious, for only by the process of classification and reclassification is there obtained group similarity; and each criterion of income, race, nationality, creed, etc., is significant only as related to all other criteria. For instance, when nationality is isolated from its various neighborhood relationships it appears to have little weight in determining consumption habits. But when placed in its neighborhood environment in relation to income, prices, and other factors, its influence is important.[14]

The study of consumers in groups is not a perfect solution to the problem of determining their needs and wants. Yet it is sufficiently valuable to encourage businessmen to intensify their efforts in such study.

QUESTIONS AND PROBLEMS

1   Even though demographic data frequently are inadequate for market segmentation, such data are widely used because they are available. Explain.

2   If the trend toward zero population growth persists, what products and services should be in greater demand in the year 2000 than at present? In lesser demand?

3   Among the various classification factors discussed in this chapter, list those you think would be most significant for segmenting the market for (a) canned baby food, (b) a new hot cereal, (c) life insurance, (d) sterling silverware, (e) automobile tires, (f) ski resort, (g) Caribbean cruises, (h) a new hair spray.

4   What differences in buying behavior would you expect to find among families in the various stages of the family life cycle with respect to (a) foods, (b) clothing, (c) furniture, (d) automobile insurance, (e) vacation travel.

5   Social class goes well beyond income as a useful concept for market segmentation. Contrast the occupations, education, neighborhoods, family background, and sources of income of the six social classes listed in this chapter.

6   Different life styles are manifested in the products and services people buy. Describe the life styles of the best prospects for (a) antiques, (b) fishing equipment, (c) ski equipment, (d) rare books, (e) lawn mowers, (f) pipe tobacco.

7   The adoption process that distinguishes innovators from early adopters from laggards, etc. is more pertinent to major innovations in a product category than to new brand introductions. Do you agree or disagree? Explain.

[14] John H. Cover, *Neighborhood Distribution and Consumption of Meat in Pittsburgh* (Chicago: University of Chicago Press, 1932), pp. 16, 17.

8   Of what significance to the advertiser is the trend toward increased longevity?

9   Some claim that the mother or wife is the purchasing agent for the home. How should this influence the advertiser?

10 The "Trim 'n Paster" machine described in the Questions and Problems section of the previous chapter would not have the same appeal to all groups of consumers. What group or groups do you believe would be most likely to get satisfaction from the product?

10

Product analysis

Consumers do not buy products. They buy the satisfactions they expect and experience from their use of products. They are less concerned with what the manufacturer puts into the product than they are with what they get out of it. As Charles Revson of Revlon, Inc., observed: "In the factory we make cosmetics; in the store we sell hope." It is not cosmetic chemicals women want, but the promise of seductive charm.

To win consumer acceptance the product should be designed, manufactured, and packaged in accordance with appropriate technical specifications, but that is not enough. The consumer must perceive the product in terms of the satisfactions it delivers. According to Theodore Levitt:

> The product is not what the engineer explicitly says it is, but what the consumer implicitly demands that it shall be. Thus the consumer consumes not things, but expected benefits—not cosmetics, but the satisfactions of the allurements they promise; not quarter-inch drills, but quarter-inch holes; not stock in companies, but capital gains; not numerically controlled milling machines, but trouble-free and accurately smooth metal parts; not low-cal whipped cream, but self-rewarding indulgence combined with sophisticated convenience.[1]

In effect, the product does not exist as a separate entity. *The product is what the consumer perceives it to be.*

[1] Theodore Levitt, "The Morality of Advertising," *Harvard Business Review,* July–August 1970, p. 91.

Consumer perceptions are strategically important at all stages of product development, from initial conceptualization to concept testing, to positioning, to designing, manufacturing, packaging, pricing, delivering, advertising, selling, financing, and servicing. Product analysis, therefore, embraces systematic research at all stages. The focus of such research is not on the product itself, but on the consumers and how they respond to the various alternatives at each stage.

To simplify the exposition we are drawing examples primarily from the field of consumer products, such as the tangible items found on the shelves of supermarkets, in department stores, appliance shops, and automobile showrooms. In doing so we are not overlooking the importance of the field of services, such as airlines, insurance companies, banks, and travel agents; nor the field of industrial goods, such as computers, chemicals, textiles, and lift trucks. While there are some differences in marketing strategies from one category to the next, the underlying principle of delivering customer satisfaction is the same.

Product concept testing

The introduction of new and improved products is the key to corporate growth and survival. Manufacturers who are first to offer a new product have, for a while, the entire market to themselves. They can build profitable sales before their competitors get started. Their initial momentum often propels them into a commanding lead that no competitor can overtake. Any manufacturer who relies on marketing the same old product in the same old way is not likely to survive. However, new product introductions are accompanied by a high risk of failure. In 1972, food processors introduced 417 new products in the average chain supermarket.[2] Two out of three of those products failed. A single failure can cost from $75,000 in test market to $20 million for a national introduction. Research and development costs alone can be substantial.

Why do most new products fail? Primarily because the innovation or the difference between the new product and established brands "is important only to the manufacturer and not to the consumer where it counts."[3] Therefore, the risk of failure can best be reduced by testing the concept of a new product before the product exists, even before any funds are committed to research and development. The best place to test the product concept is with the consumer, where it counts.

Inasmuch as ideas most often are communicated verbally, the simplest

[2] Richard L. Neale, "New Views of a $100 Billion Industry" (Paper presented at the Eastern Annual Conference of the American Association of Advertising Agencies, November 14, 1973).

[3] Theodore L. Angelus, "Why Do Most New Products Fail?" *Advertising Age,* March 24, 1969.

approach is to express the new product concept in the form of a statement, present the statement to consumers, and ask them to evaluate it. For example, the idea of a new carbonated beverage fortified with nutritional ingredients including vitamins, minerals, and protein would be presented to consumers in a statement typed on a card: "The product is a new, nutritionally fortified, soft drink. This carbonated beverage is fortified with vitamins that would equal 9 percent of the minimum daily requirement for an adult. Additionally, the product would contain protein and minerals and would be available in a variety of flavors."

To clarify and quantify consumer reactions, respondents would be asked to complete the following questionnaire:

1. How do you expect this new product would compare with the soft drink you buy most frequently? (Please check one—I think this new product would be. . . .
   _____Much better
   _____Somewhat better
   _____About the same
   _____Somewhat worse
   _____Much worse

2. How do you expect the taste of this new product would compare with the taste of the soft drink you buy most frequently? (Please check one—I think the taste of this new product would be. . . .)
   _____Much better
   _____Somewhat better
   _____About the same
   _____Somewhat worse
   _____Much worse

3. Would you expect this new product to contain more calories or fewer calories than the soft drink you buy most frequently? (Please check one.)
   _____Many more calories
   _____Somewhat more calories
   _____About the same number of calories
   _____Somewhat fewer calories
   _____Much fewer calories

4. Who in your family do you think would be most interested in drinking this product? (Please check only one person.)
   _____Myself   _____Child 6 to 12
   _____Husband   _____Child 12 to 17
   _____Child under 5   _____Young adult, 17 or older

5. What flavor or flavors do you think would be most appropriate for this new product?

6. Imagine you were going to buy this new product as it is described. How much do you think a 12-oz. can of it would cost?

7. How interested do you think you would be in buying this new product?
   _____Extremely interested

_____Quite interested

_____Somewhat interested

_____Not at all interested

8. The actual price of this product would be $0.19 per 12-oz. can, or $1.14 per 6-pack of 12-oz. cans. At this price, how interested do you think you would be in buying this new product?

_____Extremely interested

_____Quite interested

_____Somewhat interested

_____Not at all interested

9. Assuming this new product were on the market, would you please indicate your best estimate of how many of the next ten purchases you make would be for each type of beverage. (Please mark a zero if no purchase would be made.)

_____Canned juice drinks

_____Diet soft drinks

_____Regular soft drinks

_____Nutritional soft drinks

_____Powdered drinks

10. Now we would like to know to what extent you agree or disagree with various statements listed below. As you read each statement place an X in the box that best indicates how much you agree or disagree with it.

	Strongly agree	Agree somewhat	Neither agree nor disagree	Disagree somewhat	Strongly disagree
It is sometimes difficult to get everyone in the family to eat a balanced diet	( )	( )	( )	( )	( )
I am concerned that some people in the family don't get all the vitamins and minerals they need	( )	( )	( )	( )	( )
We supplement our family's diet with vitamins	( )	( )	( )	( )	( )
I am concerned that some people in the family don't get all the protein they need . . .	( )	( )	( )	( )	( )

Presenting a product concept in the form of a verbal statement leaves much to the consumer's imagination. This can be an advantage if the concept requires further sharpening. However, the more details the consumer has to fill in for himself or herself, the less reliable are the test results. A promising technique is to present the product concept in the form of an advertisement. The advertisement would clearly portray what the product would look like, what benefits it would confer, and whatever superiority it would offer over existing competition. Inasmuch as the new product eventually would have to be introduced in an advertisement, this form of communication is a most appropriate way to present the idea to consumers in a concept test.

A product may pass with flying colors at the conceptual stage, but ultimately fail in the marketplace. There are pitfalls at every step along the way—in designing, in manufacturing, in packaging, in pricing, in advertising, etc. The chance for error can be greatly reduced if consumer testing is an integral part of the entire development spectrum.

Product positioning

In a sense there is no such thing as a new product. Whatever the so-called new entry might be, the consumer immediately relates it to existing products. The new laundry detergent may have a "new" brand name, a "new" package, a "new" color, a "new" form, and make a "new" claim, but the homemaker fits it in among the brands she already knows. She perceives it as being more like one than another, as a more likely substitute for one than another, or perhaps as somewhat superior to any brand now available. *Perceptual positioning,* this process of "fitting into an existing scheme of things," epitomizes the principle that learning is a matter of relating to prior learning. Therefore, whatever the "new" encounter might be, it can't be entirely new because we can only explain it in terms of what we already know.

Positioning is strategically important and is viewed in different ways. One view holds that the manufacturer does the positioning—that by manipulating the product's form, ingredients, package size, price, etc. he produces a product that fills a gap among existing brands in a given product category. Literally, he positions the product on the supermarket shelf. This, however, overlooks the fact that regardless of how the manufacturer positions the product on the shelf, the ultimate positioning will be done in the consumer's mind. The manufacturer may try to tell the consumer that his product is "new and revolutionary." The consumer is more likely to perceive it as slightly better or worse than the brand she is now using.

General Foods Corporation developed a new dog food, code named PC-33. The result of a new technique in food processing (intermediate moisture technology), PC-33 was not as wet as canned and not as dry as existing dry dog foods. It did not require refrigeration either before or after the package was opened. PC-33 contained meat and was nutritionally balanced to provide a complete diet. It came in the form of individually wrapped serving size patties resembling patties of uncooked ground beef. In positioning the product the following alternatives were considered:

1. PC-33 is an entry in the *canned* dog food arena. It is a substitute for, or alternative to, existing types and brands of canned dog food.
2. PC-33 is an entirely *new, revolutionary,* independent, and dramatic *concept* in dog feeding, with no resemblance or relation to any other dog food on the market.
3. PC-33 is a super dog food, *high-nutrition supplement,* to be used in addition to your regular dog food.
4. PC-33 is a special dog food, specifically developed *for dogs five years of age or older.*[4]

A case could be made for each of these positioning alternatives, especially the second which would take sales from all entries in the dog food market. Research revealed, however, that consumers perceived PC-33, its color, texture, moisture content, form, and nutrition, as being more like canned dog food than any other kind. Positioning PC-33 against canned also made good marketing sense because this was the most profitable segment of the market, a segment in which General Foods had no successful entry. Therefore, PC-33, which subsequently was named Gainesburgers, was positioned as "The Canned Dog Food Without The Can."

Consumer perceptions of a competitive field can be useful in repositioning an established brand. For example, Life cereal during its first ten years on the market was positioned as a nutritional cereal for all members of the family. The advertising was product centered, claiming that Life contained the highest quality protein among ready-to-eat cereals and was more appetizing than other brands in the nutritional field. Laboratory tests substantiated the protein claim, and taste tests indicated that Life was somewhat sweeter than its competitors, Special K and Total. Following the strategy of the leader, Special K, the Quaker Oats Company, makers of Life, assumed that adults were the primary market for a nutritional cereal. By positioning Life for all members of the family, Quaker failed to make an effective appeal to children, who happen to consume more cereal than any other age group. When research showed that the principal reasons consumers gave for liking Life was its sweetness and crispy, crunchy texture (attributes most liked by children), Quaker repositioned the product and appealed to children. Sales increased substantially.

Perceptual mapping of a competitive field can be helpful in discovering an opportunity for introducing a new product or improving an established brand. To illustrate, beer drinkers might be asked to describe the attributes they consider important in comparing available brands. If the most frequently mentioned attributes are mildness and lightness they might be asked to rate each brand on a two-dimensional scale from "mild" to "bitter" and from "light" to "heavy." This would indicate how beer drinkers perceive existing brands, but may not reveal the combination of these attributes they would like to have. To learn the desired combination

[4] See General Foods-Post Division (B), Case M-102, Harvard Business School, 1964.

the same beer drinkers might be asked where they would place their ideal beer on the same scales of mildness and lightness. The responses to such questioning might then be plotted on a scatter diagram resulting in a distribution as shown in Figure 10–1.

The figure shows that two brands, Budweiser and Schlitz, are perceived as being relatively close, with Budweiser appearing somewhat milder and heavier than Schlitz. The larger circles represent greater densities of ideal points. As one might expect, the two largest selling brands are closest to the largest cluster of ideal points. If the center of circle 1 represents the most frequent ideal point, it might be assumed that many beer drinkers would like Budweiser to be a little less mild and Schlitz a little heavier. The cluster of ideal points in circles 2 and 7 indicate a possible opportunity

FIGURE 10–1
Distribution of consumer perceptions of beer brands and ideal points according to mildness and lightness

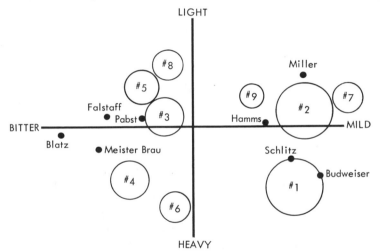

Source: Richard M. Johnson, "Market Segmentation: A Strategic Management Tool," *Journal of Marketing Research,* February 1971, p. 16.

for a new brand that would be lighter and milder than available brands. The distance of the three brands on the left from the ideal suggests they are bought because of a lower price, and this clearly demonstrates that it takes more than two attributes to explain brand purchases.

Product life cycles

Products, like people, go through a life cycle. The life of a product can be divided into four stages: *introduction, growth, maturity,* and *decline.*

FIGURE 10–2
Product life cycle

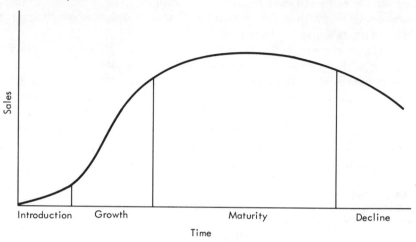

As illustrated in Figure 10–2, during the *introduction* stage, sales of the product rise slowly. If the new product is widely accepted, there is a rapid *growth* in sales. This is followed by a longer stage of *maturity* during which sales level off. Finally, the product's sales encounter a rapid or prolonged *decline*.

The life cycle concept applies to product classes (all ready-to-eat-cereals), product subclasses (high-nutrition cereals), and individual brands (Quaker's 100% Natural). The length of the total cycle and the length of each stage differ greatly from one product to the next. Hula hoops lasted 90 days. Ivory Soap seems destined to surpass 90 years. However, it should be noted that there have been so many improvements in Ivory Soap over the years that only the brand name remains the same. Most existing products are in the longest stage, the stage of maturity. Their sales are relatively stable, perhaps increasing only as much as population increases permit. A failure to meet the competition of new products or to adjust to changing consumer attitudes could quickly put them into the stage of decline. Had General Motors responded to a growing consumer prefer-ence for smaller, more efficient automobiles, they might have anticipated the sharp decline in full-size car sales that was triggered by the energy crisis in 1973.

Each stage of the product life cycle requires different advertising and promotion strategies. In the introduction stage a large number of consum-ers must quickly be told what the product is, what it does, and what benefits it offers. Building brand awareness, inducing trial, and gaining distribution in retail outlets requires heavy advertising and promotion expenditures—expenditures so heavy that it is not uncommon for them to exceed income, thereby resulting in a loss the first year. The innovating firm is willing to incur such early losses because it recognizes the advantage of momentum, that future profits are best assured by accelerating sales at the outset. If the product offers a discernible benefit—a satisfaction that consumers can readily experience when they use the product—it often makes good marketing sense to distribute free samples. This, of course, adds to the cost of introduction without adding immediately to sales. The ratio of advertising and promotion expenses to sales is highest during the introductory period, partly because extensive promotion is required and partly because it takes time for sales to catch up.

In the growth stage the innovator's sales start climbing rapidly. Many people who tried the product become repeat purchasers. Many others become triers as the product becomes more widely known. Advertising expenditures remain high, although as a ratio to sales they fall back to normal levels. Profits increase. Competitors enter the picture. Product sales now include not only the innovator's sales but all his competitors' as well. To counter competition the innovator may reduce prices, improve the product, extend the line, take a new creative approach in advertising, or make all these moves.

At the stage of maturity, sales level off and settle at the repurchase rate of the product's regular customers. Major competitors have settled into their respective positions, brands are well known, customer loyalties and market share are fairly stable. Profits have fallen to less attractive levels. Whatever innovation there might be has clearly shifted to marketing and advertising strategy and tactics. There might be attempts to increase usage among regular customers, such as the television commercials portraying a dosage of two Alka Seltzer tablets instead of one. There also might be attempts to find new uses and new users. This is a time when "creativity" in advertising is called upon to give a brand a competitive lift.

In the fourth and final stage of the life cycle, product sales decline. This may result from new, superior products replacing the old or from changing consumer preferences. If sales decline to the point where it is no longer profitable to continue, the obvious course of action is to withdraw from the market. However, in some instances, as in the case of Quaker Oatmeal, it may be possible to continue a profitable operation by holding on to a large share in a declining product category. In this stage, advertising and promotion play a minor role, mainly that of sustaining the brand in the eyes of loyal users.

Uses

Various marketing strategies might be employed to stretch the product life cycle. Levitt cites the case histories of General Foods' Jell-O and 3M's Scotch tape.[5]

[5] Theodore Levitt, *The Marketing Mode* (New York: McGraw-Hill Book Company, 1969), pp. 46, 47.

1. To promote *more frequent usage* of the product among current users, the number of Jell-O flavors was increased from six to more than twelve. Scotch tape was sold in a variety of handy dispensers that made the product easier to use.
2. To develop *more varied usage* of the product, Jell-O was promoted as a base for salads, and this use was facilitated through the development of a number of vegetable flavors. The Scotch tape line was expanded by adding colored, patterned, waterproof, invisible, and write-on Scotch tapes for sealing and decorating gifts.
3. To create *new users* Jell-O was advertised as a product with fashion-oriented weight-control appeal. Similarly, 3M introduced a lower priced tape and added a line of commercial tapes.
4. To find *new uses* a completely flavorless Jell-O was introduced for men and women who wanted to use gelatin as a bone-building dietary agent, as a means of strengthening their fingernails. 3M developed a double-coated tape to compete with liquid adhesives, a reflection tape for automobile bumpers, and marker strips to compete with paint.

In recent years, perhaps the most dramatic example of promoting an established product to a new group of users is the use of Johnson & Johnson Baby Shampoo by men. The advertising exploits the apparent incongruity by showing rugged professional athletes using the product. Also, accompanying the changing hair styles, men have become a significant market for hair sprays.

The discovery of new uses is not always the result of the manufacturer's aggressive action. Consumers themselves are inventive, as evidenced by their discovery that lemons could be used as a hair rinse, that Listerine could be used as a remedy for dandruff, that baking soda could be used to deodorize refrigerators, and that Scotch tape could be used to remove lint from clothing.

Packaging

The package, whether it be the tube from which the toothpaste is squeezed, the can from which the beer is drunk, or the carton from which the milk is poured, is an integral part of the product.

Functionally, the package protects the product in transit from manufacturer to consumer, preserves it from spoilage, and offers various conveniences for carrying, opening, and dispensing the contents. Aesthetically, the package contributes to the image of the brand. It is the most visible dimension that consumers perceive and, therefore, should clearly support and reinforce the brand's positioning. The size, shape, design, colors, graphics, name, and display features should clearly communicate the character of the brand.

Which is the best container for peanut butter?

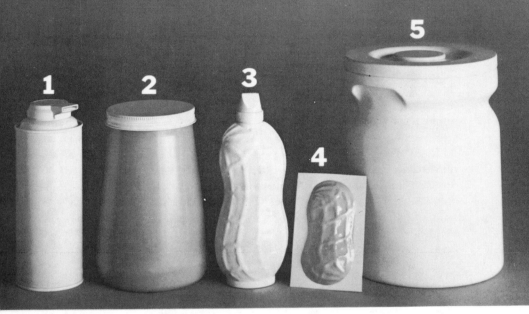

The one with the marketing plus.

We take familiar products and put them in unfamiliar packages—packages with a marketing plus built in. Take peanut butter, for example.

Number one's a pressure pack. It flows neatly, easily on crackers. Familiar package number two isn't really so familiar. It's clear plastic that looks like glass but won't shatter like glass.

Number three's a handy squeeze bottle—the type kids love—and they don't have to use knives.

Number four's an individual packet for picnic or school lunch boxes. Five's for the big family. After the peanut butter's gone, you can put in cookies.

They're all part of our experimental efforts to give familiar products new strength in the marketplace. At Continental we're continually looking for more ways like these to make products more attractive to buy and easier to sell.

Which is best? We'd like your opinion. Fill out the coupon and we'll send you a golden peanut tie-tac and our thanks.

FIGURE 10–3. How consumers help in molding the product to fit their needs or wants

To fully exploit the marketing opportunities the package affords, *laboratory tests* are conducted to assure that the package will stand up in transportation, storage, and handling; *visual tests* are conducted to assure that the graphics are legible and the colors harmonious; *dealer tests* are conducted to assure that dealers will find the package conforms to their storing, handling, and displaying practices; and *consumer tests* are conducted to assure favorable consumer reactions. Figure 10–3 illustrates how consumer opinions regarding different containers for peanut butter were sought by Continental Can Company.

Also, innovation in packaging might lead to the development of a new product. The aerosol can led to the development of hair sprays, insect repellents, and do-it-yourself spray-on paint. An improved polyethylene bag that withstands temperatures as high as 250° or as low as −100° Fahrenheit led to the development of preseasoned frozen foods that can be cooked in the package. Lightweight, inexpensive aluminum trays helped build the market for frozen dinners and pastries. An ingenious device for sustaining pressure in an aluminum container as its liquid content is removed led to the development of a keg of beer that fits in the home refrigerator. Plastic squeeze bottles hastened the entry of many liquid detergents.

The particular needs of dealers should also be considered in the development of a package. Dealers often have limited storage space and do not like packages that require a larger space than their actual contents would warrant. Odd-shaped packages that will not stack well in the warehouse, on the shelves, or in floor displays are often not desired by dealers. In the final analysis, however, the consumer is the one to choose the shape and size of the package. If he prefers an odd-shaped package, dealers will handle it.

The differentiation which a package may provide is of particular importance in the food field where a substantial part of total distribution is through self-service stores. Both the character of the container and the information printed on it are often the factors that cause the consumer to choose the product or to select one brand instead of another. In self-service outlets, all of the point-of-purchase sales burden rests with the product, its package, printed sales message, and prominence of display. It is important, therefore, to include the significant package differentiating factors in media advertising so that the association between such advertising and the displayed product will be assured.

Quality

Some manufacturers misinterpret consumer attitude toward quality. Few men and no women want clothes that will "wear forever." Producers of clothes must recognize this and try to make garments of a quality which consumers want. An automobile could be made which would be much more economical and durable than those now offered the public; but its manufacture would be justified only if consumers want such a product and were willing to pay the price for it.

The problem of incorporating all desired qualities in a given product is beyond solution in many instances because of contradictory elements. The most economical automobile does not possess the greatest pickup and speed. The following quotation emphasizes this point:

> One of the most important characteristics of merchandise from the point of view of its evaluation arises from the fact that certain product virtues are antagonistic if not directly contradictory; if a product is "best" in one respect, it commonly follows that the product cannot be best in some other respects. The breaking strengths of textiles increase up to a point as the number of threads per inch is increased, but air permeability, on the other hand, is lowered. Those soaps and cleaners that loosen dirt most quickly and easily cannot be the gentlest in their action. The most effective insect poison may not be the safest to use under conditions in which children and pets must be considered. No one blanket can combine the virtues of maximum warmth, maximum strength, and minimum weight. Those bath towels which absorb water most rapidly are not the ones which can absorb the greatest quantity of water, nor are they the strongest. No one paint can possess the special virtues of a flat finish and an enamel finish. The sheerest stockings cannot give the longest wear. Doors that open to the right cannot open to the left.[6]

While these antagonistic elements are present in many instances, the manufacturer can attempt to determine the qualities most definitely desired and concentrate emphasis on those factors. This is illustrated by the practice of the American Writing Paper Company. In making each type of paper, this manufacturer analyzes the requirements of the paper user. The following questions are asked and answered in connection with each type of paper:

1. Must the paper be nonstretchable?
2. Is it to be water-resistant?
3. Is it to be oil-resistant?
4. Is it to be chemical-resistant?
5. Is the color to be permanent or fugitive?
6. Is it to be absorbent or nonabsorbent?
7. Is it to be dense or porous?
8. Will it have considerable handling?
9. Will it have a long life or is it only made for temporary service?

---

[6] Mabel T. Gragg and Neil H. Borden, *Merchandise Testing as a Guide to Consumer Buying* (Cambridge, Mass.: Harvard University Press, 1939), p. 6.

By asking and answering questions of this sort before making a product, a quality in harmony with primary consumer needs can be produced. Costs are often reduced by following this procedure. Why add the cost of making a paper water-resistant when such a quality is not needed or desired?

Price

The price of a product will be closely related to the size of package and the quality. Under some circumstances, price will be less significant than quality or size. In other instances prices will be the dominant factor and quality and/or size should be altered to fit the price. The latter is well illustrated by items sold in variety stores. Products so sold must be built to a particular price.

In the case of the Simmons innerspring mattress, quality is more vital than price. This mattress is the leader in its field even though its price is above that of many competing products. Too often manufacturers feel that price is the dominant factor in directing consumer choice. Such is not the case in many instances. No generalizations can be made, because consumer reactions will be different for individual products. The only safe procedure is to test consumer reaction to each product before a definite decision is made.

For some products price itself is treated as the most significant indicator of quality. One manufacturer of baby powder first put his product on the market at a price somewhat lower than the leading competitive brand. Sales lagged. Without changing the quality of his product he raised the price. Sales increased sharply. One brand of aspirin has consistently led the field at a price averaging 60 percent higher than competing brands, even though all aspirin are required by law to meet U.S. Pharmacopoeia standards of quality. Apparently many people do not want to take the chance of using an inferior product when caring for the baby or their own health. They find assurance in their belief that higher price means higher quality.

Unit of sale

The unit of sale involves both the size of the packaging unit and the number of units per package. For many years Coca-Cola found the carton of six 6-ounce bottles the ideal unit of sale. Then they diversified their line to include various combinations of 6-ounce, 12-ounce, and 16-ounce bottles of 6-, 8-, and 12-unit cartons to meet the desires for different quantities of Coke per purchase. With the advent of the light-weight, aluminum, snap-top can, 6-paks of 12-ounce cans have become the most popular packaging of beer and carbonated beverages. The resealable, twist-off cap has increased the desirability of quart-size bottles.

A family of products may also be advantageously offered to fit consumer preferences. Shaving cream, powder, and lotion may be grouped to sell as a unit. Many shavers use all three and may desire to purchase them together.

The success of various products from the Kitchens of Sara Lee was partly due to the aluminum foil pan in which the item was baked, frozen, shipped, displayed, and eventually reheated in the consumer's oven. Recently the trend has been toward frozen food containers in individual serving sizes.

Brand image

What's in a name? Campbell's Soup, Ivory Soap, Kellogg, Listerine, Marlboro, Ford, Cadillac. These names are well known in American life, but to millions of consumers they mean much more than the mere identification of products. Each name signifies a unique set of properties which, having been planted firmly in peoples' thoughts and feelings, combine to form a picture of the product before the "inner eye." This mental picture is referred to as the brand image. Thus, a product may be viewed as modern or old fashioned, youthful or aged, upper crust or plebeian, feminine or masculine, distinctive or commonplace, trustworthy or questionable, etc. The image that a brand has acquired in the public mind is as important as, if not more important than any tangible attributes of the product in spelling the difference between consumer acceptance and rejection.

How is the brand image created? Through the product's design, its package, its brand name, its color, the media in which it is advertised, the television or radio shows with which it is identified, the content and style of its advertisements including pictures, layout, type faces, and art forms. These are the elements that have to be changed if the brand image has serious flaws that have been hurting sales. For example, after the makers of Marlboro cigarettes decided that the image of their product was too weak and feminine, they changed the design of their package from a nondescript white tone to a bold red-and-white flip-top box and embarked on a campaign featuring close-up photographs of virile he-men with tattoos on their hands. The strength of the new image was reflected in booming sales.

The ideal brand image is distinctive, one that gives a product stature in competition, one that is appropriate for the product and its market, and one that can be sustained over a period of years. A function of product analysis is to tell the advertiser how well the image of his brand meets these standards.

QUESTIONS AND PROBLEMS

1   If a product is what consumers perceive it to be, what is advertising's contribution to producing the product?

2   One way to present the concept of a product before it exists is to present it in the form of an advertisement. Propose a new product and prepare an advertisement that could be used to present the concept to consumers.

3   Distinguish between positioning as something the manufacturer does and positioning as something the consumer does.

4   What moves can the manufacturer take to influence the consumers' positioning of his product?

5   It might be said that there is no such thing as an entirely new product. Why?

6   From your own knowledge of competing brands in a particular product category, develop a perceptual map such as the one for beer in Figure 10–1.

7   What products can you think of that are in the growth stage of the product life cycle? In the mature stage? In decline?

8   Can you think of any products that are being used by a group of consumers for whom the product was not originally intended?

9   Why should dealer tests be an essential part of a new package development?

10   Do you believe that any change in men's hats would increase their use by college students? Why?

11   How might the construction of umbrellas be changed to make them more acceptable to college students?

12   Do you believe that consumers would readily accept an automobile that would last twice as long as those now on the market, assuming the cost to be 30 percent higher? Why?

13   Cite three cases other than those cited in this chapter where a change in package has increased consumer acceptance of the product.

14   How might the increasing popularity of frozen foods influence the advertising of canned foods?

15   It is reported that Gerber's Baby Foods were developed as a result of Mr. Gerber's having to prepare supper for the Gerber's baby daughter. The task of crushing freshly cooked peas through a strainer was not a pleasant one. As a result of this experience and subsequent observation of kitchen preparation of food for the baby, Gerber modified his puréeing machines at his cannery to strain vegetables for babies. He then introduced the famous Gerber's Baby Foods for the satisfaction of your mother and other mothers throughout the land.

   Not all product developments follow this pattern, but this example does illustrate how new products can be developed, or old ones modified, to increase human satisfactions.

   From your own experiences, or from current observations, suggest changes that might be made in at least two products of your own choice that would increase their want-satisfying ability.

Market analysis

The American market is the sum total of the needs and desires of 215 million people dispersed with varying degrees of density over a mainland area measuring 1,600 miles by 2,700 miles, plus Alaska and Hawaii. It is made up of families living in a wide variety of climates, in cities, towns, and rural areas, with differing environments, tastes, and customs. It is ever growing and ever changing.

Within this vast, diverse, and changing market no product is consumed at the same rate everywhere. Therefore, every national advertiser—the one whose product is distributed throughout the country as well as the one whose product is confined to particular regions—must view his market as an aggregate of many individual market areas each of which is different from the next. Some markets are fertile and can be cultivated profitably. Others are barren and should not be cultivated at all.

The purpose of market analysis is to locate the fertile markets and estimate their sales potential. With this information the advertiser can then distribute his effort among various market areas in proportion to their relative sales potentiality and thereby maximize the return on his advertising investment.

Distribution of population and retail sales

There are some 18,600 incorporated cities and towns, and about three million farms in the United States. However, population and retail sales are highly concentrated. As shown in Table 11–1, about 41 percent of the nation's population lives in 35 metropolitan areas. More than half of the population lives in the 74 "A," "B," and "C" markets where 56.6 percent of all retail sales are made.

The greatest population growth in recent years has been taking place in the suburbs, the areas immediately surrounding the larger cities. About 37 percent of all Americans now live in the suburbs. Accompanying the rush to the suburbs are new shopping centers, changing leisure-time activities, and expanding markets for items such as power lawn mowers and patio furniture.

For identification purposes markets are referred to by the name of the central city: the Chicago market, the Los Angeles market, the Detroit

TABLE 11–1
Distribution of population and retail sales by market size groups

		Percent of U.S. total	
Market size groups		Population	Retail sales
17	"A" Markets (populations of over 2 million) 30.3		31.5
18	"B" Markets (populations of 1 to 2 million) 11.1		11.8
39	"C" Markets (populations of 500,000–1 million) 13.1		13.3
181	"D" Markets (populations of 100,000–500,000) 19.1		19.1
Total:			
255	"A," "B," "C," and "D" markets 73/6		75.7

Source: *Sales Management, Survey of Buying Power,* July 1973.

market, etc. However, for market analysis purposes the county in which the central city is located or several contiguous counties are treated as an integral metropolitan area. To standardize the boundaries, *Standard Metropolitan Statistical Areas* are defined by the U.S. Census. The Standard Metropolitan Statistical Area (SMSA) is an integrated economic and social unit having one or more cities of 50,000 or more population, or "twin cities" having a combined population of at least 50,000. For example, the Chicago SMSA is composed of eight counties—Cook, Du Page, Kane, Lake, McHenry, and Will counties in Illinois; Lake and Porter counties in Indiana. There now are 295 such SMSAs.

Geographically, our population is concentrated in the states along our sea coasts and around the Great Lakes. The northeast section extending from the Mississippi River to the Atlantic coast includes 46 percent of total U.S. population and accounts for 44 percent of total retail sales. In fact, 41 percent of all retail sales are made in just six states: New York, California, Illinois, Pennsylvania, Ohio, and Texas.

The concentration of people and trade in relatively few areas is a boon to many national advertisers, especially those whose budgets are too small to permit blanket coverage of all areas in the nation. By concentrating their effort in the top 74 markets, they can register a telling impact where 57 percent of all retail sales are made. Of course, the same strategy would not be appropriate for advertisers of products that appeal primarily to people living in smaller towns and on farms, in which cases it may be advisable for the advertiser to avoid the big cities.

Regional differences

Climate is a basic reason for differences in regional buying preferences. Long wool underwear has a ready market along the Canadian border.

TABLE 11–2
Regional differences in the consumption of selected foods

Food group	Per person per week			
	Northeast	North Central	South	West
Fats, oils	.75 lb.	.78 lb.	.94 lb.	.77 lb.
Flour, cereal	1.08	1.20	1.95	1.31
Bakery products	2.58	2.38	2.13	2.20
Meat, poultry, fish	4.62	4.68	4.48	4.58
Sugar, sweets	.97	1.08	1.33	1.01
Potatoes, sweet potatoes	1.68	1.88	1.48	1.39
Other vegetables	3.50	3.33	3.81	3.73
Fruit.	4.18	3.76	3.20	4.01
Soup, other mixtures	.68 lb.	.63 lb.	.46 lb.	.68 lb.
Milk, cream, cheese (calcium equivalent)	4.26 qt.	4.20 qt.	3.74 qt.	4.23 qt.
Eggs.	.49 doz.	.55 doz.	.61 doz.	.58 doz.

Source: U.S. Department of Agriculture, *Food Consumption of Households in the U.S.,* July 1968.

Bathing suits are a year-round best seller in Florida. Antifreeze, a "must" in Wisconsin, is of little importance in California. Air conditioners are more readily accepted where there are sustained periods of hot, humid weather. Bright colors are more generally preferred in the sunshine areas of Florida, New Mexico, Arizona, and Southern California. Grays, browns, and navy blue are more popular up north where there are fewer warm, sunny days.

Spring moves north each year and winter moves south, gradually stimu-lating purchase of seasonal items in first one and then another climate belt. Manufacturers of outdoor sports equipment have developed seasonal maps to guide their channeling of advertising effort into different regions at the most opportune time of year.

Regional likes and dislikes also stem from habit, custom, and the tend-ency of foreign-born groups to settle in certain areas. In New Orleans the preference for coffee with a lot of chicory in it is so strong that present-day coffee manufacturers have to prepare a special blend for that one area. Ladies in New York City use almost 30 times as much makeup as those living in Vermont. The Texan's wide-brim hat contrasts sharply with the New Englander's narrow brim. Dry sausage sells best in the coastal and Great Lakes cities where immigrants from southern European countries tended to settle.

Regional differences in the consumption rates of several foods and beverages are highlighted in Table 11–2. Note how the ranking of regions differs for each product. The Northeast ranks first for bakery products but last for eggs. The South ranks first for flour, cereal, fats, and oils but last for bakery products. Some foods used in markedly larger quantities in certain regions than in others are:

Northeast . . . . Fresh whole milk, butter, lamb, veal, shellfish, fresh fruit, fruit juice.

North Central . . . . . . Fresh whole milk, cheese, butter, beef, pork, lunch meat, fresh white potatoes, commercially canned fruit, commercially frozen fruit.

South . . . . Evaporated milk, lard, vegetable shortening, pork, chicken, fish, sweet potatoes, rice, cornmeal, hominy grits, self-rising flour, syrup and molasses.

West. . . . . Skim milk, cheese, beef, fresh fruit, commercially canned fruit, dried fruit.

It is not enough for a national advertiser to note that his sales are higher or lower in some regions than in others. He should seek to learn the underlying causes. If he finds that climate or other persistent environmental factors beyond his control account for these differences, he is in a better position to segregate barren from fruitful markets and to direct his advertising effort accordingly.

The farm market

The concentration of consumers in urban areas might lead one to underestimate the importance of the farm market. Even though they are widely scattered geographically, there are approximately 2,109,000 farm families in the United States. They have an average net income of $7,192 with which they are buying products much the same as those their city cousins buy.[1] In addition, farmers are a primary market for many production items such as feeds, seeds, fertilizers, tractors, combines, corn pickers, and milking machines.

[1] *Statistical Abstract of the United States,* 1969.

The proportion of our population living on farms continues to decline. Twenty years ago one out of four persons lived on a farm. Today it is only 1 out of 18. However, this decline in numbers is more than offset by growing productivity and income. Marginal or inefficient farmers are being attracted into other industries. Their acreage is being absorbed by bigger farmers who, with greater mechanization and better farming methods, are able to produce more than enough food and raw materials for industry. As a result, today's fewer farm families represent a greater market potential for advertised products than did their more numerous predecessors.

Although they produce a substantial portion of their own food supply, farm families are good prospects for most branded food items. One study of food-purchasing habits of city and farm families indicated that the average farm family spends more money on processed foods such as flour, sugar, cereals, butter, and cheese than does the average city family. More meals served at home to bigger families with bigger appetites are factors that explain the greater food consumption per farm family. The only items for which city family purchases were reported to be materially greater were meat, poultry, milk, eggs, and fresh vegetables.

The farm market, like any other, varies in purchasing power and sales potential. For example, eight midwest states (Indiana, Illinois, Wisconsin, Iowa, Minnesota, Nebraska, South Dakota, and North Dakota) include one fifth of the U.S. farms and produce one third of the nation's agricultural income. The ranking and characteristics of other farm regions can be ascertained from the Census of Agriculture which includes data on practically all significant dimensions of farming. With this information the advertiser can single out the key farm market areas where he will be able to reap profitable sales.

Shifts in area potential

Markets are dynamic and ever changing. The Middle Atlantic and Great Lakes states for decades represented the most fertile markets; but the last several years have seen a marked increase in the relative fertility of the Mountain and South Atlantic regions. The Mountain region led the nation in the rate of population growth with an increase of 10.8 percent between 1969 and 1973. Reflecting a rapid rate of industrial growth and retirement living, effective buying income in the Mountain and South Atlantic regions increased 52.8 and 45.5 percent respectively, compared with an increase of 35.2 percent for the nation as a whole. The advertiser who notes such shifts in market potential will generally have a distinct advantage over his less observant competitor. Regional gains in population and effective buying income are shown in Figure 11–1.

FIGURE 11–1
Regional variations in market growth

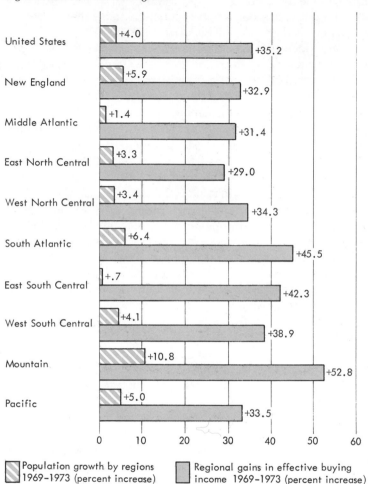

Population growth by regions
1969–1973 (percent increase)

Regional gains in effective buying
income 1969–1973 (percent increase)

Source: *Sales Management, Survey of Buying Power,* June 1970 and July 1974.

Sales potentials

Sales potential is an estimate of a market's capacity to buy a given commodity. The estimate reflects economic resources of an area and indicates the scope of sales opportunity, not the actual volume of sales that will be achieved. Stated in physical units or dollar volume or percentages, sales potentials provide a quantitative basis for adapting advertising strategy to the different sales opportunities presented by various market areas.

Sales potentials are especially useful for allocating advertising effort and selecting media.

Allocation of advertising effort   Two fundamental questions that the planner of national advertising strategy must decide upon are: To which markets should advertising be directed? How much should be spent in each market? Decisions on both of these questions should be based on sales potentials.

By ranking markets according to their respective sales potentials and selecting in rank order the number of markets to be cultivated, the advertiser will be more certain of concentrating his effort in the most promising areas. By aligning his expenditures with sales potentials he will improve his chances of realizing a maximum sales yield on his advertising investment. To illustrate, let's assume sales potentials of $100,000 in market A and $50,000 in market B. These figures do not tell the advertiser how much to spend in each market, but they do indicate that he should spend roughly twice as much in A as in B. The practice of concentrating effort in the more productive markets and balancing expenditures against potential is now generally accepted advertising strategy.

However, sales potentials should *not* be used as the only basis for allocating advertising effort.[2] They do not allow for differences among markets with respect to competition, product distribution, and merchandising support, all of which have an appreciable influence on the sales that any one advertiser can achieve. It may be advisable to spend less than the potential would warrant in a market where a competitor is solidly entrenched, or where the product is not available in enough retail stores, or where there is a lack of aggressive merchandising by dealers and distributors. Judgment still must play an important part when deciding where to advertise and how much to spend in each place.

Media selection   To deliver the required amount of impact in target areas the advertiser selects media that circulate in line with sales potentials. If he plans to use locally distributed media such as newspapers, his decision to advertise in a given market is tantamount to selecting one or more of the mediums located there. If he plans to use nationally distributed media such as magazines, he examines the coverage each medium has in various markets and selects those mediums that cover his target areas most effectively. For example, an advertiser of baking powder, sales of which are concentrated south of the Mason-Dixon Line, would select magazines that circulate mostly in the South.

[2] Sales potentials can be estimated for a variety of product groupings—total retail sales of all products, or industry sales (*coffee*), or product type sales (*instant coffee*). The last mentioned is the most common potential used—a product type narrowed down to where the next finer classification would be a *brand*. An estimate of prospective sales for a brand is generally referred to as a brand sales forecast.

DETERMINING SALES POTENTIALS

Firm's sales records

It would appear that a firm's sales, broken down by market areas, would indicate the relative sales potential of each area. If year after year a firm's sales in market X have been about 20 percent higher than in market Y, it would seem that market X has a potential about 20 percent greater than Y's. This may be so, but it would be coincidental. A firm's sales reflect the influence of many factors other than a market's capacity to consume. Competition, distribution, dealer support, personal selling, advertising, brand acceptance, and responsiveness to promotional effort—all of these factors affect sales, and they differ from market to market. Their influence may be great enough to offset a difference in potentials, with the result that lower sales may be registered in a market having a higher potential.

Then, too, a firm's sales represent past performance. They do not show what might be accomplished in the future with a new marketing mix. Therefore, a firm's sales are inadequate for estimating the relative potentials of various markets.

Industry sales data

In some industries the trade association compiles total industry sales data from reports submitted by its members. These data, broken down by market areas, give the composite experience of competitors and therefore are better suited for estimating potentials than are the sales of any one firm. Examples are the data reported by the Radio and Television Manufacturer's Association and the National Electrical Manufacturer's Association.

Industry data are subject to several limitations. Different firms are apt to report sales for territories of different sizes which would either produce inaccuracies in the compilation or result in a breakdown by only states and regions. Also, the data are restricted to past performance. Perhaps a total industry's performance measured up to potential better in some places than in others.

Census of retail trade

The most authoritative and extensive inventory of consumer purchases is that made by the United States Bureau of the Census.

Census retail figures show total sales made by each of 11 major kinds of retail business. These 11 business groups are further broken down into 66 business classifications in terms of the kind of merchandise sold. Thus, data are presented for nine different kinds of business in the apparel group: namely, men's furnishings stores, men's clothing-furnishings stores, family clothing stores, women's ready-to-wear stores, furriers and fur shops, millinery stores, custom tailors, accessories, other apparel stores, and shoe stores. The other ten major groups are similarly broken down.

Census figures, therefore, present a rather detailed inventory of consumer purchases in broad classifications. It would, of course, be more valuable if figures were available showing not only total sales of shoe stores, but also sales of each type of shoes—size, price, men's or women's, boys' or girls', sport or dress, etc. On the other hand, total sales by shoe stores provide the manufacturer with some measure of the total market for shoes and afford a base from which more detailed studies might be made through private initiative.

One of the outstanding values of the census material is to be found in its detailed territorial breakdown. Data for each of the 66 kinds of retail business are presented for each of the 50 states, the District of Columbia, and standard metropolitan areas. Data for the 11 major kinds of business

FIGURE 11–2
Market data available in *Sales Management's Survey of Buying Power*

ARIZONA

Arizona — POPULATION— 12/31/73

METRO AREA	County	Total (thousands)	% of U.S.	% White	Median Age of Pop	0-5 Yrs	6-11 Yrs	12-17 Yrs	18-24 Yrs	25-34 Yrs	35-49 Yrs	50-64 Yrs	65 & Over	Households (thou sands)	Under 25 Yrs	25-34 Yrs	35-44 Yrs	45-54 Yrs	55-64 Yrs	65 & Over
PHOENIX	Maricopa	1,147.6	.5441	94.0	27.7	10.5	11.0	12.4	12.4	14.0	16.3	13.8	9.6	380.0	9.2	22.0	17.5	17.8	14.9	18.6
TUCSON	Pima	424.5	.2013	93.1	28.0	10.3	10.3	12.0	13.1	14.2	15.6	14.1	10.4	141.0	9.9	20.0	16.5	17.5	15.8	20.3
TOTAL ABOVE AREAS		1,572.1	.7454	93.8	27.8	10.5	10.8	12.3	12.6	14.1	16.0	13.9	9.8	521.0	9.4	21.3	17.2	17.8	15.2	19.1
STATE TOTALS		2,105.2	.9981	90.2	26.9	11.0	11.1	12.5	12.8	13.7	15.8	13.7	9.4	677.9	9.2	21.1	17.3	17.8	15.6	19.0

Arizona — EFFECTIVE BUYING INCOME— 1973

METRO AREA	County	EBI ($000)	% of U.S.	Per Capita EBI	Median Hsld. EBI	Avg Hsld. EBI	$0-$2,999 Hslds	$3,000-$4,999 Hslds	$5,000-$7,999 Hslds	$8,000-$9,999 Hslds	$10,000-$14,999 Hslds	$15,000-$24,999 Hslds	$25,000 & Over Hslds	Buying Power Index	EPP (Economy Priced Products)	MPP (Moderate Priced Products)	PPP (Premium Priced Products)
PHOENIX	Maricopa	4,859,112	.5517	4,234	9,621	12,787	12.3	9.2	17.5	13.7	24.0	15.3	8.0	.5695	.5592	.5770	.5370
TUCSON	Pima	1,665,700	.1891	3,924	8,785	11,813	12.7	10.7	21.0	14.6	20.6	13.7	6.7	.1968	.2179	.1963	.1837
TOTAL ABOVE AREAS		6,524,812	.7408	4,150	9,384	12,524	12.4	9.5	18.4	13.9	23.4	14.8	7.6	.7663	.8482	.8518	.8107
STATE TOTALS		8,141,824	.9244	3,867	9,009	12,010	13.8	10.0	19.2	13.7	22.1	14.2	7.0	.9720	1.0269	.9687	.8822

Arizona — RETAIL SALES BY STORE GROUP— 1973

METRO AREA	County	Total Retail Sales ($000)	% of U.S.	Food Total ($000)	Food Super markets ($000)	Eating & Drinking Places Total ($000)	General Merchandise Total ($000)	General Merchandise Dept Stores ($000)	Apparel Total ($000)	Furn House Appl Total ($000)	Furn Home Furnishings ($000)	Automotive Total ($000)	Gas Station Total ($000)	Lumber Bldg Hdwre Total ($000)	Drug Total ($000)
PHOENIX	Maricopa	3,167,595	.6162	695,601	646,744	278,347	519,390	414,930	110,403	160,659	109,875	644,895	221,591	169,058	117,138
TUCSON	Pima	1,062,227	.2066	216,120	195,637	89,191	191,099	143,285	44,486	55,835	35,415	206,552	63,342	87,916	32,333
TOTAL ABOVE AREAS		4,229,822	.8228	911,721	842,381	367,538	710,489	558,215	154,889	216,494	145,290	851,447	284,933	256,974	149,471
STATE TOTALS		5,311,602	1.0334	1,130,553	1,007,528	488,657	851,453	584,959	195,562	250,538	163,848	1,017,168	422,444	348,620	175,765

Arizona — RETAIL SALES BY MERCHANDISE LINE—1973

METRO AREA	Groceries Other Foods Mdse Lines	Groceries Other Foods Food Stores	Cosmetics Etc Mdse Lines	Cosmetics Etc Drug stores	Women's Girls Clothing Mdse Lines	Women's Girls Clothing Dept Stores	Men's Boys Clothing Mdse Lines	Men's Boys Clothing Apparel Stores	All Footwear Mdse Lines	All Footwear Apparel Stores	Major Appliances Mdse Lines	Major Appliances Appliance Stores	Furn Sleep Etc Mdse Lines	Furn Sleep Etc FHF Stores
PHOENIX	635,195	568,306	145,709	68,174	174,218	107,467	85,525	23,185	57,017	29,478	98,195	39,358	91,860	54,168
TUCSON	202,005	179,163	43,551	19,723	63,734	32,177	32,929	10,543	19,120	9,476	37,178	15,826	36,116	16,645
TOTAL ABOVE AREAS	837,200	747,469	189,260	87,897	237,952	139,644	118,454	33,728	76,137	38,954	135,373	55,184	127,976	70,813

are given by counties and towns of 2,500 population or over. Thus, the businessman can acquaint himself with the character of consumer purchases in Ohio as compared with California or the entire nation. Or he may make similar comparisons between Cleveland and Pittsburgh, Chicago and Los Angeles, Marion County and Brown County, Podunk and Riverside.

Sales Management's Survey of Buying Power

To provide up-to-date market data during the interval between censuses, *Sales Management* magazine projects census bench mark figures and publishes current estimates in their annual *Survey of Buying Power.* For every city with retail sales of $15 million or more, every county, and every metropolitan area, the *Survey of Buying Power* presents current estimates of population, effective buying income (personal income after taxes), total retail sales, and retail sales by nine store groups. Figure 11–2 shows how these estimates are published for convenient reference.

To check the accuracy of their retail sales estimates *Sales Management* compared their estimates with the 1963 Census of Retail Trade and found their average error to be 2 percent for regions, 2.7 percent for states, and 4 percent for metropolitan areas. These margins of error are sufficiently small to indicate that the magazine's estimates are adequate for most practical purposes. As a result, the *Survey of Buying Power* is the most widely used single source of current data for keeping abreast of rapidly changing American markets.

Sample audit of retail sales

A number of private firms operate to provide continuing information of sales of specific commodities by certain types of retail outlets. The most extensive operation in this field is that of the A. C. Nielsen Company. This organization selects a sample of food and drugstores in the United States that are reasonably representative of the total. Through field representatives, bimonthly audits of food and drug items by brand and package size are made to determine the number of packages of each item that moved out of these stores to consumers.

From such data it is easy to secure a fairly accurate picture of the total amount of coffee, ready-to-eat cereal, flour, toothpaste, and similar commodities sold during a given period. In addition, sales are classified by individual brands, which thus enables individual advertisers to determine their own as well as their competitors' position in the market. This type of analysis is illustrated in Figure 11–3.

Regular bimonthly reports of the Nielsen Retail Index are available for each of nine districts: New England, Metropolitan New York, Middle

FIGURE 11–3
Market outlines of three competitive brands

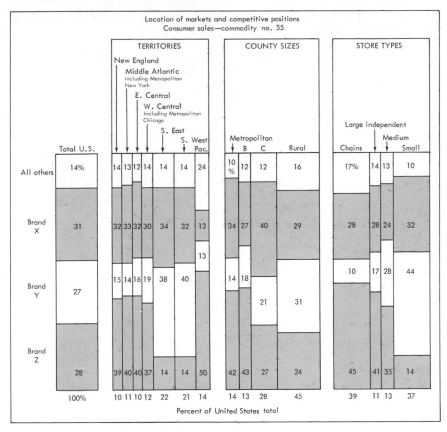

Atlantic, East Central, Metropolitan Chicago, West Central, Southeast, Southwest, and Pacific. In addition, a client may order special area breakdowns to parallel his own sales districts. Nielsen data yield ten types of information:

1. Sales to consumers.
2. Purchases by retailers.
3. Retail inventories.
4. Days' supply.
5. Distribution—number of stores carrying the brand weighted for store importance.
6. Out-of-stock—percentage of stores regularly carrying brand who do not have it in stock at time of audit.
7. Prices—wholesale and retail.

8. Special factory packs.
9. Dealer support—displays, local advertising, coupon redemptions.
10. Special observations—order size, reorders, and direct versus wholesale purchases.

With such information a manufacturer can effectively plan, control, and evaluate his marketing and advertising effort, and at the same time keep a watchful eye on his competitors' activities.

Consumer panel reports

Another approach to a measure of consumer purchases is to ask consumers to report actual purchases of specified items. The more common procedure is to select a sample of families that is reasonably representative of the market or markets to be studied. These families are asked to serve on a continuing basis and to supply detailed information about their purchases of various commodities. Such families are usually compensated in some manner for serving on the panel of "reporters."

Panel members are ordinarily supplied with forms or "diaries" on which

FIGURE 11–4
Sample diary form used by consumer panel members for reporting purchases

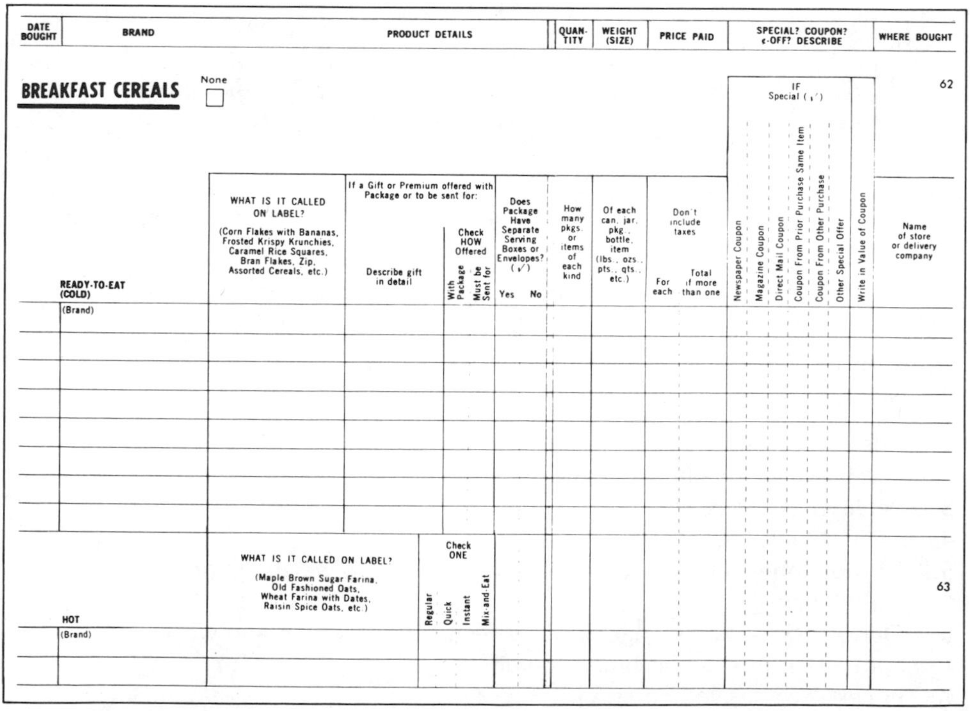
DATE BOUGHT | BRAND | PRODUCT DETAILS | QUANTITY | WEIGHT (SIZE) | PRICE PAID | SPECIAL? COUPON? ¢-OFF? DESCRIBE | WHERE BOUGHT

BREAKFAST CEREALS
None
62
READY-TO-EAT (COLD)
(Brand)
WHAT IS IT CALLED ON LABEL? (Corn Flakes with Bananas, Frosted Krispy Krunchies, Caramel Rice Squares, Bran Flakes, Zip, Assorted Cereals, etc.)
If a Gift or Premium offered with Package or to be sent for:
Describe gift in detail
Check HOW Offered: With Package / Must be Sent for
Does Package Have Separate Serving Boxes or Envelopes? (✓) Yes No
How many pkgs. or items of each kind
Of each can, jar, pkg., bottle, item (lbs., ozs., pts., qts., etc.)
Don't include taxes: For each / Total if more than one
IF Special (✓): Newspaper Coupon / Magazine Coupon / Direct Mail Coupon / Coupon From Prior Purchase Same Item / Coupon From Other Purchase / Other Special Offer
Write in Value of Coupon
Name of store or delivery company

HOT
(Brand)
WHAT IS IT CALLED ON LABEL? (Maple Brown Sugar Farina, Old Fashioned Oats, Wheat Farina with Dates, Raisin Spice Oats, etc.)
Check ONE: Regular / Quick / Instant / Mix-and-Eat
63

all purchases are to be recorded as they are made. A copy of such a form used by one research firm is reproduced in Figure 11–4. This particular diary called for a record of purchases of only ten commodity groups. The same type of diary could be used for any number of items. Some panels provide purchase data for all groceries, household supplies, and drugs.

The organization that has perhaps done the most work with consumer panels is the Market Research Corporation of America. This company operates primarily on a national and broad regional basis and provides about the same kind of geographical breakdown of data as that provided by the A. C. Nielsen Company.

The consumer panel approach, however, will give a more detailed classification of the kinds of people who buy specific types of goods and the amounts purchased by each consumer group. This is made possible from detailed personal data obtained from each panel member. Personal data can include such factors as age, size of family, education, income, religion, nationality, and occupation. Markets can thus be evaluated in terms of both geography and consumer groups. In addition, the relative number of persons in any group that uses the commodity can be determined.

When members of a consumer panel are representative of the market to be studied, commodity purchase data can be projected for the entire market. This provides a means of establishing an overall potential for each area for which separate information is available, as well as a potential for individual brands. Consumer panel data can be used to modify census figures in the same manner that data from a sample audit of retail stores can be so applied.

This method is also applicable to local markets. Because of cost, there has not been wide application on a local basis. Various agencies have experimented with local consumer panels. Included in this group are the *Chicago Tribune* and the *Cleveland Press.* Perhaps the future will see much greater use of this method at the local level. Additional reference will be made to the use of local panels in connection with testing the sales effectiveness of advertising (Chapter 27).

Home inventories

Another method of gathering information about consumer purchases is the home inventory. Newspapers have been most active in utilizing this type of study. One of the early pioneers in this has been the *Milwaukee Journal.* The *Journal* method consists of mailing a confidential questionnaire to a large number of housewives whose names have been selected at random from city and suburban directories.

The questionnaire used is not a diary, but rather a form which asks such questions as: "Do you buy muffin mix? _____"; "What brand?

FIGURE 11–5
Example of covering instructions (first page) of home inventory questionnaire

CONFIDENTIAL QUESTIONNAIRE

For a survey relating to the needs and purchases
of Greater Milwaukee families to be compiled by

THE MILWAUKEE JOURNAL
FIRST BY MERIT

Dear Madam:
A VERY LARGE SHOPPING BAG FILLED WITH PACKAGES OF WELL KNOWN
GROCERY ITEMS IS YOURS FREE *for filling in this questionnaire.*

*In order to secure this bag of grocery products you must answer the questions herein and
have your husband or the man of the house answer those questions regarding his purchases. All replies are confidential and names are not released for any purpose.*

*You must be honest in your answers and personally bring the questionnaire to the Sur-
vey Department of The Milwaukee Journal, located on the first floor of THE JOURNAL
BUILDING, AT NORTH FOURTH AND WEST STATE STREETS, on or before the
day and date printed below.*

*This bag will be filled to overcapacity. So if you have an additional sturdy bag used for
your regular shopping, be sure to bring it along.*

*The questionnaire applies only to family groups maintaining a household, and will not
be accepted from an individual living in a boarding or rooming house who does not
maintain such separate household. Your co-operation will be appreciated.*

THE MILWAUKEE JOURNAL
SURVEY DEPARTMENT

PLEASE READ THESE

INSTRUCTIONS

1. Each major question should be answered YES or NO with an "X" or other checkmark. If
   your answer to the main question is NO, do not answer any of the subquestions which follow
   and which apply to main questions.
2. PLEASE do not guess in answering this questionnaire. LOOK UP THE BRAND NAME
   if you don't remember it. List only brands you actually use.
3. Return your questionnaire early and get it checked quickly.
4. Do not return this questionnaire by mail.
5. Do not send children with this questionnaire.
6. *Please write plainly. Use ink or typewriter if possible.*
7. *If you use more than one brand of any product, list the brand you use most frequently unless
   otherwise instructed.*

You will receive a large shopping bag of grocery products if you fill in
this questionnaire and bring it to The Journal building no later than

Name_____
(You need not sign your name, but your address is essential)

Street Address_____

City, Town or Village_____

Telephone No._____

The Survey Office Hours are 9:00 a.m. to 8:00 p.m.

FIGURE 11–6
Sample page of questionnaire used in home inventory method of gathering information about consumer purchases

Do you buy rye bread? ☐ YES ☐ NO .... BRAND

Do you buy regular white bread? ☐ YES ☐ NO .... BRAND

Do you buy liver sausage? ☐ YES ☐ NO

Do you ask for any certain manufacturer's brand? ☐ YES ☐ NO .... BRAND

Do you buy pork sausages? ☐ YES ☐ NO

Do you ask for any certain manufacturer's brand? ☐ YES ☐ NO .... BRAND

Do you buy wieners or frankfurters? ☐ YES ☐ NO
(Do not include canned wieners or Vienna sausage.)

Do you ask for a certain manufacturer's brand? ☐ YES ☐ NO .... BRAND

Do you buy canned luncheon meats made of spiced ham or pork? ☐ YES ☐ NO .... BRAND
(Include only 12-oz. cans.)

Do you buy canned Chinese foods? ☐ YES ☐ NO .... BRAND

Do you buy fruit cocktail? ☐ YES ☐ NO .... BRAND

Do you buy macaroni products? ☐ YES ☐ NO .... BRAND

Do you own a dog? ☐ YES ☐ NO

Do you buy prepared dog food? ☐ YES ☐ NO
☐ Canned or loaf. Brand........
☐ Dry. Brand........

Do you buy potato chips? ☐ YES ☐ NO .... BRAND

Do you buy packaged cookies? ☐ YES ☐ NO .... BRAND

Do you buy fresh milk at stores? ☐ YES ☐ NO .... BRAND

Is fresh milk delivered to your home? ☐ YES ☐ NO .... BRAND

Do you buy canned corned beef hash? ☐ YES ☐ NO .... BRAND

Do you buy ice cream? ☐ YES ☐ NO .... BRAND

Where do you buy this ice cream? Please check.
☐ Grocery store ☐ Drugstore
☐ Ice cream store ☐ Confectionery store
☐ Other

QUESTIONS ON THIS PAGE TO BE ANSWERED BY THÉ HOUSEWIFE
Each major question must be answered Yes or No with "X" or other checkmark. Then give brand name.

Do you buy canned whole kernel corn? ☐ YES ☐ NO .... BRAND

Do you buy canned cream style corn? ☐ YES ☐ NO .... BRAND

Do you buy canned cranberries of any kind? ☐ YES ☐ NO .... BRAND

Do you buy fresh cranberries? ☐ YES ☐ NO .... BRAND

Were any rooms in your home wallpapered in 1951? ☐ YES ☐ NO

Do you know what brand of wallpaper was used? ☐ YES ☐ NO .... BRAND

Where did you purchase this wallpaper?
☐ Retail store ☐ Paperhanger
☐ Interior decorator ☐ Other

Who applied the wallpaper?
☐ Yourself or member of family ☐ Paperhanger

At what time of the year do you prefer to have wallpapering done?
☐ Spring ☐ Fall ☐ Winter ☐ Summer

Are you interested in stock and bond market quotations? ☐ YES ☐ NO

Do you read business and financial news? ☐ YES ☐ NO

Do you buy salad or cooking oil? ☐ YES ☐ NO .... BRAND

Do you buy square or oblong soda crackers in packages? ☐ YES ☐ NO .... Brand, not KIND

Do you buy paper towels? ☐ YES ☐ NO .... BRAND

Do you buy soft drinks for home use? ☐ YES ☐ NO .... BRAND

Do you buy soft drinks by the case? ☐ YES ☐ NO .... BRAND

Do you buy soft drinks by the bottle? ☐ YES ☐ NO .... BRAND

Do you buy soft drinks in 6-bottle cartons? ☐ YES ☐ NO .... BRAND

In what type of store do you usually buy soft drinks for home use?
Please check ONE:
☐ Grocery Store ☐ Delicatessen ☐ Other
☐ Drugstore ☐ Beer Depot

Do you (the housewife) have a paid job outside the home? ☐ YES ☐ NO

_____''; "Do you smoke cigarettes? _____''; "What brand are you NOW smoking? _____." Sample pages of the questionnaire used by the *Milwaukee Journal* are shown in Figures 11–5 and 11–6. Questionnaires are completed and returned to the newspaper, where tabulations are made and results summarized for the use of advertisers in evaluating the local market. Summary information in general shows the relative number of families using a particular product, total number of brands in use, relative rating of brand preferences, and relative number of users by income groups.

A modification of the mail-questionnaire approach consists in using personal interviewers who call on a representative list of families and actually check, with the aid of the housewife, the pantry shelves to determine what items are stocked. In some instances, attempts are made to determine the length of time items found on the shelves have been there. Such information can be summarized to show the relative number of families that stock a particular type of commodity and the relative position of individual brands carried in the householders' inventory. Since much can be known about the families interviewed, data can be classified by such characteristics as income, occupation, age, and size.

Home inventories are helpful in analyzing the characteristics of individual markets, but they do not have so universal an application as either retail-store audit or consumer-purchase-diary data. It is not possible to use home-inventory data to determine frequency of purchase or the total potential volume for specific commodities. Without a measure of total market potential, it is not possible to determine the dollar or quantity volume secured or expected by individual brands. This materially reduces the possibility of using such data for measuring the success of advertising effort. But even with these limitations, such studies are valuable to advertisers.

Statistical index of sales potentials

The measurement of consumer purchases helps to clarify the market picture for the advertiser. It tells what people have been buying and where. It shows that sales opportunities are greater in some markets than in others. The individual advertiser, however, wants to know not only that one market offers a greater sales opportunity than another, but also *how much greater* the opportunity is. He wants to know whether he can expect 5 percent of his total sales from territory A and 23 percent from territory B. He wants to know whether he has been obtaining from each territory all the sales volume he could logically expect. Only when he has reduced market differences to a quantitative measure can he distribute his advertising appropriation effectively.

Various statistical indexes are used to quantify market potentials. Their use is based on the idea that an unknown variable (sales potential) is so closely related to a known variable (for example, total retail sales) that differences in the size of the unknown variable from market to market can be estimated from differences in the size of the known variable.

The usual procedure is to first establish the relationship between sales of the firm's product and the index series. This can be done subjectively by relying on one's judgment, or objectively by measuring the correlation statistically. Then the index series is reduced to a percentage distribution so that the index for each market is expressed as a percentage share of the series total (100 percent) for all markets. In this way large and cumbersome figures representing a variety of units (for example, dollars, pounds, people, gallons) are reduced to a simple common denominator for easier comparison and projection. These percentages can then be applied to the firm's estimate of total potential sales to arrive at a potential figure for each market.

A firm's sales cannot serve as a basis for an index because it is probable that some territories have been returning more and others less than the potential would warrant. Hence, some other factor or factors must be found that either have a causal relationship to the firm's sales or fluctuate with them. To establish the relationship between an outside factor and a firm's sales it is necessary to compare variations in the two series among many market areas. If variations in the outside factor closely resemble the firm's sales pattern, then that factor could be used as an index of sales potentials. Since the firm's past sales performance is used as a criterion for selecting an index, it would seem that sales potentials for various markets would be established in the same relative amounts as past sales. This is not necessarily so because an index series that resembles the sales pattern in general may still reveal specific areas that do not match.

An index composed of one series of data is referred to as a single-factor index. If several series are used it is referred to as a multiple-factor index. Both types of indexes will be reviewed in the following pages.

Single-factor indexes

Any available series of data that are reliable, that are broken down by specific market areas, and that are related to sales of the product at hand might be used as a single-factor index. Population, income, and retail sales data meet these requirements in many cases, and therefore are widely used for index purposes.

Population   People make markets. Population size is the basic factor accounting for differences in sales potentials. For some products, such as table salt, that are low-priced staples with mass appeal, sales closely follow the distribution of population. If per capita consumption is not affected by economic, social, or climatic differences, population alone would be an adequate index. However, for most products per capita consumption is affected by socioeconomic and regional conditions, and therefore varies considerably among markets. In these latter instances some other factor that incorporates significant attributes of the population should be used.

Income   Total money income (after taxes) accruing to all the people living in an area might be an appropriate indicator of potential. Such an aggregate of disposable income represents a pool of purchasing power that is tapped by all sellers of goods and services. For relatively high-priced "luxury" items it would appear that the greater the income pool, the greater will be an area's potential. However, this fails to take into account differences in how the pool is distributed among the families living there. Two markets may have about the same total income, but in one market a higher proportion of the total may be concentrated in the upper-income families, whereas in the other market it may be more evenly distributed among all families.

If a product appeals primarily to upper-income families, an index based on the number of families in that group should be used. Similarly, it if appeals to middle- or lower-income groups, the number of families in these groups will be most pertinent. In any event, the income distribution will be more indicative of an area's potential than aggregate income.

Retail sales   How much people are spending for goods and services is indicated by total retail sales. Such sales data reflect not only the amount of buying power in an area, but also the people's inclination to convert that power into actual purchases.

Table 11–3 illustrates how a single-factor index based only on total retail sales can be used to estimate sales potentials in seven California metropolitan market areas. Here the index is expressed as a percent of United States total. If a company's sales were confined to a particular region, say the Pacific Coast Region, the index for each market would be expressed as a percent of total retail sales in that region. Then the percentage index for each market would be larger than those appearing in Table 11–3 because

TABLE 11–3
Illustration of use of retail sales index

Market area	Total retail sales dollars (000)	Index (percent of U.S. total retail sales)	Sales potential in dollars*
Fresno	1,036,763	0.2002	50,050
Los Angeles-Long Beach	16,200,055	3.7249	931,225
Sacramento	2,008,188	0.4278	106,950
San Diego	3,131,105	0.7179	179,475
San Francisco-Oakland	7,190,018	1.7730	443,250
San Jose	2,650,707	0.6170	154,250

* Based on firm's anticipated sales in United States totaling $25 million.
Source: *Sales Management, Survey of Buying Power,* July 1973.

a smaller total would be the 100 percent base. However, the relationship among markets would remain the same, with Los Angeles–Long Beach still having a potential about two and one-third times the potential of San Francisco–Oakland. One's own company sales, by market area, could be compared against the potential for purposes of evaluating the kind of job that had been done in individual markets and to guide the allocation of advertising dollars.

Total retail sales data, by market areas, must be considered only as a general sales index which is composed of a heterogeneous assortment of commodities. It would be merely coincidental if a firm's sales opportunities paralleled all retail sales. Some refinement may be achieved if sales by the type of store through which the company's product is distributed were used (for example, food-store sales as an index for cake mixes). But again sales of cake mixes would be such a small fraction of total food-store sales that an index based on these data would still provide only a rough approximation of potentials.

Corollary data   If sales of a company's product for which no detailed market data are available depend on sales of another product for which data are available, the company can construct an index of sales potentials for its product from the data on the other product. For example, sales of automobile tires in a market area depend on the number of automobiles in that area. The number of automobiles can be obtained from state licensing records. Thus, automobile registrations broken down by market areas can provide an index of tire sales potentials. Obviously, the same data would be useful as an index for gasoline, motor oil, batteries, spark plugs, and other replacement parts.

Another example of useful corollary data is the number of new dwelling units for which building permits have been issued in individual localities. These figures, which are compiled and published bimonthly by the Bureau of Labor Statistics, can be used to gauge market potentials for housing materials and equipment.

Multiple-factor indexes

The indexes thus far considered have been developed from a single series of data such as population, income, or total retail sales. However, differences in market potentials are due to many factors, and indexes that combine several factors should improve the quality of estimates. Some multiple-factor indexes are designed for general application, that is, to estimate potentials for consumer goods in general. Others are designed specifically for a given product.

The most widely used general multiple-factor index is the *Sales Management* Buying Power Index. This index is based on the number of people in a market area, their buying habits as revealed in total retail sales, and the amount of money they have to spend. It is a weighted average of three factors: (1) percent of United States Effective Buying Income X 5; percent of United States Retail Sales X 3; and percent of United States Population X 2. These percentages are multiplied by weights as indicated, the products added together, and the total divided by 10 (the sum of the weights). Computed for each city with over $15 million of retail sales and each county in the United States, the resulting index is published annually in *Sales Management, Survey of Buying Power.*

A general-purpose index of this type is convenient to use and may be adequate for those advertisers whose sales seem to follow the pattern of general buying power. It would not be adequate if sales are affected by differences in climate, customs, racial and ethnic groups. Woolen blankets have their heavy sale in the North, as do ice skates, sleds, heavy overcoats, etc. Outboard motors sell best in the Midwest where there are many lakes. Sales of rice are greater in the South. Sales of tomato paste are greater where foreign-born populations are concentrated. In these instances a special or custom-built index is needed.

The individual advertiser constructing his own special-purpose index is confronted with two basic problems: First, he must select those factors which explain a large part of the variation in sales potentials. Second, recognizing that every factor is not of equal importance, he must assign appropriate weights to each factor entering the computation. He should start by identifying all factors that would seem to have some bearing on sales volume. This initial listing of causal factors is mainly a matter of logical reasoning. Next, he must select the factors and weights to be used in the index. Here he can depend entirely on judgment or he can apply statistical methods that measure the correlation between sales of the product and various series of market data.

To illustrate, let's assume a manufacturer of room air-conditioning units wishes to develop a multiple-factor index of sales potentials. His listing of causal factors might include: (1) number of dwelling units; (2) per capita disposable income, (3) average temperature during June, July, and August, (4) average relative humidity during these months, and (5) average number of days per year with temperatures over 85 degrees. Then he might arbitrarily combine some of these factors and assign weights according to his best judgment, or he might measure the correlation between past sales of room air conditioners and various combinations of these factors. The statistical technique referred to as multiple correlation is ideally suited for this type of measurement. Through the use of multiple correlation he can determine what part of the variance in sales among a rather large number of markets is explained by any particular combination of factors. He may find that one combination explains 60 percent, that another combination explains 70 percent, and that still another combination explains 80 percent of the variance in sales. In the same operation he can measure the relative importance or weight of each factor. With such measurements he will be more confident that the resulting index is based on the best set of factors and weights obtainable from the data at hand. Also, he will be apprised of the index's limitations and therefore be less inclined to overrate the accuracy of his estimates.

Problem of the new company

The manufacturer just starting in business or opening up a new territory will find it difficult, if not impossible, to use the correlation method in establishing an index of sales potentials. He has no previous sales with which to correlate particular outside factors. This difficulty could be overcome in part if the total sales of representative manufacturers of the commodity involved could be obtained. This figure could be used in the absence of the new manufacturer's own sales figures. The result would give a picture of the relative fertility of sales territories, but there would be no basis for determining the probable share which the newcomer might obtain. Then, too, it would be extremely difficult, if not impossible, to obtain the sales figures of competitors.

The new company can reduce the error of guesses by considering those factors that are obviously related positively or negatively to the consumption of its product. The sale of raincoats and umbrellas is closely related to frequency and amount of rainfall. The sale of safety razors is related to sex and age groups. General buying-power indexes might be used for many products to measure the ability to buy. Questionnaire studies might be employed to measure the willingness to buy. The latter might also be used to measure willingness at different price levels, although such a method must be employed with extreme care.

No method, whether it be applied to a new or an established industry or company, can measure accurately the actual total sales possibilities of an industry, an individual company, or separate territories. Much less inaccuracy will result, however, if serious and studious attention is given to the problem. One of the foregoing methods or a combination of them can usually be employed to advantage in allocating advertising effort and in checking the returns from such effort.

QUESTIONS AND PROBLEMS

1   Even though there are some 18,600 incorporated cities and towns, the national advertiser tends to concentrate his advertising expenditures in the top 100 to 200 markets. Why?

2   Climate affects life styles which, in turn, affect purchases of goods and services. Give some examples of how this works in various regions of the United States.

3   Why are population figures alone not a reliable index of market potential?

4   A firm's sales figures, broken down by market areas, provides an adequate index of the sales potentials of those areas. Do you agree or disagree? Explain.

5   Total retail sales in a product category registered in various market areas gives some indication of sales potential in those areas, but total retail sales are largely affected by one factor. What is that factor? What would you do to the data to eliminate that factor?

6   What is the primary objection to most market analyses based upon an audit of retail sales? What kind of market data would you recommend to overcome that objection?

7   Assume you are assigned the task of constructing a multiple-factor index of sales potentials for central air-conditioning. What factors might you include?

8   Using *Sales Management*'s *Survey of Buying Power,* select the top five metropolitan areas in Ohio. Assuming total sales of $2 million for a new brand of dog food in all of those markets, what volume of sales would you set as a quota for each market?

9   Advertising effort should be distributed among various market areas in direct proportion to their sales potentiality. Do you agree or disagree? Explain.

10 People in the West and Southwest have been found to be more responsive to advertising than people in New England. What bearing, if any, would this have on advertising plans for introducing a new shampoo?

part three

The advertising message

12

Factors affecting
response

With a penetrating knowledge of the consumer's wants and the product's qualities the advertiser has the background to create messages that will *interpret the want-satisfying qualities of his product in terms of the consumer's wants.*

The advertising message thus becomes a connecting link between the producer with want-satisfying goods and the consumer with wants to be satisfied. Glenn Frank emphasized this concept admirably.

> The nature of the advertising profession, he said, is such that the advertising man is challenged to a wide knowledge of men and of materials, if he is to be more than a peddler of epigrams. The advertising man is a liaison officer between the materials of business and the mind of the nation. He must know both well before he can serve either wisely.[1]

Knowing both the consumer and the product is fundamental. However, linking the two or succeeding as an interpreter calls for some knowledge of how advertising functions as communication, as well as how it affects, and is affected by, consumer behavior.

Two views of advertising communication

A traditional view of advertising communication holds that it is something the advertiser does *to* the audience. The advertisement is viewed

[1] Glenn Frank, "The Dignity and Duties of the Advertising Profession," *Printers' Ink,* April 14, 1927, p. 81.

231

as the stimulus (*S*) that triggers the desired response (*R*). The process thus becomes "a one-way flow," $S \longrightarrow R$. The advertiser acts, and the audience *re*acts. Raymond Bauer labels this view "a model of exploitation of man by man" that is reflected in such popular phrases as brainwashing, hidden persuasion, and subliminal advertising.[2] Recognizing the influence of experimental psychology wherein rats are so often used as subjects, Bauer also notes:

> The model of a one-way exploitative process of communication . . . is probably further reinforced by the experimental design in which the subject is seen as *re*acting to conditions established by the experimenter. We forget the cartoon in which one rat says to another: "Boy, have I got this guy trained! Every time I push this bar he gives me a pellet of food." We all, it seems, believe that *we* train the *rats*.[3]

The traditional view overrates the power of the advertiser by underrating the power of the audience.

A more sophisticated view is that advertising is a "two-way flow," that it is an *interaction* between the audience and the message. It is not so much a matter of what the message brings to the audience, but more a matter of what the audience brings to the message. Instead of the message forcing a response, it *elicits* responses the audience was predisposed to make before the encounter. In other words, the audience's attitudes, beliefs, values, goals, etc. govern whether the message will be seen, heard, believed, remembered, or acted upon.

The concept of a powerful audience was introduced in the first edition of this book in 1937, when the senior author observed that the advertising message must be couched *"in terms of consumer needs and wants"* if it is to perform its interpreting function. This observation is substantiated by the recent findings of communication theorists and researchers.

Joseph Klapper, a leading scholar on the effects of mass communication, notes:

> The existing opinions and interests of people or more generally, their predispositions, have been shown profoundly to influence their behavior vis-à-vis mass communications and the effects which such communications are likely to have upon them. By and large, people tend to expose themselves to those mass communications which are in accord with their existing attitudes and interests. Consciously or unconsciously, they avoid communications of opposite hue. In the event of their being nevertheless exposed to unsympathetic material, they often seem not to perceive it, or to recast and interpret it to fit their existing views, or to forget it more readily than they forget sympathetic material. The processes involved in these self-pro-

---

[2] Raymond A. Bauer, "The Obstinate Audience: The Influence Process From the Point of View of Social Communication," *American Psychologist,* Vol. 19, No. 5 (May 1964), p. 319.

[3] Ibid., p. 322.

tective exercises have become known as selective exposure (or, more classically, "self selection"), selective perception, and selective retention.[4]

Important as it is to recognize the audience's inertia, the power of advertising should not be underestimated. This kind of communication can and does influence consumer behavior. It is more likely to do so, however, when it works with and through existing audience predispositions. Also, it is more likely to modify existing attitudes slightly than to change them sharply.

Predispositions

Attitude is the predisposition of the individual to evaluate some symbol or aspect of his world in a favorable or unfavorable manner. Attitudes include both the affective, or feeling core of liking or disliking, and the cognitive elements which relate the object to prior learning. *Opinion* is the verbal expression of an attitude, but attitudes can also be expressed in nonverbal behavior.[5]

Attitudes and opinions are usually grounded in *beliefs* which are convictions derived from perceived truths. What is perceived as true and what is in reality true may be two different things. *Values* stem from beliefs about what is desirable or undesirable, justifiable or unjustifiable, right or wrong. Values do not always express what the individual desires personally, but rather what a society considers right or wrong in a particular situation. Thus, values often reflect what ideally should or ought to exist.

Personality traits are persistent characteristics of a person's reaction pattern. Traits differ from attitudes in that they are generalized tendencies to respond in a given way without having any favorable or unfavorable reference to particular objects. When we describe a person as imaginative, flexible, venturesome, enterprising, and cheerful, we are attempting to label some of his personality traits. The *self,* or self-image, is an individual's view of the kind of person he is and how he wants others to see him. Much of his behavior is a matter of trying to be the kind of person he thinks he is or a matter of trying to project the kind of personality traits he would like others to see in him.

Group influences include those coming from a primary group such as the family, a close circle of friends, fellow workers and neighbors, and those coming from secondary groups such as social class, occupation, race, ethnic group, and opinion leaders. The concept of group identification points to an emotional tie between the individual and the group. This

[4] Joseph T. Klapper, *The Effects of Mass Communication* (New York: The Free Press, 1960), p. 19.

[5] Daniel Katz, "The Functional Approach to the Study of Attitudes," *Reader in Public Opinion and Communication (2d Ed.)*, ed. Bernard Berelson and Morris Janowitz (New York: The Free Press, 1966), p. 55.

can be a matter of the individual's incorporating group values to express his inner convictions, or it can result from the insecure person's attachment to the strength of the group to compensate for his own weakness. The concept of reference group implies less emotional attachment and suggests that many people turn to particular groups for their standards of judgment.

Elihu Katz and Paul Lazarsfeld postulated the role of personal influence in what they term the "two-step flow" of communication. Their theory states that the mass media directly influence opinion leaders, those people who are respected for their knowledge and competency in a particular field. The opinion leaders, in turn, exert their influence on those around them.[6]

Responses

Various models have been offered to explain how advertising communication works. They differ in detail and terminology, but all seek to demonstrate what happens when an advertiser tries to influence the behavior of large numbers of people by placing messages in mass media that people select voluntarily. An early model viewed the process as a sequence of audience responses moving from *attention* to the message, to *interest* in the proposition, to *desire* for the product, to *conviction* the product would yield desired satisfaction, to *action* in the form of actual purchase. Later models have tried to be more precise and more consistent with the language of.psychology. They have identified the various stages as *sensation/perception/cognition/memory/attitude change/decision.* There is a certain logic to this sequence of events. If a person is to be influenced at all by an advertisement, he must see it, understand it, remember it, accept it, and tentatively decide to buy. However, the notion that there is such a discrete series of responses obscures the importance of prior learning, which simultaneously influences all responses, particularly those labeled perception, cognition, and memory. Prior learning largely determines for each person what he will see and hear, what he will think, and what he will do.

Our model, therefore, will focus on these four, broad categories of response:

Exposure   The audience is within range and is capable of seeing and/or hearing the message.

Perception   The audience sees and/or hears the message and relates to prior learning the world/picture/sound symbols making up the message.

Integration   The audience accepts or rejects the message; believes or

[6] Elihu Katz and Paul F. Lazarsfeld, *Personal Influence: The Part Played by People in the Flow of Mass Communications* (New York: The Free Press, 1955), pp. 175–77.

FIGURE 12–1
Interaction model of advertising communication

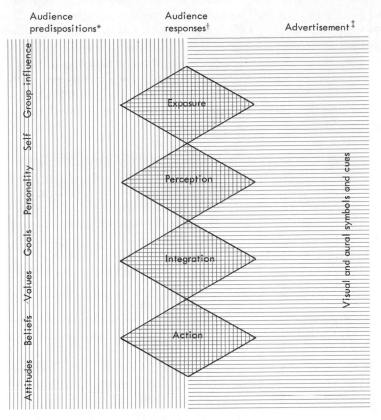

Audience
predispositions*

Audience
responses†

Advertisement‡

* Also called cognitive structure, neural trace patterns, acquired behavioral dispositions.
† Perception includes responses referred to as attention, cognition, comprehension, distortion meaning. Integration includes acceptance, rejection, memory; modification or reinforcement of attitudes, beliefs, and perceptions.
‡ A single advertisement or a series of advertisements (a campaign).

disbelieves; remembers or forgets, modifies or retains relevant attitudes and perceptions.

Action   Members of the audience buy, try, serve, repeat purchase, advocate, or openly endorse product advertised.

As diagrammed in Figure 12–1, all these response categories represent an interaction between the audience's predispositions and the advertising communication.

Exposure

A person is *exposed* to an advertisement when he is physically able to receive it. Thus, he is considered exposed to a television commercial when he is within range of seeing the picture and hearing the sound, when his eyes are focused on "the tube," and his ears are "tuned in." Of course, the sound and the picture must be sufficiently loud and clear to be readily heard and seen. Exposure to a radio commercial is less demanding. Sound can be heard in other rooms, in automobiles, and wherever small transistor radios are carried, which is just about everywhere. The radio audience member to be exposed need only be tuned in to a signal that is sufficiently loud and clear. Exposure to a print advertisement in magazines or newspapers occurs when the reader's eyes encounter the page carrying the ad. Exposure to outdoor advertising occurs when one's eyes are directed, however fleeting the glance, to the sign or poster.

Exposure to communications media tends to be voluntary and selective. It is voluntary in the sense that the person intentionally exposes himself to the medium. He turns the TV set on and tunes in particular programs or he purposely reads certain magazines and newspapers. It is selective in that he chooses only a fraction of all media available, and different people choose different things. The choices he makes, the programs, the magazines, the articles, the features he exposes himself to are likely to be those that gratify his expectations and that are compatible with his existing attitudes and opinions.

Whereas exposure to media tends to be voluntary, exposure to much advertising is involuntary, that is, the person does not seek the advertisements. The ads "come along with" the program or editorial content, and one becomes involuntarily exposed to the ads as a result of his voluntary exposure to the medium. Exceptions, of course, are exposures to classified ads, to the "yellow pages," to mail-order catalogs, and to regular sources of shopping information, such as grocery store and department store ads.

From the advertiser's viewpoint the factors affecting exposure are most significant in media decisions. He should place his messages in media that are congenial to his market's predispositions. However, he also might enhance exposure to his messages if he adopts an appealing style and consistently schedules them in appropriate media. Then the audience will be inclined to keep the line of communication open when the commercial comes on or the ad page comes in view.

Perception

To *perceive* an advertisement is to be aware of it, to see and/or hear it through the senses—and more. Perception also involves an "understanding awareness," a "relating to prior experience," or "attaching meaning" to the message. Though some psychologists assign this latter part of the process to cognition rather than perception, "the two processes are so closely intertwined that it would scarcely be feasible to consider one of them in isolation from the other."[7] We communicate, write, and think in terms of signs or symbols whose very existence is dependent on meaning. As Walter Lippmann observed: "For the most part we do not first see, and then define. We define first and then see."[8]

This concept of perception also embraces a part of the communication process referred to as attention. Gaining attention of the reader, viewer, or listener is an essential function of the advertisement. To elicit any response at all the ad must be seen or heard. Insofar as some brief time might elapse between the initial sensory experience and subsequent brain activity, a case could be made for setting attention apart from perception. However, to draw such a distinction unnecessarily complicates the process and tends to emphasize technical devices for gaining attention at the expense of incorporating meaningful substance in the message. Our interaction model, therefore, combines attention and cognition in the broader context of perception.

Perception is selective. We see what we want to see. We hear what we want to hear. Gardner Murphy explains this point of view:

> Needs determine how the incoming energies are to be put into structure form. Perception then is not something that is registered objectively, then "distorted," . . . Needs keep ahead of percepts. The needs are always controlling; perception instead of being the lawgiver, takes orders from the need . . . It is the need pattern that plays the chief role in determining *where we shall look,* to what outer stimuli we shall attend, and what other factors shall be allowed to enter the control box (selector system).[9]

Readership and listenership studies provide ample evidence of selective perception. New homeowners are more likely to read advertisements concerning lawn care. New car owners are more apt to read ads about their own make of car than about other makes. New parents are quick to see camera ads. Women with graying hair are more likely to see hair-coloring ads. People tend to see ads portraying people like themselves.

Not only do we select the message we want to perceive, we also tend to distort message content in accordance with our different beliefs, attitudes, and values. A class experiment by Bruner and Goodman[10] found that two groups of children ages 10 to 11 overestimated the physical sizes of more valuable coins (quarters and half dollars) and underestimated the sizes of less valuable coins (pennies, nickels, and dimes). More significant was the finding that the children from poor families were more inclined

[7] Floyd H. Allport, *Theories of Perception and the Concepts of Structure* (New York: John Wiley & Sons, Inc., 1955), p. 14.

[8] Walter Lippmann, *Public Opinion* (New York: The Macmillan Company, 1922), p. 81.

[9] Gardner Murphy, *Personality, A Biosocial Approach to Origins and Structure* (New York: Harper & Row, 1947), pp. 377–78.

[10] J. S. Bruner and C. C. Goodman, "Value and Need as Organizing Factors in Perception," *Journal of Abnormal and Social Psychology,* Vol. 42 (1947), pp. 33–44.

to overestimate the sizes of the more valuable coins. Another study[11] showed that people who have a greater desire to own a Volkswagen see the car as physically smaller than those who are less inclined to it. Beauty is in the eyes of the beholder.

Integration

The perceiver of an advertisement may or may not believe it, remember it, or alter his attitudes as a result of his encounter with it. The likelihood of his accepting the message largely depends on how well it fits his existing beliefs and attitudes. Thus, believing, remembering, and attitude changing are selective processes, too. All these responses are affected by one's predispositions which, in themselves, are self-protective. Not only does one's predisposition govern which message will be let in, they also govern the extent to which they themselves will be influenced by it. This part of the response sequence—the judging, evaluating, remembering, and fitting-in with existing beliefs and attitudes—we refer to as *integration.*

John C. Maloney describes integration responses as follows:

> Stimuli are integrated with memories from prior learning or experience and the effects of such integration are stored in the memory structure. They remain there until they are themselves buried (that is, forgotten) or altered by later inputs, or until they are reactivated to form a decision, a response, or a pattern of response.[12]

A person's predispositions, that is, his attitudes, beliefs, values, and goals make up his psychological world, or what is referred to as "cognitive structure." The prevailing view among psychologists is that a person strives for stability in his cognitive structure. Dorwin Cartwright states that "everyone, after the earliest stages of infancy, possesses a remarkably stable cognitive structure upon which he depends for a satisfactory adjustment to his environment."[13] When a message is inconsistent with a person's prevailing cognitive structure, it will either (*a*) be rejected, (*b*) be distorted so as to fit, or (*c*) produce changes in the cognitive structure. "Which of these outcomes will actually occur," Cartwright says, "depends upon the relative strength of the forces maintaining the cognitive structure and of those carried by the new message."

Leon Festinger, through his theory of *cognitive dissonance,* seeks to

[11] Samuel E. Stayton and Morton Weiner, "Value, Magnitude, and Accentuation," *Journal of Abnormal and Social Psychology,* Vol. 42 (January 1947), pp. 33–34.

[12] John C. Maloney, "Advertising Research and an Emerging Science of Mass Persuasion," *Journalism Quarterly,* Vol. 41 (Autumn 1964), p. 526.

[13] Dorwin Cartwright, "Some Principles of Mass Persuasion," *Dimensions of Social Psychology,* ed. W. Edgar Vinacke, Warner R. Wilson, and Gerald M. Meredity (Chicago: Scott Foresman and Company, 1964), p. 301.

explain what happens when a person is confronted with a message that conflicts with his system of beliefs. Festinger's basic hypotheses are:

1. The existence of dissonance, being psychologically uncomfortable, will motivate the person to try to reduce the dissonance and achieve consonance.
2. When dissonance is present, in addition to trying to reduce it, the person will actively avoid situations and information which would likely increase the dissonance.[14]

Dissonance is especially likely to be experienced when a new product concept is introduced. For example, for many years housewives thought that the most effective laundry soaps or detergents were those that produced the most suds—the more suds the better the cleaning action. When the Monsanto Chemical Company introduced "All," a new low-sudsing detergent, their advertising helped housewives reduce the dissonance resulting from the conflicting concept by offering a rational explanation of low-sudsing effectiveness, showing convincing demonstrations, getting washing machine manufacturers to endorse the product, and giving away samples for home trial.

Dissonance theory also suggests that it is better strategy to advertise a product on its own merits than to disparage a competitor's product. Such disparagement is not likely to switch many customers away from the competitor's brand. Perhaps the most significant contribution of dissonance theory to advertising thought is the notion that dissonance is a motivating force causing some people to strive to reconcile new ideas to their existing cognitive structure. Therefore, advertising should be designed to enhance the reconciliation.

Action

The ultimate response is consumer *action* in the marketplace. Depending on the advertiser's objective the appropriate consumer action is manifested in different ways: trying a new or improved product, shifting from one brand to another, becoming a consistent purchaser of one brand, buying more at a time, or buying more frequently. Appropriate action in response to retail advertising would be buying at a given store and becoming a regular patron. For industrial and professional advertising it would be ordering, specifying, recommending, or prescribing the advertiser's product. Satisfied customers advocating the product through word-of-mouth communication would also be acting beneficially.

Action is selective, too. After the advertiser's message or, more typically, his series of messages has filtered through exposure, perception, and integration, it still may fail to elicit the desired action. Those same predispo-

[14] Leon Festinger, *A Theory of Cognitive Dissonance* (New York: Harper & Row, 1957).

sitions continue to be in control. They may have let the message "in" and even let the person "think well" of the product, but still prevent his buying it. Attitudes supporting his present buying behavior may be too strongly held to permit a change. Or, to put it another way, the advertising may not be able to make a large enough dent in his cognitive structure to get him to try a new product, to change brands, or to switch patronage. The key point here is that it behooves the advertiser to carefully probe the relevant attitudes of his market to discover how strongly they are held. He might then find that there are some "immovable objects" and be reminded that advertising is not an "irresistible force."

The trite notion that national advertising gets people "to go down to the corner drug store right now and buy brand X" is far from reality. Buying action resulting from such advertising is a delayed response that typically takes place after many exposures to a series of advertisements over a period of weeks and months. This is not to suggest that each advertisement should not invite action. It simply means that it is naïve to expect an immediate response. Each message should be viewed as one of many nudges toward a purchase.

When the marketing objective is to introduce a new product or accelerate sales of a going product, advertising might be used along with price deals, "cents-off" coupons, contests, premiums, and other such limited-time offers to induce a more immediate response.

Most retail advertising is geared to quick action. The ads in this evening's newspaper are intended to influence tomorrow's buying. Therefore, department stores, grocery stores, and other retailers offer information that helps the consumer plan her shopping trip and make tentative choices among acceptable product alternatives on a price or service basis. Store patronage, on the other hand, is much like brand preference and comes about more slowly.

The fact that advertising seldom, if ever, is the only factor inducing buying action, and the difficulty encountered in isolating the effect of advertising on sales has led some practitioners to consider the function of advertising completed at some level of communication short of action. This level might be "awareness" of the product, "knowledge" of its selling points, "belief" in claims, or indicated "attitude change." Unfortunately, this view overlooks the pervasiveness of advertising's influence and artificially restricts its effect to responses more amenable to measurement. Reluctance to demand action responses may also be due to the small percentages of the total audience who are moved to act. Raymond Bauer reminds us that:

> . . . consistently successful commercial promotions convert only a very
> small percentage of people to action. No one cigarette now commands more
> than 14 percent of the cigarette market, but an increase of 1 percent is worth
> $60 million in sales. This means influencing possibly 0.5 percent of all adults

and 1 percent of cigarette smokers. This also means that a successful commercial campaign can alienate many more than it wins, and still be profitable.[15]

Planning of the entire advertising campaign should proceed from a statement of the specific market action to be attained, and every advertisement should be prepared with that action in mind.

Methods of gaining attention

The corollary of *selective perception* is *selective advertising.* Just as some people are more predisposed than others to seek a product's benefits and to be influenced by certain kinds of appeals, advertising that is directed specifically to those people, that is designed to appeal to their interests, has the best chance of getting through. Therefore, gaining attention is fundamentally a matter of strategy, the strategy of singling out the group or groups of people who seem to be prime prospects and addressing them in terms of their self interest.

Appeal to prospect's wants   To appeal to everybody is to appeal to nobody. Too many advertisers fail to recognize this principle. A headline such as "Men" or "The Greatest News Ever" invites the attention of all men or anyone seeking news. Such a headline should be printed in a large type, in large space, and in color, and would be noticed by many, just as the circus barker, through noise and gymnastics, arrests the momentary notice of many passers-by. If the headline or other attention-getting device is tied up with the interest of particular individuals, attention will not only be obtained but held. If instead of "Men" the headline, "To Men Who Are Dissatisfied with Their Jobs," were used, those who were stopped by the headline would read what the advertisement had to say because of an interest in finding a solution for their own particular problem.

The advertisement illustrated in Figure 12–2 uses no special layout technique to attract attention, yet it will be read by many prospective customers because of its appeal to a fundamental human interest.

Special layout   Attention to any object is at best momentary. The maximum time for which any object can hold the strict observance of a person is perhaps not more than ten seconds. An important characteristic of attention is, therefore, the element of fluctuation. This ebb and flow can be directed to some degree by the advertiser. The arrangement of various parts of an advertisement, the use of borders, lines drawn in certain directions, the focus of the eyes of persons illustrated in the advertisement, and the position of the product itself can all be utilized to guide the reader's eyes to particular parts of the advertisement. Figure 12–3 shows how design and mass are used to draw the attention of the reader to the product

[15] Bauer, "Obstinate Audience," p. 322.

FIGURE 12–2
An appeal to a fundamental human interest

The country feeling.
Live it while you can.

Lee Rider Jeans and Jackets. H. D. Lee Company, Inc., P. O. Box 440-A, Shawnee Mission, Kansas 66201 • Available Worldwide

FIGURE 12–3
Layout focuses attention on product

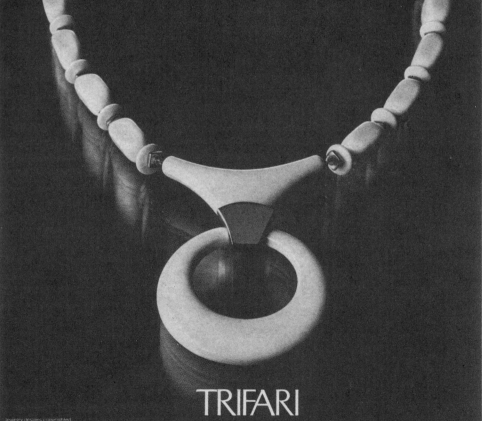

FIGURE 12–4
Without color, the visual elements are difficult to recognize

and its brand name. Care should be taken, however, to keep the special layout design from detracting from the message.

Color   The contrasts that color affords, as well as its symoblic properties and realism, can be used to gain attention. There are times, however, when color loses its attention-getting value. If the great majority of advertisements in a particular advertising medium are reproduced in color, then a black-and-white advertisement would have the advantage of contrast. Under such circumstances, color should not be used if its only function is to get increased attention.

There are, of course, other values of color. It may aid in the creation of a proper mental picture of the product if the product is one in which color is an important value factor. This will apply particularly to items like food, clothes, textiles, and furniture. Imagine how much would be added to Figure 12–4 if the lobster, shallots, tomatoes, and peppers were shown in their natural colors. To see what color adds, turn to the color advertisements in Chapter 16.

There are times when advertisers select colors that may be effective in attracting attention but actually reduce the readability of the advertisement. This may occur when a headline, or even a part of the body copy, is printed in some pastel color, or where printed material is overlaid with color. When any reading matter is printed in color, it is usually wise to select color that is sufficiently dense in tonal quality to make reading easy. Generally speaking, black is best for body copy because it is what readers are used to seeing.

Size and location   The size of an advertisement will have some influence. Various studies have been made in an attempt to measure the attention value of size. The results have indicated that attention value increases with increase in size, but not in the same ratio.

The location of an advertisement in a magazine will influence the number of persons seeing the advertisement. The most valuable location is the back cover. Pages near the covers are somewhat better than those in the body of the magazine. The amount of white space used in an advertisement will be a significant factor, a large proportion affording a contrast that will command increased notice.

Building the brand image

David Ogilvy, eloquent advocate of the image-building concept, says:

> Every advertisement must be considered as a contribution to the complex symbol which is the brand image—as part of the long-term investment in the reputation of the brand.
>
> What a miracle it is when a manufacturer manages to sustain a coherent image in his advertising over a period of years. . . . What guts it takes, what obstinate determination to stick to one coherent policy year after year in

FIGURE 12–5
One of a long series of advertisements that built a strong brand image

"To make the best, begin with the best — then cook with extra care."

This ad appeared 45 years ago...

Have you checked the price of Campbell's Tomato Soup lately?

Anyone who goes to the store or pays the bills knows what's happened to prices over the years. That's why we thought you might be interested in this advertisement that ran for Campbell's Tomato Soup on July 2, 1921.

It shows that the price was 12¢ a can. If you have a grocery store advertisement handy —or if your memory is really good, we think you'll be mildly amazed at the price today— 45 years later—for the same size can.

The same kind of price story—though in varying degree—can be told about the other Campbell's Soups.

Of course, we can't take all the credit. The happy reason that Campbell's has been able to buck the tide of rising prices is partly you, partly the grocer and farmer, and partly us. You, because there are so many more of you these days, and because you seem to like our soups more and more as time goes on. And it's the grocer and farmer, of course, because each has become increasingly efficient...the farmer in producing, and the grocer in serving you.

As for us, we just naturally like to make soup. We like to make it as good as we can, and bring it to you for as little as we can. And we find better ways to do this as we go along.

This seems like a good time to tell you that we find this a very pleasant relationship, indeed—and we thank you.

Campbell's Quality

We blend the best with careful pains
In skillful combination,
And everything we make contains
Our business reputation.

CAMPBELL'S · SWANSON · V-8
FRANCO-AMERICAN · BOUNTY
...all made by Campbell

the face of all the pressures to "come up with something new" every six months.

But what golden rewards await the advertiser who has the brains to create a favorable brand image—and to stick with it over a long period. Look at Campbell's Soup! Look at Jell-O! Look at Betty Crocker! Look at Esso! Look at Ivory Soap!

The men who have been responsible for the advertising of these immortal brands have understood that every advertisement, every radio program, every TV commercial is not a one-time shot, but a long-term investment on the total personality of their brands.[16]

Look at the Campbell's Soup ad in Figure 12–5. The straightforward product story, the style of presentation, the label, the Campbell "kid," and the signature have been used consistently for 45 years. As a result, Campbell's stands for soup, especially tomato soup, for quality, dependability, wholesome nourishment, and value. So strong and clear is the image this strategy built that no competitor has been able to threaten Campbell's leading market position. Even the chain stores have been reluctant to challenge with their own private brands.

Image building is more often associated with national brands. However, the reputation or the persistent perception of any institution becomes a significant factor in its success. A retailer should consistently portray a desirable store personality. Similarly, an industrial advertiser should project a well-defined corporate personality. Insofar as every corporation benefits if it is highly regarded by investors, employees, civic groups, and government officials, as well as by its customers, it is desirable to use every means of communication to build a favorable image. And, of course, in politics the candidate's image is vital.

Belief

The problem of believability is especially acute in highly competitive advertising that confronts the consumer with claims and counterclaims about product superiorities, about ingredients, processes, and construction features that he cannot prove on his own because he has neither the knowledge nor technical apparatus for "running a test." And when claims concern psychological satisfaction, their authenticity can only be measured in terms of peoples' attitudes and opinions. As a result, the consumer is inclined to buy on faith. The advertisements he finds easy to believe are the ones most apt to win his purchase.

Belief is not dependent upon any one factor. If it were, there would probably be much greater uniformity in the beliefs of people on such

[16] David Ogilvy, "The Image and the Brand: A New Approach to Creative Operations" (Speech before the Central Region, American Association of Advertising Agencies, October 14, 1955).

matters as politics and religion. Poffenberger summarizes the various opinions concerning the basis of belief or conviction as follows:

1. Belief is a matter of feeling and emotion rather than of reason.
2. The truth is not a primary factor in determining belief.
3. Belief is a personal matter, a fabric of *personal* experiences.
4. Belief has also a social component to be accounted for by the need for conformity with one's fellows and especially with those in authority.
5. Belief is dependent upon desire—we believe what we want to believe.[17]

The lack of uniformity in beliefs suggests that the advertiser keep in mind the audience he wants to reach and their predisposition to believe what he wants to say. As Maloney reminds us:

> *Believability is not an inherent property of the advertisement itself.* It is not a mystic something that some advertisements have and others do not have. Believability depends upon the *interaction* of each advertisement with the consumer's attitudes and memories accumulated from proper experience. . . . Different people have different expectations about the trustworthiness of various kinds of advertising; they have developed different kinds of knowledge and different types of feelings about the products or brands being advertised. This means that an advertisement completely believable to one person may not be at all believable to another. In other words, we must specify *believable to whom* when we consider the "believability" of an advertisement.[18]

Ways of gaining belief

From what we have learned about the nature of belief it is apparent that creating a believable advertisement is more difficult than merely reporting the facts. The entire strategy and manner of presentation should be designed and executed to inspire confidence. Among the many ways of gaining belief are the following.

Start with the truth   Aside from ethical considerations it is far better to tell the truth because truthful statements are generally more believable than false ones. Misleading statements, excessive exaggeration, and false claims tend to be recognized for what they are and therefore undermine consumer confidence in the product so advertised. Yet, the truth at times is stranger than fiction, and the skill with which it is told will largely determine whether or not it will be believed.

Appeal to prospect's wants   People believe what is in line with their own wants and desires. This relationship between belief and desires has

---

[17] Albert T. Poffenberger, *Psychology in Advertising* (New York: McGraw-Hill Book Co., 1932), pp. 544–45.

[18] John C. Maloney, "Is Advertising Believability Really Important?" *Journal of Marketing,* Vol. 27 (October 1963), p. 1.

been experimentally demonstrated by F. H. Lund.[19] He took 30 propositions dealing with topics of general interest selected from the fields of
religion, ethics, politics, and science and submitted them to 243 persons.
They were asked to indicate their belief in the truth or falsity of each
proposition. The result of this test showed a correlation between belief and
desire of +0.81.

A somewhat similar study was made in which propositions that were
not particularly desired were taken and evidence given to prove their
truthfulness. People were then asked to rate their belief in the propositions.
The resulting correlation between belief and evidence was only +0.42.
This would indicate that the desire to believe is a much stronger determinant of belief than evidence supporting the truthfulness of a given proposition.

This fact undoubtedly accounts in large measure for the "success" of
various patent-medicine advertising, fake stock-selling schemes, etc. People want to get well, and they want to believe that a particular medicine
will cure them. People desire to make money quickly and without effort.
They, therefore, want to believe that a particular "get-rich-quick" proposition is true. This same quality can, of course, be utilized by the advertiser
of goods with real want-satisfying qualities and remain completely in the
realm of truth.

Substantiate with reason   We are not apt to admit, even to ourselves,
that our beliefs are founded on emotions. We tend to believe what we
want to believe and then find logical reasons to justify our beliefs. Therefore, an advertisement appealing primarily to emotion is more convincing
if it also gives the prospect some "reasonable" evidence with which he
can rationalize his choice.

Note that logical reasoning plays a supporting role. It is difficult to
convince a person by the use of reason alone. All kinds of evidence might
be available to show the value of a low tariff, but such "proof" will not
be sufficient to convince the high protectionist. While rejecting the arguments of the other side he is eager to grasp at any evidence that supports
his stand.

Orient message to prospect's experience   People are inclined to
accept whatever conforms, and to reject whatever conflicts, with their
previous experience.

Many readers disbelieved one advertisement that pictured a piece of
luggage supporting a five-ton elephant, and another that showed a fountain
pen withstanding the weight of loaded busses rolling over it, and another
that claimed a phonograph reproduced the human voice so well that an

[19] F. H. Lund, *Psychology* (New York: Ronald Press Co., 1933), pp. 390–95. See also
F. H. Lund, "Emotional and Volitional Determinants of Belief," *Journal of Abnormal and
Social Psychology,* April and July 1925.

FIGURE 12–6
Effective use of testimonial

If Colgate is just a kid's cavity fighter, how come Billie Jean King won't brush with anything else?

Where she rules, Billie Jean King is a tightly controlled figure of skill, energy and concentration. But off the tennis court, with her husband and friends, her natural warmth and spirit flow effortlessly. Billie Jean likes people. That's why she brushes with Colgate.

Colgate is made for people who like people. Clinical test results show it freshens breath as long as a leading mouthwash. And the taste is brisk and clean.

Only your dentist can give teeth a better fluoride treatment than <u>Colgate</u> with <u>MFP</u>. But a great cavity fighter can be a powerful breath freshener, too.

Ask Billie Jean King. She wouldn't think of brushing with anything else.

Colgate with MFP...the breath-freshening cavity fighter.

audience could not distinguish the playback from the live voice.[20] These spectacular demonstrations probably scored well as attention getters, but they were not convincing. Even though true, such feats were too far removed from what people's experience would permit them to believe.

As is often the case, a newly developed product represents a wide departure from what people confidently have been using. Then the advertiser must recognize the inevitable gradualness of change and display a healthy respect for existing beliefs.

Talk prospect's language   The plainer the talk, the more understandable it is and the more believable it is. Words much like those the prospect himself uses, pictures of "his kind of people" and of situations encountered in "his kind of world" ring true. Unfamiliar words spoken by people who are out of touch with his way of life arouse suspicion and doubt.

The technical jargon of doctors and scientists fits popular conceptions of how people in these professions should talk and therefore is often used to add authority to testimonials. Such unintelligible language may be impressive. It is not convincing.

Use bona fide testimonials from recognized authorities   When we don't know what to believe, we are inclined to turn to an authority, someone who is expected to have specialized knowledge on the matter or who holds a position of high esteem in the public mind. Shifting the burden of decision to an expert makes up for the gap in our own knowledge and gives us a feeling of security. It requires little effort.

Doctors, successful businessmen, movie stars, and men of distinction are a few of the more popular authorities. Our tendency to believe what they have to say has been widely exploited by advertisers—perhaps too much so. However, if a testimonial is bona fide, realistic, pertinent, and from a qualified source, it can be an effective means of creating confidence (see Figure 12–6).

Other ways   In addition to those mentioned, there are other ways of gaining belief. Tell of the product's popularity. We have faith in the consensus of large numbers of people.

Display confidence, but don't brag. Confidence is contagious. Bragging is obnoxious.

Use the specific and concrete. They are more believable than the general and abstract.

Use ordinary people in story-telling photos instead of stereotyped models in obviously studied poses. The fact that ordinary people lack the habits, polish, and experience of professionals would more than likely aid in establishing the credulity of the total impression.

[20] Poffenberger, *Psychology in Advertising*, pp. 545–50.

Postpurchase reassurance and satisfaction

Every choice involves a sacrifice. The choice of one of several competing products involves giving up whatever the nonchosen products offer. The consumer who buys a Ford instead of a Chevrolet looks for reassurance that he made the "right" choice, that what he will gain from owning a Ford will be greater than what he gave up in a Chevrolet or in any other make of car that entered his deliberations. Research evidence has indicated that new-car purchasers are likely to read advertisements about the make of car they recently bought. The advertisements not only offer reassurance, they also add to the satisfaction of owning. Seeing the car portrayed to best advantage and reading about its merits not only makes the owner proud of his choice but also makes him proud of himself for having such good judgment. Also, the owner is aware of the fact that other people see the same advertisements, which indirectly tells them that he made a good choice.

Instruction books and other literature accompanying new-product purchases offer an apparent opportunity to reassure the buyer and inform him how to care for and get the most out of his purchase. Less apparent, but equally important, is the opportunity that every advertisement offers to instill pride of ownership.

A satisfied customer is not only inclined to buy again and again, he also is likely to set in motion word-of-mouth communication that multiplies the effect of the advertising.

QUESTIONS AND PROBLEMS

1   Advertising is more likely to modify existing attitudes slightly than to change them sharply. Explain.

2   The assumption that advertising is the stimulus producing a desired consumer response leads one to overrate the power of advertising and underrate the power of the consumer. Explain.

3   From your own experience cite an example of the "two-step flow" of communication.

4   The interaction model of advertising communication presented in Figure 12–1 uses the term "perception" to embrace audience responses described in various terms. What are some of these terms and what do they stand for?

5   Exposure to the advertisement is more a function of the medium than of the message. Agree or disagree? Explain.

6   Advertising campaigns include a series of advertisements designed to achieve the same communication objectives. Are audience responses to early advertisements likely to be any different from responses to later ones in the series?

7   Select three magazine advertisements that appear to recognize the principle of selective perception. Describe the audience most likely to read each advertisement and explain why they would do so.

8 List the various elements of an advertisement that can be drawn upon to build a brand image.

9 From current advertising select what you consider to be an outstanding image-building campaign. Why do you consider it outstanding?

10 What people believe is not always true, and what is true is not always believed. How can an advertiser increase the believability of his message?

11 Select two advertisements that you consider strong on believability and two others that you consider weak on this point. Contrast the content of the two groups.

12 We tend to believe what we want to believe and then look for logical reasons to justify our beliefs. How should this tendency affect the content of advertisements?

13

Advertising appeals

We have noted how important needs and wants are in motivating consumer behavior. What one buys, what he reads or listens to, what he believes, and what he remembers—all are largely determined by the needs he is consciously or subconsciously seeking to satisfy. Now, let us see how motivation theory can be put to work in advertising.

Classification of needs and wants

Thousands of motivational variables have been propounded in the brief history of psychology, but none has attained prolonged and universal acceptance. As Gardner Lindzey observes:

> For almost every set of motivational variables there has been a counterproposal to the effect that the last thing in the world that psychologists should be interested in is compiling lists of motives. Theorists who conceive of behavior as primarily motivated by benign and socially approved motives may be paired with theorists who see the chief impellents of behavior as primitive and unacceptable urges. For those who believe learned or socially acquired motives are of predominant importance there is opposition in the form of theorists convinced that the physiologically grounded and largely innate drives are of primary importance. Some have emphasized the abstract

254

or logical status of motivational constructs, while others have stressed the physical reality and concrete existence of motives.[1]

Why are there so many theories of motivation? In the first place, the study of human motivation involves the difficult task of explaining *why* people behave as they do instead of merely describing *what* they do. Secondly, motives cannot be directly observed. They can only be inferred from overt acts. This injects the idiosyncrasies of the observer-inferrer. Thirdly, all social behavior involves many interactive factors rather than a single cause-effect relationship. Lastly, there are semantic difficulties in using words with different meanings to explain phenomena for which the words are not generally intended.

Among the various classifications of needs and wants one of the most highly regarded and the one that will be used for illustrative purposes here is that presented by psychologist A. H. Maslow.[2] He believes that human needs arrange themselves in hierarchies of prepotency and that the emergence of one need rests on the prior satisfaction of a more basic or more potent need. Maslow's hierarchy of needs is arranged in the following order:

1. Physiological needs (hunger, thirst)
2. Safety needs (security, health)
3. Love needs (affection, belongingness, identification)
4. Esteem needs (self-respect, prestige, social approval)
5. Self-actualization (self-fulfillment, self-expression)

Maslow suggests that a "lower" need must be adequately satisfied before the next "higher" need emerges as a determinant of behavior. A starving man has neither a safety need, nor a love need, nor any other "higher" need. It is only after his hunger is satisfied that he turns to his safety need. Once his safety is secured he then turns his attention to love, then to esteem, and finally to self-actualization. This does not mean that a lower need must be satisfied 100 percent before the next need emerges. Actually, most members of our society are partially satisfied and partially unsatisfied in all their basic needs at the same time. To illustrate the point Maslow says it is as if the average citizen is satisfied perhaps 85 percent in his physiological needs, 70 percent in his safety needs, 50 percent in his love needs, 40 percent in his self-esteem needs, and 10 percent in his self-actualization needs. In other words, in a more affluent society the self-actualization needs are more pervasive determinants of behavior than physiological needs.

[1] Gardner Lindzey, *Assessment of Human Motives* (New York: Grove Press, Inc., 1960), p. 4.
[2] A. H. Maslow, "A Dynamic Theory of Human Motivation," *Psychological Review* (American Psychological Association, Inc.), Vol. 50, pp. 370–96.

Even though he suggests that his rank order of needs fits the behavior of most people, Maslow also recognizes exceptions. He points out that there are some people for whom self-esteem seems to be more important than love. However, such people may actually put on a front of aggressive, confident behavior as a means of gaining love rather than self-esteem itself. There are other innately creative people in whom the drive to creativeness does not seem to follow satisfaction of more basic needs, but persists in spite of the lack of such satisfactions. In other people the level of aspiration may be permanently deadened or lowered. For example, chronic unemployment may lower one's goals to simply getting enough food. On the other hand, people who have never experienced chronic hunger might look upon food as a rather unimportant thing.

A particular need does not produce a certain kind of behavior, nor does a certain kind of behavior stem from a particular need. Most behavior is multimotivated. Eating may be partially for the sake of filling the stomach, partially for the sake of pleasurable taste sensations, partially for a satisfying routine, and partially for sociability. A student may work hard at his studies not only for self-actualization, but also for prestige, for belongingness, and for security. Likewise, the purchase of a product is seldom motivated by a single need or want. Thus, the central problem confronting the advertising strategist is to select from the many relevant needs and wants those few that are most powerful in affecting his customer's purchase behavior and that are, at the same time, susceptible to arousal by advertising communication. The next problem, of course, is to design advertisements that arouse or intensify the need and that clearly present the product as a desirable means of satisfying the need.

Physiological needs

The tissue needs of the body are such that food and drink are absolute essentials to life. Our hunger and thirst prompt us to strive to satisfy our appetite. Other desires are often compared with the desire to eat. Thus the expression, "I would rather do that than eat," is often used to emphasize the intensity of a desire.

Our body mechanism automatically arouses the desire to eat and drink whenever the body requires food and liquid. Hunger, therefore, is a fundamental motivating force. However, the typical well-fed American is more likely to experience hunger pains because he habitually eats at certain hours, not because his body is starving for nutrition. Apparently the body not only knows when to order food generally, but also knows what specific kinds of foods to order. This phenomenon, referred to as homeostasis, suggests that the body seeks to maintain in the blood stream a constant content of water, salt, sugar, protein, fat, calcium, oxygen, etc. If the body lacks one of these ingredients, the individual will develop a specific appetite or hunger for foods containing that particular ingredient. Some theorists have extended the homeostasis concept and suggest that all behavior is affected by the individual's automatically seeking some sort of "balance," or "consonance," or "equilibrium" in his cognitive structure as well as his diet.

In addition to providing sustenance, eating and drinking are satisfying

FIGURE 13–1
An appeal to the desire for appetizing food

experiences in themselves. Pleasurable sensations of taste, smell, sight, touch, and even hearing can result from appetizing foods and beverages. Think of some of the foods you like most, perhaps a charcoal-broiled sirloin steak, french-fried potatoes, lettuce salad, and apple pie à la mode. Just the thought of tasty food can make the mouth water. The aroma of freshly baked bread, a turkey roasting in the oven, brewing coffee; the "eye-petizing" sight of fresh, green lettuce, ripe red tomatoes, frosty-blue blueberries; the crunch of crispy potato chips, the smoothness of ice cream; even the sound of a sizzling hamburger or the perking of a coffee percolator—all of these sensations are part of the joy of eating and drinking. And these sensations are also part of the appetites to which food and beverage advertising can appeal.

For most people the act of dining, especially "dining out," is a satisfying ritual. There is an orderliness to the sequence in which certain kinds of foods and beverages are served proceeding from the "first or appetizer course" to the "dessert course." Wouldn't it jar you to start with ice cream and finish with a shrimp cocktail? The way the table is set, the silverware, the glassware, the serving pieces—all are part of the orderly routine.

Mealtime also is a sociable time. It is the one time when all members of the family get together. It is a time for conversation, a time for companionship, a time for kinship. Having lunch with a friend or having a cup of coffee with a neighbor is a satisfying social experience that often transcends the importance of the food itself. This favorable association of sociability with dining and drinking can be effectively portrayed in food and beverage advertisements.

Safety needs

The threat of bodily harm from wild animals, criminal assault, murder, and tyranny is largely removed in our highly organized society. Fear of such attacks, while significant in the history of man, is not an active motivator in this day and age. More apparent threats to one's safety are unemployment, loss of income, loss of health, and disability. Fear of these threats is so pervasive that society has sought some protection against them through government social security programs.

Security Security for the family, for the home, and for one's self continues to be a strong motivating force in the lives of most people. Most obvious among the institutions created to enhance one's feeling of security are the life insurance companies, the pharmaceutical industry, the medical and dental professions, the police and fire departments, and other government agencies engaged in regulating the food and drug industries, building codes, and highway construction. Less obvious, but equally important, is the institution of religion, or some kind of world philosophy or science that seeks to organize the universe and man into some sort of coherent, mean-

FIGURE 13–2
An appeal to need for security

If it looks like lemonade, why shouldn't it taste like lemonade?

The best way to keep kids away from things that can hurt them, is to keep things that can hurt them away from kids.

Unfortunately, that's not always possible. Anybody who's ever tried to hide something from a child knows that.

The Travelers is trying to do the next best thing. At least as far as the companies we insure are concerned.

That's why, when we check out a product with one of our customers, we not only look at the obvious (is it poisonous or toxic?), we examine the container it comes in.

If it's tippable, breakable, flammable, or where removing the cap is child's play, we make sure the manufacturer knows what changes should be made.

When the product is, in fact, poisonous, we ask for more than a warning. We ask for an antidote. Right on the label.

Of course, household products are just one of the areas that concern our staff of more than 600 safety engineering people.

In the course of a day, they may end up testing everything from teddy bears to television sets. Trying to figure out what might possibly go wrong with a seemingly harmless product.

As an insurance company, obviously that's good for us, as well as the people whose products we insure.

It also happens to benefit somebody else. You.

THE TRAVELERS

ingful whole. Still less obvious is the institution of advertising that makes brands, manufacturers, and retail establishments more familiar and therefore more trustworthy.

While the need for security is strong, it sometimes is difficult to transfer into action. It is difficult to get people to install fire extinguishers or burglar alarms until a fire or a theft has occurred. The adage about locking the stable after the horse has been stolen illustrates the point. Many people don't use the seat belts in their automobiles and are not inclined always to obey the speed limits. Life insurance companies have found that an appeal to providing security for the family after the breadwinner's death can be less effective than a more immediate appeal to the breadwinner's self-esteem as a good provider. Part of the problem that life insurance companies encounter is man's inclination to avoid thoughts of dying. He lives as though he will live forever. Thus, life insurance plans are tied to insured mortgage payments, annuities, and retirement plans. In this vein, one company built its advertising campaign around the idea of "living insurance."

Health   The way some people complain about their ills causes one to wonder whether the joy of complaining is not greater than the desire for health. Yet this is hardly the case. Most individuals are motivated to a greater or lesser degree by the desire for health. This is true not only of those who are ill, but also of those who suffer no real sickness but who wish to remain in good health. Of course, the appeal to this desire is much more effective when directed to those who suffer from some ailment.

Our modern method of living is such that most people are below par in physical energy at some time during every year. This has led to the production and promotion of various products with health-giving claims. Physical-culture schools, health magazines, patent medicines, multitudinous devices, and diet fads have been offered the public as methods for gaining and keeping one's health. Many of these items possess no real value, but the desire for physical and mental health is so strong that many people will try anything if they think it has any possible merit. Such products enjoy wide sales and often much popular favor in spite of their worthlessness. Nature serves them as a powerful ally. Most people will get well in spite of medicines or devices used. Usually, however, the medicine rather than the healing power of time, receives the credit.

The sellers of many worthwhile products have found the health appeal effective in their advertising. This appeal has been used effectively in the sale of fruit juices, sporting goods, certain types of clothing, vacation tours, and home-ventilating and air-conditioning equipment. The Metropolitan Life Insurance Company uses the health appeal in its advertising for a double purpose. It attempts to educate the public in general toward developing better health habits. This not only builds up goodwill for the company, which results in increased sales, but also reduces the sickness and death rate by checking disease.

FIGURE 13–3
Appeal to parental affection

Closely akin to the desire for health is the desire for comfort. When people are tired, an appeal to comfort and rest is very effective. This is closely tied up with a body need and requires little effort to arouse if the effort is applied at the proper time. Many products might be advertised around this appeal. A list might include furniture, shaving equipment, automobiles, clothing, heating and air-conditioning equipment, and tobacco.

The appeal to comfort might be direct, such as the automobile advertisement which emphasized a "ride in the comfort zone" in the middle of the chassis rather than over the wheels. Good results may also be secured by a less direct approach. Indirect suggestion, through picturing a family seated in easy chairs around the fireplace or a man reclining in a lawn chair beside a pool and flowers, might be effective in arousing the desire for comfort.

Love needs

We can distinguish two kinds of love needs. First, we have the need for affectional or love relationship with other individuals. This relationship expresses itself in our society mostly between sweethearts during courtship, between husband and wife, between parents and children, and between very close friends. Secondly, we have a desire for belongingness, to have not only a close love relation with one or two or three people, but also to have a feeling of belonging to a larger group. This need is manifested in the joining of clubs, churches, unions, and political parties. It also is significant in the relationship between the individual and whatever business, professional, or organizational structure of which he considers himself a part.

Affection   The sex drive is exceedingly strong. It could be considered a purely physiological need. However, sexual behavior is multideter-mined. It is also determined by the need for love and affection. Also, the giving of love is as important as the receiving of love.

A logical appeal to the sex need suggests that one's attractiveness to a member of the opposite sex would be enhanced if he or she used the advertised product. Such an appeal is especially appropriate for advertising cosmetics, grooming aids, jewelry, and clothing. Figure 13–4 clearly portrays sex attraction that is relevant to both the product and the message. Of course, gift items can be effectively advertised as means of expressing one's affection for someone else. A somewhat different appeal to sex interest is the use of pictures displaying a scantily clad, curvacious young female. Such pictures serve as an effective attention-compelling device —and often serve no other purpose. Figure 13–5 includes a comely eye-catcher. But will it catch the right prospect's eye and will it stimulate the kind of want that can be satisfied with a furnace?

FIGURE 13–4
Sex appeal logically used

FIGURE 13–5
Sex appeal illogically used

FIGURE 13–6
Appeal to the need for belongingness

The parents' affection for the child is manifested in the protection, care, and reassuring environment they provide. Parental concern is not entirely altruistic. The mother and father welcome the child's dependence and unquestioning affection. Some parents experience personal success for themselves in the child's achievements. Some take pictures and keep an album recording growth, special events, and other milestones in growing up—not to give to the child when grown, but to help the parents recall the happy memories of rearing their offspring. Appeals to parental affection are particularly appropriate for advertising insurance, healthful foods, encyclopedias, and safety devices. Pictures of babies, of children at play, and of underprivileged children—all appeal to parental concern. The strength of this appeal in various fund-raising campaigns demonstrates the universality of affection for all children.

Belongingness   Beyond one's own family there is a desire to belong, to feel at home in the world, to have a place in the group. With a feeling of belonging one is apt to feel friendly, trusting, and tolerant of other people. Along with the feeling of being liked or loved or accepted goes the feeling of safety, security, and peace of mind. To achieve a feeling of belongingness the individual conforms to the social standards of the group and looks for ways of expressing himself that clearly identify him as a member of the group. Group identification can readily be demonstrated in manner of dress, in language or jargon, in positions taken on political issues, in stated values and goals, in places one frequents for sociability. Where one lives, the way he furnishes his home, the car he drives, all signal his membership in a particular group. Pride of ownership (a famous advertising theme for Cadillac) is largely a matter of pride in belonging to the group of owners.

Esteem needs

We all have a need to think well of ourselves and to have others think well of us, too. Self-esteem is enhanced by measuring up well against the standards set for oneself. The person seen in the mirror, his strengths, his achievements, his becoming the kind of person he wants to be and the kind of person he wants others to see—these are the bases of self-respect. The will to win, to succeed, or to compete successfully is a way of feeding one's ego. The following quotation from psychologist Donald Laird is illuminating:

> Why do small men tend to buy large automobiles? Why did an unduly large proportion of leaders come from backwoods settlements? Why are most children provided opportunities far in excess of those enjoyed by their parents? Why do at least a hundred mental patients in the United States imagine they are John D. Rockefeller? Why is it almost impossible to have your voice sound natural after an evening of bad luck at cards? Why did

FIGURE 13–7
Appeal to the need for self-esteem

You'll know where you're going when you see it our way.

Bring us your college degree and you may become an Air Force Navigator.

There's challenge in it. There's excitement in it. There's responsibility in it. And there's a secure career in it—that offers extras like a flying officer's pay, 30 days' paid vacation annually—plus a retirement package you'll wind up enjoying while still young.

And let's not forget the promotions that follow as experience grows.

How do you go about it?

Apply for Air Force Officer Training. When you qualify, you'll head for a 12-week course of specialized study that will turn you into an Air Force Officer.

Once you're commissioned, you move on to training as an Air Force Navigator.

For all the facts, mail in the coupon.

Or, for the location of your nearest Air Force recruiter, call 800-447-4700, toll free. In Illinois call 800-322-4400.

And get on course for a rewarding career.

```
Air Force Opportunities                              4-ES-44
P.O. Box AF
Peoria, Il. 61614
Please send me more information on the Air Force Navigator
Program. I understand there is no obligation.

Name_____
                    (Please Print)
Address_____

City_____

State_____Zip_____Phone_____

Soc. Sec. #_____Date of Birth_____

School_____Date of Graduation_____
```

Look up.
Be looked up to.
Air Force.

FIGURE 13–8
An appeal to the desire for social approval

EACH MONTH, as a member of The Heritage Club, you will receive one of the great classics of literature in a beautiful, *beautiful* edition. It may be a title you will welcome as an old friend, or one that you've been meaning to read. It will be a book of lasting quality, handsomely bound and designed, illustrated by a renowned artist. Often it will be freshly translated and always it will be printed in fine readable type on a quality of paper which has been tested to insure a life of at least two centuries.

You may expect fine editions like these to be very costly. Especially so, when you consider their expensive dress. Here's the good news: The Heritage Club books, despite their obvious quality, cost no more than the ordinary novels you read once and never look at again; $3.95 to members and *only $3.55 if paid for in advance*. An added PLUS is the book you receive FREE with your membership. Isn't it really a perfect plan for enriching *your* library with books that will make it a showcase of beauty and a joy forever?

MEMBERSHIP ROLLS are open once again. This is indeed a vintage year to join The Heritage Club. Each month you can look forward to the pleasure of receiving in your mail one of these beautiful Heritage editions (to mention but a few):

"Sherlock Holmes: The Later and Final Adventures." Arrangements have been made with the Estate of Sir Arthur Conan Doyle to complete our Sherlock Holmes in two volumes and this eagerly awaited set will then be available in its Heritage edition for the first time! This edition will be issued with all of the original drawings gathered from English and American sources.

"The Koran." A selection of the Suras translated for Western readers by Prof. Arthur Jeffery. Embellished with decorations in color by Valenti Angelo.

"Mont-Saint-Michel and Chartres" by Henry Adams, illustrated with photographs taken by Samuel Chamberlain following the Adams itinerary.

"The Picture of Dorian Gray" by Oscar Wilde, illustrated with drawings and portrait paintings in full color by Lucille Corcos.

"Poems of Heinrich Heine." The selection and translation by Louis Untermeyer with illustrations in color by Fritz Kredel.

IF, FOR ANY REASON, you do not want a particular title, you are given a list of some three dozen Heritage books-in-print from which you may select a substitution.

FILL OUT the coupon below and mail it promptly to The Heritage Club. You will receive a Prospectus fully descriptive of all of the books in the Twenty-second Series.

What do your books say about you?

Books are born gossipers. Sitting innocently on your shelves they reveal much about your taste and your background. Undoubtedly, you acquire books that speak well of you. Everyone who cares about books does. We feel, however, (and we may be prejudiced) that belonging to The Heritage Club is the most sensible way to collect books which will bring you tremendous reading pleasure and a warm pride of ownership.

TO MAKE ALLUREMENT DOUBLY LURING

FREE! When you become a member, choose one of these books without cost: *"Twenty Thousand Leagues Under the Sea"* by Jules Verne. Illustrated with colored gravures by that magnificent artist of the sea, Edward A. Wilson. OR: *"Peer Gynt"* by Henrik Ibsen in the authorized translation into English by William and Charles Archer. Illustrated with wonderfully imaginative paintings by the world famous Norwegian artist, Per Krohg.

TO: The Heritage Club
595 Madison Avenue, New York 22, N.Y.

Please send me your Prospectus, describing the books which you will distribute to the Members in the coming twelve months and the substitution books I may choose from. I understand you will now reserve a membership for me awaiting my application and that if I become a member, I will be entitled to have a copy of either *Twenty Thousand Leagues Under the Sea* or *Peer Gynt* without cost.

NAME_____

ADDRESS_____

CITY_____   STATE_____

the prospect sit up and start to show real interest when the salesman said, "Now, here is how this service will give you an advantage over other merchants."

Understand fully the answers to those questions and you are well on the road to knowing why most things other than strict necessities are bought. The unconscious *desire to be more adequate* is the hidden base from which these tendencies start.[3]

Insofar as glory is a reflected sort of thing we are constantly looking outward to other people for signals telling us that they see us as we would like to be—successful, intelligent, attractive, charitable, personable, gracious, friendly, sophisticated, informed, etc. The need for social approval is partly based on the need to belong, to belong to a group. It also is based on the need for esteem, the esteem of others. To win their esteem a person seeks ways of telling other people what kind of person he "really" is. To tell them verbally or directly would be immodest and embarrassing. So he resorts to indirect means of telling them. The clothes he wears, the automobile he drives, the brand of cigarettes he smokes, the way he decorates his home, the foods he serves, the kinds of liquid refreshment he pours—all are instruments of self-expression. As clearly as words they tell who he is, who he wants to be, and to what group he belongs. For example, the advertisement in Figure 13–8 says, "Books are born gossipers. Sitting innocently on your shelves they reveal much about your taste and your background." No doubt many handsomely bound books are purchased more for impressive display than for reading.

Through advertising it is possible to create the kind of product personality or brand image that will help people express themselves and gain social approval.

Self-actualization needs

Even though all the needs considered thus far are reasonably well satisfied, a nagging kind of discontent and restlessness might persist. Such discontent appears when one feels that he is doing less than his best, that he is not doing what he is fitted for or what his talents allow. What a man *can* be, he *must* be. Maslow calls this need self-actualization and describes it as the need for self-fulfillment, for the full flowering of one's capacities, to become actualized in what he is potentially, to become more and more what he is, to become everything he is capable of becoming. The specific form that these needs take varies from person to person. In one person it may take the form of the desire to be an ideal mother, in another it may be expressed athletically, and in still another by writing or painting. It is

[3] Donald A Laird, *What Makes People Buy?* (New York: McGraw-Hill Book Co., 1935), p. 35.

FIGURE 13–9
Appeal to need for self-actualization

"In the Dale Carnegie Course you discover abilities you never realized you had."

JOHN D. LEMMON, GENERAL MANAGER, MAYWOOD BELL FORD, BELL, CALIFORNIA

MRS. SUZANNE REISERT, TEACHER, HEWLETT, NY

"Nothing beats finding out that you have more abilities than you thought," says John Lemmon. "When you add the self-confidence you develop in the Dale Carnegie Course, you're on your way to realizing your goals in life.

"By learning to listen to other people, I learned how to motivate them. People sense when you're sincerely interested in them. It becomes a two-way street, and you discover the other fellow has a lot to offer you. Both of you benefit.

"My wife also took the Course and we find it's made a big difference in our lives. We really got to know one another. It probably saved us a lot of time and grief. You can't help but win when you take the Dale Carnegie Course."

Suzanne Reisert had much the same experience.

"I stopped being afraid to meet people. While I was taking the Dale Carnegie Course, I found I had a lot of hidden assets I wasn't using. Like speaking up when people want my opinion, or having the confidence to try something I know I have the talent for.

"Most of all, I enjoy relating to other people.

Putting across an idea in a dynamic way so that people want to cooperate. And then sensing that people enjoy working with me. It's a great feeling and it comes out of the Course. I get more satisfaction out of living."

People who come to the Dale Carnegie Course often leave with an entirely new concept of their own abilities. They discover hidden talents they never imagined they had and learn how to use them. The result is a more rewarding life on a day-to-day basis. You can't be very far from the Dale Carnegie Course. It's offered in more than 1,000 U.S. communities each year. Find out what it can do for you by writing for more information.

DALE CARNEGIE COURSE

SUITE 923N • 1475 FRANKLIN AVENUE • GARDEN CITY, NEW YORK 11530

not necessarily a creative urge although in people who have capacities for creative work it is likely to be so expressed.

"The ultimate motivation is to make the self-concept real," says psychologist Saul Gellerman. It is:

> . . . to live in a manner that is appropriate to one's preferred role, to be treated in a manner that corresponds to one's preferred rank, and to be rewarded in a manner that reflects one's estimate of his own abilities. Thus, we are all in perpetual pursuit of whatever we regard as our deserved role, trying to make our subjective ideas about ourselves into objective truths. . . . If there is one universal human characteristic, it is probably that everyone tries in his own fumbling, imperfect way to follow the advice of Polonius to his son: "This above all, to thine own self be true."[4]

Products and services that appeal to the need for self-actualization include educational programs, musical instruments and lessons, art shows, arts and crafts exhibits, home study courses, golf lessons, cook books, religious books, and "great books" study groups. Whatever the activity or the arena in which people strive for individual excellence, there is an opportunity to appeal to this need.

Summary

This brief discussion of motivational forces is for illustrative purposes only. The subject is far too complex to be dealt with adequately in so few pages. Maslow's hierarchy of basic needs is useful in that it consistently focuses on goals of behavior—on ends rather than means. Obviously, it is not all inclusive. Curiosity, exploration, playing, tinkering, and even loafing apparently satisfy some need. Yet they don't readily fit into the system. Perhaps they come close to being ends in themselves. In any event, Maslow reminds us that motivations are only one class of determinants of behavior. While behavior is almost always motivated, it is also most always biologically, culturally, and situationally determined as well.

As demonstrated by the advertisements reproduced in this chapter the appeal should be the central idea of the message. The picture, the headline, the proposition, the style, the tone—all should clearly portray or dramatize the need to be satisfied through use of the product. You shouldn't have to read deeply into body copy to find the appeal. It should be immediately apparent.

Every advertisement need not appeal to a basic need. The communication task at hand may only call for an announcement as in the "Yellow Pages," or a straight product display as in an industrial ad showing a cut-away section of a machine, or a detailed description of the product as in a mail-order catalog. However, in most advertising situations the

---

[4] Saul W. Gellerman, *Motivation and Productivity* (New York: American Management Association, 1963), pp. 290–91.

consumer needs to be sold, and the selling is done by appealing to his needs.

QUESTIONS AND PROBLEMS

1. Maslow's hierarchy of needs suggests that different people in different circumstances have different priorities of needs. Explain. It also suggests that the same person has different priorities at different times in his life. Explain.

2. Most behavior is multimotivated. Of what significance is this observation in developing advertising strategy?

3. Discuss several dimensions of security and relate these dimensions to advertising.

4. Contrast the need for self-esteem with the need for self-actualization. Bring to class two advertisements that demonstrate the difference.

5. Recently an executive of a men's clothing manufacturing firm, in a speech to an industry group, pointed out that American men were currently spending 20 percent less for clothing than they had spent two decades ago. He indicated that an important cause of the decline was the use of ineffective appeals in men's clothing advertising and urged the industry to "find the proper appeal."

   If you can find (from your library or private sources) back copies of some magazine that carries advertisements of men's clothing, examine those copies to see what appeals have been used in the past to stimulate men to buy clothing. Compare those appeals with ones used today. What appeals would you suggest as "proper" (that is, effective) for the industry?

6. What the consumer in the United States buys with most of his money is psychological satisfactions, not biological necessities. Discuss.

7. How can advertising create the kind of product personality or brand image that will help people express themselves and gain social approval?

8. What appeals would you consider most effective in advertising these products?
   a. Beer
   b. Stereo tape deck
   c. Antiperspirant
   d. Ski resort
   e. Tennis raquet
   f. Steel-belted radial tires
   g. Deep-freeze cabinet

9. In what age groups do you believe advertising appealing to the desire for security would be most effective? To what age groups would each of the other appeals discussed in this chapter appeal most strongly?

10. Make a portfolio consisting of one advertisement appealing to each of the needs discussed in this chapter.

11. Contrast the appeals used in advertising low-priced automobiles to those used in the high-price range.

14

Selecting the appeal

U ndoubtedly, the appeal or central idea of an advertisement is its most important element. Much thought and effort can well be devoted to selecting an appeal that will elicit the desired response. Generalizations regarding consumer motivation and behavior are useful in identifying alternative approaches. However, the problem of singling out the one approach that best fits the particular set of circumstances remains. And once the approach is settled upon, the problem is to verbalize, visualize, and dramatize the appeal in terms that will be meaningful to the audience. The need for esteem is basic, but John Jones thinks in terms of being promoted to a vice presidency.

Dewey and Humber say, "When asked which motive is strongest, the answer must always be in terms of the value systems of particular persons and particular cultures. Universally, there is no *strongest* motive."[1] Therefore, it may also be said that universally there is no *strongest* appeal.

It should thus be evident that no absolute rules can be laid down concerning the selection of an appeal for advertising a given product. Again, experimentation with various approaches to the human mind must be employed in an effort to obtain the best results.

[1] Richard Dewey and W. J. Humber, *The Development of Human Behavior* (New York: Macmillan Co., 1951), p. 193.

Identifying alternate appeals

The appeals that might be used to advertise a given product are as numerous and varied as the motives, feelings, attitudes, and opinions that move consumers to buy. The possibilities for verbalizing or symbolizing a given appeal are infinite. Therefore, when selecting the appeal a person should not jump to a hasty conclusion, no matter how obvious the merits of a particular choice appear to be. He should first seek out and identify as many alternative approaches as he can. The more alternatives he has to choose from, the better his chances of success. Then, too, the process of identifying alternatives is, in itself, a powerful stimulus to creative imagination.

Identifying alternatives is most effectively achieved through a combination of creative thinking and research. A creative person's observations, introspections, hunches, and judgments, often yield successful advertising ideas. But the scope of a person's ideas are largely limited to his own experiences, his own world, and his own subjective evaluations. Consumer research, by widening the scope of the creative person's observations and sharpening his insight into consumer behavior, often uncovers alternatives that he has overlooked entirely.

Studies of consumer motivation can be particularly useful for identifying alternative appeals because they focus on the less apparent inner determinants of human behavior. Note the character of information included in the following excerpt from a study comparing the psychological meanings of instant coffee and regular coffee which was done by Social Research, Inc., and reported in Pierre Martineau's book, *Motivation in Advertising:*

> Although instant coffee has made considerable progress, there is still a tremendous difference in psychological meaning between it and regular coffee.
>
> *a.* Regular coffee very sharply emerges as a hearty, tasty, clear, full-bodied, hot, dark, fragrant liquid. It signifies stimulation and strength, personal comfort, vigor and activity. It is a broad symbol of sociability, universally suitable for hospitality, a gesture of friendliness and graciousness.
>
> *b.* Instant coffee goes counter to virtually all these ideal qualities. In spite of its increased popularity, it is still considered an inferior substitute which can only suffer by comparison with the real thing.
>
> When people were asked to sum up the character of coffee in three words, they said:
> —Satisfying, flavorful, invigorating.
> —Fresh, priceless, stimulating.
> —Delicious, satisfying drink.
> —Strong, hot drink.
> —Rich, full flavor.
>
> These words were almost never used in describing instant coffee. Typical comments were:

__Not very useful.

__Weak, flat taste.

__Just too sweet.

__Very poor substitute.

__Easy, no aroma, flat-tasting.

c. Instant coffee stigmatizes and typifies a certain type of housewife. The housewife can serve it on occasion, of course. But any woman who goes contrary to the ideal housewife's dedication to her home and her family is neglecting her duty. If she consistently uses a product whose main claims to fame are the time and effort they save her rather than flavor and quality, she is bound to be stigmatized. She is seen as a lazy and indifferent housekeeper, not really a devoted wife.

The women who were considered to use instant coffee the least were described thus:

__She's always baking.

__The best cook of all.

__She cooks heavy meals.

__She uses recipes all the time.

d. Nevertheless the devoted housekeeper can properly use instant coffee on occasion, for example, when she is hurried, when she only wants a cup, or when she is simply at her personal leisure and wants some refreshment. When presented with the incomplete sentence, "A good homemaker uses instant coffee to . . . ," typical answers were:

__Save time and money.

__Drink when in a rush.

__Get a fast cup of coffee.

__Make small quantities.

e. The ideal cup of instant coffee really belongs to a busy housewife having herself a cup during her morning or afternoon break. It is for the working wife getting a fast breakfast before rushing out. And it is for the young housewife who is hurried, harassed, or on a tight budget. The types who received the most votes for using instant coffee were:

1. The working woman.

2. The beginner.

f. But instant coffee is a social insult. Its main drawback is that it is unaccepted for sociability. Serving it to guests is somewhat insulting, because it means that the hostess doesn't care to take the trouble to prepare "the correct thing."

g. Instant coffee's advantages are mostly practical. It does serve very imporant functions for many, readily summed up in these three-word definitions:

__Convenient, quick substitute.

__Economical, fresh, speedy.

__Good, economical drink.

__Speedy, fast, cheaper.

__Speedy, time and money saver.

Actually, these descriptions occur more often among housewives than do derogatory words. These advantages make instant coffee especially desirable for people who want only one cup or who are under pressure of work and time. There is considerable usage among older people using only small quantities.

h. And of course the position of instant coffee is changing. Its popularity is growing, which makes people believe that the product is improved. Although it is still considered a substitute, most people feel that it is getting closer to the real thing. And it is becoming more respectable socially. It definitely has these psychological assets:

1. It is recognized as a coming thing.
2. It is economical when you want only a cup or two.
3. It is time-saving and convenient.
4. It is modern.
5. It is suited to young people, rushing to get to work, progressive.

This means that they are youthful, busy, hard-working, up to date, smart, clever enough to use modern innovations.[2]

This study concluded that "as long as instant coffee stresses purely impersonal uses of speed, economy, and convenience, which are emergency uses only, it will never acquire the rich meanings of sociability, effective activity, and stimulation that still belong to regular coffee."[3] Perhaps the principal value of studies such as this is not found in the conclusions they reach but rather in the thoughts they start.

A systematic classification of potential rewards can be useful in isolating an appropriate appeal. For example, the following matrix, as developed by John Maloney, relates three kinds of product-use experiences with four kinds of rewards.

Product-use experience	Reward			
	Rational	Sensory	Social	Ego-satisfaction
Results of use 1	2	3	4	
In use. 5	6	7	8	
Incidental to use 9	10	11	12	

Hypothetical examples of each of these 12 positions are:

1. Gets clothes cleaner
2. Settles upset stomach faster
3. When you care enough to serve the best
4. For the skin you deserve to have
5. The flour that needs no sifting
6. Real gusto in a great light beer
7. A deodorant to guarantee social acceptence

[2] Pierre Martineau, *Motivation in Advertising* (New York: McGraw-Hill Book Co., 1957), pp. 55–57.

[3] Ibid.

8. The shoe for the young executive
9. The plastic pack keeps the cigarettes fresh
10. The portable television that's lighter in weight and easier to lift
11. The furniture that identifies the home of modern people
12. Stereo for the person with discriminating taste[4]

Estimating the relative strength of alternative appeals

"Use a rifle instead of a shotgun." The advertisement that concentrates on a single dominant appeal makes a deeper impression than one that peppers the consumer with a barrage of product benefits. If the consumer's attention is thinly spread over all conceivable appeals, chances are that nothing will come through sharp and clear, nothing specific will be remembered. Therefore, once the alternatives have been identified, the next step is to select the strongest appeal around which the advertisement or campaign will be built.

This does not mean that the same appeal should dominate every advertisement. If several appeals appear to be equally strong, each may be used effectively as the major theme in different advertisements. Messages directed to different consumer groups might well use different appeals. An appeal that is strong this year may be weak next year. Essentially, however, the problem of selecting a dominant appeal for a particular advertisement, directed to a given consumer group, at a given time remains the same.

Again, creative thinking and research are called for. Creative thinking is required to conjure up those meaningful words, phrases, and pictures that give proper expression to any appeal. An advertiser's experience, intuition, and judgment may guide him to the best choice. But the stakes are high. The success of an entire campaign rests on his arriving at the right answer. If his copy theme centers on a nonexistent want, or on one of small importance, he is almost certain to fail. For example, a coffee campaign that extolled the joys of drinking *really clean* coffee failed because the advertiser's hunch that people wanted *clean* coffee, while probably correct, failed to take into account that people expected all brands of coffee to be clean and this was not a deciding factor when they selected a particular brand.

Research designed to measure the relative strength of alternative appeals reduces the risk of making a wrong choice. When an advertiser learns from consumers themselves the wants that are uppermost in their minds, and the motives that exert the greatest influence on their buying behavior, he is more apt to select a powerful appeal.

A number of techniques have been developed to provide help in evalu-

---

[4] Adapted from article in *Hello!*, a publication of Leo Burnett Company Employees, February–March 1966.

ating the relative strength of specific appeals. Techniques referred to as motivation research, including depth interviewing and projective tests (the Rorschach, sentence-completion tests, thematic apperception tests, etc.), are probably more useful for uncovering and identifying hidden motives, attitudes, and feelings than for measuring their relative strength. Yet, the frequency with which a given opinion or attitude is expressed by respondents to such indirect questioning gives some idea of its importance. These techniques require lengthy interviews conducted by highly skilled interviewers. The samples are generally too small to be representative. Therefore, such research is referred to as *qualitative* instead of *quantitative*. Studies employing a questionnaire and direct questioning procedures are more appropriate for quantifying the strength of alternative appeals.

Examples of measurement

Keen competition for young college graduates, especially in science and engineering, has induced many companies to include advertising as an important part of their recruiting programs. Which appeal to you think would be most effective—starting salary or potential growth of the company? Replies by recently hired scientists and engineers to a questionnaire distributed by McGraw-Hill Book Co. are summarized in Table 14–1.

Perhaps men who are already settled in their jobs rank factors that influenced their decision differently than men who have yet to decide where they will work. But, as this evidence indicates, chances are good that a recruiting program centering on a company's growth potential and the opportunities for advancement will be more effective than one that dwells on the size of the first paycheck.

Another example of the fruitful use of a questionnaire to help select an advertising appeal is that of a manufacturer of milking machines. This

TABLE 14–1
What factors influence the job selections of young engineers and scientists?

Factors greatly influencing decision	Percent listing factor
Potential growth of company	55
Challenging opportunity	53
Company's prestige, reputation	44
Progressive research and development program	41
Geographic location	37
Permanent position	35
Starting salary	34
Educational facilities in vicinity	33
Regular salary increases	31
Chance to work on specific project or in certain field	27
Company's facilities (laboratories, technical libraries, etc.)	25
Tuition for graduate study	25

TABLE 14–2
Relative importance of milking machine qualities to dairy farmers

Milking machine qualities	Percent checking each quality
Ease of cleaning machine	67.5
Not harmful to cow	60.6
Ease of getting repairs	60.4
Ease of operation	51.1
Reputation of manufacturer	41.4
Ease of getting service	41.0
Saving of milking time	27.5
Increased milk production	21.8
Reputation of retailer	16.3
Low initial cost	6.4

Source: Farm Research Institute, Urbana, Ill.

company had a superior product which was priced below its competition. Low price was the major appeal that had been used in its advertising. Because market position was not improving, the company questioned whether it had been using the right appeal.

The company employed a research firm to help in the selection of appeals for a new advertising campaign. The firm interviewed 425 dairy farmers and asked them to select from a list of qualities the four they would consider most important in their purchase or use of a milking machine. Table 14–2 shows the relative standing of each of the milking machine qualities included on the questionnaire list.

The results from this inquiry seemed to indicate that the ease of cleaning a milking machine was a factor of outstanding importance in the mind of a user or prospective buyer. The next step was to measure the attitude of dairymen toward the specific problem of keeping milking machines clean. This was done by submitting to farmers the statements listed in Table 14–3 and asking them to check the one or ones that indicated their attitude toward the machine-cleaning problem. Answers are shown opposite each statement.

TABLE 14–3
Attitudes of dairymen toward the problem of keeping milking machines clean

Statements concerning attitude toward cleaning machine	Percent answering
Saving in milking time is worth the cleaning effort	56.4
Some brands are easier to clean than others	49.0
Not much trouble to clean	30.0
Takes too long to clean	11.6
Machine too difficult to take apart	5.2

From these studies it was concluded that an advertising campaign built around the appeal of "easy to keep clean" would be more effective than the "low-price" appeal that had been used. The brand in question was analyzed in terms of its ease of cleaning when compared with competing brands and found to be as easy to clean as any other and easier than most. It was, therefore, clear that the company could honestly use the "easy-to-clean" appeal and make that the central theme of their campaign. This they did and secured a marked increase in sales.

An imaginative approach to selecting a campaign theme for an industrial service was taken by Canteen Corporation, a firm that operates company cafeterias. At first glance it would seem that what Canteen Corporation offers its customers is menu planning, food purchasing, food preparation, and food serving. However, a more penetrating look would show that the customer receives benefits far beyond efficient food service.

To find out what these additional benefits might be, Canteen Corporation and its advertising agency, Marsteller, Inc., conducted a series of group interviews with industrial relations and management personnel in companies using food service organizations. These interviews clearly indicated that management was not merely buying food service, but rather the improved employee morale, the means of letting their people know that management cares, the recruiting advantages, and reductions in employee turnover that better food service bring about. To verify the importance of this concept of food service as a "management tool" they conducted a mail survey among readers of *Fortune* and *Business Week*. One of the research techniques used was sentence completions. One of the sentences and the frequency of words used to complete it follows:

Please fill in the word(s) you feel best complete(s) the following sentence:

"Food service is a ＿＿＿＿＿＿ tool."

	Mentions	
	Number	Percent
Management	51	14
Employee relations	29	8
Necessary	21	6
Important	8	2
Employee morale	8	2
Valuable	6	2
Time saving	6	2
Beneficial	6	2
Useful	5	1
Personnel	5	1
All others*	66	19
No answer	144	41
Total	355	100

Forty-eight other phrases received three or less mentions.

With this result and other supporting evidence, Canteen Corporation decided to concentrate their advertising on the benefits their food service offered to management. One advertisement from this series is reproduced in Figure 14–1.

It is often difficult for the advertiser to decide between the use of a positive and a negative appeal. A positive appeal dramatizes the situation to be *gained* through use of the advertised product. A negative appeal dramatizes the situation to be *avoided* through use of the advertised product.

Note the happy state of affairs in Figure 14–2. This is the positive approach portraying the comfort and satisfaction of relaxing on the flight home from a successful business trip. Figure 14–3 also appeals to the air-traveling business man, but the approach is negative. It clearly portrays the loneliness of traveling alone.

There is a considerable difference of opinion as to which approach is more effective. Those favoring the positive method of expression claim that it is much better to keep the mind of the prospect focused on the real desire to be satisfied than to call attention to unfavorable situations. Those holding an opposite view claim that some of the most powerful motivating forces are negative. They state that most people can be driven more effectively than they can be led. The fear motive is given to support their case. It is claimed that people are more easily driven to the purchase of products like patent medicines because of the fear of disease or death than are led to such purchase through the desire for health. They cite the fact that most people wait until they have a toothache before going to a dentist, instead of visiting their dentist regularly to maintain good teeth.

More subtle differences between positive and negative appeals are suggested in transactional analysis. Thomas Harris, in his book *I'm OK—You're OK,* defines four life positions.[5] They are: I'm not OK—you're not OK (the anxious dependency of the immature); I'm not OK—you're OK (feelings of inferiority, despair); I'm OK—you're not OK (strong ego); and I'm OK—you're OK (the mature adult in tune with himself and others). The positive appeal plays up the "I'm OK" position. I'm OK because I use Dial, and you're OK because you use Dial, and don't you wish everybody did? The negative appeal exploits the "I'm not OK" position. It dramatizes feelings of insecurity and impending danger.

Several studies have been made in an attempt to answer the question of the relative strength of the two approaches. D. B. Lucas and C. E. Benson made a comparison of the coupon returns from 233 advertisements of both types. These were paired into 117 comparisons, each representing a positive and negative appeal. Table 14–4 gives the results of the study.

[5] Thomas A. Harris, *I'm OK—You're OK* (New York: Harper & Row, Inc., 1969).

FIGURE 14–1
Customer research led to this appeal

Looking for an effective way to reduce employee turnover?

We have a new idea for you. Take a look at your company cafeteria. With lunch being one of the high spots of your employees' day, an outstanding cafeteria service can make them feel pretty good about the company they work for.

Think about it. An up-graded food service is a highly-visible way to tell your employees that you're really interested in them. Sure, food service isn't the entire answer. But when you have a problem as big and as costly as high turnover, every little bit helps.

If you're having problems keeping people, take a look at your cafeteria. Better yet, let Canteen take a look. We're the one company that makes food service a management tool. The kind of tool that helps solve problems in recruiting, morale, and productivity as well as in turnover. It's all in our new booklet, "Management's Guide to Food Service." Write for it at the address below.

CANTEEN

Director of Marketing, F-7, Canteen Corporation, Merchandise Mart, Chicago, Illinois 60654.
In Canada, Canteen of Canada, Ltd., Toronto, Ontario.

FIGURE 14–2
Use of positive appeal

Many happy returns.

Meet Don Richards. He's daydreaming his way home from a successful business trip. Don usually flies United. And for good reasons.

He knows that we understand the glamorous life of a traveling business man. Grabbing taxis on the run, missing meals, indifferent people, strange cities, hectic schedules, rush, rush, rush.

Often the only time he has to relax and unwind is in flight. So for a few hours when Don flies with us, we try to make it up to him with the kind of service he'd like.

A place to lean back. Some peace and quiet. A cocktail. Maybe two. Soothing music.

Magazines to read. Or just friendly conversation. Plus a schedule that sends more planes to more places more often than any other airline.

Next time you take a business trip, try United. Get the kind of service you like. And have many happy returns.

The friendly skies of your land
United Air Lines
Partners in Travel with Western International Hotels.

FIGURE 14–3
Use of negative appeal

How many trips will you make this year?
Alone.
How often will you go back to your hotel
at five? Alone.
How often will you have a late dinner?
Alone.
How many times will you call home? To
talk to your wife. And to see how the
kids are.
How long ago did you tell the family:

"We're all going to go—someday."?
To New York, to Hawaii, to Disneyland
or to see the folks.
Do you know what? You're not alone.
Thousands of businessmen have the
same dream.
"Someday on a 747."
"Someday we'll all sit together and watch
the movies on the plane."
"Someday we'll all have steak and lobster

and laugh at 'coffee, tea or milk'."
"Someday . . ."
Is this year your family's someday? After
all, next year is a lot of lonely flights away.

Getting people together.

Man was not meant to fly alone.

TABLE 14-4
Relative coupon returns for positive and negative appeals

	Coupon return comparisons			
Kind of goods	Favoring positive appeals	Favoring negative appeals	Equal	Total
Toothpaste	17	13	1	31
A food drink	19	17	1	37
A breakfast food	4	9	0	13
Sanitation articles	3	4	0	7
Total for manufactured products	43	43	2	88
Educational courses	14	14	1	29
Grand total	57	57	3	117

Source: D. B. Lucas and C. E. Benson, *Psychology for Advertisers* (New York: Harper & Row, 1930), p. 118.

These results indicate no differences in the effectiveness of one type of appeal over the other. The difference in the results of breakfast-food advertisements and of sanitation articles might be due to chance, since the sample was too small to be conclusive.

The International Correspondence School has used both types of advertising with equal success. An interesting comparison of two advertisements run by it is explained by Mr. Paul V. Barrett, its director of advertising, as follows:

Some months ago we placed two advertisements in the same issue of the same magazine. The advertisements were the same size, had the same general layout and appearance, and had occupied equally good positions. One was headed "Yes" and carried the subhead, "It's the Happiest Moment in a Man's Life." The other was headed "No!" and had a subhead, "You'll Never Get Anywhere in the World, Jack." In the "Yes" advertisement the girl was accepting the man's proposal of marriage. The text dwelt on the man's new responsibilities, and the necessity of equipping himself to meet them. In the "No!" advertisement the girl was refusing the man, for the reason explained in the subhead. The text urged the man to do something about it, by training himself for a better job.

Certainly it would be difficult to find two more clear-cut examples of the positive and negative appeal. The conditions surrounding each were as nearly identical as they could be. Which appeal was the better? Based on the business resulting from the two advertisements, and we know exactly how much business resulted from each, one appeal was just as effective as the other. Each has brought satisfactory volume of inquiries and enrolments. The negative appeal has actually produced a few more enrolments to date, but not enough to be significant.

Later returns may increase the business attributable to either or both advertisements, but they will not change the fact that so far as we can determine from this and many other tests, it does not make any difference which appeal we use. It all depends upon how we use it. And that, I suspect, is the answer to most of the arguments about which is the better.[6]

It is interesting to note that in J. L. Watkins' compilation of *The 100 Greatest Advertisements*[7] only 29 of the 100 used the negative approach. In analyzing these and other advertisements, Mr. James D. Woolf found that the negative approach seemed to be more often used when consumers were likely to be unmindful of the need for the product. Thus, the famous Listerine advertisement, "Often a bridesmaid but never a bride," was directed to a situation usually unrecognized by the consumer. Mr. Woolf concludes: "When the promised benefit is an *unwanted* benefit—when the consumer is happily ignorant of his need for the product—when the product provides a solution of an *unrecognized* problem—then it would seem that a negative approach, possibly pitched in an emotional key, is likely to be more effective than a positive appeal."[8]

The selection of either a positive or a negative appeal might well depend upon the nature of the product, the character of the consumer need, and the degree to which the consumer is conscious of the need. Results of various tests would seem to indicate that either appeal can be made effective if properly applied.

Interpreting questionnaire studies

Absolute dependence must not be placed upon the results from questionnaire studies of the strength of appeals. People do not always know what appeals will influence them most in the purchase of a particular product. A considerable amount of rationalization might take place in ranking certain appeals. Many people might check economy of use as the most vital factor in the selection of an automobile and yet actually be influenced more by a desire to possess a car that is better than one owned by a neighbor. Such people may build up a belief that the more expensive car is really more economical, reasoning that it will require less repair, can be driven longer, and will have a smaller depreciation. A partial check on such rationalization can be made by analyzing the detailed information obtained from a well-constructed questionnaire.

A serious problem is presented when two more-or-less opposite desires are rated about equally. Thus, people might rate speed and safety as equally desirable qualities in an automobile. After reaching certain levels

[6] Paul V. Barrett, "Coupons and Selectivity." *Printers' Ink,* May 30, 1935, pp. 54–56.

[7] J. L. Watkins, *The 100 Greatest Advertisements* (New York: Moore Publishing Co., 1949).

[8] James D. Woolf, "Positive or Negative Appeal? Are There Any Rules to Guide Us?" *Advertising Age,* October 1, 1951, p. 50.

of speed, any further increase will usually reduce the quality of safety. Under such circumstances the manufacturer must decide to which desire he should direct his production and advertising efforts. If careful analysis discloses that the desires for speed and safety are not present to any large degree in the same people, but rather represent the desires of two distinct groups, a different product can be made to appeal to each group.

Attempts to determine the strongest appeal have led to the use of various research techniques. These include the ranking by consumers of a product's various want-satisfying qualities as well as measuring consumer responses to specifically phrased advertising themes. A further analysis of these testing methods is to be found in Chapters 24 through 27.

QUESTIONS AND PROBLEMS

1   Psychologists who have rated the relative strength of various appeals have made the task of selecting an appeal much simpler for the individual advertiser. Agree or disagree? Explain.

2   Techniques referred to as motivation research are more appropriate for identifying alternative appeals than for evaluating the relative strength of each appeal. Explain.

3   Give an example for as many of the 12 positions relating product-use experience with four kinds of rewards (rational, sensory, social, ego-satisfaction) as you can.

4   Bring to class four advertisements, each of which fits one of the four life positions Thomas Harris outlines in his book, *I'M OK—You're OK.*

5   In some advertising situations a positive appeal is probably more effective. In others, a negative appeal may be best. Under what conditions would you recommend use of a negative appeal? A positive appeal? How might you determine which should be used?

6   Do you believe people are able to report accurately on their buying motives when responding to direct questions such as, *"Why* do you buy X brand of gasoline?"

7   Which of the following appeals do you believe is most nearly in harmony with the basic reason you are in college?

   a.   To satisfy your parents.
   b.   To have a good time.
   c.   To get a man.
   d.   To increase your social prestige.
   e.   To increase your future earning power.
   f.   To help you serve your country better.
   g.   To help you live the good life.
   h.   To make you a more useful citizen.

   If you were employed as advertising director of your college, which appeal would you use to increase the enrollment at your school?

What methods might be used to determine the stronger ones of the above appeals before you undertook your advertising campaign?

Are there any other appeals you would want to add to the list?

8 A survey among antiperspirant users revealed these ratings of product benefits:

Percent rating each item extremely important

Preventing odor 77
Keeping underarms dry 64
Providing long-lasting protection 64
Not causing a rash 63
Not staining clothing. 61
Preventing perspiration. 62
Not irritating to the skin 60
Stopping wetness 60
Being gentle to the skin 52
Making you feel fresh. 45
Not feeling sticky 44
Not being messy to use 43
Not stinging. 44
Drying quickly. 34
Killing germs 33
Not being expensive to use 31
Being easy to apply 31
Having a pleasant fragrance. 30
Not being too wet when applied. 28
Being able to apply exact amount 26
Not feeling cold when applied. 15

On the basis of these ratings what recommendations would you make for formulating and advertising a new antiperspirant?

Copywriting

Copywriting is much more than the term implies. It includes the writing of advertising messages, whether for print, television, or radio. But more than this it goes to the heart of the advertising business—the producing of ideas; ideas that embrace the total message, both pictures and words. Therefore, this chapter will deal with fundamental considerations bearing on the total message and the total thinking required, as well as the written components.

Fundamentally, an advertisement is an expression of an idea and the ultimate success of the advertisement depends on the strength of the idea it is intended to express. No matter how well it is executed in words and pictures, a weak selling idea is not likely to result in a strong message. Therefore, the quality of the advertisement is governed by the quality of the thinking that precedes the actual writing and designing. The "think before you write" stage is critical.

Facts about the consumer, about the product, about the market, and the strategic objectives are all essential information. But facts do not produce advertisements. Finally somebody has to think through all the facts and "get out an ad."

The creative process

The output of human creativity is spectacular, especially in the arts and sciences. Yet, there has been little systematic study in this area and little is known about how the creative process works. Even so, it is useful to view the process as taking place in stages.

The preparatory stage A person's creativity is enhanced when he pursues knowledge of people, of their behavior, and their world; when he exposes himself to as many life experiences as he can without conscious awareness of how useful they might be. Such general knowledge and experience are most likely to be acquired if he reads widely on many fronts and deeply on some; if he has good antennae, is a perceptive observer of the social scene, and is sensitive to people's wants, fears, hopes, and dreams.

In addition to building his general store of knowledge, the creative person tackles a specific problem by saturating himself with as much pertinent information as he can. This, of course, points to the necessity of understanding the consumer's particular motivations and behavior with respect to the product at hand and to the necessity of a penetrating knowledge of the product as primary steps in the preparation of an advertisement. The preparatory stage is most productive when the creative person keeps an open mind—when he doesn't pigeonhole information into preconceived patterns. Perhaps the greatest barrier to creative advertising is the stereotype of an ad that restricts the initial investigation and channels thought toward a preconceived mold. It is noteworthy that even after an exhaustive investigation, the creative person seldom feels he has all the information he would like to have.

The digestive stage Without pressing for an ultimate solution the creative person next works over the material he has gathered. He systematically sifts for relevancy, for appropriate combinations. James Webb Young, in describing this stage, says: "What you do is to take the different bits of material which you have gathered and feel them all over, as it were, with the tentacles of the mind. You take one fact, turn it this way and that, look at it in different lights, and feel for the meaning of it. You bring two facts together and see how they fit."[1] In this stage there is considerable merit in forcing oneself to produce alternative ideas or solutions to the problem without passing judgment on each alternative. In other words, let the mind range over the various possibilities. Getting the alternatives down on paper not only increases the supply of ideas at hand, but also increases the chances of reaching an optimum solution.

The incubation stage Apparently the age-old admonition, "sleep on it," really works. In this stage the creative person turns the problem over to his subconscious mind, which seems to be capable of working effectively without his being aware it is doing so. Turning the problem "off" for a while relieves the pressure of fatigue and frees the subconscious mind its miracles to perform.

[1] James Webb Young, *A Technique for Producing Ideas* (Chicago: Advertising Publications, Inc., 1949), pp. 42–43.

The illumination stage   "Eureka, I have found it." There is something mysterious about this stage because it suggests that suddenly out of nowhere *the* idea will appear. Irving Taylor describes it as "largely an involuntary act. The experience of insight occurs when the incubated parts form a recognizable and meaningful experience. The new organization, far superior to any of the original parts or existing stereotypes, may flash into consciousness quite suddenly—the 'subliminal uprush' for which few people are prepared and many may inhibit."[2]

Intriguing as the moment of inspiration is, let the novice beware. Inspiration is no substitute for the painstaking work required in stages one and two, the importance of which is the main reason for discussing the creative process at all.

Creative people   Psychologists tell us the creative person is characterized by his high level of intelligence, his openness to experience, his freedom from restraints, his aesthetic sensitivity, his cognitive flexibility, his independence in thought and action, and his striving for solutions to the more difficult problems he constantly sets for himself.

Don Tennant spotlighted the most telling characteristic when he said:

> *Creative people are doers.* Those people we think of as "creative" are usually people who have simply learned to go ahead and do what other people simply daydream about. They are people who have learned that the key to being creative is to *act*. The so-called "creative person" stands out in a crowd not so much for what he has done, but because of what others do not do. Creativeness is simply someone's positive attitude hard at work.[3]

Creativity in action

From the abstract to the concrete—the following is a capsule case history of a highly successful creative effort as reported by William Bernbach, president of the Doyle Dane Bernbach advertising agency:

> Let me tell you about the Volkswagen campaign. When we were awarded the account the first thing we did was to spend much time in the factory in Wolfsburg, Germany. We spent days talking to engineers, production men, executives, workers on the assembly line. We marched side by side with the molten metal that hardened into the engine, and kept going until every part was finally in its place. We watched finally as a man climbed behind the steering wheel, pumped the first life into the new-born bug and drove it off the line. We were immersed in the making of a Volkswagen and we knew what our theme had to be. We knew what distinguished this car.

[2] Irving A. Taylor, "The Nature of the Creative Process," *Creativity,* ed. Paul Smith (New York: Hastings House, 1959), p. 64.

[3] Don Tennant, *The Creative Man in the Marketing Machinery* (New York: American Association of Advertising Agencies, 1964), p. 4.

Lemon.

This Volkswagen missed the boat.

The chrome strip on the glove compartment is blemished and must be replaced. Chances are you wouldn't have noticed it; Inspector Kurt Kroner did.

There are 3,389 men at our Wolfsburg factory with only one job: to inspect Volkswagens at each stage of production. (3000 Volkswagens are produced daily; there are more inspectors than cars.)

Every shock absorber is tested (spot checking won't do), every windshield is scanned. VWs have been rejected for surface scratches barely visible to the eye.

Final inspection is really something! VW inspectors run each car off the line onto the Funktionsprüfstand (car test stand), tote up 189 check points, gun ahead to the automatic brake stand, and say "no" to one VW out of fifty.

This preoccupation with detail means the VW lasts longer and requires less maintenance, by and large, than other cars. (It also means a used VW depreciates less than any other car.)

We pluck the lemons; you get the plums.

FIGURE 15–1. A risky word boldly used

The man in the Hathaway shirt

AT long last American men are beginning to realize that it is ridiculous to buy good suits and then spoil the whole effect by wearing a cheap, mass-produced shirt. Hence the growing popularity of Hathaway shirts, which are in a class by themselves.

To begin with, Hathaway shirts *wear* infinitely longer—a matter of years. To go on with, they make you look younger and more distinguished, because of the way Hathaway cut collars—low-sloping and 'customized'. The whole shirt is cut more generously, and is therefore more *comfortable*. The tails are longer, and stay in your trousers. The buttons are made of mother-of-pearl—very big and masculine. Even the stitching has an antebellum elegance about it.

Above all, Hathaway make their shirts of very remarkable fabrics, imported from the four corners of the earth — Viyella and Aertex from England, woolen taffeta from Auchterarder in Scotland, Sea Island cotton from the British West Indies, hand-woven silk from India, broadcloth from Manchester, linen batiste from Paris. You will get a great deal of quiet satisfaction out of wearing shirts which are in such impeccable taste.

Hathaway shirts are made by a small company of dedicated craftsmen in the little town of Waterville, Maine. They have been at it, man and boy, for one hundred and fourteen years.

If you want the name of the nearest store where you can buy a Hathaway shirt, send a card to C. F. Hathaway, Waterville, Maine.

FIGURE 15–2. An advertisement that launched a successful image-building campaign

We knew what we had to tell the American public. We had to say: "This is an honest car."

This was our selling proposition. We had seen the quality of materials that were used. We had seen the almost incredible precautions taken to avoid mistakes. We had seen the costly system of inspection that turned back cars that would never have been turned down by the consumer. We had seen the impressive efficiency that resulted in such an unbelievably low price for such a quality product. We had seen the pride of craftsmanship in the worker that made him exceed even the high standards set for him. Yes, this was an honest car. We had found our selling proposition.

Was our job done? Was all we had to do now is tell the consumer "this is an honest car"? Well, I'm not going to stand here and tell you that it couldn't be done that way. But I am going to tell you it couldn't be done that way with the small budget we had. It is one thing to tell the truth. It is quite another to get people to listen to it and to accept it as the truth. As far as advertising budgets are concerned, the truth isn't the truth until people believe you.

I guess if we piled enough coins on top of that phrase "Volkswagen is an honest car" the sheer weight of those coins would eventually have pressed it into the public consciousness. But we had neither the time nor the money. We had to call in our ally, CREATIVITY. We had to startle people into an immediate awareness of our advantages in such a way that they would never forget it. That is the real function of creativity.[4]

How well this function has been performed has been amply demonstrated in the successful Volkswagen campaign. Commenting on one ad in this series, Figure 15–1, Mr. Bernbach said: "You know that this (Lemon) is the classic description for disappointment in a car. Yet, here it was used to prove memorably once again that here indeed was an honest car. For it was the ruthless VW inspector who considered this particular car a lemon because it had an almost invisible scratch. . . ."[5]

The various stages of thought thus far discussed should precede the actual preparation of advertising copy. After thus conditioning himself, the copywriter should be ready to define specific objectives, identify the audience, develop an outline of the message, and complete the ad.

Campaign strategy

"Every advertisement should be thought of as a contribution to the complex symbol which is the *brand image.* . . . Every advertisement is *not* a one-time shot, but a long-term investment in the total personality of the brand."[6] In saying this, David Ogilvy reminds us that even though

[4] William Bernbach, "Selling Proposition Isn't Enough; Creativity Must Bring the Dead Truth to Life," *Advertising Age,* May 29, 1961, p. 60.

[5] Ibid.

[6] David Ogilvy, *Confessions of An Advertising Man* (New York: Atheneum. Copyright 1963 by David Ogilvy Trustee), pp. 100–101.

FIGURE 15–3
Headline positions brand

A wealth of great taste, but stingy on the calories.

The Kellogg's® Special K® Breakfast is rich in great tastes, with everything from sip to crunch. Yet, it's stingy on the calories. It has less than 240 calories. It's 99% fat-free. And, best of all, it's 100% delicious. Some nice figures from the Special K Breakfast.

The Special K
Breakfast
4 oz. tomato
 (or orange) juice
1¼ cups (1 oz.)
 Special K
 high-protein cereal
1 teaspoon sugar
4 oz. skim milk
Black coffee or tea
(less than 240 calories)

Ⓢ Kellogg Company
© 1973 Kellogg Company

Un-Cola position established Seven Up as a unique and desirable alternative.

In a crowded and changing field such as ready-to-eat cereals, positioning is especially important. Note in Figure 15–3 how Special K, which in its early years was positioned as a nutrition cereal high in protein, is now positioned as low-calorie. Other examples of positioning statements that reflect successful campaign strategies are: "Crest is the best possible cavity-reducing toothpaste for the entire family"; "Bounty absorbs household spills faster than other paper towels"; "Shake 'n Bake is an easier way to achieve fried chicken taste"; "Crisco fries foods with no greasy taste"; "Endorsement by automatic washer makers is evidence of Tide's superior cleaning."[9]

Inasmuch as positioning is a communications concept requiring precise articulation, the professional advertising person, often a copywriter, is called upon to plan and prepare the positioning statement.

Defining objectives

It might be said that the objective of an advertisement or a series of advertisements is to increase sales. This is so broad as to be meaningless to the writer of an ad, and of course it fails to state the particular role the advertising is to play along with all the other factors that influence sales. Statements of sales and profit goals with respect to particular market segments and market areas are essential in advertising planning, but they more properly are designated marketing objectives, not advertising objectives. Once the marketing objectives are set, it becomes necessary to define the communication tasks assigned to advertising. These communication tasks can be further refined in terms of media objectives (the numbers of people in particular consumer groups to be reached—where, when, and how often) and message objectives (the effects—in terms of consumer knowledge and attitudes toward the product the messages are intended to elicit). When the message objective is clearly defined, the advertisement is more likely to be prepared as a means toward an end, not as an end in itself.

The articulation of message objectives is, in itself, a creative operation and is not easily done. Some typical objectives and additional qualifications to make them operational are as follows:

1. Create awareness of existence of product or brand.
2. Create "brand image" or favorable emotional disposition toward the brand (What kind of image?).
3. Implant information regarding benefits and superior features of brand (What information? What benefits? What features?).

[9] For other examples see the series of articles on "Positioning" by Jack Trout and Al Ries in *Advertising Age,* April 24, May 1, and May 8, 1972.

4. Combat or offset competitive claims (What claims?).
5. Correct false impressions, misinformation, and other obstacles to sales (What impressions, etc.?).
6. Build familiarity and easy recognition of package or trademark.
7. Build corporate image and favorable attitudes toward company (What kind of image? What attitudes?).
8. Establish a "reputation platform" for launching new brands or product lines (What kind of reputation?).
9. Register a unique selling proposition on the minds of consumers (What proposition?).
10. Develop sales leads for salesmen.[10]

Defining realistic and operational advertising objectives requires an intimate knowledge of the communication process, tasteful discrimination in the use of words and pictures, a sensitivity to the unique characteristics of the various media, and an empathy for the consumer.

Identify the audience

Uppermost in the writer's mind should be the people to whom he is writing. His success as an interpreter depends mainly on his ability to speak the prospects' language—not just the language of words but also the language of their needs, wants, beliefs, values, goals, etc. In fact, the whole purpose of consumer research is to identify and describe in all relevant detail that group of people to whom the advertising should be addressed. However, with all the facts at hand it still remains for the copywriter to fix clearly in his mind these distant people, to empathize with them, to put himself in their shoes. As suggested in the eight preceding chapters, he might describe them in these terms:

1. Demographic terms—age, sex, occupation, income, education, stage in life cycle.
2. Psychological terms—predispositions, attitudes, beliefs, motives, values, goals, personality traits.
3. Sociological terms—social class, status, role, reference group, life style.
4. Geographic terms—religion, climate, urban, rural, local customs.

The writer should draw on all reliable information bearing on these factors that is available. However, as often is the case, the most relevant psychological information is not available. Under such circumstances the creative writer would speculatively fill in the gaps and make assumptions. This kind of mental exploration might well yield an effective advertising idea that superficial information would only obscure. The creative person's

---

[10] See Russell H. Colley, *Defining Advertising Goals for Measured Advertising Results* (New York: Association of National Advertisers, Inc., 1961).

willingness to make assumptions, to theorize, and to test ideas logically is perhaps his greatest contribution. It would be helpful if the writer could meet and talk with several members of his desired audience before starting to prepare copy for the advertisement. In the actual writing process better copy will usually be produced if one individual member of the total consumer audience is singled out and the copy written for him. Writing would thus take on some of the warmth, directness, and meaningfulness of a personal letter. Each member of the audience who had interests similar to those of the individual the writer had in mind would also feel that the message was written specifically for him. That is an ideal situation. Note Figure 15–4 as an example of an advertisement that approaches that ideal. This advertisement was prepared especially for *Advertising Theory and Practice.*

Failure to identify the audience accurately often leads to strange and probably ineffectual copy. The headline in a hot-water heater advertisement which appeared in an issue of *Farm Journal* read, "This is the only house on the block with plenty of hot water." Another advertisement for soap in the same magazine was headlined, "She gets the *cleanest* clothes in town." Certainly the audience selected by *Farm Journal* is composed primarily of farm people. It is, therefore, somewhat incongruous to place a farm home on a "block" or to think that farm women are more interested in clothes in town than in clothes on the farm. In neither of these cases was copy written specifically to the farm audience.

The importance of directing your message to a person rather than to impersonal masses is emphasized in the advertising guide which Sears, Roebuck and Co. gives its copy staff. In that guide Sears says, "When you write Sears copy you are writing for approximately 25 million people. In writing for this vast audience . . . direct your message to *one* individual—not the 25 million."[11]

James D. Woolf expressed this same basic philosophy of advertising copy as follows: "Let us *know* those whom we would sell through the written word; let us classify our market not merely as men or women, as farmers or mechanics, but as human beings who have certain problems, feelings, and emotions with respect to the product we would influence them to buy. Let us look into census figures, geographical maps, income statistics, bank clearings, and such things by all means, but let us remember we will be missing half our data if we fail to look into—*people.*"[12]

Identifying the desired audience in terms of life style opens promising opportunities for effective advertising. For example, one study of life-style patterns of the heavy beer drinker revealed that he was a risk taker and

---

[11] *Sears Advertising Guide* (Chicago: Sears, Roebuck and Co., 1942), pp. 52–53.
[12] James D. Woolf, "Salesense in Advertising," *Advertising Age,* January 10, 1955, p. 74.

FIGURE 15–4
Do you feel that this copy is directed to you?

Did you take notes on today's assignment?

You probably jotted down a few notes for future reference and review. And the chances are you used a pen to do it.

Funny thing about fountain pens. If they really write well, they're a boon to your thoughts. But if something goes wrong, particularly in a tight spot like an exam—real trouble!

Why take a chance? Since you do so much writing, why not invest in the world's finest writing companion—the New Parker "51" Pen. It's precision-made to give absolutely dependable performance. Each easy filling of the "51" stores many many hours of smooth, skip-free writing. You can *see* the ink supply; the hooded point protects against ink smudging. Best of all, the "51" does away with blotters. It writes *dry* with Superchrome Ink. See the beautiful new "51" Pen at your dealer's. Your choice of 8 colors, all point styles, and 2 sizes: slim regular, extra-slim *demi-size.* The Parker Pen Company, Janesville, Wisconsin.

**POPULAR PARKER PENS
AT ALL PRICES**

NEW Parker "51"
with Lustraloy cap $15.00

NEW Parker "51" Special
an unusual value at $12.50

NEW Parker "51" Deluxe
with burnished metal cap $7.50

NEW Parker "21"
Octanium point $5.00

a pleasure seeker, or at least that was how he fancied himself. More than the nonuser, the heavy user tended to have a preference for a physical, male-oriented existence. He enjoyed drinking beer, which was seen as a real man's drink. "The resulting campaign was built around the imagery of the sea to dramatize the adventure of one of the last frontiers. The focus of the new campaign was on the *life style* of the men of the sea—men who live their lives with gusto and enjoy a gusto brew."[13]

Develop an outline

In the actual writing of copy an outline of what is to be included will save time and produce more effective copy. In preparing the outline the writer will be forced to set down the basic appeal to be used and the major consumer benefit to be highlighted. He will also enumerate the various product qualities that might serve to provide consumer benefits and select those to be stressed.

The sequence of ideas can be worked out in outline form before actual writing is done. It is good practice to place the most important idea first in the advertisement. Usually the most important idea will be keyed to a consumer want or benefit. Since needs and wants are the primary human motivating forces, they serve to capture attention and interest. Consumers, like all humans, are concerned most with their own welfare and care little about a manufacturer's or retailer's product except as it will add to personal satisfaction—hence, the importance of having copy start off with a consumer need or want.

Product qualities will follow consumer needs or wants in the outline. Such qualities will be developed in terms of how they will serve to bring a benefit. Notes should be included in the outline to indicate the specific qualities to be included and the amount of detail to be developed.

Use consumer viewpoint

Much has already been said about the importance of keeping the consumer uppermost in mind when preparing the advertisement, but this principle cannot be stressed too much. Kenneth Goode emphasized this principle as follows: "Hotel clerks and bank cashiers scan a signature upside down as the customer writes. A copy man requires long experience to reverse the process by writing inside out, so to speak, so that each reader unconsciously absorbs an advertisement as his *own* thought, rather than somebody else's statement to be examined and, perhaps, challenged."[14] James R. Adams, an advertising agency executive, said, "I am

---

[13] "Are Media Deciders Thinking Life Style?" *Media Decisions,* February 1974, p. 98.

[14] Kenneth Goode, *Modern Advertising* (New York: Blue Ribbon Books, 1937), p. 165.

convinced that advertising could be greatly improved in effectiveness if it were prepared exclusively from the viewpoint of the consumer."[15]

Another way of expressing this same idea is to write with the "you" approach. Such an approach is not easy for the beginner. The personal pronoun "I" is a big word in the vocabulary of most people. This would indicate that people are interested first in themselves and, when writing, are likely to write about their own actions, ideas, products, and desires. Try leaving the word "I" completely out of the next personal letter written to a friend or parent. Try, also, to think of specific interests of your friend or parent and inquire about them or pass along some new idea, an article you have read, or the experience of others you know about which would bear directly on the interests of the person to whom you are writing.

Substitution of the word "you" for "I," or the addition of "you" to a phrase or sentence, will help make copy warm and personal. Contrast "Win $100,000" with "You can win $100,000." Or compare the following pairs of sentences:

1. *a.* We are so proud of this product and its fine quality that we guarantee it to last for 20 years.
    b. You will receive an ironclad 20-year guarantee with this fine quality product.
2. *a.* This man's knowledge will save you money and give better protection.
    b. You can save money and get better protection because of this man's knowledge.
3. *a.* Crane quality—the dependable ally against high costs.
    b. You have a dependable ally against high costs in Crane quality.
4. *a.* Ceco products make for better living.
    b. You live better because of Ceco products.

The "you" approach also involves the use of consumer language. It is easy to recognize that technical product terms must be translated into words, phrases, and pictures that are understood by the prospect. It is not so easy to appreciate that even for common words, there are often vast differences in meaning to different people. Words are merely symbols and hence stand for something. That "something" for a given person will depend upon the experiences that have been associated with the symbol. Meaning thus grows out of past experiences. The following list of common words given to any group of people will have variations in meaning for each member of the group: candy, salt, milk, bourbon, coffee, and rattlesnake meat. The word "candy" to a diabetic will recall a chain of circumstances quite different from those recalled by the obese dowager. To

---

[15] James R. Adams, "Causative Action—The Vital Element" (New York: American Association of Advertising Agencies, 1956).

another it might recall that first box of chocolates which the "prince charming" brought on that first date. It is not safe for the copy man to depend upon his own word meanings—he should make every attempt to use words that stem from the consumer's frame of reference.

Headlines

In most print advertising the headline and illustration are the primary attention getters. Working together they should select from the total audience of the publication those readers who are prime prospects for the advertised product. At the same time they should promise a rewarding experience from further reading of the copy. In television and radio there are no headlines as such. However, the opening lines of the TV or radio commercial should serve a similar purpose. Without an illustration in a print ad the full burden of attracting prospects' attention and getting them to read the copy rests on the headline. In modern advertising such ads are scarce. In most cases the illustration is the dominant element and the headline serves as a caption to add meaning to the picture. In any event, picture, headline, and body text should be interrelated parts and should work together to communicate a unified message.

Self-interest is the key to successful headlines. A prospect is primarily interested in what he will get *out* of a product, not what a manufacturer put into it. Therefore, the headline that promises him a personal benefit or satisfaction is more apt to get his attention than one that proclaims the superiority of a particular product feature, or one that brags about the manufacturer's achievements. Headlines are associated with news, and news can be used to advantage in advertising. Curiosity can also be used to stimulate interest and further reading, but the risk in using curiosity headlines is that people who are merely curious may become readers while real prospects pass by.

John Caples, a veteran ad man who wrote the famous headline, "They Laughed When I Sat Down At The Piano—But When I Started To Play," suggests the following five rules for writing a good headline:

1. First and foremost, and above all else, try to get Self-Interest into every headline you write. Make your headline suggest to the reader that here is something he wants. This rule is so fundamental that it would seem obvious. Yet the rule is violated every day by scores of copy writers.
2. If you have news, such as a new product, or a new use for an old product, be sure to get that news into your headline in a big way.
3. Avoid headlines which are merely curiosity headlines. Curiosity combined with news or self-interest is an excellent aid to the pulling power of your headline. But curiosity by itself is seldom enough. This fundamental rule is violated more than any other. Every issue of every magazine and newspaper contains headlines which attempt to sell the reader through curiosity and curiosity alone.

4. Avoid, when possible, headlines which paint the gloomy or negative side of the picture. Take the cheerful, positive angle.
5. Try to suggest in your headline that here is a quick and easy way for the reader to get something he wants.[16]

By its very nature a headline is relatively brief. Depending on the idea to be communicated a headline may contain only one word or as many as 20 words. Brevity may be achieved at the expense of meaning. If it is too long it may not invite the quick reading for which it is intended. The appearance of length in a headline can be diminished by the use of sub-headlines and variations in the size of type. The use of several illustrations and captions under each illustration will also aid in getting across to the glancer the central theme developed in the copy.

Provide information

What are the want-satisfying qualities of the product? Surely, the consumer would like to know and has a right to expect the advertisement to provide such information. For many items, specific information concerning size, construction, weight, color, shrinkability, price, and credit terms would be pertinent and should be included in the advertisement.

Some writers seem to think that if certain types of information are included in copy, potential consumers would be frightened away from the product. Price is often omitted for this reason, particularly in the case of those products that are relatively high in unit cost. Those who recommend such practice suggest that the advertisement should stimulate interest in the benefit-giving qualities and let the prospect get other information at the retail store or from a salesman. The trouble is, with price information missing from the advertisement, many prospects will infer a price quite different from reality. If the inferred price is greatly lower than the actual price, the prospect will not buy when the salesman calls or when the product is examined at the retail outlet. In either case time has been wasted. If the inferred price is higher than reality, then many prospects might never seek additional information.

Information should be specific, accurate, and not misleading. The following copy was taken from an advertisement of a blanket:

> These beautiful "Keep Warms" have a scientific three-ply weave that makes use of THREE fibers instead of One—in such a way as to achieve the maximum natural advantages of ALL THREE. The Wool that accounts for half the Blanket's weight, is all fine-quality, costly, IMPORTED Wool that is finer, softer, whiter, for clearer colors and greater beauty. With it is carefully blended uniformly fine viscose Rayon fibers for even greater softness, warmth and color depth. Then this fluffy, fleecy blend is ingeniously

---

[16] John Caples, *Tested Advertising Methods,* rev. ed. (New York: Harper & Row, 1947), p. 38.

Henry VII, Elizabeth I and Mary Queen of Scots are buried in this chapel.

Tread softly past the long, long sleep of kings

THIS IS Henry VII's chapel in Westminster Abbey. These windows have filtered the sunlight of five centuries. They have also seen the crowning of twenty-two kings.

Three monarchs rest here now. Henry, Elizabeth and Mary. Such are their names in sleep. No titles. No trumpets. The banners hang battle-heavy and becalmed. But still the royal crown remains. *Honi soit qui mal y pense.*

When you go to Britain, make yourself this promise. Visit at least *one* of the thirty great cathedrals. Their famous names thunder! Durham and Armagh. Or they chime! Lincoln and Canterbury. And sometimes they *whisper*. Winchester, Norwich, Salisbury and Wells. Get a map and make your choice.

Each cathedral transcends the noblest single work of art. It is a pinnacle of faith and an act of centuries. It is an offering of human hands as close to Abraham as it is to Bach. Listen to the soaring choirs at evensong. And, if you can, go at Easter.

You will rejoice that you did.

FIGURE 15–5. Superb writing to achieve an advertising purpose

twisted around an unseen "core thread" of sturdy, long-staple Cotton that makes these NEW Blankets a full 20 percent *stronger.* This three-PLY DOUBLE WEAVE makes these NEW "Keep Warms" thicker and closer woven, for greater warmth, added softness, longer wear!

Big six feet wide by seven feet long for cozy tuck-in against winter's coldest nights. Beautifully bound in richly shimmering Acetate SATIN that gives such amazing wear. And they're TESTED AND APPROVED by the famed American Institute of Laundering as your assurance of quality and washability.

Unfortunately, this copy tries to make an asset out of a mixture of three kinds of fibers with the possible inference that they are superior to all-wool. The qualities of being "thicker" and of "closer weave" do not necessarily make for greater warmth. The phrase, "Big six feet wide by seven feet long," is also misleading since a six- by seven-foot blanket is generally minimum and could hardly be classed as big.

Readership studies and other measures of consumer reactions to advertisement support the principle of including specific and full information in copy. This, in spite of the fact that such practice will usually result in longer copy. It has been demonstrated time and again that people will read long copy as long as they are getting information they seek. When a person is thinking of buying a new automobile, rug, automatic washing machine, gas range, power lawn mower, corn shredder, suit of clothes, slide rule, fountain pen, or sweater, any advertisement for the product in mind will almost surely be noticed and all copy will be read unless the reader concludes that there is no further helpful information in the advertisement. As long as advertising copy remains interesting and helpful, it will be read by the real prospects—others do not matter.

There are those who feel that superb writing has no place in advertising; that people's everyday language and only commonplace words should be used. This notion is dispatched in the advertisement shown in Figure 15–5. It is writing at its best.

Any message intended for broad dissemination merits skill and care in its composition.

Get the audience involved

Often, the casual observer suggests that all advertising should be objective, that it should just give the "cold, hard facts." This, of course, overlooks the subjective nature of human behavior, which is guided more by personal needs for security, love, esteem, and self-expression than by cold, hard facts. Therefore, the copywriter, working with the forces of motivation, should get the audience personally and subjectively involved in the message. Personal involvement can be induced in many ways. The reader who sees in an advertisement a picture of a person just like *himself* in a situation just like *his own* speaking *his kind* of language is likely to get involved. Another approach is to build a mental picture in the reader's imagination and make it so clear that he can easily project himself into the picture. Note the vivid scene created in these opening paragraphs from the advertisement illustrated in Figure 15–5.

> This is Henry VII's chapel in Westminster Abbey. These windows have filtered the sunlight of five centuries. They have also seen the crowning of twenty-two kings.
>
> Three monarchs rest here now. Henry, Elizabeth, and Mary. Such are their names in sleep. No titles. No triumphs. The banners hang battleheavy and becalmed. But still the royal crown remains. *Honi soit qui mal y pense.*

Another way to get the audience member involved is to get him "into the action." Use second person singular and active verbs. Let each audience member participate in the experience of being there, of using the product, and enjoying its benefits. Note again how the copy in Figure 15–5 involves the reader.

> When you go to Britain, make yourself this promise. Visit at least *one* of the thirty great cathedrals. Their famous names thunder! Durham and Armagh. Or they chime! Lincoln and Canterbury. And sometimes they *whisper*. Winchester, Norwich, Salisbury, and Wells. Get a map and make your choice.

In the automobile business there is an old saying that if you can "get the customer behind the wheel" he will be well on the way to being sold. Whenever advantageous the copywriter should strive to get the audience member "behind the wheel."

Be sincere

The writer who fully believes in the merits of the product and recognizes its want-satisfying qualities is more likely to write a convincing advertisement than the writer who doubts its worth. To be sure himself he should become thoroughly informed about the product's composition, construction, performance, etc. He should digest all research reports on laboratory tests and consumer-use tests. Whenever possible he should examine the product first hand and use it himself. He might find that talking with consumers who have used it and noting their reactions as expressed in their own words will give him a sharper view of its perceived merits. Leo Burnett said there is an "inherent drama" in every product. The copywriter's job is to find that drama and stage it simply and sincerely.

Sincerity is largely a matter of respect for the other person. One is not likely to deceive one's friends. The copywriter should respect the tastes and desires of his audience even though their tastes and desires might be different from his own. Instead of writing to a mass of anonymous people he should write to an individual person, much as he would write to a friend. If he remembers that advertisements are read, heard, and/or seen by individuals, not by crowds, he might be more inclined to write as though he were writing a personal letter and as a result write more sincerely.

Consider the element of sincerity in other lines of human action, such as the host welcoming guests or bidding them goodnight; the "I do" in a mock wedding versus the same statement at the altar; the inflection of voice and facial expression of the star actor versus the amateur. Sincerity gives life and personality, as well as conviction, to the advertising message. It can be recognized in illustrations and copy alike. It may mean the difference between success and failure.

Invite action

If copy is successful, it will produce action leading to a purchase by the reader. The writer should therefore inject into copy words or phrases that will help to impel action. This may often be done by suggestion, implied or direct. Contrast the headline "El Producto Cigars" with "Smoke El Producto Cigars." The latter suggests that the reader actually smoke the advertised product. In the case of mail-order copy, the invitation to act should be direct. Action in such copy can be made easier by the use of a coupon.

The urge to action in advertising copy is not unlike the element of "closing" in personal selling. In either case, complete success has not been attained until a sale has been made. Examples of phrases that might be used to suggest action would include: "See your dealer today," "Get some this week," "Ask your dealer for a demonstration," "Send for a copy of this booklet."

Form and style

There are a number of classifications of copy that might be made. We could look at copy as either classified (want-ads) or display, retail or general, direct action or indirect action. Copy might also be classified into such forms as "reason why," emotional, news, announcements, imaginative, personal, or narrative. While copy might be so classified, such procedure often leads the writer into difficulty. Instead of focusing attention on the form of copy, consideration should be given, first, to the type of consumer to whom the message is to be directed and, then, to the preparation of the copy in terms of the characteristics and emotional makeup of that particular consumer group. True, some consumers can best be made to recognize the want-satisfying qualities of a product by reading emotional copy; others must have a logical and factual presentation of the product's qualities. Although purchases of industrial equipment will usually demand "reason-why" copy, the copywriter will obtain better results if he writes informationally to a prospective purchaser than if he follows a "reason-why" copy formula.

One successful advertising practitioner states:

> I don't . . . demand ability to write or even to recognize "Reason Why" copy. Or to differentiate "Narrative" from "News." Or "Personal" from "Poster." All this knowledge won't do you any harm. But, in practical work, it will do you astonishingly little good. . . . Not once in a quarter of a century of buying advertising, selling advertising, writing copy for myself and others, have I happened to hear anybody say, "We'll run six half-pages of didactic copy." Or "Rush me up six columns of good sound colloquial." So write whatever words will clearly and forcefully deliver your message and waste no time worrying as to what type of copy it may turn out to be.[17]

The classification of copy into types also tends to encourage the writer to follow a particular type in preparing copy for a given advertisement when, in fact, many of the most successful advertisements are a mixture of types. Reasons for purchase can be, and often are, presented in a narrative or emotional manner. Factual copy is not necessarily entirely "reason why." Therefore, do not write copy by formula, but, rather, write sincere and simple copy, keyed to the desires of a particular consumer group.

There is no single best style of writing for all advertising. A style that is appropriate for perfume would hardly be appropriate in an ad for motor oil. Just as the consumer's perceptions and attitudes are different with respect to different products so should the style of writing be different. If the product is utilitarian and thought of in rational, deliberate, and objective terms, the copy should be rational, detailed, and logical. If the product is viewed in personal, emotional, and subjective terms, then copy should be written in those terms.

Rudolf Flesch has focused attention on the element of readability through his formula for measuring "reading ease." Flesch recommends for easy reading the use of short sentences, words with one or few syllables, and high human interest. He gets the latter through the use of personal words and sentences. Formulas such as those developed by Flesch can be helpful but should not be followed blindly. It is vital, however, to ask continually: "Will this copy be easily understood by the reader?"

How long should copy be? Again it depends on the consumers' perceptions of the product category. If the product is a chewing gum or a soft drink, consumers are not seeking much information, so the copy should be short. If, on the other hand, you are advertising an electric dishwasher

---

[17] Goode, *Modern Advertising,* pp. 142–43.

or a refrigerator, give consumers the more detailed information they want. David Ogilvy makes a strong case for long copy:

> There is a universal belief in lay circles that people won't read long copy. Nothing could be farther from the truth. . . . I once wrote a page of solid text for Good Luck Margarine, with most gratifying results.
>
> Research shows that readership falls off rapidly up to 50 words of copy, but drops very little between 50 and 500 words. In my first Rolls-Royce advertisement I used 719 words—piling one fascinating fact on another. In the last paragraph I wrote, "People who feel diffident about driving a Rolls-Royce can buy a Bentley." Judging from the number of motorists who picked up the word "diffident" and bandied it about, I concluded that the advertisement was thoroughly read. In the next one I used 1400 words.[18]

If a product lends itself to objective tests, the results of such tests can often be used effectively in copy; but exact or odd, rather than round, numbers should be quoted in such cases. Thus, the statement, "19.6 miles per gallon of gasoline from a run of 100 miles at an average speed of 34.2 miles per hour," will carry greater conviction than the general statement, "about 20 miles per gallon of gasoline." Where specifications can be given in terms the consumer can easily understand, earnestness of purpose on the part of the advertiser is readily accepted by the reader.

An adroit and honest use of testimonial can often add to the feeling of sincerity impaired by copy. The forthright statement of a user of a product may well be more convincing than the same statement by the seller. That is particularly true when such statements come unsolicited and in the user's own words. This type of copy is frequently used in advertisements directed to farmers (see Figure 15–6). As O. B. Stauffer, advertising manager of the American Steel and Wire Company says, "Farmers are interested in other farmers and what they have to say. Testimonial copy has a high rate of believability with them."[19]

Comparative advertising, in which an advertiser names the names of his competitors and tells you precisely why he thinks his product is better, recently has been encouraged by the Federal Trade Commission. "Our thinking is that it's healthier to have the virtues of a product debated on the air rather than simply having advertisers use the latest sex symbol or sports figure to endorse their products," said FTC aide Gerald Thain.[20] Point-by-point comparisons can be persuasive because a challenge to a well-known brand attracts attention and places the challenger in the same league with the leader (Avis Inc.'s "We Try Harder"). However, any claim of superiority must be substantiated, which is not easy to do inasmuch as product differences, as perceived by the consumer, are largely subjective.

[18] Ogilvy, *Confessions of Advertising Man,* pp. 108–9.
[19] *Rural Marketing,* January 1952, p. 1.
[20] "So Long, Brand X," *The Wall Street Journal,* December 26, 1973, p. 1.

FIGURE 15–6
Testimonial that rings true

Robert E. Thorp, DeWitt Co., Ill., started feeding Moor-
Man's Mintrates 16 years ago. He farrows four times
a year, markets 500-600 pigs, now uses MoorMan's
Hog Feeding Program from breeding to market.

"My feed cost, $8.98/cwt., sows & pigs"

"MoorMan's makes me more profit than any other feed I've used, I'm certain of that," says Bob Thorp.

"I've tried a lot of other feeds since I started feeding Mintrates* but I always come back to Moor-Man's. My records from Illinois' Farm Bureau Farm Management Service back up my own judgment.

"I just don't see how anyone can farm today without accurate records.

Cash outlay for sow's feed only $1 per pig weaned

"Last year, I weaned 8.9 pigs per litter and marketed 491 pigs that averaged 213 pounds. Because I fed Sow Mintrate for the first time, I was anxious to see what it

cost me. Here's what my records show: *Total feed cost, including sow's feed,* $8.98 per 100 pounds pork produced. *Total sow feed cost,* breeding to weaning, $3.02 per pig weaned. $1 of this went for Sow Mintrate. The rest was the value of my corn, $1.03 a bushel. That's a mighty good investment, considering the size of litters it gave me.

Mintrates release pork-making power from corn

"*Birth-to-market feed cost,* $7.58 per 100 pounds of pork. These kinds of figures make me stick to MoorMan's program."

No matter how many times a year you farrow, good records like Bob Thorp's will prove you can

boost pig profits on MoorMan's, balancing corn with Mintrates.

Mintrates' powerful blend of the best proteins, vitamins, minerals and antibiotics helps pigs digest corn more completely . . . squeeze more pork-building power from it.

Your MoorMan Man can help you do it at low cost. He'll be glad to furnish you a free Personalized Hog Feeding & Management Program tailored to your feeding method.

More profit with your own grain and

MoorMan's*

MOORMAN MFG. CO. • QUINCY, ILL.

*Trademark Reg. U.S. Pat. Off.

No single set of criteria for comparison is used by everyone. Claims and counter claims of superiority on specific points might lead to more confusion than enlightenment.

Qualities of effective copy

Much has been written and said about what it takes to make an effective advertisement. The articulation of these specifications in itself is a perennial challenge to advertising's creative people, most of whom apparently are more successful in making ads than in talking about how they do it. As with all true craftsmen they are guided by an instinctive feel that cannot be readily explained. However, much can be learned from a craftsman's observations on his work. An excellent list of such observations is the following, which was prepared by Leo Burnett to serve as guiding principles for his agency's creative people:

1. Every message in print or over the air must have "thought-force"—a central idea that offers an advantage to the reader or listener in an interesting and plausible manner. We have no patience with doubletalk or muddy thinking.
2. The reader or listener is presumably a human being, and must be rewarded in some human manner for dwelling on your message. Much advertising, we felt, was as dull as dishwater. We decided, therefore, that we would try to make our advertising "fun to look at" or listen to. Not funny—but fun in a broad, human sense. This involves what we call the "overtones" of advertising, which are hard to describe but which make the difference between an ad that lives and one that is just so-so.
3. To plan the sale as we plan the ad—to build ads so strong in selling thought and so attractive in appearance that they would find almost automatic applications at the point of sale. We have great respect for the instinctive judgment of a good salesman regarding the advertising of his firm. If he is not enthusiastic about it, it has two strikes on it going in.
4. To observe the fitness of things in terms of all-around good taste and to keep the advertising "in character" with management thought and action.
5. To take the attitude that there is inherent drama in the product itself rather than leaning on tricks, devices, or "techniques." This also involves keeping the advertising *relevant*—shunning irrelevant approaches in headlines and illustrations, no matter how clever they are.
6. Wherever possible to make important use of the advertiser's name and package rather than trying to lure people into reading our message. They know it's an ad and they like to look at good ads. Why try to fool them?
7. To keep it simple.

8. To know the rules but be willing to break them. This involves a sense of good timing—an important factor in successful advertising.
9. To have the courage to go back to the client with a better idea whenever we can find one, even if he has already ok'd the ad and is well satisfied with it. This involves a lot of wear and tear and is often expensive, but it usually pays off.
10. To keep our place free from *prima donnas;* to subordinate pride of authorship to a better overall result to which many different people may contribute.
11. To be human without being cute or smart aleck; to be sincere without being pompous.
12. To fight for what we believe in, regardless of contrary client opinion, providing our conviction is based on sound reasoning, accurate facts, and inspired thought; to be intellectually honest.[21]

As guidelines, these principles can serve the copywriter well. Ultimately, of course, the experience he gains in his own pursuit of excellence will be his best teacher.

Writing for radio

Radio offers opportunities and imposes limitations not found in print advertising. Radio offers the human voice, the most persuasive instrument of all. It is personal. Even though the radio listener is part of a large audience he can be made to feel that the message is person-to-person, that it is directed to him alone. As a listener he can become personally involved. He can interact with the message and the person delivering it. The absence of a picture lets the listener create his own mental picture, a picture of his kind of dream house or his kind of social world.

The advertiser controls when the message will be received. He can select the exact time of day best to reach his most desirable prospects, a time when they might be most receptive. The advertiser controls the speed at which the message will be received. He can have it read faster to convey excitement, news, and immediacy; or slower to convey sincerity, warmth, and friendliness. He can repeat the central idea several times to drive the point home. He can use music, songs, melodies, jingles, and sound effects to gain attention, build identity, and reinforce memory. Radio is just about everywhere. The ubiquity of small, battery-operated radios offers the opportunity to reach different audiences at all times of the day or night.

Along with the opportunities, the radio copywriter is confronted with certain limitations. The ear cannot receive as quickly as the eye, nor assimilate as much information as the eye. The radio message is fleeting;

[21] Leo Burnett, *Communications of an Advertising Man* (Chicago: Leo Burnett Company, Inc., 1961), pp. 254–55.

THE ZIPPO—MADE BY A TOUGH, UNRECONSTRUCTED AMERICAN CRAFTSMAN—WHO BELIEVES A LIGHTER SHOULD LAST A LIFETIME.

THE INCREDIBLE STORY OF THE ZIPPO LIGHTER

—and a man who believes a lighter should work <u>forever</u>

The man who made the first Zippo, and who still runs the show, learned his trade in his father's machine shop.

He developed manual skills. He mastered the sweet science of machinery. And he learned one thing more.

He learned to love and respect workmanship for its own sake. He became a craftsman in the 19th Century American tradition—the breed of men who made things that worked. And lasted. For a long, long time.

Today, he makes a cigarette lighter that works. The Zippo. He constructs each Zippo so carefully that he is able to offer the most sweeping guarantee in the annals of American business.

If a Zippo ever fails to work—he'll fix it free!

Some modern businessmen who make products that become obsolete on a schedule don't have much respect for the Zippo man's business sense.

But he does pretty well. And he has a rare good feeling when he goes to bed each night. The feeling that comes from making a product that *works*. Every time. Year after year. Generation after generation.

Always—or he fixes it free.

ZIPPO MANUFACTURING COMPANY, BRADFORD, PA. IN CANADA: ZIPPO MANUFACTURING COMPANY, CANADA LTD:, NIAGARA FALLS, ONTARIO

FIGURE 15–7. An incredible story credibly told

here this minute, gone the next. Whereas the reader can reread the print message at will, only the sender of the radio message can repeat it. Whatever pictures are created must be created essentially with words. The radio listener usually gives only divided attention. The housewife listens while ironing, while cleaning, while sewing, while reading. Standards of broadcasting practice generally demand that the message be brief. A one-minute commercial allows about 150 words.

All the principles of planning and writing advertising copy discussed thus far also apply to radio. However, the unique characteristics of this medium call for special handling. A few points to keep in mind are:

1. *Open with an appeal to listener's self-interest.* The first words spoken must gain initial attention and promise a reward for listening further. The first few words must do what the print ad's headline and illustration do. We hear what we want to hear.

2. *Talk person-to-person.* Address your message to an individual, not a crowd. Make it like a telephone call instead of a public announcement; like a conversation instead of an exhortation.

FIGURE 15–8
Straight radio commercial

THE ADVERTISING COUNCIL, INC.

Department of Labor -- Continue Your Education Campaign

ONE-MINUTE RADIO SPOT #2

ANNOUNCER

Read any good want ads lately? Like -- "Major corporation has opening for high school graduate"? Or -- "Trainees -- Fee Paid -- High School Graduates"? Or -- "Minimum requirement -- High School Graduate"? Those companies will get their pick of graduates, too. 7 out of 10 people applying for work have finished high school. One quarter have even been to college. Sure, there are jobs for people who quit. But not many. And if you want to make real money -- forget it. To get a good job, you need a good education. You've probably heard that a million times. But it's one of those cliches that is absolutely true. So if you're in school, stay there. If you've quit, go now to your State Employment Service or Youth Opportunity Center. They'll tell you how to get more training. And if you don't think you need all the training you can get ... better read the want ads again.

---

3. *Concentrate on one theme.* It is better to develop a single idea fully and reinforce it through repetition than to touch on several ideas superficially. Keep detailed technical information to a minimum.

4. *Get the listener involved.* Describe the product, service, or experience in subjective terms, in the listener's language. Let him think along with the message as it is spoken. Make it fit readily into his world.

5. *Use the rhythm of conversation.* Use short sentences, simple structure, few qualifying clauses. Use words that are easy to pronounce, easy to hear. Read the message aloud. Does it track? Is it easy to follow, easy to understand, easy to remember?

These guidelines apply mainly to the straight commercial, the kind that is read without embellishment by one person. See Figure 15–8. Other forms include dialogue, dramatized slice-of-life, jingles, and various kinds of off-beat or humorous commercials. These other forms offer special opportunities to deliver a message in a refreshing and unobtrusive way. However, they also involve the risk of succeeding as entertainment while failing as advertising.

Writing for television

A hundred people can be involved in the production of a single television commercial, but the whole process generally begins with the copywriter. The television copywriter's contribution is his ability to think in both advertising terms and the medium's terms. He understands the marketing and communication objectives to be achieved. He develops the message idea. Then he draws on the myriad of elements of cinematography—the visual, aural, and optical elements—to plan an effective television advertisement. He functions much as a playwright or a motion picture script writer does. He not only writes what the characters in the play are to say, he also develops the plot, visualizes the scenes, plans the action, and writes instructions to the producer, the director, the performers, and the technicians who are to make his ideas come alive. One view is that writing for television is easy because there is so much to work with: sight, sound, motion, and sequential development of an idea. Another view is that such writing is difficult because there are so many variables to learn how to use. Easy or not, writing for television demands specialized knowledge and skills, far too specialized to be detailed here. Thus, this brief discussion will deal only with some of the more basic basics.

The audio portion of the television commercial should embody the qualities of an effective radio commercial. It should be personal, simple, and direct. More than this, however, the aural must work *with* the visual. Let the picture do the talking too. Let the story unfold visually with the commentary playing a supporting role. Seeing is believing.

Visual elements include the setting—whether a studio set or "on location''—the visual props, the performer, his movements, gestures, and facial expressions. Of course, how the product is to be displayed or demonstrated is a vital visual consideration.

The camera is a versatile instrument. It serves as the eyes of the viewing audience, looking where the writer wants the audience to look, seeing what he wants them to see. Inasmuch as he writes camera instructions, the writer needs to understand the language of the camera and what it can do. The basic unit of camera usage is the *shot*. A shot is as long as or as short as a single viewpoint is sustained. Some of the more commonly used camera shots are:

1. *Establishing shot*—a view of the whole set or location to establish in the viewer's mind the place, time, and situation.
2. *LS* (*long shot*)—taken from a distance showing a panoramic view or large sweep of background.
3. *MS* (*medium shot*)—a closer view concentrating on one subject head to feet.
4. *CU* (*close-up*)—head and shoulders or equivalent.
5. *ECU* (*extreme close-up*)—head alone or even closer, concentrating on one feature or detail.
6. *Dolly in or dolly out*—the camera moves slowly in toward action or slowly backs away.
7. *Trucking shot*—the camera moves along parallel to the action such as moving along side a person walking or a moving automobile.
8. *Pan*—the camera remains stationary but scans horizontally from one side to the other.

A change from one shot to another may be to change the point of view on the same action, or to change the scene. Changing the shot and/or the scene may be essential to telling the story. It also adds interest and movement to the message. Too many scene changes, however, will confuse the viewer and splinter his attention. Some typical transitions are:

1. *Cut*—an instantaneous change from one camera to another.
2. *Dissolve*—one scene fades out as another fades in. Is less abrupt than a cut and establishes a more continuous, quieter mood.
3. *Fade to black*—one scene fades out completely until screen is black and then another scene fades in. Makes a strong break between the two.
4. *Wipe*—wiping one picture off the screen as another picture appears. Many wipe patterns are available. The wipe can move from left to right, top to bottom, edges to center, center to edges, etc.

In addition, a wide variety of optical effects such as dissolves, fades, and wipes can be used to complicate or simplify the task, depending on one's attitude toward gadgetry. A danger, of course, is that the gadgetry might detract from the message.

FIGURE 15-9
Storyboard for one in a series of outstanding television commercials

FIGURE 15-9 *(Continued)*

The most widely used form of script presentation is the *storyboard*. As illustrated in Figure 15–8, a storyboard is a series of small sketches with accompanying description of action and the words to be spoken or sung. The sketches show only the major scene changes. The verbal copy is complete. The storyboard forces the copywriter to think visually as well as verbally and to coordinate the two. With the help of an artist who refines the sketches, the copywriter uses the storyboard to present his ideas to the advertiser. Once approved, the storyboard serves as a guide to the producer, director, set designer, film editor, etc., whose interpretations are critical to the commercial's success. Because of a rather rigid division of labor along the long route from writer to eventual broadcast, it is important that the storyboard portray the writer's ideas as clearly as possible. At the same time, the writer should not be so specific that he stifles the creative contributions of the various specialists along the way.

As any television viewer knows, there are many kinds of TV commercials. Without attempting to name them all, they basically are live, filmed, or taped. A live commercial is seen on the viewer's screen at the same time it is taking place before the television camera. A filmed commercial is recorded on sound motion picture film for subsequent broadcast. Filmed commercials can be either live action or animation. A taped commercial is recorded on magnetic or "videotape." The Green Giant commercial depicted in Figure 15–8 is an example of animation with a live-action long shot of a real person portraying the Green Giant in the fourth frame. To produce this scene a miniature valley was built of styrofoam hills, artificial grass, and crepe paper cornstalks. Then the real person was photographed standing in the miniature valley. He could move his arms, shoulders, and head. He could bend over to pick something up. He could smile and go "HO HO HO." But he couldn't walk.

The Green Giant advertising strategy has been eminently successful. As stated by the creative director on the account, Robert Noel of the Leo Burnett Company, the strategy is simply to "try to create a strong television personality for the brand, and sell the individual items for their specific appeals within the framework."[22]

Huntley Baldwin has developed a useful model for creating television commercials. He has organized selling ideas, basic tones or approaches, techniques of demonstration, and production techniques in a chart he refers to as "Select-A-Spot."[23] The chart and his description of various techniques of demonstration are reproduced here.

[22] Robert J. Noel, *The Big Idea, Nine Case Histories of Successful Advertising Campaigns Based on Big Creative Ideas* (New York: American Association of Advertising Agencies, 1966), p. 28.

[23] H. Huntley Baldwin, *How Television Commercials Are Made* (Evanston, Ill.: Department of Advertising, Northwestern University, 1970), pp. 17–22.

"Select-a-Spot"—A handy chart for starting commercial ideas

A. The Selling Idea (What to Demonstrate)

1. New product concept	12. Quality
2. New product model	13. Economy
3. New product feature	
4. New form, size, package	14. "Creating" problem
5. Ingredients	15. Results of not using
6. Manufacturing process	16. Results of using
7. Company (image)	*a.* tangible
8. Where product is made	*b.* intangible
	17. Users' life style
9. Major use(s)	18. Users' dedication/loyalty
10. Versatility	19. Users' satisfaction
11. Convenience	20. Number of users

B. Basic Tone or Approach

1. Straightforward   2. Lightly humorous   3. Wildly exaggerated

C. Technique of Demonstration

1. *Product alone.* The simplest way to demonstrate what a product can do is to show the product doing it. This can be done in a natural setting (shampooing a rug on the floor of a home) or in "limbo," free of background or atmosphere, where all attention is clearly focused on the product. (See Tums commercial on pages 326 and 327.)

2. *Spokesman.* Generally, there will be some kind of "off camera" spokesman accompanying a "product alone" demonstration, explaining what is happening on the screen. But the spokesman can take a more prominent role and appear on camera. He can be an announcer or not-really-familiar face (Avis, for example); he can be "real folks"; he can be a celebrity (for example, Arthur Godfrey speaking for Axion); he can be a corporate symbol (for example, Pillsbury's dough boy). (See Vicks Vaporub commercial on pages 328 and 329.)

3. *Before-and-after.* "See this dirty stain? . . . Watch while we add our product . . . there . . . stain's gone!" *Before,* women were not allowed to smoke, but then *after* (many years and the introduction of Virginia Slims) "you've got your own cigarette now, baby. . . ."

4. *Torture test.* The diver plunges from the cliffs of Acapulco and his Timex watch comes up ticking. A Bic pen is attached to the heel of an ice skater, skated around the rink, then stuck in an open flame and still "writes first time, every time." A rod attached to the wheel of a Ford truck shatters a row of light bulbs while the

rod attached to the cab (insulated by Ford shock absorbers) leaves its row of bulbs untouched. (See American Tourister commercial on pages 328 and 329.)

5. *Side-by-side.* A commercial for RCA color television begins with a close-up of a girl's face which then splits in half vertically. The "RCA half" of the screen remains clear while the "Brand X half" of the screen demonstrates common types of interference. A Volkswagen commercial begins with a shot of two suburban houses. The owner of one pulls up in his brand new $3,000 car, then looks on while a series of deliverymen wheel expensive appliances into his neighbor's house. Finally, the neighbor arrives in his brand new Volkswagen which he was able to buy with the money left over from his $3,000 after buying all the appliances. (See Commonwealth Edison commercial on pages 326 and 327.)

6. *Slice-of-life.* This is the dramatized situation in which the product saves the people from their real-life problem. "Big date tonight but about my breath"—"Don't worry, Charlie, gargle with this. . . ."—(That night, at the prom) "Thanks for the tip, pal, my love life is great again." The friendly advice can come from a wife or neighbor or a continuing character who is an expert on the subject (Josephine the plumber, Madge the manicurist, Wanda the witch, for example). (See Cheer commercial on pages 326 and 327.)

7. *Vignettes.* Instead of a long look at one person's problem, try a series of short (usually amusing) looks at a lot of different people's problem—The disadvantages of Benson & Hedges, the overweight people for Diet Rite Cola ("What've you got to lose?"), the people "covering up" embarrassment for Right Guard deodorant.

8. *Testimonial.* This is a variation on the "spokesman" approach. In this case the "spokesman" may interview a satisfied user who becomes the real spokesman, such as Ed Reimers talking with satisfied Allstate policy holders. The testimonial can be "unsolicited" and "unstaged" (such as talking to airline passengers about their flight as they arrive at the airport), or it can be delivered by a known personality (sincerely or tongue in cheek).

9. *Documentary.* This approach can be used to dramatize the problem (for example, "When there's no man around, Goodyear should be") or to document the product's performance (for example, the Mobil Economy Run and similar events). The camera seems to be reporting on real people rather than observing a minute drama. (See Volkswagen commercial on pages 328 and 329.)

10. *Symbolism.* If the idea or appeal is abstract or intangible, the demonstration may have to be symbolic rather than literal. Tupperware, for example, demonstrated "locks in freshness" by putting a combination lock on a ham, a zipper on an ear of corn, etc. Bayer Aspirin used light music and lacy-line animation to symbolize happiness and a menacing black shape to show headache pain.

11. *Fantasy.* In the world of exaggeration, almost anything is possible. Hai Karate after shave has such a passionate effect on women that the men who use it have a special training ground to learn self-defense. The Green Giant and his helpers live in a world of fantasy. And did ye ever hear the one about the dove who thought he was a hand lotion . . . ?

12. *Analogy.* Again, you can't actually show the effect of the product so you compare it with something you can show. "Cleans like a white tornado," "like sending your sinuses to Arizona," light up and "it's springtime."

D. Production Technique

1. Live action   2. Animation   3. Stop motion
4. Combinations   5. Special effects

A primary factor in selecting the kind of commercial is cost, which can vary from less than a hundred dollars for a single live commercial to a hundred thousand dollars for a spectacular production using expensive sets and expensive talent. Ultimately, however, the cost should be measured in terms of sales results, a standard of performance that always should be uppermost in the copywriter's mind.

TUMS	CHEER	COMMONWEALTH EDISON
Audio: 30 sec.	Audio: 60 sec.	Audio: 20 sec.
(A) VO: If you ever suffer from acid indigestion, this little tablet contains one of the most effective medicines ever discovered for it.	Mother: OK, Harold. When you go away to college you'll have to wash all your crazy clothes. Harold: I thought you just put them in the machine. Mother: There's more to laundry than that. Today's clothes have changed. Look at these things. These fabrics. These colors. You've got to use the right temperature.	Anncr: These two big roasts started out even.
(B) In tests at a famous college, it proved to neutralize excess acid in a matter of seconds.	Harold: Sure, Mom. Mother: You see this tag? Harold: Sure, it goes on all my clothes.	Both the same cut, the same weight.
(C) Prepared for a little shock?	Mother: No, this one---permanent press. Wash it in warm water. This crazy things's a bright color, and I don't want to see it all faded. Use cold water. Harold: When do I use hot water? Mother: You use it on white things. Harold: I need three detergents?	The one on the right was cooked in an electric oven.
(D) It's Tums.	Mother: No, Harold. Three temperatures, one detergent. All temperature Cheer. It's specially made to really clean in all those temperatures. Hot, warm or cold, use all temperature Cheer. Do it evenly. Don't stop!	It's kept more of its weight ...more of what you pay for by the pound.
(E) Now in five flavors.	Harold: Hey, Mom, it did work in all temperatures. This shirt looks groovy. Mother: You're a good son, Harold.	When there's a lot less shrinkage in your roast, that's electric cooking.
(F) It'll make your stomach feel better....now!	Anncr: All temperature Cheer for the way you wash now. Mother: All temperature, Harold.	Commonwealth Edison... concerned for your total environment.
(music under)		(music under)

TUMS   CHEER   COMMONWEALTH
                                    EDISON

VICKS VAPORUB Audio: 30 sec.	VOLKSWAGEN Audio: 60 sec.	AMERICAN TOURISTER Audio: 30 sec.
(A) Anncr: Night falls on a congested child. He's miserable. Nose clogged...chest bothers him too. He can't sleep.	(SFX. Stamping of boots, slamming of car door, starting of engine, car driving through snow)	(SFX of a gorilla in the background)
(B) Many cold medicines aren't recommended for young children.	Anncr: Ever wonder how the man who drives the snowplow drives to the snowplow?	Anncr: Dear clumsy bellboys....
(C) Vicks Vaporub is.	This one drives a Volkswagen.	Brutal cabdrivers.... Careless doormen....
(D) It relieves congestion for up to eight hours.	(SFX of a car door slamming)	Ruthless porters.... Savage baggagemasters....
(E) Your child breathes better ...feels better.	(SFX of snowplow starting)	And all butterfingered luggage handlers all over the world:
(F) Vicks Vaporub...an effective decongestant for the miseries of colds.	So you can stop wondering.	Have we got a suitcase for you!

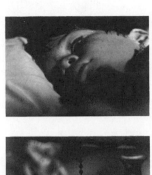

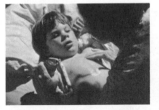

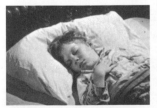

QUESTIONS AND PROBLEMS

1 How does positioning differ from image building?

2 Select two advertisements in the package goods field that position the product clearly. Select two that do not do so.

3 Clip three advertisements that are product centered and three that are user centered. Contrast the copy of each group.

4 Knowledge of the life-style patterns of the intended audience can be very useful to the copywriter. Explain and demonstrate.

5 Under what circumstances would you recommend a straightforward approach for a television commercial? A lightly humorous approach? A wildly exaggerated approach?

6 Among the television commercials you recall having seen, cite examples of the various techniques of demonstration included in Huntley Baldwin's chart.

7 Discuss the meaning and significance of "writing inside out."

8 Write an advertisement for the writing instrument you are now using.

9 You undoubtedly have a close friend, relative, parent, teacher, or school official whom you believe should be doing something that is not now being done. Maybe you want a friend to go camping or hiking with you, your parents to take a vacation for their own pleasure, a teacher to give fewer quizzes or examinations, or a school official to grant a longer Thanksgiving or Easter vacation. There is a possibility, too, that you might want some one of your friends or associates to recognize the logic and wisdom of your beliefs concerning a political party, a religious faith, racial tolerance, freedom of business enterprise, the beauties of music, or the fundamental values of advertising.

In any event, select some topic or idea about which you hold strong personal beliefs. Pick out, in your own mind, some one person that you know personally and who you think would increase his or her own happiness by accepting your belief.

Write a personal letter designed to convince him or her of the benefits that would follow the acceptance of your ideas. Let your letter be as long and as persuasive as you wish, keeping in mind always the personality of the individual to whom you are writing.

10 From each of the following pairs of advertisements select the one which you think was more effective in generating inquiries or producing sales.

Pair 1

Pair 2

Photos courtesy of Schwab, Beatty, & Porter, Inc.

Pair 3

Photos courtesy of Schwab, Beatty, & Porter, Inc.

Pair 4

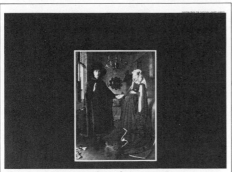

Pair 5

Pair 6

16

Illustrating the advertisement

Early attempts of mankind to transmit ideas consisted of drawing pictures in the sand and scratching pictures on rocks. Today, with the technological achievements of the graphic arts and television industries, pictures have become the most universal language. Frequent exposure to the visual media—especially television, the most visual medium of all—has made us a visual-minded people. The places we have seen, the people we know, the things we have encountered are pictured in our memories. Even the places, people, and things we have seen only in the media become part of our visual record of experience.

"Seeing is believing"; "A picture is worth a thousand words"—expressions such as these attest to the importance of this form of communication. Whereas words are abstractions, pictures represent reality. Seeing is more convincing than being told. The chances of being deceived by a picture are thought to be less than by words. In fact, many words and verbal descriptions are intended to create a mental picture. Just as we are concerned about appearances—how we appear to others—we judge products, services, and their sellers by how they appear to us. Obviously, the visual content of advertising is vitally important.

Visual content

First and foremost, the visual content of the print ad or television commercial should sustain the total impression intended. It should work with

FIGURE 16–1
West Michigan's story told in words

FIGURE 16–2
Wisconsin's story told in pictures

WEST Michigan is the BEST Michigan

It's a delightful playground that stretches along 400 miles of Lake Michigan coastline, from the state's southern boundary to the Straits Of Mackinac and Mighty Mac Bridge. It's a 31-county area with thousands of inland lakes and hundreds of miles of sparkling rivers and streams — an area that abounds with clean well-kept parks, countless places of historical and scenic interest, festive summer events by the dozens. It's a vacation land that boasts excellent accommodations to fit any budget, and that offers recreational facilities to please every taste. All it really lacks is YOU!

SEND TODAY FOR CAREFREE DAYS
FREE
VACATION GUIDE TO WEST MICHIGAN

172 Pages Packed with Information and Ideas

• Recommended Motels, American Plan Resorts, Cottage Resorts • Recommended Restaurants • Calendar of Festive Events • Places to Go and Things to See • Golf Courses • Fishing Information • Summer Theaters

7-1

WEST MICHIGAN TOURIST ASSOCIATION
Dept. 11, 107 Pearl St., N.W., Grand Rapids, Mich. 49502
Please send me my CAREFREE DAYS.

Name_____

Street_____

City_____

State_____   We must have
                        your Zip Code_____
          (Please type or print)

WISCONSIN IS:
everything you expected...

and then some!

Wisconsin has scenery in such variety that it literally overflows its boundaries. There are Great Lakes seascapes, rolling dairylands, remarkable river dells, kettle moraines, the great Mississippi valley, forested highlands, huge wildlife refuges, and an unspoiled peninsula that's a ringer for New England.

The Indians called our state the "land of the gathering waters." (We have 8,700 lakes and 20,000 miles of rivers and streams.) Our lusty heritage of fur trading, lumber camps, and the circus world is still apparent in many worthwhile historical attractions.

Accommodations range from lavish resorts where creature-comforts are unsurpassed to wilderness campsites that will set your spirits soaring.

This summer, let your family discover Wisconsin. It's the land that was made for vacations!

You'll like it here!
SEND FOR FREE VACATION KIT. 32-page brochure with 130 full-color photos, guide maps to points of interest for the nine Wisconsin vacation areas, information about state parks and forests, things to see and do the year 'round. Also, latest highway map and sources of regional information.

WISCONSIN VACATION AND TRAVEL SERVICE
Room 86H, Box 450, Madison, Wis. 53701
Please send free Wisconsin Vacation Kit to:

Name _____

Address _____

City _____ State _____ Zip Code _____

the verbal and aural elements in carrying out the planned strategy. Functions frequently assigned to the visual element are:

1. Display the product in a setting or in use, focus on the package or label
2. Demonstrate how the product works, what it does, the results of its use
3. Highlight a product feature or features
4. Dramatize the benefit the product confers, such as greater convenience, pleasing sensation, ego gratification, social acceptance
5. Create a problem, the situation to be avoided, the situation before use of the product
6. Show the problem solved, the situation gained, the situation after use of the product
7. Portray the users, the kind of people who use the product, their lifestyle, the user image
8. Build the image of the brand, endow it with subjective values, give it a personality, position it perceptually
9. Build the image of the maker, the store or service institution, the corporate image.

Less apparent, but equally important, is the mood or feeling the picture sustains. The mood may be confident, secure, authoritative; or it may be serene, peaceful, comfortable; or stable, old, reliable; or exciting, new, adventuresome; or warm, friendly, personal; or factual, objective, scientific; and so on. Visual and verbal elements should project the same mood, and of course the mood should fit the need or desire the product fulfills as well as the attitudes of the intended audience toward such products.

In some instances the selling story is told visually (Polaroid, Benson & Hedges, Coca-Cola); in others it is told verbally. Contrast the advertisements reproduced in Figures 16–1 and 16–2. Each appeals to the same audience and advertises the recreational facilities of competing states. One depends almost entirely on pictures to tell its story while the other depends on interesting type faces in a reverse cut to bring the reader's attention to its headline and to the copy that expounds the thousands of lakes, rivers, and streams, plus the mighty Mac bridge, which is one of its main attractions. The only illustration used is one of the cover of the brochure offered free to interested readers. The words in the Wisconsin advertisement, on the other hand, merely explain in more detail the sightseeing attractions and leisure-time activities that the pictures have already shown.

Factors to consider in selection of pictures

Pictures are of little value unless they assist in getting the advertiser's story across to the reader. To do this, pictures should:

1. Be keyed to the self-interest and understanding of the reader.
2. Include all or some detail of the product.
3. Be relevant to the product and copy theme.
4. Be accurate and plausible.

Keyed to self-interest and understanding of reader   This element is the very heart of all advertising. To ignore it is to invite failure. The principle of self-interest discussed in earlier chapters applies with equal force to the selection and use of illustrations. Pictures are often as valuable as headlines in stopping readers, but only the headline or picture keyed to consumer self-interest will serve adequately to attract an appreciative audience. Note the selection of pictures in Figure 16–2 and how each one tells the vacationist of the enjoyment to be found in Wisconsin.

Pictures must also be chosen in terms of the reader's background of experience if they are to be meaningful, for they can convey as little meaning to some as a foreign language. What would a geology map, a germ culture under the microscope, or an unlabeled map of the starry heavens mean to the layman? Yet some pictures used in advertisements hold as little meaning for the reader. If the product advertised is unknown, it must be explained in words and pictures that are known by the reader.

Empathy, the imaginative projection of one's own consciousness into another human being, can be effectively used in advertising art. The reader or viewer is more apt to project himself or become emotionally involved in illustrations that depict his kind of people doing true-to-life things in familiar situations. Playing upon the advancement of women's rights, the pictures in the Virginia Slims ad (Figure 16–3) quickly dramatize the difference between ''her'' world ''then'' and ''now.''

Include all or some of the product   Keyed advertisements have demonstrated that a picture of the product, in whole or in part, is productive of the greatest returns. There are exceptions in the case of products that are entirely new, or in the case of services where there is nothing to reproduce. Most people wish to see what they are buying and wish sales arguments (aids to buying) built around the product. Such illustrations may be in terms of what the product will do, how it will perform, how to use and care for it, etc. But in all such cases, there seems to be value in getting the reader's attention and interest focused on the product itself. The experience of any mail-order house will bear rich testimony to the importance of accurately illustrating the product.

When the product offers a benefit as obvious as the one portrayed in Figure 16–4, choice of illustrations is a relatively simple matter. Showing Foster Grant's Spectra-Shades in three kinds of light—indoors, cloudy, and sunny—clearly demonstrates ''the brighter the light the darker they get.''

Note also the manner in which the construction of Atlas Steelcron tires is illustrated in Figure 16–5. Understanding and, hence, believability are

FIGURE 16–3
Pictures dramatize copy theme

"When the after dinner cigars were passed and the political discussions began,
she would rise gracefully and lead the ladies to the sitting room."

Now you can sit through dessert,
coffee, and long after
with your own slim cigarette.

Virginia Slims.

This is the slim cigarette made just
for women. Blended with the kind
of flavor you'll like. Full, rich Virginia
flavor. Tailored slimmer than the fat
cigarettes men smoke. Extra long.
In the distinctive striped pack.
Regular or Menthol.

You've come
a long way, baby.

FIGURE 16–4
Product benefit clearly portrayed

FIGURE 16–5
Cross-section view shows product construction

Atlas® STEELCRON:
THE FIRST SECOND-GENERATION STEEL BELTED TIRE.

NOT JUST STEEL CORD.
BUT 2 BELTS OF
BRASS COATED STEEL CORD.
FOR EXTRA PROTECTION.
LONGER LIFE.

NOT JUST CONVENTIONAL
MOLDING. BUT
CONCAVE MOLDING.
TO PUT MORE
WIDE-TREAD TO
WORK FOR YOU.
FOR LESS SHOW
AND MORE ROAD
CONTACT.

NOT JUST FACE TREAD
BUT SIDE TREAD TOO.
FOR EXTRA CONTROL
WHEN YOU NEED
IT MOST.

NOT JUST QUALITY
CHECKED, BUT ELEC-
TRONICALLY CHECKED
FOR MINUTE FORCE
VARIATIONS. FOR AN
AMAZINGLY SMOOTH
RIDE AT ALL SPEEDS.

Cured in
concave
mold.

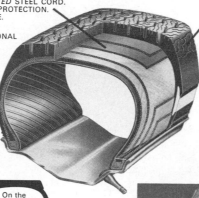

On the
road you have
maximum road
contact.

The Atlas Steelcron Tire. Now you can feel a
new sense of security. A new riding comfort. Because
we didn't rush to be first with a steel belted tire.

We waited, then tested, evaluated, and created what we
call the first second-generation steel belted. With the
best features of the first generation. And with second
generation advances to give you even better
performance.

So now put the second-generation steel belted tire on
your car. The Atlas Steelcron. See your Standard
Dealer. And charge it with your Standard Credit Card.

STANDARD

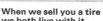
**When we sell you a tire
we both live with it.**

SO Standard Oil Division of Amoco Oil Company

FIGURE 16–6
Illustration and copy theme only remotely connected

A good letterhead reflects your most outstanding qualities.

Everyone has something that makes him stand out a little from the next person.

Take Cyrano's nose. It's not beautiful by a long shot. But one look at his letterhead and you know who he is.

A good letterhead is like that. It says something about the sender, even before the letter itself says a word.

And your company letterhead should do the same. After all, your letterhead is you.

That's why it's so important to make sure that it makes a good impression.

Of course, good letterheads begin with the paper they're printed on. Which is why Hammermill Bond is a great way to begin.

It's beautifully white and clean. Impressively opaque. And gives off an important crackle to the touch.

Ask your printer to show you samples. In white and 16 colors (all with matching Hammermill Bond envelopes), three finishes, and a wide range of weights.

Look for the Hammermill Bond watermark, it's our word of honor to the public.

Hammermill Paper Company, Erie, Pennsylvania 16512.

FIGURE 16–7
One of a series effectively visualizing campaign theme

FIGURE 16–8
Illustration dramatizes copy theme

enhanced by providing a cross-section view. Construction details are effectively described in picture and words.

Relevant to the product and copy theme   Too often advertisers have looked upon pictures as a means of attracting attention and nothing else. Selection has often been made in terms of what would be most likely to attract a large audience rather than what would attract an audience interested in the advertised product. Pictures should support the copy theme and not detract from it.

It is assumed, of course, that the copy theme is well chosen and is worthy of support. When that is not the case, both theme and illustration might be changed with profit. Note the illustration in Figure 16–6. In an obvious attempt to be clever, there is only a remote connection between Cyrano's nose and Hammermill Bond letterhead. Contrast the advertisements in Figures 16–7 and 16–8 with the Hammermill Bond ad. Benson & Hedges' visual play-on-words is consistent with the tone of a lightly humorous campaign. The illustration in Figure 16–8 clearly dramatizes the theme, "Gentlemen prefer Hanes."

Accurate and plausible   Every detail of a picture should be checked to see whether it is technically accurate, plausible to the reader, and in harmony with the reader's background of experience. Women do not, as a rule, wear high-heeled shoes and silk dresses when washing, cleaning house, cooking, or performing other household duties; yet, some advertisements picture them in such attire. The majority of farm folk do not attend parties in formal clothes; yet some advertisements in farm magazines picture people in formal dress. Such illustrations do not accurately portray the idea the advertising man was striving to get across to the reader.

If the picture is one of the product, care must be exercised to make it a faithful reproduction. A mail-order house had an exceptionally large number of shoes returned because the color was significantly different from that reproduced in the catalog. Nurseries selling fruit trees have lost business because the trees would not produce the kind of fruit pictured in the catalog. Pictures are more understandable than words, and exaggeration in them is more disastrous than similar exaggeration in words.

Color

The use of color in products offered the consumer has increased tremendously during the past few years. Color has come into the home and office as well as into the fields of pleasure and recreation. This increased use of color is in harmony with fundamental human attributes. It has enabled manufacturers to increase the want-satisfying qualities of products by adding life, spirit, attractiveness, warmth, coolness, and formality to them according to the color combinations employed. Color influences the

JAMAICA

The near place–with faraway pleasures.

Pack a bag and run away to Negril where you'll find 7 deserted miles of beach. Plus rum punch, lobster and a hammock.

Here's the place to feel unpressured.

And young.

At Negril, you laze on isolated sands. Nibble simple foods. Play in a tropical sea. (We're *south* of the Bahamas.)

The only businessman in sight is a seashell-seller.

It's a hamlet of scattered dwellers. With no phones.

No floor shows.

There are just 2 hotels.

You can go barefoot. *Not* dress all day. Beachcomb. Watch sunsets. Rent a tree house!

Try a little Negril.

Then drift around to our other beaches.

We have sleek hotel beaches. Coves to "discover." Beaches near golf, ten-

nis. Beaches to scuba from, Sailfish from, lunch *on*.

Even beaches to go to parties on. At night. With lanterns. Suckling pigs. Stars. Guitars. The works.

And—*wonderful*.

For more about our wonders (beaches to mountains to starry nights), see a travel agent or Jamaica Tourist Board.

Faraway Pleasures Are Far More Inviting in Color

KRAFT SALAD DAYS ARE HERE!

It's the time of year for ripeness, the time of year
for goodness. Fill your bowls with freshness . . . and celebrate!

Colorful Salads Appeal to the Eye as Well as the Appetite

Look closely and you'll even find vanilla and chocolate.

After all, man cannot live on pistachio
ice cream alone. Or rum raisin. Or
toasted almond. So Louis Sherry spices
up life with 26 varieties of French ice cream.
Including some of your old favorites.

Louis Sherry

Color Distinguishes Ten Delicious Flavors

emotional behavior of individuals; hence, if properly used, it adds measurably to the value of goods offered for sale.

Color can be used with equal profit in advertisements. Its possible functions include: (1) attracting attention, (2) assisting in the interpretation of the product, (3) giving life to an otherwise bleak-looking advertisement, and (4) emphasizing or highlighting a distinctive trademark or symbol. Note how color is used to perform these functions in the advertisements for Jamaica Tourist Board, Kraft Salad Dressings, and Louis Sherry Ice Cream.

Most emphasis has been placed on color as a factor in increasing the attention value of an advertisement. This, however, is perhaps the least valuable attribute of color, particularly in magazines where half or more of the advertisements are reproduced in color. We have already observed the overemphasis placed on the single problem of attracting attention to an advertisement. Attention is important only to the degree that readers interested in the product are attracted to the advertisement. The possible increase in attention value afforded by color is probably not worth the extra cost occasioned by its use, unless color gives some additional value to the advertisement.

The primary value of color in an advertisement is to aid in a more effective interpretation or translation of the want-satisfying qualities of a product. The qualities of many products cannot be adequately portrayed in black and white. Consider how much color can add to the import of illustrations of such foods as bacon and eggs, cakes, oranges, Jell-O, salads, and strawberries and cream. Add to these such items as women's dresses, men's ties, automobiles, paints, wallpaper, decorations for the home, flowers, and oriental rugs, and a keener appreciation of the interpretative quality of color is afforded.

Mail-order houses have found colored advertisements to be much more effective than black and white in selling certain products. One house a few years ago issued half of its catalogs in black and white, and half with color plates for those products lending themselves to the use of color. The latter sold about 15 times as much merchandise as the former. Other advertising is not unlike that of mail-order houses. In a sense, every advertisement in a magazine or newspaper is a page in a catalog from which consumers make purchases, or are influenced to investigate the products illustrated and described.

In those cases where the product does not lend itself to the use of color, it may be placed with profit in a colorful setting, or the results of its use illustrated in color. Baking powder is white, but the cakes in which baking powder is used may be shown in color. Electric refrigerators can be illustrated with an open door and filled with foods reproduced in natural color. Certain food products, somewhat dull in appearance, can be shown in combination with more colorful food and add both to their appearance and meaning to the consumer.

In selecting colors, care should be exercised in using those that bring out the natural qualities of the product. Yellow will make an object seem larger, black on yellow will improve legibility, red possesses a maximum of attention value, and blue is preferred by most men, but all these characteristics are secondary. If a product is green, it should be so pictured, even though green has less abstract attention value than red. Under such circumstances, green will interpret the product with fidelity and perhaps attract the attention of more interested readers than would red or some other color.

Art in advertising

Untold dollars have been placed on the altar of advertising art, with little reward outside of self-satisfaction, the muffled thanks of commercial artists, and occasionally a medal or blue ribbon as a prize in some exhibition. Too often, emphasis has been placed on art for art's sake rather than on art as an aid to a more accurate and complete unfolding of the qualities of the advertised product. Annual awards given by this and that organization have helped to set up false guideposts. Awards for the best direct-mail drawing, most distinctive illustration, best black-and-white drawing, best color photograph, etc., have influenced artists to point greater effort toward winning the applause of professional judges than increasing sales of the advertised product. So successful have advertising artists been in these efforts that their works have found their way into art galleries.

No wonder, then, that many an advertising artist works primarily with the thought that his creations may win him a medal in the next exhibition. His justifiable pride in his work is not to be criticized; but from the advertiser's point of view, it is the wrong standard of achievement. In advertising, the function of art is to provide an assist in the total job of communicating a message to prospective buyers of a product, service, or idea. Fred Ludekens, famous artist and illustrator and creative director of a large advertising agency, says,

> Pictures are a language. The very idea of a language is to communicate thoughts and ideas clearly. I do not believe pictures—either photography or the various art treatment—should be abstract or vague. Often . . . artists and photographers get 'carried away' and strain to be different. Many ideas are lost before they finally reach their intended audience. . . . My point is to be rational; to think out an illustrative problem in terms of people. Ask yourself, can the other fellow understand *precisely* what I am saying?[1]

Abstract art is intended to communicate, but it is more apt to focus on what the artist intends than what the viewer understands. Figure 16–9 is

[1] Fred Ludekens, "A Plague on Art for Art's Sake," *Advertising Age,* November 11, 1957, p. 109.

a case in point. What does the illustrator mean? The mystic symbols of abstract art are less apt to influence buying behavior than a faithful interpretation of the product's merits.

Whether pictures are reproduced in black and white or color, or are drawn by the most expert artist, the factor of outstanding importance is

FIGURE 16–9
Abstract art. What does it mean?

"Sing and dance together and be joyous, but let each one of you be alone."
KAHLIL GIBRAN

Hammond's exclusive Harmonic Drawbars put a full orchestra and thousands of tonal combinations at your fingertips.

You'll find many other exclusive

features as well, in over seventy different models . . . from $555.00 to $10,000.00.

At your Hammond Organ dealer.

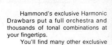
HAMMONDORGAN Ⓗ
Division of Hammond Corporation.

FIGURE 16–10
Illustration effectively symbolizes product benefit

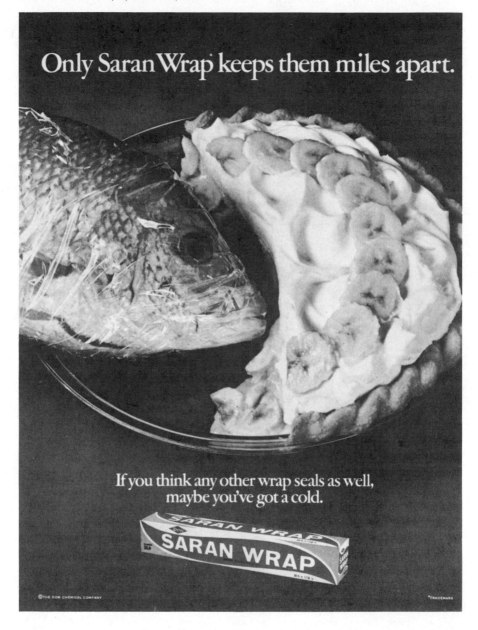

FIGURE 16–11
Illustration symbolizes copy theme

After you've harvested the noblest grapes...after your winemaster
has worked his magic...after you've done everything you can to make a fine wine,
you need one thing more to make it great: time.

Nothing good happens fast.
Paul Masson

© Paul Masson Vineyards, Saratoga, California, since 1852.

an ability to keep the point of view of the prospective purchaser. The artist should know the fundamental purpose of the illustration and figuratively look through the eyes of the consumer in visualizing the effect desired. Consumers in general do not understand art; hence, real art is usually less effective in penetrating human understanding than pictures and drawings modeled in terms of the experience of consumers. One would not rate the crayon scratching of a youngster as art; yet the announcement, "Lemonade—1¢ a glass," scratched on a board will probably attract more customers to a child's lemonade stand than a banner with real artistic qualities. It should not be inferred from this that illustrations are not to be done well, but that the subject matter chosen be related to the level of consumer understanding.

In this connection note the subject matter chosen to illustrate the products shown in the advertisements reproduced in Figures 16–10 and 16–11. The art treatment is excellent in both cases, but the vital element is the choice of subject matter that is closely related to the level of consumer understanding. These pictures meet the admonition of artist Ludekens that "advertising pictures should be 'heard' as well as seen. Advertising pictures should be participating."[2]

IDENTIFICATION MARKS

Importance of identification marks

The advertiser has a product or service whose merits he attempts to explain to the consuming public. In order that the consumer might be able to procure the specific items whose merits have been convincingly presented, it is necessary to place a name, symbol, or other mark of identification on the product or its container. Such a mark also separates the product from similar items manufactured by competitors. "By this mark you shall know me and my products," must be the advertiser's motto.

Identification marks fall into one of three general groups: (1) firm or trade name; (2) brand name; and (3) trademark. From the standpoint of the manufacturer, the firm or trade name is perhaps least valuable as a mark of identification. It is more important to identify a soap as Ivory, Camay, Cheer, etc., than merely as a product of the Procter & Gamble Company. There may be some value, however, in associating a family of products with the name of the producer, particularly if some members of the family enjoy a wide and favorable reputation. If the advertisement is designed to solicit inquiries of any kind, the firm name and address must, of course, appear in the advertisement.

The retailer, on the other hand, must consider the firm name as of paramount importance as a mark of identification. He may emphasize certain trademarked or branded merchandise in his advertising, but his

[2] Ibid.

primary motive is to attract trade to his store. He usually has no merchandise of his own to offer the public, but rather a service in the way of convenient location, courteous and efficient clerks, delivery of goods, reasonable prices, quality merchandise, etc.

Brand names

This is perhaps the most common means of identifying products. Estimates of the number of brands entering the channels of modern commerce range from one-half to one million. An analysis of brands offered for sale in any market area will emphasize their importance in terms of numbers. We have seen that in Milwaukee in 1973 there were 20 brands of laundry soap, 12 brands of canned peas, 13 brands of package coffee, 14 brands of women's girdles, etc. Too many writers place undue emphasis on trademarks as a means of identification, and they underemphasize brand names.

A brand name may often be registered as a trademark; but whether it is or not, its primary function remains the same. In general, a brand name serves more effectively than either a firm name or trademark in making it easy for customers to ask for a particular product. Relatively few people would recognize the Indian-head insignia as identifying the American Tobacco Company, but few would fail to recognize the name Lucky Strike.

A number of tests have been made of the degree to which potential consumers are familiar with the brand names of products in a particular generic group. The most notable of such tests were made by Professors Hotchkiss and Franken of New York University. Similar tests have been made by advertising agencies and advertising media. The technique of these studies in brand-name association consisted of submitting to a group of consumers a questionnaire with the names of such products as hosiery, watches, soap, coffee, toothpaste, cigarettes, hats, typewriters, etc., and asking the respondent to write under the name of each general commodity all the names of specific brands that could be recalled.

The Psychological Corporation has carried this type of test a step further by including in its questions to consumers the basic advertising theme along with the name of the general commodity. Thus, it will ask: "What soap advertises: 'Stop Those Runs in Stockings'?" Inclusion of the advertising theme in testing seems to be more logical. A consumer is more inclined to purchase a given brand if the brand name recalls or is associated with a sellling theme.

Gene Seehafer has classified brand names as *functional* names and *fanciful* names. Under each classification he lists several types. See Figure 16–12.[3]

[3] Gene Seehafer, "Classification of Brand Names" in Steuart Henderson Britt, *Consumer Behavior and the Behavioral Sciences* (New York: John Wiley & Sons, Inc., 1966), pp. 378–79.

FIGURE 16–12
Classification of brand names

Functional Names

a. *Promise of results*
Spic'n Span
Glo-Coat
Duz
Deepsleep
Silver Curl
Sight Savers
Beautyrest
Ditto

b. *Ease of application*
Pin It
Quick
Zippo
E-Zee-Freeze
Magic Chef
Kwikeeze
Easy-Off
Minit-On

c. *Standard of quality*
Gold Seal Glass Wax
Gold Medal Flour
Royal
Perfection
Ideal
Miracle Tuft
Old Gold
Capitol

d. *Description of product ingredient*
Wheaties
Coca-Cola
Hotpoint
Ry-Krisp
All-Bran
Almond Joy
Yello Bole
Green Mint

e. *Description of product use*
Bisquick
Sani-Flush
Py-O-My
Blim

Fanciful Names

a. *Pleasant-association names*
Breeze
Jubilee
Joy
Lux
Flying A
Prince Matchiabelli
Tide
Pet

b. *Promise of reward*
Pride
Gleem
Odorono
Breath-o-Pine
Fresh'nd Aire
Softskin
Prom

c. *Meaningless, but easily remembered*
Babo
Ajax
Drax
Kodak
B.V.D.
Tek
Vel

Trademarks

The Lanham Trademark Act which went into effect in July 1947 states that "the term 'trademark' includes any word, name, symbol, or device or any combination thereof adopted and used by a manufacturer or merchant to identify his goods and distinguish them from those manufactured or sold by others."[4] Thus, a trademark is somewhat broader than a trade name and, in addition, is supported by statutory law.

A trademark under the new law need not be physically affixed to the product or its container. To be kept alive, a mark must be used, but the Lanham Act states that a mark to identify goods will be considered in use "when it is placed in a manner on goods or their containers or the displays associated therewith or on the tags or labels affixed thereto and the goods are sold or transported in commerce."[5] This would seem to indicate that the inclusion of a trademark in advertising would not be sufficient to establish use, but that the mark must be associated in some way with the physical product and not merely with a picturization of it.

The 1947 law also recognized service marks, or marks used to identify services offered by individuals and firms. The act defined a service mark as one "used in the sale or advertising of services to identify the services of one person and distinguish them from the services of others and includes without limitation the marks, names, symbols, titles, designations, slogans, character names, and distinctive features of radio or other advertising used in commerce."[6] By this action, service firms such as hotels, accountants, advertising agencies, banks, public utilities, and research firms may secure the benefits of the trademark law.

Registration of marks

Trademarks, service marks, and certification marks (like the *Good Housekeeping* seal of approval) can be registered with the United States Patent Office. Such registration serves as: (1) constructive notice of claim of ownership, (2) prima-facie evidence of registrant's exclusive right to use the mark in commerce, and (3) conclusive evidence of registrant's exclusive right to use the mark in commerce under certain circumstances.

The incontestable right in a mark is secured after the mark has been filed with the Commissioner of Patents within the time prescribed, and providing that there are no action spending which contest the registrant's claim of ownership. Professor Borden suggests that this "incontestability provision may possibly work hardship on small business concerns which may not be aware of the importance of registration and of vigilance in

[4] Lanham Trademark Act, Sec. 45.
[5] Ibid.
[6] Ibid.

protecting their marks and thus may unwittingly lose their rights in their marks to another user."[7] On the other hand, this feature should protect valid users from "ambush" by later users.

Factors to consider in choosing an identification mark

Aside from the legal problems involved in the selection of a mark to identify a given product, there are other problems of equal or greater magnitude. The keynote of any mark should be distinctiveness. Such a quality will make it stand out and will increase its memory value. Association value can be enhanced if the symbol, word, name, or device chosen for a mark is suggestive of the product or certain of its qualities.

While a trademark should not be descriptive, it can be suggestive. Furthermore, certain explanatory words can be woven around the trademark without being a part of the legal instrument, yet enhancing its identification and association value. Note the marks reproduced in Figure 16–13.

If names are to be used, they should not only be relatively easy to pronounce but also be pronounceable in only one way. Such words as "Pall Mall," "Gargoyle," "Clicquot," and "Unguentine" violate the above principle. They have grown into valuable marks, but the same amount of effort placed upon some other word might have produced still greater results. Certainly, in the selection of a new mark, it is not advisable to start with a handicap that is avoidable.

With the growth of giant diversified corporations and an increasing necessity for "selling" the corporation itself to various publics such as investors, government, potential employees, etc., the demand for corporate symbols has increased greatly. The corporate symbol serves as visual shorthand for the company's formal name.

Alfred Politz says that "a trademark's effectiveness rests largely on the verbalization of the words or letters used in the symbol. By creating a symbol that can be easily pronounced, or identified by a few simple words, an advertiser automatically gets his product introduced to the ear as well as the eye of the consumer."[8]

The United States Trademark Association lists the following as desirable characteristics in a trademark:

> Brevity.
> Easy to remember.
> Easily readable and speakable.
> Easily adaptable to any media.
> No unpleasant connotations.

[7] Neil H. Borden, "The New Trade-Mark Law," *Harvard Business Review,* Spring 1947, p. 305.

[8] "Trademarks Must Sell, Not Just Identify," *Advertising Age,* May 20, 1957, p. 1.

Suitable for export.
Lends itself to pictorialization.
Subtlety.[9]

Caution should also be exercised in the adoption of a surname as a mark of identification. A person may have a justifiable pride in his family name and may like to see it indelibly associated with every unit of merchandise produced. Surnames, however, violate the ideal of distinctiveness and encourage imitation if the name becomes well known. Outstanding instances of such imitation are found in the names of Williams, Rogers, Dobbs, Baker, and Stetson.

The use of a surname may provide a satisfactory mark when associated with another word, a symbol, or written in a distinctive manner. The mark reproduced in Figure 16–14 illustrates all three types of association. It further illustrates how a company may alter its mark without changing its basic format and utilize such alteration to symbolize and call attention to the modern and progressive character of the company.

Protection afforded by identification marks

The advertiser is afforded both common and statutory law protection for identification marks that meet certain requirements and that have been used by the company in its advertising or on its products. In the case of trademarks, service marks, and some others, the law provides for registration with the U.S. Patent Office, which affords definite protection. For other marks, protection is found both in the laws dealing with unfair competition and in courts of equity for violations of common-law rights.

Important as legal protection may be, of still greater importance is the protection of favorable consumer attitudes toward the mark and a proper association between the mark and the advertised product. Emphasis must always be placed on the value of a mark as a means of helping the consumer to select the merchandise whose want-satisfying qualities have been explained and interpreted through advertising.

Protection which identification marks afford consumers should not be ignored. They provide a means whereby consumers can duplicate the purchase of products that have given satisfaction, or avoid those that have not. Thus, to the manufacturer this may prove a double-edged sword. It therefore behooves the advertiser to offer to the public merchandise that is not only good but is also uniformly good. Identification marks can thus serve as a partial guide to intelligent buying.

Clowry Chapman has summarized in admirable fashion the relationship of identification marks and advertising and their value to both the producer

[9] United States Trademark Association, *Trademark Management* (New York, 1956), pp. 17–19.

FIGURE 16–13
Some well-known marks of identification

FIGURE 16–14
Alteration of a trademark to symbolize progress

which of these two
trademarks would YOU pick
for a big corporation ?

1. **Thompson Products**

this? ↑ *or this?* ↓

2. *Thompson Products*

STYLES CHANGE...that's for sure! In clothing ... in cars ... in industry ... *even in trademarks* which are intended to reflect the products and the personalities of the companies they represent. The Thompson Products trademark is a case in point.

Thompson has grown tremendously in the past 20 years...has multiplied its sales from three million dollars to more than three hundred million a year! And Thompson research, development, production methods, products and markets have grown at the same pace.

Now it's time for the Thompson trademark to change and reflect the modern trend of the company's many operations.

If you picked *No. 2* of the above two trademarks, you've agreed with the design experts who chose it from more than 100 trademarks submitted. This is the new Thompson Products trademark that you'll be seeing from now on. No. 1, incidentally, is the old trademark which No. 2 replaces, after thirty years.

You can expect still greater improvements in Thompson engineering, products and parts as new challenges come up through the years. 20 years from now...maybe sooner...you might be looking at a still newer Thompson trademark! Thompson Products, Inc., General Offices, Cleveland 17, Ohio.

ATTENTION, ENGINEERS! Contact us about joining our company, which has contributed importantly to the development of the airplane as well as the automobile, since their early days. We are now also expanding in the fields of electronics, hydraulics, pneumatics, nuclear energy and general industry. Write Ray Stanish, Manager, Central Staff Placement, Thompson Products, Inc., Cleveland 17, Ohio. Phone: IVanhoe 1-7500.

and consumer. His use of the term "trademark" could be broadened to include all identification marks: His statement follows:

> Trademarks will always need the help of other advertising, for at best the trademark is but a form of advertising, a very abridged or tabloid form of advertising—a word, a symbol, a phrase. Too much should not be expected of it alone, but, when helped by other advertising its service is amazing —identifying, reminding, fixing responsibility, increasing pride of production and morale, reassuring and insuring—insuring future markets for the product; reassuring customers that standards have been upheld. It inspires better morale among workers and greater pride in the product, making the manu-facturer stand squarely behind the product. It reminds customers of what they know or have learned, guides and protects them in their marketing by identifying what they have set out to get and warding off the frauds that lie in the wake of confusion.[10]

QUESTIONS AND PROBLEMS

1 What implications for advertising do you see in the observation that "people are visual minded?"

2 What implications for advertising do you see in the proposition that "seeing is believing"?

3 Only nine men have walked on the moon, yet millions of people shared the experience visually. How might such "mediated experience" be used in advertising?

4 Bring to class nine advertisements demonstrating the functions assigned to the visual element as listed on page 336.

5 Bring to class four advertisements projecting different moods.

6 A person is more apt to project himself or herself into advertisements depict-ing his or her kind of people. Bring to class two ads in which you think the illustration depicts the intended audience.

7 Frequently advertisements are referred to as being either product centered or people centered. Under what circumstances do you think each would be more appropriate?

8 Bring to class one advertisement in which you think the illustration is not relevant to the headline or copy theme.

9 What is the danger of overemphasizing art in advertising? What is its proper function?

10 "Pictures are of little value in an advertisement unless they assist in getting the advertiser's story across to the reader." Analyze this statement critically.

11 Fred Ludekens says, "Do not put the visual message in an idiom *people* cannot understand." Comment on this statement by Ludekens.

---

[10] Clowry Chapman, *How Advertisements Defeat Their Own Ends* (New York: Prentice-Hall, Inc., 1931), pp. 19–20.

12   What protection is afforded through the registration of a trademark? What other types of protection are afforded the advertiser against infringement of trademarks, brand names, and firm names?

13   How might an advertiser's mark of identification protect the consumer?

14   Changes in consumer tastes and buying preferences often produce problems for manufacturers who have built too restricted a meaning into their product identification marks. An example of this difficulty is found in the experience of the Iron Fireman Manufacturing Co.

This company was one of the leaders in the development and promotion of mechanical stokers for coal-burning home heating units. It achieved high popularity among consumers as a result of its quality product and its effective advertising. Its trademark consisted of an energetic, coal-shoveling robot, and it adopted the trade name "Iron Fireman." In the minds of many consumers the symbol of the shoveling robot and the name Iron Fireman became synonymous with coal stokers.

During the past several years consumer fuel preferences for home heating have undergone radical changes. There has been a rapid switch from coal to oil and gas. The Iron Fireman Company has made no attempt to influence people not to switch from coal to some other fuel. Instead, the company has kept abreast of this change by adding oil- and gas-burning heating units to its line of products. It is well equipped to meet the heating needs of the modern home regardless of the type of fuel used.

The company, however, has been faced with a serious problem in respect to its identification marks. As one official stated, "Our trademark and brand names are known from coast to coast, but they are still associated in the minds of too many people with coal stokers only."

The old mark and name have been promoted for over a quarter of a century. Strong and lasting associations have been developed with these marks. Should they be kept to cover all heating equipment of the company? Should they be kept only for coal-burning equipment and new marks and names be created for oil and gas equipment? Should the company attempt to persuade consumers away from oil and gas and toward coal stokers? What recommendations would you make?

17

Preparing the layout

The visual composition of an advertisement, the arrangement of illustration, headline, body copy, and logotype into a unified message is referred to as the "layout." The layout serves as a means of communication among the several people involved in the creative process. As a visual representation of the finished ad it is submitted to the client for his approval. It also serves as a blueprint for the printer, comparable to the architect's blueprint furnished the builder.

The layout should be designed to provide a logical, clear, unified presentation of the advertising message. Elements that are intended to attract attention and stimulate interest should be prominent in the layout. These elements usually are the illustration and headline. The design should always be in terms of consumer reaction rather than beauty, although one may be attained without sacrificing the other. A somewhat broader view of layout preparation includes visualization of the central idea of the advertisement as well as the arrangement of elements. Therefore, the layout artist and copywriter should work closely together.

Procedure in making layouts

The layout artist should first determine the exact dimensions of the finished advertisement. The page sizes and column widths of different magazines and newspapers can be checked in *Standard Rate and Data*

360

Service. After this has been determined, the outside dimensions of the advertisement should be ruled on a piece of paper, and space indicated for border or margin of white space. The space to be occupied by each part of the advertisement is then blocked in or indicated by lines or other marks.

Most layouts follow a fairly standard pattern of headline, illustration, copy, and standing details such as identification mark, coupon, or other instructional lines. This affords a logical presentation in terms of meaning as well as structure. Nevertheless, there are sufficient variations to be considered so that the layout man can well afford to work first with thumbnail sketches. Thumbnail sketches are in the nature of thinking on paper. They afford a basis for getting one's ideas into form. As many as a dozen or more such sketches may be drawn before one feels that a satisfactory design has been developed. Even then, when the chosen sketch is worked into a rough layout, it may prove unsatisfactory.

The amount of detail included in the layout and the precision of the rendering determines whether it is a *rough layout* or a *comprehensive layout*. To the layman's eye a rough layout might appear rather smooth. It clearly shows the use of space, the form of the various elements, a sketch of the people or objects to be portrayed, hand-lettered headlines, and the logotype or other identification feature. Body copy is indicated with straight lines showing the weight of the type matter and where it will appear. Figure 17–1 is a rough layout. It is an excellent example of layout and copy theme working closely together. The visual clearly communicates the idea, "He Walks Tall and Packs Two Peas." Of course, if this layout were reproduced here as it actually was rendered, the "Giant" would be "Green."

A comprehensive layout is a faithful rendering of the advertisement as it eventually would appear in print. The illustration would be precisely drawn or a print of the proposed photograph would be inserted. Lettering would be carefully done. Body copy might even be set in type and pasted in. Due to the expense and time required to turn out such a finished piece of work, comprehensive layouts are seldom used. The layout artist concentrates on making roughs and leaves the preparation of finished art to artists and photographers specializing in that kind of work.

The amount of detail going into the layout varies somewhat with the dependence placed upon the printer. Some advertising men insist that nothing be left to the discretion of the printer and, hence, include in the layout specifications of type style and size, how much leading is to be used between lines, the exact space to be occupied by copy, the extent of paragraph indentions, etc. This procedure is to be preferred when the layout man is thoroughly familiar with type faces and sizes and can visualize how the advertisement will look when reproduced. When he is not familiar with these matters, better results will be attained if some depen-

FIGURE 17–1
Layout portrays central idea

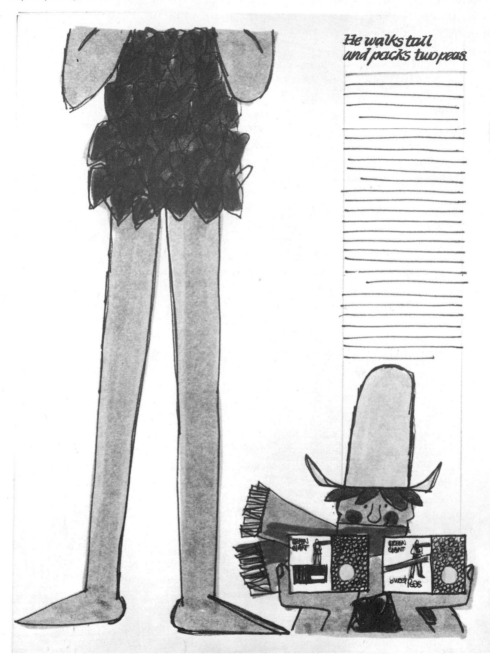

Courtesy: Leo Burnett Company Inc.

dence is placed on the printer, with the provision that proofs be submitted. With proofs at hand, an evaluation of the readability, appearance, and unity of the finished product is easy, and changes can be made if the printer's selection of type is not satisfactory.

Fundamental in the preparation of a layout is the idea to be visualized. Stephen Baker, a leading art director, draws a distinction between *arranging elements on a page* and *visualizing an idea.* "The former is a designer's (or layout man's) feat; his innate sense of composition, balance, color is brought fully into play. On the other hand, presenting the clearest visual interpretation requires a strong desire to communicate with the audience, a flair for the dramatic, the ability to think in pictorial terms (usually referred to as "visual sense"), and, probably most significant, a firm understanding of the advertiser's goal."[1]

Qualities to be considered in layouts

No formula can be given that will assure successful layouts; but fewer failures will be recorded if the factors of balance, contrast, proportion, motion, and unity are considered.

Balance Balance is the arrangement of elements to achieve a pleasing distribution of visual impression. The weight of visual impression is determined by size, color, shape, and density of the particular element. Generally, the bigger something is the heavier impression it makes. A dark blue square appears heavier than a light yellow square the same size. A square looks heavier than a vertical rectangle enclosing the same area. Black looks heavier than gray.

There are two kinds of balance; formal and informal. Formal balance is achieved by distributing objects of equal weight on either side of the "optical center" of the advertisement. The optical center is slightly above the mathematical center. A line drawn from top to bottom through the optical center divides the space into the equal segments. Thus, two objects of equal weight would be formally balanced when they are equidistant from the imaginary vertical line. Informal balance is attained by placing elements of different size, shape, or density at different distances from the optical center. Much like a teeter-totter, a heavier object near the center can be balanced by a lighter object farther from the center.

Formal balance communicates a feeling of security, stability, dignity, dependability, and conservatism. Informal balance is more exciting, more refreshing, and more dynamic. Each, however, has its place.

Figures 17–2 and 17–3 illustrate good usage of formal and informal balance, respectively. The type of balance used in each is in harmony with

[1] Stephen Baker, *Advertising Layout and Art Direction* (New York: McGraw-Hill Book Co., 1959), p. 3.

FIGURE 17–2
Formal balance in a layout

FIGURE 17–3
Informal balance

Our pants can even stand kneeling.

If your legs can take it, Pants That Fit can take it. Without getting baggy knees. Or saggy wrinkles. That's because our pants are trim without being tight. And they're Perma-Prest fabric of polyester and silk doubleknit. They come in sizes 8 to 20, proportioned to height. You'll find our skinny little tops hard to pass up, too.

In Misses Sportswear. At most Sears, Roebuck and Co. larger stores.

Similar styles in catalog.

Sears

PANTS THAT FIT

the products advertised. The elegance of Chanel No. 5 is enhanced by the classic simplicity of the bottle and label placed in such a formal setting. Sears "Pants that Fit," on the other hand, are for the active person. The layout appropriately conveys a feeling of informality and casualness.

Contrast   The appearance of an advertisement will be improved and its attention value and readability enhanced if its parts are arranged to provide contrast. This can be attained by combining different sizes, shapes, densities, and colors. Headlines and subheads in larger type than body copy or printed in a different color provide contrast. Where several visual elements are used, contrast is achieved by varying their size and shape. The dominant element should stand out at first glance. Figure 17–4 exemplifies an effective use of contrast. Note how the symbolic figure and the soup in the spoon over the bowl stand out from the field. The white headline contrasts with the dark background.

Much of the contrast in Figure 17–4 is achieved by using a *reverse*. A *reverse* means "the image is defined by the ink surrounding it, or the areas that ordinarily are black become white."[2] Figure 17–1 also is in reverse. A reverse not only provides a contrasting background for the graphic elements of the individual advertisement, it also makes that ad stand out from the many others employing a white background in the same publication.

Another device for achieving the benefits of contrast while at the same time registering dramatic impact is the *close-up*. The close-up shot so frequently used in television has its counterpart in print. The close-up eliminates diversionary background details. Instead of showing people from head to toes, the close-up (as illustrated in Figure 17–5) captures the character, individuality, and mood of the subjects as revealed in their eyes. Insofar as other advertisements in the same publication place products and people in various settings, the close-up stands out in that field.

Proportion   One of the more intangible qualities of good designing is proportion. Proportion involves the relationship of objects to the background in which they appear and their relationship to each other. Subconsciously things "in proportion" are more pleasing to the eye than things "out of proportion." The Greeks found that two areas held a pleasant relationship to each other when one was between one half and two thirds the area of the other. Thus, good proportions would be 3 to 5, 2 to 3, 4 to 6, 8 to 10, and so on. The eye cannot measure these ratios easily, yet they break the appearance of monotony. Having an eye for the "fitness of things" is one of the artist's more important contributions.

Gaze-motion   A harmonious arrangement of parts is desirable. Headline, illustration, copy, and identification mark, in that order, will usually

[2] William Bockus, *Advertising Graphics* (New York: Macmillan Publishing Co., 1974), p. 144.

FIGURE 17–4
Effective use of contrast in layout

Campbell's Chicken & Stars Soup.
If kids had their wish,
the stars would all come out at noon.

Kids love the chicken soup that gives them hundreds of twinkling stars to wish upon. And what more could a mother wish for in a lovable lunchtime soup than tender pieces of chicken, a sprinkling of carrots and celery, and enriched macaroni stars in a golden broth made rich and flavorful with two chicken stocks. Keep plenty of Campbell's Chicken & Stars, and also Chicken Vegetable and Chicken 'n Dumplings Soup on hand. Then you'll be ready to serve your kids a quick and easy lunchtime treat whenever you wish.

M'm! M'm! Good!

FIGURE 17–5
Effective use of close-up

The past is only a beginning

For four generations we've been making medicines as if people's lives depended on them.

FIGURE 17-6
Example of a "C" layout

provide a logical follow-through from the interest-arresting part of the advertisement to the close. It is often desirable, however, to alter this orthodox arrangement.

Some advertisers like to provide an arrangement that will tend to direct the vision of the glancer from the headline through the illustrations and to the identification mark at the close, thus to some degree eliminating copy as a barrier to a tie-up of the headline message with the name of the advertiser and his product.

The types of layouts used to obtain such results can be classified in general by letters of the alphabet, as C, S, Z, and V. To these should be added the use of arbitrary lines and the position and shape of the product itself as a means of directing the reader's attention. The C layout may use a number of pictures and illustrations, starting from the right-hand side of the advertisement, back to the left, and down the left side to the bottom. The top illustration may pull the gaze of the reader to the left by having the persons in the picture looking toward the left, the product moving in that direction, or by lines drawn in the illustration for that purpose. Figure 17–6 illustrates a "C" type of layout. The eye is drawn from the headline through the curve of the illustrations to the name of the product and the text.

Gaze-motion is important, but it must be handled with care. Arrangement to capitalize on this force should not be so obvious as to attract attention to the technique rather than to the product or service being advertised.

Unity   The well-designed advertisement creates an impression of completeness. The qualities of balance, contrast, proportion, and gaze-motion should be employed to develop unity of thought, appearance, and design in the layout. Copy should be written and illustrations chosen to present a message in logical fashion. The layout artist should assist in maintaining and, if possible, improving a logical and unified presentation. Coupons, for example, will not be placed at the beginning of an advertisement unless the copy theme is built around the idea of clipping the coupon. If reference to the coupon is entirely secondary, unity would be destroyed by placing it at the top.

Perhaps the surest way of achieving unity is to keep the layout simple. Attesting to this principle is the overwhelming popularity of the simplest layout of all—one illustration followed by one headline, followed by one block of body copy. The greater the number of elements the greater is the fragmentation of attention. Another way to get visual unity is overlapping. A cut of the product overlaps into the main illustration or, if several items are displayed, one overlaps the other. Typographic unity helps tie an ad together. Generally, it is a good idea to use the same type-face or style throughout the ad.

Judicious use of white space

There is no uniform conviction concerning the value of white space in advertisements. One school of thought emphasizes brief copy and a great deal of white space, holding that this procedure will secure a maximum number of readers and that the reverse will scare readers away. The opposite school of thought maintains that unless a complete message is presented, little value will be obtained from the advertising. Its adherents claim that the kernel of the message can be presented in headlines and

Think small.

Our little car isn't so much of a novelty any more.

A couple of dozen college kids don't try to squeeze inside it.

The guy at the gas station doesn't ask where the gas goes.

Nobody even stares at our shape.

In fact, some people who drive our little flivver don't even think 32 miles to the gallon is going any great guns.

Or using five pints of oil instead of five quarts.

Or never needing anti-freeze.

Or racking up 40,000 miles on a set of tires.

That's because once you get used to some of our economies, you don't even think about them any more.

Except when you squeeze into a small parking spot. Or renew your small insurance. Or pay a small repair bill. Or trade in your old VW for a new one.

Think it over.

FIGURE 17–7. Effective use of white space

illustrations and the rest of the space utilized to its fullest extent in presenting details for the interested reader. They cite mail-order experience to support their belief in the value of long copy and a minimum of white space.

Stephen Baker summarizes in the following statement his attitude toward the use of white space: "Many layout men become so preoccupied with the illustration and the handling of the copy that they forget that blank space is a very significant part of the overall pattern. An overdose of it at the wrong spot can throw the composition off balance, just as an improperly placed illustration can. White space can also be considered a tool for separating the advertisement from its competition, for making an illustration more prominent."[3]

Figure 17–7 is a classic example of the effective use of white space. What better way to dramatize the idea, "Think Small"?

Use of small space in layouts

Making a layout for a small advertisement is often more difficult than making one for a full page. The small space ad is likely to be positioned on a page along with several other ads. To gain attention the design should be simple and bold. A single idea, a single illustration, a short caption, clear display type provide the needed simplicity. Masses of black and white give the ad the boldness to stand out on the printed page. And, of course, the limited space demands a brief message. Figure 17–8 shows a series of layouts demonstrating different uses of small space.

The large amount of black space used in these small layouts increased attention value and made the one-sixteenth page of space used do extra duty. However, since some magazines restrict the amount of black space in a given advertisement, *Standard Rate and Data Service* should be consulted for such restrictions before a layout is prepared.

Advertisements to be run in newspapers can often be drawn to such proportions that a smaller amount of space will provide greater value than the actual space used. Thus a half-page advertisement in an eight-column newspaper may be five columns wide and reach considerably above the horizontal center of the page. This will leave part of the advertisement showing, regardless of how the paper is folded, and will, in general, dominate the entire page. It will almost guarantee reading matter next to the advertisement.

Storyboards

A storyboard serves as a "layout" of the television commercial. Just as the layout visualizes the finished print advertisement, the storyboard

---

[3] Baker, *Advertising Layout,* p. 47.

FIGURE 17–8
Four arrangements of a small-space advertisement

conveys a visual impression of the finished commercial and guides the people involved in its creation, approval, and production. However, it is much more difficult to imagine the finished commercial from looking at a storyboard than to imagine a finished magazine ad from looking at the layout. There are so many more dimensions in television—time, movement, scene changes, sound, music, etc. A static, oversimplified series of drawings can only provide a rough approximation of the eventual experience. It is not uncommon, therefore, for the storyboard to be used as a visual prop for "acting out" the proposed commercial.

Film goes through the projector at a rate of 24 frames per second. In a 30-second commercial there would be 720 frames. A key problem in drawing a storyboard, therefore, is to decide how many frames and which frames to show. The number of frames to show depends largely on the number of scene changes. If there is to be an on-camera spokesman with few, if any, scene changes, a storyboard with three or four frames would be adequate. If the commercial is more complicated, involving a cast of several characters, an evolving plot, considerable action, and several scene changes, more frames will be required. The number of frames should be sufficient to communicate the essence of the commercial, but not so many as to confuse the total impression. Which frames to show will depend on which scene changes, which characters, which action, which ideas are essential to the flow of thought the ultimate viewer is intended to experience. Huntley Baldwin states the problem succinctly:

> Storyboards must tread the line between being too vague to be any guide at all and being too specific or comprehensive to permit any creative latitude in final production. If they are too sketchy or ambiguous they run the risk of being misunderstood by the client. If the client does not know what the creative people are trying to achieve (or worse, if they don't know themselves), the odds are increased that he will be surprised, disappointed, or angered by the results.[4]

The actual drawing of the individual storyboard frames calls for all the principles of good design discussed earlier, plus the ingenuity and skill of the professional artist.

QUESTIONS AND PROBLEMS

1   When preparing a layout, which is more important—arranging elements on a page or visualizing an idea? Explain.

2   List some products and services for which you think formal balance would be appropriate. Clip some examples that support your list. Do the same for informal balance.

[4] H. Huntley Baldwin, *How Television Commercials Are Made* (Evanston, Ill.: Department of Advertising, Northwestern University, 1970), p. 34.

3   Contrast is not only a desirable quality to achieve within the advertisement, but also within the field in which the advertisement is to appear. Explain with examples.

4   Clip two advertisements: one that fails to use a close-up and another that effectively uses a close-up.

5   Find an advertisement that you think is an excellent example of unity in design. Trace the outline of the visual elements in the ad. What observations would you make about the design as revealed in your tracing?

6   A storyboard is a static interpretation of a motion picture idea. Explain. What difficulties does this pose for the storyboard artist?

7   Layouts often vary according to the medium in which they are placed. Compare layouts in the following media and write down any significant differences that you believe were influenced by the medium: newspaper, general magazine, professional journal, business or trade magazine, outdoor poster board, car card, direct mail.

18

Reproducing the advertisement

After the typewritten text, the drawings and charts, and the layout have been prepared and the photographs and other art work secured, the advertisement must still be reproduced in sufficient numbers to reach the audience of consumers, often numbered in the millions, to which its message is directed. Aside from radio and television and a few minor forms of advertising, the message is delivered through a printed medium such as a newspaper or magazine or mailing piece. The operations by which the advertisement is put in printed form are known collectively as *mechanical production*. Involved in this process are various phases of the graphic arts.

In large organizations, one or more individuals specialize in mechanical production and are required to be familiar with all its details. The small and medium-sized advertisers and agencies, however, usually cannot afford to employ full-time specialists but must depend upon an outside organization for advice and service. Still, advertising men in such organizations will find it advantageous to understand, at least in a general way, the mechanical methods and skills used in reproducing advertisements. One need not become an expert, but a fair knowledge of production will be useful in various ways. It will facilitate the handling of the preliminary steps of copy writing, layout, and art work, and it will make possible more efficient and economical purchasing of all the elements of production.

It is true that some phases of production will not be within the control of the advertiser. Advertisements placed in such media as newspapers and magazines, unless furnished as "inserts," will automatically be printed by the same methods the media employ. But again, unless the advertiser understands something about the methods to be used in each case, he will be handicapped in supplying the advertisement in the form required.

The advertiser needs, therefore, to have a general knowledge of mechanical production. This means that he must become acquainted with these basic graphic arts processes: typography and type composition; photoengraving and platemaking; and printing. He will still need the help of the specialists, but he will be able to deal more effectively with them if he has this basic knowledge.

TYPOGRAPHY AND TYPE COMPOSITION

In one sense, typography refers to the physical composition or setting of the type; in another, it is the art of selecting and arranging for printing type faces, spacing, and decorative materials. Today, composition, in the sense of transforming original copy into a form suitable for printing or platemaking, consists of more than the setting of movable type or hot metal; it also includes photosetting, video character generation, and composition by various strike-on typewriter-like machines for reproduction by lithographic or planographic processes. We shall discuss printing methods later, but the initial problem is the selection and arrangement of type, or the effective application of the art of typography. We begin by becoming acquainted with type faces.

Type faces

A single piece of type, the unit of most type composition, has a definite anatomy. The accompanying illustration (Figure 18–1) names and illustrates the parts of a piece of handset metal type. Note particularly the point body and the serifs.

All except the newest typewriters have only one kind of type face. In printing, however, there are thousands of type faces. The nomenclature and measurements of this array of types are often ambiguous, and their very abundance creates difficulties of selection. But it also offers opportunity to those who know how to use them.

Type faces vary in weight, design, and in body size (see Figure 18–2). A type *font* is a complete assortment of characters of one face and size, including capitals, small capitals, lowercase letters, numbers, punctuation marks, and so on. A type *series* may run from 6-point to 72-point size in uppercase and lowercase. A type *family* is made up of different series, such as roman, italic, condensed, extended, boldface, boldface italic, and so on, of the same general design of type. Many type families are amaz-

FIGURE 18–1
Anatomy of a single piece of type

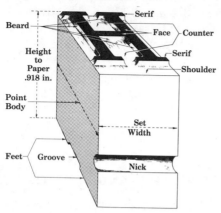

ingly versatile and complete. Among such type families are Caslon, Bodoni, Garamond, Janson, Caledonia, Baskerville, and Cheltenham.

Type faces may be classified further into groups of related faces. Some systems of classification are based on variations in historical development, often minor, rather than upon visual factors. The descendants of the earlier types, based in the beginning on manuscript writing or patterned after the first Roman alphabet, are called "Old Style." In these faces there are usually slanted serifs and the strokes flow easily from thick to thin. Examples of Old Style faces are to be found in the Garamond and Caslon families, among others.

Transitional faces are sometimes considered a separate group. These are the faces designed in mid-18th century, such as Baskerville and Bulmer. Compared to Old Style faces, these faces have sharper contrast between thick and thin strokes and straighter serifs. The *Modern* faces carry the characteristics of the Transitional further in the direction of accentuating the contrast between thick and thin strokes. Serifs and the other square strokes become straight. Bodoni is an example of a Modern face. These type faces, although called "Modern" really are historically only slightly more recent than the Transitional, having been designed soon after them, and the distinction is often ignored, all being classified as Modern.

The trouble with the historical classifications of type is that they cut across family lines. Many type families contain faces representative of both Old Style and Modern, making classification of today's type faces on the basis of historical development rather meaningless. For the purposes of the advertiser, therefore, it is more convenient and practical to classify type not according to historical origin, but on the basis of easily recogniza-

Ornamental Type

GOLD RUSH
MANDARIN
Cloister Text
LOMBARDIC

Caslon Old Style Type Family, 18 pt. size

Caslon roman
Caslon italic
Caslon boldface
Caslon boldface italic
Caslon Bold Condensed
Caslon Open Face

Italic and Cursive Type

Garamond Italic
Deepdene Italic
Raleigh Cursive
Bernhard Cursive
Bank Script
Brush Script

Block Letter Type

Univers (Sans-serif)
Stymie (Square-serifed)

Roman Type

Caslon Old Face (Old Style)
Baskerville (Transitional)
Bodoni (Modern)

8 pt. Garamond Font

ABCDEFGHIJKLMNOPQRSTUVWXYZ
ABCDEFGHIJKLMNOPQRSTUVWXYZ
abcdefghijklmnopqrstuvwxyz fi fl ffi ffl
[]%†‡¶*()$,.-;:'!?& 1234567890

ABCDEFGHIJKLMNOPQRSTUVWXYZ
abcdefghijklmnopqrstuvwxyz fi fl ffi ffl
[]%†‡¶()$.,;:'!?& 1234567890*

Caslon Old Style No. 337 Type Series, 6 pt. to 72 pt.

aA aA aA aA aA aA aA aA aA aA aA aA aA

ble visual characteristics. Such a grouping would place types into these four broad classes: roman, block letter, cursive, and ornamental. (See Figure 18–2.)

The *roman* letter is characterized by serifs and graduated thick and thin strokes. A roman type may be either Old Style or Modern. The Modern roman letter emphasizes contrast in weight of lines and has strong level serifs. The Old Style roman has less contrast and smaller, often sloping, serifs. Roman type is adaptable to many purposes. It is possible with it to secure contrasting effects without switching to another type design. It is the easiest face to read, even in smaller sizes. Both Caslon Old Style and modern Bodoni are classified as belonging to the roman group.

The *block letter,* also called sans-serif, gothic, grotesque, and contemporary, is of two general types: (1) sans-serif, and (2) block-serifed. The sans-serif letter lacks serifs entirely. The block- or square-serifed letter has serifs, but these consist of short strokes of the same weight and thickness as the main parts of the letter, and there are no brackets. In both, the strokes forming the letters are of uniform weight throughout the letter. This uniformity and the lack of serifs make block letters harder to read than roman letters. Examples of sans-serifed type are Futura, Helvetica, and Univers; examples of square-serifed type are Beton, Karnak, or Memphis.

The basic features of *cursive* are the slanted letters and their appearance of being connected and continuous. The two main classifications of cursive types are italics and scripts. Italic is the familiar slanted form of faces in the Roman group; scripts are those faces drawn to look as if handwritten. Scripts may vary from very formal, fine-line types like Bank Script to very informal brushwriting such as Brush Script. These types are all harder to read than either roman or sans-serif. Used injudiciously in a headline, for example, they can conceal rather than reveal the message. Some of them offer, however, a convenient means of conveying such qualities as informality or the feminine touch.

Ornamental types are usually embellished forms of other classes of types. They are used essentially for decorative or atmospheric purposes. A common earlier form of decorative type was Black Letter or Old English, which was based on European handwriting in Medieval times. It is hard to read but is still used occasionally today to suggest antiquity or religious themes. Ornamental faces are often used to suggest the atmosphere of a particular time, place, or culture. Examples are Rustic, P. T. Barnum, Lombardic, Gold Rush, Old Bowery, and Mandarin.

Selection of type faces

When the advertiser approaches the problem of selecting specific type faces for his advertisement, he will find all of the classes of type mentioned above available in almost bewildering abundance in the type books put out by his typesetters. The problem is complicated by ambiguities in current nomenclature and type measurements, and by the practice of different type foundries issuing varying versions of a type face under the same name. There are, for example, numerous Caslons, Bodonis, Garamonds, and Baskervilles. Also, type faces designed for use in the numerous new photographic and electronic typesetting devices are most often inexact copies of older faces given different names. San-serif faces range from the older Spartans and Futuras through the numerous Gothics to Optima, Helvetica, Venus, and Univers. Square-serifed faces go under various names from Stymie to Memphis and, like the sans-serifs, may be very condensed or quite extended. There are numerous cursives, including the special cursive designed for use in the Electra family because the Electra oblique italic lacked cursive feeling. The number of ornamental faces available is abundant, indeed.

Type measurement and fitting type to space will be discussed later, but type size need not usually place restrictions on selecting type on the basis of other considerations, because most faces are available in an adequate number of sizes. To find his way through the complexities of type selection, the advertiser needs to be guided by a few simple principles, pending his development through time and experience of a competence, and perhaps a personal style, in this field. Following such guidelines he will find the problem of selection to be diminished; but in the end the advertiser, unless he turns to the specialists, will have to depend on his own good taste and sensitivity to atmosphere and appropriateness to solve his problems.

The most important principle of all is to select type faces on the basis of their *legibility*. Type is meant to communicate, and the more legible it is, the clearer and faster will be the communication. Scientific research has made contributions to understanding of the bases of legibility, but the findings are not complete or conclusive. Legibility and readability are relative terms. What is legible to one person in one situation may not be so to others. Legibility is affected by the characteristics of the type selected, the degree of familiarity of the reader with the type face, the size of the type, the length of the line, the leading or space between lines, and the use of white space in the advertisement. In selecting a type for legibility, all of these factors should be taken into account. Other considerations than legibility, important as they may be, are secondary to the ability of the type to communicate the message quickly and clearly.

In combining type faces for an advertisement, the question arises as to the relative importance to place upon *harmony* and *contrast*. Perhaps the safest procedure is to use the same type face throughout, creating close harmony, but a judicious combination of faces to employ both harmony and contrast is most effective. Variations in style and size of type help in meeting the needs of different parts of the advertisement and in making clear the relative importance of different elements. Relative importance should not be left in doubt but should be made absolutely clear by relative weights of the type chosen.

Relative weights of type will be affected not only by the size of the type but also by its style; weight; whether italic, boldface, all capitals, capitals and small capitals, or lowercase roman; and position on the page. A large type, of course, outranks a smaller one of the same style. Ornamental faces make a stronger impression than regular faces. Italic is more emphatic than roman and boldface outranks both. In the same sizes and styles, all-capital lines are stronger than those set in capitals and small capitals, and both are stronger than those set in capitals and lowercase. Position on the page also indicates the importance of a line of type.

Within the possibilities compatible with the basic requirements of legibility and emphasis, consideration should be given to type selection on the basis of feeling or atmosphere. It is usually possible to discern the differences between types in their degree of femininity and masculinity, although this and similar distinctions are subjective, and reactions may vary from person to person. Some types are felt to be rugged and masculine, others delicate and feminine. Likewise, a type may be felt to be sturdy, stable, and businesslike; warm and informal or cold and formal; elegant and aristocratic or rustic; fussy, dramatic; or just plain neutral. These qualities felt to be present in type faces may be the basis for selecting one type rather than another for a particular purpose. Occasionally an ornamental type may be chosen, as has been mentioned, to match a particular historic, geographic, or cultural atmosphere.

However, in selecting type, the advertiser should be careful to avoid trick or freak hard-to-read faces, even though such faces might attract attention because they are different. One should never lose sight of the fact that advertising space costs a great deal and the message must be read if a profitable return is to be obtained from such investment. Legibility should be kept in mind at all times; the measure of good typography is its ability to make the advertising story easy to read. Generally, the type should not call attention to itself.

Type measurement

Printers have a system of measurement which differs from the common one of measuring in inches and fractions of an inch, and it is not the metric system either. It is relatively easy to understand and apply in production work. Its essential features are as follows:

Point system The unit of measurement of type and spaces or leading between lines of type is the *point*. For all practical purposes 72 points equals 1 inch. The point measures type *height* only, not its overall dimensions, and it measures not the height of a single letter but the height of a line of the type in question measured from the bottom of the descenders, or extensions downward from the body of the type, to the top of the ascenders, or extensions upward from the body of the type. The width of a single letter depends on the style of type face—whether fat or thin, extended or condensed—and on the proportions of the letter—whether, for instance, it is a *w* or an *i*.

Standard type sizes and the ones frequently used are 5, 5½, 6, 7, 8, 9, 10, 11, 12, 14, 18, 24, 30, 36, 48, and 72 point. Before specifying sizes, however, consult the printer's type book or list. Five point, 5½ point, 7 point, and even 9 and 11 point, and all of the larger sizes above 12 or 14 point may be missing from the face you wish to use. The smaller size may be brought in from a matching or similar face, and the larger sizes may be found among the "display" sizes of the same type or selected from the many available display faces created especially for this purpose. Comparisons of type sizes are shown in Figure 18–3. The text of this book is set in 10 point Optima.

The layout man may specify on the margin of his copy the size and kind of face to be used, or he may leave this to the printer. In the case of the copy shown in Figure 18–4 (pages 385–86), the agency layout man specified both the size and style of type.

Leading   Leading is also expressed in points, as, for example, 12 point type leaded 1 point (also expressed as "12 on 13"). A type face 12 points high will not measure exactly 12 points since the face of the letter itself is not as high as the base on which it is mounted. This provides a small amount of white space between lines when set solid, but usually not enough for easy reading. Additional white space is provided by leading. Type can be leaded to the number of points desired. The text of this book is 10 point type with 2 points leading between lines. This gives an equivalent of 12 points in depth; thus, six lines measure 72 points or exactly one inch in depth.

Pica   A pica is equal to 12 points, and there are 6 picas to an inch, making it quite simple to translate picas into inches and vice versa. The pica is used to measure type horizontally, and a significant measure is the number of characters of a particular type face there are in a pica, on the average, and consequently in a line of type a certain number of picas wide. There are approximately 2.67 characters per pica in this 10 point Optima you are reading. Dimensions of lines and blocks of type are given in picas and half picas, or, if less than 6 picas, may be given in points. Illustrations and margins, however, are usually measured in inches, as are paper sizes.

Agate line   The term "agate" was originally applied to a size of type (5½ point). The size of type to which it now refers is slightly smaller than

FIGURE 18–3
Illustration of various sizes of type

6 Point Garamond

The medieval seclusion from the concerns of the current world, which marked all but a few colleges until 1930, has happily been broken down.

8 Point Garamond

The medieval seclusion from the concerns of the current world, which marked all but a few colleges until 1930, has happily been broken down.

10 Point Garamond

The medieval seclusion from the concerns of the current world, which marked all but a few colleges until 1930, has happily been broken down.

12 Point Garamond

The medieval seclusion from the concerns of the current world, which marked all but a few colleges until 1930, has happily been broken down.

14 Point Garamond

The medieval seclusion from the concerns of the current world, which marked all but a few colleges until 1930, has happily been broken down.

18 Point Garamond

The medieval seclusion from the concerns of the current world, which marked all but a few colleges until 1930, has happily

24 Point Garamond

The medieval seclusion from the concerns of the current world, which marked all but a few col-

30 Point Garamond

The medieval seclusion from the concerns of the current world, which

FIGURE 18–4
Copy with type specifications for the printer

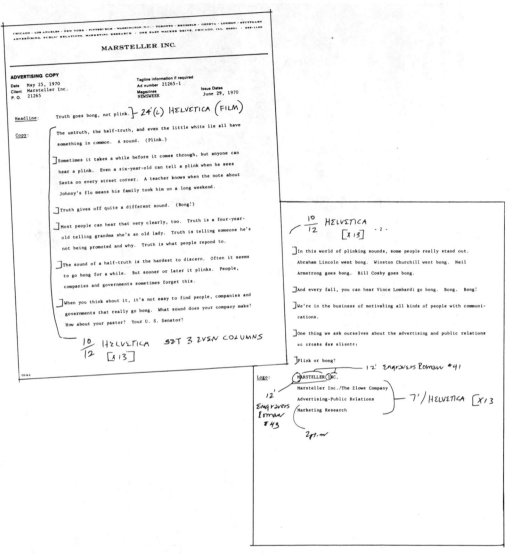

5½ point, measuring 14 lines to the inch. Today, its use is generally confined to measurement of space in newspapers and magazines. Practically all papers, large and small, compute their national advertising rates on the agate line basis. One agate line, one column wide, is the unit. Originally, most newspapers had a uniform column 13 picas wide, but in recent years the column has been narrowed until today we find that most

FIGURE 18–4 (*Continued*)

Truth goes bong, not plink.

The untruth, the half-truth, and even the little white lie all have something in common. A sound. (Plink.)

Sometimes it takes a while before it comes through, but anyone can hear a plink. Even a six-year-old can tell a plink when he sees Santa on every street corner. A teacher knows when the note about Johnny's flu means his family took him on a long weekend.

Truth gives off quite a different sound. (Bong!)

Most people can hear that very clearly, too. Truth is a four-year-old telling grandma she's an old lady. Truth is telling someone he's

not being promoted and why. Truth is what people respond to.

The sound of a half-truth is the hardest to discern. Often it seems to go bong for a while. But sooner or later it plinks. People, companies and governments sometimes forget this.

When you think about it, it's not easy to find people, companies and governments that really go bong. What sound does your company make? How about your pastor? Your U.S. Senator?

In this world of plinking sounds, some people really stand out.

Abraham Lincoln went bong. Winston Churchill went bong.

Neil Armstrong goes bong. Bill Cosby goes bong.

And every fall, you can hear Vince Lombardi go bong. Bong! Bong!

We're in the business of motivating all kinds of people with communications.

One thing we ask ourselves about the advertising and public relations we create for clients:

Plink or bong?

MARSTELLER INC.
Marsteller Inc. / The Zlowe Company

Advertising · Public Relations
Marketing Research

Chicago · Los Angeles · New York · Pittsburgh · Washington · Brussels · Geneva · London · Paris · Stockholm · Stuttgart · Toronto

large dailies have an 11½-pica column and the smaller papers a 13-pica column. The number of agate lines in a given space is the depth in inches, times the number of columns, times 14. Thus, a newspaper advertisement 6 inches deep and 3 columns wide would represent 252 agate lines (6 X 3 X 14).

Fitting copy to space

It is important to fit copy to available space because if you do not do so, and it turns out that the copy when set in type is either too long or too short to fit the layout, you will either (1) have to change to a different style of type (fatter or thinner); (2) choose a type with a larger or smaller point size; (3) reduce or increase the leading; or (4) arrange for a larger or smaller type area. Since all of these alternatives are inconvenient and costly, you would probably prefer to cut the copy or add to it. And this, too, is expensive after the copy is set in type: It is much better to make sure that the copy fits the layout *before* you have it set in type.

Considerations of fit will also affect to some extent the original selection of a type face, not only in point size but also in type style or design. Different type styles of the same point size may vary considerably in width of the letters. Types may be compared in this respect by comparing their *alphabetic lengths,* a measurement of length in points of a complete lowercase alphabet, as given in type books. If you know that you are going to have difficulty securing a fit, either because the copy is long or short for the space, you can take a first step toward solving the problems by selecting a face with an appropriate alphabetic length. For example, the alphabetic length of 10 point Primer is 150 points, while that of 10 point Garamond is only 125 points, as shown below:

abcdefghijklmnopqrstuvwxyz
abcdefghijklmnopqrstuvwxyz

There are two commonly used methods of determining the amount of space a given amount of copy will occupy. When only a rough approximation is required, the "square-inch" method may be used. For more accurate copy fitting, the "character-count" method is indispensable.

Square-inch method In this method the number of words in the copy is counted, and this number is divided by the number of words per square inch that can be set in types of particular sizes, as given in standard tables, similar to Table 18–1.

This method will indicate roughly and in a preliminary way the number of square inches the copy will occupy in a given point size leaded a given number of points. However, it does not take into account the differences between widths of types of varying degrees of fatness or thinness, and it could be quite inaccurate if the type chosen is either very extended or very condensed. Also, the method will be inaccurate if the copy contains an unusual number of long or short words.

The character-count method Obviously more accurate is the character-count method, which ignores word lengths and is based on counting the number of characters (letters, spaces, and punctuation marks) in the

TABLE 18–1
Estimated number of words to the square inch

Type size	Words per square inch	
	Solid	Leaded 2 points
6 point................47		34
8 point................32		23
10 point................21		16
12 point................14		11
14 point................11		9
18 point................ 7		6

copy and relating this to the number of lines of a given length the copy will make when set in a specific size and style of type. The basic information needed is the number of characters in the typewritten copy and the average number of characters per pica in the type chosen. In estimating the manuscript copy, it is helpful to know that copy typed in pica type will have 10 characters to the inch and copy typed in elite type will have 12. Printers, type foundries, and manufacturers of typesetting machines supply copy-fitting guides and tables that give the average number of characters per pica in the various type sizes and styles. This information is similar to that shown in Table 18–2.

Note that the same type face and size in different typesetting systems may have different character counts per pica. It is important to do your copy-fitting calculations in the systems that will be used in setting your copy.

To illustrate copy fitting by the character-count method, let us assume

TABLE 18–2
Characters per pica in different sizes and styles of type

Type size and style	Characters per pica	Type size and style	Characters per pica
Century Expanded (Linofilm)		Garamond (No. 3) (Linotype)	
8 point 2.80		8 point 3.20	
9 point 2.50		9 point 3.00	
10 point 2.30		10 point 2.85	
12 point 1.95		11 point 2.65	
14 point 1.90		12 point 2.50	
		14 point 2.15	
News Gothic (Videocomp)		Caslon Old Style (Monotype)	
8 point 3.10		7 point 3.50	
9 point 2.80		8 point 3.20	
10 point 2.50		10 point 2.60	
11 point 2.30		12 point 2.25	

Note that the same type face and size in different typesetting systems may have different character counts per pica. It is important to do your copy-fitting calculations in the systems that will be used in setting your copy.

that you have counted the number of characters in a typewritten block of copy which according to the layout is to occupy a space 4 inches wide (or 24 picas) by 5 inches deep (or 30 picas). You find that you have 1,500 characters, and you would like to set this copy in 12 point Garamond No. 3, leaded 1 point. The additional steps necessary to determine whether or not your copy will fit are as follows:

1. By reference to a type book or a copy-fitting guide giving information similar to that given in Table 18–2, you ascertain that 12 point Garamond No. 3 sets 2.50 characters per pica. Since your line is to be 24 picas wide, you multiply 2.50 by 24 and determine that there will be 60 characters per printed line.
2. You divide the number of characters in the copy (1,500) by 60. This gives you the number of printed lines, or 25.
3. Now, you multiply the number of lines by the point size plus leading (12 plus 1 or 13) and divide by 72 (the number of points in an inch). This will give you the vertical space required in inches, or about 4½ inches. In picas this would be a little over 27.

You are short but still fairly close to having a fit, and you could add a few lines of copy to fill or you could settle for a bit more white space in the layout.

A helpful technique is to type your copy originally the same number of characters per line as will be contained in a line of type in the size and style you have chosen. Bear in mind that tables giving average number of characters per pica in various type sizes and styles do not apply to display lines set in all capitals, capitals and small capitals, or ornamental faces. Here it is necessary to compare the copy letter for letter with the type face chosen.

Methods of composition

Composition—the transforming of original copy into a form suitable for printing or making printing plates—has made significant advances in recent years. There are today five principal methods in use: (1) setting metal type by hand; (2) setting metal type by machine; (3) setting copy on a typewriter or typewriterlike machine such as the IBM Composer, the Justowriter or the Varityper; (4) photocomposition; and (5) Cathode Ray Tube (CRT) composition. The traditional hot metal typesetting systems have rapidly been giving ground in recent years to various photocomposition systems, with their greater flexibility and speed, in the creation of type for advertising text and display. Machine composition has been made faster and more efficient by the introduction of paper or magnetic tape and the use of the computer automatically to hyphenate and "justify" lines faster than the operator can on the keyboard.

Hand setting   As its name indicates, this is strictly a hand operation in which individual metal (rarely, wood) characters and spaces are assembled one at a time, set in a "composing stick," and spaced out to the desired measure. Its use is limited today to display purposes and to occasional small blocks of type. Hand setting may employ any one of three kinds of type: (1) foundry, (2) Monotype, and (3) Ludlow. Foundry type, used mainly for display, is purchased ready-made from the type foundries by the compositor. Monotype consists of individual characters cast as needed in the Monotype machine. Ludlow is cast on a Ludlow machine as a slug rather than as individual characters, but it is classed as hand composition because the mats for the characters must first be assembled by hand. This method is used primarily for casting display lines.

Setting metal type by machine   Three machines are available to set metal type; Monotype, Linotype, and Intertype (see Figures 18–5 and 18–6). The Linotype and Intertype machines are virtually identical. In describing Linotype, therefore, we shall also be describing Intertype. All three machines are essentially devices for pouring molten (hot) metal into small molds (mats or matrices), to form type characters in accordance with instructions fed into the machine. The instructions are given by an operator typing the copy on the keyboard of the machine or by punched tape from a teletypesetter or computer, or in the case of Monotype, from a perforated roll of paper produced by an operator on a separate keyboard machine.

In Monotype, as the perforated roll is fed into the casting machine it causes the matrix case to move so that individual characters are in position to receive the molten metal and in rapid sequence form a line of type of individual characters and word spaces. Justification of each line so it reaches its full measure is accomplished by control punches in the perforated roll that set the width of word spaces. The lines are discharged onto a galley tray. Monotype is cast of harder metal than that used for Linotype. Its main advantages, however, are greater flexibility in setting difficult material such as tables and mathematical formulas, and less difficulty and expense in making corrections.

The Linotype machine combines keyboard and caster in the same machine, linked by a magazine containing mats. When the key for a given character is pressed, the corresponding mat is released and drops into position in a rack on which the desired length of line in picas is controlled. The mats continue to drop into their places in the line until the operator decides that when spaces are put in, it will be filled to the desired measure. Then he sends it to the casting element, where the line of mats is justified. The device that makes justification possible is the spaceband, a small, wedge-shaped piece of metal about 4 inches in length placed between words as the mats are assembled (see Figure 18–7). As the line comes into

FIGURE 18–5
Linotype machine

position to be cast, a bar moving from below pushes the spacebands until the line is wedged out to full measure. Then the line is cast as a solid slug, trimmed, and ejected into a galley tray. The mats are returned automatically to the magazine for reuse.

Each mat can have two—and no more—characters on it. Usually this will be the roman and italic forms of the same character, but it may be roman and boldface, or even the same letter from two different type faces. Changing from one character to the other is accomplished by moving a lever which operates like the shift key on a typewriter. The limitation of

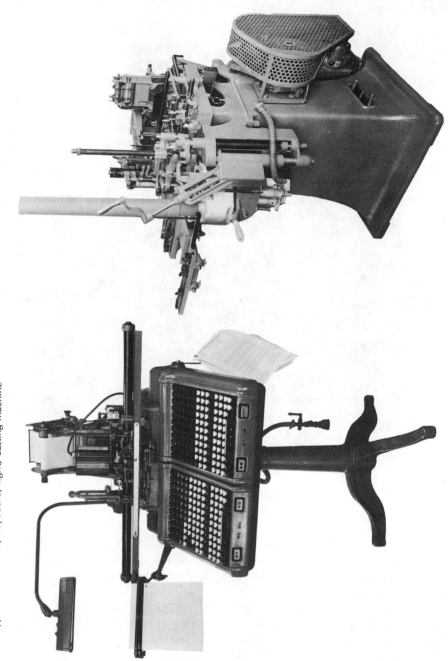

FIGURE 18-6
Monotype machine—*left*, keyboard; *right*, casting machine

FIGURE 18–7
Line of Linotype mats assembled with spacebands
between words

being able to have only two characters on a mat is overcome by the use of a Linotype Mixer, which provides two to four extra magazines of different fonts to which access can be obtained by the operator by the shift of a lever. For greater speed some linotype machines are driven by perforated paper tape prepared on a teletype style typewriter keyboard.

Linotype and Intertype are faster, and therefore less costly, than Monotype. However, corrections are somewhat more difficult to make and cost more.

Typewriter (cold type) composition   Machines similar to typewriters, such as the IBM Composer, the Justowriter, and the Varityper, may also be used to compose type which can be transformed into printing plates. They provide a typescript like an ordinary typewriter, but they have devices for spacing out lines, or justifying right-hand margins. Also, the characters vary in width like hot metal characters, and it is possible to secure a variety of type styles. The typescript can be further varied by the use of art type that can be pasted in for display lines. These machines provide a sharper image than the ordinary typewriter does and give good results when the typescript is made into a printing plate by a photochemical process. This form of composition offers substantial savings, and it is used when economy is a primary consideration.

Optical character recognition   OCR devices, using fiber optics, phototransistors, or laser beam, scan specially typed copy and produce perforated paper tape or magnetic tape to drive hot metal or phototypesetting machines. The typed copy carries typographic function codes, the phototypesetting equipment does the hyphenation, justification, and typographic formatting, or a computer can perform these latter functions in producing paper tape for hot metal setting.

A Video Display Terminal (VDT) may be put into the system following the OCR operation. This device looks like a hybrid television set and typewriter. The device reads the coded tape and brings copy onto the screen. An editor or newspaper mark-up man can make corrections and insert typesetting command codes for a news story, display, or classified ad.

Phototypography   With the printing industry shift from letterpress to offset printing, the fastest growing typesetting method uses photography rather than molten metal to form characters. The final product is a film or photographic paper positive or negative image which is used directly to make offset printing plates or photopolymer letterpress plates.

Development in the 1950s and 60s was rapid and complex. By the mid-1970s there were well over 100 different phototypesetting machines for setting text or display or both. We will touch on a few of those more widely used in advertising.

In general, equipment such as the Alphatype, Linofilm, and Photon can produce type in a greater range of sizes, can mix and align more type fonts, produce sharper images, simplify ad makeup, and provide more spacing flexibility (leading, character fit, kerning) than earlier systems. The machines are capable of extremely fast output. Input speeds (keyboarding) are the limiting factor. Corrections are more complex, slower, and more costly.

The Alphatype keyboard produces "hard copy" for proofreading and magnetic tape for driving the photounit. A high level of typographic quality, usually demanded by advertisers, is assured by the use of a separate type font in each size up to 18 point in the photounit. The 168-character type font typically contains the roman-italic combination of 84 alphabet characters. These characters are negative images in a photographic film "grid." The grids for different type faces and sizes are mounted in the photounit as required. Up to five grids can be "mixed" at a time. Light, flashing through the font characters as directed by the coded magnetic tape, exposes letters, words, and lines of type on photographic film which when developed is used to make offset or photopolymer letterpress plates.

Usually, various chunks of text and display photocomposition are assembled with film of line and halftone art in proper position and "stripped" together for platemaking.

The Linofilm keyboard unit produces hard copy for proofreading and a punched paper tape for driving the photounit. The codes punched into the tape control type face and size, line length, and leading. The Linofilm grid contains 88 characters, and up to 18 grids can be mounted in the photounit at one time. By means of a lens system, more than one type

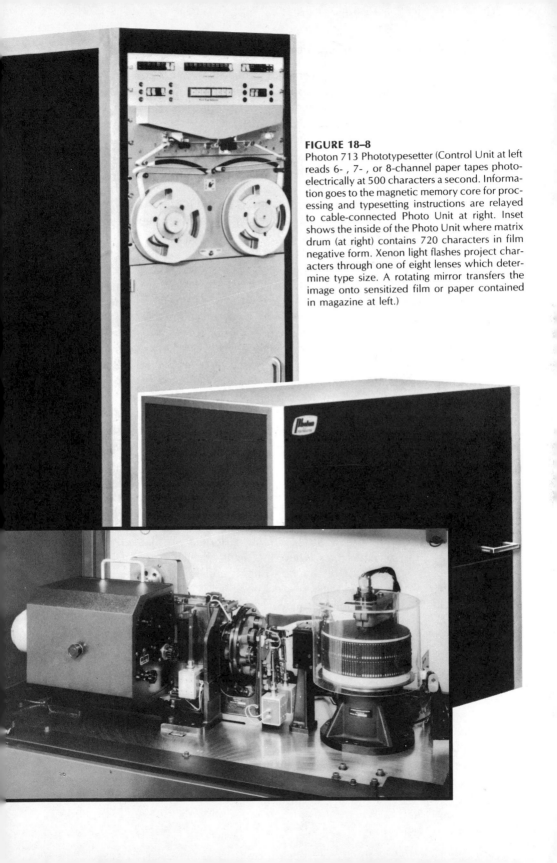

FIGURE 18–8

Photon 713 Phototypesetter (Control Unit at left reads 6-, 7-, or 8-channel paper tapes photoelectrically at 500 characters a second. Information goes to the magnetic memory core for processing and typesetting instructions are relayed to cable-connected Photo Unit at right. Inset shows the inside of the Photo Unit where matrix drum (at right) contains 720 characters in film negative form. Xenon light flashes project characters through one of eight lenses which determine type size. A rotating mirror transfers the image onto sensitized film or paper contained in magazine at left.)

size is produced from a given grid. Three different grids of a face are used to produce sizes from 6 to 36 point. Light flashing through the grids and lenses onto photographic film or paper produces positive copy for stripping or paste-up into the ad.

The Photon machine widely used in newspaper typesetting has a photounit in various models operated by paper or magnetic tape, carrying 8 to 32 fonts of 90 or 96 characters capable of producing from 8 to 23 type sizes from 4½ to 72 points up to 54 picas wide. (See Figure 18–8.)

By the beginning of 1974, according to the International Typographic Composition Association, 62 percent of typesetters used metal composition, down from 95 percent in 1960 and 81 percent in 1970. The trend to photocomposition had accelerated.

CRT   Cathode Ray Tube typesetting devices are electronic rather than photographic in nature. One version of the machine has a computer memory which stores fonts of type. Properly keyboarded magnetic tape is combined with type selection and other programmed formatting information often stored on a disk memory. The resulting new tape triggers the character-generating functions, and characters and lines of type are rapidly formed on the face of a cathode ray (TV) tube and exposed to a strip of photographic film. Drawings and photos can be scanned. Computer programming of the device can produce fully made up book and catalog pages on the initial pass through the equipment. Speeds range up to 10,000 characters per second, but input keyboarding speeds are comparatively very low. The movable type of Gutenberg has become movable electronic dots.

PHOTOENGRAVING AND PLATE DUPLICATION

Photoengraving is a process by means of which photography can be used to create a printing surface. Its basic principle is that actinic light can change the physical properties of a light-sensitive surface, such as its solubility in water or resistance to acid, and this differentiation can be further enhanced and utilized to create either (1) a relief plate (engraving), in which the nonprinting surface is etched away, or (2) its reverse, a gravure or intaglio plate in which the printing parts of the surface are etched away, or (3) a lithographic plate in which the material on the plate that is to be printed differs chemically from the nonprinting areas so that the printing areas attract the greasy ink while the nonprinting areas, when dampened, repel it.

Through the photoengraving process, art work—line charts, drawings, photographs—and paste-up of type can be transferred to a negative photochemically, and the image on the negative can be transferred to a metal plate for printing. While photoengraving is most commonly used to reproduce art work of all kinds, it can also be used to reproduce combinations of illustrations and type or even of type alone, or the products of photocomposition. We shall discuss photoengraving as it relates to (1) line plates and halftones; (2) combination plates and those using Ben Day and its variations; (3) color plates and color separations; and (4) duplicate plates, including electrotypes, stereotypes, and plastics. There will be additional discussion of plates in connection with the discussion of printing methods.

Line plates and halftones

The photoengravings used in reproducing art work for letterpress printing are of two kinds: line plates and halftones. Line plates are also called "zinc" etchings, although they may also be made today of magnesium or a special alloy called Micrometal. Line plates are used when the copy to be reproduced is single tone; when the copy is multitone, halftones are required, since line engravings do not show continuous tones in gradations from solid black through grays to white. The line engraving prints from solid lines or areas. Thus, a line chart of a pen-and-ink sketch can be reproduced by a line cut, but a photograph cannot.

Halftones reproduce shadings and gradations of tone by breaking up the copy into thousands of dots. This is done by photographing the copy through a glass or plastic film plate or screen on which appears a grid of fine lines. The individual size of the resulting dot is in proportion to the amount of ink to be printed in its position on the printed version. This gives the illusion of varying tones, corresponding to those of the original. Larger dots with less intervening white space produce darker tones. Smaller dots with more intervening white space produce the lighter tones. Generally speaking, a halftone consists of three tones: the very light ones, or highlights; the grays or shadows; and the dark tones of lowlights. Variations in size of dots is shown in Figure 18–9.

The size and distance apart of the dots, and therefore the quality of the illusion, depends upon the fineness of the screen. This is designated as the

FIGURE 18–9
Cross-section of a halftone showing variations in the size and character of dots that serve as the printing surface (reproduced by permission of the Colton Press and the Regensteiner Corporation)

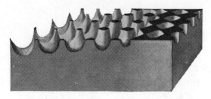

FIGURE 18–10
Halftones showing the effect of photographing the same subject through 65-line screen, 110-line screen, and 133-line screen

number of lines the grid has to the inch. For example, a 65-line screen will have 65 parallel lines to the inch each way. Screens are commonly available in a range from 50 line to 150 line, though coarser and finer screens exist. Variation in fineness of screen is necessary because the paper on which the halftone is to be printed may be coarse and absorbent of ink or smooth and glossy. The paper on which newspapers are printed requires a coarser screen; slick-paper magazines will take a fine-screen halftone. Figure 18–10 shows the effect different screens have on the reproduction of a photograph. In the coarser screen, the dots can even be seen with the naked eye.

After the subject is photographed through a screen, and the film negative developed, it can be transferred to a sensitized metal plate which is then etched with acid to produce a raised printing surface (halftone engraving) for letterpress printing. The negative (or positive) will be handled in a different way to produce gravure or lithographic printing surfaces, and it, by itself, also bears the name "halftone."

Combination plates and Ben Day

Line and halftone techniques can be used jointly to produce a combination plate. Such a plate will print varying shades of tone, as does a halftone, and the solid blacks, as does a line cut. Although more costly than an ordinary halftone, the combination facilitates prior combination by the advertiser of text and illustrations in a single plate or pieces of film to send to a printer.

Some of the tonal effects of the halftone, and a variety of shadings and patterns, can be included in a line cut by using the Ben Day process or its variations. These are mechanical methods of applying dots, lines, stipple effects, and a wide variety of patterns, either on the art work by the artist or later by the engraver. Available to the artist are various commercial types of paste-on material consisting of shading, stippling, crosshatching, and so on which may be applied directly to the art work. The engraver has in stock numerous Ben Day screens by means of which the dots and patterns can be transferred photographically to the negative and later to an engraving. Ben Day lends itself both to black-and-white and color reproduction.

Color plates

The method of making four-color process engravings is based on the principle that all colors can be printed by combinations of three primary colors—yellow, red, and blue. Black is added to give density and detail to the reproduction. In any four-color process printing, there must be a separate impression for the black and for each of the three primary colors. In letterpress printing, separate halftone engravings are made for the black and for each of the colors. These are made by the same process as regular halftones.

The first step, however, is to produce color separations. This is done by photographing the subject four times. The copy is photographed with a special lens to secure the black, and each of the three primary colors is isolated by means of filters on the camera. The end result is four separate halftone plates, each screened at a different angle. Tiny clusters of halftone dots of the four colors in varying sizes on the printed page then give to the eye the illusion of seeing the many different colors of the original photograph or painting. For good results, four-color process printing requires that each impression be registered or aligned with precision. Otherwise the subject will be blurred.

To aid the printer in matching the quality of the original as closely as possible, each color plate is proofed separately in the exact ink and on the paper to be used in the regular run of the advertisement. The printer is also furnished with a set of "progressives," proofs that show not only the individual color printings but also the color sequence in printing and the result as each additional color is added.

If the advertisement is to be printed by gravure or lithography, color-separated positive or negative film is furnished rather than plates. These are color corrected, that is, improved by hand work, and transferred to the type of printing plates used in each method.

Scan-A-Color, and other electronic scanning devices, provide color separations, producing a set of color-corrected separations in less than an hour. These separations are on film and may be used with letterpress, lithographic, or gravure printing. Scan-A-Color has a computer that electronically relates the factors of density range, hue, brightness, and saturation for optimum results.

Besides process color printing, simple, flat, color printing may be done. This may consist of line color for printing selected lines of type or rules, borders, ornaments, and so on, or the Ben Day areas in illustrations. Or it may consist of overprinting—printing one transparent color on top of another. Halftones may also be printed in a single color or as duotones, a combination of two halftones, one black, the other in color, so treated in the photographic process as to secure an effect of contrast and depth not possible by printing a halftone over a panel of solid color. For a simple color plate, the advertiser starts with black-and-white copy—one copy for each of the colors if they overlap. If they do not overlap, a single black-and-white copy is used as a key, and the other colors are pasted on as transparent acetate overlays.

In preparing advertising folders, catalogs, and so on, for which the entire process of production can be controlled by the advertiser, it is possible to use the paper itself to provide one color, thus securing a two-color effect with one printing impression.

Duplicate plates

Most advertisers find duplicate plates advantageous and even essential, for several reasons. If the advertisement is to appear in several periodicals simultaneously, duplicate plates are an obvious necessity. Also, with duplicates the same material can be run at the same time on more than one press.

A duplicate *electrotype* or electro is made by preparing a negative mold of the original type and engravings in vinyl plastic, or the now rarely used wax or lead, and using an electrolytic process to deposit a shell of copper on it. This, when properly backed up, becomes a duplicate printing plate. Electros used mainly for long, letterpress runs are often chrome plated for extra wear.

For letterpress newspapers, the advertisers usually supply mats. These are papier-maché impressions made by pressing the original plate into cellulose pulp, producing a negative mold. The newspaper casts a positive plate called a *stereotype* from this mold by placing it in a casting box and pouring molten metal over it. The quality of reproduction to be secured from the stereotype is inferior to that obtainable from the electro, but the stereos are less expensive and, since the mats are light in weight, shipping costs are reduced.

Stereotyping offers an economical and rapid method of supplying multiple plates of an advertisement. When an advertiser wishes to run an advertisement in, say, 100 newspapers, it is easy and economical to supply mats and let the papers make their own casts.

If the newspaper prints by the offset method, the advertiser supplies reproduction proof (repros). These are merely very high quality prints of the type pulled on enamel paper for the best quality result. The paper would then make film negatives or positives, strip in a screened film of the illustrations, and expose his printing plate.

Other molded letterpress plates are made of rubber or plastic under heat and pressure. The letterflex photopolymer plates for letterpress are made through photography and use a photosensitive plastic to form the raised printing surface.

PRINTING

There are four basic printing processes in common use today: letterpress; gravure; lithography, especially offset lithography; and screen process printing, often called silk screen.

Letterpress

The oldest method of printing is by letterpress. In letterpress printing, ink is applied to a raised (relief) surface and transferred to paper by direct pressing onto the paper. This may be done from metal type, but more commonly it is done from plates in which the portions to be printed are in relief.

Although there is a distinct trend toward offset lithography, most newspapers and a variety of advertising materials are printed by letterpress. The presses used in letterpress are of three types: (1) platen, (2) cylinder, and (3) rotary.

On a *platen* press there are two flat surfaces—one the bed, which holds the type form, and the other the platen, which holds the paper. These open and close much like the jaws of a clamshell. Ink is applied to the form, as the jaws open and close, by a roller which alternately passes over it and a flat ink plate behind it. At the same time a sheet of paper is fed to the platen, usually from an automatic feeder. When the jaws close, the sheet is printed, and when they open again, the printed sheet is delivered and a new sheet is fed in. Platen presses are relatively slow and are most useful in job printing and for short runs.

On *cylinder* presses the printing form is placed on a large, flat bed while a rotating cylinder applies the pressure. Ink rollers and sheets of paper carried by the cylinder alternately pass over the printing form held in the bed. There are also *perfecting* flat-bed presses which print simultaneously

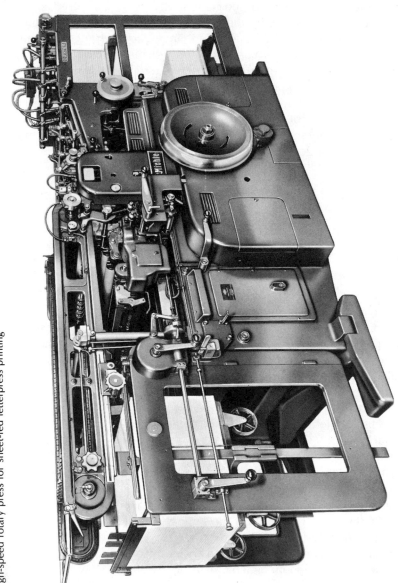

FIGURE 18–11
High-speed rotary press for sheet-fed letterpress printing

on both sides of the paper by means of two flat beds and two cylinders. Cylinder presses are much faster than the platen presses.

By far the fastest and most efficient of the presses for letterpress printing are the rotary presses (see Figure 18–11). On these, both the printing surface and the paper are on cylinders, and the plates used—generally electrotypes or stereotypes—must be curved to fit the cylinder. The printing impression is made as the two cylinders roll together. Ink rollers ink the printing surface with each revolution of the cylinder. The paper may be fed in sheets or from a continuous roll or "web" of paper. Perfecting web-fed rotary presses print both sides of the paper at the same time by means of additional cylinders. Multicolor web-fed rotary presses make possible the high-speed printing of numerous colors at the same time.

A development designed to make letterpress competitive in price with offset lithography is wrap-around letterpress. In this type of printing, a one-piece shallow-relief plate of full press form size is made and wrapped around the plate cylinder like an offset plate. This adapts a plate with a relief surface to faster rotary speeds and affords a saving in make-ready and plate costs.

Gravure

The principle of gravure or intaglio printing is the reverse of that of letterpress in that the printing surface, instead of being raised, is etched into the plate and is depressed. Ink is laid into minute receptacles in the printing surface and transferred to paper by pressure and suction.

Gravure plates are made by a somewhat more complicated process than that for letterpress plates. The copy is photographed to produce two separate films—one for line copy and the other for halftone copy. The negatives are combined into one continuous film positive. Color separations are made in the same way as for letterpress and offset. In conventional gravure, the image is transferred to a copper cylinder by the use of a sensitized medium called carbon tissue, or Du Pont's Rotofilm may be used. A method adapted especially to color reproduction is the News-Dultgen process which differs in some details from conventional gravure. Another development is the direct transfer method, by means of which the cylinder itself is made light sensitive through the application of a coating. After processing this permits the cylinder to make a direct printing impression.

Gravure is essentially a rotary method, easily adaptable to web-fed printing. The printing cylinder revolves in a trough of ink which not only fills the wells and depressions of the printing surface but also deposits ink over the entire surface. As the cylinder emerges from the ink trough, the surface is wiped dry and free of ink by a "doctor blade," leaving the ink only in the recesses etched into the cylinder. The ink is then "lifted" out of the recesses by the paper as it is pressed against the cylinder. The inks used are quick drying.

Rotogravure presses print long-run newspaper supplements and catalogs at high speed and are web-fed. For shorter runs, sheet-fed gravure presses are also available.

Lithography

In lithography, the printing surface is on the same plane as the nonprinting surface, instead of being raised, as in letterpress, or depressed, as in gravure. Printing in this way is made possible by first processing the surface of the plate in such a way that the areas to be printed become grease receptive while the nonprinting surface becomes water receptive. Water and grease, of course, do not mix. When the plate is moistened with water, therefore, the water-receptive (nonprinting) areas repel the greasy ink when it is spread over the plate, while the grease-receptive (printing) areas pick up the ink. When the plate is brought in contact with paper, a printing impression results.

The first lithographic plates were slabs of limestone, and stone remained in use until the beginning of the 20th century. The images to be printed were drawn on the stone by hand. Today lithographic plates are commonly thin sheets of metal and are of three main types: (1) surface, (2) deep etch, and (3) multimetal.

Surface plates are coated with a light-sensitive, ink-receptive substance so that on exposure, the light coming through a photographic negative hardens the printing area where the light hits; the nonprinting parts stay soft. When the soft parts are washed out and a coating of water-receptive substance is applied, the plate is divided into ink-receptive printing parts and ink-repellent nonprinting parts. Surface plates are designated, according to their materials and processing, as albumen, presensitized, and wipe on.

Deep-etch plates are those in which the plate is processed so that the printing areas are minutely below the surface of the nonprinting areas. These plates are more durable than surface plate and are used for longer runs.

Multimetal plates are those that receive an extra coating of metal through an electrolytic process. Bimetal plates have an ink-receptive metal base on which a light-sensitive coating is placed. On development, the coating is removed from the nonprinting parts and these parts are given a water-receptive metal coating electrolytically. A second bath washes away the remaining light-sensitive coating, leaving bare the ink-receptive base metal (the printing area). Or the process can be reversed so that the base metal is the nonprinting area, and the plated areas are the printing parts. Trimetal plates are those in which the entire plate is metal plated. Bimetal plates are very durable, and trimetal plates are even more so.

FIGURE 18–12
An offset lithography press

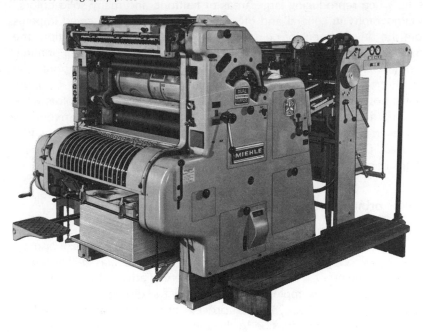

Multimetal plates are, of course, more expensive than any others described, and are used for long runs only.

The images to be printed are placed on the plates by a photochemical process similar to photoengraving. In photographing the copy, line and halftone copy are shot separately. The lithographic camera employs screens to break up tone copy into dots as in the production of any halftone. After the negatives or positives are made, line copy and tone copy are pieced together (stripped) into a single flat. Thus, the lithograph plate contains all the type matter and the illustrations, and it is not necessary to assemble individual cuts and metal type into page forms as in letterpress.

Direct lithography—printing directly from plate to paper—has largely given way to *offset lithography,* the fastest growing printing method of our day. In offset an intermediary cylinder picks up the image from the lithographic plate and transfers it to the paper. Offset presses have three cylinders of the same size: a plate cylinder, a blanket cylinder, and an impression cylinder. The inked and dampened plate on the first cylinder prints on the rubber-blanketed cylinder, which in turn "offsets" onto the paper held on the third or impression cylinder (see Figure 18–12). The use of rubber for the blanket makes it possible to print fine designs and photographs on fairly coarse paper, since the flexibility of rubber will adapt the printing surface to the rough paper surface. Offset lithography is especially useful when reproducing large areas of halftone and many solid colors.

Lithography in general and offset in particular have received impetus from the development of cold-type and photographic composition, the products of which are particularly well adapted to this method of printing. Also, lithography has advantages over letterpress in that it can print type and illustrations with little more effort and cost than type alone. Until the 1940s, however, lithography produced a gray, flat tone, and colors were dull and muddy, which made the result look cheap. Many improvements have been made in presses, inks, and paper so that a first-rate job can now be turned out consistently. The high-speed web offset presses of today set a hard competitive pace for any other process to match.

Screen process printing

Screen process printing, also called "silk screen," is a stencil process in which ink is forced through a mesh screen onto various kinds of printing surfaces—wood, glass, metal, plastic, fabric, and others, as well as paper. This makes the process useful for a wide variety of advertising and packaging purposes. For example, it can be used for displays, banners, and 24-sheet billboards. Today, screen process printing can also be used for longer runs than formerly, due to the introduction of faster presses.

The screen used in screen process printing may be a piece of silk, nylon, Dacron, or metal mesh. The screen is stretched tightly over a wooden or metal frame and serves to hold in place the mask or stencil which has been attached to it. The stencils may be hand cut from film specially designed for this purpose or may be prepared photographically from any drawing or printed design. Ink is squeezed through the screen by a squeegee (a rubber-edged bar) sliding across the surface, causing a printing impression to be made. In color printing, a separate mask or stencil is usually made for each color.

An interesting feature of screen process printing is the ink used. A heavy film of ink can be deposited by this process—even ten times as heavy as that possible with letterpress—and the flow of the ink can be controlled in a way not possible with other methods. The ink can be built up until it looks like embossing. Formerly the ink took a long time to dry, slowing the process, but now there are new types of quick-drying inks and hot-air dryers which have speeded things up.

SELECTING GRAPHIC ARTS SUPPLIERS

In many instances the advertiser does not have control over the mechanical production of the advertising message. He sends copy (on which specifications may or may not have been marked), layout, and art work or art copy to the media, and it is processed from there on by whatever methods the media normally uses; or the advertiser may be in control up to the point of providing film, mats or stereos, electros, or color separations and progressives, or even four-color process plates. The advertiser may or may not have full-time specialists in his employ. His art department, if he has one, will vary in the extent to which it is qualified to do finished art work. It may do the whole job, or it may be necessary to have the work done by the printer or an outside art studio.

Most advertisers do, however, on occasion, particularly in direct-mail advertising, find it necessary to select graphic arts suppliers—engravers, composition houses, binders, and complete printers, as well as art studios. In doing this, certain typical problems arise, and certain principles serve as guidelines in making selections.

The first question that arises is: To what point can we carry the job ourselves and at what stage do we turn it over to the graphic arts specialists? This question largely answers itself, but it is important that the advertiser avoid amateurish experimentation on his own and that he turn the job over to the experts at any point where such specialized skill is not available in his own company.

A second question that must be answered early is: Which is more important in this particular job—speed of production, quality, or cost? Frequently it is not possible to have all three; something of one must be sacrificed to achieve the others. An appropriate balance among these factors for the job in question should be sought.

A third consideration is: Shall we turn the job over to a printer having complete creative and production facilities or shall we deal with separate art studios, engravers, compositors, and even binders if the advertising piece is to have hard or even soft covers? Today, the graphic arts services are highly specialized, although complete printing houses are numerous. Greater economy and better quality may be possible through judicious selection of specialized suppliers. However, this takes more of the advertiser's time in securing estimates and in coordinating the work of the specialized services. It may result in a slower schedule.

A fourth consideration is: By what method shall the advertising message be produced? This choice requires relating the method appropriately to the job from the standpoints of speed, quality, and economy. It will be helpful to bear in mind the following advantages and disadvantages of the various methods.

1. *Letterpress.* This method still gives great assurance of sharp detail and good quality. It does not produce as smooth a tone in illustrations as offset, and it necessitates the use of coated paper stock for fine halftones. It is more expensive than offset.

2. *Gravure.* Gravure does not produce as sharp an impression as letterpress because the entire plate is screened, and the cost of preparing

gravure printing cylinders is high. But it produces excellent results at reasonable cost in runs of 100,000 or more.

3. *Offset.* This is the most economical method for extremely small runs and also is competitively at some advantage in long runs on modern sheet-fed perfector and web offset presses. Offset permits printing of halftones on a wider range of paper stocks and provides smoother tone. It makes it possible to reproduce previously printed copy and typewriter composition as well as various kinds of art work without resetting or redrawing. It is especially well adapted to the use of the products of photocomposition. It eliminates the need for separate cuts of illustrations.

4. *Screen process printing.* The chief advantages of this method are its versatility and the effects that can be achieved through the inks used. Through the screen process, it is possible to print on a large variety of materials besides paper. The inks used give rich effects. The disadvantages are mostly in the slowness of the process relative to the speeds that can be attained by other methods.

Having made, at least tentatively, the foregoing basic decisions about the job, the advertiser should proceed systematically to secure cost estimates. Perhaps he has a printed form available for requesting estimates. In any case it is essential to cover completely what the advertiser expects the supplier to do and to provide exact specifications as to quantity, number of pages, size, number of colors, illustrations, paper stock, and so on. Unless it is possible to describe the job exactly, it will also be necessary to accompany the request for estimate with the actual copy, layout, and perhaps a dummy. A first principle in securing estimates is: Give each supplier exactly the same specifications and the same complete descriptions of what is wanted. Then make sure that the bids are exactly comparable—that is, cover precisely the same services.

In making the final choice of a graphic arts supplier, a few principles will serve as guides:

1. What is the supplier's reputation and past record—especially his past performance with the advertiser's own jobs? Has the supplier been in business long enough to have established a reputation for reliability and good work? If a new firm, are the firm's principals sufficiently experienced and well enough backed financially to inspire confidence? Few things are more frustrating than to have a supplier go broke in the middle of a job or botch the job through incompetence.

2. Will the supplier give you the kind of schedule you want and can he be relied upon to keep his promises on delivery, provided you hold up your end?

3. Is his cost-estimating system sound so that you can have confidence in his estimates? Does he stand by his estimates or does he come around later and beg to be rescued from a bad guess?

4. Does he have all the skills and equipment he needs to do the job?

FIGURE 18–13
Live-action production

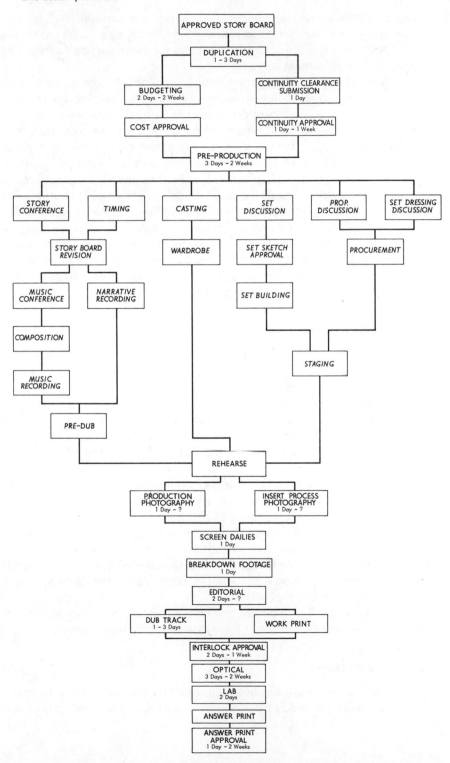

This may include creative services; all the type faces and special characters wanted—either he has them in his own type library or is willing to secure the mats elsewhere; the right kind of presses for the job; a good composing room and proofreading services.

5. Does he have a large amount of special-priority government work or a few large customers for whom he will put your job aside if necessary?

A final word: Always insist on seeing proofs and check them carefully. The battle against errors is a never-ending one, and one frequently lost. Nothing is more embarrassing than to discover gross errors in type or illustrations after the advertisement has been printed. Errors may destroy the entire value of the advertisement or lead to costly complications, as when the price is wrong or the terms of sale are distorted. On the other hand, in proofreading, the high cost of alterations should be kept in mind and balanced against the importance of the change. The layman has little idea of the number of costly operations needed to change even a punctuation mark. To change art elements might require making an entirely new cut or plate. The advertiser can save much time and money by getting the copy and art work right in the first place.

TELEVISION PRODUCTION

The production of a typical live television commercial is relatively simple—simple, that is, if one takes the marvel of television broadcasting as a going system requiring no further explanation. The commercial is simply transmitted and reproduced electronically on the screens of millions of receiving sets in millions of homes at the very instant it is being enacted in the studio. Producing a live commercial is mainly a matter of preparing the studio set, selecting whatever props are to be used, and rehearsing the performance.

Production of a film commercial is considerably more complicated, too complicated to be fully described in these few pages. However, this type of commercial is so predominant in national advertising that the student should have a working knowledge of the basic steps. Also, much of the creative work on a film commercial is done in the production phases. Hooper White, Creative Manager at the Leo Burnett Company, suggests that television production is an "interpretation" rather than a mere execution of writers' and artists' ideas.

This section will outline the production phases of a live-action film commercial. See Figure 18–13 for a flowchart of these phases.

Preproduction operations

Once the storyboard has been approved by the client, the advertising agency's producer sends the storyboard and accompanying production

FIGURE 18–14

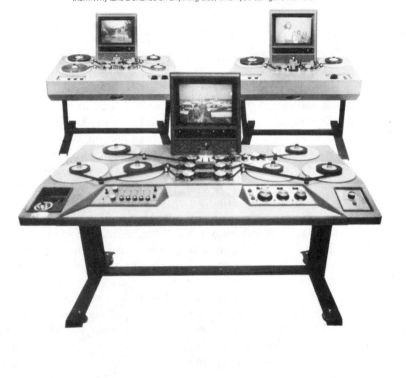

MOVIOLA
When it comes to flatbeds, nobody else cuts it.

Because nobody else in the world knows your film cutting needs like Moviola. That's why our new six-plate, four-plate and two-plate flatbed editors can save you time and money in a way nobody else can match.

They're simple, fast, flexible and precise. With solid, practical features you won't find all together anywhere else. Like picture/sound interlock at ten times sound speed · Electronically controlled picture/sound inching and single-frame viewing · Immediate stop on a precise frame at sound speed with no spillage or tension loss · Frame/footage or second/minute display · Clear and sharp 8½" x 11½" viewer that provides full viewer brightness with no film damage · Integrated circuit audio system · And more.

Remember, we've been a basic, everyday part of the American motion picture industry for more than fifty years. And that kind of on-the-job experience is the reason why our new flatbeds will outperform anything put up against them. Why take a chance on anything else, when you can get a Moviola?

Courtesy of magnasync/moviola corporation

notes, such as announcer preference, set sketches, ideas for props, and music requirements to several producing studios and asks them to bid on the job. After a contract is signed with the winning studio and before the actual shooting schedule begins, the producer gets involved in:

1. Casting sessions to select the actors and/or the announcer.
2. Set design sessions to work out exactly how the background will look.
3. Location discussions, or actual survey trips, to decide where the commercial will be shot.
4. Prop sessions to decide on various articles to be used such as glassware, tableware, furniture, and art objects.
5. Music sessions, if music is required, with composers, singers, performing groups, etc.
6. Arranging shooting schedules, recording sessions, and completion dates.
7. Seeing that all of the above get done.

Filming and editing

Filming a television commercial is much the same as filming a Hollywood movie. In fact, many are done in Hollywood. The individual scenes usually are not shot in the sequence in which they will appear in the final version. Visual and sound tracks may not be recorded at the same time. Several different angles and views of each scene are taken to give the film editor a choice of best possible shots when putting the commercial together.

After the shooting begins, the film is quickly developed, often overnight, to provide *rushes* or *dailies* which are hurried prints of inferior quality. Rushes give the director an opportunity to screen the preceding day's work, to select the best shots, and to decide whether any retakes are needed before the set is torn down and the cast disbanded.

In the "postproduction" phase of film making, the sound track is completed, the picture cut or edited, and finally the two are "married" or printed together for the first time on an answer print.

Usually the sound or audio part of the spot is completed first. All of the individual sound tracks that will make up the completed or mixed track are transferred to magnetic sprocketed film. This may include separate tracks of lip-synchronized footage already filmed on stage or location, voice-over narration, one or more music tracks, and one or more sound effects tracks.

A sound cutter "lays in" or arranges these tracks so that they can be mixed. At the mxing session, an audio engineer operates a console with a "pot" or dial that controls the volume of each track. Therefore, he can make one sound "underscore" another or cause one sound to fade or segue into another.

Often the audio mixing is done to a rough cut of the picture. Or the editor may cut the spot to a completed mixed track.

The editor uses a "workprint" made from the original footage. Frame-by-frame, using a Moviola, the selected scenes or shots are arranged to work with each other and the sound track. Optical effects are indicated in grease pencil on the workprint.

At an "interlock" the workprint is projected in "sync" with the audio track to see how the spot "works" and for client approval before expensive optical work is done.

Edge numbers on the workprint and the original footage allow the "conformist" to cut together the scenes of original footage exactly as they have been selected by the "editor."

Effects such as multiple images, type supers, dissolves, fades, and wipes are made on an optical printer.

When work is completed on the picture part of the spot, it is finally combined with the master sound track to produce the answer print. From storyboard to answer print, the production of a standard, live-action commercial takes seven to eight weeks.

After the answer print has been approved, an appropriate number of release prints are prepared and these are shipped to the networks and/or individual stations for broadcast.

QUESTIONS AND PROBLEMS

1   Bring to class five advertisements each of which projects an atmosphere or character that is: (1) feminine, (2) masculine, (3) elegant, (4) rugged, (5) old fashioned.

2   Type faces are classified into fonts, series, families, and groups or classes. Define each.

3   What factors should be considered in the selection of type faces?

4   How many agate lines are there in a newspaper advertisement 10 inches deep and 4 columns wide?

5   Even though typographic composition has shifted rapidly in recent years from metal to film the knowledge, skill and craftsmanship of expert typographers is still required. Explain.

6   Contrast halftones and line plates in terms of the mechanics of manufacture and their usefulness in reproducing illustrations.

7   What principles underlie four-color process as a means of reproducing color photographs and paintings?

8   What are the differences between various types of lithograph plates?

9   What factors should be considered in selecting a graphic arts supplier?

10   As advertising manager, you have been handed a manuscript of 10,000 characters to be set in type for a direct-mail pamphlet, which will measure

in page size 6 X 9 inches. This type is to be set in 10-point with 2-point leads in an area 4½ X 7¼ inches on each page.

a)   What are the minimum number of pages which are required for printing this manuscript in the design of type you prefer?

b)   Inasmuch as the economical cuts for the paper that would be used to make a booklet of this size fold into 4, 8, 16, and 32 pages, what recommendations would you make?

11   Production of a television commercial has sometimes been referred to as "creative interpretation." Why?

part four

Advertising media

Media planning

The advertising medium is the carrier of the advertising message. Before the days of the printing press, about the only means the advertiser had for transmitting his message were signs and town criers. Today, our vast array of printed publications, radio stations, and television stations offers the advertisers so many ways of communicating his message to the public that the problem of developing a media plan, including choosing an appropriate medium, is of major importance. The principal media may be classified as follows:

1. Newspapers
2. Magazines
   - a. Consumer magazines
   - b. Business publications
   - c. Farm publications
   - d. Professional journals
3. Radio
4. Television
5. Direct mail
6. Outdoor
   - a. Signs
   - b. Posters
   - c. Painted bulletins
   - d. Electric displays
7. Transit
8. Others
   - a. Dealer displays
   - b. Packages, labels, and inserts
   - c. Films
   - d. Specialties
   - e. Directories
   - f. Sampling

TABLE 19–1
Advertising expenditures in the United States in 1972 and 1973

| Medium | 1972* | | 1973 | | |
	Millions	Percent of total	Millions	Percent of total	Percent change
Newspapers					
Total	$ 7,008	30.3	$ 7,705	30.7	+10.0
National	1,103	4.8	1,150	4.6	+ 4.0
Local.	5,905	25.5	6,555	26.1	+11.0
Magazines					
Total	1,440	6.2	1,470	5.9	+ 2.0
Weeklies.	610	2.6	580	2.3	− 5.0
Women's	368	1.6	370	1.5	+ 1.0
Monthlies	462	2.0	520	2.1	+12.0
Farm publications	59	0.3	65	0.3	+10.0
Television					
Total	4,091	17.7	4,565	18.1	+12.0
Network	1,804	7.8	2,020	8.0	+12.0
Spot	1,318	5.7	1,460	5.8	+11.0
Local.	969	4.2	1,085	4.3	+12.0
Radio					
Total	1,555	6.7	1,625	6.5	+ 5.0
Network	75	0.3	70	0.3	− 5.0
Spot	400	1.7	380	1.5	− 5.0
Local.	1,080	4.7	1,175	4.7	+ 9.0
Direct mail.	3,350	14.5	3,580	14.2	+ 7.0
Business papers	781	3.4	855	3.4	+ 9.0
Outdoor					
Total	292	1.3	310	1.2	+ 6.0
National	192	0.8	200	0.8	+ 5.0
Local.	100	0.4	110	0.4	+10.0
Miscellaneous					
Total	4,554	19.7	4,965	19.7	+ 9.0
National	2,418	10.5	2,590	10.3	+ 7.0
Local.	2,136	9.2	2,375	9.4	+11.0
Total					
National	12,940	55.9	13,840	55.1	+ 7.0
Local.	10,190	44.1	11,300	44.9	+11.0
Grand total	$23,130	100.0	$25,140	100.0	+ 8.7

* Revised.
Source: *Advertising Age,* December 17, 1973, p. 114.

Estimates of total advertising expenditures in the various types of media during 1971 and 1972 are shown in Table 19–1. Expenditures for newspaper advertising are 30 percent of the total. Television advertising expenditures, which increased dramatically during the 1960s, now usually account for around 17 to 18 percent of the total volume and thus are in second place. Direct mail, the importance of which is often overlooked, is third. Whereas retail or local advertising is heavily concentrated in newspapers, national advertising is more widely distributed among a number of media.

ELEMENTS OF THE MEDIA PLAN

In the development of a media plan, the advertising strategist should take into account various strategic elements. Before discussing some of these elements, however, it will be helpful to examine several basic media concepts.

Reach is a term used to designate the number of different homes or individuals exposed to a given medium or combination of media over a period of time. Reach is expressed as a percent of all the homes or individuals comprising the market involved. When two or more issues of the same media vehicle or when two or more vehicles are used, there is likely to be some "duplication," that is, some homes or individuals will be reached by both issues or by both vehicles. For example, the reach of a single issue of a weekly magazine might be 25 percent of all U.S. homes. With three issues, the magazine's reach might extend to, say, 37 percent (these figures are for a hypothetical magazine; each magazine, such as *Time, Good Housekeeping, Playboy,* and the like, has its own pattern of duplication). For television, the term *reach* generally is used to designate the number of different homes (expressed as a percent of total homes) exposed over a four-week period. A major network television program, such as "All in the Family," will typically reach over 50 percent of U.S. homes with four telecasts. Even though reach deals with an unduplicated audience, duplication need not and generally cannot be avoided. Repetition can be a good thing.

Frequency refers to the average number of times different households or individuals are reached by a particular media schedule within a period of time. For example, the frequency attained with three issues of a weekly magazine might be 2.2 times. In other words, in the 37 percent of U.S. homes reached by at least one of the three issues of such a magazine (from our example in the preceding paragraph), an average of 2.2 issues are read. Frequency of impressions is depended upon to reinforce the image, to remind, and to sustain a share of the customer's mind. The greater the frequency, the greater the probability that the message will make a deep and lasting impression.

Reach and frequency, taken together, provide a third basic concept— *gross rating points* (GRP). This is merely the gross weight or the total tonnage that is being directed toward a particular market during a period of time. The GRP level is derived by multiplying reach by frequency. For example, if a media plan seeks to reach 40 percent of a particular target an average of five times, the GRP level of the plan is 200 (40 X 5). By knowing the GRP level, a planner can make useful comparisons among media alternatives.

Continuity refers to the overall pattern of message deliveries over a period of time. Insertions and/or broadcasts may be scheduled at about

FIGURE 19–1
A total media plan

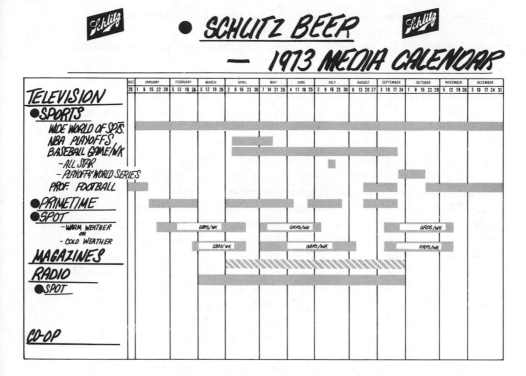

the same frequency the year around, or they may be concentrated in particular seasons. Continuity may also pertain to the way a specific medium is used. A continuous schedule in the same medium provides repeated impressions on the same audience. Shifting from one medium to another tends to sacrifice continuity in favor of wider coverage. The media plan in Figure 19–1 illustrates the patterning of media usage over a 12-month period.

Size of the message, measured in space units for print media and time units for broadcast media, affects the strength of each impression. It is generally assumed that a two-page spread makes a stronger impression than a single page; that a full page makes a stronger impression than a half page; that a one-minute commercial makes a stronger impression than a thirty-second commercial, etc.

When planning media expenditures the advertiser must deal with reach, frequency, continuity, and size as interrelated and interdependent elements that can be combined to form many different message delivery patterns. The interdependence of these elements and the variety of possible combinations are indicated in the following alternatives:

1. Greater reach at the expense of frequency, and/or continuity, and/or message size.
2. Greater frequency at the expense of reach, and/or continuity, and/or message size.
3. Greater continuity at the expense of reach, and/or frequency, and/or message size.
4. Larger message size at the expense of reach, and/or frequency, and/or continuity.

It should be apparent that there is no single combination of these elements that is ideally suited to every advertising situation. Each advertiser, within the limitations of his budget, must develop the pattern of reach, frequency, continuity, and message sizes that he deems best to achieve his own objectives. If he does not deliver messages broadly enough, or in sufficient number, or with sufficient regularity, his advertising dollars will be largely wasted.

Having introduced the basic media concepts, attention now can be directed to the strategic elements to be considered when designing a media plan. These elements, discussed in the following pages of this chapter, are (1) the market, (2) extent and character of distribution, (3) creative strategy, (4) circulations, (5) audiences, (6) costs, (7) editorial or program content, and (8) advertiser usage.

The market—type of consumers

The first task of the advertiser in developing his media plan will be a thorough and definite understanding of the market for his product. An advertising medium is a carrier of a message. The sender of the message can select the carrier with intelligence only after he knows the type or class of consumers to whom the message is to be directed. Is the message to be aimed at all types of consumers or to women, children, professional people, sport lovers, businessmen, farmers, blacks, or some religious sect? If to businessmen, what kind of business—manufacturing or trading? If to the former, what particular kind of production—steel, lumber, food, automobile, glass, pottery, textile, or novelty? What kind of men in the manufacturing field are to receive the message—executives, plant superintendents, foremen, purchasing agents, or laborers?

Most of this information will have been collected in the consumer-research studies carried on by or for the advertiser. It is important that media be selected that will reach the desired group. Newpapers, magazines, radio stations, and other media are not all alike. One newspaper will have a different following from another. One will be conservative in its editorial and news policy; another liberal. One will have the laboring class as its heaviest subscribers, while another will attract the "white-collar" classes.

Magazines have a much more selective audience than newspapers. In the field of sports there are special magazines for the hunter and trapper, the golfer, the fisherman, and the tennis player. Every well-established profession has its own journal written in the language of the profession. A special group of magazines is available for those wishing to advertise to youth. There is a religious press appealing to people of each particular faith.

Radio and television stations also have their own type of audience. This is especially true of radio stations where selection is made on the basis of the character of the stations. Some stations will emphasize educational programs, in-depth news analysis, symphonic music, operas, and theatrical productions. Others will have their time predominantly filled with currently popular music and news headlines. Each kind of program attracts a different audience, the character of which can be determined by analysis. This is often done by the station, and the information made available to the advertiser.

The type of consumer to whom advertising is to be directed is often predetermined by the character of the product. Farm machinery is not sold to the public in general. It would be folly to advertise such products in a general magazine such as *TV Guide*. Industrial goods will usually not be advertised in general consumer magazines but in those that reach a particular buyer group.

Since the real purpose of an advertising medium is that of a messenger, strong emphasis must be placed upon the necessity for knowing the direction the messenger takes. A merchant in Chicago would not think of shipping a package destined for New York City on a train going to Denver. Yet there are advertisers that put an advertisement "aboard" a particular medium not knowing whether the medium goes to the type of consumer that should logically be interested in their products. This situation can be remedied only by knowing, first, the type of prospect and, second, the ability of the medium to reach that prospect.

Extent and character of distribution

Advertising will be of little or no value in getting people to buy merchandise unless such merchandise is placed within easy reach of them. It is usually unwise to use the *Podunk Journal* as a medium if no dealers in Podunk handle the advertised goods. Likewise, it would be wasteful to use a medium covering the entire United States if there were dealer distribution in only that section east of the Mississippi River and north of the Ohio River. There are times when a local medium may be used in the absence of dealer distribution in order to bring pressure on dealers to stock the advertised product. Such procedure is rare and, when used, is only a temporary expedient.

Distribution might be classified as national, regional, or local. There are some media, like magazines and network broadcasting, that specialize in covering the national market. Other media, such as newspapers, can be applied nationally by using a sufficiently large number of them. There are a few media that serve particular regions. The *Prairie Farmer* and *Ohio Motorist* are examples. Media serving local areas are exceedingly plentiful. Every town of any size has its daily or weekly newspaper. Radio and television stations serve local and regional markets. Billboards can be rented on a local basis. Signs are distinctly local.

Even though an advertiser has national distribution, he may wish to work some territories more intensely than others. The results of a market analysis may have revealed some districts as more fertile than others, thus meriting more sales effort. In such cases, national media may be supplemented by media serving the richer areas only. New products might also be offered in a small territory to test their reception. Here, again, local media will serve best.

Dealer distribution may at times depend not so much upon the size of the advertiser as upon the character of the market. If the market is a "thin" one, dealers will logically be few in relation to total population. Under such circumstances, a medium should be selected that reaches the few, but important, prospects.

Persons in the distribution system often exert considerable influence on the national advertiser's use and choice of local media. They are inclined to want more local advertising support. Being "on the spot" they feel better qualified than the remote advertiser and agency personnel to decide which of the community's newspapers, radio or television stations do the best job. The national advertiser, of course, cannot heed all of their wishes. Yet, when making his media decisions the importance of keeping his dealers happy cannot be overlooked.

Creative strategy

In many instances the copy approach or technique of presenting the message requires a particular medium for proper expression. If top quality four-color reproduction is needed, magazines would have the edge on newspapers. Product demonstrations and personal sales deliveries are uniquely suited to television. New product introductions require the sense of urgency and newsworthiness so characteristic of newspapers, radio, and television. If creative strategy seeks to inspire confidence or dispel doubt, a medium such as *Good Housekeeping* magazine with its highly respected editorial content and Seal of Approval would be appropriate.

If the advertisement is designed to build and sustain a certain brand image or product personality, it should be placed in media having personality traits that complement and reinforce the desired image. Some me-

FIGURE 19–2
An advertisement which appeared in a farm magazine (word choice and illustration not in harmony with farm setting)

dia—notably magazines, television programs, and radio programs—have distinct personalities that may be described in such terms as masculine or feminine, modern or old fashioned, high-brow or low-brow, homey or worldly, serious or frivolous. These media that have the kind of personality that is right for the product tend to strengthen the effectiveness of the image-building advertisement.

Copy that is to appear in a given medium should be written in terms that will be understood by readers of the publication. Thus, an advertisement appearing in *The New Yorker* might not be appropriate in *True Story* or *Movie World*. The readers of the former have social, cultural, and economic interests that differ from those of the readers of the latter magazines. The advertiser should talk to each audience in its own language. More important differences will, of course, be noted among the readers of magazines serving special interests. *Western Canner & Packer* attracts an audience greatly different from that attracted by *The Atlantic*.

Many advertisers believe that the same copy and illustrations can be used in all the media selected for products having an almost universal appeal, such as tobacco, furniture, automobiles, soap, and canned foods. The probabilities are that greater effectiveness will be obtained if different copy is written for each medium where differences in audience are discernible. Use the farmer's language when advertising tobacco to him through a farm magazine and he will buy more of your tobacco than he would if you used the language of *The New Yorker*.

Figure 19–2 is a reproduction of an advertisement that appeared in *Farm Journal*. The creator of an advertisement to be carried in a magazine with such concentrated circulation among farm people could have been more effective in his communication to farmers than he was with the advertisement illustrated. The headline, "She gets the cleanest clothes in town," does not focus attention on the farm and the problem of getting farm clothes clean. The illustration is even worse. Surely a farm scene with farm clothing could have been used. What farm woman sends her husband off to work in a white shirt and with a dinner pail in his hand? In many respects this advertisement implies that Tide is for town women and is not to be used for overalls and other farm clothing. Surely this advertisement could not have been created with the *Farm Journal* audience in mind.

Circulations

The circulation of a newspaper or magazine can be clearly defined. It is the total number of copies of an average issue that are distributed to people. The unit of measurement is a *copy*. Then what is the circulation of a radio or television station, of outdoor posters or transit advertisements? The obvious answer is that these media have no circulation which is directly comparable to the circulation of a newspaper or magazine because they do not distribute *copies.* Yet, the term "circulation" has been used to describe various dimensions of all types of media and has had a different meaning for each type. To avoid the kind of fuzzy thinking associated with loose definition of terms, media analysts in recent years have restricted the circulation concept to newspapers and magazines. They measure the advertising opportunity offered by other media in terms of audiences, a concept which will be discussed later in this chapter.

Circulation figures as applied to newspapers and magazines are factual, regularly reported, and easily understood. They give the advertisers an indication of (1) how many people are reached by a publication, (2) where these people live, and (3) the degree of interest people have in the editorial content.

If magazine A circulates twice as many copies as magazine B, it is logical to assume that magazine A is reaching many more people than magazine B. However, the actual number of *readers* may not be twice as great. Magazine B may reach more readers per copy. Also, one magazine may be read more thoroughly than another, with the result that the advertiser's message may be exposed to a larger share of the readers of one magazine than of another. Even though the number of copies circulated is not a direct measure of the number of people reached, circulation is generally accepted as the basic standard for estimating the advertising value of newspapers and magazines.

A geographic breakdown of circulation shows the advertiser how well a publication fits his distribution pattern. When he knows how many copies of a magazine go into the various states, counties, and metropolitan areas, he can see to what extent the magazine's circulation is concentrated in his most promising markets. When he knows how many copies of a newspaper are sold within the immediate city zone, within the surrounding trade zone, and in nearby counties and towns, he can make significant inferences about the composition of the market reached by that newspaper. City-zone circulation includes most of the copies sold to apartment dwellers, commuters, and office workers. The retail trading zone reaches out to suburbia where younger and larger families reside. Copies going outside of the trading zone can be expected to reach more families living on farms.

Reader interest in a publication's editorial content can be inferred from the trend of circulation and the methods used to build circulation. A consistently growing circulation may indicate greater reader interest. A declining circulation suggests less reader interest. However, circulation growth may be the result of using gimmicks instead of providing the kind of editorial content that wins readers on its own merit.

Since rates charged for space are primarily dependent upon volume of circulation, it is to the advantage of media to obtain as large a subscription list as possible. This has led to many methods of increasing the circulation figures. One method is that of offering a group of magazines at reduced subscription prices. One popular magazine is often included, and others, less popular, are taken because of the low price.

Door-to-door canvassing is a common method employed by some publishers or subscription associations. Few housewives have not heard the pleas of some young "college student" working his way through school by selling magazines. Certainly the "lady of the house" would not begrudge ten cents a week for such a worthy cause. Then, there is the regular subscription salesman who offers valuable premiums in the way of maps, globes, shrubbery, or books with each order of a number of periodicals. Others obtain the endorsement of the parent-teachers' association, churches, or other local organizations to make selling easy. Often these organizations are promised a commission on all sales. Such tactics place emphasis upon factors other than the publications, and they often result in building up a list of subscribers that are not materially interested in the magazine.

Many publishers give special prices for short-term subscriptions in the hope that, when the trial period is over, the person will become a regular subscriber. Some will continue the short-term rates regularly. Bulk subscriptions are also used to increase sales. Schools are solicited for such orders where the publications can be used in classes.

There are also publishers who do not cancel a subscriber from the list when the subscription date has expired. Several months will often elapse before cancellation is effected. Some indication of the interest which a reader shows in a publication can often be obtained by checking the percentage of renewals.

Audit bureaus   The mad scramble of publishers for large circulations, together with the practice of some of falsifying their published circulation figures, led to the establishment in 1914 of the Audit Bureau of Circulations (A.B.C.). This bureau was sponsored by national and local advertisers, advertising agencies, and publishers desirous of protecting themselves against those whose statements could not be relied upon. Control of the bureau is vested in a board of directors consisting of 27 members: 12 advertisers, 3 advertising agencies, 6 newspapers publishers, and 6 magazine publishers. Note that the buyers of advertising space are in the majority.

Presently, only publications having 70 percent or more paid circulation are eligible for A.B.C. membership and audit. Paid circulation is roughly defined as those copies that people have paid for at not less than one-half the established basic prices. If the basic single-copy price is $0.20, then only those copies for which the buyer paid $0.10 or more can be included in net paid circulation. If the basic annual subscription price is $7.00, then only those subscriptions for which $3.50 or more was paid can be included in net paid. The A.B.C. treats the payment of money as substantial

FIGURE 19–3
An Audit Bureau of Circulations form for reporting circulation figures

AUDIT BUREAU OF CIRCULATIONS
123 NORTH WACKER DRIVE • CHICAGO 6, ILLINOIS
[This statement is subject to audit by the Audit Bureau of Circulations. For Audit Report refer to latest white paper form.]

Publisher's Statement — Newspaper
6 months ending March 31, (year)

Chicago (Cook County), Illinois
The Chronicle (Evening)
See Par. 9

8. Average net paid circulation:	Evening
	See Par. 9
CITY ZONE	
Carrier Delivery by independent carriers filing lists Par. 28(a)	21,742
Dealers & Carriers not filing lists	3,283
Street Vendors	21,266
Publisher's Counter Sales	9
Mail Subscriptions	
Total City Zone Population 1950 Census 3,684,491	46,300
RETAIL TRADING ZONE	
Carrier Delivery by independent carriers filing lists	5,115
Dealers & Carriers not filing lists	24,821
Mail Subscriptions	1,497
Total Retail Trading Zone Population 1950 Census 1,816,168	31,433
Total City & Retail Trading Population 1950 Census 5,500,659	77,733
ALL OTHER	
Dealers & Carriers	11,862
Mail Subscriptions	9,600
Total "All Other"	21,462
Subscriptions to Armed Forces (orders for 11 or more only)	
TOTAL NET PAID excl. Bulk (For bulk sales, see Par. 10)	(a)99,195
AVERAGES BY QUARTERS:	
October 1 to December 31, (year)	96,365
January 1 to March 31, (year)	102,025

(a) Includes predate edition, see Pars. 9 & 28(b).

9. Net Press Run & time of editions: Evening Issue for Thursday, March 18, (year)

Edition	Press Time	Date Printed	Issue Dated	Net Press Run	Sales Release See Note	Approx. Distribution City Zone	Retail Zone	All Other
1st	9:00 AM	3/18	3/18	3,000	A–C	56%	12%	32%
2nd	11:00 AM	3/18	3/18	3,740	A–C	60%	29%	11%
3rd	1:30 PM	3/18	3/18	16,250	A–C	83%	16%	1%
4th	3:30 PM	3/18	3/18	75,000	A–C	42%	41%	17%
Predate	6:00 PM	3/18	3/19	9,000	C	0%	10%	90%

For explanation see Par. 28(b).

Note: A Immediate sales release in City.
C Sales release on arrival at destination in Retail Zone and All Other.

10. Average bulk sales in all zones: 123.

11. Average unpaid distribution:	Evening
Arrears Over Three Months	
Short Term Subscriptions in Arrears	
Credit Subscriptions in Arrears	
Total Arrears	
Service Copies, Local Advs., Employes, etc.	893
Advg. Agencies, Complimentary, Samples, etc.	1,380
Other Not Qualifying as Paid	1,963
Total Arrears, Service Copies, etc.	4,236

12. (a) & (b): See reverse side.

13. (a) Basic Prices:	By Mail in Retail Trading Zone 1 Yr.	6 Mos.	3 Mos.	1 Mo.	By Carrier in City Zone 1 Yr.	6 Mos.	3 Mos.	1 Mo.	1 Wk.	Single Copy
E. only	$9.00	$5.00	$2.75	$1.00	$15.60	$7.80	$3.90	$1.30	30c	5c

(b) **Basic price by mail in city zone:** None.
(c) **Basic price by mail in all other zone:** Same as by mail in Par. 13(a).
(d) **Basic price to R. F. D. subscribers in retail trading zone:** Same as by mail in Par. 13(a).
(e) **Basic price to R. F. D. subscribers in all other zone:** Same as by mail in Par. 13(a).
(f) **Basic price by carrier in retail trading zone:** Same as by carrier in Par. 13(a).
(g) **Basic price by carrier in all other zone:** Same as by carrier in Par. 13(a).
(h) **Basic price to motor route subscribers in retail trading zone:** Same as by carrier in Par. 13(a).
(i) **Basic price to motor route subscribers in all other zone:** Same as by carrier in Par. 13(a).
(j) **Special reduced prices:** By mail, during January (year), 1 year $6.00.
13 (k) & (l): For prices higher than basic and prices lower than basic see Audit Report.

14. (a) **Were returns accepted?**
Dealers and street vendors in city zone were allowed 15% return privilege and dealers in retail trading zone and all other were allowed 10% return privilege.
(b) **Were these deducted, so that only net paid is shown in Par. 8?** Yes.

evidence that the buyer is sufficiently interested in the publication to read it.

The A.B.C. performs three important functions: (1) audits the circulation figures of member publishers and certifies to the accuracy of publishers' statements, (2) establishes standards for reporting the quantity, quality, and distribution of circulation, and (3) serves as a clearing house, gathering statements from member publishers and disseminating circulation reports to advertisers and agencies. Figure 19–3 shows a publisher's statement to the A.B.C.

Not all publishers are members of the A.B.C. The bureau has had its influence on them, however, since many advertisers are skeptical of figures not certified by some recognized agency. Nonmembers often make sworn statements of their circulation. If most copies are mailed out, such statements can be checked with the post office for accuracy. The work of the A.B.C. has made advertisers more conscious of the importance of accurate

FIGURE 19–4

First page of form used for reporting distribution of a controlled circulation magazine

For 6 Month Period Ending

DECEMBER. 19—-

MASS TRANSPORTATION

Controlled Circulation
is Qualified Circulation

FORM A

PUBLISHER'S STATEMENT

Subject to Audit

BUSINESS PUBLICATIONS AUDIT OF CIRCULATION, INC.

420 Lexington Avenue   New York 17, N. Y.

Formerly Controlled Circulation Audit, Inc.   No. 12351P

1. MASS TRANSPORTATION
   Name of Publication

2. Hitchcock Publishing Company
   Publishing Company

3. 222 E. Willow Avenue   Wheaton, Illinois
   Address

4. ....1904....
   Established

5. ....Monthly....
   Frequency

6. FIELD SERVED AND DEFINITION OF RECIPIENT QUALIFICATION

MASS TRANSPORTATION serves the field of public passenger transportation.

Those eligible to receive MASS TRANSPORTATION are persons on the executive or super-
visory level in companies operating:

    1) City and suburban transit service - using buses, trolley
        coaches and/or street cars.

    2) Intercity bus service.

    3) School bus service.

    4) Charter bus service.

    5) Sight-seeing bus service.

    6) Airport limousine and bus service.

    7) Passenger air line service.

    8) Passenger railroad service.

Also eligible are men in allied occupations serving the companies operating the
above services, such as manufacturers and suppliers of equipment and supplies used
by these companies, government officials, investment and financial houses, transportation consultants and research organizations.

7. AVERAGE TOTAL CONTROLLED AND NON-CONTROLLED FOR PERIOD

Average Controlled Circulation — single copies (Mailed in separate wrappers or otherwise separately addressed)	11,612	Advertisers, Agencies, Advertising Prospects	740
		Samples	810
Average Controlled Circulation—bulk	48	All other	264
		Average Total Non-Controlled	1,814
AVERAGE TOTAL CONTROLLED	11,660	AVERAGE TOTAL CONTROLLED AND NON-CONTROLLED	13,474

MASS TRANSPORTATION
DECEMBER 19—-

figures and has thus greatly reduced the number of false statements by nonmembers.

Publications that confine their distribution to special groups on a free basis are not now eligible to have their circulation figures audited by the A.B.C. Such papers may be audited by the Business Publications Audit of Circulations, Inc. (B.P.A.). A Business Publications Audit report is reproduced in Figure 19–4. The term "controlled circulation" refers to the number of copies that are sent to those groups of business or professional people who are most apt to be interested in the publication's editorial content. Note, from the data presented for *Mass Transportation,* the extent to which circulation is limited to persons engaged in mass transportation.

Audiences

An audience is defined as those people whose minds are reached by the medium carrying the advertiser's message. Whereas circulation is measured in numbers of *copies,* an audience is measured in numbers of *people.*[1] Whereas circulation figures are *indirect* evidence of how many and what kinds of people a medium reaches, audience data are *direct* evidence obtained from sample surveys of the people themselves.

As one would expect, the total number of people reached by a magazine or a newspaper is greater than the number of copies circulated. This difference is clearly indicated in the comparison of circulation and audience figures shown in Table 19–2.

Composition of a medium's audience is often more important than its size. If an advertiser's market is concentrated in particular consumer

TABLE 19–2
Comparison of circulation and total audience of selected magazines

Magazine	Average paid circulation	Total audience 18 years of age and older
Newsweek.	2,642,820	13,984,000
Time.	4,339,516	20,832,000
TV Guide.	17,612,589	38,997,000
Reader's Digest.	18,232,277	42,107,000
Better Homes & Gardens.	8,060,606	23,019,000
McCall's.	7,533,669	18,139,000
Sports Illustrated.	2,207,546	11,417,000
Playboy	6,613,978	17,927,000

Sources: *SRDS, Consumer Magazine and Farm Publication Rates and Data,* January 1973; *Simmons Study of Selective Markets,* 1973.

[1] Audiences are also measured in numbers of households (groups of people) and numbers of television or radio sets tuned to a station or network (assumes people are viewing or listening).

TABLE 19–3
Female audience composition of two women's magazines

Adult audience classification	Good Housekeeping (percent)	McCall's (percent)
Age		
10–17 years	18.4	17.7
18–24	17.6	16.5
25–34	17.2	15.5
35–49	22.0	22.6
50–64	15.5	17.4
65 and older	9.3	10.3
Education		
Grade school or less	6.9	9.2
Some high school	16.3	16.4
Graduated high school	45.2	42.6
Some college	18.9	18.2
Graduated college	8.9	8.7
Some postgraduate	3.8	4.9
Marital status		
Married	72.3	70.5
Race		
White	94.9	93.9
Nonwhite	5.1	6.1
Annual household income		
Under $5,000	14.8	15.7
$5,000–6,999	7.3	8.3
$7,000–9,999	19.9	21.4
$10,000–14,999	28.3	26.4
$15,000–24,999	23.2	22.0
$25,000 and over	6.5	6.2

Source: *Starch Continuing Media/Market Service,* 1972.

groups, he wants to know to what extent a medium's audience is concentrated in those groups. For example, an advertiser considering *Good Housekeeping* and *McCall's* as possible choices is in a better position to determine how efficiently these magazines reach his best prospects when he has the kind of information included in Table 19–3. He could infer from the editorial content of these two magazines that their readers are predominantly women, but any assumptions he might make about their readers' ages, incomes, and education levels are likely to be erroneous if he doesn't have factual evidence reflecting such characteristics. Having the data that are included in Table 19–3, he can determine with reasonable accuracy that the female readers of these magazines are mostly under 50 years of age, have not gone to college, and have annual household incomes of less than $15,000.

The similarity in the composition of these two audiences suggests that either the readers of *Good Housekeeping* are much the same as the readers of *McCall's,* or the readers are different; but the classification factors used here are inadequate for highlighting the differences. The latter circumstance is probably true, and this points to a current frontier in audience research. Studies have shown that sociopsychological factors reveal significant audience differences that do not appear when the traditional socioeconomic factors (age, income, education, occupation, etc.) are used. For example, the Simmons study classifies readers according to their "willingness to try new products." In a recent report, 20.5 percent of all the people who always or often try one or more new listed products read an average issue of *Time*.[2] Another magazine, *House Beautiful,* refers to its readers as "the beautiful families" who do things—parties, vacations, gardens, interiors—beautifully.

Lack of standards in audience measurement   In practice, there is no single definition of an audience that is appropriate for all types of media. Communication channels differ. People *read* newspapers and magazines. They *listen* to radio. They *view* or *watch-while-listening-to* television. Readers, listeners, and viewers are all people, but they are people receiving different forms of communication under different circumstances. If a magazine's audience is defined as all those people who report reading at least one item in a given issue, how should a radio station's audience be defined? Should it include all those people who listen to the station at least once a week, or only those who listen once a day? Whereas reading of one item in a magazine implies exposure to all items, listening to one of the programs broadcast by a radio station by no means indicates exposure to all of its programs. Without laboring over these differences, the point is that exposure to a tangible, space-organized, printed publication has no direct counterpart in exposure to a time-organized broadcast medium.

Audiences exposed to outdoor and transit media are defined in terms to traffic: those people who, during a given period of time, were in a position to see the outdoor sign or transit advertisement. For outdoor advertising, automobile and pedestrian traffic passing by places where signs are located reflects the size of audience. In the case of transit advertising placed in subways or busses, the audience is defined in terms of the number of passengers using the vehicles over a period of time.

Thus, each channel of communication functions in a different way, and the audience each reaches must be defined in different terms.

Even when measuring audiences of the same medium various research techniques employ various criteria for qualifying a person as a member of an audience. One technique uses *recognition* as a criterion for determining whether or not a person read a particular issue of a magazine: "Readers" are those who, when shown the cover, claim they saw or read part of that issue; if they aren't sure, they are permitted to look inside. Another technique uses *aided recall:* "Readers" are those who are able to describe an item in the magazine after being shown only the cover. As

[2] W. R. Simmons and Associates, *Selective Markets and the Media Reaching Them* (New York), 1972.

one would expect, the more rigorous criterion, recall, produces a smaller audience than the less rigorous criterion, recognition. One study that measured the size of audience (age 18 and up) reached by an issue of a weekly magazine using both criteria found 12, 241,000 readers when aided recall was used and 18,785,000 readers when recognition was used.[3]

Depending on the research technique used, radio- and television-station audiences are variously defined as those people who respond to a mail questionnaire, or those who report in a personal interview, or those who reply when telephoned, or those who record in a diary, or those in whose homes an electronic device automatically records that they received a station's broadcast. Each technique gathers *different* information in *different* ways from *different* samples of *different* populations. Therefore, even though they set out to measure the same audiences, no two techniques yield the same results. Radio and television audience measurement methods currently used will be discussed in greater detail in Chapter 21.

Confronted with such a variety of definitions and measurement standards, the media analyst must be cautious when he uses audience data. He is on safer ground when he compares audiences reached by media of the same type (two or more magazines, two or more television stations, etc.) and uses data arrived at through the same research procedure. He is on weaker ground when he compares audiences of different media types (magazine versus television, etc.) or uses data arrived at through different research procedures.

For planning purposes the advertiser is interested not only in the size and character of audiences reached by individual media vehicles, but also in the audiences reached by combinations of media. Several research firms provide information in this area. For example, W. R. Simmons & Associates annually issues a study entitled, "Selective Markets and the Media Reaching Them." This report describes the audiences of approximately 70 magazines and all network television programs in terms of their demographic characteristics and usage or ownership of more than 500 products and services. In addition to average-issue and average-telecast data, the Simmons report indicates cumulative and repeat audiences across multiple issues and telecasts. Such information allows the media planner to determine reach and frequency levels for various media combinations. Planners are thus greatly assisted in establishing workable and measurable objectives.

Media costs

The common expression, "You get what you pay for," is as true in the purchase of space or time in advertising media as in buying commodities.

[3] *Printed Advertising Rating Methods Study,* Advertising Research Foundation, Inc. (New York, 1956).

It is therefore important to compare costs with the ability of the medium to render the kind of service desired. Since the advertiser is interested in using a carrier that will deliver his message to his prospects with a minimum of waste, the first task of selection is that of measuring such abilities. A number of media may qualify as possibilities. Then, when appraising this select group the advertiser must deal with two basic questions: How much will I have to pay for the space or time? What do I get for what I pay?

Most newspapers quote their rates in terms of a standard unit of space referred to as a *line*. A line (short for *agate line*) is one fourteenth of an inch deep and one column wide. A comparison of line rates tells the advertiser how much more he will have to pay for space in one paper than in another but does not reveal the differences in advertising value he will receive. To illustrate this point, in St. Louis there are two daily newspapers each of which also publishes a weekend or Sunday edition. Recent line rates were as follows:

Newspaper	Line rate
Globe-Democrat, morning	$1.14
Globe-Democrat, weekend	1.14
Post-Dispatch, evening	1.48
Post-Dispatch, Sunday	1.92

On the basis of line rates alone, the Sunday *Post-Dispatch* is the highest-priced medium. This comparison, however, does not take into account the number of people reached by each paper. A family would expect to pay more rent for an eight-room house than for a four-room house, other things being equal. A trucker would be willing to pay a higher rental for a two-ton truck than for a one-ton truck. Likewise, an advertiser would be willing to pay a higher price for space in a newspaper circulating 100,000 copies than for space in one circulating 50,000 copies. A glance at the circulation figures of the papers mentioned above will give a picture of their value as carriers of advertising messages. Recent circulation figures for these papers as certified by the A.B.C. were as follows:

Newspaper	Circulation
Globe-Democrat, morning	300,183
Globe-Democrat, weekend	300,027
Post-Dispatch, evening	320,646
Post-Dispatch, Sunday	523,147

In the light of these circulation figures, the rate of $1.92 per line for the Sunday *Post-Dispatch* does not appear so unfavorable.

The usual procedure for comparing prices of different quantities is to reduce the prices to a common denominator of one unit, the price per unit. However, the rate per line per copy circulated is an unwieldly fraction of a cent ($0.000004 for the first of the papers listed). Multiplying this small fraction by one million moves the decimal six places to the right and thereby produces a dollars and cents figure. Thus, we arrive at the most widely used yardstick for comparing newspaper rates, the "milline rate." The formula for figuring the milline rate is:

$$\frac{\text{Line rate} \times 1,000,000}{\text{Circulation}} = \text{Milline rate}$$

This converts the rate charged by each paper to a common standard—the rate per line per one million circulation.

Milline rates for the St. Louis newspapers turn out to be:

Newspaper	Milline rate
Globe-Democrat, morning	$3.79
Globe-Democrat, weekend	3.80
Post-Dispatch, evening	4.62
Post-Dispatch, Sunday	3.67

As a rule, the greater the circulation of a newspaper the lower is its milline rate; the smaller the circulation the higher is its milline rate.

If the advertiser were interested in reaching only those people living within the city and retail trading zones, he might omit the circulation going outside of this area when comparing rates. The city and trading zone circulation of the St. Louis papers varies from 64 percent of the total for the Sunday *Post-Dispatch* to 78 percent for the evening *Post-Dispatch.* When the standard rate of comparison is based on this part of total circulation, it is referred to as the "truline rate."

The same general problems involved in comparing space costs in newspapers are present in magazine cost comparisons. The common unit of space for which magazine rates are quoted is a page or fraction of a page rather than the agate line, although the latter is often included on the rate card. The most widely used standard for comparing magazine rates is the cost-per-page-per-thousand circulation, or as it is more simply called, "cost-per-thousand" (often written as C.P.M.). The formula is:

$$\frac{\text{Page rate} \times 1,000}{\text{Circulation}} = \text{Cost-per-thousand (C.P.M.)}$$

In recent years, the availability of a greater number of studies reporting size of magazine audiences has permitted advertisers to compare rates on the basis of people reached as well as copies circulated. To figure a magazine's cost-per-thousand readers, its total audience would be used in the above formula instead of its circulation. In effect, as demonstrated in Table 19–4, this modifies a rate comparison based on circulation by allowing for differences in the number of readers per copy.

If the advertiser is primarily interested in reaching a particular group of

TABLE 19–4

Comparison of cost-per-page-per-thousand based on circulation and total audience

Magazine	Rate per four-color page	Cost-per-thousand	
		Circulation	Total Audience
Newsweek................	$26,680	$10.10	$1.91
Time......................	38,190	8.80	1.83
TV Guide.................	51,000	2.90	1.31
Reader's Digest..............	61,765	3.39	1.47
Better Homes & Gardens.......	45,985	5.70	2.00
McCall's....................	40,500	5.38	2.23
Sports Illustrated.............	23,475	10.63	2.06
Playboy	42,950	6.49	2.40

Sources: *SRDS, Consumer Magazine and Farm Publication Rates and Data,* January 1973; *Simmons Study of Selective Markets,* 1973.

readers, say men between the ages of 30 and 45, he might compare rates on the basis of the number of such readers in each magazine's audience. This more nearly approaches the ideal standard for comparing media costs—the cost of reaching a thousand real prospects.

Media analysts in a leading advertising agency have evaluated farm publications in terms of cost-per-thousand hogs on farms reached by various publications. They have evaluated television stations in terms of cost-per-thousand dairy cows within station coverage areas. They have evaluated magazines in terms of cost-per-thousand cake bakers and cost-per-thousand cakes baked per month.

A media planner also may be interested in comparing magazines according to how they are used by readers or by the attitudes readers hold toward the publications. For example, he might compare a group of magazines on *how thoroughly* they were read. Assume a situation in which a planner is considering three magazines:

Magazine	Number of readers	Page rate	Cost per thousand readers
A	20,000	$200	$10.00
B	30,000	275	9.17
C	40,000	375	9.38

On a straight cost-per-thousand basis, magazine B is the best buy. Further assume, though, that research was done in which readers indicated "how thoroughly" they read each magazine:

Magazine	Readers who claimed reading "most thoroughly"
A.........	10,000 (50% of readers)
B.........	12,000 (40% of readers)
C.........	16,000 (40% of readers)

The planner could now refigure cost-per-thousands on the basis of those who "read most thoroughly:"

Magazine	Cost per thousand readers who read "most thoroughly"
A	$20.00
B	22.92
C	23.44

Thus, if the planner places high importance on the thoroughness of reading a magazine (on the likely assumption that advertising exposure is increased), magazine A outscores its competitors.

Television and radio rates are quoted for units of time—one minute, 30 seconds, 20 seconds, etc. To compare rates charged by different stations or networks, an appropriate standard is the cost-per-commercial-minute-per-thousand viewers or listeners. However, at the present time, use of such a standard is mainly limited to comparing rates of a few stations in major cities and of the nationwide networks, audiences of which are regularly and rather well measured. Reliable and standard audiences measurements are not currently available for many individual markets. Therefore, when buying time on many stations rate comparison is often a matter of subjective evaluation.

Space or time should never be purchased solely on a price basis. Other factors are also important. It may happen that the publication with a relatively high cost-per-thousand should be the first choice because it provides a better climate, more favorable reader attitudes, or better advertising associations. However, when a number of specific media possess about equal merit in everything but price, the advertiser would probably depend on cost comparison to indicate the most economical medium.

Standard Rate and Data Service   The one source of information most often referred to by media buyers is *Standard Rate and Data Service.* Published monthly, *SRDS* lists current rates, circulations, mechanical requirements, issuance and closing dates, contract and copy regulations, sales offices, and pertinent market data for media grouped as follows:

1. Newspapers (all U.S. daily and Sunday newspapers)
2. Consumer magazines and farm publications (825 consumer magazines and 220 farm publications)
3. Radio stations (approximately 7,000 AM and FM stations)
4. Television stations (all U.S. television stations)
5. Radio and television networks
6. Business publications (2,400 business papers in 159 market classifications)
7. Transit advertising (450 transportation advertising facilities)

Obviously, with all this information available for handy reference, the planning of media strategy and the buying of space and time for national advertising is greatly expedited.[4]

Editorial or program content

Less susceptible to measurement, but no less important than other dimensions of a medium, is the quality of its editorial or program content. It is logical to assume that the environment in which an advertiser's message appears has an appreciable influence on the effectiveness of the advertisement itself. A magazine's editorial content may center on subject matter into which the advertiser's product readily fits, thereby conditioning readers to be more receptive to his message. (This is particularly true of business publications such as *Rock Products, Railway Age,* etc.) Or, the editorial content may provide a backdrop of prestige and authority that "rubs off" on the advertiser's product. Or, the magazine's articles and stories may be the kind with which readers identify themselves and get personally involved, thereby becoming more responsive to an advertisement reaching them when they are in such a mood. These are but a few of the many possible relationships between a medium and its audience that can work in the advertiser's favor. Therefore, it behooves the advertiser to carefully appraise the editorial content of newspapers and magazines, and the programing of television and radio stations before making a selection.

Evaluating content is mainly a matter of judgment. However, a few studies employing the techniques of motivation research have sought to analyze media content as reflected in the attitudes and feelings of readers, viewers, and listeners. One such study was conducted by Social Research, Inc. for *Good Housekeeping.* Some of the findings of this study are illustrated in Figure 19–5. In the light of the later demise of the *Post* and *Life* it would appear that editorial emphasis on practical concerns provided the most beneficial environment for advertisers.

Television or radio program content and station programing practices are often the basis for selecting a broadcast medium. Without detailed audience data the advertiser can only infer from the program itself how well it attracts a particular type of customer. This can be risky business as evidenced by the popular, but erroneous, assumptions that classical music appeals primarily to upper-income groups and that "westerns" appeal only to youngsters.

[4] Rates published in *SRDS* for newspapers, radio stations, and television stations are those charged national advertisers and are generally higher than those charged retail advertisers. Retailers generally obtain rate information and other data direct from representatives of the media serving their local community.

FIGURE 19-5

Comparison of satisfactions received from three magazines

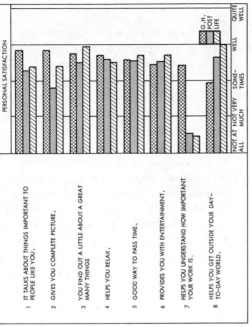

PERSONAL SATISFACTION

1 IT TALKS ABOUT THINGS IMPORTANT TO PEOPLE LIKE YOU.

2 GIVES YOU COMPLETE PICTURE.

3 YOU FIND OUT A LITTLE ABOUT A GREAT MANY THINGS

4 HELPS YOU RELAX.

5 GOOD WAY TO PASS TIME.

6 PROVIDES YOU WITH ENTERTAINMENT.

7 HELPS YOU UNDERSTAND HOW IMPORTANT YOUR WORK IS.

8 HELPS YOU GET OUTSIDE YOUR DAY-TO-DAY WORLD.

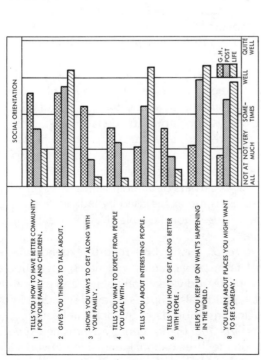

SOCIAL ORIENTATION

1 TELLS YOU HOW TO HAVE BETTER COMMUNITY FOR YOUR FAMILY AND CHILDREN.

2 GIVES YOU THINGS TO TALK ABOUT.

3 SHOWS YOU WAYS TO GET ALONG WITH YOUR FAMILY.

4 TELLS YOU WHAT TO EXPECT FROM PEOPLE YOU DEAL WITH.

5 TELLS YOU ABOUT INTERESTING PEOPLE.

6 TELLS YOU HOW TO GET ALONG BETTER WITH PEOPLE.

7 HELPS YOU KEEP UP ON WHAT'S HAPPENING IN THE WORLD.

8 YOU LEARN ABOUT PLACES YOU MIGHT WANT TO SEE SOMEDAY.

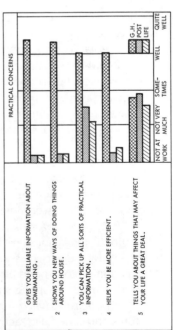

PRACTICAL CONCERNS

1 GIVES YOU RELIABLE INFORMATION ABOUT HOMEMAKING.

2 SHOWS YOU NEW WAYS OF DOING THINGS AROUND HOUSE.

3 YOU CAN PICK UP ALL SORTS OF PRACTICAL INFORMATION.

4 HELPS YOU BE MORE EFFICIENT.

5 TELLS YOU ABOUT THINGS THAT MAY AFFECT YOUR LIFE A GREAT DEAL.

Source: *The Meaning of Good Housekeeping and Its Advertising to Its Readers,* prepared by Social Research, Inc. for *Good Housekeeping* (New York: The Hearst Corporation, 1956).

Advertiser usage

The extent to which other advertisers use a given medium is often used as an indicator of its effectiveness. A medium that consistently carries a greater total volume of advertising is presumed to be the one that advertisers generally consider more effective. However, the total volume carried is less significant to an individual advertiser than is the amount of advertising for his type of product. A food advertiser, for example, is most interested in the volume of food advertising carried.

When selecting local media such as newspapers, national advertisers are inclined to favor those preferred by their local retail dealers. For example, in Los Angeles the *Los Angeles Times* consistently carries about 75 percent of all the advertising placed by women's shoe stores in the major metropolitan papers. This indicates that women's shoe retailers in Los Angeles, who are in a position to observe sales resulting from their advertising day by day, generally favor the *Times.* Chances are, therefore, that most national advertisers of women's shoes would also choose to place the major portion of their Los Angeles newspaper space in the *Times.* A further refinement of this type of evidence would be the records of media usage by individual retailers.

An advertiser's selection of media should not be governed by his competitor's choices, but where and how competitors place their advertising should be considered. A competitor's marketing strategy and tactics can be rather well determined from records showing the extent to which he uses specific media.

Media Records, Inc. measures and reports the advertising linage carried by 244 daily and Sunday newspapers in 83 cities. A Media Records Report gives each newspaper's linage broken down by various classifications. Retail classifications include department stores (by departments), clothing stores (men's, women's), drugstores, grocery stores, etc. National classifications include passenger cars, gasolines and oils, grocery products, sporting goods, etc. From these figures an advertiser can quickly see how newspapers in a given city rank as carriers of different kinds of advertising. A Media Records Report also gives the linage used by individual national advertisers in each newspaper. These figures enable an advertiser to check the linage of his competitors.

Publishers Information Bureau, Inc. (P.I.B.) reports expenditures in national magazines, national farm publications, and newspaper supplements by industry classifications, by individual companies, and by brands. In addition to expenditure data, P.I.B. also reports detailed schedule information such as space sizes and insertion dates in each publication.

Broadcast Advertising Reports, Inc. (BAR) reports advertising expenditures and scheduling activity on the three national television networks and the three national radio networks, ABC, NBC, and CBS. It provides gross time costs by advertisers and individual brands. BAR also supplies similar information on spot television usage by national brands in the top 75 spot markets.

Rome Report gives advertising expenditures for a limited number of business publications.

Leading National Advertisers (L.N.A.) provides a useful summary report, "National Advertising Investments," which gives dollar expenditures by company and brand in magazines, newspaper supplements, network and spot television, network radio, and outdoor.

The media-selection problem

The individual advertising situation largely determines the complexity of media selection. A retailer in a small town where there is only a weekly newspaper doesn't have much of a problem. However, a retailer in a major metropolitan area has the problem of choosing media from among newspapers, radio, television, outdoor, transit, and direct mail.

The complexity of the problem of media selection is even more discernible in the case of the national advertiser who sells to a broad nation-wide market. What *types* of media should he use? Magazines? Newspapers? Television? Radio? Outdoor? If magazines, what *classes?* General interest magazines? Women's magazines? Romance magazines? If women's magazines, which specific ones? *Ladies' Home Journal? McCall's? Good Housekeeping?* If newspapers, in which cities? If there are several newspapers in a selected city, which specific newspapers? If television, should he use a nationwide network or select stations for local coverage in individual markets? What network? What stations?

There are no rules-of-thumb or pat formulas for solving these selection problems. Each advertising situation presents its own unique set of circumstances. Each type of medium has its own character and each specific medium, in turn, differs from the next. There is no single "best" medium for all advertising situations. Each media decision must be made in light of the particular requirements of a particular situation. Even competitors selling nearly the same products to nearly the same markets employ different media strategies. As shown in Table 19–5, there are noticeable differences in the way three petroleum companies distribute their advertising expenditures among types of media.

A limiting factor that always must be taken into account is the budget or amount of money available for advertising. There is never enough money to fully exploit all the media opportunities available. Therefore, the advertiser must be selective. He seeks to maximize the return on his advertising investment by selecting those media that will deliver the messages most efficiently and effectively. His chances of making the right choices are greatly improved when he has carefully analyzed all available

TABLE 19–5
Distribution of advertising expenditures among five media for three petroleum companies, 1971 (by percent)

Medium	Gulf	Shell	Texaco
Magazines..............	3%	19%	10%
Spot television	18	43	4
Network television	67	31	72
Radio.................	10	7	13
Outdoor	2	—	1
	100%	100%	100%

Source: *Advertising Age,* August 28, 1972.

facts bearing on his marketing situation and his media alternatives. The decision-making process, however, should be creative. Characteristics of a creative media decision are described by Brown, Lessler, and Weilbacher as follows:

> A creative media decision is made when all the factors operating in a given market situation are combined with media experience and sound judgment and imagination to determine a media strategy or a media choice. To the extent that any policy factor is ignored, to the extent that the marketing realities reflected in allied marketing strategies are ignored, to the extent that applicable objective research findings are ignored or misinterpreted, a media decision is not truly creative. Furthermore, to the extent that executive judgment and imagination do not actively assimilate these factors and find a unique media solution, media decisions are not creative.[5]

Summary

Reach, frequency, gross rating points, continuity, and message size are concepts considered by the media planner in developing objectives. How these variables are interrelated is a decision area of keen importance.

To develop a media plan and select media that will carry his messages most efficiently to the people comprising his market, the advertiser should carefully analyze all available facts bearing on his marketing situation and media alternatives.

Who are the people who buy the product, who influence the purchase, where do they live, where and how is the product distributed—all of the questions that pinpoint the marketing task must be answered, and they must be answered in terms of the particular product in question.

[5] Lyndon O. Brown, Richard S. Lessler, and William M. Weilbacher, *Advertising Media* (New York: Ronald Press Co., 1957), p. 7.

The creative strategy to be employed, the mood or product-image the advertising is designed to emphasize, the need for color, for demonstration, for news, for authority—all are essential considerations.

Audited circulations and available audience data indicate how many and what classes of people a medium reaches.

How much does the space or time cost? What do you get for what you pay? The "milline rate" and "cost-per-thousand" are widely used standards for comparing the cost efficiency of alternative media.

Editorial or program content reflect the kind of environment in which the advertiser's message will appear. The volume and types of advertising a medium carries reflect how other advertisers view its worth.

But facts and figures are not enough. Sound judgment and imagination are required to exploit the unique advertising opportunities offered by any medium.

QUESTIONS AND PROBLEMS

1   The fact that more money is spent for newspaper advertising than for advertising in any other medium is substantial evidence that newspapers are the most effective medium. Do you agree or disagree? Explain.

2   Table 19–1 lists advertising expenditures for a recent period, with the percent of total for each major medium. What might these "percent of total" figures be in, say, ten years? Why do you think such changes, if any, might occur?

3   In the development of a media plan certain strategic elements or factors should be considered. What factors are involved in such a decision? Provide a brief explanation of these and discuss ways in which *interaction* among factors may occur.

4   Media planners often describe alternative media buys in terms of *reach* and *frequency*. How are these concepts useful in making a media decision?

5   Assume that a particular media buy reaches 60 percent of a target market and delivers a frequency of 3.5. What does such a buy provide in terms of gross rating points? If an alternative media buy more gross rating points, would it be better? Why or why not?

6   Discuss the ways in which *continuity* relates to reach and frequency when making media decisions.

7   From a continuity standpoint, what do you think the advertiser was trying to accomplish with the scheduling pattern shown in Figure 19–1?

8   Would it be good policy for a company to run identical advertisements in the *Ladies Home Journal, Time,* and *Successful Farming?*

9   Distinguish between *circulation* and *audience* as measures of media values.

10   Why should the advertiser be interested in how the circulation of a medium has been built up?

11   Composition of a medium's audience is often more important than its size. Why?

12   Observe the data for *TV Guide* and *Reader's Digest* in Tables 19–2 and 19–4. Since *TV Guide* has the lower cost-per-thousand (for both circulation and total audience), a media planner would always recommend *TV Guide* over *Reader's Digest*. Do you agree or disagree? Explain.

13   Which of the following newspapers is more reasonably priced?

Newspaper	Line Rate	Circulation
A $0.06		16,000
B............. $0.05		12,500

14   One way to make general cost-per-thousand figures more meaningful is to determine the number of readers who read a publication "most thoroughly." What other variables can you suggest that might be useful for such analyses?

Newspapers and magazines

A number of factors of importance in planning media were discussed in the preceding chapter. A more detailed discussion of the characteristics of the various media available to advertisers will be considered in this and following chapters.

NEWSPAPERS

There are several kinds of newspapers available to advertisers in the United States. To simplify the evaluation of their character, they can be roughly divided into five groups: (1) daily, (2) Sunday, (3) weekly or community, (4) shopping news, and (5) special interest.

Daily and Sunday newspapers make up the great majority of the total circulation of all newspapers. About 1,761 daily newspapers with a combined circulation of 62,510,242 are published in the United States. There are 603 Sunday papers circulating a total of 49,338,765 copies. Of the total number of dailies, about eight out of ten are evening papers.

The weekly or community newspaper is a product of the small, rather homogeneous community. In fact, many of these newspapers are issued more than once a week, often two or three times weekly. Such "weekly" newspapers are available in many small towns throughout the United States as well as serving suburban communities of major metropolitan areas. There are 7,553 of them, with a total circulation of almost 32

445

million. The average circulation is, therefore, only around 4,000 copies per issue. Publishers of such papers often depend heavily on sources of revenue other than subscriptions and advertising space, otherwise many could not operate profitably.

Community papers generally have an interested local following, perhaps born from the closeness of the community served. Studies that have been made for such papers show substantially higher readership than for metropolitan dailies.

The shopping-news type of newspaper is unlike either the regular metropolitan daily or the community weekly in that it carries little or no news and is distributed free. Its space is often wholly devoted to advertisements. The term "news" is associated with it on the grounds that advertisements are news of a vital type desired by many people. That this claim is true can hardly be denied in light of readership figures for advertisements in orthodox papers which show many advertisements read by vastly more people than many of the regular news items in the paper. The shopping newspaper is distributed free, and thus its circulation can be controlled by the publisher. It can, and often is, distributed only to certain sections of a town or to selected types of households.

Special-interest newspapers may be dailies or weeklies, but they deserve a separate classification because of their selection of an audience. Such newspapers serve groups that have common ties in the realm of religion, labor, race, language, trade, finance, and production. These papers often take on many of the characteristics of magazines but follow the format and publishing policy of newspapers.

Community acceptance

The newspaper has become an integral part of the life of almost every community. It takes its place alongside the church, school, bank, and department store as a necessary adjunct to living. The newspaper at the breakfast table and while commuting to and from work is a familiar part of the American scene. In the few instances when communities have been temporarily without newspapers because of strikes, the intensity of feeling toward such loss has been observed and partially measured.

The daily papers in Rockford, Illinois, were strikebound for 71 days in 1970 and 1971. A typical response of a sample of persons contacted during the strike was, "I miss the Rockford newspapers, especially the news and ads."[1] The study of newspaper readers in Rockford, conducted by Market Research Studies, asked if the lack of newspaper ads affected shopping. Forty-nine percent answered "yes" to this question, and half

---

[1] "Newspapers Retain Readers' Loyalty in 2 Surveys Made During Absence," *Editor & Publisher,* January 23, 1971, p. 7.

FIGURE 20–1
Newspaper acceptance by a particular segment of the market

How do you get to Philadelphia women?

Nice and easy. When you take The Bulletin.

Because you'll reach more women than you could reach with the other two Philadelphia newspapers together.

You'll reach 7 out of 10 Philadelphia women* with The Bulletin.

That's 755,000 compared to 671,000 in the other two papers.

You'll get 434,000 exclusive readers with us. 84,000 more than the other two.

You'll also reach 199,000 women with at least some college. 42,000 more than the other two.

And you'll get 345,000 women in households with incomes of $12,500 or over. 102,000 more than those other two.

With all our women, does it really add up to add another paper or two?

Take The Bulletin. The first place to go for Philadelphia women.

Nearly everybody reads The Bulletin.

*DAILY READERS OF PHILADELPHIA NEWSPAPERS IN THE EIGHT-COUNTY SMSA. SOURCE: "PHILADELPHIA: MEASURE OF A MARKET" BY BELDEN ASSOCIATES-'72.
MEMBER MILLION MARKET NEWSPAPERS, INC.

Take The Bulletin.
Evening and Sunday

of these mentioned they had missed sales, bargains, and specials in stores, both before and after Christmas.

During a two-week shutdown of the Pittsburg *Post-Gazette* and the *Press* in 1971, a study by Ketchum, MacLeod & Grove advertising agency revealed that newspaper readers turned to radio and television for news; but "they felt that neither the quality nor the credibility of TV advertising matched that of the printed ads, and they failed to get much of the news they find in the papers."[2] Among those interviewed, 47 percent rated the quality of newspaper advertising best in comparison with 35 percent so rating television advertising; 13 percent voted for magazines, and radio received 5 percent of the response.

Another measure of community acceptance is the percentage of the residents who subscribe to a local paper. That percentage is exceedingly high, ranging from 70 to 95 percent for the great majority of papers. Figure 20–1 reproduces an advertisement of the Philadelphia *Bulletin* which dramatizes the high acceptance factor among women, especially those with particular demographic characteristics.

A motivational study analyzing the role the newspaper plays in the daily lives of its readers reported these observations:

1. People identify themselves with the community through newspapers.
2. The newspaper helps a person guard against feeling isolated, . . . against being shut out from the world and from the local community.
3. The authority of the newspaper is reinforced by a belief that, to a much greater extent than media which use the perishable spoken word, the newspaper is somehow accountable for what it prints.
4. Newspaper advertising is familiar . . . has a strong connotation of immediacy. The image that is firmly entrenched is that newspaper advertising is practical for immediate use.
5. Dependence on the newspaper as a shopping guide is indicated by a housewife's statement: "I go over the ads every day. It's part of reading the paper. I like to keep well up on prices, and I'm always on the lookout for clothes buys, what with three children."[3]

Customer selectivity

The newspaper serves a local and highly concentrated market. Any area that can support a daily newspaper must have a rather high degree of centrality and fairly active trade. The map reproduced in Figure 20–2 shows the counties in the United States in which daily newspapers are published. They represent only one third of all counties in the country; yet they correspond closely to population concentration, income-tax re-

---

[2] Ibid.

[3] *People Speak Their Inner Minds about Newspapers* (New York: Bureau of Advertising, American Newspaper Publishers Association, Inc., 1956).

FIGURE 20–2
Counties in the United States in which daily newspapers are published

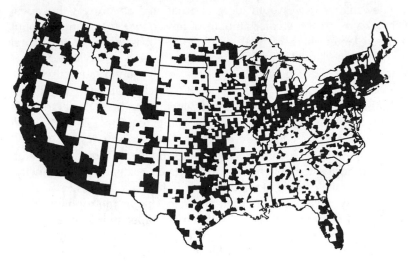

turns, retail sales, and other factors indicative of the more fertile markets.

Newspapers, however, do not generally select their readers to the same degree as many magazines. In Chicago, newspaper readers must choose from three general papers. This means that the subscribers of a particular paper will usually be a heterogeneous group. The newspaper-reading population of Chicago will subscribe to scores of magazines, according to the particular interest served by a magazine. A newspaper advertisement must, therefore, appeal primarily to a mass audience. It would be extremely wasteful to use newspapers to reach a small specialized group. Appeals directed only to doctors, lawyers, musicians, or carpenters should, in general, find no place in newspapers. Selection of the better territorial markets is admirably done by newspapers, but they do not select particular consumer groups for the advertiser wishing to appeal to such groups, except in the case of the relatively few special-interest newspapers.

Since newspapers do reach a heterogeneous group, attempts are made to produce a paper which will meet varied interests; and material success has been achieved in performing this difficult task. The paper is divided into sections of news, sports, homemaking, comics, etc. An increased circulation among satisfied subscribers has resulted. But some buy a given paper because of its comic strip; others, because of its sports news. Advertisements appearing in other sections of the paper will have little chance of even being seen by some individuals.

Use by retailers

The newspaper serves both local and national advertisers, but local retailers take by far the greater amount of newspaper space and account for a much larger share of total expenditures. It is estimated that total advertising expenditures in newspapers in 1972 was $6.96 billion. Of that total, retailers accounted for $5.72 billion, and national advertisers accounted for $1.24 billion. Thus, about 82 percent of total newspaper advertising expenditures are made by retailers. It has been projected that total newspaper advertising expenditures will increase to $10.377 billion by 1978, with $8.687 billion (84 percent) by local users.[4]

The newspaper is an ideal medium for most retailers. Its circulation area generally conforms to their trading areas. Even retailers located in the suburban shopping centers of major cities usually have access to a suburban community newspaper. In addition, many major metropolitan daily newspapers offer "zone editions," whereby a paper's circulation is split into geographic areas or zones. In this way, a retailer serving only a part of the metropolitan area can beam his advertising into this area.

Daily publication readily fits into the day-to-day selling and quick action promotions that characterize most retailing. A print medium effectively carries pictures of the merchandise, product specifications, and prices. Consumers have a habit of turning to their newspapers for shopping information. The wide range of space sizes and insertion schedules that can be bought gives small as well as large retailers an opportunity to advertise profitably. It's no wonder that the newspaper is the only mass medium used by many retailers.

Department stores are the largest single users of newspaper space and account for about one third of all local advertising linage.

Use by national advertisers

National advertisers in 1972 allotted almost 10 percent of their total national advertising investment to newspapers. Until 1941, newspapers received a greater share of the national advertiser's budget than was received by any other medium. From 1941 to 1951 the lead fluctuated between general magazines and newspapers. But now television holds the lead. These figures are based on direct expenditures of national advertisers; however, they do not include the substantial sums contributed by national advertisers to retailers for cooperative advertising.

Whether newspapers or some other medium stands first does not matter. The significant fact is that national advertisers find newspapers, which are essentially a local medium, of value as a means of reaching specific

---

[4] J. Walter Thompson Advertising Agency, 1973.

TABLE 20–1
Top 20 national newspaper advertisers, 1971

Rank	Advertiser	Expenditures*
1.	General Motors Corporation	$24,022,500
2.	Ford Motor Company	21,189,570
3.	Philip Morris Company	14,866,100
4.	R.J. Reynolds Industries Inc.	14,684,190
5.	Chrysler Corporation	14,360,270
6.	American Brands	14,323,020
7.	Distillers Corporation—Seagrams Ltd.	10,725,930
8.	British-American Tobacco Company, Ltd.	9,572,050
9.	Trans World Airlines Incorporated	6,830,340
10.	RCA Corporation	6,191,940
11.	Pan American World Airways, Inc.	5,967,990
12.	Delta Airlines	5,815,400
13.	American Airlines	5,713,040
14.	General Foods Corporation	5,640,010
15.	UAL Incorporated	5,274,540
16.	Rapid-American Corporation	5,133,430
17.	American Motors	4,990,490
18.	Walker-Gooderham & Worts Hiram Ltd.	4,733,675
19.	Eastern Airlines	4,705,450
20.	Kraftco Corporation	4,696,630

* Figures represent *only* expenditures for the actual space used in newspapers measured by Media Records, Inc.
  Source: Newspaper Advertising Bureau, A.N.P.A., April 1973.

markets and use them extensively for that purpose. Newspapers emphasize that all markets are local. Advertisers can achieve national coverage
by using many newspapers. However, the cost is considerable. To place
a one-page, black-and-white ad in the top paper in each of the top one
hundred markets costs $228,377. This amounts to about $9 per thousand
circulation. These markets include only 60 percent of all U.S. households,
and the top paper averages about 50 percent coverage in each city.

Table 20–1 shows the expenditures of the top 20 national newspaper
advertisers. Note that automobile manufacturers and airlines were significant users of the medium. In total, these 20 companies accounted for over
20 percent of the total dollars invested in national newspaper advertising.

Territorial flexibility

The newspaper offers great flexibility in the territorial distribution of
advertising. Although most communities that support a daily newspaper
are better markets than those that do not, there is a great difference even
among those communities having a newspaper. Advertisers who wish to
concentrate their sales efforts on the better markets will find newspapers
an adaptable medium.

Professor Borden emphasizes this element of flexibility when he says:

"Newspapers as a basic coverage medium are particularly suitable for those companies which for one reason or another need to adjust their advertising and promotion from market to market in order to avoid waste in effort and gain greatest effectiveness."[5]

Some markets are good today and bad tomorrow. Local business depressions are often occasioned by drought, labor troubles, recession in an industry which dominates a community, or other factors that do not spread to other regions. The newspaper advertiser can avoid such markets. If he has been working such a territory, he can cancel it from his total budget and transfer his efforts to other sections. This can be done on short notice. In the case of magazine advertising, cancellation orders must often be given months in advance.

Figure 20–3 illustrates the territorial flexibility afforded by newspapers. A northern market can thus be covered by an advertiser of winter merchandise without waste on southern circulation. Efforts can be focused on Detroit when the automobile business is good and reduced in San Francisco during a strike.

When new advertising ideas are to be tried out on a small scale or when new products are to be introduced, newspapers will generally be used. This procedure reduces the investment in experimentation. It also provides a means whereby those advertisements with greater effectiveness can be discovered prior to their use on a larger scale. Closer supervision can also be given such trial efforts.

FIGURE 20–3
Newspaper advertising can be concentrated where desired

[5] Neil H. Borden and Others, *National Advertising in Newspapers* (Cambridge, Mass.: Harvard University Press, 1946), p. 185.

Newsvertising

The time flexibility of newspapers is demonstrated in the opportunities which they give the advertiser to tie his advertising message in with the national or local news of the moment. An advertisement for a newspaper needs to be presented for publication only a few hours before press time. Thus, it can be almost as fresh as the news printed in the same paper. This characteristic of newspapers allows the advertiser to adapt his advertisement to outstanding happenings of the day if such incidents are relevant to the product being advertised. The seller of rain apparel can place his advertising more or less in harmony with the weather. If a disaster like a flood, fire, or tornado hits a particular city or community, it might serve

FIGURE 20–4
An effective use of "newsvertising"

as the theme for advertising copy. Such advertisements can appear a few hours after the disaster. The same thing is applicable to national news. Newspapers call this quality of their medium "newsvertising." It permits the advertiser to capitalize on current events.

The bank advertisement reproduced in Figure 20–4 illustrates an effective use of "newsvertising." The ad is a "thank you" to the fire fighters who saved the bank building from a disastrous fire next door. The ad reached readers in the same issue of the paper that carried a banner front-page headline and report of the fire.

Life of a newspaper

Newspapers have a very short life. They are usually read as soon as they are received and then thrown away. Some are kept for more than a day, but this is not the common case. Because of this short life, newspaper advertisements are not exposed to the readers for any length of time. If an advertisement is not seen during the time of the first reading of the paper, it probably will not be seen at all, since the first reading is usually the last reading. Magazine publishers are quick to point to this weakness of newspapers. Newspaper publishers claim that the characteristic is valuable, pointing out that newspapers offer a *daily* opportunity to reach the entire reading public. A fresh message is provided every day instead of one that presumably lasts a week or a month. Most national advertisers, however, do not use the newspaper every day. This means that the old advertisement does not last until the new one appears.

Services for advertisers

Newspapers provide a number of services for retail advertisers. Most small retailers, and many larger ones, have either no advertising department or an inadequate one. Most daily newspapers have facilities to help such retailers create individual advertisements or plan complete campaigns. This service will include writing copy, preparing layouts, and minor art work.

For the national advertiser, newspapers will often provide merchandising service to support national advertisements. This may involve getting retailers to display the products advertised by the manufacturer, encouraging retailers to time their own advertising with the manufacturer, or helping the manufacturer secure adequate distribution for his product locally.

Research studies are made by many newspapers which have value to both the local and national advertiser. Such studies include a measure of consumer buying habits, consumer patronage of different types of retail outlets, the flow of goods (by brands) from the retail stores or into consumer homes, and linage data for different kinds of advertising. There are studies to show the quality and character of the market served by the

FIGURE 20–5
Newspaper use of market data to attract advertisers

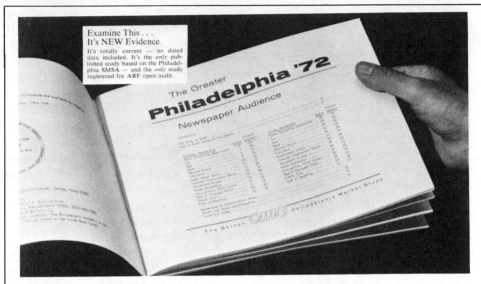

Proved: In Philadelphia

*Just One Paper—*The Bulletin*—Is*

indispensable

SEND for the new Belden study of the Philadelphia market. It makes one thing perfectly clear — *you only need one daily newspaper, the Bulletin,* to reach your best prospects in the entire Philadelphia SMSA.

The Belden study covers both Daily *and* Sunday — both the 8-county Metro area and the wider 13-county primary market.

It covers scores of different market measurements and indicators — including people who

> Own 2 or more cars
> Own 3 or more cars
> Took 5 domestic flights last year
> Rented car twice last year
> Took vacation trip outside U.S.
> Own one or more credit cards
> Own gasoline credit card
> Own stocks, bonds, or mutual funds
> Traded stocks, past 60 days
> Served Canadian whisky past 30 days
> Ditto Scotch, bourbon, vodka, gin
> Ditto imported wine
> Have income over $15,000
> Are College Graduates

. . . and in almost every case, the same pattern prevails —

1: **The Bulletin alone** covers three-quarters of the total number of your prospects who read a Philadelphia daily paper.

2: If you add another Philadelphia daily, *more than half* of your dollars are spent to *duplicate* Bulletin coverage — yet your reach is increased by less than a third!

3: If you add a second Philadelphia daily, the prospects you add cost you *three times as much* as the prospects you reach through the Bulletin.

For food advertisers, too, the Bulletin is dominant in all the key indices which identify best grocery prospects — with 71% more women in households of $10M plus income — 89% more women in households of five or more persons — 94% more women with children in the household.

Recent new combination rates don't alter

the unshakeable fact — in Philadelphia the Bulletin is indispensable.

LIKE the Philadelphia Bulletin, every independently-owned, independently-edited newspaper in the Million Market Newspaper group is *indispensable*.

1. Indispensable Markets: Just as the Bulletin is the key to Philadelphia, each MMN newspaper is the key to a marketing area far greater than the city itself.

2. Indispensable Medium: In each of these markets, the local businesses who ultimately *sell your product for you* spend more money in newspapers than in any other medium.

3. Indispensable Coverage: It is impossible to cover Philadelphia without the Bulletin — New England without the Boston Globe — Milwaukee without the Journal and Sentinel — the Bay Area without the San Jose Mercury-News — Washington without the Star-News, St. Louis without the Post-Dispatch.

Million Market Newspapers
"The Indispensables"

newspaper. These include the assemblage of population and economic data pertinent to the market, and circulation figures to show the degree of newspaper penetration of the market. Figure 20–5 shows the emphasis that one paper placed on such data in an advertisement designed to influence national advertisers to purchase space. Professor McClure has pointed out that most newspaper research is designed to "fulfill one or more of three functions: (1) to serve as a basis for improving the content of a newspaper; (2) to accumulate information about the market, consumers, and media for use by business firms in planning their merchandising programs; and (3) to develop information that the sales department can use in selling space in the newspaper."[6]

Various organizations are employed or sponsored by individual newspapers to facilitate the purchase of space by national advertisers or their agencies. The newspaper representative is a general salesman who maintains offices in the major cities where advertisers and agencies are found. He will represent a number of newspapers and has the power to contract with advertisers for space in the papers he represents.

Space in weekly and college newspapers can be purchased through the specialized press associations supported by those papers. This is of material value to an advertiser who wishes to reach the nonurban or college markets but does not wish to contract for space directly with each of the hundreds or thousands of papers involved.

Rates

You'll see the terms *flat* and *open* used in newspaper rate cards. If a newspaper quotes a *flat rate,* the advertiser is charged the same rate per line regardless of the quantity of space he buys. Whether he buys 50,000 lines a year or only 100 lines the advertiser is charged the same rate.

Open rate signifies that the newspaper is offering discounts to advertisers for buying greater quantities of space or for advertising more frequently. The open rate is the maximum price charged. As the number of lines purchased increase, the rate gradually steps down. The following is a typical example of such a sliding-scale rate structure:

Lines per year	Line rate
Open	$0.43
1,000 lines	0.42
2,500 lines	0.41
5,000 lines	0.40
10,000 lines	0.39
20,000 lines	0.38
30,000 lines	0.37
50,000 lines	0.36

[6] Leslie W. McClure, *Newspaper Advertising and Promotion* (New York: Macmillan Co., 1950), pp. 174–75.

TABLE 20–2
Cumulative circulation and rates of leading daily newspapers in top 100
metropolitan markets

Metro markets	Total circulation (000)	Open line rate	Black-and-white page cost
Top 10...........	8,060.2	$ 22.70	$ 52,691
Top 20...........	11,323.9	41.20	81,787
Top 30...........	14,695.7	52.72	109,756
Top 40...........	17,603.4	63.60	134,946
Top 50...........	19,702.2	71.90	154,161
Top 60...........	21,434.6	79.80	173,598
Top 70...........	23,258.7	87.16	191,345
Top 80...........	24,584.8	93.14	205,995
Top 90...........	25,562.4	98.17	218,272
Top 100..........	26,336.0	102.38	228,377

Source: Newspaper Advertising Bureau, A.N.P.A., January 1973.

The quantities involved in most sliding-scale plans pertain to the linage
used in a year's time. The advertiser signs a contract for the volume of
space he expects to use, and each month he pays for the space he actually
uses at the contract rate. If at the end of the year he has used less space
than he contracted for, he will receive a *short-rate* bill from the newspaper
for the difference between the contract rate that he paid and the higher
rate that he actually earned.

For example, using the above sliding-scale plan, assume that an advertiser contracted for 20,000 lines but by the end of the year he has used only
15,000 lines. In accordance with the contract, he paid $5,700 (15,000
lines X 38¢). For the quantity of space used he should have paid $5,850
(15,000 lines X 39¢). Thus, he will receive a *short-rate* bill for $150.

If, under the same contract, this advertiser had used 30,000 lines, he
would receive a *rebate* of $300 for the difference of one cent per line that
he paid (38¢) and the rate he earned (37¢).

Some newspapers avoid the problems of short rating and rebating by
eliminating contracts and billing the advertiser according to the rate he
earns each month.

Table 20–2 provides an overview of the cost to advertise in the top 100
metropolitan markets, assuming that the advertiser chooses the leading
paper in each market. Thus, a full-page, black-and-white advertisement
in the top ten markets would cost $52,691, when calculated on the basis
of the open line rate. The same space would cost only $43,586 if the
advertiser used sufficient space to qualify for the 50,000-line discount
(16.28 percent) suggested in the example cited above.

Rate differentials

Newspapers do not operate on a strict one-price policy. A majority of
newspapers charge the national advertiser substantially more than the

local or retail advertiser. This differential will average from 35 to 70 percent. In a number of instances the national rate will be as much as double the retail rate. Whereas retailers are offered liberal sliding-scale plans, national advertisers are often charged a flat rate.

Newspapers justify this higher rate for general or national advertising on the grounds that high commissions or brokerage fees are entailed in the sale of such space. A 15 percent commission is allowed the advertising agency; and, when space is sold through a publisher's representative or a press association, an additional 15 percent is paid. Thus, many newspapers receive only 70 percent of the rate quoted to national advertisers.

The variance between local and national rates has caused advertising agencies and national advertisers not only to use methods to take advantage of the lower local rates, but also to urge a reduction of the discrepancy. National advertisers have increased their practice of having newspaper advertising placed by their dealers so that the lower local rate might be obtained. Such practices have caused some newspapers to revise their rate policy and place general advertising in a less unfavorable position. Most recently, there has been a slight trend for some newspapers to offer the same rate to both local and national advertisers; it is still too early to determine how extensively this "one-rate" policy will develop.

Newspapers also maintain rate differentials for different types of advertising. A given amount of space used for advertising amusements would not cost the same as the same space used for a political announcement or a financial advertisement.

Rate variations are made also for space purchased by retailers. These differences are in the form of discounts for quantity of space used and for frequency of insertion. Such discounts are often substantial.

Space and color selection

Most advertising in newspapers is placed ROP (run of paper). It is possible, however, to buy a special position in some papers, although such position will not always be guaranteed. A particular section of the paper may be requested by the advertiser, with fair assurance of obtaining a position in that section. Most daily papers have such sections as automobile, resorts and travel, real estate, teens, finance, sports, comics, foods, etc. Many Sunday papers also have a magazine section. Consideration might well be given to the purchase of space in such specialized sections.

The development of comic-strip advertising is most impressive. A majority of all daily newspapers accept comic-strip advertising for regular issues, and most Sunday papers accept color advertising in their comic sections. In many instances, space in such sections can be purchased through one sales agency for a group of newspapers.

The use of ROP color in daily papers has also had a rapid development in recent years. As of March 1973 some 1,499 daily papers would accept "spot color" (ROP in black and one or two colors), while 1,156 would accept four-color ROP.[7] The extra cost of such advertising is illustrated in Table 20–3.

In addition to ROP color, many newspapers accept "preprint" color advertising, whereby the printing of the color advertisement is done away from the newspaper plant and shipped to the newspaper. There are three types of such preprints: (1) roll-fed ("hi-fi"), (2) in-register ("Spectacolor"), and (3) multipage inserts. Hi-fi color is printed on one side of a newsprint roll; the color side is of a high-quality paper, and the net result is a color advertisement of "magazine quality." The newspaper uses the unprinted side, which is of regular newsprint quality, for regular copy. Because of

TABLE 20–3
How color adds to advertising cost (average percent ROP color premium over B/W costs)

	Full-page ads		1,000-line ads	
Market group	1 extra color	3 extra colors	1 extra color	3 extra colors
Top 100. 17		29	35	62
Second 100. 18		33	35	68
Third 100 18		35	36	71

Source: Newspaper Advertising Bureau, A.N.P.A. April 1973.

the varying "stretch" of newsprint, the layout for hi-fi is done in a "wallpaper" design. There are 1,550 dailies that accept hi-fi.

Spectacolor is the same as hi-fi except that the wallpaper format is eliminated by using an electric-eye system to automatically cut the advertising page at the proper point. Presently, only 432 newspapers have such a system.

Multiple inserts are tabloid-size pages which, likewise, are printed in color away from the newspapers and shipped to the newspaper plant where they are inserted into the regular paper.

Information as to which papers accept color preprints, costs, mechanical requirements, closing dates, etc. is available in a special section of Standard Rate & Data Service, Inc.'s *Newspaper Rates and Data.*

Color certainly adds to the attention value of an advertisement. This is particularly true in newspapers, where relatively few advertisers use it. The extra cost, however, can be justified only on the grounds of increased sales; hence, tests should be run to determine the influence on sales. In an experiment designed to measure the effectiveness of color versus black-and-white advertisements, the *Milwaukee Journal* found that the addition

[7] Newspaper Advertising Bureau, A.N.P.A., May 1973.

of color increased readership 77 percent among men and 55 percent among women. Retention was 125 percent greater for men and 67 percent greater for women.

Reading habits

Newspapers reach a broad array of the population of a market area. A recent survey for the Newspaper Advertising Bureau by Audit and Surveys, Inc. showed that 77 percent of the people interviewed indicated

TABLE 20–4
Daily newspaper readership, by demographic characteristics

Characteristic	Percent who read a daily newspaper "yesterday"		
	Total	Male	Female
Total	77	79	76
Education			
8 years or less	70	74	65
9–11 years	72	73	72
Completed high school	77	77	77
Some college	84	86	82
Completed college	88	92	83
Income			
Under $5,000	67	66	68
$5,000–7,499	69	72	67
$7,500–9,999	81	83	79
$10,000–14,999	88	92	83
$15,000 and over	79	75	84

Source: "Facts About Newspapers—1973," Newspaper Advertising Bureau, A.N.P.A.

reading a daily newspaper. As shown in Table 20–4, this readership was heavier among those with a college education and income between $10,-000 and $14,999.

The study further revealed that a vast majority of readers were rather thorough in going through a newspaper, thus providing an advertiser with high exposure opportunity for an advertisement. The average page, exclusive of the classified section, stood an 84 percent chance of being opened by a reader. Other studies have shown, though, that daily newspapers are read hastily, generally in an average of about 20 minutes. Thus, although exposure opportunity is high, the short reading time must be considered in designing and writing a particular advertisement. Newspaper copy is usually prepared to conform with these hasty reading habits by keeping copy to a minimum for the amount of space used.

New techniques

In order to maintain their position as a leading advertising medium, newspapers have introduced a number of technological innovations. Presently, about 70 percent of the weeklies and 42 percent of all daily newspapers are produced by offset printing (lithography). Such printing allows for better ROP color and generally improves the appearance of the newspaper.

A process whereby full-color drawings and photographs are reproduced as line engravings was recently introduced. The technique, known as color *mezzotint,* results in a much better reproduction on newsprint than conventional ROP color.

Flexform advertising allows the advertiser to combine any unorthodox space layout with editorial copy. An advertisement can run up, down, or across the page; it can form a letter or symbol or can float in the middle of the page. For example, a soft-drink ad may be in the shape of the bottle, with editorial matter surrounding it. Flexform thus eliminates the rectangular appearance of ads and increases attention-getting value. Presently, only around 200 newspapers offer this technique.

In order to increase the advertising coverage of a particular advertisement some newspapers are experimenting with *total market coverage* (TMC). With this development a newspaper delivers an advertisement to *every* home in a market area and not just to subscribing families. Nonsubscribers are sent a copy of the ad either through direct mail or by having newsboy carriers deliver copies at home. This virtually allows an advertiser to cover an entire market area.

Newspaper supplements

The newspaper supplement offers the advertiser another way to expose his advertising to newspaper readers. These supplements are distributed in most Sunday or weekend papers and are either nationally syndicated or locally edited. For example, *Parade*—a national supplement—is distributed through 100 newspapers and reaches an adult audience of over 33 million people.[8] An advertiser could thus contract with only one source, *Parade,* and have his advertisement appear in the 100 markets. A full-color, full-page ad in this vehicle costs $78,895.

Local supplements are purchased in much the same way as a daily newspaper—that is, an advertiser buys space in this special section of a particular paper serving a specific market. These supplements range extensively in terms of their appearance and content. Some are similar to the national supplements in that they include high-quality color editorial mat-

[8] J. Walter Thompson, *Media Information,* 1972–73.

ter and advertising. The Denver *Post's* locally edited "Empire" is produced by the rotogravure method on magazine-quality paper. Local supplements also include less elaborate vehicles. For example, many newspapers publish a once-a-week television section which is inserted into a regular issue of the paper.

Comic supplements are likewise available on a national, syndicated basis or through local newspapers. *Puck—The Comic Weekly* can be purchased nationally in 96 newspapers at a cost of $91,663 for a full-page color advertisement. Rate and circulation data for supplements are available in *SRDS, Newspaper Rates and Data.*

MAGAZINES

In his book, *Magazines in the Twentieth Century,* Theodore Peterson says: "The magazine industry shared in the expansion of the American economy as a whole in the 20th century, just as did manufacturers of automobiles, refrigerators, and dentifrices, and such other communications media as newspapers and broadcasting."[9] Magazine advertising expenditures climbed from less than $100 million in 1933 to $379 million in 1946—and to an all-time high of almost $1.5 billion in 1972. The figure

TABLE 20–5
Top 20 magazine advertisers, 1972

Rank	Advertiser	Expenditures
1.	General Motors Corp.	$29,117,371
2.	Philip Morris Inc.	26,653,067
3.	British-American Tobacco Co. Ltd.	25,151,924
4.	R. J. Reynolds Industries, Inc.	24,376,257
5.	Ford Motor Co.	24,276,097
6.	Sears Roebuck & Co.	23,058,754
7.	Distillers Corp.—Seagrams, Ltd.	22,762,406
8.	Bristol-Myers Co.	20,981,515
9.	American Brands Inc.	16,811,042
10.	Loews Corp.	16,448,978
11.	Time Inc.	16,185,052
12.	General Foods Corp.	15,755,617
13.	Norton Simon Inc.	12,709,090
14.	U.S. Government	12,088,959
15.	Columbia Broadcasting System, Inc.	11,945,979
16.	RCA Corp.	11,515,599
17.	Chrysler Corp.	11,026,332
18.	Colgate-Palmolive Co.	11,016,584
19.	General Electric Co.	10,627,787
20.	American Telephone & Telegraph Co.	10,588,664

Source: Magazine Publishers Association, Inc., 1973.

[9] Theodore Peterson, *Magazines in the Twentieth Century* (Urbana, Ill.: University of Illinois Press, 1964), p. 45.

FIGURE 20–6

Quintile reading of magazines among men and women who are college educated and whose household income is $10,000 and over

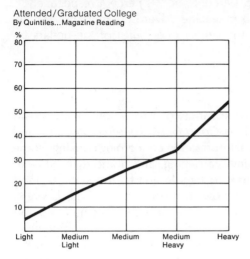

Attended/Graduated College
By Quintiles... Magazine Reading

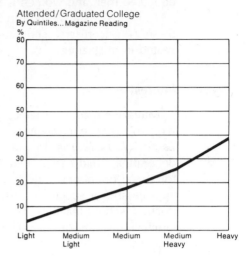

Attended/Graduated College
By Quintiles... Magazine Reading

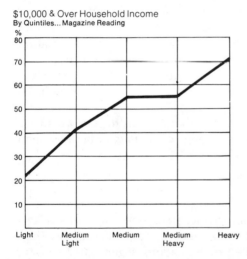

$10,000 & Over Household Income
By Quintiles... Magazine Reading

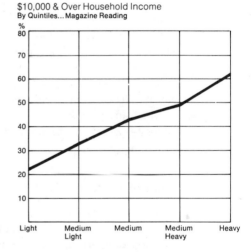

$10,000 & Over Household Income
By Quintiles... Magazine Reading

is expected to rise to over $2 billion by 1978. Circulation of consumer and farm magazines has increased in the past 20 years from 151.5 million an issue to 242.5 million an issue, a gain of 60 percent. A growing population, a growing economy, greater personal income, more education, and more leisure time are all factors contributing to the rapid growth of magazine circulation.

The degree of magazine reading, as related to household income and college attendance, is graphically illustrated in Figure 20–6. Among men with $10,000-and-over household incomes, 71 percent are heavy readers (62 percent among women). Heavy magazine reading by college-educated men and women is 55 percent and 38 percent respectively.

Table 20–5 shows the top 20 magazine advertisers in 1972. Totally, these 20 advertisers accounted for almost one fourth of the dollars invested in magazines.

Reader interest

Magazine reading provides a wide variety of satisfaction. Women read women's service magazines, such as *Good Housekeeping, McCall's,* and *Ladies' Home Journal,* for practical information concerning cooking, home decorating, child care, entertaining, gardening, and home management; for social orientation, such as how to handle guests, the kinds of food appropriate for specific occasions, how to meet and deal with lawyers, doctors, school teachers, and how to get along with one's husband and family; for the personal satisfaction of daydreaming, escaping from routine, relaxing, identifying one's self, and finding means of self-expression.[10]

Along with the entertainment they provide, our modern large-circulation magazines are opening up new worlds of knowledge and ideas to their readers. Well-known, authoritative articles on science, economics, philosophy, and art—the kind of article found only in small, specialized journals in the past—are now regular fare in general interest magazines. Stanley High, a senior editor of *Reader's Digest,* reports: "As recently as 1930 the average large-circulation magazine was 70 percent fiction. Today it's 70 percent *non*fiction."

Most any person can find a magazine that appeals to his own special interest—whether it be hot rods or beekeeping, boating, or business management.

Classification of magazines

Standard Rate and Data Service divides magazines into three groups: consumer magazines, farm publications, and business publications. These are then divided into more detailed classifications. Figure 20–7 shows a detailed classification of consumer magazines and farm publications.

The detailed classification for business magazines is not given here because *SRDS* lists 159 classes for the some 2,400 magazines of this type. These numbers should, in themselves, indicate the high degree of specialized interests served by such magazines. Practically every industry, trade and profession is included.

[10] *Women and Advertising, A Motivation Study of the Attitudes of Women Toward Eight Magazines* (New York: Good Housekeeping Magazines, 1954).

FIGURE 20–7

Consumer Magazines Classified

Airline, inflight
Almanacs and directories
Art and antiques
Automotive
Aviation
Babies
Boating and yachting
Brides
Business and finance
Campers, recreational vehicles,
    mobile homes and trailers
Camping and outdoor recreation
Children's
Civic (male)
College and alumni
Comics and comic technique
Crafts, hobbies, and models
Dancing
Detective
Dogs and pets
Dressmaking and needlework
Editorialized and classified adver-
    tising
Education and teacher
Entertainment guides and programs
Epicurean
Fashions
Finance
Fishing and hunting
Fraternal, professional groups, serv-
    ice clubs, veteran's organiza-
    tions, and associations
Gardening
General editorial

Health
Home service and home
Horses, riding and breeding
Labor-trade union
Literary, book reviews, and writing
    techniques
Mechanics and science
Men's
Metropolitan
Military and naval
Movie, radio, TV, and recording
    personalities
Music
Mystery, adventure, and science
    fiction
Nature and ecology
News
Newspaper comic supplements
Newspaper distributed magazines
Photography
Physical sciences
Political and social topics
Professional
Religious and denominational
Romance
Senior citizens
Society
Sports
Travel
TV and radio
Women's
Women's fashions, beauty, and
    grooming
Youth

Farm Publications Classified

Dairy and dairy breeds
Diversified farming and farm home
Farm education and vocations
Farm electrification
Farm organizations and cooperatives
Field crops and soil management

Fruits, nuts, vegetables, and special
    products
Land use, irrigation, conservation
Livestock and breed
Newspaper distributed farm publi-
    cations
Poultry

These classifications help to show the wide variety of magazines in all fields available to advertisers. A specific advertiser, however, will have to analyze the individual magazine and the character of its market penetration.

Customer selectivity

The detailed classification of magazines listed in the preceding section should help emphasize the very high degree of selectivity of audience which magazines provide. In the case of advertisers wishing to reach the farm market, magazines are available that will offer a general farm audience, or a highly specialized one in terms of specific farm interests (dairying, bee raising, vegetable growing) or, in some cases, restricted geographic areas. If it is the total farm market that is to be cultivated, then some general farm magazine like *Successful Farming* or the *Farm Journal* might be selected. If a more narrow or "thin" market is to be reached, a wide range of possibilities is presented. As shown in the previous section, there are 11 general divisions of the farm market, each served by specialized magazines. In each field, from 2 to 50 or more magazines are available. A manufacturer of poultry supplies may select the *Poultry Press* or the *Turkey World,* according to the specialized character of the product.

Selectivity on a geographical basis is provided to a lesser degree. A number of the farm papers concentrate their circulation in a given state or region; but such territorial selectivity is much less pronounced than in the case of newspapers, billboards, radio, direct mail, etc. *Standard Rate and Data Service* provides state or regional circulation figures for magazines that are members of the Audit Bureaus of Circulations. Such figures can be used to determine the territories in which a message will be carried. These data can be compared with the distributive outlets of the advertiser to check possible waste circulation. The *Ohio Farmer* had an average net paid circulation of 106,740 for the period ending June, 1972. Of this total, 104,876 subscribers were in Ohio. The remainder were divided among the bordering states of Pennsylvania, Indiana, Michigan, West Virginia, New York, and Kentucky. *Hoard's Dairyman* does not appeal to a special group confined to one territory but, rather, to all dairymen, wherever located. It had a net paid circulation of 320,328 as of June 30, 1972. There were subscribers in every state. Over 50 percent of the circulation, however, was in the East North Central and West North Central regions where there is a concentration of dairy farming. The coverage of the magazine, therefore, parallels the dairy industry which it is designed to serve. Similar comparisons could be made of other magazines serving different groups.

Business magazines are equally selective. Some go so far as to refuse subscriptions from persons not closely associated with the field served by the magazine. Controlled-circulation (free distribution) papers are de-

FIGURE 20–8
High audience selectivity offered by a business magazine

TRANSPORT TOPICS is unique in every sense of the word, which accounts for our leadership (Number 1 in linage) over other trucking industry publications. ■ We're BIGGEST IN THE BIG TRUCK MARKET because our editorial content caters to the "must know it now" needs of the Big Truck operators. ■ We are a NEWS NOW publication, weekly as opposed to monthly. ■ We are the only paid circulation publication in the field ($20.00 a year with a renewal rate of 81.07%. ■ We deliver the ACTION AUDIENCE, decision-making management people who can provide the advertiser with buying response. Advertisers who seek unique results can get them in TRANSPORT TOPICS. A captive audience of buyers reads the publication because it provides the unique kind of information they need to keep their business running smoothly. ■ Write for a copy of the PROFILE OF THE BIG TRUCK MARKET.

 If you have read this far, you no doubt are a potential advertiser. As such, you are entitled to a free gift of a TRANSPORT TOPICS CAT PIN. This attractive pin can be found at leading jewelers. It's yours simply by writing to us on your letterhead. Our representative will deliver your pin and, at the same time, give you the complete TT story. Write today, your best girl will be glad you did.

TRANSPORT TOPICS
BIGGEST IN THE BIG TRUCK MARKET
1616 P STREET N.W., WASHINGTON, D.C. 20036

yes, we're unique

signed to ferret out business and industrial groups with common specialized interests and limit their distribution to such persons. Obviously, in the case of business papers, there is little or no emphasis placed on territorial selection. Trades and professions are not generally confined to a particular area; but, in the few cases where such is true, the occupation rather than the address of the reader is of primary importance. Figure 20–8 illustrates an advertisement emphasizing the specialized audience reached through a business magazine.

General magazines select their audience more on the basis of general social and cultural interests than in terms of occupation. Mass-circulation magazines, such as *Reader's Digest* and *TV Guide,* emphasize general circulation throughout the United States, but circulation that varies, area by area, with variations in purchasing power of consumers. Thus, these magazines claim to pick out of each community those families that provide the richest opportunities for cultivation by advertisers. Magazines like *Fortune* and *Newsweek* claim to offer the "cream of the mass market" to advertisers.

A survey of males who read *Playboy* showed that 19.6 percent were college graduates, 59.2 percent were 18 to 34 years of age, and 29.2 percent were single.

As one might expect, over three fourths of the readers of *Seventeen* are high-school girls.

The Macfadden publications, particularly the "true story" women's group, emphasize sociological as well as economic factors in detailing the character of audience. Emphasis is placed on its high concentration among wage-earner families and women under middle age.

Time restrictions

Magazine advertising cannot be tied to day-by-day events. Occasionally this is tried, but the news element is stale by the time it reaches the reader. Generally, magazine advertising which does capitalize on recent events, such as the winner of the Indianapolis "500," serves merely as a testimonial.

The nature of magazine publication militates against the early appearance of an advertisement after it has been submitted for printing. Many magazines are published in great quantities, requiring days to complete the run. The preparation of the forms takes a great deal of time. The use of color prolongs the completion of printing. The widespread distribution of the magazine requires time to get it from the publisher to distant points. This period is lengthened still further when magazines are shipped in bulk in carload lots to central points and then distributed to dealers. When a publication is to appear on the newsstands simultaneously all over the country, the areas near the printing plant must wait until the distant areas are supplied before distribution is made available to prospective buyers of the magazine. All this means that an advertisement must be in the hands of the publisher weeks before it is received by prospective customers. *Reader's Digest* magazine requires that all copy, plates, etc., for a four-color advertisement be in its hands eight and one-half weeks before publication date.

Regional editions

The flexibility of consumer magazines has been greatly increased through regional editions which enable advertisers to place ads in copies circulated in particular market areas. *Look* (now defunct) pioneered regional editions in 1959 with its Magazone plan that then divided total circulation into eight marketing zones, each of which was available individually or in any combination.

As a current example of such flexibility, *Newsweek* permits regional advertising in 11 different geographic editions. These editions are composed of several contiguous states. In addition, an advertiser can buy one or more of 39 metropolitan markets. This service is illustrated in Figure 20–9.

Regional editions enable smaller advertisers whose distribution is confined to part of the country to benefit from the prestige of national publications. Large national advertisers benefit, too, in that they can promote products whose popularity is restricted to one section of the country. Regionals are also finding favor among makers of items whose markets are determined by climate, as well as proving useful for test marketing and advertising experimentation.

Regional advertising is likely to continue its substantial growth rate, as more and more magazines begin to offer regional breakouts. One hundred and seventeen consumer magazines were offering regional editions as of January 1973. As shown in Table 20–6, regional advertising in 1972 represented 18 percent of total magazine dollars, an all-time high.

A further refinement of regional editions is "demographic advertising." To give advertisers an opportunity to reach certain income and/or occupation groups, a select number of magazines offer a separate edition that is delivered only to subscribers in those particular demographic classifications. *Time* magazine, for example, has four demographic editions singling out doctors, educators, college students, and businessmen. The college student edition circulates to over 500,000 subscribers; a full-color, one-page advertisement can be purchased for $7,860 (compared with a $38,-190 cost for the full run of 4,339,516 circulation).

FIGURE 20–9
Regional advertising offered by *Newsweek*

NEWSWEEK REGIONAL ADVERTISING SERVICE
Versatility to meet nearly every advertising requirement

Newsweek offers an ever-wide range of flexibility to enable marketers to allocate their advertising investment more effectively, consisting of 11 Regional Editions; 11 Metro Group I Editions and 28 Metro Group II Editions; plus a Student Demographic Edition, a growing market of today and of tomorrow; plus 5 "group plans" to cover sections of the country for either geographic or seasonal needs. These combinations make for concentration and for advertising efficiencies.

In 1971, advertisers, ranging from local businesses to giant corporations, placed more than 25,000 pages in Newsweek's Regional and Metro Group Editions.

1973 National Rate Base: 2,725,000. One Page, Black & White, 1 Time: $17,155.

11 REGIONAL EDITIONS
—basic regional configurations that can be broadly adapted—individually or collectively—to seasonal and geographic sales efforts.

	Rate Base	One-Time B&W Page Rate
Eastern	845,000	$ 6,920
New England	225,000	2,105
Middle Atlantic	620,000	5,275
East Central	705,000	5,925
West Central	205,000	1,865
Southern	485,000	4,230
Southeast	310,000	2,820
Florida	80,000	1,200
Southwest	175,000	1,710
Western	495,000	4,210
Pacific Northwest	120,000	1,180
Pacific Southwest	375,000	3,325
California	300,000	2,910

11 METRO GROUP I EDITIONS
—to concentrate advertising support in the country's topmost consumer, business, and industrial markets.

	Rate Base	One-Time B&W Page Rate
New York	265,000	$ 2,410
Los Angeles	180,000	1,965
Philadelphia	125,000	1,575
San Francisco	120,000	1,515
Chicago	110,000	1,405
Washington/Baltimore	110,000	1,405
Boston	90,000	1,250
Detroit	75,000	1,130
Pittsburgh	75,000	1,130
Cleveland	70,000	1,055
Atlanta	29,000	710

28 METRO GROUP II EDITIONS
—to enable the advertiser to concentrate in the remaining major U.S. markets.

	Rate Base	One-Time B&W Page Rate
Buffalo	21,000	$ 820
Cincinnati	19,000	785
Columbus	21,000	820
Dallas	17,000	755
Dayton	14,000	690
Denver	21,000	820
Hartford	17,000	755
Honolulu	15,000	710
Houston	22,000	830
Indianapolis	18,000	765
Jacksonville	23,000	840
Kansas City	19,000	785
Miami	27,000	890
Milwaukee	22,000	830
Minneapolis/St. Paul	31,000	915
New Haven	19,000	785
New Orleans	16,000	735
Omaha	15,000	710
Phoenix	21,000	820
Portland	23,000	840
Providence	13,000	665
Rochester	16,000	735
San Antonio	16,000	735
San Diego	23,000	840
Seattle	32,000	920
St. Louis	34,000	930
Syracuse	12,000	640
Tampa/St. Petersburg	19,000	785

For further details, call or write your nearby Newsweek salesman, or: Robert H. Golden, Regional Advertising Manager, 444 Madison Avenue, New York, N.Y. 10022. Phone: (212) 350-2253.

Newsweek
the world's most quoted newsweekly

INTERNATIONAL EDITIONS
(See International Section)

TABLE 20–6
Dollar magazine volume in regional editions

Year	Dollar volume	Percent of total magazine dollars
1959.......	$ 42,629,531	5.4
1960.......	71,020,830	8.3
1961.......	93,427,865	11.2
1962.......	114,381,512	13.1
1963.......	134,747,597	14.5
1964.......	147,545,332	14.8
1965.......	163,760,729	15.1
1966.......	184,769,900	15.8
1967.......	195,462,571	16.8
1968.......	199,963,964	16.7
1969.......	206,872,695	16.6
1970.......	202,547,128	17.0
1971.......	222,722,985	17.8
1972.......	233,916,071	18.0

Source: Publishers Information Bureau, Inc.

Mechanical and quality characteristics

Magazines are usually printed on good paper that will allow for excellent reproductions of art and color work. Halftones can be used effectively for either black-and-white or color illustrations. Some magazines are even prepared to print advertisements in metallic ink in different colors. To achieve the maximum use of page area, a magazine ad may often be designed to bleed off the page on one or more sides. An example of this is shown in Figure 20–10 where the picture is carried to the very edge of the paper at top and sides. To accomplish this, the original illustration had to exceed the page dimension so that some of it was actually cut off when the page was trimmed, hence the use of the term bleed or bleed edge.

The life of a magazine is an important quality. An old issue is often kept some time after a new issue has been received. This gives to an advertisement a greater opportunity of being seen and read. The reading habits of magazine subscribers are also favorable to an advertisement. Most magazines are not read at one sitting but are picked up and read at various intervals between issues. A research study estimated the average number of days that a reader reads an issue of the following magazines one or more times.[11]

Magazine	Average reading days
Reader's Digest.........................	5.3
Good Housekeeping....................	4.1

[11] *A Study of Seven Publications,* conducted by Alfred Politz Research, Inc. for *Reader's Digest* (Pleasantville, New York: Reader's Digest Association, Inc., 1956).

She's just completed the analysis of 131 electronics companies and selected two for inclusion in her portfolio.

She does it the easy way—by having Bank of America's experienced professional managers take care of all her investments. These men work full-time researching, analyzing and selecting stocks, bonds, real estate and other investments. They can tailor an individual portfolio for maximum performance in growth, income or tax-free holdings.

This Investment Management Service—which takes care of all details and paperwork—is available for you and your family today. Just see the manager at your local Bank of America branch or stop in soon at any of our District Trust Offices.

BANK OF AMERICA
NATIONAL TRUST AND SAVINGS ASSOCIATION • MEMBER FEDERAL DEPOSIT INSURANCE CORPORATION

FIGURE 20–10. Magazine production quality not feasible in newspapers

Rates

Magazine space is generally sold in units of a full page or a fraction of a page. For example, *Better Homes and Gardens* quotes rates for one page, three-fourths page, half page, quarter page, and eighth page. Small-space ads are sold by the agate line. Fractional-page units vary according to the number of columns on a page. A magazine with a three-column page quotes rates for full, two-thirds, and one-third pages. *Reader's Digest* does not accept ads measuring less than one-half page.

The variation in page sizes among magazines might be considered important. However, a full page in a magazine with a small format will possess the same relative dominance as a full page in a magazine of larger size. Page size is probably more significant as a factor influencing the design of the advertisement than as a factor affecting the value of the space.

Most magazines make an additional charge for certain preferred positions. The cover pages are highly desirable because of their greater attention-getting value. *Time* charges the same for the second and third cover pages as for a regular four-color page ad, which was $38,190 in January 1973. The fourth cover (back cover) carries an additional cost of 26 percent over other color pages, and thus costs $48,050. A full-page ad in black and white costs $24,640 about one half of the charge for the back cover. Those magazines that accept orders for bleed pages generally charge extra, usually 15 percent.

Many magazines offer discounts based on the amount of space used and a number of other critieria. For example, *Playboy* quotes the following bulk space discounts:

Pages per year	Discount (percent)
6	5
12	10
18	15

As demonstrated in the preceding chapter, magazine rates are usually compared on the basis of cost-per-thousand circulation. The following cost comparisons indicate some significant characteristics of magazine rates:

	Rate per page B/W	Circulation	C.P.M.
Reader's Digest	$51,375	18,232,277	$ 2.82
New Yorker	4,800	476,618	10.07
Fortune	7,510	580,242	16.39
Advertising Age	1,995	65,968	30.24

The wide range of costs-per-thousand among these four magazines indicates differing degrees of selectivity, differing buying power per audience member, and differing influence per audience member on business purchases. *The New Yorker's* circulation is more concentrated among higher-income families than is the circulation of *Reader's Digest. Fortune* and *Advertising Age* reach businessmen whose decisions influence large-scale business buying. Generally speaking, the greater the selectivity, or the greater the buying potential per person reached, the higher is the cost-per-thousand.

Copy and contract requirements

Advertisements are, in general, accepted subject to the approval of the publisher. Thus, no guarantees are given to print any copy that is submitted. Many magazine publishers assist the advertiser by setting up specific standards to which copy must conform.

The majority of publishers specify certain contract requirements. Those dealing with ethics are reproduced here:

24. All advertisements are accepted and published by the publisher on the representation that the advertising and/or advertising agency are properly authorized to publish the entire contents and subject matter thereof. When advertisements containing the names, pictures and/or testimonials of living persons are submitted for publication, the order or request for the publication thereof shall be deemed to be a representation by the advertiser and/or advertising agency that they have obtained the written consent of the use in the advertisement of the name, picture and/or testimonial of any living person which is contained therein. It is understood that the advertiser and/or advertising agency will indemnify and save the publisher harmless from and against any loss, expense or other liability resulting from any claims or suits for libel, violation of rights of privacy, plagiarism, copyright infringement and any other claims or suits that may arise out of the publication of such advertisement. All copy, text, and illustrations are subject to the publisher's approval before execution of the order; and the right is reserved to reject or exclude copy which is unethical, misleading, extravagant, challenging, questionable in character, in bad taste, detrimental to public health or interest otherwise inappropriate or incompatible with the character of the publication, or that does not meet with the approval of the Federal Trade Commission; whether or not the same has already been accepted and/or published. In the event of such cancellation or rejection by the publisher, the advertising already run shall be paid for or billed at the rate provided for in the order.
25. Acceptance of advertising for any product or service is subject to investigation of the product or service, and of the claims made for it

upon its package, labels and accompanying material, and in the advertisement submitted for publication.[12]

QUESTIONS AND PROBLEMS

1   Why do some newspapers charge more for national than for local advertising?

2   In preparing a newspaper schedule, what factors would influence your selection of morning, evening, or Sunday newspapers?

3   If given an appropriation to be spent in *Time,* either (1) in a series of four black-and-white, full-page advertisements or (2) in two, four-color cover advertisements, which would you choose? Why? How much would each series of ads cost?

4   The specialized business or trade magazine assembles for the advertiser a number of people with similar business or trade interests. This provides a high degree of homogeneity, at least in respect to certain interests. Does this high degree of homogeneity make this type of magazine a highly desirable medium for advertisers? Would it be more desirable for some than for other advertisers? Explain.

5   Newspapers emphasize that "all markets are local." Magazines place emphasis on the quality aspects of markets, in terms of kinds of people reached rather than their territorial location. Is it safe to generalize on the relative values of those two claims? What is your evaluation of these claims? Be specific and give examples supporting your observations.

6   The satisfactions people get out of reading their daily newspapers are different from the satisfactions they receive from reading magazines. Do you agree or disagree? Explain.

7   Compare the "milline" rates of the following newspapers: *Cincinnati Enquirer, Cincinnati Post and Times-Star, Chicago Tribune,* and *Chicago Daily News.*

8   Why are milline rates generally higher for small-circulation papers than for large-circulation papers?

9   Compare the cost per black-and-white page per thousand circulation of the following magazines: *Time, Newsweek, Madison Avenue,* and *Sales Management.* What factors probably account for these cost differences?

10   Compare the editorial content of any two magazines in a particular classification. What qualitative differences do you observe that you think might have some bearing on the value of each magazine as an advertising medium?

11   Magazines cover so many specialized fields that their use makes it possible to reach markets profitably in a manner not possible by the use of newspapers. Do you agree? Why?

12   You have been asked to buy some space in the daily newspaper which you read (or believe you should read) regularly. You are to buy space equivalent to 4 columns by 12 inches. This space is to be used by a national advertiser.

[12] "Contract and Copy Regulations," *Consumer Magazine and Form Publication Rates and Data, Standard Rate and Data Service,* January 27, 1973, p. 22.

How much will this space cost if you were to use the same amount of space once a week for 52 weeks?

Is there a possibility that this space would cost less if it were to be used by a local retailer? How could you find out whether that is true?

13 Assume you are a newspaper publisher. What new techniques can you think of, not now offered by newspapers, that might be of value to an advertiser? What would you suggest for a magazine publisher?

Television and radio

A s channels of communication, television and radio are fundamentally different. One combines sight, motion, and sound. The other depends entirely on sound.

Yet, these media also have much in common. Both use the airwaves to broadcast messages which are received instantaneously in the home. Both depend on the public's voluntary investment in receiving sets to complete the communication channel. Both are regulated private enterprises and are licensed to operate by the same government agency, the Federal Communications Commission. Both are time organized. They schedule programs and commercials by the hour of the day and sell units of time to advertisers. Both provide nationwide networks of stations for simultaneous broadcasting in all parts of the country. Both use the same methods of audience measurement. Both belong to the same trade association, the National Association of Broadcasters.

Whether he is buying television time or radio time, the advertiser is dealing with media that are organized, operated, and sold in much the same way. Therefore, these two media are treated together in this chapter.

Advertising volume

Television is the fastest-growing medium. In the short span of 25 years, expenditures for television advertising grew from zero to about $4.1 billion

FIGURE 21–1
Growth and composition of television and radio advertising

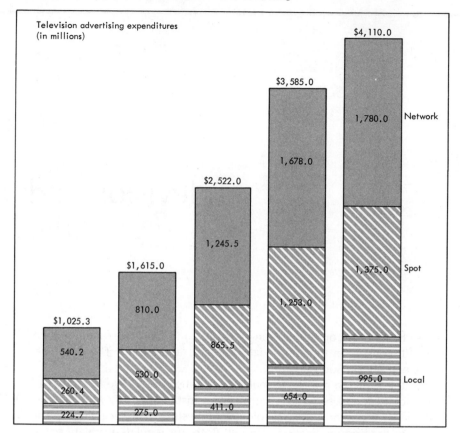

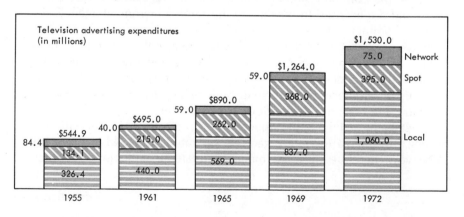

dollars annually. With national advertisers spending about $3.2 billion in 1972, television is the leading national advertising medium. It is estimated that volume in 1978 will reach $6.4 billion, of which $4.7 billion will be national.[1]

Radio, in the wake of television's impact, declined from a volume of $624 million in 1952 to $545 million in 1955. However, from the mid-1950s radio expenditures have had a consistent upward trend, with 1972 volume at $1.5 billion. Expenditures in 1978 are expected to reach $2.4 billion.

Network television, which provides simultaneous coverage of a nationwide market, accounted for 43 percent of total television advertising expenditures in 1972. *National spot* television, which involves national advertiser's selecting individual stations to reach individual markets ("spots" on the map), accounted for 34 percent of the total. *Local* television, the use of local stations by retailers, accounted for 23 percent. These relationships are illustrated in Figure 21-1.

Radio advertising expenditures in 1972 were 69 percent *local,* 26 percent *national spot,* and 5 percent *network.* Thus, radio today is primarily a local medium with strong support coming from national spot. This has not always been so. Before the advent of television, network advertising accounted for the major share of radio advertising expenditures. However, as more and more people began watching network television programs during prime evening hours, the value of network radio as an advertising medium declined.

Facilities available

Advertisers are naturally interested in knowing what facilities a medium can offer for reaching prospective customers. Physical facilities offered by television and radio are represented by the number of stations, networks, and receiving sets.

Number of stations   In January 1973, there were 696 commercial television stations on the air. Of these stations, 510 were VHF (very-high-frequency—channels 2 through 13) and 186 were UHF (ultra-high-frequency—channels 14 through 83).[2]

Further expansion of television broadcast facilities largely depends on the number of new stations that will be added in the UHF range, where most of the unassigned channels are available. However, several factors have limited the growth of UHF facilities. During the first five years of

---

[1] J. Walter Thompson Advertising Agency, 1973.

[2] The VHF range is from 54 to 216 megacycles. UHF range is from 470 to 890 megacycles. Each channel assigned for television broadcasting is 6 megacycles wide. Twelve of the VHF channels are allocated for commercial broadcasting, and the others are for use by military and other services.

commercial television all the stations on the air were VHF and all the receiving sets sold were equipped to receive only VHF broadcasts. Most of these early stations were located in the densely populated metropolitan markets. Thus, by 1952, when the Federal Communications Commission began licensing UHF stations, the system of television broadcasting had been fairly well established in the VHF channels. As a result, there was little or no incentive to construct UHF stations in the major markets where practically all the receiving sets received only VHF. In smaller markets where both V's and the U's went on the air about the same time, the networks and national advertisers favored the V's, thereby making the operation of a UHF station unprofitable. Obviously, would-be UHF broadcasters were not eager to seek a license to lose money. Now, however, as a result of a congressional law passed in 1964, all television sets shipped in interstate commerce must be able to receive both UHF and VHF channels. Presently, about 85 percent of U.S. television households are equipped for all-channel reception. In 1973, almost all commercial stations were equipped to carry some form of color programming.

There were 7,330 radio stations on the air in 1973. Of this number, 4,410 were AM stations, 2,920 were FM.[3] The majority of these stations are low-power local outlets and are located in the smaller markets. Radio blankets the United States. Anyone with a receiving set, regardless of where he might be, can be assured of radio service. In the vast majority of localities, listeners can choose from a half dozen or more stations at will.[4]

Networks   There are three national television networks and four national radio networks, with one radio network broken into four systems. Columbia Broadcasting System (CBS), National Broadcasting Company (NBC), and American Broadcasting Company (ABC) operate both television and radio networks. The Mutual Broadcasting System operates a radio network only. The total number of interconnected stations offered by each network in 1973 is shown at the top of page 481.[5]

The networks perform several important functions: (1) they assemble the network by negotiating station affiliation agreements and arranging for American Telephone and Telegraph facilities (coaxial cables and microwave relays) by which affiliated stations are interconnected for simultaneous broadcasts; (2) they provide physical facilities, such as studios, cameras, microphones, scenery, sets, etc., for originating network pro-

---

[3] The AM broadcast band ranges from 535 to 1,605 kilocycles and consists of 107 channels, each 10 kilocycles wide. The FM band ranges from 88 to 108 megacycles (1,000 kilocycles) and consists of 100 channels, each 0.2 megacycle wide.

[4] Radio stations are generally classified as *local, regional, or clear channel.* Local stations operate with power not in excess of 250 watts and have an average daytime range of 15 to 20 miles. *Regional* stations operate with power not in excess of 5,000 watts and have an average daytime range of 40 to 65 miles. *Clear channel* stations operate at 50,000 watts and have an average daytime range of 100 to 125 miles.

[5] Standard Rate & Data Service, Inc., *Network Rate and Data,* January 10, 1973.

Network	TV stations	Radio stations
CBS 210		251
NBC. 212		234
ABC. 178		
Contemporary		309
Entertainment		340
FM		217
Information		430
Mutual.		567

grams; (3) they produce programs; and (4) they sell network time periods and programs to advertising agencies and advertisers.

Networks offer advertisers the opportunity to reach nationwide audiences during specific time periods at a low cost-per-thousand figure. By making it possible to distribute talent and program production costs over many markets, the networks enable advertisers to benefit from the popularity, prestige, and publicity of high-priced talent and expensive shows.

Even though the number of television stations has increased greatly since the infant stage of the industry, the number of television networks decreased from four to three. Claims that network practices were stifling competition and preventing the formation of new networks led the Federal Communications Commission to undertake a special study of television networks. In the report of the FCC's network study group, which was issued in 1957, it was noted: "The high concentration of control exercised by networks, the barriers to new network entry, the strong bargaining position of the networks in their relations with stations in many markets, and the limited opportunity for nonnetwork groups to compete represent in combination a serious problem for the realization of the objectives of the commission."[6]

Until the existing structure of television broadcasting is considerably modified it would appear that there is little prospect for more networks. In fact, with the growth of communications satellites it is difficult to assess the future of network television. Not only will television become more international as a result of satellite relay, but the entire method of beaming network programs into the home through local stations is subject to change.

Number of receiving sets An analysis of the number and location of stations provides a picture of the facilities for getting messages into the airwaves. Such an analysis must be combined with a measure of the number of receiving sets capable of reproducing those messages for consumers.

In 1973, there were almost 66 million homes equipped with one or

[6] *Report of the Network Study Staff to the Network Study Commission,* Federal Communications Commission, 1957.

more TV sets. This included 96 percent of all homes. By 1978, the penetration is expected to be 98 percent. Of these 66 million TV households, 42 percent have more than one set. The coverage of multiset homes has more than doubled since 1965.

Over 60 percent of TV homes had a color set in 1973, a substantial increase over the 39 percent who could receive color programming in 1970. The penetration of color TV homes is projected to reach 84 percent in 1978. As can be noted in Figure 21–2, television usage in color set households tends to be higher than in those with only a black-and-white set. The margin of difference ranges from 4 percent more usage during weekday daytime to 28 percent more during weekend daytime.

FIGURE 21–2
Comparison of television usage by color set and black-and-white set households

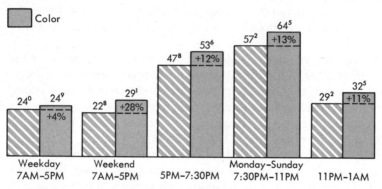

Source: Nielsen Television Index estimates, December 1972.

The expression "radio is everywhere" is close to the truth. In 1973 there were an estimated 67 million radio homes, 98.6 percent of all homes in the United States. There are almost 370 million radio sets in working order, of which over one fourth are in automobiles. The average household thus has somewhat over five sets, and 99 percent of all automobiles are equipped with radios. The ubiquity of radio was dramatically increased with the development of battery-powered, transistorized, lightweight, portable receiving sets. Whereas transistor set sales were 11 million units in 1962, over 33 million per year are presently being sold. As would be expected, teen-agers are the group with the largest degree of ownership of transistor radios—75 percent of them own such a set.

The degree of FM set penetration has increased dramatically over the past several years. Less than half of all homes had an FM set in 1966, but presently the penetration level is 88 percent and is projected to be 97 percent by 1978.

Community antenna television (CATV)

CATV uses a master antenna to receive signals from both nearby and distant TV stations and then distributes the signals to subscriber homes by cable. CATV, or "cable television," began as a service to communities where regular television reception was poor or where channel availabilities were minimal. Thus, cable television has primarily served small towns and rural areas. Presently, however, CATV is on the threshold of development in the major metropolitan areas of the United States.[7]

As can be seen in Table 21–1, cable television has grown consistently over the past 22 years, with 11 percent of TV households subscribing to a system in 1973. This growth is projected to continue at a steady rate, with approximately 15.3 million subscribers (21 percent of TV homes) as early as 1978.

The distribution of cable systems is uneven throughout the United States, with the greatest degree of coverage in rural and mountainous

TABLE 21–1
CATV operating systems and subscribers

Year	Operating systems	Total subscribers	Percent of TV households
1952	70	14,000	0.1
1953	150	30,000	0.1
1954	300	65,000	0.3
1955	400	150,000	0.5
1956	450	300,000	0.9
1957	500	350,000	0.9
1958	525	450,000	1.1
1959	560	550,000	1.3
1960	640	650,000	1.4
1961	700	725,000	1.5
1962	800	850,000	1.7
1963	1,000	950,000	1.9
1964	1,200	1,085,000	2.1
1965	1,325	1,275,000	2.4
1966	1,570	1,575,000	2.9
1967	1,770	2,100,000	3.8
1968	2,000	2,800,000	4.9
1969	2,260	3,600,000	6.2
1970	2,490	4,500,000	7.6
1971	2,570	5,300,000	8.7
1972	2,770	6,000,000	9.6
1973	3,00	7,200,000	11.1

Source: *Television Digest,* January 1 of each year.

[7] See Walter S. Baer, *Cable Television: A Handbook for Decisionmaking* (Santa Monica, Calif.: Rand Corporation, 1973).

regions. For example, penetration into the counties containing the 25 largest metropolitan areas (so-called "A" counties) is less than 4 percent of TV homes, whereas those counties with population between 35,000 and 150,000 ("C" counties) have a penetration level of 24 percent.[8] As indicated above, though, it is likely that future development will occur in major metropolitan areas.

Much of the long-range growth of the medium is predicated on technological capabilities of CATV systems. In addition to offering subscribers local programming such as continuous weather news, telecasts of municipal events, and educational services, there is the likelihood of broadcasting first-run movies and live sporting events which would be available to subscribers for an additional fee ("pay TV"). The ability of viewers to communicate through their sets with a host of service activities (two-way communication) should enhance the desirability of cable. Two-way communication involves such things as remote shopping in retail stores, banking by television, and information retrieval services.[9] One of the most significant implications for advertisers of the growth of cable television is that viewing may become substantially more selective and fragmented, and the opportunity to reach large audiences with single telecasts may be rare.

Audiences

In the course of a week about 64 million U.S. families make some use of their TV sets. Household viewing, cumulatively for all members of the household, averages 6 hours and 12 minutes per day.[10]

Television audiences are big. For example, the movie "The Ten Commandments," aired in February 1973, was viewed by almost 32 million homes; "All in the Family," a top-ranked program in 1972 and 1973, often reaches an audience of 20 to 25 million homes and 58 to 72 million persons. The largest audiences are assembled when all three networks cover the same event, such as a presidential address.

Obviously, television viewing is influenced by time of day and season of the year. Changes in the hour-by-hour activities of various members of the family influence the number of viewers per home and the composition of the audience by age and sex. School, job, and household routines are reflected in the TV audience. As illustrated in Figure 21–3, through the early daytime hours the number of families viewing television increases steadily to a high between 1 and 2 P.M. After a slight dip in mid-afternoon the viewing audience again increases hour by hour to reach its peak for

[8] *Nielsen Television '73.*
[9] Baer, *Cable Television.*
[10] A. C. Nielsen Co., 1973.

FIGURE 21–3
Hour-by-hour and seasonal pattern of television viewing

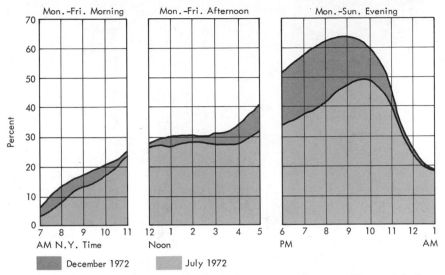

Source: Nielsen Television Index estimates, July and December 1972. Times of TV usage: NYT, except in Pacific territory, NYT plus 3 hours.

TABLE 21–2
Weekly reach of radio by sex and age

Characteristic	Weekly cumulative audience (by percent)		
	Mon.–Sun.	Mon.–Fri.	Sat.–Sun.
Persons 12+	96.6	96.0	87.4
Teens 12–17	99.3	99.2	96.1
Persons 18+	96.1	95.4	85.8
Adult men 18+	96.6	95.9	86.1
Men 18–34	99.4	99.2	92.8
Men 18–49	98.3	97.9	88.7
Men 25–49	97.8	97.3	86.1
Men 35–49	96.9	96.3	83.3
Men 35+	95.0	93.9	82.1
Men 50+	93.5	92.0	81.2
Adult women 18+	95.5	95.0	85.5
Women 18–34	99.5	99.1	90.7
Women 18–49	98.1	97.8	88.2
Women 25–49	97.4	97.1	86.6
Women 35–49	96.3	96.0	84.7
Women 35+	93.4	92.8	82.6
Women 50+	91.5	90.5	81.1

Source: *Radio's All Dimension Audience Research (RADAR)*, 1972.

FIGURE 21–4
Composition of national television audience, by time of day and season of year (average minute of daypart)

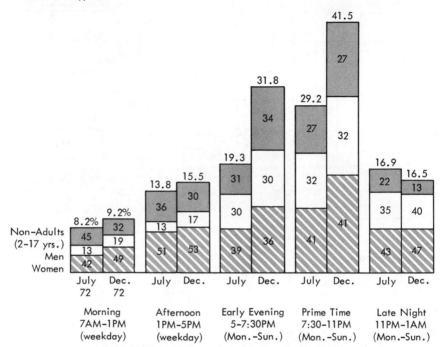

Source: Nielsen Television Index estimates: Based on NYT, except in Pacific territory, NYT plus 3 hours.

the entire day at mid-evening. Summer viewing is noticeably lower than winter levels between 4 P.M. and 10 P.M.

Composition of the television audience at different hours of the day according to season of year is shown in Figure 21–4. Nonadults are the biggest viewing group during summer mornings. Women are the biggest group watching at all other time periods, although early evening and prime time audiences are fairly evenly distributed among the three groups. It should be noted, however, that these figures are national averages. Composition of audiences reached by specific programs may differ greatly from the average.

Radio, likewise, has a large reach potential. In a typical week, 96.6 percent of all persons 12 years old and over are reached by the medium. As can be noted in Table 21–2, the highest weekly reached levels are among men and women in the 18 to 34 age category, as well as by teens. Weekend listening is consistently lower than weekday.

The hour-by-hour pattern of listening is shown in Figure 21–5. Listening reaches its peak for the entire day between 7 and 8 A.M., with over 35 percent of the total population tuned in. Listenership decreases until mid-

FIGURE 21–5
Hour-by-hour pattern of radio listening (average quarter-hour ratings Monday–Friday, 6:00
A.M.–midnight)

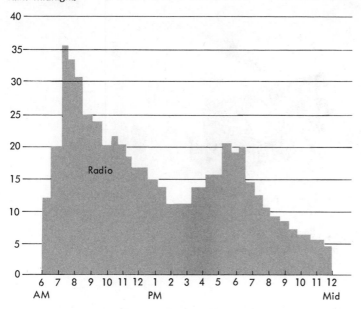

afternoon; then another buildup occurs between 3 and 7 P.M. reflecting
the surge of automobile travelers returning home from work. Due to the
mobility of receiving sets, total radio listening remains fairly constant in
both summer and winter.

Measuring size of specific audiences

Advertisers, of course, are interested not only in the pattern of total
listening and viewing, but more particularly in the number and type of
people tuned to a particular program. Just as some magazines and newspapers have high and low readership, so do similar differences exist among
radio and TV programs. Since such differences are so important to advertisers, much attention is given to measuring the size of specific program
audiences.

There are a number of methods employed to measure audience size
and character. The *Nielsen Audimeter* (see Figure 21–6) is an electronic
device about the size of an automobile battery which is installed somewhere out of sight in the home. It makes a minute-by-minute record on
photographic film—24 hours a day, all year—of the set tuning of all
television receivers in the home. It thus provides a continuous record of
the time periods when a set is turned on, the specific stations to which

FIGURE 21–6
The Nielsen Audimeter

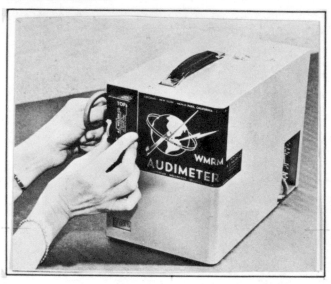

the set is turned, the dialing from one station to another, and the length of time spent with each station. The film cartridges are sent in every two weeks by panel members to the Nielsen organization where the data are tabulated and matched against the program schedules of the television networks involved. While the Audimeter provides a precise record of set tuning, it does not show how many people were viewing or listening, nor does it show which members of the family were doing so.

The *coincidental telephone* method consists of telephoning homes and asking whether a radio or television set is turned on and, if so, to what station or program. This method is used extensively in local market areas. It is relatively inexpensive.

The *roster-recall* method is used in a number of the larger metropolitan areas. It consists of having personal interviewers present to people a roster of all stations and programs readily available in the area and asking people to check those programs or stations which they recall having heard or seen. People are generally asked to recall a time period of only a few hours. The method is especially valuable for use among nontelephone homes and where there are significant ethnic differences in the population.

A somewhat more qualitative picture of listening or viewing can be secured from use of the *diary* method. This consists of placing either a family diary or individual diaries in the hands of a sample of people and asking them to record listening and viewing in the diary at the time such activity occurs. This method can supply data related to different age, sex, and occupational groups as well as out-of-home listening and viewing. This latter factor is especially important with the great number of automobile and portable radios.

To combine the advantages of the Audimeter and diary methods the A. C. Nielsen Company supplements its Audimeter homes with a matched sample of homes in which family members keep a diary, known as an *Audilog,* of their program viewing. To verify the accuracy and completeness of Audilog entries, Nielsen installs a *Recordimeter* which automatically records the total minutes of set usage daily.

Commonly used measurements of television and radio audiences are: (1) sets-in-use, (2) program rating, (3) share-of-audience, (4) projected audience, and (5) audience composition.

Sets-in-use is the percentage of all homes in the sample where a receiving set was turned on.

Program rating is the percentage of all homes in the sample tuned to the program.

Share-of-audience is the percentage of homes with a set turned on that was tuned to each program. (If sets-in-use were 60.0 and program rating were 15.0, then the program's share-of-audience would be 25.0.)

Projected audience is the number of homes reached by the program. (If there were 300,000 homes in the area sampled and the program rating were 15.0, then the projected audience would be 45,000 homes).

Audience composition is the percentage distribution of the total number of people viewing or listening by sex, age, education, or other classification factors.

Program ratings are the most widely publicized measurement of television and radio audiences, but a comparison of programs on the basis of rating alone does not take into account differences in the number of viewers per set and difference in the composition of audience. For example, a program rated at 20.0 with three viewers per set has a larger audience than a program rated at 25.0 with only two viewers per set. Similarly, a program rated at 10.0 may reach many more *adult* viewers than a program rated at 15.0 which has a greater appeal to children. Thus, the total number of people viewing a program and the composition of the audience are more meaningful measures to an advertiser than the program rating.

Nationwide network audiences have been measured extensively for many years. The A. C. Nielsen Company and Videodex report on the performance of network programs. A page from a National Nielsen Television Report is reproduced in Figure 21–7. Since the Audimeter, which is used to gather these data, keeps a continuous minute-by-minute record, it is possible to determine the total number of homes tuned to each program sometime during the broadcast. The number of such homes is referred to in this report as *total audience* and is somewhat larger than the *average audience,* which is the number of homes tuned in during an average minute of the program.

FIGURE 21–7
Excerpt of a page from the National Nielsen Television Report

NATIONAL *Nielsen* TV AUDIENCE ESTIMATES   EVE. · SUN. FEB. 18, 1973

TIME	7:00	7:15	7:30	7:45	8:00	8:15	8:30	8:45	9:00	9:15	9:30	9:45	10:00	10:15	10:30	10:45	11:00

ABC TV

TOTAL AUDIENCE (Households (000) & %): 31,560 / 48.7
Program: ANDY WILLIAMS GOLF (5:15–7:15PM)[1] — The Ten Commandments (0:00–12:25AM) (2)

AVERAGE AUDIENCE (Households (000) & %): 21,510 / 33.2 26.7* 31.6* 33.2* 34.8* 35.1* 36.1*
SHARE OF AUDIENCE %: 54 41* 47* 48* 51* 53* 59*
AVG. AUD. BY ¼ HR. %: 12.4 25.3 28.1 31.1 32.0 32.9 33.5 34.7 34.8 35.1 35.0 36.3 35.9

CBS TV

TOTAL AUDIENCE (Households (000) & %): 13,280 / 20.5   11,530 / 17.8   12,180 / 18.8   10,240 / 15.8
Programs: Dick Van Dyke Show — M*A*S*H — Mannix — Barnaby Jones

AVERAGE AUDIENCE (Households (000) & %): 11,660 / 18.0   10,300 / 15.9   10,110 / 15.6 15.6*   9,010 / 13.9 13.7* 14.2*
SHARE OF AUDIENCE %: 30 24 23 23* 23* 21 20* 23*
AVG. AUD. BY ¼ HR. %: 17.5 18.4 15.5 16.4 15.5 15.8 15.6 15.7 15.7 13.5 13.9 14.2 14.1

NBC TV

TOTAL AUDIENCE (Households (000) & %): 18,140 / 28.0   14,060 / 21.7
Programs: The Wonderful World of Disney "RASCAL" PART II — NBC Sunday Mystery Movie "MSC RAMSEY" (8:30–10:30PM)

AVERAGE AUDIENCE (Households (000) & %): 13,540 / 20.9 23.2*   10,300 / 18.6* 15.9 15.7*   16.3*   16.4*   15.3*
SHARE OF AUDIENCE %: 33 38* 28* 23* 23* 24* 24* 23*
AVG. AUD. BY ¼ HR. %: 23.1 23.4 19.4 17.8 15.8 15.6 16.2 16.3 16.7 16.1 15.6 15.0

ABC TV

TOTAL AUDIENCE (Households (000) & %): 14,640 / 22.6   21,900 / 33.8
Programs: The F.B.I. — ABC Sunday Night Movie "PAINT YOUR WAGON" (9:00–12:05AM) (2)

AVERAGE AUDIENCE (Households (000) & %): 10,300 / 15.9 13.8*   13,410 / 20.7 18.4*   21.3*   22.0*   23.6*
SHARE OF AUDIENCE %: 24 21* 27* 38 27* 32* 34* 43*
AVG. AUD. BY ¼ HR. %: 13.3 14.2 17.8 18.4 18.0 18.9 21.1 21.6 22.1 21.8 23.8 23.5

CBS TV

TOTAL AUDIENCE (Households (000) & %): 10,500 / 16.2   12,700 / 19.6   16,910 / 26.1   17,760 / 27.4
Programs: Dick Van Dyke Show — M*A*S*H — Mannix — Barnaby Jones

AVERAGE AUDIENCE (Households (000) & %): 9,270 / 14.3   11,280 / 17.4   12,440 / 19.2 18.0*   15,810 / 24.4 24.1* 24.7*
SHARE OF AUDIENCE %: 23 27 28 27* 30* 37 36* 39*
AVG. AUD. BY ¼ HR. %: 13.7 14.9 17.2 17.7 17.6 18.3 19.8 21.2 23.2 25.0 25.2 24.3

NBC TV

TOTAL AUDIENCE (Households (000) & %): 22,550 / 34.4   22,230 / 34.3   13,670 / 21.1
Programs: Highlights Of Ringling Bros. And Barnum & Bailey Circus (7:30–9:30PM) — Country Music Hit Parade (8:30–9:30PM) — Jack Lemmon-Get Happy (9:30–10:30PM) — Interview With Henry Kissinger (10:30–11:00PM)

AVERAGE AUDIENCE (Households (000) & %): 17,760 / 27.4 26.1*   17,370 / 28.6* 26.8 27.0*   9,850 / 26.6* 15.2 17.0* 13.4*
SHARE OF AUDIENCE %: 43 41* 44* 39 40* 39* 23 26* 21*
AVG. AUD. BY ¼ HR. %: 25.6 26.5 28.4 28.9 27.1 27.0 27.2 26.0 18.2 15.8 13.9 12.6

TV HOUSEHOLDS USING TV	7:00	7:15	7:30	7:45	8:00	8:15	8:30	8:45	9:00	9:15	9:30	9:45	10:00	10:15	10:30	10:45
WK 1	56.0	57.8	60.0	62.1	64.7	66.6	67.2	67.4	68.8	69.4	68.3	67.7	66.9	66.1	62.2	61.3
WK 2	56.7	60.2	62.7	63.3	64.8	66.1	67.1	67.1	68.0	68.7	67.0	66.3	65.5	62.8	56.0	52.6

U.S. TV Households: 64,800,000   * Half-hour ratings (for immediately preceding and subject quarter-hours).   (R) Repeat, see page 8.
(OP) Other Programs: See pages A34–A39.
(1) FOR REM, RATINGS SEE PAGE A-32.   (2) FOR REM, RATINGS SEE OP PAGES.

EVE. · SUN. FEB. 25, 1973

Network audience measurements do not reflect differences in program performance in individual markets. A given network program may go over great in New York but not so well in San Francisco. Furthermore, national spot advertisers and retail advertisers are concerned with the audiences reached by individual stations, not network audiences. To bridge this gap in audience measurement the A. C. Nielsen Company offers another service, the *Nielsen Station Index,* which reports periodically on the audiences reached by individual stations in over 200 markets. The American Research Bureau offers a similar service in the form of their *ARB Local Market Reports.*

Radio and television programs

Both radio and television stations operate under license from the Federal Communications Commission. Licensees agree to operate in the public interest. Programs represent the very heart of radio and television so far as the public is concerned. Those who have any responsibility in the development of programs should never lose sight of the public interest factor.

This is of special concern to advertisers who use radio or television, since many stations and networks have permitted advertisers either to build their own programs for sponsorship or to exercise substantial influence over the character of programs developed by others. There is no fundamental reason why public interest cannot be served with programs that also offer specific values to advertisers.

The basic function of a program from the point of view of the advertiser is to provide an audience that will be receptive to a commercial message hitched to, or sandwiched in with, the program. Either the size or the character of the audience, or both, might be important to the advertiser. If the product or service to be advertised is one of broad universal use, the size of the audience might be more important than character or quality, since practically all people would be prospective customers. If the item has a specialized market (farm tractors, dog food, fishing tackle), then the character of the audience should rate above size in importance.

Specialized audiences can be selected by the type of program used. Opportunities along this line are almost unlimited. Examples of program types that will attract people with special-product interests would include classical music, sports, science, religion, labor news, foreign-language broadcasts, book reviews, and farming.

The history of broadcasting indicates that advertisers have tended to place heavy emphasis on reaching a mass rather than a class audience. Programs have been built with such an objective in mind. Variety shows, popular music, light drama, general news, and popular sports have tended to dominate the scene. Audience-measurement services have been keyed to that emphasis. The size of the program rating (percentage of families listening) has often been the factor guiding program selection and promotion.

Television has had a significant influence on changing the emphasis of radio on mass appeal for most of its programs. Television has adopted the mass-appeal approach and is successfully pulling a high percentage of entertainment seekers to it and from radio. As a result, radio has become a much more selective medium. In time, the growth of UHF-TV, as well as CATV, will also likely make TV a more selective medium.

Building the audience

Radio and television programs can be promoted the same as any other service. There is no reason to believe that all interested people will be aware of new programs soon after they are introduced or even old programs that have been on the air for some time. The promotion or advertising of both new and old programs can acquaint people with such programs, where and when they can be found, and give enough detail about them so that people can estimate their possible want-satisfying qualities.

The promotion of programs that are designed for some specialized group (farmers, sports fans, etc.) can often increase materially the number of listeners. The cost of such promotion then becomes an investment and not an expense. Once new people have been attracted to a program, many will continue as regular or semiregular members of the audience if the program lives up to its claims. This larger audience is then available to the advertiser for his commercial messages at no greater time cost than for the original smaller audience.

Too many advertisers and station managers have believed that special-interest programs cannot draw an audience sufficiently large to warrant either sponsorship or promotion. There is now a considerable amount of evidence which indicates that significant numbers of people can be drawn to specialized programs. An experiment at the University of Illinois shed some light on this question. That experiment consisted of promoting four, specialized, educational type programs in a one-county area. The four programs were (1) a homemaker's half-hour, (2) chamber music, (3) semi-classical "pops" music, and (4) a university classroom literature hour.

These programs were promoted over a short period of time (two months). Careful measurements were made of audience size before, during, and after the periods of promotion. Results showed more than a threefold increase in audience size during and immediately after promotion. Thirteen months after promotion was stopped the audience was still more than twice the size of the original. Each of the four programs attained a "rating" comparable to the vast number of standard radio programs.[11]

Television and radio rates

Television and radio rates are quoted for various units of time: one minute or less, five minutes, ten minutes, quarter hour, half hour, and one hour. Units of one minute or less are referred to as *announcements.* They are placed between programs or within *participating programs,* such as disk-jockey shows, that carry announcements of several advertisers. Participating programs function much as magazines and newspapers in that advertisers have no direct control over the program's content. *Station*

[11] C. H. Sandage, *Building Audiences for Educational Radio Programs* (Urbana, Ill.: Institute of Communications Research, 1951).

breaks are announcements that are broadcast by network-affiliated stations between network programs.

Program time units may be sold for *exclusive, alternate,* or *shared sponsorship.* Through exclusive sponsorship, a single advertiser gains the full benefit of being identified with the program, but he also must bear the full cost. To provide some of the advantages of sponsorship without requiring an advertiser to bear the full burden of a costly program, especially a network television program, alternate and shared sponsorship arrangements have been developed. Through alternate sponsorship, two advertisers sponsor alternate broadcasts of a regularly scheduled program. Through shared sponsorship, two or more advertisers buy particular segments of a program.

In an attempt to adjust their rates to reflect the differences in audience size at different times of the day, television and radio stations classify various time periods as AA, A, B, C, and D. Classes of time are based primarily on total sets in use. Thus, Class AA television time includes those evening hours when the maximum number of TV sets are turned on. A typical television station in the Central Time Zone lists the following classes of time and 30-second announcement rates:

Class AA.	$1,800
6:29 P.M. to 10:30 P.M. daily	
Class A.	$ 700
5:00 P.M. to 6:29 P.M. daily	
10:30 P.M. to midnight daily	
Class B	$ 400
3:29 P.M. to 5:00 P.M. daily	
Class C	$ 250
8:59 A.M. to 3:29 P.M. daily	
Class D	$ 120
Sign-on to 8:59 A.M. daily	
Midnight to sign-off daily	

A glance at Figure 21–3 on page 485 will show the logic behind these time classes. Class AA represents the evening peak. Classes A and B represent time periods when the audience is building up to, and dropping off from, the peak. Class C includes the daytime hours.

All stations do not classify their time the same way. For example, small market stations have fewer time classes than big city stations.

Reflecting the influence of television, many radio stations quote the same rate for all hours of the day. The larger stations in major metropolitan areas, however, have rate schedules that reflect the variation in listenership patterns. For example, WLS in Chicago has the following rates for one-minute announcements:

Class AA. $200
    6 A.M. to 10 A.M. Mon.–Sat.
    3 P.M. to 7 P.M. Mon.–Fri.
    10 A.M. to 7 P.M. Sat.
Class A $140
    7 P.M. to midnight Mon.–Sun.
    10 A.M. to 7 P.M. Sun.
Class B $125
    10 A.M. to 3 P.M. Mon.–Fri.
Class C . . . . $ 50
    5 A.M. to 6 A.M. Mon.–Fri.

An ideal rate structure might be one in which rates varied directly with the actual audience reached by a station or network during each specific time period. This would more nearly approach charging for what is actually delivered, but it would require continuous audience measurement and would complicate pricing and billing practices. The idea of a "guaranteed audience," which involves giving a rebate to the advertiser if the audience reached was smaller than that on which the rate was based, has been proposed, but it has gained little support.

Television and radio rates are subject to a wide variety of discounts. The usual practice, however, is to charge a lower rate per minute for longer time segments and for greater frequency of broadcasts. For example, a radio station might have a rate schedule for a particular class of time as follows:

| | Announcements per week | | |
Length of commercial	1 time	6 times	12 times
1 minute.	$200	$190	$180
30 seconds.	160	152	144
10 seconds.	100	95	90

Network rates are based on a composite of rates charged by the individual stations making up the network. Discounts depend on the number of stations the advertiser uses, the number of consecutive weeks he uses the network, weekly billings for time, and annual volume of business done with the network. The ultimate price an advertiser pays for network commercials, however, is usually the result of negotiation. Agency media buyers, representing their advertiser clients, deal with network sales people in arriving at a rate for a particular buy.

The cost to advertise on network television ranges substantially, depending largely upon the size of audience that is likely to be delivered by a particular program. Whereas 60-second commercials placed in daytime television programs typically cost between $5,000 and $15,000, the same commercial in a prime time program is likely to cost between $50,000 and $70,000. These are *average* costs, and it is quite possible to buy commercials for more or less. For example, a 60-second commercial during a Super Bowl game will cost in excess of $200,000.

Budgets

Radio and television are major advertising media and budgets should be planned in such terms. Advertisers can probably secure maximum benefits from any major medium only when a substantial percentage of the total advertising is allocated to the medium.

Some evidence to support the above recommendation came from an intensive study of the use of radio by retailers. Their budgeting practices were correlated with their success from radio. From that analysis it was concluded that retail "firms with annual advertising expenditures of $50,-000 or more generally should expect to spend at least 15 percent of their total budget on radio if they wish high success, and that smaller firms should expect to spend as much as 20 percent of the total advertising budget on radio for high success."[12] It would seem logical to apply this same reasoning to national advertisers and also to the use of major media other than radio.

Users of television and radio

Producers of mass-consumption items have been the largest users of television and radio. As can be noted in Table 21–3, the 20 leading network television advertisers in 1972 were manufacturers of food products, automobiles, toiletries, drug items, and soap products. These same product categories accounted for the major share of national spot television. Procter & Gamble, a firm that produces a broad line of soap products, toiletries, and food products, has consistently been the leading user of television. In addition to the $116 million Procter & Gamble invested in network television, they bought over $72 million in spot markets. It should be noted that prior to 1971, cigarette brands were advertised heavily in radio and television, but Congress banned such advertising as of January 1, 1971.

Table 21–4 lists the top 20 users of spot radio. Included are many of the same product categories advertised on television and, indeed, 7 companies appear in the top 20 of both network television and spot radio.

[12] C. H. Sandage, *Radio Advertising for Retailers* (Cambridge, Mass.: Harvard University Press, 1945), p. 13.

TABLE 21–3
Top 20 network television advertisers, 1972

Rank	Advertiser	Expenditures
1.	Procter & Gamble................	$116,032,400
2.	American Home Products	61,195,000
3.	Sterling Drug....................	56,398,200
4.	Bristol-Myers....................	55,901,100
5.	General Foods...................	50,578,300
6.	Ford Motor Co...................	50,185,900
7.	General Motors..................	39,311,900
8.	Warner-Lambert	36,618,100
9.	Sears, Roebuck & Co.............	36,355,600
10.	Gillette Co......................	36,162,900
11.	Colgate-Palmolive...............	35,516,500
12.	S. C. Johnson & Son.............	31,152,000
13.	Lever Bros.	30,743,200
14.	Nabisco Inc.....................	28,682,800
15.	General Mills....................	28,477,400
16.	Kellogg Co......................	25,442,600
17.	Chrysler Corp...................	24,343,000
18.	Ralston Purina...................	24,253,400
19.	Miles Laboratories	22,481,400
20.	Carter-Wallace	20,443,800

Source: Television Bureau of Advertising, 1973.

TABLE 21–4
Top 20 spot radio advertisers, 1972

Rank	Advertiser	Expenditures
1.	General Motors..................	$17,739,000
2.	Ford Motor	17,231,000
3.	Chrysler Corp...................	14,802,000
4.	Sears, Roebuck & Co.............	11,438,000
5.	American Home Products	11,214,000
6.	Anheuser-Busch	11,116,000
7.	Coca-Cola Co.	9,373,000
8.	PepsiCo........................	6,895,000
9.	Bristol-Myers....................	5,372,000
10.	AT&T..........................	4,800,000
11.	Humble Oil......................	4,504,000
12.	American Oil	4,396,000
13.	American Airlines	3,898,000
14.	Wm. Wrigley Jr. Co..............	3,754,000
15.	Sterling Drug....................	3,625,000
16.	Mobil Oil.......................	3,322,000
17.	Kraftco.........................	3,244,000
18.	Eastern Air Lines.................	3,194,000
19.	TWA	3,014,000
20.	Texaco*.......................	2,961,000

* Includes $300,000 for the Texaco sponsored Metropolitan Opera broadcasts not reported by RER.
   Source: Radio Advertising Bureau and Radio Expenditure Reports, as reported in *Advertising Age,* July 9, 1973, p. 40.

Interestingly, petroleum companies and airlines are heavy users of spot radio.

Although newspapers continue to be their primary medium, retailers spent over $1 billion for radio advertising and $955 million for television in 1972. Thus, retailers invested around 20 percent of their advertising budget in broadcast. This is a noted increase from a 15 percent level in 1960.

Advertising values of radio and television

Each of the mass media communications offers advertisers effective opportunities to present specific commercial messages. Maximum effectiveness can be obtained from utilizing the particular strengths of each medium.

Radio and television provide timeliness to an even greater extent than do newspapers. This can be of particular value in the case of very sudden changes in conditions. During rain or snow storms, floods, outstanding news happenings, or sudden changes in temperature, the radio commercial can be given almost simultaneously with the event. A department store planned its outstanding promotion of the year to celebrate its 25th anniversary. The evening newspapers on the night before the "big day" carried pages of advertising by the store. Morning papers duplicated the previous evening emphasis. Unfortunately, the morning was shrouded in the worst rainstorm in the history of the city and the weather report offered no hope for relief. To meet this situation the store purchased all radio time available to talk with local residents about the storm and what the store was offering in its big sale that day. Special inducements in respect to transportation and lunch were offered, too. As a result of this timeliness, the store had a tremendously successful day.

"Tennessee Ernie" Ford, when he was a radio announcer in Bristol, Tennessee, "had all the fires sold." Whenever there was a fire, the station would cut in with an announcement telling where the fire was, advising listeners not to foul up the traffic trying to get there, and then follow up with a one-minute commercial for a fire insurance company.

Radio and television are, or can be, more personal than any other medium. They provide the warmth of the human voice and come closer than any other medium in matching personal selling. In the case of television, the ability to demonstrate visually the advertised items is added to the personal factor.

Radio is highly flexible territorially. Television is, too, up to the limit of the number of markets served and the number of stations in each market. Both TV and radio provide, through networks, combined market coverage on a simultaneous basis. Both media provide local market selectivity. A national advertiser can use spot TV or spot radio for seasonal promotions, for saturation campaigns, for bolstering weak markets, for launching new products, for localizing appeals, for pretesting messages, and for complementing network advertising.

The opportunity to reach selective audiences is offered by both TV and radio through choice of program and time of broadcast.

Limitations

All advertising media have some limitations. The life of a radio or television advertisement is no longer than the time it takes for presentation. If an announcement is broadcast at a time when few prospects are listening, it is lost forever so far as most prospects are concerned, unless word-of-mouth publicity occasioned by listeners or viewers is developed. An advertisement in a magazine has a chance of being seen and read as long as the magazine remains in the home. In addition to the fleeting nature of the broadcast message, listeners and viewers often engage in some other activity while the set is on. This might consist of reading, performing household tasks, playing cards, dancing, or carrying on a conversation with guests. Such activity reduces the effectiveness of the advertising message.

A serious limitation is the fact that there are only 24 hours in a day, some of which must be spent in sleep. And people cannot listen to more than one program at a time. Thus, television advertising on a large scale cannot be employed by a great number of advertisers. One national network could accommodate only 64 advertisers for 15 minutes each, if every 15-minute period between 8 A.M. and midnight were taken. When a number of networks are organized to carry the message of other advertisers, the audience of each network is diminished.

Of course these limitations do not necessarily impair the effectiveness of individual radio and television advertisements but, rather, indicate limitations of facilities to meet all possible advertising demands.

QUESTIONS AND PROBLEMS

1   Television is generally considered to be a "mass" medium—that is, it reaches a broad cross-section of the public. What is the likelihood that television will become a more selective medium in the future? What factors or conditions might relate to the situation?

2   Do you foresee any cultural patterns that may affect television viewing and radio listening in the near future? What effects, if any, might such patterns produce?

3   Television and radio can be used to reach particular consumer groups efficiently. How would you use these media to reach (1) teen-agers, (2) homemakers, (3) office workers, (4) farmers?

4   The total number of people viewing a television program and the composition of the audience are more meaningful measures to the advertiser than the program rating. Explain.

5   How would you assess the future of cable television? What factors, if any, are likely to contribute to future growth?

6   Distinguish between the following: exclusive sponsorship, shared sponsorship, and alternate sponsorship. What advantages and disadvantages do you see in each of these buys?

7   Within a given time classification the size of audience reached by specified programs may vary considerably, yet advertisers are often charged the same rate for any time they buy during the hours included in that time class. Wouldn't it be more appropriate to base rates on program ratings instead of time classifications? Support whatever position you take on this question.

8   Can you offer an explanation for the fact that a number of airlines use spot radio extensively in their media plans?

9   Look up the cost to broadcast a 30-second commercial on a television station in your hometown. Note how costs vary by time of day and by station (if more than one in the city). Do the same thing for local radio stations. Is there more variance in rates among the radio stations than the TV stations? If so, can you explain?

22

Direct mail

A dvertising media previously described offer space or time on a contract basis to manufacturers, retailers, and other advertisers who wish to have their message distributed on a mass basis. Those mass media have already selected the groups to whom they will deliver the advertiser's message, and the advertiser has no control over that selection.

In the case of direct mail, the advertising message is carried directly from the advertiser to individuals selected by him. The Direct Mail Advertising Association defines such advertising as "a vehicle for transmitting an advertiser's message in permanent written, printed, or processed form, by controlled distribution, direct to selected individuals."[1]

Because it employs the principle of *selected* rather than *mass* distribution of the advertisement, direct-mail advertising has often been described as the "rifle," in contrast to the "shotgun," method of conveying a sales message. Agency media specialist Paul M. Roth has described direct mail as "the only medium which permits the advertiser to pinpoint recipients of his advertising communication with a minimal amount of waste circulation."[2]

Scope of direct mail

The term "direct mail" does not adequately cover all of the advertising usually included under that name. While this term is used here because

[1] Direct Mail Advertising Association, 230 Park Avenue, New York 10017.

[2] Paul M. Roth, "Uses of Direct Mail and Out-of-Home Media," *Handbook of Advertising Management,* ed. Roger Barton (New York: McGraw-Hill Book Co., 1970), pp. 21–23.

500

of its long acceptance, a more accurate designation would be "direct advertising." This latter term would include *direct-mail* and *nonmailed-direct* advertising. Most direct advertising is distributed by mail, but a substantial and increasing amount is passed from door to door or to pedestrians in a limited area, placed in parked automobiles, handed to customers in retail stores, inserted in packages or bundles, presented by salesmen or messengers, or in some other way conveyed directly to the intended recipient. Giveaway novelties, if they bear an advertiser's message, also belong in the category of direct advertising, provided they reach the prospect by one of the above methods, mailed or nonmailed.

Closely associated with *direct-mail advertising,* and therefore often confused with it, is *mail-order selling.* This latter term is properly used to describe that type of merchandising operation which depends upon orders

FIGURE 22–1
Use of direct-mail advertising to encourage purchase by mail order

coming through the mail, without aid of personal salesmanship. In seeking orders and advertising its goods, the mail-order firm need not, and, indeed, scarcely ever does, depend entirely upon direct mail to carry the sales message. One expert pleads, "Let's recognize mail order as merely a way of doing business, in regard to *how* orders come back—regardless of what type of advertising was used to persuade people to send in the orders."[3] Mail-order selling by letter, folders, catalogs, and order forms is employing direct-mail advertising; mail-order selling by means of space advertisements and television or radio commercials is not. Figure 22–1 is an example of *mail-order selling* in which the advertisement was delivered by *direct mail.* Recipients of the offer were individuals who owned the World Book Encyclopedia.

Expenditures for direct mail

In compiling data on the expenditures of direct mail, the statistician's task is obviously complicated by the widespread local use of this form of advertising, especially by small enterprisers. Unlike other major media, direct-mail's advertising volume is neither measured nor reported regularly. Estimates of the total volume are generally arrived at by determining direct-mail's share of total postal volume and by adding an amount to cover costs of producing the pieces mailed.

McCann-Erickson Advertising Agency estimated the volume of direct-mail advertising in 1972 to be $3.4 billion. This represented 14.5 percent of the total for all media. Among all media, then, direct mail was third, following newspapers with 30.2 percent, and television with 17.9 percent.[4]

Characteristics

The factors of selectivity of audience and flexibility of territorial coverage, which every advertiser looks for in choosing a medium, are the basic characteristics of direct advertising. The Direct Mail Advertising Association, the Mail Advertising Service Association, and other advocates of direct advertising as an effective sales-promotion medium, have long emphasized these qualities of selectivity and flexibility. The D.M.A.A. lists the following ten points as the advantages of direct advertising:

1. Direct advertising can be directed to specific individuals or markets with greater control than any other medium.
2. Direct advertising can be made personal to the point of being absolutely confidential.

[3] Harrie A. Bell, "Should *Mail* Be Dropped from Direct Mail Advertising?" *The Reporter of Direct Mail Advertising,* March 1948, p. 2.

[4] *Advertising Age,* February 19, 1973, p. 64.

3. Direct advertising is a single advertiser's individual message and is not in competition with other advertising and/or editorial.
4. Direct advertising does not have the limitations on space and format as do other mediums of advertising.
5. Direct advertising permits greater flexibility in materials and processes of production than any other medium of advertising.
6. Direct advertising provides a means for introducing novelty and realism into the interpretation of the advertiser's story.
7. Direct advertising can be produced according to the needs of the advertiser's own immediate schedule.
8. Direct advertising can be controlled for specific jobs of research, reaching small groups, testing ideas, appeals, reactions.
9. Direct advertising can be dispatched for accurate and in some cases exact timing, both as to departure of the pieces as well as to their receipt.
10. Direct advertising provides more thorough means for the reader to act or buy through action devices not possible of employment by other media.[5]

The ultimate clue as to whether direct-mail advertising is suited to the advertiser's needs lies in the fact that it is the most personal, the most intimate of all forms of advertising. Edward N. Mayer, Jr., past president of D.M.A.A., says: "You address your customer or prospect individually by the most important word he knows—his name. Basically, you seek to create the impression that you know who he is and what he is like. In most direct-mail copy you talk to him as you would if you were face to face. Therefore, direct-mail advertising is best suited to situations where it is logical and likely that you should so approach your prospects."[6]

The high degree of selectivity and adaptation to individuals and to groups which is inherent in this medium is realized as an asset, however, only when the advertiser is sure the right people have been reached. The relatively high per-contact cost of direct advertising is justified only when the advertiser knows his message has reached the hands of those for whom it was written. A brochure costing nearly $2 each, for instance, sent to approximately a thousand steel and foundry executives to sell a furnace installation costing $750,000, was not considered an out-of-line expense when the mailing brought in $7 million worth of orders.

In the 1972 presidential campaign, George McGovern's organization used direct-mail advertising most effectively. One particular mailing, which cost $20,000, was a letter seeking contributions. Attached to the letter were four bank checks with the recipient's name and address preprinted on them and dated for four consecutive months (August 1 through

[5] Direct Mail Advertising Association, Manual Fiel #1201.
[6] Edward N. Mayer, Jr., "Direct Mail Advertising," *Harvard Business Review,* July 1951, p. 48.

November 1). Respondents were encouraged to mail in their contribution each month. The mailing produced almost $1 million from 25 percent of those receiving the letter. Bob Stone, a direct-mail expert, analyzed why the letter was so successful:

1. There were two great ideas in the letter: (1) All contributors were made to feel very much a part of the campaign through enrollment in the McGovern Million Member Club, and (2) an ingenious plan was developed for precommitment of monthly contributions through the medium of four postdated checks.
2. The computer was utilized in a unique way to provide the vehicle for making the contributions.
3. The clincher was the offer of a free sterling pin with preaddressed shipping label provided.[7]

Functions and uses

Media/scope magazine, in their "Check List For Direct Mail Advertising," lists the following circumstances as to when to use direct mail:

1. When sampling would be both practical and desirable.
2. When the advertising message is too complicated or too detailed to be conveyed efficiently in other media.
3. When a specific, selected market is desired and other media can provide it only at the cost of waste circulation.
4. When personal, personalized, or confidential communication is desired.
5. When the format or color that an advertiser's marketing strategy requires can't be carried in other media.
6. When a specific market area needs to be covered with a minimum of slop-over into adjacent areas.
7. When specific timing or frequency of contact is desired.
8. When couponing is desirable.
9. When controlled research is called for (for example, measuring of effectiveness within certain markets; ascertaining prospect profiles; or testing price, packaging, or logical users for new products).
10. When a controlled mailing is desirable (mailings will go only to certain income groups, owners of certain makes of cars, boat owners, etc.).
11. When mail order (sale of the product directly to the prospect, without retailers, dealers or other media) is desirable.
12. When you want to accomplish the following jobs in the marketing process:
    A. Obtain responses indicating interest (as in "securing leads")—
       a. to be followed up by more direct mail.
       b. to be followed up by salesmen.

[7] *Advertising Age,* June 4, 1973, p. 77.

   B. Put the prospect into position for personal selling (as in "traffic building")—
- *a.* in a retail outlet or showroom.
- *b.* in front of an exhibit of products—particularly those which salesmen cannot take to the prospect for demonstration.

   C. Create a receptive atmosphere for salesmen—
- *a.* through cordial-contact mailings which build an "image."
- *b.* through institutional types of direct mail (for example, mailings such as the paper and printing companies use to illustrate the product features or the company's abilities).
- *c.* through the "impact" created by any type of mailing sent out. Any mailing will create some kind of impression. Well-executed mailings will identify the advertiser favorably.

   D. Influence selected groups to action—
- *a.* building salesman incentive.
- *b.* obtaining credits and collections.
- *c.* building mailing lists.
- *d.* developing political campaigns.

   E. Make more effective the impact of advertising in other media—
- *a.* by gaining the cooperation and building the enthusiasm of all persons involved with your advertising efforts, through keeping them properly motivated and informed.
- *b.* by helping to convert impressions created by other advertising media into sales through—
  - (1) bringing the prospect and product together at the point of sale.
  - (2) following up inquiries developed by other media.
  - (3) using ads from newspapers or magazines as a mailing piece or part of a mailing unit to precede or follow up the issue of the magazine or newspaper in which the ad appears.[8]

To carry out these functions of direct advertising, a myriad of styles and forms are at the disposal of the advertiser. Let us look at some of them.

Forms of direct mail

In style of copy, direct advertising parallels the other media. The principles of language choice, psychological patterns, emotional appeals, and layout discussed elsewhere, therefore, need not be discussed in detail here. In personalized letters and postal cards, of course, the forms acceptable in business correspondence prevail. In "circular" letters and in all other types of pieces, the headline and body-copy style of presentation is usually followed. The same semantic theories and readability principles hold for

[8] *Media/scope,* Vol. 10 (June 1966).

FIGURE 22–2
Front and back of a common type of mailing card

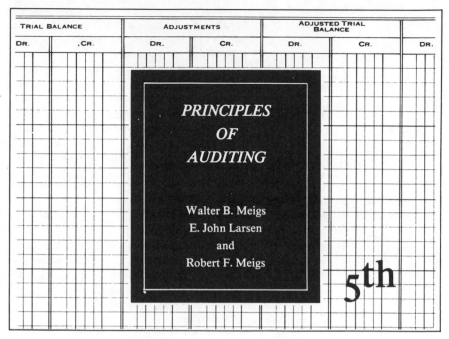

FIGURE 22–3
Nonpersonalized direct-mail letter

Bell & Howell Company
Business Equipment Group

Ditto INCORPORATED

6800 McCORMICK ROAD • CHICAGO, ILLINOIS 60645 • 539-7300

Have a cup of coffee.
(It's on us!)

Insert Dime

Be our guest for your morning coffee!

And, while you're enjoying the steaming brew, we'd like some important information which only you can provide. Your answers to the questions below will enable us to be more selective in the materials we mail to you--and to make certain you are getting only information of immediate and direct value to you. To make it easy for you we enclose an addressed postage-paid envelope for your reply.

Total estimated time: three minutes. (And that should leave you a few extra minutes to enjoy your coffee, undisturbed!)

Cordially,

[signature]

Director, Advertising
and Sales Promotion

1. Do you know how many separate writings you require to get your
   orders shipped and billed . . . . ? Yes__ No__
2. Are the orders sent in by your branch offices or salesmen
   rewritten in your office . . . . ? Yes__ No__
3. Are shipping addresses retyped on your bills of lading . . . . . ? Yes__ No__
4. Are these same addresses again rewritten on your tags and labels ? Yes__ No__
5. Are your invoices written separately from your shipping orders. . ? Yes__ No__
6. When a partial shipment is made, do you write a new shipping
   order to cover items back-ordered . . . . ? Yes__ No__
7. Do you write a new set of billing copies covering each back-
   order shipment . . . . ? Yes__ No__
8. Do you post each individual invoice to your accounts receivable
   ledger . . . . ? Yes__ No__
9. May we send folders illustrating how you can eliminate all re-
   typing, on original and back-orders, simplify stock picking
   and inventory control and eliminate posting to accounts
   receivable . . . . ? Yes__ No__

Name_____ Title_____

Firm_____ Address_____

City_____ County_____ State_____ Zip_____

BUSINESS EQUIPMENT GROUP

MICRO-DATA DIVISION • MICRO PHOTO DIVISION • BAUMFOLDER DIVISION • DITTO, INCORPORATED • PHILLIPSBURG DIVISION • ROCHESTER FILM DIVISION
Microfilm Equipment   Microfilming Services   Folding Machines   Duplicating Products   Mail Inserters   Microfilm & Graphic Arts Film

the copy of this medium. The copy appeals are slanted to the same basic buying motives employed successfully in other copy.

While this similarity of copy style holds for direct advertising, the *physical* forms which it may take are innumerable. Size, shape, typography, color, and illustrations are not nearly so predetermined here as in other media; therefore, the design they take is determined by the advertiser's needs for each separate occasion. He can use any kind of paper or ink, die cut a piece to resemble the shape of his product, emboss to simulate the feel, or perfume to imitate the odor.

The following list has been presented by Mayer as representing the most commonly used forms or types of direct advertising:

Letters	Programs
Folders	Sales, research, and informative
Broadsides	bulletins
Booklets	Charts
Brochures	Posters
Self-mailers	Blow-ups
Postal cards	Coupons
Mailing cards	Calendars
Catalogues	Reprints
House magazines	Memorandums
Blotters	Printed novelties
Price lists	Business cards
Sales and informative manuals	Order forms
Invitations	Reply cards and envelopes[9]

Figures 22–2 and 22–3 illustrate two of the more widely used types of mailing pieces. Figure 22–2 is a mailing card, 5¼ by 8 inches, with self-contained postage-prepaid reply form. Figure 22–3 is a typical nonpersonalized letter with the headline taking the place of salutation.

Securing and maintaining the mailing list

The keystone in the arch of direct-advertising effectiveness is the list. If the advertiser is going to reach prospects rather than mere suspects, and thereby hold mailing waste to a minimum, he must start with a carefully built list. As Mayer says: "Your copy can sparkle, your layout and format be an art director's joy, your printing good enough to win a Graphic Arts top award, and your postage can be the newest and hardest-to-get commemorative stamp, but if your mailing piece is directed to people who are not prospects and cannot buy the product, your entire effort will be an expensive bust."[10]

[9] Edward N. Mayer, Jr., *How to Make More Money with Your Direct Mail* (New York: Funk & Wagnalls Co., 1950), p. 29.

[10] Ibid., p. 189.

FIGURE 22-4

Sources of names as suggested by the Addressograph-Multigraph Corporation

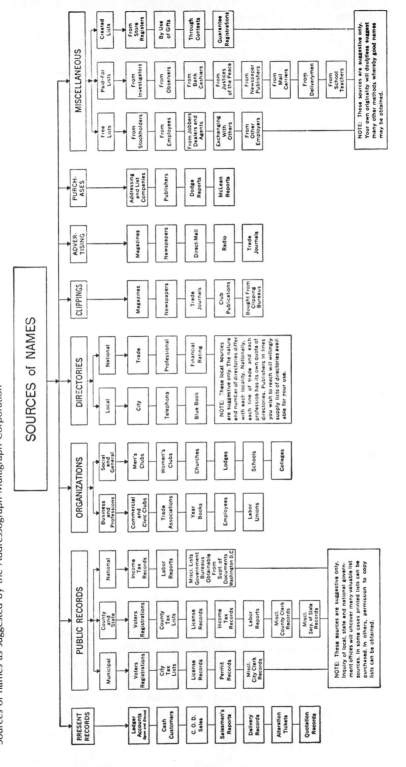

Mailing lists are composed of the names of people who are prospective customers for the goods or services the advertiser has to offer. Once the advertiser has defined the group he wishes to reach, the sources of a mailing list of such persons are practically unlimited. As a rule, lists are obtained by one of the following methods:

1. Build your own.
2. Trade or exchange with others.
3. Rent from a broker.
4. Buy from a list house.
5. Arrange to use expiration list of a periodical.

Figure 22–4 represents many specific and detailed sources of lists available to the direct-mail user.

Building one's own list is indeed a job to be performed with extreme care. A well-trained person is needed to use directories discriminately so that they yield only the kinds of prospects being sought. The lowest cost and often the most profitable names available are those to be had in the present list of customers, from inquiries, and from reports of salesmen's daily calls. The standard sources for mailing lists are telephone and city directories; trade directories; trade reports; commercial rating books; tax lists; club-membership lists; and the records of state, county, and city officials. More limited in usefulness, but frequently used, are press clippings, court proceedings, real estate sales records, stock-ownership records, credit-agency reports, social registers, and lists of charity contributors. It must be borne in mind that the cost of a list of names varies with the amount of labor involved in compiling and checking them.

Today businessmen lean heavily on professionally compiled lists. These may be purchased either through a broker or direct from a list-compiling firm. The list broker concentrates on knowing where to obtain lists which the advertiser might wish. When the broker receives a request for a particular kind of list, he obtains one from the best source he can, adds a brokerage fee, and delivers it to his client.

The list company is a far more complicated operation. In its files are contained the names and addresses of business executives, shoe shops in the Bronx, wealthy widows, Hudson Bay trappers, and millions of other persons and establishments. The more popular lists are ready-made and ready for immediate delivery. Specialized lists have to be made on order.

Figure 22–5 shows a page from *Standard Rate and Data Service, Direct Mail List,* a semiannual publication which contains mailing lists from thousands of suppliers. Included are sections for list brokers, business lists, consumer lists, farm lists, and co-op mailing firms.

A list is supplied to the buyer in one of several ways. It may consist merely of names and addresses typed on sheets of paper or listed on a computer printout. The list house may, however, address envelopes or gummed labels. One of the largest list companies is R. L. Polk & Company of Detroit, specializing in lists of automobile owners, but also furnishing many other types of lists gleaned from the many city directories it publishes. In New York, Dun & Bradstreet, Inc., publishes a large alphabetical catalog of the lists the company is prepared to furnish. The leading list-sellers in Chicago include Buckley-Dement Company and Reuben H. Donnelley Corporation.

The maintenance of lists is costly, painstaking, and continuously neces-

FIGURE 22–5
Page from the consumer lists section of *SRDS, Direct Mail List*

sary. People are constantly moving, getting married, divorced, having children, dying. Business firms fail, merge, change name, or move. In the United States during normal times an estimated 4,000 to 5,000 firms daily go out of business or otherwise move, requiring change of address. The whole task of minimizing wastage in direct-mail advertising hinges upon keeping the list constantly up to date. Commercial list houses and private list-users alike must continually be on the alert for changes. Checking of returned mailing pieces against the most recently issued address information is a most important phase of maintenance activity. First-class mail is automatically returned to sender with directory notations provided by the post office. Third-class mail, since it travels at a lower rate, is not entitled to this service unless the sender imprints on each mailing piece "Form 3547 Requested"; then the sender pays for each form returned bearing the most recent post office directory information. Where lists are used frequently, one or the other of these methods must be employed periodically to assure accuracy of the list. Mailers may also use a questionnaire-type postal card from time to time to see whether the name and address being used is correct.

In recent years, the use of electronic computers has greatly improved the ability to maintain lists. With a computer's phenomenal memory capacity, firms are better able to keep their lists current and process updated information on respondents. In addition, the computer allows for the opportunity to provide greater selectivity in targeting and to personalize sales messages.

Direct-mail costs

The factors of cost which the direct advertiser must consider are those of the mailing list, production and handling, and distribution.

Rental fees for mailing lists are normally quoted on a "cost-per-thousand-names" basis, and the costs vary greatly according to the specialized nature of the lists. General-type lists usually average around $20 to $25 per thousand. Special lists, requiring extensive research to compile, can cost as much as $0.50 a name. Most lists are guaranteed to reach a certain percentage of the names on them, usually varying from 90 to 100 percent. The company refunds postage on all undelivered mail below the percentage guarantee.

Very little can be said here about production and handling costs such as printing, folding, assembling, and envelope stuffing. These vary with the form of the mailing, quality of printing and paper, quantity produced, and facilities for handling distribution. Estimates of production costs for each direct-mail undertaking should be secured from a printer before it is undertaken. The printer can often make suggestions for reducing costs.

Since postal rates and regulations change frequently, no attempt is made to quote them specifically. The user of direct mail should always consult his postmaster before undertaking any mailing, no matter how large or small. Usually the advertiser finds third-class more advantageous than first-class because of the favorable bulk rates for mailings in excess of 200 identical pieces (or 20 pounds). There are times, of course, when the first-class letter or postal-card rates are paid because the added prestige and attention value of this kind of postage are desired.

Since costs in direct advertising are extremely flexible, they must be judged entirely in relation to results. Accordingly, it is often wise to judge the effectiveness of a direct advertising effort on a "cost-per-order" basis. The cost of the mailing is divided by the number of orders received so as to obtain a cost-per-order figure. Where traceable sales results are an objective of the direct advertising campaign, the cost-per-order figures can be used to measure the relative efficiency of the advertising.

Given the variability of costs—list, production, and distribution—the total cost for a particular direct mailing is highly unique to the situation. Nevertheless, it may be helpful to not some overall averages which were compiled in 1971 by the mail-order division of Ogilvy & Mather Advertising Agency. The following price ranges are based on a mailing of 100,000 and include printing, list, production, assembly, and third-class postage costs:[11]

Type of mailing	Average cost range (cents each)
Self-mailer	6–8
Envelope, letter, reply card	8–10
Envelope, letter, reply card, reply envelope, two-color brochure	12–15
Envelope, four-page letter, reply card, reply envelope, four-color brochure	15–25
Computer letter personalized with variable body copy	30

To estimate current costs for such mailings, one would have to take into consideration any postage increases, along with general price increases for labor, materials, and printing due to inflation.

QUESTIONS AND PROBLEMS

1   A dealer in medium-price automobiles, contemplating a direct-mail campaign, has two possible sources for his mailing list: One is the city directory, giving names and addresses of people by sections of the city, so that people living in the better sections of the city could be selected; the other is a company which tabulates automobile registrations by make of car owned, and which will furnish lists of owners of any make of car in any territory for $0.03 per name. The dealer reasoned that since he had free access to a city directory, it would be to his advantage to use it. Do you agree? Why?

2   It is often said that direct mail provides advertisers with the most selective medium of all. Do you agree with that point of view? Support your stand with examples.

3   Assume that after you graduate you set yourself up in a direct-mail advertising service business. You offer to plan and execute direct-mail advertising campaigns for retailers, local clubs, hospitals, community chests, and other local institutions. At lunch one day a local businessman told you that he thought most of the money spent in direct mail was wasted. He pointed out that most of that type of mail which came to him was immediately thrown in the wastebas-

[11] *O&M Pocket Guide to Media,* 4th ed., p. 53.

ket. He was confident that the same practice was followed by the great majority of people. If that were true, he reasoned, then it would be foolish to spend much, if any, money in direct mail. He advised you to close up your business and get into something else.

How would you answer your luncheon partner?

4 Many of you will be looking for a job when you graduate. When that day approaches you will have an opportunity to develop your first real advertising campaign. You will have the problem of "interpreting your own personal qualities to a prospective employer in terms of his needs or desires."

You are asked to prepare such a campaign now, depending completely on direct mail as your medium. As a part of this assignment, bring to class the following:

a. A statement of specific sources you would use in compiling a mailing list.

b. A detailed listing of the kinds of information, if any, you would want to obtain about each name on your mailing list before preparing a specific advertising letter or folder.

c. How you would proceed to secure the desired information. Name specific sources of information.

d. A detailed outline of your campaign procedure, including such things as what kind of material you would mail, in what form, to how many people, at what time, and whether follow-up mailings would be made if there was no response from your first mailing.

e. A one-page "sales" letter designed to (1) show how the prospective employer could benefit from having you on his payroll and (2) to secure a personal interview for you.

f. A statement of the estimated cost of your campaign, broken down into (1) money to be spent and (2) number of hours of your time required to plan and execute the entire campaign.

23

Other media

In previous chapters, consideration was given to the types of media that claim the major portion of the advertiser's dollar. Other media available to the advertiser will be treated in the following pages.

The use of outdoor advertising is one of the oldest methods employed by advertisers to get their message before the public. Outdoor advertising, as used in this chapter, consists of the following types: (1) signs, (2) posters, (3) painted bulletins, and (4) electric displays. The most pervasive of these is the outdoor poster which accounts for over three fourths of the volume in this medium.

The expenditures in outdoor advertising in 1972 were $290 million, or 1.3 percent of total advertising investment. Of this amount, 65 percent was by national advertisers. It is estimated that both local and national advertisers will be spending about $414 million for this medium in 1978.[1]

Outdoor advertising provides a medium to reach people when they are out of doors or traveling, rather than when they are in the home or office. The copy requirements of outdoor are different from those of magazines, newspapers, direct mail, or radio. In the former, the message must be

[1] J. Walter Thompson Advertising Agency, 1973.

515

presented so that pedestrians and motorists can get its meaning in a very short space of time. Brevity is a necessity in copy, and pictures are highly important in gaining attention. Because of these limitations, outdoor advertising can be used effectively for only those products or services whose sales message can be told in pictures and brief copy. It can be used to remind people of the merits of known products and where they can be secured.

In our highly mobile society, outdoor advertising is seen by a large proportion of the population. Studies have shown that a typical showing reaches over 80 percent of the adults in a market during the first week of exposure. By the end of a normal 30-day posting, 89.2 percent of the adults will have been exposed to the advertiser's message, and the frequency of exposure will be 31 times.

Since the passage of the Highway Beautification Act of 1965, the outdoor industry has been faced with a number of restrictions. Although the act is primarily concerned with the placement of outdoor bulletins and posters along interstate highways (placement cannot be within 660 feet of the highway), states and municipalities increasingly have enacted their own legislation. For example, many cities now limit the extent of outdoor advertising to certain areas or "zones," and quite a number also place restrictions on the use of business signs.

Store signs

The purpose of store signs is to identify a place of business. For most stores, such signs should emphasize the kind of merchandise sold or service rendered rather than the name of the proprietor or company. Passers-by are more interested in locating a place where food, drugs, or clothing can be purchased than where John Smith operates a store. But department stores are somewhat of an exception, since reputation is a factor in patronage and the vast window-display space provides a method for informing the public concerning the kind of merchandise sold.

Store signs are either on the building itself or on boards or metal overhanging the street. They may be painted or electric. Electric signs have increased in popularity with the introduction of the neon sign. This has permitted a wide range of attention-getting techniques.

Outdoor posters

Posters lining our streets and highways are one of the most common forms of outdoor advertising. They appear in various sizes, but the most common panel measures 12'3" high by 24'6" in length, including frame. The amount of space available for copy depends upon which of three types are used; the 24-sheet, 30-sheet, or bleed-size poster. The copy

FIGURE 23–1
Copy areas for three standard-size posters

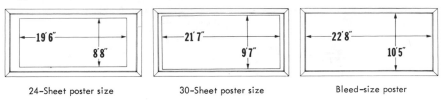

24-Sheet poster size   30-Sheet poster size   Bleed–size poster

areas for these posters are shown in Figure 23–1. The 30-sheet size offers 25 percent more copy area than the 24-sheet board; and the "bleed" size, using all of the area within the frame, provides 40 percent more area. There also are three-sheet posters which have a printing surface 82 inches high and 48 inches wide. They are most often used near the point of sale as last-minute reminders. Popular places for such signs are grocery and drugstores located at street intersections.

The use of large outdoor posters along streets and highways developed with the growth of automobile traffic. Any medium that will provide an economical means for reaching the vast numbers of automobile drivers will be of value to the advertiser of many types of products. The potential value of poster boards is therefore measured in terms of the number of persons passing during a given interval of time. To provide an authentic measure of such traffic, the Traffic Audit Bureau has been established to do for outdoor advertising what the Audit Bureau of Circulations does for newspapers and magazines.

Buying poster space Poster-board advertising space can be purchased in some 11,000 city and town trading areas. National coverage can be attained by combining many local areas, or coverage can be spotted in those areas where added advertising emphasis is desired. In fact, space on a single board can often be purchased by a local advertiser who wishes to reach a very limited area.

The principal item of cost is the rental of space. Such costs vary a great deal according to the volume and character of traffic past the board. The use of fluorescent ink does not increase the space cost but does increase the hours of visibility and thus increases the advertising value of such posters.

Space is usually purchased in terms of relative coverage. Until recently, purchase coverage was designated by numbers 50, 75, 100, 150, and so on. A No. 100 coverage was the accepted standard of full coverage in a given market and meant that an advertiser's message would appear on the number of boards considered necessary to reach the entire mobile population within a 30-day period. Thus, the number of boards required for a No. 100 coverage varied from market to market, depending on the

FIGURE 23–2
Location of boards within a city

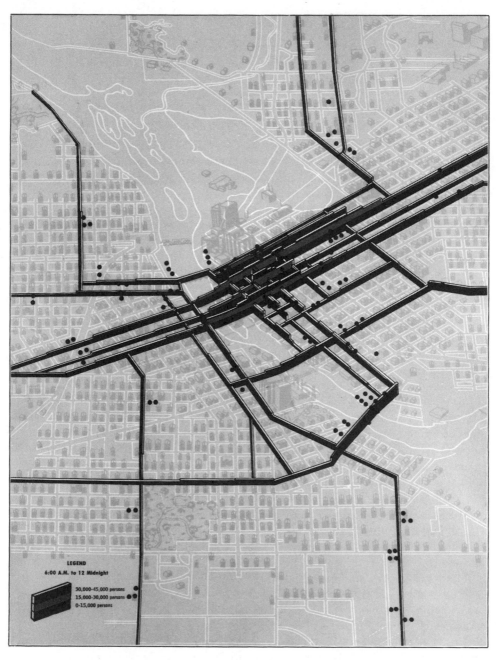

LEGEND
6:00 A.M. to 12 Midnight

30,000–45,000 persons
15,000–30,000 persons
0–15,000 persons

market's population and number of traffic arteries. In most markets about 80 to 90 percent of the traffic moves over 10 to 20 percent of the streets. Accordingly, plant operators build most of their panels along these arteries. An example of such concentration can be observed in Figure 23–2.

Presently, the outdoor industry refers to market penetration in terms of *gross rating points* (GRPs), which are defined as "the sum of the circulation of each of the panels in a showing, estimated from half-hour traffic counts." Thus, when an advertiser buys 100 GRPs, he is provided the boards necessary to give him, in a single day, the number of exposures equal to 100 percent of the population in a given market. Seventy-five GRPs provide 75 percent coverage, and so forth.

Rates for various GRP levels are quoted on a monthly basis. The data

TABLE 23–1
Cost of outdoor advertising in selected metropolitan areas

Market	Population	Number of boards for 100 GRPs		Monthly cost/mkt.
		Nonilluminated	Illuminated	
Chicago, Ill.*	6,408,300	68	224	$39,056
Seattle, Wash	1,436,400	26	60	10,020
Sacramento, Cal	813,100	18	36	6,984
Greenville, S.C	303,100	16	16	2,760
Champaign, Urbana, Ill.	102,000	7	5	840

* 75 GRPs.
Source: *The Buyers Guide to Outdoor Advertising,* January 1973.

in Table 23–1 reflect the cost of outdoor advertising in a few selected cities.

National advertisers generally place their outdoor campaigns through advertising agencies. The agencies, in turn, are likely to use the services of the National Outdoor Advertising Bureau, Inc. (NOAB), an organization which is cooperatively owned and maintained by advertising agencies. Functioning as a middleman between the agencies and the widely scattered plant operators, the NOAB assembles cost estimates for outdoor space, draws up contracts, bills the agencies, handles payment to plant operators, and provides field inspection services.

Local advertisers or other small users of outdoor space place their orders directly with the plant operators.

Regardless of the channel through which purchase is made, the plant operators assume responsibility for posting the advertisements and keeping them in repair for the full 30 days before the advertisement is changed and new sheets provided. If a portion of the advertisement is torn or marred during the 30-day period, the local plant is responsible for repairing the damage if the advertiser has furnished extra sheets.

FIGURE 23–3
Possible layout arrangement of sheets for 24-sheet poster

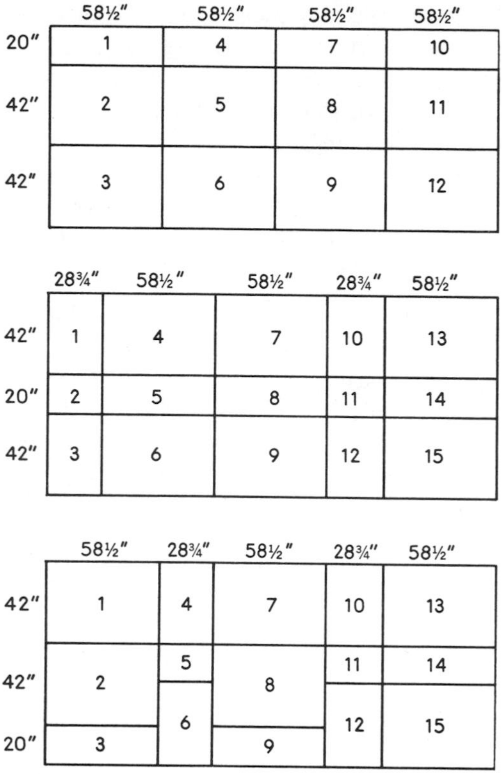

	58½"	58½"	58½"	58½"
20"	1	4	7	10
42"	2	5	8	11
42"	3	6	9	12

	28¾"	58½"	58½"	28¾"	58½"
42"	1	4	7	10	13
20"	2	5	8	11	14
42"	3	6	9	12	15

	58½"	28¾"	58½"	28¾"	58½"
42"	1	4	7	10	13
42"	2	5	8	11	14
20"		6	9	12	15
	3				

Printing is also an important item of cost in the use of posters. Printing is usually done by the lithographic process and will average around $4 per board, although for large runs the cost may be somewhat lower. Costs of printing can often be reduced by a careful arrangement of color in illustrations, so that a minimum of color sheets needs to be run. While large posters are referred to as "24-sheet posters" (because that was at one time the number of sheets printed for each board), larger sheets are printed today. The usual number is 10, but these can be cut so as to be arranged in 12 or 15 pieces for more economical and practical manufacturing. Three suggested layouts are given in Figure 23–3. Other arrangements are possible according to the design of the poster, subject to the one restriction that the sheets must be so cut as to necessitate no more than five separate sections lengthwise of the board, and these sections must run from top to bottom in vertical lines.

Since the same design remains on a board for 30 days, it is important that colors be used that will not fade readily when exposed to sunlight.

Pinks, purples, and certain types of blues and greens should be used sparingly because of their tendency to fade.

Advantages of poster advertising   Poster boards constitute a primary advertising medium. The enterprise is well organized, making it easy for the advertiser to avail himself of its facilities. Although this form of advertising is limited in its application for the reasons already set forth, its advantages for certain products and services are numerous. According to "Essentials of Outdoor Advertising," published by the Association of National Advertisers, outdoor is bought because:

1. It can deliver a message simultaneously across the country, giving the medium the characteristic of national magazine, network radio and TV.
2. Outdoor can be used to cover individual markets and can be bought market-by-market.
3. While used on a national scale, it also can be tailored in frequency and coverage to meet special sales problems in individual markets.
4. A truly mass medium, it is exposed to all economic and social groups, delivering messages to people on their way to work, to play, to shop.
5. Outdoor is unique in that other media deliver primarily during a period of indoor activity.

TABLE 23–2
Top outdoor advertisers—1971

Advertisers	Expenditures
1. R. J. Reynolds Industries	$11,294,400
2. Distillers Corp.-Seagrams Ltd.	9,398,100
3. Loews Corp.	8,863,500
4. Brown & Williamson Tobacco	8,025,700
5. Philip Morris Inc.	7,848,700
6. Liggett & Myers	4,530,400
7. National Distillers & Chemical Corp.	4,022,000
8. Heublein Inc.	3,040,700
9. Rapid-American Corp.	2,794,700
10. General Motors Corp.	2,557,100
11. Ford Motor Co.	2,209,300
12. Volkswagen of America	2,028,100
13. Bankamerica Corp.	1,870,200
14. Norton Simon Inc.	1,715,000
15. Brown-Forman Distillers	1,665,300
16. General Motors (Local Dealers)	1,574,700
17. Coca-Cola Co.	1,491,100
18. Hiram Walker-Gooderham & Worts	1,393,500
19. Ford Motors (Dealer Assns.)	1,304,400
20. Seven-Up Co.	1,190,100
21. Northwest Industries	1,184,800
22. Schering-Plough Inc.	1,124,400
23. American Airlines	1,114,900
24. Standard Oil of New Jersey	930,100
25. PepsiCo Inc.	928,600

Source: *Advertising Age,* August 28, 1972, p. 98.

6. Outdoor must speak quickly, memorably, and repeatedly.
7. Its low cost enables it to be used as an impulse-trigger, for it delivers at the time the prospect is apt to recognize his need for the product.[2]

National advertisers account for two thirds of total outdoor advertising expenditures. Advertisers of automobiles, cigarettes, soft drinks, and liquor are the principal users of this medium. A listing of the top 25 outdoor advertisers and their expenditures can be noted in Table 23–2.

Painted and electric displays

The same general principles that apply to poster boards apply to painted displays, for the two are comparable in matters of circulation and copy requirements. Painted displays appear on buildings, bulletin boards, and wall panels. Farm buildings often afford a site for a painted display. Wall panels are comparable to the 3-sheet poster, and painted bulletins to 24-sheet, 30-sheet, and bleed-size posters, except that bulletins are usually larger than poster boards and may be built in special shapes and designs. Figure 23–4 is an example of a specially shaped bulletin.

Copy remains without change for a longer period of time on painted displays than on posters, the period varying from four months to one year, according to type of display and location. The most common period is six months. Location and the presence or absence of illumination are the principal factors influencing cost.

To give advertisers the impact of a big painted display plus wider coverage of a market than would be possible with one or a few fixed position displays, outdoor plants in several cities now offer a *rotary plan.*

FIGURE 23–4
Painted display in which the design is extended above the rectangular board area

[2] *Advertising Age,* "The World of Advertising," January 15, 1963, p. 131.

Under the rotary plan, one or several movable display units are rotated every 30, 60, or 90 days on a series of choice locations.

The most imposing of all outdoor-advertising media are the large electric displays erected at heavy traffic centers in our larger cities. In the daytime they compete with other street signs, but at night they have the field more or less to themselves. Their cost is enormous, owing to the scarcity of choice locations and the expense of operation and maintenance. World-famous electric displays are located in New York's Times Square area, where monthly rental costs alone often run $25,000.

TRANSIT

As a medium for reaching the millions of people who depend on commuter trains, subways, or buses to take them shopping or to work and bring them home again, transit advertising is unequaled. The medium actually consists of three types: (1) *car cards,* found on the inside of public transportation vehicles; (2) *outside displays,* located on the fronts, backs, and sides of vehicles; and (3) *station posters,* placed in and around vehicle stations (as a subway station).

Transit advertising is carried by more than 70,000 vehicles throughout urban areas of the United States. Advertisers currently invest over $35 million per year in the medium.

Car-card space is generally sold on the basis of full, half, or quarter showings. Full service provides one card in every vehicle in a fleet; half or quarter service is scaled proportionately. An occasional advertiser will buy a "double" showing which provides two cards in each vehicle. Purchase can be made in one of three ways: (1) direct from the local franchise holder, (2) through an advertising agency, or (3) from a national representative of local operators.

Statistics concerning ridership and readership are supplied from studies made for the Transit Advertising Association and the American Transit Association. For example, in markets of 250,000-and-over population, almost 28 million adults ride a transit vehicle in an average month.[3] This represents 36 percent of the population in such markets, with women a noticeably larger percent of the total than men (41 versus 31 percent). The average length of ride is almost 23 minutes.

A study of outside displays on buses in Philadelphia revealed that a full showing reached 17 million people in a 30-day period. The audience consisted primarily of pedestrian traffic (92 percent), with only 8 percent viewing from vehicles. The heaviest exposure occurred later in the day, between 3:30 P.M. and 8:30 P.M.

Readership of car cards averages higher than for newspapers but does

[3] See George T. Clarke, *Transit Advertising* (New York: The Transit Advertising Assoc., 1970), p. 77.

FIGURE 23–5
Typical car cards

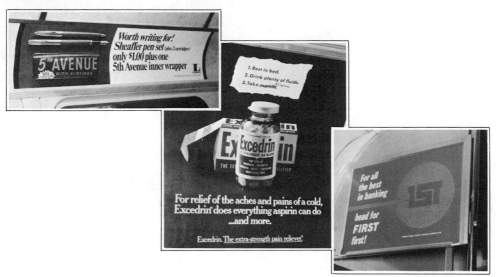

not show the extremes found in the latter. It is doubtful whether any car cards would ever have as low a readership as 1 percent, which is common for some newspaper advertisements. An average readership of around 25 percent is common for car cards. This is not surprising, in view of the average length of time each rider spends in a vehicle and the fact that cards remain in the car for 30 days before they are changed. With car cards, as with other printed media, readership is influenced by the interest people have in the product advertised, character of the card, size, and location in the car.

Rates for car-card advertising vary with the number of riders but will average from four to five cents per thousand monthly rides. Space can be purchased for one month but usually not for a shorter time. The more common practice is to contract for space for one year. Discounts are generally provided if space is used for three months within one year. The production cost of cards is not a part of the space cost. The cost of cards varies materially with the quality of stock and printing. Rates, number of monthly rides, size requirements, and other valuable information relative to all types of transit advertising are found in *SRDS's Transit Advertising Rates and Data*.

The most common size for car cards is 11 inches high by 28 inches long. Two other lengths (42 and 56 inches) are also considered standard, but these latter two are in the distinct minority in use. Figure 23–5 shows some examples of car cards.

Standard sizes for the outside of the vehicle are:

King-size: 30″ × 144″
Queen-size: 30″ × 88″
Traveling display: 21″ × 44″

These are placed along the side of a vehicle. In addition, most transit systems offer a variety of rear-of-vehicle signs. Some also offer ''Bus-O-Rama,'' which is a roof-top, illuminated panel backlighted by means of fluorescent tubes. Examples of outside displays are shown in Figure 23–6.

Transit advertising is flexible. Its use can be confined to one city or expanded to include almost any combination of markets desired. It cannot, of course, reach the farm and village market; but for metropolitan areas intense coverage is provided.

The audience delivered is a large one and includes all economic groups. George Clarke summarizes the functions of the transit audience as follows:

> Transit advertising affords both national and local advertisers low-cost penetration and coverage of selected markets. It provides frequency and continuity of ad impressions to repeat audiences of working riders. It extends advertising exposure potential through continuing presence and visibility to

FIGURE 23–6
Examples of outside displays

mass-transit users. The medium is used by national and local advertisers for both broad and selective market coverage. It affords varying positional and size options in markets with concentrations of retail outlets and shopping centers stocking branded items and packaged goods. . . . Transit advertisements reach specific audiences: workers, both men and working wives traveling to and from employment, housewives during daytime shopping hours, school and college students.

For the local advertiser, transit's flexibility permits shifting of advertising weight in relation to specific markets to reach riders along transit routes passing particular retail outlets. Transit also provides retailers low-cost, volume exposure close to point of sale. . . . For both local and national advertisers transit advertisements are attractive in themselves in format, impression value, makeup and content. Products can be displayed in one or more colors or in black and white to full advantage. The medium offers creative latitude in format, illustration, and color to add interest and originality for prospect-winning attention.[4]

SPECIALTIES[5]

According to early records, the specialty advertising industry began in the United States in 1845. It was then that an anonymous insurance salesman placed calendar pads on his advertising signs. Calendars and other simple promotional items characterized the early history of the medium. By 1900 specialty advertising encompassed such things as horse blankets, wagon umbrellas, and wooden gasoline measuring sticks. Some early items, as yardsticks and pencils, are still extensively used today.

Specialty advertising is an advertising medium employing useful articles, known as advertising specialties, that are imprinted with the advertiser's name, address, and/or sales message. Specialties are utilized to reach a preselected audience and are given without cost or obligation, thus serving as items of goodwill and reminder values. The specialty advertising industry consists of approximately 4,400 manufacturers, distributors, and direct selling houses. Volume is estimated to be around $1 billion annually.

Advertising specialties are generally divided into three main categories: calendars, imprinted specialties, and business or executive gifts.

Calendars account for about one third of the total business done by the advertising specialty industry. They are used by virtually any business, ranging from the small retailer to the giants of American industry. For example, the Ford Motor Company distributed over three million Norman Rockwell-illustrated calendars during their 50th Anniversary celebration. Surveys have shown that 75 percent of all calendars produced and dis-

---

[4] Ibid., pp. 66–67.

[5] Information in this section comes largely from the Specialty Advertising Association International, 740 N. Rush Street, Chicago, Illinois 60611, and especially a pamphlet, *Specialty Advertising,* by Walter A. Gaw, The reader is also referred to George L. Herlpel and Richard A. Collins, *Speciality Advertising in Marketing* (Homewood, Ill.: Dow Jones-Irwin, Inc., 1972).

tributed are kept by the recipients. Some examples are shown in Figure 23–7.

There are more than 10,000 different types of imprinted specialties, including such typical items as ash trays, cigarette lighters, thermometers, key chains, ballpoint pens, memo pads, paperweights, rulers, and balloons. Several examples are shown in Figure 23–8. Often such novelties are used to tie-in with a campaign theme carried in other media.

Business or executive gifts are primarily distinguished from other specialities by price. It is usually a more prestigious item given personally on a selective basis. It may be imprinted or personalized, but usually is not. Business gifts range in price and variety, including such things as attaché cases, luggage, and desk sets. Changes in the tax law have a bearing on what can properly be placed in this category. Presently, business gifts that cost more than $4 or which are not imprinted are fully deductible for the first $25 per recipient.

Advertising specialties, as all other media, are characterized by both advantages and limitations. Probably the greatest limitation of the medium is the limited amount of space available for a sales message. Often, the imprint consists of no more than the advertiser's name and address. Also to be taken into consideration when using specialties is the limited circulation generally affordable. Cost of the specialty and distribution expenses normally preclude the building of large audiences which are obtainable in some media.

The specialty advertising industry recognizes the fact that a specialty has certain intrinsic value as merchandise, but they prefer to emphasize their *advertising* value. Accordingly, the following advantages are generally credited to the medium.

FIGURE 23–7
Examples of imprinted calendars

FIGURE 23–8
Some examples of imprinted specialties

1. *Ad specialties are useful items of value given without obligation.* The recipient is actually getting a useful item in return for being exposed to the advertiser's message.
2. *Ad specialties are received with appreciation and are usually kept and used frequently.* They have lasting value and, most importantly, repeat advertising exposure and impact without repeat cost.
3. *Ad specialties zero in on their target.* The market can be completely controlled by the advertiser because specialties can be created to reach a preselected audience at a specifically selected time. The advertising message is told directly to the target audience.
4. *Ad specialties can achieve preferred position.* They can be placed permanently in places such as purses, pockets, office walls, inside or on top of desks, in the home, and even in the boudoir, where no other advertising medium normally reaches.
5. *Ad specialties are welcomed by their recipients and received gratefully,* creating an atmosphere of goodwill and appreciation.
6. *Ad specialties, in addition to getting the advertising message read on initial impact, provide multiple impressions as the gift is kept and used as well as shown and exposed to others.*
7. *Ad specialties are inexpensive* whether created for a selected or mass market and because they are not competitive with other media, can be integrated into campaigns which use a variety of media.
8. *Ad specialties aid and complement other advertising and promotional methods,* and they provide the vital element of direct and personal impact.

DEALER DISPLAYS

The retailer's display space is probably worth more than many other types of advertising he might use. The Point-of-Purchase Advertising Institute estimates that over $2.25 billion was spent on dealer-display advertising in 1972. As can be noted in Table 23–3, the leading users of point-of-purchase included manufacturers of automobiles, beer, soft drinks, liquor, and packaged goods (foods, drugs, soap products, and toiletries). In terms of the percentage of the advertising and sales promotion budget spent for point-of-purchase advertising, major industry users were:

	Percent of advertising and sales promotion budget
Beer	21.7
Cosmetics	19.0
Liquor	17.2
Soft drinks	12.4
Petroleum products	10.0
Foods	7.9
Automobiles	5.0

TABLE 23–3
Top point-of-purchase advertisers—1971

Advertisers	Expenditures
1. General Motors Corp.	$44,000,000
2. Coca-Cola Co.	16,000,000
3. Distillers Corp.-Seagrams.	13,450,000
4. Procter & Gamble Co.	9,100,000
5. Bristol-Myers Co.	7,942,000
6. Warner-Lambert Co.	7,300,000
7. American Home Products Corp.	7,245,000
8. Ford Motor Co.	7,100,000
9. PepsiCo., Inc.	6,858,000
10. Chrysler Corp.	6,400,000
11. Anheuser-Busch.	5,500,000
12. National Distillers	5,200,000
13. Goodyear Tire & Rubber	4,950,000
14. Eastman Kodak Co.	4,900,000
15. Joseph Schlitz Brewing Co.	4,800,000
16. Beatrice Foods Corp. (food & medical companies only)	4,450,000
17. Heublein Inc. (Smirnoff Beverage & Import Co., consumer products & United Vintners)	4,200,000
18. Gillette Co..	4,150,000
19. General Foods	4,000,000
20. ITT	4,000,000
21. Schering-Plough.	3,950,000
22. Lever Bros..	3,805,000
23. Brown & Williamson	3,750,000
24. R. J. Reynolds Industries	3,700,000
25. Brown-Forman Distillers	3,600,000

Source: *Advertising Age,* September 18, 1972, p. 98.

Most point-of-purchase materials are distributed free (79.3 percent), although 5.7 percent are sold at full cost. Another 5 percent are distributed by charging a small fee, and 9 percent are provided without cost when the dealer purchases a specified amount of the product.

In the sale of most consumer goods, the retailer is the last link in the chain of distribution from manufacturer or producer to consumer. He therefore holds an exceptionally strategic position at the point of sale. Manufacturers that can get their merchandise on display at the point of sale, where it may be seen by consumers in a buying mood, will usually be rewarded by a generous increase in sales.

Traffic

The traffic exposed to dealer-display material consists of the number of people, within a given period of time, who pass and who have an opportunity to see the display. In general, only pedestrians passing on the near side of the street would be included in traffic figures for window displays; and only those coming into the store, for interior displays. The traffic for a given store will vary according to the size of town and location in the town.

Both the volume and character of traffic are vital items in determining advertising value. In measuring character or quality of traffic, consideration should be given to sex, age, and income groups passing the displays and the reasons for their walking past the store (going to or from work, bus, theater, or on a buying trip). Certain types of stores located near a commuter station will have a volume of pedestrian traffic far out of proportion to its quality as measured in terms of potential customers of that store. Furthermore, people going to and from work are generally not in a receptive mood to buy merchandise.

Kinds of dealer displays

Dealer displays can be classified into two general groups—window displays and inside displays. A wide variety of material is regularly sent to the dealer for use both in the windows and inside the store. Many display pieces can be used in either place; hence, a careful distinction between the two major groups is unnecessary.

Often the most valuable of all display material is the product itself. As has been emphasized, pictures of the product in magazine and newspaper advertisements produce better results than almost any other kind of picture. In the case of dealer-display space, the product itself, rather than merely a picture, can be shown—and shown at the point of sale. Around the product can be placed various kinds of lithographed cards, posters, and cutouts, to explain various features of the product, how it can be used, what it will do, and its price. In addition to material built around the product itself, other material stating the kind and brand of merchandise sold and containing a brief sales message may be used.

Cutouts   These consist of lithographed cardboard displays in various sizes and shapes usually constructed so they will stand without support. In their construction, dies are used to cut and crease the boards. The large displays often consist of three panels that can be used as a background for a complete window display. Since the windows of most small retail stores are open in the back, such displays are popular, although they should be sufficiently low to allow passers-by to see into the store. The background display can serve to create an atmosphere for one of the featured products as well as for related products. For example, a background for shotguns may serve for a window of hunters' equipment and supplies.

Cutouts usually have high attention-value; and if they are designed so that not only the particular product advertised, but also related products, can be displayed, their life as useful display pieces will be lengthened. In designing and using this type of display, primary consideration should be given to displaying the merchandise itself, using the printed panel to increase the general attractiveness of the window and to help in a logical arrangement of merchandise.

Display cards   These are usually plain-shaped, medium- or small-size cards that can be used in the window or on a counter or wall. They may be reproductions of magazine or newspaper advertisements, to be used as a means of point-of-sale tie-up with other advertising efforts, or they may merely feature a brief selling message, a special offer, or a special price. If they are too large, the retailer will not use them because of space requirements. The advertiser will also find that more of them will be used if printed on both sides. Those printed on one side only provide good cardboard on which the retailer can paint his own message.

Comparable to display cards are name plates designed to be hung on walls. Of such plates, the ones most used are those that tie in with the needs of the retailer. A plate for a proprietary product may carry the term "Prescription Department" above the advertised product and thus encourage the druggist to use the plate to call attention to the location of that department. One should never lose sight of the fact that the retailer is the final judge as to what display material is to be used, and one must remember that he has much more material available than he can use.

Counter displays   While display cards may be used on counters, the usual counter display has greater utility than a card. It usually provides a method for displaying the merchandise itself. It is particularly valuable for so-called "impulse goods," where purchase is often made on sight. Quite often the package itself is designed to serve as a counter display. Examples include candy, gum, cigarettes, cigars, and cheese. Usually, only merchandise with a high turnover will rate a counter position, although occasionally long-profit items will be accorded such a place. Figure 23–9 illustrates a counter display for Arrow handkerchiefs.

Cabinets and racks   Serving the same function as counter displays, but designed for more permanent use, are fine metal, wood, and glass cabinets and racks. Some are designed for use on the counter and some for use on the floor. These displays are expensive but perhaps provide as great or greater return to the advertiser as any other form. Their very costliness emphasizes their value to both the retailer and the advertiser. Consequently, the latter is careful in his distribution of such material, often requiring a certain volume of business from the retailer before providing him with a permanent cabinet or rack. The retailer, in turn, thus impressed by the value of the material, will usually give it a preferred position. Examples of products displayed in permanent racks and cabinets include electric-light bulbs, motor oil, certain types of men's clothing accessories, crackers and cookies, jewelry, and fountain pens.

Window strips   These are perhaps the least expensive of all dealer display material but often are quite productive when the retailer can be

FIGURE 23–9
A counter display which holds a sizable quantity of the product

induced to use them. They consist of strips of paper of various sizes to be stuck on the windowpane. They are usually gummed on the edges to facilitate sticking. They should, of course, be designed so their use will not obstruct the view of products displayed in the window. Smaller stores are the most common users of this kind of material.

The decalcomania window sticker provides a more permanent and attractive strip. Dealers are naturally reluctant to allow many such signs to be placed on their windows, limiting them to signs for products that are popular or that carry a large profit margin. Among the types of products advertised by this kind of sign are tobacco, soft drinks, hardware items, and paint. Their principal value is to tell the public where the particular brand of goods in question can be purchased.

Getting display material used

The advertising value of space in retail stores and windows is well recognized by most retailers and manufacturers. So great, however, is the competition for such space that more material is supplied than can possibly be used. This, together with the kind of material supplied and the method used to distribute it, often reduces the percentage of material used from any given manufacturer to a small part of the total. Some studies indicate that when no particular effort is exerted by the manufacturer to get his material displayed, only from 1 to 20 percent of it is used; but with emphasis on how, when, and why to use it, plus help in installation, as much as 80 percent will be used.

Naturally, some products will get more display space and attention than others. Sugar, flour, and similar grocery staples will not be displayed as much as fresh fruits and vegetables. The producer should study the practices of retailers in this respect before preparing his displays. For those products that do lend themselves to display, a number of methods might be employed to increase the use of display material. Manufacturers may promote window-display contests, offering monthly prizes for the best window. Helps may be given the dealer in checking the results in terms of actual sales of different display material. Once the retailer can see values in terms of dollar sales and increased profits, he will be ready to give greater attention to display material.

Methods of distributing material   In the final analysis, the extent to which material is used depends largely on the methods employed in placing it in the hands of retailers. Possible distributive agencies and methods would include: (1) manufacturers' salesmen; (2) packed with merchandise itself; (3) mail; (4) wholesalers or jobbers; and (5) display crews, either in the direct employ of the advertiser, or of a regular professional display-service organization.

Of the various methods listed, the first and last will give better results. Many retailers are not expert in the art of dressing windows or arranging inside displays and, hence, welcome expert assistance. If such assistance results in a noticeable increase in the sales of displayed items, the advertiser will continue to receive valuable display space. The salesman or professional display man should provide the retailer with a well-rounded display, not insisting that all space be devoted to the particular product in question.

Further suggestions concerning dealer displays

In developing any display, attention should be given to the character of the goods and the type of consumer to whom they might appeal. In general, goods that are popular and attractive are best for display purposes, since they will stop a greater number of passers-by. Thought should also be given to the particular buying mood of consumers. This is difficult to ascertain, but certain days and seasons give an indication of probable buying attitudes. Rainy days should encourage displays of umbrellas, raincoats, and perhaps magazines, scrapbooks for youngsters, games, and other items for inside use. Particular kinds of commodites are associated with Easter, Thanksgiving, the opening of school, etc., and should be emphasized at those times.

The type of commodities to display, however, is not the only factor making for effectiveness. The manner of arrangement, the number of items included, and color combinations are factors of importance. There is as much value in testing the sales effectiveness of window and inside displays as in testing the effectiveness of newspaper, magazine, and other forms of advertising.

PACKAGES, LABELS, AND INSERTS

The problems of package design were discussed in Chapter 10, where emphasis was placed upon presenting products to the public in a form to meet consumer desires. People prefer packaged merchandise and, consequently, they get it. But packages are more than safe and attractive containers for goods—they are also a medium for carrying an advertising message.

The audiences reached by packages as a whole, when duplication and repetition is not considered, run into untold millions. The primary audience of the packages of a given manufacturer can easily be determined. Furthermore, this audience includes consumers that have demonstrated, through purchase, a definite interest in the product.

Advertising copy on packages must be brief and pictorial. It should usually be limited to the brand name, perhaps a picture of the product itself or in use, and a statement concerning its qualities, variety of uses, and methods of use. Packages are often examined and copy on them read by potential buyers before a final choice of brand is made. It is therefore highly advisable to include a brief message to help consumers judge the want-satisfying qualities of a product in their effort to make a choice. This is particularly true today when self-service is the rule in many lines of retailing. Figure 23–10 shows a variety of packages. Note the use of photographs.

Some items are distributed in two packages, particularly liquid and other products put up in glass containers. In such cases, the label on the inside container should carry an advertising message similar to that on the cardboard box. These items will be of value to the purchaser and, in addition, may attract the attention and interest of nonusers who may be introduced to the product through satisfied customers. Packages thus have a secondary circulation value that should not be ignored.

Package inserts   The package insert has practically as great a circulation as the package itself and, in addition, affords a means of presenting a different kind of advertising message. There is no less costly method of

FIGURE 23–10
Use of packages to communicate product identity and qualities

carrying a piece of direct advertising to consumers. Furthermore, the audience is a very selective one because the purchase of the product itself indicates the character of its interest. The potentialities of the insert as a means of reaching a preferred list of consumers has probably not been adequately appreciated.

The package insert has been very poorly handled by many advertisers. It has too often been used as a piece of paper in which to wrap a bottle being placed in a cardboard container. Too little thought has been given to the appearance, readability, and simplicity of the insert. If the insert were keyed to the self-interest of consumers, it would have a larger audience. The great majority of users of the insert try to put a long sales story on a minimum amount of paper; they fold it in a difficult manner; and then they expect to get effective results. The same insert is included in every package, month in and month out, without thought of changing it to give repeat customers a different sales message.

Inserts could be made more profitable by—

1. Printing in legible type.
2. Emphasizing one copy theme.
3. Changing the sales message occasionally. (Shredded Wheat obtains variety by changing inserts regularly and obtains interest and continuity by encouraging consumers to look for the recurring inserts and use them in a scrapbook.)
4. Making greater use of pictures and briefer copy.
5. Judicious folding. (Fold them so that an interest-arresting picture or headline appears on the front and so that the unfolding process will be easy and logical.)
6. Printing on substantial paper and, if possible, in a form that encourages keeping (recipes on cards that can be filed, etc.).

As to the kind of information that might be included in package inserts, Paul Hillery many years ago suggested that the advertiser consider:

1. How best to use the product. (If this is a long story, as in the case of recipes, follow the plan of changing the package insert frequently. Make it a serial story, even though the customer may miss some of the installments: that's better than having her miss the entire message.)
2. How to correct troubles that may develop when using the product—service tips
3. How other items in your line will also serve to increase her happiness
4. How to fit your product in with other items with which it is naturally related
5. About new, novel, unusual uses for the product
6. About special offers which you may be making, such as premiums
7. How to make the product last longer or last better
8. How to use package leftovers
9. Use the insert as a reminder to order a new package—put the insert toward the bottom of the package[6]

These suggestions are still valid today.

SAMPLING

Sampling is based on the idea that a product will sell itself if once used. To get people to use the product, a small- or regular-size package is

---

[6] Paul Hillery, "The Neglected Package Insert," *Advertising and Selling,* October 8, 1936, p. 34.

distributed to potential consumers. Naturally, this form of advertising is limited to merchandise of relatively low cost, with a large amount of repeat business. It is most effective in introducing a new product or in building distribution in a new territory. Breakfast food, candy, gum, soap, and toilet articles lend themselves to sampling.

There are four general methods of sampling: (1) direct delivery to consumer or home, (2) distribution of coupons that can be redeemed at local retail store, (3) demonstrations in retail store, and (4) sampling in connection with other forms of advertising.

Direct delivery is usually accomplished through the use of regular crews that go from house to house, handing out small packages of the product. Better results are usually obtained if the package is handed directly to the housewife with a statement of the purpose of the sampling as well as a brief statement concerning the merits of the product. An alternative method is to distribute coupons, having the distributor give a brief sales talk concerning the product and explaining that the coupon can be redeemed at the local store. This method obtains the cooperation of the dealer, which is usually quite important.

Certain types of products can best be distributed in the store itself. This is particularly true where some sort of preparation is necessary before using the product. Soup can be heated and served to customers; cookies, crackers, sandwich spreads, and preserves can be served with tea or some other drink; coffee can be made before the customer. In this way, the product is sampled in its proper form and the advertiser is sure the product has reached the consumer.

A great deal of sampling is done in connection with other forms of advertising. Many newspaper and magazine advertisements carry coupons which, if sent directly to the advertiser or presented to the dealer, will bring the consumer a sample of the product. Television advertising directed to children has employed sampling to a high degree. Much of this kind of sampling is not free but, instead, requires that the consumer send money to "cover costs of packing and mailing." Contest and premium advertising may be a form of sampling where such advertising requires the submission of proof of purchase before qualifying in a contest or receiving a premium.

Sampling is also accomplished through car-card advertising by attaching a package of coupons or "take-ones" to the card. Riders are thus invited to help themselves to the "take-one" literature and send in the coupon for a sample of merchandise.

FILMS

Advertisers have long recognized the inherent value of sound motion pictures as a means of selling ideas and goods. This medium combines sight with sound and motion. In addition, and of extreme value, motion pictures obtain the undivided attention of the audience. The major problem associated with this medium is that of obtaining an audience.

Methods of distributing films

There are two major methods of distributing advertising films: (1) theatrical and (2) nontheatrical. The first method gives the advertiser a large audience without much effort on his part. Such an audience, however, is interested in entertainment rather than advertising. This dictates extreme care in the preparation of the advertising film. It must, in general, follow the television technique.

Two types of advertising films are in general use. One type is comparable to a movie short consisting of one reel of film. This type must be entertaining or educational in nature if it is to be accepted by the audience. The "commercial" must be short, as in broadcast advertising. The second type of theatrical film is the minute, or trailer, movie. This is comparable to the advertising of "coming attractions" regularly shown in most movie houses. Such trailers take from 45 to 90 seconds to run. They are spliced on the end of some part of the regular movie program. There is no attempt to disguise the fact that they are pure advertisements.

About 80 percent of the 10,000 or so movie theaters accept theater-screen advertising. Virtually all of an additional 4,000 drive-ins accept screen advertising. In a special study of this medium and its audience, the J. Walter Thompson Company found that during a sample week in the summer, over 56 million people saw advertising on the screens of theaters and drive-ins. For many products in this country, theater-screen advertising is the lowest cost advertising available. In many foreign countries it is virtually the *only* mass sight and sound medium available.

Nontheatrical distribution has the problem of building an audience for the film. Audiences are solicited through schools, clubs, lodges, women's organizations, churches, conventions, etc. Longer films are usually used and a pure entertainment movie often run in connection with the advertiser's film.

This type of distribution may be developed through: (1) film-distributing agencies, (2) film libraries, or (3) the advertiser's own organization.

Film-distributing agencies take the responsibility of finding the audience and showing the picture. An advertiser may contract with such agencies for a certain volume of distribution. Regular reports will be furnished the advertiser.

Film libraries provide a means whereby organizations having their own projection equipment may borrow films to show to their own group. Schools and clubs make extensive use of these facilities. Advertisers can deposit prints of their films with these libraries and have them included in the library's listing.

OTHER MEDIA

Other methods of getting an advertising message or the name of the product to the public include stunts, skywriting, bus-stop benches programs, directories, and many more.

Of these, perhaps the use of directories has the widest application. Various industrial and trade directories provide a valuable means of advertising certain products and services. Classified sections of telephone directories are particularly valuable.

For example, a study done for the National Yellow Pages Service revealed that 83.5 million adult Americans use the Yellow Pages. The average number of references per user was 44 in a year, and 93 percent of such references were followed up with action—phoning, visiting, or writing the advertiser.

QUESTIONS AND PROBLEMS

1   A number of municipalities in the United States have passed or have considered legislation to restrict the size and character of signs used to identify a place of business. If you were a merchant in such a municipality, how would or should you react to such legislation?

2   In the same vein as question 1, how would or should you react, if you were a national advertiser, to the legislation restricting the use of outdoor posters along interstate highways? Would you react differently if you were a lay citizen that had no interest in any national advertiser?

3   Discuss the question of waste in dealer displays and suggest methods for reducing this waste.

4   Discuss the place of sampling in advertising.

5   What factors determine the number of poster boards needed to secure 100 GRPs in a market?

6   Would you design an advertisement for a car card differently than an outside display? Why?

7   Some have argued that specialty advertising is ineffective because much of it is thrown away. Discuss the circumstances under which specialties can be an effective advertising medium.

8   The Tom Sawyer company, a small producer of potato chips in a metropolitan area, sought to find a way to compete with large producers who could spend as much as thousands of dollars weekly for television and other media. The Tom Sawyer company was on a limited budget of about $2,000 a month.

   The agency hired by the company undertook extensive research. Three members of the agency spent several days in the factory observing the process of making potato chips. In fact, it was during one of these tours that a basic idea for the campaign took shape.

   It was observed that white clouds were rising from the potatoes during the preparatory process; these clouds were strarch being washed out of the potatoes. In planning conferences later, "Starch Reduced" became the selling theme and the keynote of the campaign.

Agency representatives also spent a day with each of the salesmen on trucks to get market and grocer reaction to the products, observe merchandise displays, and note the type of selling being done by competition at point of purchase.

Observation of consumer purchases disclosed that 67 percent of the potato chip purchases were being made on impulse. The company then thought it logical to place major stress on a point-of-purchase campaign with a distinct attempt made at dramatizing the Tom Sawyer packages replete with the "Starch Reduced" slogan and laid out on special fluorescent displays.

After the new packages and displays had been in markets for two weeks, sales records showed a 37 percent increase over sales before the point-of-purchase campaign started.

Evaluate the use of point-of-purchase advertising for this and other types of goods. Is such advertising more valuable for impulse goods than for other types? How would you compare the relative value of the appeal "starch reduced" with that of the advertising medium used as causes for major increases in sales?

part five

Testing advertising effectiveness

The rationale
of testing

Researching the consumer, the product, and the market, as discussed in earlier chapters, enlarges the advertiser's knowledge about what consumers want and why, about the want-satisfying qualities inherent in the product, about who and where his prime prospects are. Such research is useful in planning advertising strategy, in deciding what should be said to whom through what types of media to accomplish what objectives. Another kind of research generally referred to as testing is used to measure the performance of specific elements of an advertising program or of the entire program itself.

Why test?

How well a particular advertisement or campaign performs is largely determined by the knowledge and skill of the people preparing it. People who are sensitive to the marketing situation and proficient in the art of communication are more likely to produce effective advertising. However, even the most successful copywriters sometimes forget that they are more sophisticated than their audience. They are literate and verbal and sometimes don't fully realize that the average person doesn't recognize the fine nuances in the writer's words. Copywriters seek and find small product differences that seem important to them but are of little consequence to anyone else. They often are upper-income males who find it difficult to empathize with a lower-middle-income housewife.

The experts don't always agree. Their evaluations are subjective, reflecting different criteria. The preparation of advertising seldom is a one-man show. In the chain of events leading from the conceptualization of an ad, writers, artists, media specialists, plans board members, client executives, and occasionally clients' wives all get in the act. As it so often happens, different people with different ideas resolve their differences in different ways—arguing it out, majority rule, turning to higher authority. A reasonable approach, and often an expedient one, is to marshal as much evidence as possible on the relative merit of each alternative. Such evidence, if it is obtained through sound testing procedures, may not be decisive, but it should give the best alternative a better chance to prevail.

Some creative people view testing as a threat to their particular role. Some feel that it stifles creativity. Others treat it as unwarranted interference. In the quest for certainty where perhaps there is no certainty, it is conceivable that testing might be overdone. Leo Burnett refers to excessive research on the creative product as "a banana peel in the path of advertising" and clarifies his position as follows:

> I am one who believes in going the limit in research in trying to find out what people want and why, and how best to serve them. But I believe that in its creative aspects a lot of advertising today is being analyzed, engineered, researched, and nit-picked within an inch of its life.
>
> The guiding principle in many quarters today, both among advertisers and agencies, seems to be, "Play It Safe."
>
> The search for the unique selling proposition, or whatever you want to call it, has become so intense and so scientific that the same tense, tightened-up type of thinking tends to carry over to the words and pictures. The result is a lot of very expensive advertising that is irrefutably rational, but hopelessly dull.[1]

There is no precise way to determine the cost of a mistake. A single advertisement scheduled for national media typically requires an expenditure of $125,000. A single idea destined to become a campaign theme often calls for an expenditure of millions of dollars. In terms of out-of-pocket cost alone, it is obvious that the prudent businessman would want every assurance available that he will get maximum results. But the cost of running inferior advertising is greater than the out-of-pocket cost. The additional sales that would have been generated by superior advertising would be lost. A competitive advantage would be lost. Time would be lost. And ultimately, some profits would be lost. The loss of opportunity to do

---

[1] Leo Burnett, *Communications of an Advertising Man* (Chicago: Leo Burnett Co., Inc., 1961), p. 11.

the job better must be reckoned as part of the cost of advertising that is less than the best attainable. In other words, it pays to test not only because advertising costs money, but because it makes money.

The greater the possible loss and the greater the chance of such loss occurring, the more sense it makes to spend whatever is required for an adequate test. This is likely to be a consideration when introducing a package-goods item on a national scale. Suppose, for example, that a firm estimates its maximum possible loss would be $1.5 million if its new product fails and assumes the odds of the failure's occurring to be one in ten. Then the anticipated loss for going national would be $150,000 ($1.5 million x 1/10). If the cost of an adequate test were estimated at $200,000, it would hardly pay to undertake the test. If, on the other hand, the odds of the failure's occurring were set at 50 percent, the anticipated loss would be $750,000 ($1.5 million x 50/100). Then, paying $200,000 for the test does make sense.

Over the years many researchers have had high hopes that testing might be employed to test hypotheses bearing on the general problem of explaining how advertising works. Instead of limiting tests to solve immediate problems encountered in isolated situations they have advocated conducting tests within a conceptual framework and pooling the results for the benefit of all advertisers. Peter Langhoff, a leading researcher, supports this point of view this way:

> Tests must be employed to aid in the development of increased communications efficiency. We need to know more about the symbolic power of words, colors, and pictures—why one phrase catches on, becomes part of our folklore, while another, apparently no less clever, dies on the printed page. Copy tests, as part of an orderly copy research program, can teach us how to write and talk more effectively to consumers.
>
> This is by way of saying that copy development and copy testing should work as an organic unit. Measurement makes possible the collection, storage, and use of past experience. It should build a body of usable experience which is banked in the library and in the creative bloodstream rather than starting afresh at every decision point.[2]

The fact remains that no industry-wide, systematic collection and storage of test experience has been undertaken. Perhaps with the computer's speed and efficiency in reporting marketing data we shall see more experimentation to enlarge our store of knowledge.

To summarize, the principal reasons for testing are: *to avoid costly mistakes, to predict the relative strength of alternative strategies and tactics, and to increase the efficiency of advertising generally.*

---

[2] Peter Langhoff, "Should the Agency Test Copy?" (Speech before the Eastern Annual Conference of the American Association of Advertising Agencies, November 3, 1960).

What to test

Theoretically, any variable subject to the advertiser's control might appropriately be tested. In practice, several factors tend to restrict testing to a small fraction of its potential. These limiting factors are: the role assigned to this kind of research, time, cost, and the efficacy of known testing techniques.

When the assigned role is to provide a quality control check of finished or nearly finished advertisements before they are scheduled for publication or broadcast in costly media, individual messages are tested rather quickly at relatively low cost per test. Such measurements are limited to visual characteristics and text matter that can be handled in assembly line laboratory checks or in speedy field trials. When the assigned role is to guide strategic planning, then many variables inherent in media choices, scheduling, and budgeting, as well as in the message, are tested. Such strategic research requires considerable time, much money, and elaborate experiments.

Message variables   Deciding which variables to test in the advertising message depends on the way the message itself is viewed. If it is treated as a composite, made up of several parts with the strength of the completed structure being no greater than the total strength of the parts, then the variables to be tested in a typical print advertisement would be the headline, the illustration, the body text, the layout, and the typography. This is a mechanistic view that fails to take into account the way the reader, who is not an ad maker, sees the advertisement. The reader is apt to see it as a single entity apart from its technical components.

If the message is treated as a dichotomy, with a distinction being made between "what it says" and "how well it says it," then the variables to be tested would be the selling ideas, the information, and symbolic content on the one hand and the various verbal and visual devices used to impart the content on the other. This, of course, is a fictitious distinction, because ideas cannot be considered apart from the means used to communicate them. A given proposition presented as a single sentence on a three-by-five-inch card can hardly be considered the same as when it is presented in the context of a finished advertisement.

If the message is treated as a gestalt or a totality greater than the sum of its parts, then the variables to be tested would always be presented in the context of an entire advertisement. Time and cost factors in pretest situations, especially for television commercials, might prohibit the preparation of finished ads, but the nearer the finished form the better. Then, any of the variables—appeals, themes, propositions, rhetorical style, symbolic content, visual devices, format, typography, illustration technique, etc.—would be manipulated to measure performance differences in the total message environment.

The farther one gets away from finished ads, the less certain he is that his test results are predictive of the actual results that would be obtained in the marketplace. Rough-cut TV commercials on sound film provide less certainty than do tests of finished commercials; tests of slide films synchronized with a sound track are not as certain as rough cuts; and tests of storyboards narrated by the interviewer are still less certain. There are no simple rules for determining how rough the ad or commercial can be and still yield meaningful test results. For mood commercials the values added by production, staging, casting, music, and sound effects may be crucial. Finished photography may be essential when appetite appeal is the key to influencing consumer attitudes.

Media variables   The alternatives encountered at four levels of media decisions mark the wide range of media testing opportunities.

First, the advertiser must decide which among broad classes of media (newspapers, television, magazines, radio, outdoor, direct mail, etc.) he is to use.

Second, he must decide on the subclasses of media. What kind of newspapers: Daily? Sunday? Evening? Morning? What kind of television or radio: Spot? Network? Regional? What kind of magazines: Women's? Shelter? General? Farm?

Third, he must select specific media vehicles: Which newspapers in Chicago? Which television stations in St. Louis? Magazine A, B, or C? Or all three? What combination of vehicles is to be used?

Fourth, he must specify space units: Full page? Half page? Spread? And broadcast time units: Thirty seconds? Twenty seconds? Sixty seconds? And position: Back cover? Front of book? Sports section? ROP? And television program environment: In what program? Between what programs?

Considerable data bearing on these alternatives are available in the form of circulation reports and audience measurements. Such data are useful, but they do not fully explain differences in media performance. The so-called "qualitative factors" are significant too. Short of testing, the advertiser can only infer the effect of these factors by examining editorial and program content.

Obviously, advertising has to be placed in media to test media alternatives. This can be costly. The cost can be kept down, however, by experimenting in local markets and in regional editions of national magazines. If seemingly sound alternatives are tested, there should be some advertising value received for the space and time costs incurred.

Scheduling variables   Important, but seldom researched, variables are timing, frequency, and continuity. Consumer behavior is influenced by time—season of the year, week of the month, day of the week, and hour of the day. Seasonal influence is obvious in the case of Christmas gift items, Easter bonnets, antifreeze, and swim suits. And good judgment would suggest that advertising of these items be heaviest in the peak buying seasons. But how far ahead should the season be anticipated? We've seen Christmas selling moved ahead to the first part of November. For some gift items perhaps year-round advertising would be more effective than a concentrated schedule in only the gift buying seasons. Not so many years ago grocery advertising in newspapers was heaviest on Friday, the day before the biggest sales day of the week. Now such advertising is heaviest on Thursdays. In other words, traditional assumptions that have guided the timing of advertising are not necessarily valid.

Should the schedule be concentrated in an intensive burst or should it be spread out over a longer period? Should continuity be sacrificed for frequency or vice versa? For the same expenditure should a smaller number of consumers be exposed to the advertising many times or should a larger number be exposed fewer times? The strategic importance of these variables and the paucity of research on them makes scheduling a promising area for testing in the future.

Budgeting variables   How much should be spent for advertising? How should the total be allocated to markets, to media, to sales territories, and to specific items in the product line? These are the most complicated questions of all, not only because the budget affects all other advertising variables but also because all other variables affect the budget. The economizing advertiser recognizes that there can be as much waste in spending too little as in spending too much. But how much is too little and how much is too much? Without some measure of the various yields from various increments of advertising, budget decisions are mere speculations.

Operations research has produced models or theoretical statements of the relationship between budgeting variables and profit yields. Individual advertisers, however, must actually measure these relationships through testing or experimentation before they can be of much use in making budget decisions.

When to test

Testing is appropriate at any stage of the advertising process. In the planning stage it may be used to test the efficacy of alternative appeals or themes. In the execution stage it may be a matter of testing alternative means of presentation. In the quality control stage advertisements may be tested to see that they meet predetermined standards of performance. In retrospect, campaigns may be tested after they have run to determine what results were achieved.

Pre-testing and post-testing are popular terms to distinguish between testing done prior to publication or broadcast and testing done afterwards. Since the variable inherent in selecting media, scheduling, and budgeting cannot be tested without actually running the advertising, the terms pre-testing and post-testing apply only to the measurement of messages. Pre-testing increases the likelihood of preparing the most effective messages before media costs are incurred and before profitable business is lost by failure to run the best advertisements available. Pre-testing should be to advertising what the proving ground is to the automobile manufacturer. It should eliminate weaknesses before consumers force such elimination either by indifference or by negative response to inferior advertisements.

Post-testing requires a greater expenditure of money and time, but it permits testing of advertisements under actual running conditions and overcomes the artificiality of pre-test situations. Some of the advantages of both post-testing and pre-testing can be enjoyed when advertisements are run on a small scale in a few test markets before embarking on a full-scale national campaign.

When the stakes are high—when millions of dollars are invested in an advertising program or in a single theme, when thousands of dollars are spent to run a single advertisement, when advertising is the only or the dominant selling force in the marketing mix—these are times when testing would seem to be most appropriate. Yet, it would behoove the small-scale advertiser to test, too. Efficiency is a relative concept. The dollar amount may not be as great in small business, but the importance of efficiency may be even greater. As we shall see in subsequent chapters, simple, inexpensive tests can be tailor made for the small advertiser, just as more elaborate ones can be designed to meet the more complex problems of the big spenders.

Testing may be done sporadically or continuously depending on the role assigned to it—sporadically, if only called upon when the experts disagree or when the client demands; continuously, if used for quality control or as an approach to seeking optimum solutions to advertising problems.

How to test

There is no single best way to test. Different techniques have been developed to test different advertising variables in terms of different aspects of effectiveness. We have seen, for example, that pre-testing techniques are well suited to measuring message variables but are not appropriate for measuring media, scheduling, and budgeting variables. Also, it is apparent that television and radio messages call for techniques different from those used in testing magazine advertisements. Since the ultimate purpose of most advertising is to increase sales profitably, it would seem that a test which would tell us how sales would be affected by alternative strategies would be the "best" test. This would be true if there were enough time, enough money, enough importance attached to the problem, and enough confidence in the experimental design to undertake a sales results test. These conditions are prerequisite to such a test because there is no quick and easy way to control all the many factors influencing sales of a product. Seldom do these conditions exist. Usually, the advertiser wants quick answers to immediate problems whose solution he does not consider important enough to warrant the investment of a large sum of money.

Since direct measures of sales effectiveness are so seldom practical, researchers have turned to "intermediate criteria" of effectiveness. Reasoning that advertising must function as communication before it can influence a sale, they have designed various tests to measure communication performance in terms of getting attention, arousing interest, transmitting information, building an image, being understood, inspiring confidence, engendering favorable attitudes, registering selling points, portraying benefits, and making a lasting impression. Assuming that persuasion is a gradual process and that the function of advertising is to *predispose* people toward buying, researchers have designed still other tests to measure awareness of the advertised product, knowledge of what it has to offer, attitudes toward it, preference for it, and willingness to buy it. Advertising managers are becoming more concerned with what people think of the *product* as a result of advertising, not merely with what people think of the *advertising* itself:

> The purpose of an advertisement is not just to get itself seen. It is not just to get itself heard or read. The purpose of an advertisement is to convey information and attitudes about a product (service, company, cause) in such a way that the consumer will be more favorably disposed toward its purchase.
>
> . . . Obviously, an ad must be seen before it is read. Obviously a viewer must physically be present to receive a television announcement. *Traffic counts* of the number of people who are exposed to ads, who stop, look and read, or listen, are necessary and helpful. But they do not go far enough. In addition we need to know—
>
> . . . How many *more* people are *more acutely aware* of our brand or company name after being exposed to our advertising?
>
> . . . How many more people comprehend the features, advantages and benefits of the product because of the advertising?
>
> . . . How many more people are favorably disposed (rationally or emotionally) toward the purchase of the product?
>
> . . . How many more people have gone the whole route—taken action by asking for, or reaching for, the product?[3]

In a sense, every test is an experiment to measure the relationship between advertising variables on the stimulus side and changes in perception, knowledge, attitudes, predispositions, and other relevant behavior on the response side. In the ideal experiment the research works on the

[3] Russell H. Colley, *Defining Advertising Goals for Measured Advertising Results* (New York: Association of National Advertisers, Inc., 1961).

stimulus side with one variable at a time or with several variables the interactions of which he precisely controls, and on the response side with measures that clearly isolate the effects of the stimulus variable. Such ideal experimental conditions seldom, if ever, are obtained in advertising where causation is multiple, complex, and simultaneous—where each stimulus variable produces many effects and each effect is the result of many causes. The researcher, therefore, must exercise considerable judgment in deciding which measure of response is to be used.

> If he tries to measure too many aspects of advertising performance at once he will end up in a state of confusion. If he measures only one or two peripheral aspects of advertising effectiveness very neatly, his results will seem too sterile and unrealistic to those who must use the test results for decision making. If he uncritically equates recall with impact or attitude change with sale in the mind he may often be making wholly unwarranted leaps of faith.[4]

Sound sampling procedures should be used in testing as in all forms of advertising research. Test results can only be generalized to real life if the people on whom the test is conducted are representative of the advertiser's market. When pre-testing messages that are designed to reach a particular market segment through a particular medium, the sample should be made up of people in that segment who are likely to be exposed to that medium. When experimenting in test market areas, the areas selected should be representative of the broader market which the advertising eventually will reach. Size of the sample should be governed by the purpose of the test. For quality control purposes—to avoid mistakes, to check on comprehension of specific phrases, to check on believability of claims—relatively small samples may be adequate. If 25 out of the first 30 respondents get a wrong impression from a proposed advertisement, it should not be necessary to complete 100 interviews to discover that something is wrong with the ad. On the other hand, the testing of alternative themes for a major campaign may require a relatively large sample to assure selection of the strongest theme. In post-testing, a large number of interviews may be necessary to reach an adequate subsample of respondents who were exposed to the advertising in question.

Where to test

Where is the test to be administered: In a laboratory or in the field? How are the advertising variables to be exposed to respondents: Artificially or naturally? How are responses to be obtained: Forced or voluntary?

In laboratory testing, consumers are brought individually or in a group

---

[4] Leo Burnett Co., Inc., Research Department. Unpublished report on advertising pretests.

into a studio or auditorium where they are confronted with some form of advertising—print, television, or radio. Print ads are handed to them separately, or bound in a dummy magazine, or projected on a screen, or shown through some kind of apparatus to vary the illumination, distance, exposure time, or visual field. Television commercials are projected on a large screen or transmitted via closed-circuit to a regular television set. Taped radio commercials are piped through a studio sound system or through standard receiving sets. Responses to the material presented are obtained in various ways—through direct questioning, written questionnaires, rating scales, preexposure to postexposure changes in attitudes and brand preferences, or through various kinds of laboratory apparatus, such as opinion-voting machines, eye cameras, the psychogalvanograph, the tachistoscope, and binocular rivalry test equipment.

Laboratory testing offers the advantages of speed, low cost, and a high degree of control. The researcher can be sure that the respondents saw, read, or heard the material in question. He can control the way they were exposed. He can measure responses immediately, before confusion and forgetting intervene. He can use technical apparatus for presenting the material and measuring response. He can pretest some material, television commercials for example, that could not be as readily presented in the field. However, the validity of laboratory findings is questionable. Forced exposure in such a setting does not square with "real life." The people who agree to serve as subjects for such tests may not be representative of the advertiser's market.

Testing in the field does not necessarily overcome the obstacles of the laboratory. If a respondent in her home is shown some advertisements, or is asked to look through a magazine, or to watch a commercial, the exposure is forced and artificial. Some researchers have sought to reduce artificiality by inserting test ads in a dummy magazine or in a limited number of copies of a regular magazine and by leaving these magazines in the home for normal reading. On the response side, whether a respondent is questioned in the laboratory or in the home, his or her reaction to the advertisement is likely to be different than it would be in the normal course of events. However sophisticated the measuring device, it "always represents a less-than-perfect means of *inferring* something about the respondent's reaction to the advertisement. The research has no *direct* way of observing whether or not the correspondent is more or less aware of, interested in, or apt to buy the product. This automatically means that any reaction obtained to the advertisement includes reactions to both the advertisement *and* the test."[5]

Controlled experiments, in which the advertising is actually published or broadcast and the voluntary responses of consumers are objectively

[5] Ibid.

observed, offers the most promise for testing under "real" conditions. Such experiments are designed so that one sample of consumers is exposed to the advertising variable and another sample is not. If a significant difference in the active response of the two samples is observed, the difference is attributed to the advertising variable. The exposed and nonexposed samples can be achieved in advance by using split run or by selecting several local market areas, some of which will get the advertising and the others won't. Or, the two samples can be isolated through audience-tracing techniques after the advertising has run. Differences in the overt responses of the two groups are registered in the form of inquiries, mail orders, or product purchases. Controlled experiments will be discussed further in Chapter 27.

Considering all the various combinations of exposure techniques and response measures, it is no wonder that such a wide variety of tests are used. For classification purposes the response side has dominated. Thus, tests are generally classified as those based on opinion and attitudes, those based on recognition and recall, those based on inquiries, and those based on sales results.

Criteria for testing the test

We have noted that instead of a single test there are many different techniques to test different variables in terms of different aspects of effectiveness. It is apparent, therefore, that testing itself poses challenging problems in decision making, the very process it is intended to serve. The skilled researcher should be called upon to design and execute most tests, especially the more complicated ones. However, the decision maker, whatever his particular role in advertising, should be well enough informed to evaluate test results in terms of their validity, reliability, and relevance.

Validity   The most important question that needs to be raised regarding any test concerns its validity—does the test actually measure what it purports to measure? The question is not intended to cast doubt on the researcher's integrity, although this might be appropriate at times, but rather to challenge the test itself. The determination of validity requires some criterion of the performance the test is designed to predict. For example, if a pretest is designed to predict the sales effectiveness of alternative themes, some criterion of ultimate sales effectiveness would be required to validate the test. But sales resulting from an advertising theme are exceedingly difficult to trace. Consequently, tests usually resort to compromise measures (attention, comprehension, believability, memorability, etc.) and are formulated in terms of *inferred* psychological functions for which no objective verification is available. The tests are validated "logically," but not "empirically."

Empirical validation would involve the comparison of two sets of data, test scores, and criterion measures, on the same advertising variable. A high correlation between test scores and criterion measures would indicate a high degree of validity for the test. For example, to validate a consumer opinion test to be used by a mail-order advertiser in selecting selling themes, ultimate mail-order sales would be the criterion. Test scores would be obtained for several different themes. Then all the themes would be used in a split run and records would be kept on the volume of mail orders produced by each theme. A high correlation between test scores and mail orders would signify that the themes which scored high on the test had been relatively successful in producing mail orders, while those scoring low on the test had been inferior producers of orders. A low correlation would indicate little correspondence between test scores and criterion measures, and hence poor validity for the test.

Reliability   The reliability of a test refers to the consistency of results obtained when the same advertising variable is tested again and again. If the results varied sharply from one application to the next, the testing technique would be in doubt. In its broadest sense, test reliability indicates the extent to which differences in test results are attributable to errors of measurement or to factors not controlled in the test. Thus, when the researcher tries to maintain uniform testing conditions by controlling the sample, the testing environment, the instructions to respondents, the wording of questions, the recording of responses, time limits, and other such factors, he is seeking to make the test results more reliable. The most obvious method for determining reliability is to repeat the same test of the same advertising variable on successive matched samples of respondents. The higher the correlation from application to application the greater is the test's reliability.

Relevance   Since it is not practical to test every aspect of advertising performance every time, careful attention must be given to the relevance of the variables and response measures selected. Whenever possible the test should go to the heart of the most important decisions. It should not dwell on peripheral matters that might be neatly measured but which contribute little to overall efficiency. Perhaps too much testing time has been devoted to mechanical details such as the logotype, the typography, the layout, the size, position, color versus black-and-white, and not enough to the underlying proposition, the symbolic content, and the meaningfulness of the message. Media costs represent the biggest outlay of funds, but relatively few substantial tests of media variables have been done. It may well be that the more important the matter, the more difficult it is to test. But if difficulty is permitted to overrule importance there can be little progress.

The test should be relevant to the particular advertising objectives at hand. If the objective is to launch a new product or a new improvement in an established product, the test should focus on the news value, excitement, and brand identification in the advertising. If the objective is to obtain new users of the product, the test should focus on attitude change among nonusers. If the objective is to offset competitive claims, the test should focus on the strength of the appeal and believability. If the objective is to build an image, that is what the test should measure. In other words, tests should be designed to fit the problem, problems should not be cut to fit existing testing techniques.

QUESTIONS AND PROBLEMS

1   One view states that each advertising situation represents a unique combination of circumstances. If so, what value would there be in storing test results for future use?

2   If a firm estimates the maximum possible loss it might incur in mounting a new national advertising campaign to be $4 million and assumes the chances of such a loss occuring to be 1 in 20, how much would you recommend they spend on testing?

3   William Bernbach maintains that "execution is content," that the way an idea is executed in the finished advertisement largely determines what the idea is. What bearing should this have on designing a test of alternative television commercials?

4   Media costs on the average represent about 80 percent of total advertising costs. Therefore, testing alternative media plans is the most expensive testing of all. Do you agree? Explain.

5   Distinguish between pre-testing and post-testing. What are the merits of each?

6   What response measures other than sales do you suggest for testing the communication effectiveness of alternative magazine advertisements?

7   The director of research in one of the leading advertising agencies uses the term "copy research" instead of the term "copy testing" when referring to the agency's work in attempting to predict the relative effectiveness of alternative copy approaches. Which of these two terms do you think would be more acceptable to copywriters?

8   It has been said that if the researcher "measures only one or two peripheral aspects of advertising effectiveness very neatly, his results will seem too sterile and unrealistic to those who must use the test results for decision making. . . ." How can the researcher solve this problem?

9   How might it be possible to find out if advertising test measures themselves are really impartial and accurate?

10   Do you think people behave differently when they are being asked questions about their behavior than they would normally? Why? How could this affect test results?

11   Would it be better to measure the consumer's attitude toward the advertisement or the consumer's attitude toward the product after seeing the advertisement? Why?

12   It is said that "any reaction obtained to the advertisement includes reactions to both the advertisement *and* the test." Is there some way to separate these reactions for measurement? What would it be?

25

Opinion and attitude tests

How well alternative advertisements ultimately perform in generating sales is determined by how well they perform in communicating to the people they are intended to influence. On the assumption that the people to be influenced can be helpful in selecting the advertisement most likely to influence them, various tests have been designed to tap this source of intelligence. The principal methods for obtaining consumer reactions are (1) those that ask for rankings, (2) those that employ a series of direct questions, (3) those that seek to measure attitudes through the use of rating scales, and (4) those that probe for underlying reactions through indirect questioning or projective techniques. Whichever of these methods is used, the first step is to select an appropriate sample of consumers.

Selecting the test group

In selecting a test group of consumers, as in selecting any sample, the first question to be answered is: What large group of consumers is the relatively small test group intended to represent? Or, in other words, what universe is to be sampled? A partial answer might be that the test group should represent the consumers to whom the advertising is addressed. But to *what* consumers is the advertising addressed? To present buyers or prospective buyers or both? To a narrow, well-defined market segment or a broad anonymous public? To consumers who are regular users of the

558

medium which will carry the message or to consumers who seldom, if ever, are exposed to the medium? It would seem that the target audience, and therefore the universe, should be composed of prime prospects whose characteristics are well defined and who are regular users of the scheduled medium. However, for many products such prime prospects are not clearly identified, and, even if they were, the individual members of such a universe could not be readily isolated for testing purposes. As a result, test groups of respondents are apt to be selected by judgment sampling instead of probability sampling methods.

Selecting respondents for personal interviews is relatively simple when the advertiser's market is highly concentrated geographically or when it is so widespread that a high percentage of the general public can be considered prospects. Selection is most difficult when the advertiser has a thin national market. If the test is to be conducted by mail, which is especially appropriate for industrial advertisers, the difficulty of selection depends on the quality of available mailing lists.

The problem of sample bias or lack of representativeness is ever present when selecting test groups. Some consumers are more available and more willing to serve as respondents than others. Women generally are more available than men. People who have a high regard for their own opinions are more apt to serve than those who are not so sure of things. On the assumption that it does not significantly affect validity of the test some researchers are willing to tolerate a biased sample. However, the possibility that selected respondents do not reflect the opinons of all prospects should not be overlooked.

Size of the sample often is governed by the responses registered in successive interviews. If a high degree of consistency is noted in the early opinions expressed, a relatively small sample, perhaps 30 to 40, is likely to be considered adequate. If opinions are more evenly divided, a larger sample is used. However, consistency alone should not be the determinant of sample size. Early interviews might be concentrated among a narrow segment of prospects whose similar reactions do not reflect the wider differences of opinion that would be expressed by segments not yet reached. Sample size should be determined by balancing factors such as the heterogeneity of the advertiser's market, the variance in anticipated responses, the probable error to be tolerated, the time available, and the funds provided for the test.

Rankings

The most direct approach to gauging consumers' reactions is to show them a few proposed advertisements and ask which one they think would be most effective. In the early days of testing this is what was done. The method was called the "consumer-jury test," reflecting the role of jurors rendering a verdict. The idea of going to the consumer has prevailed, but some refinements have been made in the criteria for judging effectiveness.

As indicated in the following questions different criteria might be used:

1. Which advertisement do you *like* best?
2. Which advertisement do you find most *interesting?*
3. Which advertisement *convinces* you most of the superiority of the product?
4. If you were looking through a magazine, which advertisement would you most likely *notice* first?
5. Which advertisement would you most likely *read* first?
6. Which advertisement would most likely cause you to *buy* (name of product)?

The first three questions involve immediate reactions—*liking, interesting, convincing.* The last three questions are hypothetical and require the respondent to speculate what his behavior would be if he were exposed to the advertisements in the normal course of events sometime in the future. The first three are likely to yield more valid results, but are not as relevant to ultimate buying behavior. The last question is the most relevant, but the least likely to produce valid results. Researchers tend to favor the immediate, nonhypothetical, nonspeculative criteria. They question the ability of people to predict ultimate responses to advertisements encountered in artificial test situations.

Dissatisfaction with a single criterion has led some researchers to seek opinons on several bases—interest, comprehension, believability, personal pertinence, etc. For example, each respondent might be asked to rank the advertisements on the basis of three or four of the above listed questions. However, once he has registered his opinion on the first criterion, chances are he will rank the ads in the same order on subsequent criteria. He is apt to rank the best-liked ad highest in all respects. Psychologists call this the "halo effect."

Whatever criterion is specified, there is no assurance that it will be interpreted by respondents as the researcher intends, or that it will be used at all in reaching an opinion. Asking consumers to rank ads on the basis of believability in no way guarantees that their choices will be made on the basis of believability. Some kind of undefinable feeling may be the controlling factor. Also, respondents tend to vote against negative appeals and hard selling copy, yet such approaches often are effective in advertising.

Ranking techniques

When more than two advertisements are tested, it is desirable to have the respondent select not only the best, but also the second best, the third best, and so on. Two methods used to facilitate comparison and ranking are: (1) order-of-merit and (2) paired comparisons.

Order-of-merit method In the order-of-merit method the respondent is handed the several proposed advertisements and asked to arrange them in rank order. Score sheets indicating the rankings by each respondent are compiled to obtain a composite picture of the rankings by the entire test group. Table 25–1 illustrates the composite score sheet from a test involving 8 advertisements and 25 respondents. By averaging the scores the relative standing of each advertisement can be observed. Thus, ad F in first place with an average score of 2.52 fared considerably better than ad H with an average score of 6.04.

When asked to rank more than six or seven advertisements, several of which appear to have nearly equal merit, the respondent finds that the task is rather difficult. The paired comparisons method, to be described next, makes the task somewhat easier.

TABLE 25–1
Opinions of 25 respondents concerning the relative merit of eight advertisements

Respondents	Advertisements							
	A	*B*	*C*	*D*	*E*	*F*	*G*	*H*
1	1	5	7	8	3	4	2	6
2	4	7	6	3	2	1	5	8
3	1	8	5	3	4	2	7	7
4	6	4	2	1	5	3	8	7
5	2	7	4	6	3	5	1	8
6	5	8	3	2	4	1	7	6
7	2	7	6	5	4	1	8	3
8	7	6	5	4	1	2	3	8
9	2	5	7	8	6	1	4	3
10	4	6	8	5	1	2	3	7
11	3	2	1	4	7	5	6	8
12	5	7	6	2	4	3	1	8
13	3	8	7	1	6	2	5	4
14	4	7	8	5	3	2	6	1
15	2	4	8	6	3	1	5	7
16	4	3	6	1	8	7	2	5
17	1	3	7	6	4	2	5	8
18	1	2	8	3	6	4	7	5
19	6	7	2	5	1	3	4	8
20	5	8	7	2	6	1	3	4
21	4	1	2	7	8	5	3	6
22	1	6	3	5	7	2	8	4
23	5	7	3	4	2	1	6	8
24	5	2	7	4	3	1	6	8
25	4	8	6	1	7	2	3	5
Total	84	138	134	101	108	63	118	151
Average	3.36	5.52	5.36	4.04	4.32	2.52	4.72	6.04
Rank	2	7	6	3	4	1	5	8

TABLE 25–2
Individual scorecard in paired comparison test

	A	B	C	D	E	F	G	H
A	—							
B	A	—						
C	C	C	—					
D	A	B	C	—				
E	E	E	C	E	—			
F	A	B	C	D	E	—		
G	G	G	C	G	G	G	—	
H	A	B	C	D	E	H	G	—

Paired comparisons method This method consists of comparing each advertisement with every other advertisement in the group. At any one time, only two advertisements are being judged. As each comparison is made, the winner of the pair is listed. Then another pair is compared and the winner listed. This procedure is continued until each advertisement has been paired with each of the others. The number of comparisons necessary increases rapidly as the number of advertisements increases. The number of comparisons is equal to

$$\frac{n\,(n-1)}{2}$$

where n equals the number of advertisements. Thus, where 8 advertisements are to be ranked, 28 comparisons will be necessary. This is about the upper limit for number of advertisements. If the number is any larger, the procedure becomes too burdensome.

Table 25–2 shows how a scorecard would look after a respondent had completed the comparisons for eight advertisements. A letter representing each ad is listed along the top and at the side of the card. Ad A is compared with B and the winner of these two is listed in the square opposite B. Then A is compared with C and the winner listed opposite C. After A has been compared with all others, B is compared with the remaining six, then C with the remaining five, and so on. A single count of the number of times each ad won would determine the ranking. For the score card in Table 25–2 the ranking is as follows:

	A	B	C	D	E	F	G	H
Number of times a winner.........	4	3	7	2	5	0	6	1
Rank...........................	4	5	1	6	3	8	2	7

To reduce the "halo effect" in the paired comparison method an advertisement from one pair would not be used in the next succeeding pair. When comparing five or more ads it is possible to arrange a sequence of different pairs—AB, CD, AE, BD, AC, DE, BC, etc. The sequence should be rotated through successive interviews. Another refinement would be to alternate each ad between left-hand and right-hand position as it is presented to the respondent. This would reduce position bias.

The rankings compiled in any opinion test should be subjected to appropriate statistical tests of significance to determine whether or not the differences among scores are due to respondent opinions or to chance.

Evaluation

Opinion rankings are open to question on several counts. Do respondents report their own reactions or do they turn "expert" and try to estimate other people's reactions? Are the reactions reported in an interview situation apt to be the same as those occurring in normal exposure? Are the criteria used by respondents relevant to advertising effectiveness? Are opinion tests discriminating enough to establish significant differences between advertisements of similar quality?

Chances are that many respondents do assume the role of "expert" or "critic," a role they are not asked to fill. There is a strong possibility that respondents employ irrelevant criteria, such as "cleverness" or "cuteness," and seek to make favorable impressions on the interviewer by ranking rational, pleasant, neutral advertisements ahead of emotional, negative, intrusive ones. The few attempts that have been made to check the validity of opinion tests have indicated that such tests are successful in discriminating between extremely good and extremely bad advertisements, a distinction the advertiser himself generally has little difficulty in making. However, they are not as successful in differentiating ads of similar quality, the kind of task the advertiser is most likely to assign to testing. In other words, opinion tests function well when least needed, and not so well when most needed.

Consumer opinions can serve a useful purpose, however, and they still are sought, but more often for checking on particular strengths or weaknesses in individual advertisements than for ranking alternative ads.

Direct questioning

To avoid the pitfalls of rankings but still gain the benefit of consumer reactions, a series of questions might be asked to elicit a fuller range of responses to the advertising in question. What does the advertising say? What does it mean? What effect, if any, does exposure to the advertising have on perception of the product? What uniqueness, if any, does it give the product? Is it believable? Is the message relevant to the consumers' needs and wants? For example, in testing a proposed TV commercial for Ban spray deodorant in which there was a demonstration to show that "Ban goes on dry and stays dry," the following questions were asked.

1. What was said in the commercial? (Probe)
2. What was shown in the commercial? (Probe)
3. In your own words what do you think the manufacturer was trying to tell you in order to get you to try Ban deodorant?
4. Did the commercial say anything new or different about Ban?
5. If "yes," ask: What was new or different? (Probe)
6. The commercial you saw compared Ban to another leading deodorant. What do you think is the main difference between the two deodorants?
7. How did the commercial say and show Ban is better than other deodorants?

From the consumers' answers to such questions and the accompanying verbatim comments the researcher can infer how well the message communicated the key copy points. In the "verbatims" the researcher can detect more subtle reactions. Also, in the language of consumer comments there often can be found language that is appropriate for advertising. For example, some of the verbatim comments elicited in the test of the Ban commercial were:

> Women in the elevator with a man wearing glasses. The glasses are removed and each lens is sprayed with a different deodorant. Ban leaves the lens clear and the other one makes the lens filmy.
>
> Judy and her girl friend went into an elevator, I think, and pulled out two cans of spray deodorant. Judy had Ban and the other girl had some other brand. They started discussing them. Judy yanked off a poor defenseless man's glasses. She sprayed one deodorant on one side of the glasses and Ban on the other. One deodorant was runny. Ban was almost dry. It's not sticky.
>
> The gals were taking off a guy's glasses and spraying their deodorants on them. One was wet and the other was dry. Ban was the one that was dry. The other deodorant was drippy. Ban is dry . . . not drippy.
>
> Ban sprayed on dry—not wet. Keeps you dry. Ban wasn't messy or runny. You get comfort plus protection with Ban.
>
> It's new dry Ban that has some feature to keep you dry all day long. It prevents the wetness you get sometimes under your arms. They sprayed it on eyeglasses and one was foamy and fogged up, but the Ban didn't because of the new ingredient. I'd say that it has been improved.

To capture the tone and inflections of verbatim comments and to observe the interaction among several respondents when exposed to the same advertising at the same time, many agencies conduct "focus group interviews." A small sample of consumers, usually not more than ten, are assembled in a "home like" room furnished and decorated much like a typical living room. The proposed commercials are projected on the screen of a standard television set. Then an interviewer encourages the group to respond freely to what they have seen as well as to what other members of the group have to say. The interviewer's questions are open ended and serve mainly to give some direction to the discussion. Ordinarily, to enhance uninhibited responses the interviewer does not record the discussion. A concealed microphone and tape recorder are used to serve that purpose. Occasionally, a two-way mirror is installed as part of the room's decor to permit observers outside the room to see, as well as hear, the group's reactions. While it may not always be the practice, it would seem appropriate that the group be advised that they are being recorded and observed.

Direct questioning is useful for diagnostic purposes, for discovering *why* one strategy or tactic is better than another. Questions can be asked to examine each strategy in depth—to discover its sources of strength or weakness, to see the essence of its appeal, or to reveal the root of its potential failure. Direct questioning is especially effective for testing alternatives in the early stages of development. In effect, this asks consumers to be participants in ad making at a time when their reactions can best be acted upon. Once creative work progresses to the point where professional reputations have been put on the line and substantial funds have been committed to nearly finished production, test results are likely to be accepted only if they confirm decisions that already have been made.

ATTITUDE MEASUREMENT

An attitude is defined as a predisposition to react in an evaluative way—to like or not like, to feel "it's for me" or "it's not for me"—toward a designated class of stimuli. As such, attitudes cannot be directly observed, but must be inferred from overt behavior, both verbal and nonverbal. Attitude scales in general use are designed to provide a measure of a person's relative position along a continuum from favorable to unfavorable concerning a particular issue or object. The respondent is confronted with a number of statements which are relevant to the behavior in question and asked to indicate his position on the scale. Positions on the scale are numbered or assigned numbers in scoring. Statement scores can be combined to get a group score. Attitude information also is obtained through nonscaling methods such as depth interviewing and projective techniques.

On the assumption that advertising should engender favorable attitudes toward itself as well as the product, some form of attitude measurement is incorporated in many test designs. Some tests deal with attitudes toward components—themes, messages, media, etc. Others deal with attitudes toward the overall advertising effort. Still others deal with attitudes toward the thing advertised—the product, the brand, the corporation. Researchers who feel compelled to stop short of measuring sales results are inclined to treat attitude change as an appropriate measure of advertising effectiveness.

A survey of research directors of the 50 largest advertising agencies revealed that attitude tests are highly valued as a research tool. Attitude was the highest rated criterion for determining *campaign* effectiveness, and was considered to have "high" value for testing single advertisements.[1]

Rating scales

A popular scaling device is the *semantic differential,* which requires respondents to make repeated judgments against a series of bipolar-adjectival scales. To see how this works, look at the picture of the man in Figure 25–1. Is he sad or is he cheerful? Is he worried or unworried? The advertiser knew what kind of mood he wanted this picture to project, but would consumers see it that way? To find out, he ran a test using the semantic differential. Respondents were shown the picture and rating scale and asked to "rate where this man fits on these scales."

The majority of respondents rated the man in the mood that was intended and the picture was used with the headline, "Peaceful Outlook Pictured Here."[2]

The principal advantage of the semantic differential is its simplicity. Also, when administered quickly, it might elicit the kind of spontaneous responses that reveal underlying attitudes more clearly than would lengthy deliberation. In its simplicity, however, lies its weaknesses. Some attitudes cannot be verbalized. The adjectives used may not reveal the most important attributes of the thing judged. Words have different meanings and the intervals on the scales are perceived differently by different people.

Another scaling technique, sometimes referred to as a *three-dimensional* or *trivariant* test, is especially appropriate for evaluating a relatively large number of possible advertising themes. Each theme is typed on a 3 x 5 card. The cards are shuffled and handed to the respondent one at a time. The respondent is asked to rate each theme on a scale according to a particular criterion, such as *desirability* of the claimed feature or benefit. Then the cards are shuffled again, and the respondent goes through the deck again rating each theme according to another criterion,

[1] Lee Adler, Allan Greenberg, and Darrell B. Lucas, "What Big Agency Men Think of Copy Testing Methods," *Journal of Marketing Research,* Vol. 2 (November 1965), pp. 339–45.

[2] Persham C. Nahl, "Speedy, Inexpensive Pretests of Ads—Capsule Case Histories," Proceedings, Fourth Annual Conference, Advertising Research Foundation (New York: October 2, 1958), p. 55.

FIGURE 25–1
Is he sad or is he cheerful? Is he worried or unworried?

                                               Average

Rich	(——)	(——)	(——)	(——)	(——)	(——)	(——)	Poor
Short	(——)	(——)	(——)	(——)	(——)	(——)	(——)	Tall
Healthy	(——)	(——)	(——)	(——)	(——)	(——)	(——)	Unhealthy
Worried	(——)	(——)	(——)	(——)	(——)	(——)	(——)	Unworried
Likeable	(——)	(——)	(——)	(——)	(——)	(——)	(——)	Unlikeable
Cheerful	(——)	(——)	(——)	(——)	(——)	(——)	(——)	Sad

FIGURE 25–2
Three-dimensional evaluation—coffee claims

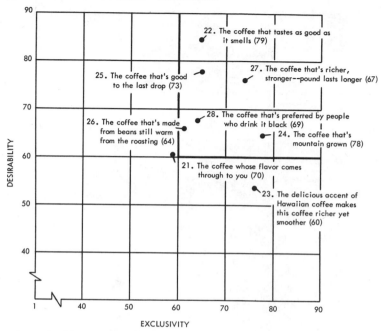

Note: Believability scores are in parentheses.

exclusivity or *uniqueness*. The same procedure is followed to obtain ratings in terms of a third criterion, *believability*. Those themes that score high on all counts are then considered to be most promising.[3]

A trivariant test of eight themes for advertising coffee yielded results as graphed in Figure 25–2.[4] Those themes appearing in the upper right-hand part of the graph were rated best on the two dimensions of desirability and exclusivity. The numbers in parentheses indicate the believability scores. The proposed theme, the subject of the test, was number 23: "The Delicious Accent of Hawaiian Coffee Makes This Coffee Richer Yet Smoother." It ranked among the top three themes in terms of exclusivity, but it ranked lowest on desirability and believability. It should be noted, however, that the top four themes had been heavily advertised over a considerable period of time prior to the test. The high ranking of these themes might have resulted from successful advertising, as well as any

[3] Dik Warren Twedt, "New 3-Way Measure of Ad Effectiveness," *Printers' Ink,* September 6, 1957, pp. 22–23.

[4] William A. Mindak, "Selecting Copy Themes or Appeals Via the Use of Trivariant Analysis" (Paper delivered to Association for Education in Journalism annual convention, August 29, 1961).

merit in the themes themselves. Perhaps with equally heavy advertising the proposed theme would have scored among the leaders on all counts. This, of course, is one of the imponderables encountered when testing an unadvertised, unfamiliar idea against those that have become well known through successful advertising. Also, it should not be assumed that desirability, exclusivity, and believability are equally important in every advertising situation.

Changing, building, or maintaining the image that consumers have of a product, a brand, or a company is an important function of advertising. Inasmuch as the image is a composite of attitudes, feelings, and perceptions, scaling techniques are used to delineate images and to measure changes resulting from advertising exposure. For example, the Curtis Publishing Company's research department sought to measure what influence the first two advertisements in a Pontiac campaign would have on the

FIGURE 25–3
Attitude changes after exposure to Pontiac advertisements

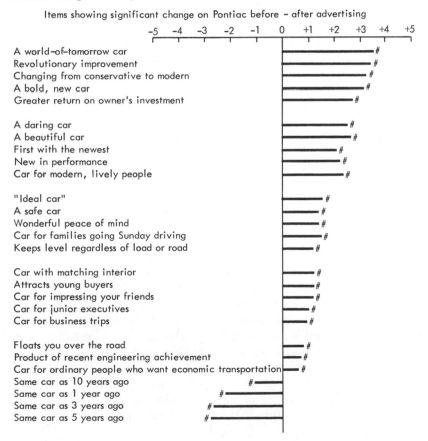

Pontiac image. They developed a list of 51 phrases about automobiles and asked respondents to rate Pontiac on each of the phrases. Then the respondents were shown a magazine containing articles, fiction, and the two advertisements. After exposure to the advertisements, respondents again were asked to rate Pontiac on the same list of phrases. As shown in Figure 25–3, the image profile changed most on the phrases "a world-of-tomorrow car," "revolutionary improvements," "changing from conservative to modern," "a bold new car." These also were the main ideas stressed in the two advertisements which were headlined "A New Kind of Car Is Born" and "Bold New Pontiac." Thus, it was concluded that the two advertisements succeeded in changing the Pontiac image in the desired direction. One might question whether these results indicated attitude changes, or merely that there had been some learning and recall of the advertised themes. Most conjectures on attitude formation suggest that attitudes are not changed so expeditiously.

Brand preferences

Brand preferences, expressed in some manner short of actual purchase, represent another form of attitude measurement. Respondents are asked to rank competing brands prior to exposure to alternative advertising presentations and again after exposure. The presentation that results in the greatest shift of preferences to the advertised brand is presumed to be most effective.

The Schwerin Research Corporation developed a unique procedure for testing television commercials on the basis of brand preference changes. About 350 people are invited to a theater to see some filmed television shows and commercials. Upon entering the theater each person is handed a ticket, the stub of which is torn off and deposited in a box for subsequent drawing in a lottery. Before any testing starts each person is asked to indicate on a check list which brand of a particular product—instant coffee, for example—he wishes to receive a year's supply of if he is the winner in the drawing. Next, the audience is shown the commercial for the brand in question, either in the advertiser's own show or in a special program. Following the viewing of the program and the commercial, the audience is told that as an added gesture of appreciation, a second drawing will be made, and the participants are asked to indicate their choice for the second draw. In this way the difference in the percentage of people choosing the advertised brand before and after exposure to the commercial is observed. Different commercials are tested in separate sessions with different audiences which are intended to be matched samples. The commercial producing the greatest increase in percentage of respondents preferring the advertised brand is assumed to be most effective.

Referring to this technique as a "pre-post" theater test, Fred L. Schlinger, creative research director at the Leo Burnett Company, noted:

> On a purely practical basis, it seems to work better for new products than for established ones. For many established products, these tests are simply not very sensitive. The number of cases where a real and actionable difference can be found is often disappointingly small. We are frequently dealing with small percentage-change scores, and in these cases there is often a serious question about the reliability of the differences.[5]

In addition to brand preference changes, the Schwerin technique requires respondents to record whatever they remember having seen and heard in the commercials.

The chance of winning a year's supply of a brand places some monetary value on the choice decision and presumably encourages more careful deliberation than a simple no-cost, no-reward statement of preference. However, choices made in a lottery can hardly be considered equivalent to choices made in the marketplace. Artificiality of the test situation and the assumption that a single exposure can significantly alter established brand preferences are other weaknesses in the Schwerin technique.

PROJECTIVE TECHNIQUES

We have noted that direct questioning of consumers about the efficacy of alternative advertising ideas forces them to assume the role of expert, to judge on the basis of inadequate criteria, to restrict their responses to the relatively few that can be verbalized, to conceal some of their reactions, and to deal with advertising in a way entirely different from the way they encounter it in everyday life where it influences people without their being particularly aware of it, without their making it the object of a critical analysis. To overcome some of these limitations, depth interviewing and projective techniques are used. Among the more common applications of these techniques in testing are the following: (1) to find out if the proposed advertising conveys the intended image, (2) to determine the emotional impact of the message or the degree to which it stimulates self-reference ("it's for me"), (3) to ascertain the connotations of words and phrases (do they mean what they are intended to mean?), and (4) to see if particular themes or illustrations induce positive or negative reactions.

In a depth interview the respondent is shown the advertising material in question and encouraged to talk freely about it. Instead of seeking specific answers to specific questions, the interviewer stimulates discus-

[5] Fred L. Schlinger, "The Measurement of Advertising Communication: Some Considerations," *Journal of Advertising,* Vol. 3, No. 1 (1973), pp. 12–15.

sion by improvising leading questions as the interview progresses and lets the respondent determine what features of the advertisement are worthy of comment or elaboration. If the respondent is kept talking, it is assumed that eventually traces of his unconscious underlying reactions will come to the surface to be perceived by the interviewer. Such interviews are time consuming and expensive. And so much depends on the competence of the interviewer that lack of competence is a constant threat to reliability. "In fact, the findings of depth interviews are so dependent upon the interpretive abilities of the analyst that some wonder whether the interviews are not merely used as a vehicle for expression of the opinions the analyst has already formed from his accumulated knowledge of human behavior."[6] Yet, when competently done, depth interviewing can provide important insights that are not obtainable through direct questioning and attitude scaling.

On the assumption that people talk more freely in a group and react to the stimulus of comments by others, some researchers use group interviewing for test purposes. Advocates of this technique suggest that respondents enjoy greater security in a group situation and therefore are more apt to express their private views. On the other side it is argued that they may become even more secretive about their true reactions because they would be exposing their inner selves to a number of people rather than to a single interviewer. And there is some likelihood that group discussions are dominated by people who like to hear the sound of their own voices. Here again, however, the skill of the interviewer or psychologist-leader is the critical factor.

Many variations of the projective techniques used in clinical psychology have been applied to the testing of advertising, especially in the developmental stages. Such techniques include word associations, sentence completions, role playing, and, perhaps most dramatic of all, the thematic apperception test (T.A.T.). In the standard thematic apperception test respondents are shown a patented set of pictures of people in an ambiguous form of action and are asked to tell the story of each picture. The idea is that the respondent will project his own true, and perhaps deeply hidden, feelings into the story he tells about the characters in the pictures.

A simple derivation of the T.A.T. is to show respondents a proposed illustration for an advertisement and ask them to tell a story about it. The purpose here, of course, is not to analyze the respondent but rather to test the illustration for self-reference or person pertinence. Is the illustration one in which the respondent readily identifies himself and his kind of people? Does it induce the kinds of reactions the advertiser intended?

Another derivation of T.A.T. is the cartoon technique as demonstrated

    [6] Harry Deane Wolfe, James K. Brown, and G. Clark Thompson, *Measuring Advertising Results* (New York: National Industrial Conference Board, Inc., 1962), p. 151.

FIGURE 25-4
Cartoon test used by Granite City Steel Company

in Figure 25–4. The Granite City Steel Company prepared these cartoon pictures of two farmers talking to each other, with a question in the balloon over one farmer's head and a blank balloon over the other's head. Respondents were asked to imagine what the second farmer would say and give the first answer that came to their minds. It was hoped that the respondent would project his own thoughts into the words he concocted for the second farmer. Using this technique the company learned that their advertising had been effective in informing farmers about the advantages of not accepting substitutes for steel.[7]

Evaluation of any test employing projective techniques must necessarily turn to the qualifications of the researcher. In the hands of skilled, insightful, and professionally trained psychologists such techniques have produced meaningful results. There is ample evidence that they serve the objective of obtaining unguarded responses revealing hidden or subtle reactions. However, the results are difficult to quantify, the tests are not readily duplicated, and the samples are remarkably small. Darrel B. Lucas and Steuart Henderson Britt comment on reliability and validity as follows: "The values of projective techniques in forecasting human behavior can best be understood by admitting that reliability is likely to be low, and that validity is unknown. Even in the clinical applications, for which these methods were invented, projective analysis is not the most precise predictor of subsequent behavior."[8]

But, then, no opinion or attitude test in popular use is noted for its validity. The various techniques for seeking consumer reactions would seem to substitute one kind of uncertainty for another—the uncertainty in testing for the uncertainty in advertising decision making. Again it must be remembered that testing is an aid to, not a substitute for, judgment. The test of reasonableness must be applied to all test results. Insofar as opinion and attitude tests reduce the chances of making costly mistakes and insofar as they give the advertiser greater confidence in the decisions he makes, they serve a useful purpose. Advertising is still an inexact speculation. Testing cannot make it otherwise, only less so.

QUESTIONS AND PROBLEMS

1 An agency research supervisor hands you two ads and says, "Go down to the lobby and ask 30 people what they think of these ads." What would you think of such an assignment?

2 Asking consumers to rank ads on the basis of believability doesn't guarantee that their choices will be made on the basis of believability. Why not?

3 In the respondents' verbatim comments the researcher can detect a wide range of reactions to the advertisement in question. Explain.

4 Clip three different advertisements for the same product and test them in a "focus group interview" using direct questioning.

5 A weakness of the semantic differential is that some attitudes can not be verbalized. Explain and give examples.

6 Pre-post brand preference tests seem to work better for new products than established products. Why?

[7] Ibid., pp. 54–57.

[8] Darrel B. Lucas and Steuart Henderson Britt, *Measuring Advertising Effectiveness* (New York: McGraw-Hill Book Company, Inc., 1963), p. 152.

7   Discuss some ways of reducing or compensating for the halo effect.

8   Which is more important—to find out if people like an advertisement, or to find out how people's attitudes toward the product have been changed as a result of an advertisement?

9   Is it better to find out what a respondent thinks, what he thinks he should think, or what he thinks other people think? Which responses are most likely to be obtained in opinion testing?

10 What advantages, if any, do you see in the use of attitude scales and depth interviewing instead of direct questions calling for such generalized answers as "like" or "dislike" when conducting an opinion test?

11 *Use of an opinion test by a milk company:*

A large New England milk company, with branches in small towns, was meeting sales resistance because it was looked upon as being an "outside" firm. To counteract this negative attitude, the company decided to run an institutional campaign featuring pictures of a different routeman each week and emphasizing the fact that he was a local resident and an active citizen of the town.

A series of 11 ads, spaced one week apart, was to be run in one small town as a test campaign. Each ad with a news story format would also contain quotes concerning the quality of the company's products. If the campaign in this one town produced the desired results, the company planned to expand its use to the other branches. Therefore, it was necessary to find some way of measuring the impact of these advertisements on the townspeople.

Management felt that door-to-door interviewing would prove of little value in measuring effectiveness, and so the group opinion test was chosen.

Procedure:

A group of 26 women, members of a local Women's Club of the town, was selected. The only inducements offered were an opportunity to be of service in furthering basic advertising research and reimbursement for the cost of refreshments served at their weekly meetings.

The actual testing was performed under the name of the advertising agency handling the account, in order to avoid any bias that might be created by revealing the company's name.

The advertisement for the milk company, plus one similar advertisement from each of three competing milk companies were mounted on cardboard. Each woman was asked to rate the ads on readership, sincerity, believability, general feelings, and objective of the company's campaign.

After the rating sheets were filled, discussions with two groups, one rating the campaign "high," the other "low," were led by trained interviewers. A recording was made of the reactions of the respondents as they justified their ratings.

Conclusions:

An analysis of the data revealed: (1) the milk company's ad had comparatively good readership; (2) the purpose of the campaign was identified correctly; and (3) the milk company ad's was rated as less sincere, less truthful, less reasonable, and less friendly than the ads of competitors.

Comments of respondents revolved around a feeling: (*a*) of being tricked by news story format: (*b*) that routemen were not a voluntary part of the advertising campaign; (c) of "corny," crude, simple, undignified, highly emotional appeals; (d) of general negative reaction toward photographs and general tenor of campaign.

As a result of these findings, management decided not to use this type of advertising in other small towns. They also agreed that the ads had failed principally because attempts to create goodwill and sell products in the same advertisement apparently created suspicion and antagonism with many people.

Problem:

1. Do you agree with the decision of the management? Why?
2. Do you think the evidence disclosed by the opinion test was sufficient?
3. Was interviewing respondents as a group, rather than on an individual basis, satisfactory?
4. Evaluate the opinion test in this case for validity and reliability.

26

Recognition
and recall

Whatever its purpose an advertisement must first get itself seen, read, or heard. In the competition for attention one ad might get 80 percent of a magazine's readers to stop, look, and read while another might attract less than 5 percent. Such differences in readership were documented by George Gallup in 1931 in his *Survey of Reader Interest.* Since that time advertisers have been interested in finding out how many people read their ads.

Purchase of the advertised product typically is a delayed response. To bridge the time-lapse between perception of the ad or a series of ads and purchase of the product, lasting impressions must be made, impressions that will be retained long enough to influence behavior at the point of sale. Looking at it another way, advertising is intended to bring about learning, and learning is inseparable from memory.[1] Therefore, the memorability of an ad has long been considered an appropriate index of its effectiveness.

This chapter deals with recognition and recall as measures of ad readership and remembrance.

THE RECOGNITION METHOD

Recognition is simply a matter of identifying something as having been seen before. The aid to memory is the thing to be remembered. To deter-

[1] For a discussion of the implications of memory in advertising see James Playsted Wood, *Advertising and the Soul's Belly* (Athens, Ga.: University of Georgia Press, 1961).

mine whether or not a person saw or read a given advertisement he is shown the ad and asked if he had previously seen or read any part of it. If the answer is "yes," it may be assumed that a previous encounter actually occurred. Yet, as we shall see, such an assumption is open to question.

The staunchest advocate and principal user of the recognition method is Daniel Starch and Staff, who established a syndicated Advertisement Readership Service in 1932. In the course of 43 years of surveys of most leading magazines, Starch ratings have had a considerable influence on copy and layout techniques. The method, as practiced by the Daniel Starch organization, is as follows:

Personal interviews are conducted with a national quota sample of 100 to 150 readers per sex, of each magazine included in the service. To give respondents time to obtain and read their copy, interviewing begins three days after the on-sale date for weekly and biweekly magazines and two weeks after the on-sale date for monthly magazines.

The first step in the interview is to determine if the respondent qualifies as a reader of the issue. He is shown the cover and asked if he has seen or read any part of that particular issue. If he is not sure, he is allowed to look through it to establish whether or not he read it.

After qualifying as a reader of the issue, the respondent goes through it, page by page, with the interviewer and is questioned about each advertisement one-half page or larger in size. Starting points are randomized to equalize the fatigue element in long interviews. The respondent is asked, "Did you see or read any part of this advertisement?" If yes, he is asked to indicate what was seen or read. All data resulting from the interviews are recorded on standardized questionnaires and made available to Starch subscribers in final tabulations as illustrated in Figure 26–1. Results are expressed for three levels of readership: *Noted* is the percent of issue readers who reported they had seen the advertisement in the issue being studied. *Associated* is the percent of issue readers who reported they had seen or read any part of the ad containing the name of the product or advertiser. *Read Most* is the percentage of issue readers who reported they had read 50 percent or more of the reading matter.

When comparing advertisements of different sizes (full page versus half page), or that use a different number of colors (four colors versus black-and-white), or that appear in different media, allowance should be made for the difference in cost. Starch uses the common denominator "readers per dollar," which indicates the number of primary readers attracted by the ad for each dollar invested in space cost. This is calculated by projecting the "noted" score (the percent of issue readers who reported having seen the advertisement) to the total primary readers and dividing by the space cost.

$$\frac{\text{Percent noted} \times \text{Magazine's primary readers}}{\text{Space cost}} = \text{Readers per dollar}$$

FIGURE 26–1

Section from a Starch readership report on *Time*

TIME   FEBRUARY 26 1973   MEN READERS

PAGE	SIZE & COLOR	PRODUCT CATEGORIES / ADVERTISER	COST PENNIES PER READER	RANK IN ISSUE BY NUMBER OF READERS	RANK IN ISSUE BY COST PER READER	PERCENTAGES NOTED	PERCENTAGES ASSOCIATED	PERCENTAGES READ MOST	READERS PER DOLLAR NOTED	READERS PER DOLLAR ASSOCIATED	READERS PER DOLLAR READ MOST	COST RATIOS NOTED	COST RATIOS ASSOCIATED	COST RATIOS READ MOST
		PROFESSIONAL SERVICES												
56	H1/2P4	INTERBANK MASTER CHARGE CARD	1.6	15	2	44	36	11	75	62	19	163	172	238
		BANKING/FINANCE												
53	1P	CARLISLE DECOPPET	3.4	30	24	38	18	6	61	29	10	133	81	125
77	1P	WADDELL & REED	4.8	31	28	17	13	4	27	21	6	59	58	75
		FIRE/CASUALTY INSURANCE												
1	1P	ALLSTATE AUTO INSURANCE	2.2	19	8	41	29	13	65	46	21	141	128	263
3	1P2	TRAVELERS INSURANCE GEN PROM	2.8	21	16	34	28	5	43	36	6	93	100	75
		OFFICE MACHINES/EQUIPMENT												
29	1P2	PITNEY BOWES POSTAGE METER	3.6	25	25	32	22	6	41	28	8	89	78	100
84	1S	GTE INFORMATION SYSTEMS	5.3	23	29	37	24	6	29	19	5	63	53	63
		MAGAZINES/NEWSPAPERS												
88	1P	PSYCHOLOGY TODAY MAGAZINE	3.3	29	22	26	19	6	41	30	10	89	83	125
		PASSENGER CARS/VEHICLES												
32	X 1S4B	CADILLAC ELDORADO CARS	3.3	3	22	62	53	11	35	30	6	76	83	75
39	1P B	FIAT 128 CARS	1.8	11	3	48	40	10	66	55	14	143	153	175
55	1P4B	BUICK CENTURY REGAL CARS	2.1	3	7	59	53	12	53	47	11	115	131	138
64	1P4	FORD PINTO WAGONS	2.0	8	5	55	48	11	57	49	11	124	136	138
69	1P B	AMERICAN MOTORS CORP G P	2.3	17	11	34	31	10	47	43	14	102	119	175
82B	1P	MAZDA CARS	1.3	7	1	54	49	17	86	78	27	187	217	338
		TIRES/TUBES												
25A	1S4	GOODYEAR TIRES	3.1	1	19	69	62	16	35	32	8	76	89	100
		PASSENGER TRAVEL												
10	1P4B	UNITED AIR LINES	2.5	9	13	59	45	11	53	40	10	115	111	125
		RESORTS/TRAVEL ACCOMMODATION												
34	1P4B	WESTERN INTERNATIONAL HOTELS	5.3	26	29	34	21	5	30	19	4	65	53	50
		PERSONAL HYGIENE PRODUCTS												
93	1P	COLGATE DENTAL CREAM	2.5	22	13	29	25	4	46	40	6	100	111	75
		HAIR PRODUCTS												
11	H1/2P2	TEGRIN MEDICATED SHAMPOO	2.0	24	5	32	23	4	68	49	8	148	136	100
		LIQUOR & WHISKEY												
26	1P4B	SEAGRAM'S 7 CROWN WHISKEY	3.2	16	21	49	35	6	44	31	5	96	86	63
41	1P4	CANADIAN CLUB BLENDED WHISKY	1.9	6	4	63	51	10	65	52	10	141	144	125
74	1P4B	GALLIANO LIQUEUR	2.8	11	16	49	40	8	44	36	7	96	100	88
3C	1P4B	JOHNNIE WALKER BLACK LABEL	2.2	5	8	59	52	29-	53	46	26	115	128	325
		TOBACCO/TOBACCO PRODUCTS												
2C	1P4B	BENSON & HEDGES MULTIFILTERS	2.9	14	18	48	39	6	43	35	5	93	97	63
25	1P4	RALEIGH FILTER KINGS/LONGS	2.4	11	12	47	40	5	48	41	5	104	114	63
42	1P4B	KENT FILTER KING SIZE/100'S	3.6	17	25	38	31	9-	34	28	8	74	78	100
72	1S4	WINSTON FILTER KING SIZE	4.3	10	27	49	44	12-	25	23	6	54	64	75
78	1P2B	PALL MALL FILTER EXTRA MILD	3.1	19	19	32	29	2	35	32	2	76	89	25
4C	1P4B	MARLBORO MENTHOL/KINGS/100'S	2.5	2	13	66	57	57-	47	40	40	102	111	500
		- FEWER THAN 50 WORDS IN AD.												
		JEWELRY/WATCHES												
87	1P4B	DE BEERS DIAMONDS	5.3	26	29	38	21	8	34	19	7	74	53	88
		MISCELLANEOUS												
40	2/3P	CHRISTIAN CHILDREN'S FUND	2.2	28	10	31	20	4	69	45	9	150	125	113
		MEDIAN READERS/DOLLAR							46	36	8			

READERS PER DOLLAR ARE BASED ON 4,070,000 MEN READERS AND PUBLISHED ONE-TIME SPACE RATES. READER FIGURES ARE OBTAINED FROM 4,329,535 U.S. A.B.C. CIRC. TIMES PRIMARY READERS PER COPY FROM STARCH MEDIA STUDY.

FIGURE 26–2
Starch readership scores

For example, if full-page advertisement A had a noted score of 25 percent, and half-page B had a noted score of 17 percent; if ad A cost $20,000, and ad B cost $11,000; and if both ads were run in the same magazine which reached 8 million primary readers; the half-page ad would have been more efficient, having attracted 124 readers per dollar as compared to the 100 readers per dollar attracted by ad A.

For quick comparison of ad ratings against par for the issue Starch includes *cost ratios* which express the relationship between readers-per-dollar for each ad and the median average readers-per-dollar for all half-page or larger advertisements. A cost ratio of 175 would mean that the ad scored 75 points above par.

In addition to the information described above, Starch also provides his clients with a copy of the magazine tested and in which each tested advertisement is "tabbed" showing the scores of various *components of the ad.* Thus, the percent of readers (men and women) seeing the *illustration* is given, as well as other components such as the *headline* and *signature.* These "tabs" can be noted in Figure 26–2.

Usefulness of readership scores

More ingenious than the method itself are the many ways that readership data have been used. Without attempting to catalog all the possible analyses here, the following questions are the principal ones that the Starch organization suggest their data be used to answer: To what extent is my advertisement seen and read? Are my present advertisements better read than previous ones? Are my advertisements better read than those of my competitors? Is the reading of my current campaign increasing or decreasing? How can I tell my ad story so that it will be better read?

Most widely used of the Starch data are the "noted" scores. This perhaps reflects many advertisers' preoccupation with getting attention as well as their uncertainty about the meaning of other measures. In any event, "noted" scores are likely to be affected by a number of factors other than the content of the advertisement itself. Some of these factors are: (1) the proportion of the publication's readers who have an interest in the product—readership of an automobile ad placed in *Time* generally would be higher than readership of a cash register ad placed in the same magazine; (2) the number of advertisements in the issue—the greater the number of ads, the lower the average score, such a decrease resulting from respondent fatigue or boredom in the interview situation as well as from the greater competition for attention in the reading situation; (3) degree of reader interest generated by issue's editorial content; (4) time spent reading each issue; (5) position of advertisement in the book; (6) degree of interest in adjacent pages; and (7) exposure to same or similar advertisements in other media. Therefore, when comparing readership scores of different advertisements every attempt should be made to control such outside variables.

Insofar as possible, comparisons should be limited to advertisements for the same type of product appearing in the same medium. Also, determining an advertisement's performance readership-wise is much like establishing a golfer's handicap. Both require an average of many scores.

The typical Starch survey does not classify readers beyond the groupings of men and women. This impairs the usefulness of the data for advertisers who wish to reach a particular market segment. Such advertisers are interested in finding out how many prospective buyers read their ad, not how many men or how many women. It might be assumed that the higher the "noted" score the greater the number of prospects included in the noting group. But this is not necessarily so. Donald R. Murphy demonstrates that it isn't in his book, *What Farmers Read and Like*.[2] Reporting on 20 years of readership research done by two farm papers, *Wallaces' Farmer* and *Wisconsin Agriculturist,* Murphy shows that some ads are more successful than others in attracting likely prospects even though overall "noted" scores indicate otherwise. For instance, two hog feed ads in *Wallaces' Farmer* were noted by about the same number of men readers. But when the readers were classified by ownership of spring pigs, the record for the ads was as follows:

	Total noting	Readers with no pigs	Readers with 1–74 pigs	Readers with 75 pigs or more
Ad X	65	21	14	30
Ad Y	67	6	21	40

It is evident that ad Y attracted considerably more prospects than ad X.

Evaluation

The primary virtue of the recognition method is its simplicity. Available on a syndicated basis, readership data are current, continuous, and inexpensive, costing each subscriber to the Starch service only $25 to $50 per report. The method focuses on pertinent aspects of advertisement performance. The fact that it has been used for so long a time suggests it is serving a useful purpose. Yet, it is a perennial target of much criticism.

Controversy over this and other methods of measuring advertisement reading and remembrance led the Advertising Research Foundation to undertake an elaborate field experiment to test the methods. The ARF's

[2] Donald R. Murphy, *What Farmers Read and Like* (Ames, Iowa: Iowa State University Press, 1962).

Study of Printed Advertising Rating Methods,[3] known as the PARM study, found that the Starch method was reproducible, that sampling procedures were adequate, that it was not overly sensitive to interviewer skill, and that noted scores were not significantly affected by elapsed time since reading, by time spent reading, by age, education, and socioeconomic level of respondents. These findings would seem to represent an endorsement of the method. But to some researchers they were an indictment. Shouldn't "noted" scores decline with the passage of time?[4] Shouldn't they be affected by differences in interviewer skill and by differences in the education level of respondents? If they aren't so affected, are "noted" scores truly a measure of recognition?

The Starch organization agreed that scores should drop with the passage of time and stated that their own studies showed this to be the case, thus casting doubt on the PARM study.[5] Resuming the attack based on PARM data, two researchers, Appel and Blum, reasoned that "since conventional ad recognition methods do not conform to what might be expected either on the basis of learning theory or common sense there was reason to believe that a substantial portion of the variance among advertisements of such recognition measures is attributable to factors other than exposure of a particular ad in a particular magazine issue."[6] They subjected this hypothesis to experimental test and reached the following conclusions:

1. The noted score is not an uncontaminated measure of ad recognition. Only part of the noted score variance is attributable to ad recognition *per se.* The remaining variance is attributable to such factors as consumer interest in the product advertised, nearness to purchase of the brand advertised, etc.
2. There are certain consumers who have a higher tendency to note ads and there are other consumers who have a lesser tendency toward ad noting, regardless of whether they were actually exposed to the ad.
3. This noting set, or tendency to note ads, is related to multimagazine readership. Multimagazine readers are more likely to note ads falsely than nonmultimagazine readers.[7]

It frequently has been demonstrated that some respondents claim to have seen advertisements they could not possibly have seen. The usual

[3] Advertising Research Foundation, *A Study of Printed Advertising Rating Methods* (New York: Advertising Research Foundation, 1956).

[4] Darrell B. Lucas, "The ABC's of ARF's PARM," *Journal of Marketing,* Vol. 25 (July 1960), pp. 9–20.

[5] D. Morgan Neu, "Measuring Advertisement Recognition," *Journal of Advertising Research,* Vol. 1 (December 1961), p. 21.

[6] Valentine Appel and Milton L. Blum, "Ad Recognition and Respondent Set," *Journal of Advertising Research,* Vol. 1 (June 1961), p. 13.

[7] Ibid., p. 14.

FIGURE 26–3

"It may not sell your product, but think of the readership!"

procedure for detecting false claiming is to insert bogus ads among those that actually appeared in the copy of the magazine shown the respondent. Some of the more commonly accepted causes for false claiming are: genuine confusion with other advertising, guessing when uncertain, deliberate exaggeration, deduction that advertisement was seen based on recognition of surrounding material, deduction of likely noting based on memory or knowledge of one's own reading habits, eagerness to please interviewer, hesitation to appear ignorant, misunderstanding of instruction given by interviewer.[8] To these causes might be added the respondent's desire to make a favorable impression on the interviewer. Thus some housewives might be less inclined to report they read a beer advertisement and more inclined to report they read a baby-food ad.

What all this adds up to is considerable confusion about the meaning of readership scores. Yet, the surveys continue to be made and the scores continue to be used. No doubt the users assume that such data reflect something about the attention-getting power of advertisements and therefore can be used to isolate those elements that get more people to stop, look, and read. It was on the basis of readership data that the picture-caption layout and the cartoon technique became widely adopted in advertising. One large food advertiser switched to cartoons and watched readership figures soar, only to find that sales figures did not develop in the same fashion. The company substituted a straight appetite appeal. Readership fell, but sales did well.

[8] Darrel B. Lucas and Steuart Henderson Britt, *Measuring Advertising Effectiveness* (New York: McGraw-Hill Book Co., 1963), p. 60.

It is difficult to assess the long-range utilization of the recognition method as a test of advertising effectiveness. Research directors of the 50 leading advertising agencies were queried relative to their feelings about current testing methods. Although their reactions were varied, there was considerable agreement that "recognition ratings and those methods requiring consumers to judge the effectiveness of copy have only minor value."[9] Thus, this method may give way to other measuring techniques.

LABORATORY TESTS OF RECOGNITION

Recognition has long been used by experimental psychologists to measure perception, learning, and memory. Perhaps the most sophisticated recognition tests of advertisements in a laboratory setting were conducted by HRB-Singer Inc. for the Du Pont Company and the Advertising Research Foundation.[10] The purpose of these tests was to measure the visual efficiency of advertisements having different physical characteristics —different layouts, designs, colors, and typographic treatments. Visual efficiency was measured in terms of how near, how brightly, and how long the ad must be exposed to be subsequently recognized. A fourth measurement was how well the ad competed against other ads for readers' attention.

An apparatus, illustrated in Figure 26–4, was devised to carry out all four visual tests. Apparent distance between subject and ad was controlled by two zoomar lenses. Illumination was controlled by neutral density filters. Exposure time depended on the shutters, which were synchronized and controlled by a solenoid. Binocular rivalry was achieved by presenting two advertisements simultaneously through separate lens systems.

The tests were given to 24 students with normal vision from the Pennsylvania State University. In the distance test, each student viewed 36 different ads in random order under three different settings of apparent distance. The greatest distance was used first, and the shortest last. The three settings were selected so that most ads would not be recognized at the greatest distance. Illumination and exposure time were held constant.

The illumination test was similar to the distance test, except that three levels of illumination, rather than distance, were used. Time and distance were held constant.

The time test was also similar, except that the three presentations varied in length while illumination and distance were held constant. Exposure times used were a fiftieth, a tenth, and a fifth of a second.

In the binocular rivalry test, each presentation consisted of flashing two

[9] Lee Adler, Allan Greenberg, and Darrell B. Lucas, "What Big Agency Men Think of Copy Testing Methods," *Journal of Marketing Research,* Vol. 2 (November 1965), p. 344.

[10] *The Measurement and Control of the Visual Efficiency of Advertisements* (New York: Advertising Research Foundation, 1962).

FIGURE 26–4
Apparatus for testing visual efficiency of advertisements

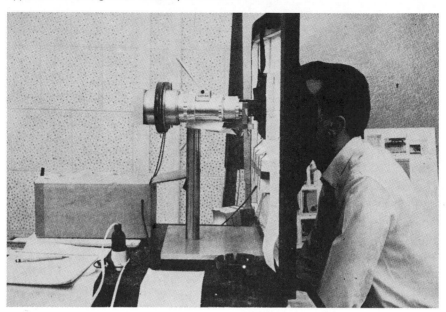

ads simultaneously, one to each eye. Under these conditions a subject usually sees first one of the ads, then the other. Then the first reappears and the second vanishes, and so on. A problem that had to be considered in this test was that of eye dominance. Almost everyone has one eye that sees better than the other, and this could have biased the results. To control this effect, each subject was presented all possible comparisons a second time. On the second presentation of each pair, the ads were switched so that the one formerly presented to the right eye was then presented to the left. Each ad was given a score on this test equal to the number of times it was recognized in preference to the competing ad.

The response required from each subject in each of these tests was simply recognition. After each presentation the subject scanned a large card showing reproductions of the 36 ads plus 6 dummies. The subject then identified the ad he thought he had seen.

Results of these tests indicated that an advertisement to be easily recognized should:

1. Contain a small number of perceptual units for its area
2. Have a dark illustration
3. Have an illustration no more than two or three times as large as its copy area
4. State its headline message directly
5. Have its largest single color darker than the rest of the ad.

These results were no great revelation to experienced advertising men who know the importance of simplicity, contrast, dominance, color, etc. in layout and design. However, by confirming some well-established principles, the laboratory apparatus and procedures developed in these tests should continue to be useful for predicting visual performance of alternative advertisements. The fact that visual performance is only part of the communications spectrum within which advertising functions should never be overlooked.

RECALL TESTS

As a test of memory, recall is more demanding than recognition. Recall involves questioning the respondent about what he has seen or read without having the ad in front of him while he is answering.

Various recall tests differ in the subject matter they deal with and the aid to memory they supply. Some deal with messages that have circulated in either print or broadcast media: How many people recall seeing or hearing the ad? How much and what do they remember about it? Some deal with campaign themes and slogans: How fast and how widely is the theme registering? Some are designed to pretest advertisements prior to circulation: How well are test ads recalled after controlled exposure in a dummy magazine or in a portfolio of ads? Others are designed to find out what people have learned about the product, the company, or the service advertised. The aid to memory or the amount of help given the respondent ranges from merely limiting the field of inquiry to supplying successive cues until little remains to be remembered.

Principal methods currently used are (1) Gallup & Robinson's Impact Post-test, (2) dummy magazine test, (3) portfolio tests, (4) television recall tests, (5) association tests, and (6) knowledge or awareness tests.

Gallup & Robinson's Impact Post-test

Gallup & Robinson's Impact data are gathered through personal interviews which probe magazine readers' ability to describe the ads they have seen and to play back the ideas that the advertiser tried to register.

The respondent is shown the magazine cover and asked if he has read that particular issue. If he reports that he has, he is asked to describe something in it he remembers having seen. If he correctly describes at least one item, he qualifies as an issue reader.

With the magazine remaining closed, the respondent is then handed a deck of cards bearing names of brands and advertisers included in the issue and asked to state which ads he remembers having seen. When this stage of the interview is completed, the respondent is asked to "play back" everything he can remember about each of the ads he mentioned. What did the ad look like? What did it say? Did it increase interest in buying the product? Interviewers are instructed to probe in a neutral fashion, in order to obtain complete information about each ad recalled.

Next, the interviewer opens the magazine to the ads mentioned and asks if these were the ads the respondent was thinking of. The percentage of all qualified issue-readers who successfully associated the brand or advertiser with some specific feature or sales point of the advertisement is referred to as "Proved Name Registration" (PNR).

A unique feature of this method is getting readers to "play back" the main ideas of advertisements. These playbacks provide material for detailed analyses of the ads' strengths and weaknesses.

As one might expect, the PNRs produced by Gallup & Robinson's aided-recall technique are much lower than the "noted" scores produced by Starch's recognition method. How great the difference is was demonstrated in the Advertising Research Foundation's *Study of Printed Advertising Rating Methods.*[11] The average PNRs and noting scores for the same group of ads were:

Proved Name Registration 3.0%
Noting 21.7%

Perhaps the most significant conclusion drawn from the data provided by this study is that the recognition method is more expedient for gathering *quantitative* evidence of advertisement readership, but aided recall with playback gathers more *qualitative* information from the relatively few people who can supply it.

Dummy magazine tests

Dummy magazines are used to pretest advertisements under conditions approximating normal exposure. Gallup and Robinson also pioneered this type of research, and the organization bearing their names conducts regularly scheduled tests in its *IMPACT—The World Today.* This is a dummy magazine containing standard editorial material in which are inserted ads to be pretested as well as a number of control ads which already have been tested in a regular issue of one of the consumer magazines. Interviewers distribute copies of *IMPACT* to a sample of households and ask the recipients to read it some time that day as they ordinarily would read any magazine. The next day the interviewer returns and conducts an aided-recall test as described above.

To test its client's ads, Young and Rubicam advertising agency publishes its own magazine, *New Canadian World,* and follows much the same procedure as Gallup & Robinson. To save the cost of producing a dummy

---

[11] Advertising Research Foundation, *Study of Advertising Rating Methods.*

magazine some agencies obtain advance copies of a real magazine and bind test ads in these copies before distributing them to respondents.

Dummy or altered magazines, in addition to assuring a quasi-natural exposure of test ads, make it possible to control the sample, the number and location of ads in the issue, the editorial environment, and the time interval between exposure and response. Under these circumstances alternative ads for a given product can be inserted in the same page position of alternate copies and tested among matched samples of respondents. Against these advantages must be weighed the fact that exposure is somewhat forced, with the result that recall scores are likely to be higher than they would if obtained after normal exposure.

Portfolio tests

The portfolio test makes no pretense of duplicating normal exposure. This method places the test ad in a folder which also contains a number of control ads. The respondent is handed the folder of ads, asked to look through it and to read just what interests him. When he has finished, the folder is closed and returned to the interviewer. Beginning with a question such as, "What brands and products do you remember seeing ads for?" the interviewer establishes which ads are recalled. Due to the absence of cues this part of the interview is referred to as *unaided recall*. Additional questions, narrowing the inquiry to specific products and brands, are asked to verify recall and to find out what the respondent got out of the ads. Such recall measures typically are expressed as a percentage of respondents who can remember the brand advertised, the principal selling points, or the pictorial and copy elements.

The relative merit of alternative ads can be measured by changing only the test ads in successive interviews. A comparison of recall scores for test and control ads gives some indication of the test ad's performance. Validity of such comparisons, however, depends on the neutrality or consistency of scores for the control ads. Finding that recall scores for control ads varied more than recall scores for test ads in several experiments, one researcher concluded that variations in recall scores "result from the fact that people are most likely to notice and least likely to forget ads for those brands and products in which they are most interested or which they know the most about."[12] This suggests that the portfolio should include only advertisements for the same type of product. However, the similarity of advertisements of competing brands might further contaminate the recall scores. These are problems that could be met by using larger samples than those ordinarily used in portfolio testing.

[12] John C. Maloney, "Portfolio Tests—Are They Here to Stay?" *Journal of Marketing,* Vol. 25 (July 1961), pp. 32–37.

Television recall tests

Recall is used to test television commercials that were actually broadcast and received under normal viewing conditions. Burke Marketing Service offers advertisers the opportunity to test television commercials in any of 25 cities. The day after the test commercial is broadcast telephone interviews are conducted with a sample of housewives or other pertinent group to determine (1) whether or not they viewed the program in which the test commercial appeared, (2) what products they recall seeing advertised on the program, (3) what they recall about the commercial's content, and (4) what they thought of the commercial. It is assumed that the numbers of respondents who remembered seeing the commercial, and remembered its content, and were favorably impressed are indicators of its effectiveness.

Gallup & Robinson's Total Prime Time Television Research measures all television commercials appearing in both program and station-break positions between the hours of 7:30 and 11:30 P.M. on 28 nights in the Philadelphia metropolitan area. Personal interviews are made with the aid of a program roster. Respondents are asked to plot their TV viewing pattern during the previous evening for any half-hour segment in which they were actively watching all or nearly all of the time. Then, using a roster of all the commercials identified by brand name that appeared in those segments the previous evening, respondents indicate which commercials they recall seeing. For each commercial recalled, open-end questions are asked to determine if the respondent can prove recall and to measure levels of idea communication, attitudinal reactions, and persuasiveness.

A possible danger in relying too heavily on recall tests is that the advertising will tend to take on a particular "look" or "style." As Fred Schlinger observed: "It is relatively easy to spot on the air advertising that has been selected on a high-recall basis . . . it tends to be actor-dialogue, problem solution, slice-of-life."[13]

Association tests

Association, the connecting of one fact or experience with another, is implicit in learning and remembering. Getting consumers to associate a satisfaction with a brand name is a fundamental function of advertising, and the extent to which consumers make the intended association is sometimes used as a measure of advertising effectiveness.

The *triple-associates* test, as developed by Henry C. Link, consists of asking respondents this type of question: "What brand of watch is advertised as 'The World's Most Honored Watch'?" Such a question gives the

[13] Fred L. Schlinger, "The Measurement of Advertising Communication: Some Considerations," *Journal of Advertising,* Vol. 3, No. 1 (1973), pp. 12–15.

respondent two associates, (1) the generic product (watch) and (2) the theme or slogan ("The World's Most Honored Watch"), and asks for the third element, (3) the brand name, which in this case is Longines. The percentage of respondents who correctly identify the brand provides a measure of how effective the advertising has been in registering the theme and brand association in consumers' thinking. Typically, a triple-associates test included themes for several products and brands, thus permitting a comparison of competitive standings. To estimate the rate at which a new theme is registering on consumers, the test is given at successive intervals during the introductory campaign.

Being a test of themes, selling propositions, or slogans, the triple-associates test has limited value. It measures only a little bit of learning and is useful only in those advertising situations that depend heavily on such abbreviated messages. Such brevity is prevalent in the advertising of cigarettes, soaps, dentifrices, and beverages. Again, it must be remembered there is no assurance that completion of the desired association will result in favorable action. The respondent might disbelieve the claim or react negatively to it.

Awareness and knowledge tests

The extent to which people have become aware of a product's existence and the knowledge they have of its want-satisfying properties are often considered appropriate measures of advertising performance. Obviously, creating awareness is most important when introducing a new product and when opening a new market for an established product. Getting more prospects to be more knowledgeable about a product's attributes is a more universal concern.

The variety of questions asked to test consumers' knowledge of advertised products and services is as great as the variety of quizzes encountered by the college student. Open-end questions, multiple choice, true-false, fill-in-blanks, and check lists are just a few of the questioning techniques used. For example, the Sun Oil Company tested consumer knowledge of its new gasoline blending system by asking these questions:

1. Have you ever heard of a gasoline pump that dispenses more than one grade of gasoline through the same hose?
2. What gasoline company uses that kind of pump?
3. How many different grades of gasoline does that pump dispense?
4. Have you ever heard of "custom blended" gasoline?
5. What gasoline company sells "custom blended" gasoline?

If advertising were the only means of communications used, the amount of knowledge people have of the company and its products could readily be attributed to advertising. But this seldom is the case. Typically, many kinds of communication—personal selling, packaging, labeling, and store display—are employed. To isolate advertising's contribution to consumer knowledge, an appropriate experimental design must be used. To serve any diagnostic purpose, knowledge tests would have to be conducted for alternative advertising strategies.

As criteria of advertising effectiveness, recognition, recall, awareness, association, and knowledge have one thing in common. All are indicators that some degree of communication was achieved. Until there is much more experimental evidence of the relationship between such intermediate effects and buying behavior, the ultimate influence on sales can only be inferred from the nature of the communication itself.

QUESTIONS AND PROBLEMS

1. Starch "noted" scores are not an uncontaminated measure of ad recognition. What are some of the contaminants?

2. Do you think it is possible to prepare television commercials that will score well in recall tests but score poorly in generating sales? If so, explain.

3. What advantages might community antenna television (CATV) or cable television offer for conducting television recall tests?

4. What elements of an advertisement are best suited for visual efficiency tests in a laboratory setting?

5. Among the people who "noted" a particular automobile advertisement, would you expect to find many or few people who recently bought that car? Why?

6. Contrast the recognition test with the aided-recall test, with respect to qualifying issue-readers and determining advertisement readership.

7. The recognition method is more expedient for gathering *quantitative* evidence of advertisement performance, but aided recall with playback gathers more *qualitative* information from the relatively few people who can supply it. Explain.

8. When comparing the scores of individual advertisements appearing in different issues of a given magazine, each score should be related to the average score of all ads in the issue. Why?

9. Prepare a triple-associates test for six advertisements appearing in current magazines or newspapers. (Sample: What cigarette advertises "Tastes Good Like a Cigarette Should"?)

27

Controlled
experiments
in the field

A ll of the tests discussed thus far involve some degree of artificiality. Whenever people are forced to examine advertisements in an interview situation or in a laboratory setting, whenever they are forced to respond to questions bearing on some aspect of communication, the conditions are different from those under which advertising works in real life, where people select media and messages voluntarily, where they form opinions and attitudes without submitting to interrogation, where they respond in the marketplace without giving much thought to how their buying behavior was influenced. Also, the aforementioned tests focus primarily on the message. They do not deal with the many important variables inherent in media selection, scheduling, budgeting, and spending strategies.

To approximate reality a test should be conducted in the field. The experimental variable should be introduced in a natural setting—that is, the advertising should actually be placed in the media so that it will reach people during their normal reading, viewing, or listening. Exposure should be voluntary. Response in the form of overt behavior should be objectively observed. Under these conditions there can be little doubt that test results would be sustained in actual practice. Under these conditions it is possible to test media, schedules, and budgets, as well as messages.

Testing under conditions of reality, however, poses a real problem.

How can the effect of advertising variables be isolated from the effect of all other variables that influence consumer behavior? This can be done through controlled experiments. In the simplest of such experiments one group of people is exposed to the advertising variable and a comparable group is not exposed. If the response—say, purchase of the advertised product—is significantly greater among the exposed group than among the nonexposed group, it can logically be inferred that the advertising variable was the causal factor. More complicated experimental designs permit the simultaneous testing of several variables and several applications of each variable—for example, different media and different levels of expenditure in each medium. Some of the designs that are particularly appropriate for advertising experiments are discussed here.[1]

SALES TESTING

Ideally, the advertiser would like to know which among alternative strategies and tactics would increase sales and profit the most. He may attach significance to measures of communication efficiency, to how well his advertising performs in gaining attention, in transmitting information, in modifying perceptions, in creating brand awareness in changing attitudes, etc., but he is constantly reminded that the payoff is sales. The fundamental question remains: How many dollars does he get for the dollars he spends?

Paradoxically, little research has been done on the fundamental question. It would seem that researchers have been overawed by the task of isolating the advertising effect from the effect of all other variables operating in the marketplace. They have been quick to point out that sales are the result of many factors: the product, the package, price, distribution, display at the point of purchase, personal selling, all the elements in the marketing mix that are subject to the advertiser's control. In addition, there are the activities of competitors, dealer support, economic conditions, the capriciousness of consumer behavior, the weather, and all the environmental factors over which the advertiser has no control. To these complicating circumstances are added the further observations that the effects of advertising are delayed and cumulative, that a change in advertising today does not produce a change in sales tomorrow, that even a continuing change in advertising may not produce a perceptible change in sales because the passage of time multiplies the effect of other variables as well. Yet, impossible as it may seem, the task is not hopeless.

Some researchers are facing up to the challenge. Their views are typified

---

[1] The reader who desires a more detailed investigation of experiments may wish to refer to Seymour Banks, *Experimentation in Marketing* (New York: McGraw-Hill Book Co., 1965).

in the following statement by Paul Gerhold, president of the Advertising Research Foundation:

> The question of measuring dollar returns from dollar advertising expenditures is a problem that can be solved if any substantial portion of the industry's brain power can be diverted from preparing rationalizations on why the problem cannot be solved to active work toward its solution. Those who argue that dollar returns from dollar investments are unmeasurable would, I suspect, also have us believe:
>
> —that we cannot measure the effect of the moon on tides, because the moon is far away and uncontrollable, and because the level of the water is influenced by the action of the winds and passing ships and similar uncontrollable variables.
>
> —that we cannot determine the effect of spark plugs on the performance of an automobile, because spark plugs, after all, are only a small part of the complex system that moves a car.
>
> —that we cannot evaluate what soil enrichment does for agriculture because the enrichment takes place at one time, and the crops come along a lot later.[2]

A recent survey of large-agency research directors asked the question, "Can sales be the criterion of campaign effectiveness?" Adler, Greenberg, and Lucas report that:

> The answers to whether sales effects of campaigns are obtainable were emphatic, in that 27 of the 37 committed responses indicated they are obtainable. Statements by the majority point out that sales effects have been measured, that case histories are available, that controlled experiments have continually proven their potential, and that it is merely a question of enough time and money to do account ability studies properly. In other words, it appears that suitable sales data may not be generally available, but that such data can presently be obtained.[3]

The control problem is not unique to advertising. The social scientist is faced with a host of highly variable social, economic, and psychological factors that he cannot change at will. The agricultural experimenter must contend with variability in weather conditions and soil characteristics. The presence of factors not readily manipulated by the researcher does not rule out the possibility of isolating the influence of test factors. The presence of side variables simply calls for the use of a well-designed and carefully executed experiment.

---

[2] Paul E. J. Gerhold, from his part in a panel discussion on "Measuring What We Pay For," presented at the 1962 American Association of Advertising Agencies Annual Meeting.

[3] Lee Adler, Allan Greenberg, and Darrell B. Lucas, "What Big Agency Men Think of Copy Testing Methods," *Journal of Marketing Research,* Vol. 2 (November 1965), p. 343.

Single-variable experimental design

Let us assume that a national advertiser is planning to add spot television to his present media lineup. He wants to know if spot TV is going to increase sales enough to warrant the additional cost. To test this medium using a simple experimental design he would select several market areas totally isolated from one another. For a period of time—say, two months— during which advertising proceeded as usual without spot TV he would record retail sales of his product in all the selected markets. Then, during the next two months he would add spot TV advertising in half of the markets while at the same time continuing his regular media schedule without spot TV in the other half. During this second period he would continue recording sales in all markets. Then, he would compare the change in sales volume from the first period to the second period in the *test* markets, those where spot TV was added, with the change in sales

TABLE 27–1
Single-variable experimental design

	First period	Second period
Test markets	No spot TV	Spot TV
Control markets	No spot TV	No spot TV

volume registered in the *control* markets, those where spot TV was not added. This single-variable experimental design is diagrammed in Table 27–1.

In such an experiment it is assumed that "all other" variables exerted a similar influence in all markets. Therefore, if there is a significant difference in sales changes between the test and control markets, the difference would be attributed to the spot TV advertising. A simple comparison of sales changes in test and control markets is illustrated in Table 27–2. In this hypothetical case the sales increase of 5 percent in the control markets indicates that sales in the test markets would have increased about $37,500 without spot television advertising. However, sales increased 8 percent in the test markets, suggesting that the difference of 3 percent, or $22,500 in sales, was due to the effect of spot TV. If we further assume that an appropriate statistical test of significance showed that this difference of 3 percent would be expected on a chance basis less than five times in a hundred, the advertiser could be reasonably certain that spot TV did increase sales. But was the increase enough to justify the expenditure? If, in this case, a 3 percent increase in sales returns a profit of $10,000, and the cost of spot TV was $85,00, it can be said that this advertising returned $1,500 in profit.

Conceivably, sales in the test markets might decline. Insofar as such a

TABLE 27–2
Comparison of test and control markets

	Sales before spot TV	Sales during spot TV	Percent change	Sales change attributed to other factors	Sales change attributed to spot TV
Test markets	$750,000	$810,000	+8	$37,500	$22,500
Control markets. . . .	600,000	630,000	+5		

decline resulted from a seasonal drop, from competive activity, from weakening economic conditions, or from other extraneous factors, the depressing effect of these factors would also be registered in the control markets. If sales declined less in test markets than in control markets, the difference would reflect a positive effect from the experimental variable. To illustrate, let's change the figures around in the hypothetical test of spot TV. Let's say that instead of increases we found a 5 percent decrease in sales in the test markets and an 8 percent decrease in the control markets. Here again, spot TV would have been effective, for it prevented sales from going down an additional 3 percent. Again, assuming the same profit relationship, the use of spot TV prevented a loss of an additional $10,000 in profit.

To measure the delayed response or cumulative effect of advertising, the experiment might be continued for another period of time during which the experimental variable would be withdrawn from the test markets. However, posttest data lead to conflicting interpretations. If sales continued at or near the level attained during the test period, it might be assumed that this demonstrated the cumulative effect of the advertising variable. On the other hand, if sales declined when the advertising was stopped, was the decline due to a lack of cumulative effect or a lack of continuity?

A single-variable experiment, as the name implies, involves the testing of one variable at a time. In the above hypothetical case the variable was the medium, spot television, not alternative uses of the medium. To control scheduling variables the medium should be used "normally" or as it eventually would be used in the firm's overall advertising program. To do otherwise, to hypo sales through overuse of the medium, or to subject it to an acid test through curtailed use, would make it impossible to project test results to future operations. The number of stations, the timing, and frequency of broadcasts scheduled in test markets should parallel the kind of schedule the advertiser would be likely to sustain on a broader scale. It is advisable, therefore, to plan the ultimate use of the medium before planning the test schedule.

To test alternative schedules, such as concentrated frequency versus longer continuity, one schedule would be used in one group of markets, the other schedule would be used in another group of markets. Insofar as all other factors were operating similarly in both groups the difference in sales observed would be attributed to the scheduling difference. In like fashion, different budgets, different spending strategies, and different campaign themes can be tested in single-variable experiments. Ordinarily, different message components—headlines, illustrations, and copy treatments—are not apt to produce significant differences in sales and, therefore, are more appropriately tested through techniques discussed earlier.

Selection of test and control markets

The selection of market areas for sales testing is essentially a sampling problem. The relatively few local markets selected should be representative of the advertiser's total market. Ordinarily, the number of markets included in the experiment is not great enough to permit the use of random selection procedures. Therefore, purposive selection, the selection of markets that best conform to predetermined criteria, is generally employed. Size, location, population characteristics, social customs, economic structure, distribution patterns, competition, and media availabilities, all are factors that must be taken into account in the selection process. And all of these factors must be considered in light of the purpose of the particular experiment.

Number and size of markets   There is no standard number of markets to be used. The greater the number used in the experiment, the greater the chance they will adequately represent the advertiser's total market and the greater the confidence that can be placed in the findings. However, if too many markets are used the purpose of experimentation, which is to discover on a small scale what is likely to happen on a large scale, is defeated. In view of the relatively small amounts of money advertisers have been willing to invest in this kind of research, it would seem there is greater danger in using two few instead of too many markets. Clearly, one test and one control are too few. There is little or no likelihood of finding one market that is representative of the whole. And there is too much risk in "putting all your eggs in one basket." If anything went wrong in one market all would be lost. While there may not be any particular magic in the number "three," it would seem that the minimum number of markets should be three test and three control. Four or five of each would be more appropriate in most cases. Of course, if the value placed on test results and the level of confidence required were high enough, the number of test and control markets might well be 20.

As in any sampling problem, the greater the variation in sales fluctuations among markets from one time period to the next, the larger the number of markets required to yield reliable findings. But how can one know what the market-to-market variation will be before conducting the experiment? On the assumption that sales variations in a particular product category tend to persist, Valentine Appel suggests that these variations can be estimated from a retabulation of market data gathered in previous years.[4] Such data may be found in the advertisers' files or can be obtained from the A. C. Nielsen Company which, for a reasonable charge, will retabulate store audit figures from previous years.

Each market should be large enough to provide a diversity of economic activity, a well-developed retail trade, and a variety of advertising media. Yet, it should not be so large that media costs and the costs of measuring sales would be unnecessarily high. The right size markets for experimental purposes are most likely to be found among those with populations ranging from 100,000 to 200,000. Each and every market selected need not meet the criteria of representativeness. It is the combined characteristics of each group, test and control, that should approximate the characteristics of the advertiser's total markets.

Location factors   To prevent any spill-over of the experimental variable into control areas and to relate sales results to a known advertising input, all markets should be isolated geographically one from another. Each should be a discrete trading area, neither a suburb of nor a satellite to a major metropolitan area. Otherwise there could be no assurance that recorded sales were not subject to outside promotional effort or that sales resulting from the experimental variable were not registered elsewhere.

Test and control markets should be spotted in different regions to match the regional distribution of the advertiser's product and to include regional differences in climate, styles of life, and consumer preferences.

Social and economic factors   Local habits and customs stemming from different climates, different ethnic backgrounds and religious beliefs produce marked differences in sales of many products. For example, Salt Lake City would not be satisfactory for testing coffee or Postum. It has an antipathy for the former and an affinity for the latter. The experiment should not be loaded with test markets where people are unusually receptive to the advertiser's product unless, of course, these are the only places in which he sells. Nor should the experiment be treated as an acid test including only those markets where exceptional opposition is encountered. Both types of situations should be represented or a happy medium should be struck between the two.

Markets having a diversity of industry should be sought. Such markets enhance the representativeness of the sample and reduce the risk of invalidity in the experiment because of a local industrial disturbance. The

---

[4] Valentine Appel, "Suppositions and Sales Tests," *Proceedings: 18th Annual Conference, Advertising Research Foundation* (New York: Advertising Research Foundation, Inc., 1972), pp. 31–37.

one-industry town, such as a mining town, a railroad town, or a steel town should be avoided. A variety of occupations—factory workers, office workers, tradesmen, professional people, etc.—should be represented.

Distribution factors   Only markets in which the advertiser has adequate distribution should be selected. Obviously, his product should be readily available in the types of retail stores through which he regularly distributes. Inventories and prices should be maintained at normal levels. Dealers and salesmen should not be informed about the test. If they knew about it they might feel compelled to give the product more prominent display or to sell harder than usual to make a good showing. "Business as usual" should prevail. If dealers departed from usual practice by cutting prices or running special promotions, there would be no way to determine whether changes in sales volume were due to the national advertiser's experimental variable or to the dealer's promotional activity. Markets in which such unusual activity occurred during the test would have to be discarded when compiling the final results

Competitive factors   The advertiser's competitive position in test and control markets should approximate his position nationally. Markets where his share of market is unusually high or unusually low should be avoided. Where his share is high he might be benefiting from exceptionally weak competition. Where his share is low he might be up against exceptionally strong competition. In either situation, sales gains registered during a test are apt to be atypical.

The activity of competitors should be carefully observed during the test. If a competitor cuts prices or runs a special promotion in some of the test or control markets, sales of the product involved in the test are likely to be depressed in those areas. If a competitor notes the entrance of another firm's test advertising in a particular market, he might counter with increased advertising of his own. This, of course, would impair the usefulness of test results.

Media factors   When the purpose of the experiment is to test strategies involving the use of local media—newspapers, spot television, spot radio, outdoor—it is not particularly difficult to find markets in which these facilities are available. The problem becomes more complicated when the purpose is to test strategies for ultimate use in national media, such as network television or national magazines. If network television is involved, test markets should have three television stations in order to reproduce network competition. If national magazines are involved, test markets should have a local roto supplement that offers magazine-type format and color. The availability of regional editions of national magazines makes it possible to select markets for actual magazine coverage at reasonable cost. The soundest approach to translating a national media plan into local media is to equalize delivered impressions. This requires the scheduling of sufficient broadcasts or insertions in the test markets to match the reach and frequency that probably would be achieved by the anticipated national media schedule.

Measuring sales

Ordinarily, a manufacturer's sales records do not reveal week-to-week or even month-to-month retail sales in individual markets. His records indicate shipments to distributors, but do not show the extent to which inventories at the wholesale or retail level are being built up or depleted over short periods of time. Therefore, some means must be employed to provide a standardized audit of retail sales in test and control markets.

Retailers should not be counted on to furnish a record of their own sales. Some could not give accurate information on a particular item's sales and others would not do so. If they knew their store was being used in a test, some retailers would be tempted to create the impression that they were superior outlets for the product in question. They might devote greater than usual effort to the item or they might overstate its sales.

The local media, especially newspapers, often are willing and able to check sales. They also should not be counted on, for they might be tempted to make their medium look good in the test. Similarly, the company's own sales force might work overenthusiastically if they knew a test was on in their territory. Therefore, they also should not be asked to check sales.

Generally, the most efficient way to get current retail sales data is to buy such information from an independent research firm specializing in this service. Best known of these firms is the A. C. Nielsen Company, which regularly audits retail sales of food and drug items in various markets and sells standardized reports of these data on a syndicated basis. If the markets selected for an experiment are not included among those regularly audited, the Nielsen Company is prepared to send their investigators into the selected areas to gather the necessary sales data. Cost of the Nielsen service is apt to be less than what it would cost the advertiser to hire and train investigators to obtain the information on his own.

An acceptable procedure for auditing sales, and the one used by the Nielsen Company, is as follows: A sample of the types and sizes of stores carrying the advertised product is selected for audit. At the start of the experiment investigators check the quantity of the product each store has on hand. At regular intervals, preferably every other week, the investigators return to each store, check the invoices showing the quantity of the product purchased since the last visit, and check the stock on hand again. With this information each store's sales during each period of time between visits can be readily calculated.

(Beginning inventory + Purchases) − Ending inventory = Sales

A cumulative record of product sales in the sample of stores in test and control markets prior to introduction of the experimental variable establishes the benchmark figures. Totals for the test period during which the experimental variable is operating are arrived at similarly. With these data the before-after comparison can be made and sales resulting from the experimental variable can be inferred.

Instead of checking the flow of his product out of retail stores, the advertiser may prefer to measure the flow into the homes of consumers. This can be done by using consumer panels and product purchase diaries as explained in Chapter 11.

Retail audits do not tell the advertiser whether his product is being purchased infrequently by a large segment of consumers or frequently by a small segment. Nor do such audits tell him what kinds of people are responding to the test advertising. When data are gathered through consumer-purchase diaries, the advertiser can classify his customers according to age, family size, income, occupation, or some other relevant factor. If he finds that increases in sales result from purchases made largely by a particular consumer group, he can exploit the marketing opportunity such prime prospects represent or he can modify his advertising program to more effectively cultivate other segments.

The ubiquitous computer offers a new channel for monitoring consumer purchases. Some retail stores are replacing cash registers and written sales slips with computer terminals that record individual transactions, handle credit checks and account charges, and automatically control inventories. As a by-product, such point-of-sale terminals also deliver each morning a complete record, store-by-store and market-by-market, of yesterday's consumer purchases. Some researchers see in this innovation the opportunity "to monitor at the retail level the purchasing behavior of hundreds of thousands of consumers" and thereby be able "to track day-by-day the buying response to a new ad, a new medium, a new level of brand advertising expenditure."[5] One might hope that in their zeal to collect data these researchers not overlook the possibility of intruding on the consumer's privacy.

Multivariable experimental design

More sophisticated experimental designs, in which several variables are tested simultaneously, are now being used in advertising research. Such designs not only make it possible to measure the sales effect of each variable, but also take into account the *interaction* between variables. The interaction may produce a combined effect that is greater than the

[5] Paul E. J. Gerhold, "The Coming Emphasis on Measuring Payout," *Proceedings: 18th Annual Conference, Advertising Research Foundation* (New York: Advertising Research Foundation, Inc. 1972), pp. 50–53.

TABLE 27–3
Sixteen-area multimedia experimental design

	No newspapers				Newspapers			
	No radio		Radio		No radio		Radio	
	No TV	TV	No TV	TV	No TV	TV	No TV	TV
No outdoor 1	2		3	4	5	6	7	8
Ourdoor 9	10		11	12	13	14	15	16

algebraic sum of the separate effects. For example, a given expenditure on television and radio together may yield greater sales than the same expenditure on either one of the media separately. Multivariable experimental designs offer the most promise for testing alternative advertising strategies under conditions of reality.

A design used by the Ford Motor Company to test various combinations of 4 media in 16 market areas is illustrated in Table 27–3.

George H. Brown commented on this experiment as follows:

> A brief study of this design will show that for any single medium, eight geographic areas have been exposed and eight have not been exposed. Thus it is possible to execute the basic test-control, before-after analysis inherent in an elementary design. It is also possible to observe how each medium behaves alone and in all possible combinations with other media. (See Table 27–4.)
>
> If identical dollar expenditures (at national rates) are established for each

TABLE 27–4
Media combinations contained in 16-cell design

Combination	Area number
No media	1
TV only.	2
Radio only	3
Newspaper only.	5
Outdoor only	9
TV—radio.	4
TV—newspaper	6
Newspaper—radio	7
Outdoor—TV	10
Outdoor—radio	11
Outdoor—newspaper	13
TV—radio—newspaper	8
Outdoor—radio—TV	12
Outdoor—TV—newspaper	14
Outdoor—radio—newspaper	15
Outdoor—TV—radio—newspaper	16

TABLE 27–5
Factorial design for testing two media at three levels of expenditure

I	II	III
$5M Radio $5M Television	$10M Radio $5M Television	$15M Radio $5M Television
IV	V	VI
$5M Radio $10M Television	$10M Radio $10M Television	$15M Radio $10M Television
VII	VIII	IX
$5M Radio $15M Television	$10M Radio $15M Television	$15M Radio $15M Television

medium, area No. 1 will receive no advertising expenditures, areas, 2, 3, 5, and 9 will receive advertising at the same dollar rates; areas 4, 6, 7, 10, 11, and 13 will receive advertising at twice this dollar rate; areas 8, 12, 14, 15 at three times as much dollar advertising, and area 16 at four times this dollar expenditure. The information-producing potential of such a design is obviously quite great.[6]

Whereas dollar expenditures in each medium were held constant in the Ford experiment, the factorial design illustrated in Table 27–5 permits the testing of three levels of expenditure. In this design each of nine markets receives a different mixture of radio and television advertising. A single experiment of this type provides useful results. Predictability, however, can be considerably improved by rotating the combinations among the same nine markets or by reproducing the experiment in different sets of markets. Insofar as such experimentation enables the advertiser to predict sales returns from alternative spending strategies, it increases the likelihood of his maximizing profit on the media investment. Similarly, the same type of experiment could be used to evaluate alternative scheduling patterns with respect to frequency, continuity, and space and time units.

The design and analysis of complex experiments is a branch of applied mathematics and will not be dealt with further here. The above examples are intended to demonstrate the logic of such experiments and to indicate that techniques are available for measuring the particular effect of advertising variables on dollars and cents sales.

Matched samples of exposed and nonexposed groups

Instead of isolating test and control groups prior to introducing the advertising variable, audience-tracing techniques may be used to isolate

[6] George H. Brown, "Measuring the Sales Effectiveness of Alternative Media," *Proceedings: 7th Annual Conference, Advertising Research Foundation* (New York: Advertising Research Foundation, Inc., 1961), pp. 43–47.

exposed and nonexposed groups after the advertising has run. The logic of such ex post facto experiments is simply that some people will voluntarily expose themselves to the media carrying the advertising in question and others will not. Some will see a given television program, others won't; some will read a given magazine, others won't; some will listen to radio at a given time, others won't. Once viewers and nonviewers, or readers and nonreaders, or listeners and nonlisteners are identified, the difference in their purchases of the advertised product is observed, and the part of the difference attributed to the advertising is determined.

The consumer panel technique best serves the dual purpose of identifying exposed and nonexposed groups and recording purchase behavior of each group. To illustrate, let's assume the sales effectiveness of sponsoring a particular television show is under test. Panel members would keep one diary of their television viewing and another diary of their product purchases. From the viewing diaries it can be determined which panel members regularly watch the TV show and, therefore, see the advertising. If the purchase diaries indicate that those who regularly see the show buy more of the advertised product than do the nonviewers, it might seem reasonable to credit the difference to the television advertising on that show. However, the viewing group might be different from the nonviewing group, as evidenced by the fact that one group chose to watch the show while the other group did not. The show itself tends to select a particular kind of audience. The difference in purchases may be due to inherent differences between viewers and nonviewers and not due to the television advertising on that show.

The key factor in the success of this method is the adequacy with which the two groups, the exposed and nonexposed groups, can be matched. If the exposed group includes a higher proportion of upper-income families than the nonexposed group, this factor may account for part of any observed difference in their respective purchases. Therefore, the two groups should be matched by adjusting the composition of each group so that the result will be two *matched samples.* This can be accomplished by random selections within each relevant classification which will leave each group with the same proportion in various income levels, age groups, family size groups, occupational classes, purchase behavior patterns, etc. It should be recognized, however, that two groups of human beings can be proportionally matched in terms of observable characteristics, but still be different in terms of underlying personality traits. This is the principal weakness of the matched sample technique.

CATV (community antenna television) offers a unique opportunity for isolating comparable groups of consumers in the same market. Inasmuch as each CATV household is wired to receive the TV signal, the test advertising can be transmitted to some households and not to others. Or, different treatments of advertising can be transmitted to different households. The members of the respective households, not knowing which group they are in, would thereby be receiving the test advertising under normal viewing conditions. Their purchases of the product in question could be determined from periodic surveys, from diaries, or, as in the case of a large department store, from charge account records. In the event that CATV develops to the point where two-way communication is possible, members of the household could place their orders and have their purchases recorded by the same communication system that transmits the advertising.

Whatever method is used, sales testing is expensive and time consuming. It requires technical skills that are not in plentiful supply. Such experiments are most appropriate when the product is purchased at frequent intervals, when the likelihood of quick response to advertising is high, and when advertising is the dominant selling force in the marketing mix. These also happen to be the conditions when the advertising investment is likely to be high. The greater the investment the more prudent it is to employ testing procedures that measure the return in dollars and cents.

INQUIRY TESTS

The mail-order advertiser who distributes his ads by mail is an ideal situation to experiment. If he wishes to test advertisement A against advertisement B, he can send ad A to every other name on the mailing list and ad B to the intervening names. Such a distribution assures him that each ad will reach a similar group of prospects. By keying each ad, perhaps with a different address for replying, he can keep a record of the number of orders each produced. He can be assured not only that the observed difference in response is due to differences in the advertisements, but also that the better performing ad in the test is also the better producer of sales. A similar opportunity to experiment is available when using direct mail designed to secure leads for company and distributor salesmen.

Advertising which is intended to produce mail orders, or requests for a sample, a booklet, or a premium, but which is placed in published media, does not offer the same degree of controlled exposure as in direct mail. However, the inquiries may be an important element in the company's sales promotion program and may be considered an appropriate measure of an advertisement's performance.

In more typical situations, the purpose of advertising is to influence consumer purchases in retail stores, not to produce inquiries. Therefore, a critical factor in inquiry tests of such advertising is the relationship between an advertisement's ability to generate inquiries and its ability to exert a favorable influence on retail sales. The validity of inquiry tests in these situations rests heavily on the relevance of motives underlying requests for the offer to motives prompting purchase of the product.

External variables affecting inquiries

Several factors outside of the advertisement itself affect the number of inquiries received. They are seasonal differences, media differences, and differences in the nature and presentation of the offer.

Seasonal differences reflect the greater amount of time people spend reading magazines and newspapers during the winter months and their greater inclination to "send in" for things when outdoor leisure time activities are curtailed. The number of inquiries generally is highest in February and March and lowest in June and July. One exception to the winter-summer pattern of difference is December, which with its busy holiday season yields fewer inquiries.

In his *Analysis of 12 Million Inquiries,*[7] Daniel Starch found that the highest inquiry-producing month, February, stood 20 percent above the average; that the lowest months, June and December, stood 20 percent below average. This seasonal variation is portrayed in Figure 27–1. Dr. Starch's data represent the combined experience of many companies who tabulated inquiries resulting from many of their advertisements over a period of many years. Such a generalized seasonal pattern may not fit the experience of individual companies, especially industrial advertisers, for whose products there may be peak buying interest during the summer months. For example, the Republic Steel Company found that their advertisements in architectural magazines produced the most inquiries during May, June, and July.

Regardless of the pattern of variation, it is important to recognize that the seasonal factor affects inquiries and therefore must be controlled if any valid results are to be obtained through inquiry testing.

FIGURE 27–1

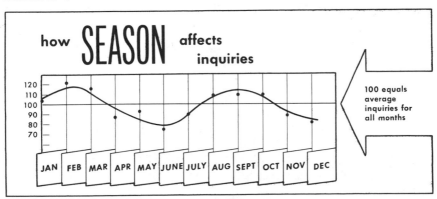

[7] Daniel Starch, *An Analysis of 12 Million Inquiries* (Evanston, Ill.: Standard Rate & Data Service, Inc., 1959).

Media differences include differences in size and character of audiences, differences in editorial content, and differences in positioning of advertisements. A large number of inquiries should be expected from a test advertisement placed in a magazine with a larger audience, with a larger proportion of prospects, and with more attention-compelling editorial content. Positioning the ad toward the front or the back of the book may or may not affect the number of inquiries, but it can be assumed that an ad positioned adjacent to a high-traffic editorial page will fare better than one buried in a low-traffic section. These observations suggest that whenever test advertisements are placed in different publications, or in different issues of the same publication, or in different positions, there can be no assurance that a difference in the number of inquiries was due to a difference in the ads.

Nature and presentation of the offer have a material effect on the number of inquiries. Frequently the offer is a sample of the product, or a booklet providing more detailed information about the product, or a premium that prospects are likely to want. Whatever is offered, the number of requests will depend on how appealing the offer is and how well it is presented. To increase the number of requests, John Caples recommends: (1) offer the sample or booklet free, instead of for 10¢; (2) set a value on the offer, such as "regular 35¢ size"; (3) describe the offer attractively by listing its good features; and (4) sweeten the offer by adding a free gift.[8]

As an example of sweetening the offer, Mr. Caples reports on a test of advertisements for airplane trips to Bermuda:

> We found that a hidden offer of a booklet pulled less than 100 replies. This was not considered sufficient.
> We sweetened the offer by including the offer of a free pair of sunglasses and free map of Bermuda, in addition to the free booklet. We called the offer a *"Free Bermuda Vacation Kit."* This offer brought more than enough replies for a copy test, namely over 400 replies per ad.[9]

A coupon generally produces more inquiries than an offer buried in the copy. An industrial advertiser compared inquiry returns from three methods of offering a booklet to those who would write the company. The relative pulling power of the method used was as follows:

Offer buried in copy 26
Word "free" and paragraph describing booklet added 100
Coupon added 185

[8] John Caples, "How to Get More Replies from Hidden Offers," *Printers' Ink,* October 11, 1957, p. 27.
[9] Ibid.

Obviously, inquiries can be boosted if the advertisement is designed to achieve that objective; if the headline, illustration, and body text focus on the offer; if the coupon is given dominant display and placed at an outer corner of the page for easy clipping. The response to such an ad, however, would merely demonstrate its power to generate requests for the item offered. Devices that succeed in motivating people to get something "free" have little or no bearing on the kind of message needed to get people to buy a product at the usual price through the usual channels.

For testing purposes the offer should be related, but incidental, to the objective of the advertisement. A recipe book, for example, is generally accepted as an appropriate offer for a food advertisement. Dominance of the offer should depend on the purpose of the test. If the purpose is to test attention-getting power, a clearly displayed, but nonintrusive, coupon is appropriate. If the purpose is to test thoroughness of readership, a buried offer is called for. These are matters requiring the exercise of good judgment. It is apparent, however, that the offer and its presentation should be the same in all advertisements involved in an inquiry test.

Split run

Split run is a technique that makes it possible to test two or more advertisements in the same position, in the same issue of the same publication with assurance that each ad will reach comparable groups of readers.

Alternate-copy or "50–50" split runs involve a mechanical technique whereby every other copy off the press carries advertisement A, and each copy in between carries advertisement B. Since the two test ads alternate throughout the press run, each reader of the publication has a 50–50 chance of receiving a copy carrying either of the two ads. Thus, readers of copies carrying advertisement A should have the same general characteristics as readers of copies carrying advertisement B. Appearing in the same position in the same issue, each advertisement is subjected to the same editorial environment and reaches both groups of readers at the same time. Under such controlled conditions it can be inferred that differences in the number of inquiries are due solely to differences in the advertisements themselves.

Some publications which cannot provide an every-other-copy or "true" split can arrange a change of advertisements midway in the press run. This has the disadvantage of concentrating distribution of the ad appearing in the first half of the run in geographic areas farthest from the place where the publication is printed. Most national magazines now offer a geographical split which permits the advertiser to insert different advertisements in different regional parts of the total circulation. This type of split, however, is more appropriate for matching advertising coverage to a firm's product distribution than for testing purposes.

Service charges for split-run insertions vary. For alternate-copy split runs the *Reader's Digest* charges $200 for black-and-white ads, $300 for two-color ads, and $500 for four-color ads.

As a technique for controlled experimentation, split run is objective, reliable, and inexpensive.

Keying the advertisement

To keep a record of the number of inquiries produced by each advertisement it is necessary to adopt some method of identifying which inquiries came from which ad. Where coupons are inserted in the advertisements, this problem is easily solved. A key number or some other identification mark placed on each coupon will allow a proper sorting. There are numerous keying devices. The address given for reply might be varied for each advertisement. Thus, one address might be 1215 Prospect Place, while another might be 1217 Prospect Place. There might be included in one address, Department C, and in another, Department D. Arrangements can be made with the Post Office for varying addresses. Where booklets are offered, the name or number of the booklet can be varied in each ad and thus serve as a key. Figure 27–2 reproduces a number of pairs of coupons keyed in different ways. Can you detect the keys?

Media tests

Inquiries may be used to measure the relative effectiveness of different media. In such tests the message and, insofar as possible, the time factor should be controlled. For example, to determine the relative pulling power of different magazines, the same advertisement would be placed in each magazine and a record kept of the inquiries received. To control whatever effect different seasons, months, or weeks might have on response, the ads would run at the same, or approximately the same, time.

The magazine with a higher circulation might be expected to produce more inquiries. To equalize circulation differences the inquiry count would be related to some standard unit of circulation, say, 100,000 circulation. If magazine A with a circulation of 200,000 produced 240 inquiries and magazine B with 130,000 circulation produced 195 inquiries, magazine A scored 120 and B scored 150 per 100,000 circulation.

A more meaningful standard of comparison would take into account the difference in space cost. Thus, if cost of the space used in magazine A above were $720, and the cost in B were $480, the cost per inquiry would be $3.00 for A, and $2.46 for B. In this comparison the magazine producing the fewer inquiries was the more efficient.

FIGURE 27–2

Pairs of coupons illustrating methods of keying advertisements

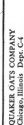

Evaluation

Inquiry testing offers several advantages. The advertisements actually run in published media and reach people in the course of their normal reading. Therefore, exposure is voluntary and takes place in a natural setting. The response is a voluntary act, which at the very least indicates the person saw the ad and was motivated to take a positive action. If the offer is buried in body text, a reply is substantial evidence of thorough readership. If the offer requires sending a coin for a sample of the product or for a premium, there is further evidence that the person was motivated to spend something for the item offered.

Split run is ideal for controlled experiments. The experimental variable in the advertisements can be manipulated with assurance that all other variables are adequately controlled. Such experiments are easy to conduct. They can provide quick results at relatively low cost. No interviewing or elaborate laboratory apparatus is required. It is simply a matter of counting replies and applying statistical tests of significance to the data. Cost is limited mainly to the cost of the offer, its handling and mailing, and the extra charge for the split run, which we have noted is minimal. Assuming that only advertisements of recognized merit would be included in the test, some advertising value is received for the production costs and space costs incurred. These costs, therefore, should not be charged against the experiment. Also, if the offer has value as a sales promotion device, such as a cook book that includes recipes calling for use of the advertised product, the cost of the offer should not be borne entirely by the experiment. In the final analysis, split run is the least expensive technique for controlled experiments in the field.

On the negative side, critics of inquiry tests say that respondents are apt to be bargain hunters looking for anything free, or chronic coupon-clippers who are not typical of prospects for the advertised product. No doubt many such people do respond, but when split run is used they are equally divided between the two groups exposed to each ad and therefore do not affect the difference in response. In this connection it should be remembered that the number of inquiries provides a comparative measure of each ad's performance, one versus the other, not an absolute measure of effectiveness. The purpose is to test one treatment against another and to infer from the difference in inquiries which one worked the better. Through systematic and consistent experimentation much can be learned about the efficacy of alternative message strategies.

The most serious limitation of inquiry testing concerns the relationship between motives leading to requests for the offer and motives leading to purchases of the advertised product. When these motives are highly related, test results can be projected with confidence to regular advertising practice. Otherwise, the results would merely indicate that one ad scored better than another in achieving some kind of communication and in prompting some kind of response that may or may not be effective in promoting sales of the product. Therefore, the usefulness of inquiry testing is limited to those situations in which the advertising is intended to produce mail orders, sales leads, or requests for additional information and to those situations in which a relevant premium or sample offer is feasible.

QUESTIONS AND PROBLEMS

1 Reviewing the previous chapters on advertising testing techniques, how do the exposures to the ads and the responses to them differ from real life?

2 Design an experiment for sales testing a new advertising campaign for an established brand of dog food. Support each recommendation you propose.

3 If a product's sales are subject to considerable seasonal variation, should the sales test be conducted in the season when sales are high or the season when sales are low? Why?

4 What factors would you consider in deciding how long a sales test should run? Under what circumstances should the period tend to be longer? Shorter?

5 How might computer terminals that replace cash registers in retail stores enhance sales testing?

6 How might community antenna television (CATV) be used in sales testing?

7 Sales in test cities A, B, and C were 3,400 cases in the period before advertising and 6,200 cases after. In control cities X, Y, and Z sales were 4,600 cases for the first period and 4,830 for the second. What increase in sales was logically attributable to advertising?

8 Sales testing is best suited for products which are purchased by consumers at frequent intervals? Do you agree or disagree? Explain.

9 An inquiry test merely measures the ability of an advertisement to produce inquiries. It does not measure the advertisement's ability to produce sales. Do you agree or disagree? Explain.

10 What variables that might influence the results of an inquiry test are controlled by a split run?

11 How would you design an inquiry test to measure the relative effectiveness of two different magazines?

part six

The advertising
organization

The advertising agency

The advertising agency has evolved to provide the specialized knowledge, skills, and experience needed to produce effective advertising campaigns. It provides a quality and range of service greater than any single advertiser could afford or would need to employ for himself.

Operating outside the advertiser's own organization, the agency is in a position to draw on the broad experience it gains while handling the diverse problems of different clients. Also, as an outsider it can approach the advertiser's problems with an objective point of view.

The agency functions *mainly* in the "national" field, handling the advertising campaigns of manufacturers who distribute nationally or regionally rather than in the local field of retail advertising. There are, however, agencies in many cities, even in cities of less than 100,000 population, that provide service to local retailers and service organizations.

The agency has come to represent the core of the advertising profession, and "Madison Avenue," an area in New York where several large agencies are located, has become a symbol of advertising to the nonadvertising world.

History

The development of the advertising agency can be divided roughly into four periods:

1. Period of early growth: 1841–65
2. Wholesaling period: 1865–80
3. Semiservice period: 1880–1917
4. Service period: 1917–present

Period of early growth   The first advertising agency on record in the United States was Volney B. Palmer. In 1841, Palmer organized a newspaper advertising and subscription agency. By 1849 he had established offices in the cities of New York, Boston, Baltimore, and Philadelphia.

At this early date, there were no directories of newspapers and no published rates for space to be sold to advertisers. Palmer acted as an informatory agent in these matters to prospective advertisers. In essence, he served as a salesman of space for publishers; and they, in turn, gave him a commission of 25 percent of such sales. The publishers found this method of selling more effective than trying to sell direct, and advertisers wishing to reach more than one territory found value in such service.

Palmer seems to have been the only agent for advertising space until 1848, when one of his employees left him and started a similar business for himself. Competition increased, and the usual price cutting occurred. Success seemed to depend upon one's ability to bargain with the publisher and the advertiser. The natural result of this policy was a general reduction in profits to the agency; this led to a search for new competitive tools which would return a profit.

Wholesaling period   The new competitive tool was supplied by George P. Rowell, who opened an agency in 1865. Rowell contracted with 100 newspapers to sell him a column of space each week for a year. By contracting for such large amounts of space for a period of time, Rowell was able to obtain a greatly reduced price from the publishers. In addition to the lower price obtained from buying space in quantity, he also received the 25 percent agency commission. He resold space to advertisers in one-inch units. The price he charged was not necessarily a uniform one; nor was it the price which he paid the publisher, less his 25 percent. His plan was successful, the main element of success being the principle of buying in wholesale lots and reselling to small buyers.

Throughout the wholesaling period, the agent continued as a seller of space for publishers. This took on different forms, one of which was the exclusive right to sell space in certain publications. Thus, one agency developed a controlled list of religious papers, another a "List of Thirty" household magazines. Any advertiser wishing to buy space in any of the controlled publications was forced to buy through the exclusive wholesaler for that paper.

Semiservice period   The wholesaling phase of agency work was checked when publishers began to establish their own sales departments for selling space. Some of these departments sold direct to the advertiser; others, to the general advertising agency. Thus, the agency was forced to turn its attention somewhat away from the particular function of selling or peddling space for a publisher and toward the function of buying space for the advertiser.

This about-face at least changed the surface character of the agency business. It tended to make it a semiservant of the advertiser. Emphasis was placed upon the value of obtaining space in the proper publications, and the agency represented itself as being capable of choosing the proper publications.

Early in the semiservice period, agencies offered to write the copy for the advertiser, thus giving added weight to their claim of being servants of the advertiser. This concept of service was slow to develop; but in the early part of the 20th century, agencies began to emphasize strongly this "free" service. One agency in 1905 advertised that it paid $28,000 a year for a copywriter. These methods increased the agency business and forced most space sales to be made through them.

Service period By 1917 the idea of service had grown until not only was copywriting done for the advertiser but many other things as well. During the service period, many agencies have grown to the position of advertising and marketing counselors for advertisers. Market research, media testing, merchandising service, layout construction, art work, the supervision of engraving, etc., now constitute regular agency service.

The service element has solidified the position of agencies to such a degree that radio and television networks and magazine publishers have come to depend upon them as the primary channel though which time and space are sold. Publishers claim to have had an important part in the encouragement of agencies to provide extra service to the advertiser. By providing advertisers with the kind of assistance that will improve the effectiveness of advertising, more time and space naturally will be sold.

Functions of a modern agency

The modern advertising agency ranges in size from a one-person agency to a large organization employing hundreds of people to carry on its work. The functions performed by these agencies vary to a considerable degree. Some concentrate major attention on the preparation and placing of advertisements. Many, however, have organized themselves to perform the broad functions of marketing and advertising. To perform such functions well requires a keen understanding of the complete marketing and merchandising problems of the advertiser, as well as a knowledge of markets, media, and consumer psychology. The older service functions of writing copy and designing the form of a finished advertisement are thus only a part of the total work of most modern agencies.

The American Association of Advertising Agencies emphasizes the service function its members perform for clients and points out that such service consists primarily of interpreting to a specific public or publics the advantages or want-satisfying characteristics of a product, service, or idea. The association offers the following seven-point program as necessary for an adequate job of interpretation:

1. A study of the client's *product or service* in order to determine the advantages and disadvantages inherent in the product itself, and in its relation to competition
2. An analysis of the *present and potential* market for which the product or service is adapted:
   a. As to location
   b. As to extent of possible sale
   c. As to season
   d. As to trade and economic conditions
   e. As to nature and amount of competition
3. A knowledge of the factors of *distribution and sales* and their methods of operation
4. A knowledge of all the available *media* and means which can profitably be used to carry the interpretation of the product or service to consumer, wholesaler, dealer, contractor or other factor. This knowledge covers:
   a. Character
   b. Influence
   c. Circulation
      Quantity
      Quality
      Location
   d. Physical Requirements
   e. Costs
5. *Formulation of a definite plan* and presentation of the plan to the client
6. *Execution of plan:*
   a. Writing, designing, illustrating of advertisements, or other appropriate forms of the message
   b. Contracting for the space, time, or other means of advertising
   c. The proper incorporation of the message in mechanical form and forwarding it with proper instructions for the fulfillment of the contract
   d. Checking and verifying insertions, display, or other means used
   e. The auditing and billing for the service, space, and preparation
7. Cooperation with the client's sales work, to insure the greatest effect from advertising

   In addition to strictly advertising service, there is a willingness among many agencies today to assist the client with his other activities of distribution. They do special work for the manufacturer in such fields as package designing, sales research, sales training, preparation of sales and service literature, designing of merchandising displays, public relations, and publicity.[1]

[1] Frederic R. Gamble, *What Advertising Agencies Are—What They Do and How They Do it* (New York: American Association of Advertising Agencies, Inc., 1970), pp. 6 and 7.

Some perspective on the breadth of agency services beyond the traditional functions of planning, creating, and placing advertising can be gained from the following list of "extra" services now provided by advertising agencies:[2]

Marketing
- Pricing policies
- Distribution policies
- Sales policies
- Sampling

Merchandising Pieces
- Wall banners
- Package inserts
- Counter, floor, and window displays
- Shelf tape
- Talking displays
- Counter giveaways
- Sampling cards
- Dispensers

Trade Promotion
- Dealer promotions
- Dealer contacts
- Convention exhibits
- Catalogs
- Sales literature
- Bulletins
- Broadsides

Public Relations
- Employee-employer relations
- Consumer relations

Publicity
- News stories
- Product promotion
- General

Miscellaneous
- Annual reports
- Testimonials
- Contests
- Recipes

Research
- Consumer panels
- Audience and readership analysis
- Market research
- Copy research

Sales Training
- Sales meetings
- Sales portfolios
- Visual sales aids
- Slide films
- Demonstrations

Product Analysis
- New product development
- Product design and styling
- Brand name development
- Trademark design
- Labeling
- Packaging
- Pretesting
- Motivational studies
- Recipe testing

Direct Mail
- Letters
- Folders
- Booklets
- Envelope stuffers
- Return cards
- Brochures
- Couponing and sampling
- Reminders—calendars, desk gifts, etc.
- Instruction booklets
- House organs
- Premiums
- Cookbooks

[2] "Growth of Advertising Agency Services," *Printers' Ink,* January 27, 1956, pp. 21–30.

Any organization performing a number of these services might properly be called a "marketing agency" instead of an advertising agency.

Agency organization

In harmony with the expansions of service, agencies have generally developed an internal organization based upon functions performed. The scope and character of organization vary according to the size of agency. A typical advertising agency organization chart is illustrated in Figure 28–1.

Research The research department gathers, analyzes, and interprets facts concerning the *consumer*—his motivations, opinions, attitudes, and buying behavior; the *product*—its want-satisfying qualities and competitive selling points; the *market*—its location, composition, and potentiality; the *competition*—their positions and marketing practices; and the *effectiveness of alternative advertising strategies.* The work of this department is more fully explained in Parts Two and Five of this book.

Media The planning and selection of media is very important. Should magazines, newspapers, radio, television, direct mail, or some other medium be used to carry the advertising message to the consumer? If magazines, what kind of magazines—women's, general, trade, or professional? And, most importantly, how does such a selection relate to the advertiser's marketing and advertising goals?

It is the function of the media department to answer these and many other questions. A close harmony should exist between this and the research department. A satisfactory answer to the above questions can come

FIGURE 28–1
A typical advertising agency organization chart by functions

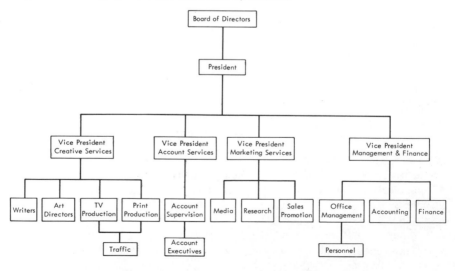

FIGURE 28–2
Newspaper schedule

LEO BURNETT COMPANY · INC.
ADVERTISING
PRUDENTIAL PLAZA · CHICAGO, ILL.   60601
TELEPHONE CEntral 6-5959

SCHEDULE OF ADVERTISING
NEWSPAPER

CLIENT	SCHEDULE NUMBER	REV	SCHEDULE NAME	MARKETING AREA	DATE	PAGE
JOS SCHLITZ	72-76A-0201-8260	1	BEER ROP CINCINNATI MCA #6615		10/13/72	2

ED	C S	INSERTION DATES	PROD CODE	SPACE	RATE	ADDITIONAL CHARGE	COST PER INSERTION	C D	FOOT NOTES	CANCEL DATE	PAYMENT DATE

SPECIAL INFORMATION

LINEAGE

CINCINNATI ENQUIRER		0	189,993						
M	6/30	1000	LI B/W	.6200		620.00			
M	9/24	1000	LI B/W	.6200		620.00			
		BENGAL OPENER SECTION			1,240.00	*		2000	*
CINCINNATI HERALD		0							
ST	7/08	1000	LI B/W	.2000		200.00	2%		
	9/23	1000	LI B/W	.2000		200.00	2%		
						400.00	*	2000	*
CINCINNATI PST TMS STR		0							
E	6/29	1000	LI B/W	.7500		750.00	2%		
E	9/21	1000	LI B/W	.7500		750.00	2%		
						1,500.00	*	2000	*

	GROSS	C/D	NET
GRAND TOTAL	3,140.00	32.30	3,107.70 *

THESE FIGURES ARE ESTIMATED COST BASED ON
LATEST QUOTATIONS AND SUBJECT TO CHANGE.
FORM 6 0/ PRINTED IN U S A 3-69

SCHEDULE
APPROVED BY_____   DATE_____

only from a knowledge of the location of prospective customers, their tastes, and their living and buying habits. The extent of dealer representation for the advertised product must also be considered.

The media department will be charged with the responsibility of knowing not only all the available media and means which can be used to carry the message of the advertiser, but also the cost and probable effectiveness of each. After a selection has been made, a detailed media schedule should be drawn up, including the names of the media to be used, the exact dates the advertisements are to appear, and the exact size of the advertisements (if to be printed) or length of time to be used (if broadcast). This schedule will serve as a blueprint to be followed in the preparation and insertion of advertisements. Figures 28–2, 28–3, and 28–4 illustrate media schedules for newspapers, spot television, and spot radio.

After media have been selected, checking on their relative effectiveness in doing the job becomes an important function of the agency. This, again, requires a close working arrangement between the research and media departments. Reference should be made to Part Four of this book for more detailed material dealing with media.

Sales promotion   Sales promotion, or merchandising, includes developing favorable dealer relations, providing dealer aids, keying the advertising program to other promotional activities of the advertiser, planning retail promotions, etc.

FIGURE 28–3
Spot television schedule

JOS. SCHLITZ BREWING COMPANY
Current Announcement Schedule—Spot TV

Brand: Schlitz Beer   Dates 3/6-3/26, 4/3-6/4
Station & Channel: WCAU - Ch. 10
City of Origin & Net. Affil.: Phildelphia - CBS   MCA: Philadelphia
Rating Source: F/M '71, May '71, Nov. '71 ARB   Division: Eastern

DAY	TIME	LENGTH	ADJACENT PROGRAMS PRECEDING/FOLLOWING	ADI. RTG.	HOMES (000)	Men 18-49 (000)	MEN 18-34 (000)	Dates	
Sun	7:30-9:30P	Various	CBS Sunday Movie	20	391	179	99	5/14, 5/28, 6/4	
Sun	9:30-10:30P	:30	Cade's County	10	213	123	76	7/2	
Mon	10-11P	:30	Sonny & Cher	11	229	110	71	6/19	
Thur	9-11P	:60	CBS Thursday Movie	18	386	173	85	5/25, 6/1	
Fri	9-10:30P	:60	CBS Friday Movie	16	357	150	68	6/16, 6/30	
M-F	11:30-c	:60	Late Movie	8	160	69	46	3/6-3/26	4/3-6/4
Sun	11:30-c	:60	Name of the Game	8	160	66	42	3/6-3/26	4/3-6/4
M-Su	6-7P	:60	Early News	11	224	68	36	3/6-3/26	4/3-6/4
Sun	Various	:60	NHL Game of the Week	4	102	53	24	3/6-3/26	4/3-6/4
Various		:30	Prime Orbit	23	506	168	106	3/6-3/26	4/3-6/4
Thur	9-11P		CBS Thursday Movie	21	483	200	113		
Sat	10-11P		Mission Impossible	20	435	200	116		
Wed	9-10P		Medical Center	26	590	173	105		
Tues	8:30-9:30P		Hawaii Five-0	23	215	170	90		
Various		:30	Prime Orbit	17	386	165	96	3/6-3/26	4/3-6/4
Sat	8-8:30 P		All In The Family	38	850	375	201		
Sun	9:30-10:30 P		Cade's County	10	213	123	76		
Mon	8-9 P		Gunsmoke	14	325	110	65		
Fri	8-9 P		O'Hara U. S. Treasure	12	273	105	68		

Creative services Included in creative services are copy, art, TV and radio production, and mechanical production. There are those who consider the copy department the most important part of an agency. It is, insofar as it interprets to prospective buyers the product or service being advertised in terms of its want-satisfying ability. The copywriter is usually supplied with the results of research to determine the strength of particular appeals, the medium in which the copy is to appear, and the amount of copy to write. He is governed, also, by the advertising plan that has been established by the client and the agency's account people. An effort is then made to develop copy that will assist in the effective execution of the planned program.

It is being recognized more and more that such qualities as beauty of expression, snappy slogans, and clever phrases in copy should not be the goal of the copywriter. He or she should attempt, instead, to ascertain the

FIGURE 28–4
Radio-spot buying preview for Jos. Schlitz Brewing Company

Brand: Schlitz Beer
Region: Southern
MCA: Mobile
Confirmation No.: 9617–S
Flight dates: 7/23–10/21 (10/13)

AVERAGE WEEKLY MARKET TOTALS

Weekly GRPs/spots: 6/144
Homes: NA
Men 18–49: 290
Men 18–34: 280
Number of spots: 144
Percent weight in 60s: 100
Percent weight in 30s: 0
Percent weight in prime: 0
Average weekly cost: $765.24

PROGRAM DETAIL

Station	No. spots/wk.	Length (seconds)	Day part
WLOX-A 24		60	7 P.M.–midnite
WTAM-F 12		60	3 P.M.–7 P.M.
	12	60	7 P.M.–midnite
WBOP-A 24		60	3 P.M.–7 P.M.
WABB-A 6		60	7 P.M.–9 P.M.
	18	60	9 P.M.–midnite
WGOK-A 24		60	3 P.M.–7 P.M.
WBSR-A 24		60	7 P.M.–midnite

NA = Not available.

fundamental characteristics of the consumer and to determine the most effective avenues of approach to his consciousness. It is not copy for copy's sake, but copy that will sell goods. Results from tests of copy effectiveness are being used more and more as a guide to the copywriter. Some copywriting principles and techniques of testing copy effectiveness were given in Parts Three and Five.

Art in advertising is valuable in dramatizing the product and its want-satisfying qualities. This consists of not only determining the type of illustrations to use in an advertisement but also the development of a plan of physical arrangement for the entire advertisement. Thus, this department is responsible primarily for developing more-or-less rough sketches of layouts and illustrations. The finished art work is usually done by an outside artist. Layouts sufficiently clear to guide the printer are all that will be necessary, unless a more comprehensive one is needed to show the client a close approximation of what the finished advertisement will be like. The important function is the effective coordination of all parts of an advertisement into a complete and unified selling message. The employees in this department should be consumer conscious as well as art conscious. It is their function to arrange a selling message in effective form rather than to produce great art.

The production of television and radio commercials requires different talents and procedures than are required for producing print advertisements. Therefore, agencies doing much television and radio work have separate creative departments for these media.

The mechanical production department is responsible for converting art work and copy into the printing plates, typography, and mats used to reproduce the finished advertisement in print media.

Account services   After a new account has been obtained, a contact person or account executive is assigned to serve as the liaison between agency and client. It is usually through the contact person that the various services of the agency are made available to the advertiser. It is his or her responsibility to obtain the client's acceptance and approval of the agency's campaign plan, individual advertisements, media plan, etc. The account executive may take part in the research and marketing activities of the advertiser. In fact, he or she is supposed to be thoroughly familiar with all of the marketing and advertising problems of the client and capable of presenting suggested solutions to these problems in such a way that they will be accepted by the advertiser.

Internal services   As in most business enterprises, an advertising agency requires accounting, financial control, personnel management, office management, secretarial work, and clerical help.

Business getting   The agency, like the advertiser, has something to sell. If the agency is to give the service expected, a volume of business compatible with its facilities for service must be maintained. It is, therefore, quite logical to set up a group of people charged with the responsibility of getting new business to replace accounts that have been lost, to balance declines in the business of present clients, and to secure new accounts where an increased volume of business is desired.

The agency has an opportunity, through the work of this group, to demonstrate its ability to do an advertising and selling job. No "client" is present to veto a proposed program. The sales problem is strictly an individual one. All the merchandising, research, copy, and art facilities of the agency are available for the development of an effective sales program. A challenge should be laid down to do for itself the kind of selling job it claims to be able to do for a client.

Methods followed in obtaining new business are determined by the individual agency. Competition for new business is based largely upon service, rather than price, because of the rather intangible nature of that which is being sold.

Coordination of complete campaign

The advertising agency may be referred to as a collection of specialized business brains. The functional organization of the agency is designed to facilitate the work of these specialists. It is vital, however, that the work of each person be directed toward one common goal—the successful planning, development, and execution of the complete campaign.

The basic plan underlying a given campaign will usually be determined by the account executive serving as contact person with the client, other key executives, and certain members of important departments. Upon the work of this committee or plans board will depend much of the success of the campaign. In many respects, this is the very heart of the agency's operation—the creative application of its specialized knowledge and experience to build a successful advertising *plan* for the product. Molding the work of specialists in research, copy, art, media, and production into a harmonious and coordinated program is the particular task of agency management.

It is important that the work of various departments or functionaries be scheduled in a manner that will make possible the completion of an advertisement in ample time to meet media deadlines. Here, again, the coordination efforts of management are vital. Production schedules somewhat comparable to assembly-line techniques are often necessary. Plates cannot be made until art work is finished, the printer must wait for finished copy, insertion orders cannot be placed until media have been selected and approved by the client, etc. Delays in one department must thus be made up in another if the advertisement is to be in the hands of the publisher before the closing of forms. Good management will see that there is a minimum of delays and conflicts.

New developments

In the evolution of the advertising agency, there continually have been notable developments which have affected various aspects of agency organization and operation. Presently, a number of developments appear to be of special significance and shall be discussed briefly.

The growth of so-called media "middlemen" or independent media-buying services has been a new development of importance. Middlemen serve advertisers and agencies through the performance of the media-buying function. They operate mainly in the broadcast area, buying time on radio and television stations. In fact, independent services now handle 12 percent of all radio and television billings.[3]

---

[3] *Media Decisions,* July 1973, p. 30.

FIGURE 28–5
An advertisement for agency offering "modular" service

YOUR BIGGEST PROBLEM
AGENCY AND HOW

Every advertiser has a different concept of "full service." For you, it's that specific combination of advertising services that fits your needs. Maybe that means the traditional "package" provided by an ordinary full-service agency. But maybe it doesn't. And that's when you have a problem.

INTRODUCING CUSTOM-DESIGNED ADVERTISING

At Gardner, we think you should be able to get full service from a professional advertising agency without having to buy more services than you really need.

So we've developed something pretty unusual for an advertising agency. The ability to operate united—or divided. This means we can serve you in the traditional way, if that's what you require. Or we can divide ourselves into individual "modules." Each one an independent service. Functioning separately. Separately priced. So we can pull together precisely the services that will meet your needs. That's what we mean when we say we can custom-design your advertising program.

WE IMPROVED THE WHOLE BY IMPROVING THE PARTS

But, frankly, all of this reorganizing wasn't just for your benefit. We had another motive. We reasoned that dividing up our agency into individual modules would not only allow us to provide an advertiser with the specific services he needs, but would also make us a better full-service agency. Because if each department was to be aggressively marketed, each one had to develop something extraordinary to sell.

To illustrate, here is a sampling of Gardner's modules and the innovative services we can now give you:

ADVANSWERS MEDIA/PROGRAMMING, INC.

Our media module. You'll find Advanswers' approach several years ahead of the rest of the industry. Six years of R & D work have resulted in the use of powerful scientific computers to produce more effective methods of exposing advertising. For example, one of our systems accurately forecasts the minimum going rates for TV, by market, for two years into the future. This system can help you plan more productive media investments. And save you money in the process.

GARDIAN PRODUCTIONS, INC.

Our film production module. Designed to give you high quality production for a sensible price, Gardian bases all billing on three simple but revolutionary principles. Our markup is a constant 20%, compared to the 30 to 60% industry norms. Our fee is fixed—it won't go up if your job goes over-budget. And our books are open—you know exactly how much you're paying for what you're getting.

WESTGATE RESEARCH, INC.

Our research module. Westgate offers several exclusive services. Like the most advanced approach to small-sample qualitative research in the country. And a way of testing your commercials on air before you spend money producing them. We can show you how this testing procedure could save you thousands of dollars every year.

VANGARD COMMUNICATIONS, INC.

Our technical module. If yours is a "technical" field, whether agribusiness, industrial, or service-oriented, Vangard can give you a complete range of the marketing communications services you'll need—from sales incentive programs to consumer television commercials. Specifically structured to serve your kind of account, you'll enjoy Vangard's small-agency flexibility coupled with its large-agency resources.

FIGURE 28–5 (*Continued*)

WITH THE FULL-SERVICE WE SOLVED IT.

GARDNER CREATIVE

Modularization has added a new dimension to our creative department as well. In operating a la carte, our creative people have had to take a broader view of the creative process. They have become more intimately involved in product positioning, the marketing environment, and all the other realities of communicating to the right people in the right way to sell your product.

Another development has added greatly to creative's new vitality. That's the addition to our staff of some of Wells, Rich, Greene's top creative talents. Their enthusiasm and striving for creative excellence have greatly improved the way we work, the way we think, and the quality of our output.

The best proof of this? The clients we serve. Among them:

Anheuser-Busch
Banquet Foods Corporation
Cessna Aircraft
Deere & Company
Eli Lilly/Elanco
General Dynamics
ITT/Financial Services
Jack Daniel Distillery
Brunswick/Mercury Marine
Northwest Industries/Velsicol
Ralston Purina
Southwestern Bell
Sun Oil

HOW DOES ALL THIS HELP YOU?

Now you can have an advertising plan tailored to your needs by a professional, highly competent full-service agency. And your projects will be staffed with a team from our more than 200 employees—most of whom have worked with some of the country's top 30 advertising agencies.

On the other hand, if you're one of the great majority of advertisers who still requires full-service capabilities, you'll find our reorganization means improved service for you too. Because, in the process of strengthening each individual department's services to sell them modularly, our full-service performance has become more disciplined, more businesslike, more clearly defined. That's meant more efficient output for every client.

Finally, it makes sense to us that just as services should be custom-tailored to the advertising problem, so should compensation be tailored to the situation. So we now offer a variety of compensation systems in addition to the standard 15%-of-media commission, including a flat-fee system, a commission plus-fee system, and a project-bid system, among others. So in addition to getting only the services you need—you'll pay only for what you get.

So whether you buy Gardner's services modularly or on a full service basis, you'll be giving your product its best chance in every way. From positioning it, to pinpointing its market. From exposure of messages in the media, to creation of those messages. In these and all the steps in between, you'll be getting advertising that gets attention, evokes a reaction, and most importantly, sells your product.

Gardner Advertising. Tell us *your* advertising problems. We'll analyze your needs and custom-design the advertising program to solve them. Call Barry Loughrane in St. Louis at 314-444-2000 or in New York at 212-759-8940.

UNITED WE STAND. DIVIDED WE STAND.

GARDNER ADVERTISING COMPANY
NEW YORK, ST. LOUIS, HOLLYWOOD

In serving a client, either advertiser or agency, middlemen claim they can do a better job of buying than the agency's media department. By "better" they usually mean securing either cheaper rates or more desirable broadcast spots. A basic question here is: Why did such an organization come into existence? There are many explanations offered for the origin of middlemen, but one of the most salient is that agency media departments were not as efficient as required by the marketplace. The growth of middlemen, however, has allowed agencies to reexamine their media function and, where necessary, to improve the service offered to clients. Middlemen, though, will continue to function by serving advertisers who prefer not to use agencies and agencies who prefer not to have a media department.

Closely related to the development of media middlemen has been the emergence of specialists in the creative function—creative "boutiques." These organizations usually operate as small agencies and limit their client service to creative planning and execution. They leave other advertising functions—for example, media, research, and merchandising—to either the advertiser or to other specialists such as the media middleman. The handling of advertising in this way—that is, by independent specialists— has led to the term "à la carte" which contrasts with the concept of a full-service agency providing a multitude of functions.[4]

The desire of some advertisers to have closer control over the advertising function has resulted in the use of "in-house" agencies. This development is where an advertiser establishes his own agency rather than using an existing one. The purposes typically are to provide a greater control over the advertising function and to better coordinate advertising and marketing. As to whether these goals are actually achieved is a moot point. Often, advertisers setting up a house agency do so because they believe they can save money by so doing. In fact, the increase in such organizations since the middle 1960s has been attributed to the profit squeeze situation.[5] There are a substantial number of companies using house agencies for brands in the early stage of market development. This is done in order to retain the greatest possible control and confidentiality for a test brand; then, once the brand is launched on a larger scale, the advertiser uses the services of an outside agency.

The growth of media middlemen, creative boutiques, and in-house agencies has caused much soul searching on the part of full-service agencies. As mentioned, this often has meant a reexamination of specific functions and improvement of the quality of services. It also has resulted in some agencies modifying their organization to the extent that they can offer client service on an à la carte or "modular" basis. The advertisement

[4] For a complete discussion, see Barton A. Cummings, "Full Service Agencies vs. A la Carte," *Journal of Advertising,* Vol. 2, No. 1 (1973), pp. 12–15.

[5] Ibid.

for the Gardner Agency in Figure 28–5 provides a good explanation of this development.

Although not directly related to the developments discussed above, one additional situation merits comment. In recent years a number of advertising agencies have become "public" corporations by offering their stock for sale to the general public. In 1973 there were some 20 agencies listed on one of the stock exchanges or their stock sold on an over-the-counter basis. An agency may go public for a number of reasons, perhaps the primary one being increased liquidity. A public agency, though, also may achieve benefits through wider publicity and by acquiring subsidiary companies. The opportunity for employees to purchase stock easily is available and can contribute to better morale and incentive. Although agency stocks have not done especially well in the market, it is still likely that more and more agencies will be publicly owned in the future.

Protection of ideas

Ideas and the ability to make them articulate and alive constitute the primary properties of the advertising agency. The character of ideas used in advertising often encourages persons to submit suggestions to agencies for possible use, with the hope of monetary reward. Likewise, the agency will at times submit ideas to a prospective client in the process of soliciting new business. The agency thus has the dual problem of protecting itself against the use of ideas belonging to others and protecting its own ideas from being appropriated.

In the past, and to a considerable degree today, primary protection is afforded by the integrity of those involved in the commerce of ideas. In 1935, however, two cases were tried in U.S. courts in which theft of advertising ideas formed the basis of the litigation. One of these cases was *Ryan and Associates* v. *Century Brewing Association,* tried in the Superior Court of King County, Washington, and affirmed by the Supreme Court of Washington.[6] The plaintiff, How. J. Ryan & Associates, Inc., had previously solicited the account of the Century Brewing Association. They had outlined various advertising suggestions in the one and one-half hour presentation made to the company. These suggestions included the slogan, "The Beer of the Century." An agency other than How. J. Ryan & Associates obtained the account. Some time later, however, when the advertising of the Century Brewing Association appeared, the slogan, "The Beer of the Century," formed a prominent part.

The plaintiff brought action against the brewing company. During the trial they were required to establish three points: (1) that the slogan was

---

[6] *Ryan and Associates* v. *Century Brewing Association,* Washington Reports, Vol. 185, p. 600.

first conceived by the plaintiff, (2) that it is customary in advertising agency practice for the agency to receive compensation for its ideas if used by the advertiser, and (3) that the Century Brewing Association received value from the use of the slogan in question. The verdict was in favor of the plaintiff. A sum of $7,500 was granted them by the court. The legal basis for the decision was the common law doctrine of unjust enrichment.

The other case decided in 1935 was somewhat different. It was brought by a man who had written a letter to Liggett & Myers Tobacco Company in which he suggested a certain advertising theme for billboard advertising and asked for compensation for the idea. The tobacco company did not acknowledge the letter in any way. Some two years after receipt of the letter, Liggett & Myers used advertising which was similar, but not identical, to the suggestion sent in by the plaintiff.

Court action was brought, and a verdict in favor of the plaintiff was handed down. A judgment of $9,000 was awarded. The decision in this case was based upon an implied contract rather than unjust enrichment. An offer was made by the plaintiff when he mailed the letter. He had at no time withdrawn the offer, and the company had not rejected it. The use of the idea by the company, even though some two years later, was construed as an acceptance of the offer.[7]

The problem of protecting ideas is a delicate one and is difficult to handle. Many agencies and advertisers have adopted the policy of refusing to receive ideas from anyone until a clear understanding of possible liability has been established.

Methods of paying the agency

The methods by which the agency receives compensation for work performed have been the subject of much discussion. It is therefore pertinent to inquire into both method and philosophy.

Commission plan   The most common method by which the advertising agency receives compensation for its services is the so-called "commission plan." It is, in essence, a discount from list price given the agency by the medium in which space is purchased. In other words, the medium—newspaper, magazine, radio, etc.—pays the agency.

An example will illustrate the general procedure. Company A contracts with Agency X to have X engineer an advertising campaign for the company. A total of $500,000 has been appropriated for this campaign. Agency X will perform a part or all of the functions set forth above. Let us assume that space amounting to $450,000 is contracted for in magazines and newspapers. These media will bill X for the $450,000, less the regular discount allowed agencies, usually amounting to 15 percent. This

---

[7] *Meyer* v. *Liggett & Myers Tobacco Co.,* 194 N.E. 206.

leaves a net bill of $382,500, which X will pay the various media. Agency X will bill the advertiser for the full $450,000.

Commissions from advertising media provide some 65 percent of agency income, on the average. The larger the agency, the higher is the proportion of income accounted for by commissions. But even among the largest agencies between 10 percent and 25 percent of their income comes from other methods of payment.

Other methods of payment   In addition to the commissions received from media, agencies also receive direct payment from advertisers for materials and services, such as engravings, finished art, comprehensive layouts, TV storyboards, producer's services for TV commercials, research, and publicity. Various methods of charging advertisers are used. For some materials and services the advertiser is charged the *cost* to the agency. For others the charge is *cost plus 15 percent,* to compensate the agency for service in connection with specifying, controlling, and consummating the purchase. For still others a *flat fee* is charged.

There is no standard practice to determine what services are performed in consideration of commissions received from media and what services are charged for separately. It seems obvious, however, that a fixed percentage commission will cover the cost of more services for an advertiser spending $1 million a year than for one spending only $50,000. In many respects, it is as costly to produce an advertisement to be placed in a small-circulation magazine as it is to produce an ad to be placed in a large-circulation magazine; yet, the former provides a much smaller commission than the latter. Thus, the smaller the agency and the smaller the

TABLE 28–1
Principal methods of compensating agencies

Method	Percent advertisers using different compensation methods						
	1 media com- mission only	2 fee, plus media com- mission	3 fee, media com- mission credited	4 flat fee	5 at cost to agency	6 cost to agency plus per- centage	Total
Type of service							
Copy (magazines, newspapers)	66.6	17.6	4.3	3.7	2.1	5.7	100
Copy (direct mail, display)	21.5	15.1	3.9	23.9	9.6	26.0	100
Finished art	9.1	17.1	1.0	13.9	12.4	46.5	100
Marketing research	9.1	9.1	.6	41.5	19.6	20.1	100
Publicity	8.2	8.9	1.1	40.5	23.8	17.5	100
Engravings, typography	10.5	13.2	1.1	8.3	13.0	53.9	100

Source: "Frey Report On Agency Services and Compensation," *Advertising Age,* November 4, 1957, p. 132.

account, the greater is the dependence on fees and service charges as sources of income.

In cases of direct mail, dealer display, and some business publication advertising, the fee basis is often most advisable. Certainly, the commission plan cannot be depended upon for direct-mail and dealer-display work, since these media are noncommissionable.

Charging the advertiser an annual retainer—or "professional fee" is another method used by some agencies. Under this method, commissions granted by the media are usually credited against these fees, although some agencies work for a minimum annual retainer and add commissions from media to this. This works well where the bulk of the advertising is done through noncommissionable media.

An agency's work on a campaign to introduce a new product can become a losing proposition if the product fails. To protect the agency from this kind of loss, one client, the Lever Brothers Company, pays a fee "for a large portion—but not all—of the direct cost of new product work; with these fees recoverable from subsequent agreed levels of billing if the product succeeds, and retained by the agency if it does not."[8]

The relative importance of various methods of compensating agencies for different types of service is indicated in Table 28–1.

Qualifications for agency commission

Allowance of commissions to advertising agencies is the method developed over the years by advertising media to promote the sale and more effective use of their space and time. In effect, the 15 percent commission operates as a *functional discount* granted to agencies for performing functions that benefit media. Agencies promote advertising as a marketing instrument. They develop new business. They increase the productivity of advertising. They centralize the servicing of many accounts. They reduce the publisher's cost in the mechanical preparation of advertising. They reduce credit risk.

To qualify for the commission an agency has to meet certain requirements. Prior to 1956, media granted commissions only to "recognized" agencies. Recognition was a function performed by individual media owners and their trade associations, such as the American Newspaper Publishers Association, Publishers Association of New York City, Associated Business Publications, Periodical Publishers Association, and Agricultural Publishers Association. To secure recognition an agency had to meet the following requirements:

1.   Be a *bona fide* agency—that is, free from control by an advertiser, in order that it may not be prejudiced or restricted in its service to

[8] Milton C. Mumford, *The Advertising Agency As A Business Institution* (New York: American Association of Advertising Agencies, 1966), p. 4.

all clients; free from control by a medium owner, in order that it may give unbiased advice to advertisers in the selection of media.

2. *Keep all commissions* (that is, not rebate any) received from media owners, in order to maintain their rate cards and to devote the commissions to such service and development of advertising as the individual media owners desire.

3. Possess *adequate personnel* of experience and ability to serve general advertisers.

4. Have the *financial capacity* to meet the obligations it incurs to the media owners.

On May 12, 1955, the Department of Justice filed a civil antitrust suit against the American Association of Advertising Agencies and the five media associations listed above. In the complaint it was alleged that the defendants in violation of the Sherman Act, engaged in "unlawful combinations, conspiracies, understandings, and agreements" with particular reference to the uniform standards for recognition of advertising agencies, the withholding of commissions from agencies not recognized, the charging of gross rates to direct advertisers, and the fixing of the commission at 15 percent of the gross rate.

On February 1, 1956, a consent decree was entered in the U.S. District Court in New York City enjoining and restraining the A.A.A.A. from engaging in the alleged practices. Similar consent decrees were entered later for the defendant media associations involved in the suit. It should be noted, however, that this suit dealt entirely with acts by the associations and did not relate to individual arrangements between an agency and a medium or between an agency and its clients.

Considerable speculation followed the settlement of this suit. Did it spell the end of the 15 percent commission as a standard of agency compensation? Would there now be many house agencies? Would there be widespread rebating? Would advertisers be able to buy at net rates? As of 18 years later, no major changes along these lines have taken place, although "house" agencies today are generally able to secure the 15 percent commission. The traditional recognition procedure, especially the role played by the associations, has been abandoned, but individual media continue to grant the 15 percent commission much as they have in the past. The associations continue to furnish "credit ratings" of advertising agencies to their members. In the case of A.N.P.A., an agency applying for credit rating may be required to demonstrate that it:

1. Itself assumes sole liability for the full performance of its contracts with newspapers;

2. Makes prompt payments;

3. Is morally responsible;

4. Is engaged in the business of developing, servicing, and placing national advertising in newspapers; and

5. Maintains a minimum of 25 percent of its average monthly billing in liquid capital and surplus.

Appraisal of the commission system

The commission system has been the subject of controversy for many years. Major criticism has hinged around the unique client-agency-medium relationship. The agency, instead of being a vendor for the publisher as it once was, is now a "close-working partner" of the advertiser, but the compensation system has not been changed to meet these new conditions. There is strong feeling among advertisers that they—the agency's "clients," not the various media—should be the ones to pay the agency for its services. They suggest that media should sell to the advertiser at net rates so that the advertiser can negotiate with the agency to arrive at a mutually satisfactory compensation.

Principal objections to the commission system concern (1) the fixed percentage of media cost and (2) the client's lack of control over services paid for through the commission.

A fixed percentage of the cost of space and time provides the agency with compensation that may or may not be related to the cost of services performed. The agency's cost of producing an advertisement to appear in space costing $40,000 would probably not be ten times the cost of producing an ad to appear in space costing $4,000. Yet, the agency's compensation would be ten times greater for the former than for the latter. Also, on a fixed percentage basis, the more the client spends the more the agency makes. This creates the suspicion that the agency has no incentive to hold down the cost of advertising.

Lacking control over the services covered by the commission, the advertiser is compelled to negotiate for these so-called "free services." Is he getting all of the services to which he is entitled? Is he being forced to pay for services that he would not order if he controlled the amount and kind of work done on his account? Are the fees that he pays over and above the commission justified? Many advertisers feel that they do not have a large enough part in planning what the agency is to do for the commission it receives.

Supporters of the commission system claim that it is a means of rewarding agencies in direct proportion to the use that is made of their creative work. This is a "box office" approach to determining the value of an agency's service. It assumes that the value of an advertisement depends on the size of audience it reaches, not on the cost of producing it. However, most agencies would be quick to point out that they allocate more time and higher-salaried creative people to producing advertisements for big audiences than for small audiences, thereby also adapting the cost of production to the size of audience to be reached. To further reduce possible inequities arising from a fixed commission on media expenditures, agencies generally include more "free services" on big billings than on small billings.

Other arguments in favor of the commission system are that it places agency competition on a creative service basis instead of a price basis, that it has worked satisfactorily, though imperfectly, through the years, and that it will have to do until a better system comes along.

Both the Association of National Advertisers and the American Association of Advertising Agencies have made studies of the merits and shortcomings of the commission system. The former has, in general, questioned the wisdom of the method, while the latter has considered it superior to any other as a basic method of compensation. The latest study of agency services and compensation was commissioned by the A.N.A. and was conducted by professors Albert Frey and Kenneth Davis. This study indicated that a majority of all advertising managers, agencies, and media found the commission system satisfactory, but about one third of the advertising managers believed that a system involving net rates, no commissions, and fees fixed by negotiation between agency and client would be a better system.[9]

Agencies in international marketing

With the growth of world advertising expenditures to a present level of approximately $35 billion, it is to be expected that advertising agencies—both U.S. based and those from other countries—would be heavily involved in international marketing. In fact, the ten largest U.S. agencies in 1972 derived over 40 percent of their total billings outside of the United States.

Although a few U.S. agencies have had foreign branches for many years (J. Walter Thompson opened a London office before 1900), it is only since the rapid growth of international business during the 1960s and 1970s that such agency expansion has occurred. Of the 50 largest agencies in the United States today, 32 have billings in foreign countries. Table 28–2 shows these 50 agencies in terms of their United States and world billings. Many companies whose products are distributed internationally prefer to use the same agency throughout the world. The reasons usually given for this preference are:

1. The agency can coordinate the planning and preparation of advertising and promotional programs;
2. The agency can transfer creative materials from one location to another;

[9] Albert W. Frey and Kenneth R. Davis, *The Advertising Industry; Agency Services, Working Relationships, Compensation Methods* (New York: Association of National Advertisers, Inc., 1958), pp. 298, 299.

TABLE 28–2
World and U.S. billings of leading agencies, 1972

Billing rank			
World	*U.S.*	*World billing*	*U.S. billing*
1	1	J. Walter Thompson Co. $767.0	$393.0
2	8	McCann-Erickson* 625.0	207.7
3	2	Young & Rubicam 563.5	357.7
4	4	Leo Burnett Co. 471.2	313.4
5	6	Ted Bates & Co. 457.8	252.8
6	9	Ogilvy & Mather International. 399.2	200.0
7	3	Batten, Barton, Durstine & Osborn 370.1	323.2
8	5	Doyle Dane Bernbach 323.0	259.1
9	7	Grey Advertising. 314.0	247.0
10	17	SSC&B. 269.4	134.7
11	10	Foote, Cone & Belding Communications 266.5	194.3
12	11	D'Arcy-MacManus & Masius. 231.0	181.0
13	16	Benton & Bowles 225.7	160.2
14	13	Needham, Harper & Steers 205.9	171.5
15	12	Dancer-Fitzgerald-Sample 183.0	178.0
16	21	Compton Advertising 177.3	102.3
17	27	Norman, Craig & Kummel. 168.9	67.7
18	14	William Esty Co. 165.0	165.0
19	15	N. W. Ayer & Son 163.0	163.0
20	20	Kenyon & Eckhardt Advertising. 126.7	107.0
21	18	Wells, Rich, Greene 118.3	112.4
22	22	Ketchum, MacLeod & Grove. 116.3	99.8
23	19	Campbell-Ewald Co.* 112.0	112.0
24	25	Marsteller Inc. 99.8	81.9
25	23	Clinton E. Frank Inc. 86.8	86.8
26	24	Cunningham & Walsh 85.2	85.2
27	26	Campbell-Mithun 76.0	76.0
28	28	Ross Roy Inc. 60.3	60.3
29	29	Bozell & Jacobs 60.1	60.1
30	30	Gardner Advertising 59.0	57.7
31	35	Warwick, Welsh & Miller 57.0	53.0
32	31	Post-Keyes-Gardner 56.4	56.4
33	33	Tatham-Laird & Kudner 56.3	55.3
33	32	McCaffrey & McCall 56.3	56.3
35	34	Griswold-Eshleman Co. 55.0	54.0
36	38	Carl Ally Inc. 48.6	45.3
37	36	Marschalk Co.* 47.2	47.2
38	37	Doremus & Co. 46.9	46.9
39	39	Rumrill-Hoyt 42.3	42.1
40	40	Fuller & Smith & Ross 38.8	38.4
41	41	Albert Frank-Guenther Law 38.1	38.1
42	42	Honig-Cooper & Harrington 36.0	36.0
43	43	Della Femina, Travisano & Partners 35.3	35.3
44	44	DKG Inc. 34.2	33.0
45	48	Sudler & Hennessey 34.0	31.0
46	54	Wunderman, Ricotta & Kline. 33.9	28.3
47	46	Daniel & Charles 32.3	31.8
48	45	W. B. Doner & Co. 32.0	32.0
49	47	John F. Murray Advertising 31.5	31.5
50	48	William Douglas McAdams Inc. 31.0	31.0

* Part of Interpublic Group of Cos., whose agency units last year billed an estimated world aggregate of $893,099,000.
Source: *Advertising Age,* February 26, 1973.

3. Small accounts in some countries receive services that on an individual basis might not be profitable for the agency—that is, the advertiser receives service that he could not get from another agency; and
4. The agency can furnish periodic reports on the services it has performed for subsidiaries.[10]

The increased involvement of agencies in international advertising is highly likely to continue well into the 1980s. Many of the top U.S. agencies will get at least half of their advertising volume from abroad, and most of these agencies will get even a higher percentage of their profits from foreign billings.[11]

Future of the advertising agency

The future of the advertising agency can be exceedingly bright. Its substantial growth and success in the past have resulted in large measure from the increased degree to which it has turned from a mere peddler of space to a true servant of the advertiser. Today, the opportunity awaits the agency to broaden its scope of service. It does now, in a number of instances, and can in the future in many more instances, serve as an efficient marketing and advertising counselor to business.

There were 5,700 advertising agencies in the United States in 1972. However, total agency billings, a measure of the business done by agencies for their clients, are highly concentrated in relatively few agencies. *Advertising Age* estimated that 63 agencies, each billing over $25 million a year, accounted for total billings of $8.6 billion in 1972. These 63 agencies accounted for 75 percent of all agency billings. The top ten agencies, each billing over $250 million, billed a combined $4.6 billion or 41 percent of the total.

The small agency will, of course, find it difficult to provide the same breadth of service as that afforded by the large integrated agency. On the other hand, the large agency seldom makes its services available to the small advertiser, and hence the latter is deprived of that outside counsel unless the small agency is accepted. Recent developments in the form of agency networks have given the small agency some of the values of integration afforded by the large agency. A network consists of the grouping of many small agencies in all parts of the country for purposes of exchanging ideas, pooling research undertakings, trading operational data, and exchanging pertinent information in respect to successful campaigns. This development holds much promise for the small agency as well as the small advertiser.

---

[10] Gordon E. Miracle, "International Advertising," *Handbook of Advertising Management,* ed. Roger Barton (New York: McGraw-Hill Book Co., 1970), pp. 31–42.

[11] See E. B. Weiss, "The Shape of the Agency Business Beyond 1980," *Advertising Age,* June 26, 1972, pp. 61–68.

QUESTIONS AND PROBLEMS

1   The commission method of compensating advertising agencies has often been questioned. What are some of the reasons for questioning the method? What do you recommend as a method of payment? Why?

2   What is meant by the term "wholesaling" in connection with advertising agencies?

3   Explain how the research department of an agency might best serve an advertising client. How should the research function relate to other functions within the agency?

4   Outline the organization of a modern advertising agency by departments. What effect does the size of the agency have upon its functions?

5   What protection does the creator of ideas have when such ideas are offered to an advertising agency? Why is this so important to the agency?

6   What differences do you see in the *recognition* procedure, as practiced by media trade associations prior to 1956, and the furnishing of *credit ratings* such as those provided by the A.N.P.A. after 1956?

7   The advertising agency has increased its functions over the years until it is now a potent factor in developing merchandising and selling ideas for the advertiser. What changes in agency practice would you recommend as a means of increasing still further the services rendered the advertiser?

8   "When we are ill, we call in a doctor. When we have legal difficulties, we call in a lawyer." Is it therefore logical that when we have product promotional problems, we call in an advertising agency? Should we place the same faith in the agency that we place in the doctor or the lawyer? Explain in detail.

9   The account services person provides the necessary liaison between the advertising agency and the advertiser. What kind of qualifications do you feel are necessary to perform this task efficiently? What educational background is most helpful to such people? Why?

10   "Media middlemen and creative boutiques are just a fad and will die out in a few years." Do you agree or disagree with this statement?

11   Why would a U.S. agency want to open offices in foreign countries?

12   After ten years with a nationally known advertising agency, Bob Peterson has finally been able to return to his first love—his own agency in his own home town in Indiana. The town is small, a little under 50,000 population, but Peterson knows every retail establishment there.

In fact, he hopes to serve retailers primarily. In his town these include 2 "department" stores, about 15 specialty shops, 6 supermarkets, and a number of stores of other types.

Peterson knows how to write copy, make layouts, and has worked in the media department in an agency. He has been able to get two other men, both able to perform most of the services offered by larger advertising agencies, although not on the same scale and perhaps not as expertly.

Peterson is aware that most agencies avoid retail clients as much as possible because of their unique merchandising situations, but he thinks that by having as many noncompeting retailers as possible he can make a go of his business.

Many policy-making problems present themselves. One problem is the selection of a method of compensation that is satisfactory to the retail stores and to himself. He bears in mind that his is the first agency of its kind in this area and that he has to prove himself.

Recently, there has been a great deal of talk about an "agency network," a cooperative organization of small agencies who band together for legal, accounting, and research advice. Individually a small agency could not undertake these services, but spread over a number of them the cost would be relatively small. Peterson has been approached by a representative of such a network and must make a decision.

What sort of advice would you give Peterson concerning his problems? If you were offered an opportunity to join his agency, would you take it? Why?

29

The advertising
department

At one time the advertising policies and all advertising work carried on directly by the advertiser were the responsibility of the sales department or the president's office. More recently, most large-scale advertisers and many of those operating on a smaller plane have established a separate department in which all advertising problems are centered. The top advertising executive in a company typically is given broad responsibility for the planning and execution of the advertising task. In many instances this executive will be at the vice presidential level, thus indicating advertising's importance in the company structure.

Organization of the advertising department

To promote more effective integration of advertising management functions within corporate organizations, various associations (such as the Association of National Advertisers) and management consultants have studied the methods of representative firms. For example, Russell Colley, a well-known management consultant in the advertising field, has pointed out that surveys among hundreds of leading national advertisers indicate that advertising organizations can be classified into six basic types:

1. Advertising is one of several functions reporting to the chief executive.
2. Advertising is one of several marketing functions reporting to the chief marketing executive.

642

3. Advertising reports to the chief sales executive (or at a level below this position).
4. In a multidivision corporation, advertising is a centralized operating department.
5. In a multidivision corporation, advertising is decentralized, operating at the division level.
6. In a multidivision corporation, advertising is decentralized at the operating division level, with a centralized advertising department at the corporate level to provide staff services to the operating divisions, and with line responsibility for corporate advertising.[1]

In deciding exactly which type of advertising organization to utilize, Colley suggests that a company deal with some fundamental questions:

1. What is advertising's purpose and function in the company?
2. Should advertising and sales promotion be under a single head or under separate heads? Should advertising and public relations be combined?
3. In a multiproduct or multidivision corporation, should there be a central advertising department serving all products and divisions or a separate advertising department for each autonomous division or product group?
4. What are the pros and cons of the product manager type of organization?[2]

Once advertising's position within the corporate structure is established, there are further decisions relative to the internal organization of the advertising department itself. Although there are numerous formats for organizing the department, five basic approaches will be considered.

One method is to organize the advertising department according to the *subfunctions* of advertising. Thus, we might find the advertising executive coordinating such tasks as creative, art and production, media, and advertising research. Figure 29–1 shows a department organized along these lines.

Secondly, a company might organize the advertising department by *product*. This method is, of course, available only to a multiproduct company. There are at least two options to this approach, depending upon whether the advertising department is centralized or decentralized. Figure 29–2 indicates a product approach for a centralized operation, whereas Figure 29–3 shows the decentralized method in which there is a corporate advertising function to provide staff assistance to product managers. This latter method is quite typical in a brand manager or product manager type of organization.

The advertising department also can organize internally according to *market* or *end user*. Structurally this format is the same as that shown in

---

[1] Russell H. Colley, "Organizing for Advertising," *Handbook of Modern Marketing,* ed. Victor P. Buell (New York: McGraw-Hill Book Co., 1970), pp. 8–79.
[2] Ibid.

FIGURE 29–1
Organization of the advertising department according to subfunction of advertising

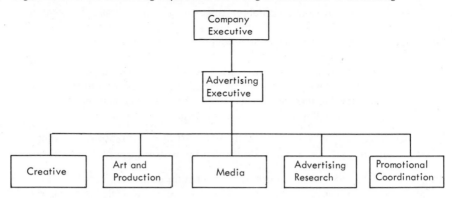

Figure 29–2, with market divisions substituted for product. For example, a marketer of a detergent product might subdivide the department into institutional users (hospitals, hotels, restaurants), industrial users (manufacturing plants), military installations, and ultimate consumer market.

A fourth organizational format is according to *media.* Although not used extensively, it is a method that can be useful for an advertiser with a product requiring unique treatment on a medium-by-medium basis. Figure 29–4 indicates this structure.

Lastly, a marketer can structure the advertising department by *geography.* This would be similar to Figure 29–2, with various geographical areas (Northeast, Central, South, West) in place of individual products.

The five methods mentioned can, of course, be combined in any number of ways. Each company must establish that organizational format which is most workable for its needs at a particular point in time. The

FIGURE 29–2
Centralized advertising department organized by product

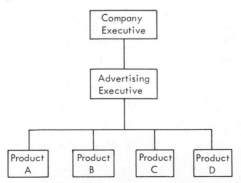

FIGURE 29–3
Decentralized advertising department organized by product, with staff advertising assistance provided to product managers

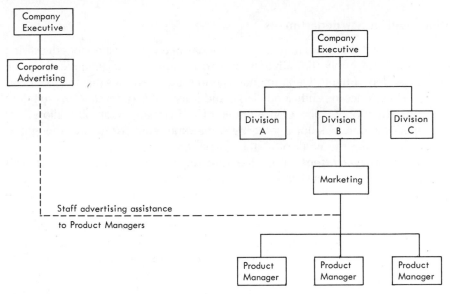

FIGURE 29–4
Advertising department organized by media

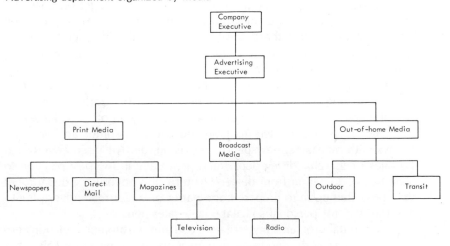

proper functioning of the department must constantly be appraised, and the alert marketer changes or modifies the format as conditions warrant.

Relations with other departments

The fact that a separate department has been established for advertising should not imply that advertising is to be operated independently of all other departments. Departmentalization usually signifies that the particular field has become sufficiently large and important to demand the full time and attention of one or a number of individuals. Such size allows for specialization of labor but, at the same time, calls for greater thought in coordinating the work of all the specialists.

Sales department   The advertising department will need to work with the sales department more than with any other. It must always be remembered that advertising is one type of selling. True, it is of such importance that it often needs to be separated from the direct supervision of the sales manager. However, the same fundamental principles that govern one should govern the other. There are certain kinds of data that each department will want collected, although the use made of such data may differ. The measurement of sales possibilities, both in total and by territories, will be of value to both departments. Both will be interested in determining an effective appeal or appeals in presenting the sales message to prospective customers by personal salesmen, by radio or television, or by the printed word. The basic appeal should be used by all sales agencies.

Those data and ideas that are used cooperatively might be collected cooperatively. Many companies have established a marketing research department to perform these common tasks. In the absence of such a separation of function, common supervision of such work by those interested in the results may be advisable.

There are other matters in which the degree of success attained from the work of one department is dependent upon the work of the other. Thus, the effectiveness of an advertising campaign can often be increased materially by getting dealers to time the use of counter and window displays with magazine, newspaper, television, and/or radio advertising. The sales or merchandising department is usually in the best position to solicit this cooperation from dealers. In turn, the advertising department might be called upon to prepare trade-paper or direct-mail advertising to pave the way for personal solicitation by salesmen.

These mutual problems necessitate close and harmonious relations between the sales and advertising departments. In some companies, the advertising manager or his assistants spend part of their time traveling with the salesmen or visiting dealers to know selling problems firsthand. Conversely, a few concerns include in their training of new salesmen a period of work in the advertising department.

Production department   There is also a close relationship between the advertising and production departments. The advertiser might like to have the product restyled, changed in color, standardized as to size, improved in its operation, or packaged differently. The sales and advertising departments together should be charged with the responsibility of finding out what people want and the extent to which the products they have to sell meet these consumer wants. Their findings must be reported to the production department if any changes are desired, and conferences held to determine whether such changes are technically possible and economically feasible.

Executive department   The executive department usually passes on all matters of policy before work is undertaken on a project or program. This department also acts as the coordinator of all functional divisions of the company. The advertising department, therefore, must clear all major problems with the executive offices. In instances where advertising is a part of the marketing function, the chief marketing executive coordinates advertising with other related functions and also serves to implement company policy in advertising matters.

The advertising department will initiate ideas, draw up proposed advertising campaigns and strategy, outline the kind of research that might be carried on, figure the monetary needs in carrying out a given program, and suggest the methods by which such proposals might be accomplished. The use of an advertising agency might be recommended. All such matters will be taken to the executive department for final approval. Thus, a selling job within the organization must be performed before real work is started. This task is not to be underestimated. Advertising is a field in which problems must be scientifically handled if satisfactory results are to be obtained. It is also a field in which everyone thinks that he knows what should be done and, hence, gives advice and criticism freely. Those in the executive offices are often of this type. It therefore requires tact, as well as much objective evidence, to obtain the executive's stamp of approval on a proposed program. Changes which an executive may feel to be minor may often prove disastrous if made. Thus, the relationship between the advertising and executive departments is both a difficult and vital one.

Other departments   There are other divisions with which the advertising department will have dealings from time to time. The purchasing department may be called upon to buy supplies of various kinds. If no advertising agency is employed, the volume of supplies to be purchased will be increased. Specific instructions as to the kind and quality of material desired must accompany any requisition.

If engravings or dealer-display materials are to be sent out, the advice of the shipping department should be sought. The same should be done when a new package is designed. The shipping department can often offer suggestions concerning the shape of a new package which will reduce the packing and shipping costs, although such suggestions should not be accepted if they would force a change in design out of harmony with probable human desires. Quite often, however, both needs can be met if the needs are recognized before the package is designed.

The accounting department might be called upon to keep the record of advertising expenditures in a particular way, especially when detailed cost figures are desired. A running record may be desired for expenditures by type of medium, for mechanical costs, overhead, research, etc. Such record will usually be of value, particularly where careful budgeting is done or where careful checks are made on the monetary value of particular media or advertisements.

The legal department is often a very important ally of the advertising division. A competitor may attempt to copy the company trademark, or a suit might be brought against the company for trademark infringement. The recent court decisions granting judgments against advertisers for using ideas of others without compensation might tend to multiply such suits in the future. Under such conditions the legal department will be called upon to defend the company. This department may also be called upon to render an opinion upon the legality of proposed new trademarks, package designs, etc. If any advertisements are copyrighted, the responsibility for having this done usually comes under the jurisdiction of the legal department. With the current emphasis by federal regulatory agencies, such as the Federal Trade Commission, on false and misleading advertising, the legal department is often used extensively to review creative ideas.

Functions of the advertising department

The relationship between the advertising department and other departments as outlined here might lead the reader to believe that the other departments do all the advertising work—that the advertising department merely gets ideas and orders others to execute them. Such, however, is not the case. There is plenty of work for the advertising department to do.

If the services of an advertising agency are utilized, the advertising department will be relieved of much of the work of planning and executing product advertising in mass media. The functions performed or activities engaged in, aside from product advertising, are many. The management-consulting firm of McKinsey & Company obtained from 202 companies, who were members of the Association of National Advertisers, an accounting of the various activities, other than product advertising, engaged in by the advertising department. These firms reported 33 separate activities for which the advertising department was wholly responsible or in which it assisted other departments. That list of activities is given in Table 29–1 together with figures showing for each activity the percentage of

TABLE 29–1
Activities engaged in by advertising department

Activity	Percentage reporting advertising department	
	Fully responsible	Assisting others
Handle institutional advertising	86.6	6.4
Prepare displays for dealers or distributors	85.6	4.9
Prepare exhibits and other material for shows, conventions, etc.	79.7	19.3
Handle publicity releases	73.2	11.9
Develop visual sales material, such as easels and portfolios	72.3	16.3
Prepare catalogues	68.8	8.4
Prepare motion pictures or sound slides for use in sales departments	56.9	14.8
Prepare easels, slides, etc., for speeches by others	55.4	18.8
Edit house magazines for dealers	52.0	3.9
Edit consumer house organs	49.5	14.5
Handle dealer cooperative advertising	48.5	6.9
Do package design work	47.5	26.7
Do market research	47.5	31.2
Prepare motion pictures or sound slides for use in strengthening public relations	47.0	11.4
Edit employee publications	42.1	12.3
Hold consumer meetings or schools	36.6	8.4
Handle ceremonies such as "E" awards, etc.	35.6	26.7
Prepare internal posters for employee morale building	35.2	26.7
Provide facilities for public functions	32.6	20.3
Prepare material for interpreting company policies to employees	32.2	25.7
Advertise company's products and/or policies direct to stockholders	31.2	14.8
Hold dealer meetings	31.2	28.7
Do sales analysis work	28.2	27.7
Handle pretesting of products	27.2	28.8
Prepare speeches for others	26.7	42.1
Prepare motion pictures or sound slides for use in strengthening employee relations	23.3	17.8
Prepare releases and bulletins to stockholders	22.7	23.3
Handle company drives, such as bond and community fund	21.8	39.6
Arrange employee affairs, such as athletics, parties, etc.	15.8	24.2
Prepare annual reports	15.3	40.1
Advertise for new employees	14.8	58.4
Prepare material for use in dealing with the government	13.3	27.2
Prepare material for stockholders' meetings	7.4	18.3

Source: Paul B. West, "How the Advertising Department is Organized and What It Does," *Advertising Handbook,* ed. Roger Barton (New York: Prentice-Hall, Inc., 1950), p. 815.

firms where the advertising department (1) had full responsibility or (2) assisted other departments.

From a review of the activities listed in Table 29–1, it should be obvious that the advertising department of a large advertiser is concerned with many aspects of the company operation. It should be expert in the art of communications and thus serve as the informational and interpretative arm of the firm.

Of course the major and primary job of advertising for most companies is to sell or help to sell products or services. Generally, either the advertising department itself is responsible for planning and executing the entire product advertising program, or it is responsible for selecting an agency to serve the company. Most large advertisers use an advertising agency and have the advertising department work with the agency to present company policy and coordinate agency operations with those company activities that relate to product advertising.

Choosing the agency

The results of an advertising program may depend to a considerable degree upon the care with which an agency is chosen to carry out the details of the program. Before a choice is made, the definite purpose that advertising is to accomplish should be recognized. A selection should be made on the basis of the probable ability of an agency to help carry out a program that will bring the results desired. This may occasion the choice of two or more agencies, each equipped to render a particular, although different, service.

While the selection of an agency cannot be reduced to scientific rules, the advertiser will benefit by weeding out all agencies unsuited to his needs. He should first draw up a preliminary list of likely agencies. Then he should set up yardsticks based on what he desires from the agencies. The agencies then usually prepare presentations for the solicitation and call on the advertiser's executives to make their presentations. From these the advertiser can decide where to award his account.

Mack Hanan, a management consultant, suggests that six specific criteria be examined during the process of agency selection:

1. Are the agency candidates truly available to the advertiser, representative of a broad spectrum of agency service, and compatible with advertiser philosophy?
2. Are the agency account teams creative, catalytic among themselves, and conscientious?
3. Are the agency performance records successful, planned in advance, and well researched?

4. Are the agency's client relationships standardized, codified, and vigorously adhered to?
5. Are the agency investments required of the advertiser affordable by him, yet adequate and motivational to the agency?
6. Is the agency partnership likely to be permanent, responsible, and responsive over time?[3]

Turning to a specific advertiser's approach to agency selection, the General Electric Company uses the following check list and rating scale when selecting an agency:

Criteria	*Rating points*
Agency history	
1. Growth	1
2. Experience	5
3. Account history	5
4. Man power	7
5. Marketing concept	2
Total	20
Marketing services	
6. Campaign planning	10
7. Creative	11
8. Media	5
9. Sales promotion	7
10. Research	7
11. Merchandising	7
12. Product publicity	5
13. Production	3
Total	55
Handling of our account	
14. Personnel	15
15. Technique	5
16. Contact	5
Total	25

Under each of these criteria, General Electric Company executives look for such things as:

1. *Growth.* Have growth and billings been sound and consistent or having billings been up one year and down the next? Why?
2. *Experience.* In what fields of industry do its accounts lie? Has it demonstrated extreme versatility in all product areas or does it have particular strength in an individual product classification area?
3. *Account History.* What is its average age of service to its clients; what has been its account turnover?
4. *Man Power.* Here we look at the depth of experience and the number of people on second and third levels as well as the top level; here, too, we look at turnover.

---

[3] Mack Hanan, "Criteria for Advertising Agency Selection," *Handbook of Modern Marketing,* pp. 13–25.

5. *Marketing Concept.* Here we ask for the agency's philosophy of business operation. Is it progressive or conservative? Does it treat each problem individually or does it stick pretty close to a rigid formula? Does it reveal a keen appreciation of the place of business in its economic, social and political environment?

6. *Campaign Planning.* Here we judge the ability of the agency to secure, analyze and interpret all the facts and conditions affecting the marketing problem and their ability to develop advertising objectives and competitive strategy that form the essence of the campaign.

7. *Creative.* This is the judgment of the agency's ability to create essentially good ideas—applying imagination to the problem and developing sound ideas of unique value with great competitive impact.

8. *Media.* Here we are judging the evidence of thoroughness and soundness in media research, the preliminary media recommendations, relative cost compared to budget, and so on.

9. *Sales Promotion.* As used in this appraisal, this is that part of the campaign plan designed to stimulate, persuade and inform all people who sell the product; department salesmen, wholesalers and their salesmen, retailers and their salesmen.

10. *Research.* This means primarily evaluating the resources to collect and interpret facts for a campaign plan that will help determine and achieve the sales and advertising objectives. Here we evaluate the abilities of the agency in the many forms of research such as copy research, motivation research, product planning research, package research, and others.

11. *Merchandising.* This is an evaluation of the ideas devised and materials that an agency can provide to make all forms of selling pay off at the point of purchase.

12. *Product Publicity.* This service need not necessarily be performed by *any* agency, especially if other means for clearing news of Company operations is maintained.

13. *Production.* This is an evaluation of the agency's resources to produce or supervise production of all types of advertising, promotional and merchandising material. This will include slide films, motion pictures, radio and television programs and commercials, if they should be an essential part of the advertising campaign.

14. *Personnel.* This is the number and quality of the people who will be assigned full time to the account—the most important factor in agency service. In a sense, we want to regard these people as being a part of our organization and thus their personalities and attitudes, as well as their planning and creative abilities, should be of a nature that will work well in harness with our people.

15. *Technique.* Here we evaluate the mechanics of getting a job done. Who does what, when, and how, must be planned, controlled, and communicated to all who are affected both within the client's organization and that of the agency.

16. *Contact.* This means the availability of agency personnel for personal

contact with the frequency desired; the convenience and speed of contact for both regular and emergency purposes.[4]

Working with the agency

It takes more than an agency to conduct a successful campaign. There must be close cooperation between the agency and advertiser. The advertiser must be willing to furnish the agency with records, tests run on the product, quality characteristics of the product, and other information which is available and desired by the agency.

A most important element in modern advertising is product, market, and consumer analysis. Often, such research projects are carried out through the cooperation of the agency and the advertising department of the advertiser. The agency might draw up the form for questionnaires and send them out, while the advertiser takes over the responsibility of tabulating and summarizing the results.

In some instances, the advertiser chooses to do a major portion of all research work. Thus, General Motors Corporation maintains its own research organization as a part of its advertising department. It is there that the General Motors consumer studies have been made; but once these studies are completed, the results are given to the advertising agency to be used as seen fit in the conduct of a campaign.

The agency should have the primary responsibility for an effective presentation of the advertising message, but it is the advertiser who should assume the primary responsibility for determining what that message should be. In arriving at his decision the advertiser should consider and respect his agency's opinion, but he should make the decision.

Checking on work of agency

When an agency is selected to do a particular job, confidence is usually placed in its ability to perform the task satisfactorily. Under such circumstances it would appear unnecessary to check or supervise its work in any way. Some draw an analogy between the work of a lawyer or a physician and an advertising agency. A patient usually would not advise the doctor; nor would a lawyer's client attempt to direct his plan of procedure.

In both these cases, however, the parties paying the bills would want to check the results obtained. They might even observe the degree to which the lawyer or the physician seemed to place the client's or patient's

[4] C. J. Coward, "Effective Methods for the Selection of An Advertising Agency," *New Understanding in the Agency-Client Relationship* (Milwaukee, Wisc.: Bureau of Business and Economic Research, Marquette University, 1957).

interests and welfare ahead of all else. To an even greater degree might the advertiser check the sincerity of the agency.

As has already been pointed out, the advertising agency often receives its pay, not from its client, but from various media. This might lead to advising a greater appropriation than might be necessary. It might result in the choice of media not suited to the advertiser's needs, purely because such media carried the 15 percent discount; effective media might be left out of consideration because of the absence of a commission. Likewise, since the agency often receives no extra remuneration for the research work done, such work might be done in a very superficial manner. But

TABLE 29–2
Documentation required from agency

Client classification	Marketing strategy (percent)	Creative strategy (percent)	Research results (percent)
All types	50	75	40
Industrial	45	70	35
Package goods	50	90	60
Durables and services	50	75	30
Small	40	60	25
Medium	55	80	35
Large	50	85	60

these things do not necessarily happen. Undoubtedly, most agencies work earnestly and effectively for the advertiser. They may even sacrifice a possible increased income in order to increase the profits of their client. But to avoid the continued use of an agency of the other type, it behooves the advertising director of the manufacturer to keep a continual check on the work of the agency. Of course, this should be a constructive check rather than one designed to pry into the affairs of others. The advertiser does not wish to catch the agency betraying the trust placed in it but, rather wishes to keep it conscious of the advertiser's interests.

The advertising department will usually check all detailed work of the agency and approve it for release. Sometimes suggestions for changes will be made in the choice of media as well as in the finished advertisement itself. In general, however, matters pertaining to the construction of an advertisement are left to the judgment of the agency because they are technical in character, and the technician will usually be better qualified to pass judgment than a layman. This is not true of the results of research, the basic appeal used in an advertisement, the use of certain media, or the methods employed to measure advertising effectiveness.

In a study of the creative approval process the Association of National Advertisers found that 50 percent of the clients surveyed require a marketing strategy statement, 75 percent require a creative strategy statement, and 40 percent require research documentation when the agency submits creative work for approval. As shown in Table 29–2, package goods advertisers and large advertisers are more inclined to require creative strategy statements and research documentation.[5]

Control of advertising expenditures

The problems incident to determining the amount of money to spend for advertising and the ways in which it will be spent are of vital importance. Chapter 31 is devoted to a consideration of this subject.

After the budget has been established, it becomes the duty of the advertising department to direct the expenditure of all sums thus provided. Effective supervision will involve a careful breakdown of expenditures into classes representing the character of services purchased. These classes may represent media by types, overhead expense, mechanical costs, etc. True, the budget will carry a total figure for each of these items for the entire year. It becomes the duty of the advertising department, however, to follow these expenditures by the week or month. This may be done graphically on a chart or by noting the total figures. The value of such a continual check is found in its currentness. Without it, the total allotment might be spent long before the end of the year.

The breakdown and charting of expenditures are not so important for amounts spent on major advertising schedules in magazines, newspapers, etc., because these are easily determined accurately in advance or are controllable at any time. The opposite is true for the expenses of display, sampling material, and certain types of direct mail. The number of coupons received cannot be predetermined, and most coupon returns necessitate the sending of some type of material. It is this kind of expenditure that necessitates constant checking and charting in order to keep within the overall advertising budget.

In addition to charting expenditures for each type of advertising used, a record should also be kept of expenditures by territories. As changes in sales possibilities occur, owing to weather conditions, strikes, floods, changes in general business activity, activities of competitors, etc., changes in the amount of advertising money allotted to such territories should be made to harmonize with changed conditions. This function is discussed further in Chapter 31.

Getting new ideas

Every progressive manufacturer is looking for new ideas which will improve his product or make his selling or advertising appeal more effec-

[5] Association of National Advertisers, *The Creative Approval Process* (New York: Association of National Advertisers, Inc., 1966), p. 3.

tive. The advertising department is usually the contact point between the manufacturer and those having new ideas to give.

One company saved $50,000 a year, merely by changing the name on the shipping boxes; thus, the product fell in a different freight classification, calling for a lower rate. The idea came from outside. Another company adopted a new name, suggested by an outsider, for a golf ball. This name was passed on to the agency serving the company, and a successful campaign was built around it.

Changes in package design have often resulted through suggestions made from outside sources. If contests are conducted for the express purpose of getting new ideas, it is the advertising department that will receive and study their possibilities. The work involved in supervising a contest and digesting the returns is often very great, and the value of contests depends to a considerable degree upon the manner in which the returns are handled. The alert advertising department, in supervising consumer research relative to the effectiveness of company advertising, often can uncover workable ideas from consumer responses. One company added a pouring spout to their cereal product as a result of several respondents in a copy test remarking about this feature.

The court decisions granting a judgment against an advertiser for using ideas without compensation increases the burden upon the advertising department. Extreme care must be taken to protect the company against unreasonable claims from those offering new ideas. Too much encouragement to get the layman to send in ideas without proper safeguards to both the advertiser and the layman might be disastrous.

QUESTIONS AND PROBLEMS

1   Assume that you are employed as manager of the advertising department of a manufacturer of men's suits. Draw up an organization chart that you would recommend. Show the flow of communication "up," "down," and "sideways" from your position as advertising manager.

2   One of your responsibilities as advertising manager is to select an advertising agency to handle your national advertising. Prepare a report for the executive officers of your company setting forth the criteria you recommend as a guide to selection.

3   How much dependance would you place on your advertising agency to perform or direct consumer, product, and market research for you?

4   If sufficient care is taken in selecting an agency, is there any need for checking the agency's work?

5   What advantages accrue from a long-term contract with an advertising agency?

6   In what way does the breakdown and charting of expenditures for magazine and newspaper advertising differ from that for display and direct-mail advertising?

7 Why can a company not accept new ideas for the betterment of its product indiscriminately from the general public?

8 "Because of the greater degree of specialization attained in the advertising agency, more powers are delegated to it, thereby decreasing the need for the advertising department in the business organization." Do you agree? Why?

9 Do you think it a good policy to select more than one advertising agency as a means of increasing the degree of specialization in functions performed? Why?

10 A large cosmetic producer has developed a new nail polish remover for which it makes the following claims:

  a. Since it contains lanolin it does not dry out the nails and thus keeps them from becoming brittle and easy to break.

  b. It is guaranteed to remove polish on the first application.

  c. It is packaged in a self-sealing tube and therefore does not evaporate as quickly as other polish removers.

  d. Because of the self-sealing feature of the tube, the remover will last twice as long as competing brands.

  While this new product is apparently much superior to competing brands, the cost of production is such as to require a price approximately three times that of competitors' products.

  The product is new and hence unknown to the public. The company is small and has only a moderate amount of capital. It is not sure what the public reaction would be to the new product, especially with the premium price that is necessary.

  The company questions whether it should undertake to do its own advertising through its advertising department or to solicit the services of an agency. It also wonders whether any consumer research should be undertaken before launching an advertising campaign, and if research is done, whether it should be done by its own advertising department.

  What advice would you give the company? Support your recommendations.

30

Retail advertising

The importance of retail advertising is often underestimated. It does not present the glamour of national advertising, nor does it get the criticism that is often leveled against the advertisements of certain branded and trademarked products. For the most part, general advertising agencies devote a minimum of time to serving retail accounts. And yet, retail or local advertising accounts for close to 50 percent of the total annual advertising bill.

The nature of retailing

Retailing, as used here, relates to business firms that maintain physical establishments for the purpose of selling products or providing services directly to consumers. Such firms are, therefore, local in nature, although local outlets may be tied together as a regional or national chain.

Retail and service establishments that are substantial advertisers include department stores, furniture and home furnishings stores, food stores, building materials outlets, automobile dealers and service shops, drugstores, apparel and accessory stores, motels and hotels, eating establishments, and amusement places. Generally such establishments invest from something less than 1 percent to 3.5 percent of sales in advertising. Leaders in relative advertising expenditures are amusement places, furniture stores, department and apparel stores.

658

Retail establishments might also be classified according to pricing practices, organizational structure, or location. Each such classification will have a bearing on advertising strategy. Thus discount houses will follow a different strategy than full-service stores, and chain stores will differ from single proprietorships. The development of shopping centers has also had a significant influence on the character of retail advertising and promotion.

Character of retail advertising

Retail advertising is distinctly local in character. It can, therefore, tie the products being advertised directly to the store handling them. In this respect, it is a focused type of advertising. Direct action can be emphasized much more than in national advertising. "Buy the XYZ radio at your nearest retailer," does not possess the same tone or carry the same weight as "Buy your XYZ radio from the John Jones Radio Store, Sixth and Walnut Streets." This directness allows for greater ease in checking the results of retail advertisements. Many retailers keep a record of the sales of specific products before, during, and after the time they have been featured in the advertising.

The retailer must, in general, initiate his own advertising program and follow it through to completion. The large retail organizations like department stores and chain stores can afford a well-rounded advertising department. Such a department will be capable of accomplishing for the retailer what the general agency and the advertising department do for the manufacturer. The work will include development of the basic research program preliminary to advertising, selection of media, writing copy, getting art work done, putting the advertisement together, taking care of the mechanical problems incident to reproduction, checking on the effectiveness of advertisements already run and to be run, etc.

The small retailer cannot make use of specialization, and no separate department can be established for advertising. Dependence must, therefore, be placed upon the general ability of the manager, the use of certain specialized agencies, and the advertising departments of local media. The advertising departments of many newspapers and broadcast stations will provide an "agency" type service for small retailers. They will help plan strategy, write copy, design layouts, prepare or obtain appropriate art work for print or visuals for broadcast, and suggest appropriate time schedules. Local media will also have available various aids such as the *A.N.P.A. Plan Book,* advertising practices of other retailers, mat services, etc.

Working with other departments

If the retailer is large enough to justify a separate advertising department, this department's work must be coordinated with the other departments of the store, just as described in connection with manufacturing concerns. In the larger stores, the advertising department is likely to have these chief functions: preparing and planning of advertising, displaying goods within the store, preparing signs, doing advertising research, and obtaining favorable publicity about the store and its featured selling events. Its association will be particularly close with the various merchandising departments which perform the buying and selling functions.

The advertising department must learn all it can about the features of the merchandise it is promoting, and the buyers in the various merchandising departments should see that full information is provided. The advertising and merchandising executives together must determine the space to be devoted to each department and the items to be featured. The advertising staff should give valuable assistance by originating promotional ideas and by providing the customer's viewpoint. Teamwork in the store is essential, for, although advertising may draw shoppers to the store, sales will be made only if sales efforts within the store support the advertising. Leaders in the field generally agree that the failure of merchants to support external advertising with appropriate and timely inside-the-store promotion is a serious shortcoming of retail sales promotion.

Relations with advertising agencies

The retail advertiser, in general, has not used the advertising agency to plan and execute an advertising program. Several factors have helped to produce this situation. The time element is one factor. The advertising strategy to be employed by the retailer may be planned well in advance of the appearance of any advertising, but the actual advertisements are often written "against time." An advertisement may be scheduled for a given edition of the local newspaper, and yet its completion may be held up until a few hours before press time. This delay is often necessary so that full advantage can be taken of such factors as weather, competitors' activities, trend in consumer demand, nondelivery of expected merchandise, etc.

A close acquaintanceship with the problems of the retailer is necessary if an effective advertising job is to be done. The large retailer, therefore, has usually preferred to depend upon his own advertising department for all such work. The small retailer spends such a small amount on advertising that no general agency finds it profitable to solicit his business.

The differential existing between local and national newspaper and broadcast rates also militates against the use of the general agency. We have seen how newspapers, for example, grant to local advertisers a special rate that is much lower than that granted national advertisers. Usually, no agency discount is allowed on the local rate. The retailer who would like to use an agency must, therefore, pay directly for such services. The apparent additional cost often encourages the retailer to plan and execute his own advertising program without the help of the general agency.

While several factors have tended to keep the general agency out of the retail field, there are certainly no unsurmountable obstacles to the entrance of the agency into this field. This is particularly true in the top 100 markets in the United States. In most such markets there are branches of large New York or Chicago based agencies or smaller independent agencies that are equipped to provide the kind of knowledge and facilities to adequately serve the advertising needs of local business firms. Changes in the advertising and promotion strategy of national firms have stimulated the growth of local agencies. There has been a trend toward the allocation of more of the manufacturer's advertising dollar for local advertising and retail-trade promotion. This trend caused *Advertising Age* to editorialize that "the renewed emphasis on local promotions . . . gives smaller ad agencies with specialized knowledge of a market, or an industry, or a local area, a decided advantage. The larger agencies have been quick to spot this advantage and . . . have bought into smaller shops to gain this local expertise. This trend . . . is sure to continue."[1]

The local advertising agency may or may not be equipped to provide consumer and market research services. In any event the retailer will find it worthwhile to allocate part of his budget to cover the cost of such research. Certainly, the effectiveness of an advertising program for the retailer will depend upon the degree to which it is keyed to consumer desires. The location of those consumers whose needs and wants can be satisfied by the products carried for sale should be ascertained. Media should be chosen in terms of their ability to reach such consumers. Some means of checking the effectiveness of advertisements should be devised. The retailer, particularly the small one, is often not in a position to perform all these tasks. There are specialized research agencies that stand ready to perform such services, and the cost is usually not excessive. When measured in terms of values received, the expenditure is certainly not an expense but a wise investment.

Media used

The retail advertiser can use practically any medium except magazines, which are ruled out because they cover a much wider area than that served by the retailer. However, the regional edition of those magazines that split their distribution by regions for advertising purposes can be used successfully by some of the larger retail organizations. Of course chain stores can also use magazines, especially for image-building campaigns and special, organization-wide, sales events.

---

[1] *Advertising Age,* January 15, 1973, p. 14.

The following media are suggested as being of value to retail stores:

Newspaper advertising
  a. Daily newspapers
  b. Weekly newspapers
  c. Shopping news

Direct-mail advertising
  a. Letters
  b. Postal cards
  c. Circulars, booklets, leaflets,
      etc.

Radio and television advertising
  a. Spot announcements
  b. Sponsored programs

Cable television

Outdoor advertising
  a. Billboards
  b. Illuminated store signs
  c. Signs on delivery trucks

Transit advertising
  a. Streetcar cards
  b. Bus cards
  c. Suburban train cards

Motion-picture theater advertising
  a. Colored slides
  b. Commercial trailers

Advertising by personal distribution
  a. Handbills
  b. Dodgers

Classified advertising
  a. In newspapers
  b. In telephone directories
  c. In buyers' directories

Advertising confined to store itself
  a. Window displays
  b. Counter and floor displays
  c. Elevator bulletins

Transit radio
  a. Program sponsorship
  b. Special announcements

The retailer will find that advertising within the store itself, such as counter and window displays, will prove of great profit if properly used. Good windows, attractively decorated and carrying out one central idea, will prove effective. Displays should be changed often. Suggestions for displays can be obtained from manufacturers whose goods are handled and from companies that sell decorative materials.

In terms of the amount of money spent, newspapers are the most important medium for retailers. Well over 50 percent of all retail advertising is in newspapers, but use of the broadcast media is increasing. The ratio of retail expenditures in the mid-1970s in the three major media (newspapers, radio, and television) was approximately five to one to one. Harry McMahan, commenting in 1973 on the rise in television advertising by retailers, said:

> Retail television advertising started out with slides. Then there were the used-car pitchmen. And the "weather gals" turned commercial. Finally, when cigaret advertising departed and took some big bites out of revenues, the stations went to work. So now , in its 25th year, retail TV is finally coming

into its own. Next year, there's a good chance it will exceed national TV revenue, well over the $1 billion expected for this year.[2]

About one fourth of all television revenue now comes from local or retail advertisers. In the case of newspapers, the comparable figure for local advertisers is slightly more than 80 percent and for radio, about 70 percent.

The development of cable television holds promise for a significant (new) medium for retail advertisers. It can be more local than either newspapers, radio, or television. It should be of particular value to small retailers and suburban merchants.

Regardless of what media are used, it is important that all efforts be carefully coordinated. This will increase the effectiveness of each.

Budgeting expenditures

The general problems of budgeting are considered in Chapter 31. Retailers will find their budgeting problems somewhat simpler than those of some companies covering a large territory. The retailer need not divide his appropriation on the basis of sales territories. He must, however, consider the basis upon which he shall arrive at the total amount to be spent and the distribution of this amount to various media and products.

Measured in terms of sales, the expenditures for retail advertising averages from nothing at all for some types of stores to 8 or 9 percent for others. Flower and beauty shops will have an average advertising expenditure amounting to about 5.5 percent of sales. Department stores will set aside from 2 to 5 percent of sales, according to the size of the store. The percentage, in general, varies directly with the volume of sales, except for those stores doing more than $10 million business, in which cases the percentage declines. Grocery stores will, in general, appropriate about 1 percent of their sales for advertising. (See Chapter 31 for more detailed figures.)

These are average figures and have all the shortcomings of averages. But they do serve as a rough guide to what is done. Naturally, many stores spend less and many spend more for advertising than the average figures quoted. It should be recognized that the percentage of sales is not the best guide to the establishment of the advertising appropriation. A better method consists of correlating the appropriation to the task to be performed (see Chapter 31).

After the appropriation has been established, it should be divided according to the media to be used and the products to be advertised. In relating expenditures to products, thought must be given to the general popularity of the product, the season of the year, unit price, gross margin, and similar factors. It is not wise to place much advertising behind slow-

[2] Harry Wayne McMahan, "Retail TV Advertising Grows Up," *Advertising Age*, November 12, 1973, p. 63.

moving items. The fact that they do move slowly is probably an indication that consumers do not care for them. Push those items for which there is a potent demand, and better results will be obtained. It is extremely costly to change human desires; it is much better to harmonize advertising efforts with existing desires. Thus, by placing the major portion of the appropriation behind those items most desired, a greater percentage of total area sales will probably be received.

Special days, weeks, and seasons will, of course, have a direct influence on the desires of customers for given products. These periods can be anticipated and provision made in advance for extra promotional and advertising effort. Of course, such days as Christmas, New Year's Day, Independence Day, and Thanksgiving will not be forgotten. But what of Flag Day, Army Day, Candy Week, Baseball Week, Education Week, Golf Week, etc.?

The following list of special weeks and days indicates the great variety

ALPHABETICAL INDEX OF SPECIAL WEEKS AND DAYS

American Education Week
American Legion Convention
American Toy Fair in New York
Apple Week, National
Ash Wednesday (beginning of Lent)
Baseball Week, National
Better Homes Week, National
Boy Scout Anniversary Week
Business Women's Week
Candy Week, National
Cheese Week, National
Cherry Week, National
Children's Day (Commercial)
Columbus Day
Constitution Week
Cotton Week, National
Decoration Day (Memorial Day)
Defense Week, National
Dog Week, National
Easter Sunday
Election Day
Father's Day
Father and Son Week
Fire-Prevention Week
First-Aid Week, National

Fisherman's Week, National
Flag Day
Flower Shut-In Day, National
Foreign Trade Week
Garden Week, National
Girl Scout Week
Golf Week, National
Good Friday
Halloween
Hobby Week, National
Independence Day (July 4)
Labor Day
Lent
Lincoln's Birthday
May Day
Mother's Day
Music Week, National
Navy Day
Palm Sunday
Poppy Week
Red Cross Roll Call
Restaurant Week, National
St. Patrick's Day
Veteran's Day

of occasions when advertising and promotion efforts might be coordinated with national, regional, or local celebrations. Naturally, many of these days or weeks are of significance to a limited number of retail institutions; but where they do apply, an extra amount might be appropriated for advertising during such periods.

Items with a high price and large gross margin can usually sustain a larger amount of advertising than the lower-price items. Here again, attention must be given to general consumer attitudes before much is spent.

Advertising strategy

Most advertising carried on by a manufacturer is built around the promotion of an identified product. In fact, were it not for the existence of branded merchandise, national advertising would be very different and perhaps very much diminished. This does not hold for retail advertising because the retailer has no monopoly or control of branded merchandise unless he has his own private brands or an exclusive agency contract for a manufacturer's brand. Hence, retail advertising should not be built around the promotion of branded merchandise as such.

The retailer is essentially a purchasing agent for the consumer rather than a peddler of products for the producer. A multiplicity of brands is available to the retailer. Retail advertising emphasis should therefore be placed upon the general character of goods made available to the community and the type of service rendered. Such factors as style, quality, price, delivery, credit, location, honesty, and variety of merchandise are the things in which the retailer deals. The factors provided by a particular retailer should be emphasized and associated with his name. Branded merchandise might be advertised as a means of portraying the idea of quality or style; but, in any event, such factors must be associated with the name of the retailer. Note the contrast in national and retail advertising in this respect. In the latter the name of the merchant is prominently displayed, while in the former it is the brand name of the product.

Strategy will differ somewhat according to the type of retail outlet. Masis Seklemian says there are basically three types of advertising that might be used by a major retailer in a well-rounded campaign:

1. Class A advertising is action oriented, geared primarily to drawing shoppers for particular sale events. Both department stores and discounters rely heavily on this type of promotion as the mainstay of their advertising activity.

2. Class B advertising involves general traffic-building. This is the kind of advertising that presents the customer with new ideas, and new products, with tie-ins with in-store activities.

3. Class C advertising is almost totally concerned with goodwill or image building. This type of advertising sells the customer on the store, not on specific merchandise.[3]

---

[3] "Discounters pit marketing ideas vs. department stores," *Advertising Age,* June 11, 1973, p. 81.

Regardless of the type of store, the local merchant should recognize that he has an almost face-to-face association with the consumer. He should therefore focus all advertising on the needs of the customer rather than the seller.

Working with the manufacturer

The retailer has no particular interest in the products of any one manufacturer. His interest is centered on stocking and selling merchandise that his customers want. The product advertising problem becomes one of informing the public of the qualities of such products, how these qualities will meet consumer desires, and where the products can be purchased.

Too many retailers have felt that the qualities of a product need not be advertised in specific terms; that such terms as "superb quality," "outstanding value," and "bargain of the century" are adequate to draw in the buyers. This philosophy is apparently on the decline. Consumers are demanding more detailed information about the products offered for sale.

The retailer can obtain this detail from the manufacturer and should insist upon it. Quite often, much value will be received by having a representative of the advertising department visit the manufacturer in order that a more thorough understanding of the qualities of the product might be obtained before copy is written. The manufacturer also should have an interest in this procedure. If the retailer does not or cannot contact the manufacturer, the latter might send a representative to the larger retail establishments or, by mail, explain in detail the qualities possessed by products offered for sale.

A different kind of cooperation between the retailer and manufacturer is that in which the latter offers advertising allowances to retailers to pay part or all of the cost incurred in advertising a specific item on a local basis. By having the local store contract for space in the local papers, the manufacturer may receive the advantage of local rates. Such cooperation on the part of the manufacturer also places the prestige of a local establishment behind his brand and encourages the retailer to give extra promotion to specific brands. The retailer gains by receiving some compensation for his efforts in this promotion and by being able to purchase more advertising space, thus getting better quantity discounts from media. However, the retailer must not permit this inducement to detour him from his fundamental job of stocking and promoting those goods that are most desired by his customers. The manufacturer, on the other hand, should be sure that allowances granted are used for advertising purposes and, also, be wary lest such allowances constitute discrimination between dealers which would violate the Robinson-Patman Act.

The use of advertising allowances, or cooperative advertising, has, at times, been abused by both the manufacturer and the retailer. It may also encourage the retailer to turn his attention away from the consumer and toward the seller.

Herbert Strawbridge, chairman of the board of The Higbee Company department store of Cleveland, has this to say about advertising allowances:

> Co-op is too frequently used as a corrupter of the buyers by the manufacturer and by the advertising fraternity, and it isn't used to really generate sales for the store. It is used as a generation of sales of the manufacturer to the store. Now there is no good in selling the store merchandise that the store can't get rid of. You may temporarily gain a few points with your client if you are the advertising agency. But the total doesn't gain unless we can get rid of it. In the department store business today there are a number of inexperienced buyers who are new in their job and they can be snowed, and co-op is one of the worst offenders in snowing an inexperienced buyer.[4]

Mr. Strawbridge suggests that co-op advertising often corrupts the buyer, and also at times corrupts retail management and local media. It has led, at times, to double billing where the local medium issues a hiked bill to be submitted to the manufacturer and a true bill to the retailer. Such practice is illegal but, unfortunately, quite prevalent. In 1974 the Federal Communications Commission refused to renew the license of a radio station because it had been practicing double billing for a period of five years. Of course, double billing should never be practiced.

Intraindustry cooperation

The small independent retailer is, in many ways, unable to compete with the larger concerns in the use of advertising. He cannot employ specialists, and his advertising volume is not sufficiently large to give him sizable quantity discounts from newspapers. Neither can he utilize the large circulation of newspapers or audiences of broadcasting stations, whose readers or listeners largely are outside the area from which he draws trade. The large downtown retailer, and particularly the chain organizations, can obtain the services of specialists, get the more favorable rate discounts, and utilize media with broad area circulation.

When independent retailers work together in group advertising, they largely can offset these disadvantages. With stores spread throughout the community, they waste little of the circulation of newspapers. By dividing the cost among many, they can afford competent talent, can buy large enough space to be effective, and can obtain quantity rate discounts. Some of the same advantages apply to use of other media, such as handbills, direct mail, and window displays.

---

[4] American Association of Advertising Agencies, "Changes in Retailing: How they Affect National Advertising" (New York, 1973), p. 43.

Retailers may organize themselves into cooperatives for advertising and other mutual benefits, or they may join groups sponsored by wholesale concerns known as "voluntary" chains. The usual procedure in such organizations is for each member to contribute a certain sum periodically for advertising purposes. This common fund supplies sufficient money to employ efficient technicians to prepare circulars, handbills, newspaper advertisements, and other material to be used by members individually or jointly.

The development of shopping centers has brought about an increase in group advertising. Kurt Schmidt, an authority on shopping centers, points out that:

> Most shopping centers have a fund of promotional money, approximately $0.20 per square foot, contributed by tenants for their occupied space, available for overall shopping center promotion. In the centers that are being *properly* promoted, a portion of this money is used as a catalyst or seed money to generate additional expenditures by the merchants for specific merchandise advertising. The shopping center promotional program must embody certain activities that permit stores to advertise with their own advertising funds. The most common method is the special section or tabloid. This, either distributed in the newspaper or through direct mail, involves the center purchasing the cover page and individual stores buying advertisements within the section itself.[5]

Special mat and other services

The small retailer wishing to "run an ad" in the local paper often hesitates because he does not know how to prepare an advertisement. This lack of knowledge need not keep him from having a relatively good advertisement. He can subscribe for a regular advertising service, or he can obtain from his local publisher examples of advertisements from which he can choose.

The Metro Associated Services, Inc., Multi-Ad Services, Inc., and Stamps-Conhaim Senior Newspaper Advertising Service are 3 of the 40 firms preparing regular catalogs or "proof books," as they are called, of illustrations and sample advertisements. The retailer can select illustrations or complete advertisements from these books. Each illustration in the proof book is accompanied by a matrix from which the advertisement can be set up for printing. The publisher will add the retailer's name, the prices of the products advertised, and any minor items desired.

This service is usually provided by newspaper publishers at little or no cost to the advertiser; the publishers receive their income from the sale of space. The service does provide the small merchant with advertise-

[5] Kurt Schmidt, Speech given before the American Marketing Association, Urbana, Ill., September 1973.

ments which are prepared by specialists and are usually better than the ones which he might prepare himself. In addition, he saves the cost of hiring specialists to write individual advertisements.

A similar service is given by many manufacturers. The makers of laundry equipment, radios, TV sets, electric refrigerators, automobiles, etc., are interested in having their retail outlets advertise their products. To encourage such advertising and to make sure that it will be of a relatively high standard, the manufacturer furnishes retailers, either directly or through their local media, with sample advertisements. The retailer can select a particular advertisement for publication. Reproductions of suggested advertisements available in mat form from the manufacturer are given in Figures 30–1 and 30–2. These mats can often be ordered by number, as noted at the bottom of Figure 30–1.

Wholesalers and trade associations often provide mat services. Thus, the National Retail Hardware Association provides such a service to hardware dealers. Each month in the *Hardware Retailer* are shown proofs of the mats obtainable for the following month's use. Any such illustration can be obtained at small cost in either electro or mat form.

In addition to mat services, manufacturers and wholesalers may provide the retailer with definite help in conducting a direct-mail campaign, obtaining outdoor-poster advertising at low cost, and in making attractive window displays. The cost to the local operator is much less than it would be if the printing were done individually. Bundle inserts are obtainable in the same way.

The small retailer in particular can well afford to acquaint himself with these aids to more effective advertising. While his advertising appropriation will be small, results obtained from his expenditures can be increased by making use of the many free or inexpensive aids available.

Retailers who use wholesalers as sources of supply will often be able to obtain helpful assistance from such suppliers in planning advertising programs. This may be of particular value in securing point-of-purchase display material and in getting the personal assistance of the wholesaler in developing window and store displays.

The importance of advertising displays at point of purchase has become most evident with the development of self-service retailing. Manufacturers, wholesalers, and retailers are involved in the problem of getting specific brands of merchandise forcefully and dynamically brought to the attention of consumers during their self-selection of merchandise inside the store. Manufacturers and private-brand wholesalers strive to get their brands displayed in favorable spots in the retail store, and the retailer wishes to secure and maintain strong consumer patronage. The retailer can still select the specific brands of merchandise to promote actively; but, once that is done, advertising and merchandising helps should be solicited from the manufacturer or supplier of those brands.

FIGURE 30–1
Mat available to local dealer

Small Car?

The little dollar sign means a great big deal at your Ford Dealer!

The little dollar sign at your participating Ford Dealer is the sign of big savings on a group of currently available "service specials."

But that's not all . . . you'll also find that sign on spe-cially-selected '74 Fords—including our small cars, Pinto, Maverick, and Mustang II. Cars we've tagged for immediate delivery—with the kind of deal just too good to pass up.

If you're in the market for a small car, or any car, come on in and look for our dollar signs. It's the sign of a great car, and a deal to match!

See your Ford Dealer, the Professionals

(DEALER NAME)

Schedule No. **4B527**
351 lines—B & W
Newspapers, 1974
J. Walter Thompson, Chicago

FIGURE 30–2
Manufacturer's mat with blank space for retail price and store name

BONUS VALUE
on GE Portable Stereo Phonographs

3BUCKS BACK!

Now's the time to buy a high-quality GE Stereo
Portable Phonograph and get 3 BUCKS BACK.
Take your choice of any eligible model and take
great stereo sound with you, anywhere you go.

V935/936

Wildcat Stereo with 3-speed
changer, big 6″ oval speakers,
in light, easy-to-carry case.

only $00.00
and GE will refund $3.00.

T541

Trimline "500"
Stereo with
ceramic cartridge,
diamond stylus,
and four-speed
automatic, drop-
down changer.
Speakers sepa-
rate up to 12′.
Steel case with
durable vinyl
covering.

only $00.00
and GE will refund $3.00.

*Come in and see these
GE Portable Stereo Phonographs now!*
Limited time offer—Feb. 11-March 31, 1974

DEALER NAME

Truth in retail advertising

Recent federal legislation has increased the powers of the Federal Trade Commission over interstate advertising. In general, however, the authority of the Commission does not reach the retail advertiser. Perhaps the most potent forces in promoting truthful retail advertising are the Better Business Bureaus and censorship by local media.

Retailers should recognize the wisdom of using a type of advertising that carries conviction to the reader. False and exaggerated statements militate against this. It is important to keep truthful, not only one's own advertising, but also that of other retailers. Cooperation with the local Better Business Bureau will help in both cases. The publication, *A Guide for Retail Advertising and Selling*, published by National Better Business Bureau, Inc., should be in the hands of every retail advertiser. The *Guide* provides the retailer with specific standards and definitions of terms often used in retailing, which enable him to keep his advertising truthful. It gives some 300 rules on such items of general interest as comparative prices, "bait" advertising, and other factors. By following the recommendations of the bureau, retailers will have greater assurance of maintaining the confidence of customers.

QUESTIONS AND PROBLEMS

1 In what respect is retail advertising a "buyer's guide" type?

2 Bring to class three retail advertisements that do and three that do not appear to you as beneficial aids to the consumer. Point out the reasons for your appraisal.

3 In what way might co-op advertising corrupt a retail store buyer or owner?

4 Discuss the pros and cons of co-op advertising from the point of view of both the manufacturer and the retailer.

5 Who usually takes the place of the general advertising agency in the planning, preparation, and placing of advertisements and commercial messages for the retailer?

6 Why is the budgeting of the retail advertiser's appropriation often less complicated than that of the large national advertiser?

7 In your role as a consumer, what is your attitude toward retail advertising in general?

8 If you were a retailer and the newspaper in your community temporarily stopped publishing because of a strike, what would you do? Do you think such stoppage would have an adverse effect on your sales? Would it be detrimental to consumers?

9 How would you account for the increased use of television by retailers?

The advertising
budget

Advertising management is essentially a matter of setting objectives,
planning operations to achieve the objectives, putting the plans into
action, and controlling operations. The principal instrument used in performing these functions is the advertising budget. In a sense, the entire
administrative process—reviewing past operations, controlling on-going
operations, and planning ahead—centers on the budget. Budgeting encourages more precise planning. It enhances a most profitable allocation
of resources. It helps keep expenditures within predetermined limits.

An advertising budget encompasses two areas of decision: (1) the total
number of dollars to be spent for advertising, often referred to as the
appropriation; and (2) how these dollars will be spent.

SIZE OF THE BUDGET

The amount of money to be spent in advertising is of vital concern to
the company and to the agency chosen to serve the company. To both,
it serves to establish a limit to the advertising to be done during a given
period. It provides the cloth from which the advertising campaign is to
be cut; the size of this cloth should be considered carefully before the
campaign is planned and started.

The following factors are significant in determining the size of the
budget: (1) the procedure for arriving at the total number of dollars to be

spent, (2) the role of advertising in the marketing plan, and (3) the items to be charged to advertising.

Procedures for determining size of the budget

The procedure used to determine the size of the budget should not only arrive at the number of dollars to be spent. It should also provide justification for the expenditure. The more common procedures in use include the following: (1) percentage of past sales, (2) percentage of anticipated future sales, (3) percentage based on both past and anticipated sales, and (4) objective-and-task method.[1]

Percentage of past sales   Both this method and the one based on future sales justify themselves by assuming the existence of a definite relationship between the volume of sales and the volume of advertising necessary to produce those sales. Of course, they presuppose a proper coordination of advertising and all other sales activities. It is in the establishment of this proper coordination that the advertising percentage is set.

Let us assume that a given product sells for $1. Of this dollar, 20 percent goes for all selling costs. These costs include salesmen's salaries, office expense, billing and shipping expense, advertising, etc. What combination of these factors will provide the best results? Should 12 percent go for expenses of personal selling, 5 percent for advertising, and 3 percent for other selling costs? When these ratios have been worked out, the relative importance of advertising in the selling program has been established in terms of a percentage of total sales. This figure can then be applied to total sales of the previous year to get the total appropriation.

The percentage finally arrived at will differ materially for different industries and for different companies within an industry. For many years, *Advertising Age* has published the percentage of sales invested in advertising by a broad variety of industry types. Their figures, as shown in Table 31–1, are based on source material on file at the Internal Revenue Service for 217 product or service classifications (65 major groups are shown in the table).

As indicated in Table 31–1, the percentage of sales invested in advertising for all industrial groups was 1.13 percent for the 1969–70 period. This figure has been quite stable over a 15-year period. The industry category with the largest percentage invested was "soaps, cleaners, and toilet goods" (10.09 percent).

The percentage-of-past-sales method has certain distinct weaknesses. It makes no allowance for the trend of individual sales or cyclical fluctuations of business. It is based on the seeming assumption that advertising

---

[1] Less typical methods include: all you can afford, percentage of past or future profits, given appropriation per retail outlet, given assessment per market share, given amount related to a set of indicators (for example, gross national product).

is to follow sales, rather than precede sales, in spite of the theoretical assumption that this is not the case. The amount to be spent can be increased or decreased by increasing or decreasing the percentage figure. The general principle underlying this approach is that a certain relationship exists between total sales and the advertising cost of obtaining those sales. The percentage figure finally applied to sales will determine the total sum to be spent. This will be discussed later in this chapter. The method would not be particularly weak if sales were relatively stable from year to year. It does not meet the problem of altering the appropriation to harmonize with cyclical changes in business activity.

Percentage of anticipated future sales   This method involves looking forward into the future and estimating the sales volume expected for the following year. It is similar to the use of a percentage of past sales, in that it is predicated on the philosophy that a certain relationship exists between sales and advertising cost in obtaining such sales. It differs, in that advertising is applied against the sales volume which advertising is supposed to help bring in. In this respect, it tends to correct some of the weaknesses of the method just reviewed. Its strength lies in the fact that advertising is tied to the future rather than to the past; it assumes that advertising precedes, rather than follows, sales. A company that opens up a new territory with the expectation of increasing its sales volume could not logically base the advertising appropriation on past sales. The expected future sales, however, could be used as a basis for making the appropriation.

Where this method is used, the advertising budget should be revised at least every three months. This revision will result from changes in the forecast of sales. Only by chance will a given forecast be accurate. As the year for which a forecast is made progresses, the error in the forecast for the remainder of the year can be reduced.

Combination percentage method   This method attempts to bring together the strong points of the past-sales and the future-sales methods and to eliminate most of their weaknesses. Just how much emphasis is to be placed on past sales and how much on future sales will be a problem for the budget committee. In practice, the relative importance of these two factors will vary from year to year. Past-sales records can be used to provide a picture of sales stability or instability. They can give some help in directing future actions. Often, the sales records of the past five years or so are averaged in with the forecast made for future sales, in order to give a percentage base. This practice has worked well for some of those companies selling products which have a relatively inelastic demand.

Objective-and-task method   The outstanding weakness of any sales-percentage basis for setting advertising appropriations lies in the fact that sales volume does not fluctuate regularly with the ease or difficulty of the selling task. A given amount of selling effort in one year will produce a

TABLE 31–1

Percentage of sales invested in advertising, 1969–70

INDUSTRY	PER CENT	INDUSTRY	PER CENT
TOTAL ACTIVE CORPORATION		miscellaneous publishing	3.60
RETURNS	1.13	Other printing and publishing	0.52
AGRICULTURE, FORESTRY		Chemicals and allied products	3.99
AND FISHERIES	0.28	Basic chemicals, plastics,	
Farms	0.30	and synthetics	1.17
Agricultural services, forestry,		Drugs	9.10
and fisheries	0.24	Soap, cleaners, and toilet goods	10.09
MINING	0.16	Paints and allied products	1.31
Metal mining	0.07	Chemical products not	
Iron ores	0.01	elsewhere classified	1.55
Copper, lead and zinc, gold		Chemicals and allied	
and silver ores	0.08	products not allocable	2.79
Miscellaneous metal mining	0.23	Petroleum refining and related industries	0.52
Coal mining	0.07	Petroleum refining	0.51
Crude petroleum, natural gas	0.21	Miscellaneous petroleum	
Crude petroleum, natural gas,		and coal products	0.72
and natural gas liquids	0.09	Rubber and miscellaneous	
Oil and gas field services	0.42	plastics products	1.29
Nonmetallic minerals (except		Rubber products	1.51
fuels) mining	0.19	Miscellaneous plastics products	0.56
Crushed, broken and dimension		Leather and leather products	1.49
stone; sand and gravel	0.19	Footwear, except rubber	1.61
Other nonmetallic minerals,		Leather, and leather products not	
except fuels	0.17	elsewhere classified	1.24
CONTRACT CONSTRUCTION	0.20	Stone, clay, and glass products	0.61
Building construction	0.20	Glass products	0.73
General contractors, except		Cement, Hydraulic	0.28
building construction	0.12	Concrete, gypsum and plaster products	0.41
Special trade contractors	0.26	Other nonmetallic mineral products	0.81
MANUFACTURING	1.37	Primary metal industries	0.37
Food and kindred products	2.35	Ferrous metal processing and basic	
Meat products	0.50	products, and primary metal	
Dairy products	1.50	products not elsewhere classified	0.22
Canned and frozen foods	2.38	Nonferrous metal processing	
Grain mill products	3.84	and basic products	0.56
Bakery products	1.77	Fabricated metal products, except machin-	
Sugar	0.52	ery and transportation equipment	0.88
Malt liquors and malt	5.33	Metal cans	0.90
Alcoholic beverages, except		Cutlery, hand tools, and hardware	3.90
malt liquors and malt	3.10	Plumbing and heating apparatus,	
Bottled soft drinks and flavorings	5.01	except electric	1.05
Other food and kindred products	3.80	Fabricated structural metal products	0.39
Tobacco manufacturers	5.36	Screw machine products, bolts, and	
Textiles mill products	0.61	similar products	0.46
Weaving mills and textile finishing	0.56	Metal stampings	0.66
Knitting mills	0.87	Other fabricated metal products	0.67
Other textile mill products	0.52	Machinery, except electrical	0.86
Apparel and other		Farm machinery	1.02
fabricated textile products	0.79	Construction, mining, and materials han-	
Men's and boys' clothing	0.95	dling machinery and equipment	0.63
Women's, children's and		Metalworking machinery	0.84
infants' clothing	0.76	Special industry machinery	0.87
Miscellaneous apparel		General industrial machinery	0.90
and accessories	0.79	Office and computing machines	0.93
Miscellaneous fabricated		Service industry machines	1.18
textile products	0.48	Other machinery, except electrical	0.71
Lumber and wood products,		Electrical equipment and supplies	1.46
except furniture	0.40	Household appliances	1.93
Logging, lumber, and		Radio, television, and communication	
wood basic products	0.27	equipment	2.24
Millwork, plywood, and prefabricated		Electronic components and accessories	0.92
structural products	0.53	Other electrical equipment and supplies	1.17
Other wood products, except furniture	0.42	Motor vehicles and equipment	0.95
Furniture and fixtures	1.01	Transportation equipment, except motor	
Household furniture	1.08	vehicles	0.31
Furniture and fixtures,		Aircraft, guided missiles, and parts	0.22
except household furniture	0.87	Ship and boat building and repairing	0.79
Paper and allied products	0.80	Transportation equipment not else-	
Pulp, paper, and board	0.92	where classified	0.58
Other paper and allied products	0.62	Scientific instruments, photographic	
Printing and publishing	0.91	equipment, watches and clocks	2.13
Newspapers	0.28	Scientific and mechanical measuring	
Periodicals	0.30	instruments	1.03
Books, greeting cards, and		Optical, medical, and ophthalmic goods	3.18

Source: *Advertising Age,* July 16, 1973, p. 34.

TABLE 31–1 (*continued*)

INDUSTRY	PER CENT	INDUSTRY	PER CENT
Photographic equipment and supplies	2.12	mutual savings banks	1.29
Watches and clocks	4.26	Credit agencies other than banks	1.49
Miscellaneous manufactured products,		Savings and loan associations	1.71
and manufacturing not allocable	2.25	Personal credit agencies	2.35
Ordnance, except guided missiles	0.87	Business credit agencies	0.51
Miscellaneous manufactured		Other credit agencies, and	
products, except ordnance, and		finance not allocable	0.98
manufacturing not allocable	0.23	Security and commodity brokers,	
TRANSPORTATION, COMMUNICATION,		dealers, exchanges and services	1.39
ELECTRIC, GAS, AND		Security brokers, dealers,	
SANITARY SERVICES	0.53	and flotation companies	1.39
Transportation	0.68	Commodity brokers and dealers;	
Railroad transportation	0.12	security and commodity	
Local and interurban passenger		exchanges, and allied services	1.42
transit	0.67	Holding and other investment companies	0.22
Trucking and warehousing	0.27	Regulated investment companies	0.00
Water transportation	0.45	Small business investment	
Air transportation	2.45	companies	0.45
Pipe line transportation	0.04	Other holding and investment	
Transportation services not		companies	0.53
elsewhere classified	0.56	Insurance carriers	0.36
Communication	0.49	Life insurance	0.26
Telephone, telegraph, and other		Life insurance, stock companies	0.29
communication services	0.45	Life insurance, mutual companies	0.24
Radio and television broadcasting	0.74	Other life insurance companies	-0.35
Electric, gas and sanitary services	0.32	Mutual insurance, except life or	
Electric companies and systems	0.39	marine and certain fire or	
Gas companies and systems	0.30	flood insurance companies	0.45
Combination companies and systems	0.29	Other insurance companies	0.51
Water supply and other		Insurance agents, brokers, and service	1.79
sanitary services	0.23	Real estate	1.66
WHOLESALE AND RETAIL TRADE	1.02	Real estate operator (except develop-	
Wholesale trade	0.43	ers) and lessors of buildings	0.62
Groceries and related products	0.32	Lessors of mining, oil,	
Machinery, equipment, and supplies	0.48	and similar property	0.02
Miscellaneous wholesale trade	0.46	Lessors of railroad property,	
Motor vehicles and		and of real property not	
automotive equipment	0.86	elsewhere classified	0.14
Drugs, chemicals, and		Subdividers, developers, and	
allied products	0.36	operative builders	3.06
Dry goods and apparel	0.43	Other real estate and combinations	
Farm product-raw materials	0.18	of real estate, insurance,	
Electrical goods	0.69	loan, and law offices	4.00
Hardware, plumbing		**SERVICES**	1.61
and heating equipment	0.35	Hotels and other lodging places	2.02
Metals and minerals, except		Personal services	1.62
petroleum and scrap	0.13	Business services	1.45
Petroleum and petroleum products	0.30	Advertising	1.15
Alcoholic beverages	0.62	Business services, except advertising	1.59
Paper and its products	0.15	Automobile services and miscellaneous	
Lumber and construction materials	0.18	repair services	0.87
Other wholesale trade	0.65	Auto parking and repair services	0.92
Retail trade	1.51	Repair services except auto	0.70
Building materials, hardware,		Amusement and recreation services	3.31
and farm equipment	0.79	Motion picture production,	
General merchandise stores	2.60	distribution and related services	3.37
Food stores	1.10	Motion pictures	5.51
Automotive dealers and service stations	0.91	Other amusement and	
Automobile and truck dealers	0.86	recreation services	2.68
Gasoline service stations	0.81	Other services	0.98
Other automotive dealers	1.37	Offices of physicians and surgeons	0.07
Apparel and accessory stores	2.12	Other medical services	0.34
Furniture, home furnishings,		Educational services	6.51
and equipment stores	3.13	Legal services	0.36
Eating and drinking places	1.50	Services not elsewhere classified	0.61
Miscellaneous retail stores	1.17	Nature of business not allocable	0.38
Drug stores and proprietary stores	1.27		
Liquor stores	0.43		
Other retail stores	1.26		
Wholesale and retail trade not allocable	0.73		
FINANCE, INSURANCE, AND REAL ESTATE	0.84		
Banking	1.24		
Mutual savings banks	0.86		
Banks and trust companies, except			

NOTE: Except for eight major and minor categories related to insurance, the computations for the Finance, Insurance and Real Estate classifications are percentages of total compiled receipts, which include interest, dividends, royalties, rents, etc., in addition to sales.

certain sales volume. Increased activity of a competitor in one territory will force either a decrease in the company's sales or an increase in the selling effort applied to that territory. The sales-percentage method will not allow for this difference in difficulty of selling except by altering the percentage figure to be applied to sales.

The objective-and-task method offers perhaps the best basis for determining the size of an advertising budget. It focuses attention on the objectives to be reached and on the role to be played by advertising. It treats advertising as a cause of sales instead of a result of sales.

The first step when using this method is to define objectives, such as the volume of sales and profits to be attained, the share of market to be won, the consumer groups and market areas to be cultivated, and the nature of the consumer responses sought. Next, the tasks—or advertising strategy and tactics—deemed necessary to attain the objectives are planned. Then, the estimated cost of the required advertising program becomes the basis for setting the size of the budget.

J. F. Engel, H. G. Wales, and M. R. Warshaw say of this method:

> The objective-and-task approach is simple to describe. All one must do is spell out objectives realistically and in detail and calculate costs necessary to accomplish the objectives. Often financial liquidity will enter as a constraint on the upper limit of the budget. It is assumed that research has been done to specify the tasks necessary to attain the objectives, and all that remains is to put dollar estimates on these efforts.
>
> On the face of it, one cannot argue with this approach. Truly it epitomizes the thinking of marginal analysis in that it forces a striving for the intersection of marginal cost and marginal returns. It avoids the arbitrary thinking and the illusory certainty of other approaches and generates research-oriented analysis consistent with a modern philosophy of promotional strategy.[2]

This method, too, requires a periodic revision of the budget. If the advertising campaign results in greater returns than were expected, then expenditures can be reduced. Increases might be made where results are less than expected. Consider the example of advertising in which coupon returns are solicited; here, the cost per inquiry can be measured. The objective may be the receipt of 50,000 coupons during a year. The cost per inquiry may be estimated at $2. This would call for an appropriation of $100,000. If the first three months of advertising bring in inquiries at a cost of $1.50 each, then the budget can be reduced, since the objective established can be reached for less than $100,000. This same procedure can be followed where the objective is an increase in total sales, or in the number of customers, regardless of sales volume, or in the unit of purchase.

[2] J. F. Engel, H. G. Wales, and M. R. Warshaw, *Promotional Strategy,* rev. ed. (Homewood, Ill.: Richard D. Irwin, Inc., 1971), pp. 204–5.

Advertisers are giving more and more attention to this procedure in setting advertising appropriations. The effectiveness of the method is more easily demonstrated in cases where particular advertisements or advertising campaigns can be measured for their ability to accomplish the end desired. The advance in the techniques of measuring advertising results has increased the use of the objective method. A recent study indicated that 29 percent of the budgets prepared in the consumer goods field used this method; the figure for industrial advertisers was a substantial 43 percent.[3]

Role of advertising in the marketing plan

Advertising is only one part of the total marketing process. The marketing process includes product design, pricing, distribution, personal selling, merchandising, sales management, etc. All of these functions are interrelated. Should any one of them break down, the danger to the business would be great. It is advisable for a company to determine, as accurately as possible, the most profitable combination of these various marketing elements. Decisions on this point will influence the size of the advertising budget.

Some companies require advertising to carry the full burden of generating sales. Other companies depend almost entirely on personal selling. Other things being equal, the greater the selling burden placed on advertising, the larger the budget tends to be.

New or established product   The introduction of a new product generally requires a heavier advertising budget than is required to sustain an established product. The cost of launching a new product in a highly competitive field may very well wipe out any gross profit for the first year. A spectacular example of this was Proctor & Gamble's launching of Gleem toothpaste. The product and copy were tested in local markets for almost a year; and when it went into national distribution the first-year budget was around $15 million. Yet, other products, Dial soap for example, achieved success with saturation campaigns in a few key local markets before going national. When a company's financial resources are inadequate for a heavy introductory campaign on a nationwide scale, a market-by-market campaign is often the best strategy.

Product differentiation   If the product possesses distinct qualities which the buyer can readily observe, the amount of advertising needed would probably be less than that required for a product not so easily differentiated. When there are no apparent differences among competing brands, the budget should allow for a kind of "investment spending" that is designed to build a long-term capital asset referred to as the "brand image."

[3] Ibid., p. 206.

Profit margin per unit and volume of purchases   Profit margin and volume of purchases are inseparable considerations. If the profit margin is substantial, even though volume is relatively light there is considerable leeway in establishing the size of budget. We see this demonstrated in the case of automobiles. Car makers spent an average of $29.37 in measured media in 1970 to sell one car. Advertising cost for selling each Lincoln that year was $52.37.

On the other hand, a small profit margin per unit may be more than made up for by a large volume. Because volume of purchase is so high, cigarettes, soap, and detergent products can afford to spend a large amount on advertising. With sales of 84.5 billion Winston cigarettes in 1972, the Reynolds Company was able to spend almost $22 million to advertise Winstons that year. Yet, this amounted to an advertising cost of only 5.2¢ per carton.[4]

Extent of the market   Obviously, more money should be budgeted to advertise to a mass market on a national scale than to advertise to a class market that is geographically concentrated. The problem is to scale the size of the budget to the size of the market to be reached.

Advertising of competitors   Strangely enough, many companies follow the lead of the larger advertisers in their field, a situation which to some degree results from that more or less blind faith in advertising which so many possess. Apparently the reasoning is that, if the leaders advertise a great deal, they must be leaders because of their advertising; therefore, if one also wishes to become big or to be recognized as a leader, he must advertise extensively. This is fallacious reasoning, but common nevertheless.

A more valid viewpoint would be that of considering advertising effectiveness in terms of sales rather than in terms of the amount of advertising done. In that sense a competitor's advertising might profitably be studied in terms of its ability to sell goods and not in terms of its size alone.

Cigarette advertising appears to have been built to some degree upon the policy of the leader. When an advertising-minded president of one of the large companies increased advertising appropriations and obtained the largest sales volume of any cigarette manufacturer, the easy conclusion as to the cause was found in advertising volume. This led to increases in appropriations by other companies.

Trend of business   Professor Jules Backman has commented on the question of advertising and business fluctuations in the following manner:

> The trends during the course of the business cycle also underline the fact that advertising is a result rather than the cause of the levels of economic activity. When the level of economic activity grows less rapidly or turns down, company executives press to curtail advertising expenditures. . . .

[4] *Advertising Age,* November 5, 1973, p. 41.

Thomas Dillon, president of Batten, Barton, Durstine & Osborn, was quoted as stating: "The lag reflects cost-cutting efforts by companies hit hard by the sales and profit squeeze." Similarly, Samuel B. Vitt, senior vice president of Ted Bates & Company, noted: "When the business outlook is bright, an advertiser will boost outlays based on pure optimism, but when the economy slows up, it takes a lot more than a predicted upturn to bring ad spending back to its former levels."[5]

It is perhaps easier to get advertisers to maintain or increase advertising efforts in periods of recession than to curtail appropriations during "spending sprees" by consumers. Yet, if restraint were practiced during business peaks, recessions might be modified. Concerted efforts along these lines might be necessary for adequate results.

A number of persons and agencies in the advertising field have made recommendations designed to encourage business to curtail advertising expenditures during periods of prosperity and to establish reserves during such periods to be used in recession years. Some government men recommended a tax on advertising in order to reduce its amount and thus relieve some inflationary pressures in the market.

S. R. Bernstein in an editorial in *Advertising Age* proposed a plan which would encourage business not only to reduce advertising expenditures during boom times, but also to increase expenditures in periods of slow business. His proposal would have the United States Treasury allow individual business firms to divide advertising appropriations into two parts: (1) money to be spent during the current year and (2) a contingency for future years. Both parts of the appropriation would be treated as a deductible expense for the year when appropriated. This would encourage businesses to add monies to the advertising contingency or reserve fund when selling was relatively easy (consumer demand high) and have such funds available for use when consumers need strong urging to buy. Such a program would seem to have some promise for modifying extremes of a business cycle.

Size of the company   The size of the company will influence materially the total amount spent for advertising. Not only will the small company have less money to spend, but it will have a smaller selling job to do. Consideration must also be given to the production capacity of the company. There is no value in advertising for the sake of advertising. Neither is there value in advertising to increase sales when such increase can neither be readily produced nor handled properly. Perhaps some individual business concerns would be better off if more emphasis were placed on reducing selling costs and stabilizing sales than in using all possible selling tools to increase sales.

---

[5] Jules Backman, "Advertising in the National Economy," *Handbook of Advertising Management,* ed. Roger Barton (New York: McGraw-Hill Book Co., 1970), pp. 2–5.

TABLE 31–2
Top ten national advertisers, 1972

Rank	Company	Advertising expenditures	Advertising as percent of sales
1	Procter & Gamble....................	$275,000,000	7.0
2	Sears, Roebuck & Co.*...............	215,000,000	2.2
3	General Foods Corp.	170,000,000	8.6
4	General Motors Corp.................	146,000,000	0.5
5	Warner-Lambert Pharmaceutical	134,000,000	14.6
6	Ford Motor Co......................	132,500,000	0.7
7	American Home Products	116,000,000	9.4
8	Bristol-Myers Co.	115,000,000	12.0
9	Colgate-Palmolive Co.	105,000,000	12.1
10	Chrysler Corp.......................	95,415,400	1.3

* Sears also spent $250 million in local advertising.
Source: *Advertising Age,* August 27, 1973, p. 28.

Twenty-two companies marketing drugs and cosmetics spent a total of $1.13 billion on advertising in 1972. Eighteen companies marketing food and grocery products spent $862 million. Five companies in soaps and cleansers spent $509 million, whereas six automobile manufacturers spent $461 million.[6] These 51 companies alone accounted for almost 23 percent of all national advertising expenditures. Table 31–2 shows the top ten national advertisers in 1972, along with their advertising investment and percentage of sales in advertising.

Character of items to be charged to advertising

The size of an appropriation will depend somewhat on the items to be charged to the advertising account, and practice in this respect differs. Some companies include as advertising any sales-promotion expenditure which cannot conveniently be placed in other recognized accounts. Where, for example, should contributions to the United Way, the firemen's ball, Christmas presents to employees, liquor for parties, sales-convention expense, and similar expenditures be placed? The phrase, "Charge them to advertising," has become all too common. The advertising account, however, can be divided into these four major divisions: (1) media costs; (2) advertising production, or mechanical costs; (3) administrative overhead; and (4) research.

Figure 31–1 shows the recommendations of *Printers' Ink* in respect to the items to be charged to advertising. Too often, items included in *Printers' Ink's* black list are charged to advertising.

Media costs represent the largest part of the advertising dollar. They

[6] *Advertising Age,* August 27, 1973.

FIGURE 31–1
Printers' Ink white, black, and gray lists of charges to the advertising account

What charges belong in the advertising account?

- Printers' Ink guide to allocation of the advertising appropriation
- Charges that belong in the advertising account: white list
- Charges that do not belong in the advertising account: black list
- Charges that are borderline: gray list

WHITE LIST

(These charges belong in the advertising account)

SPACE:
(Paid advertising in all recognized mediums, including:)
Newspapers
Magazines
Business papers
Farm papers
Class journals
Car cards
Theater programs
Outdoor
Point of purchase
Novelties
Booklets
Directories
Direct advertising
Cartons and labels (for advertising purposes, such as in window displays)
Catalogs
Package inserts (when used

as advertising and not just as direction sheets)
House magazines to dealers or consumers
Motion pictures (including talking pictures) when used for advertising
Slides
Export advertising
Dealer helps
Reprints of advertisements used in mail or for display
Radio
Television
All other printed and lithographed material used directly for advertising purposes

ADMINISTRATION:
Salaries of advertising de-

partment executives and employees
Office supplies and fixtures used solely by advertising department
Commissions and fees to advertising agencies, special writers or advisers
Expenses incurred by salesmen when on work for advertising department
Traveling expenses of department employees engaged in departmental business
(Note: In some companies these go into special "Administration" account)

MECHANICAL:
Art work

Typography
Engraving
Mats
Electros
Photographs
Radio & TV production
Package design (advertising aspects only)
Etc.

MISCELLANEOUS:
Transportation of advertising material (to include postage and other carrying charges)
Fees to window display installation services
Other miscellaneous expenses connected with items on the White List

BLACK LIST

(These charges do not belong in the advertising account although too frequently they are put there:)

Free goods
Picnic and bazaar programs
Charitable, religious and fraternal donations
Other expenses for good-will purposes
Cartons
Labels
Instruction sheets
Package manufacture
Press agentry
Stationery used outside advertising department
Price list
Salesmen's calling cards
Motion pictures for sales use only
House magazines going to factory employees
Bonuses to trade
Special rebates

Membership in trade associations
Entertaining customers or prospects
Annual reports
Showrooms
Demonstration stores
Sales convention expenses
Salesmen's samples (including photographs used in lieu of samples)
Welfare activities among employees
Such recreational activities as baseball teams, etc.
Sales expenses at conventions
Cost of salesmen's automobiles
Special editions which approach advertisers on good-will basis

GRAY LIST

(These are borderline charges, sometimes belonging in the advertising accounts and sometimes in other accounts, depending on circumstances:)

Samples
Demonstrations
Fairs
Canvassing
Rent
Light
Heat
Depreciation of equipment used by advertising department
Telephone and other overhead expenses, apportioned to advertising department
House magazines going to salesmen
Advertising automobiles
Premiums

Membership in associations or other organizations devoted to advertising
Testing bureaus
Advertising portfolios for salesmen
Contributions to special advertising funds of trade associations
Display signs on the factory or office building
Salesmen's catalogs
Research and market investigations
Advertising allowances to trade for co-operative effort

This chart is based on the principle that there are three types of expenses that generally are charged against the advertising appropriation.

The first charge is made up of expenses that are always justifiable under any scheme of accounting practice. These have been included in the white list of charges that belong in the advertising account.

A second type consists of those charges which cannot and should not under any system of accounting be justified as advertising expenses. These have been placed on the black list.

There is a third type of expense which can sometimes be justified under advertising and sometimes not. Frequently the justification for the charge depends upon the method used in carrying on a certain activity. These charges have been placed in a borderline gray list.

The chart is the result of the collaboration of the editors of PRINTERS' INK and several hundred advertisers. It has been revised for a third time for publication in this Annual, with the aid of advertising and accounting men. It may be considered, therefore, to represent sound, standard practice.

TABLE 31–3
Type of expenses charged to advertising by industrial advertisers

Expense item	Number reporting expense	Percentage charging to advertising
1. Direct mail	124	100
2. Mechanical costs for ads—artwork, engraving, etc.	145	100
3. Television advertising	12	100
4. Publication advertising	144	99
5. Commissions and fees to advertising agencies	128	98
6. Catalogue advertising	120	97
7. Dealer helps	87	97
8. Radio advertising	19	95
9. Directory advertising	128	95
10. Counter and window displays	62	95
11. Reprints of advertisements	134	94
12. Posters	34	94
13. Booklets	111	91
14. Company catalogues	127	90
15. House organs going to dealers or consumers	49	88
16. Car cards	6	83
17. Publicity	107	82
18. Novelties	72	79
19. Outdoor advertising	13	77
20. Maintenance of mailing lists	116	72
21. Display racks	42	71
22. Advertising portfolios for salesmen	73	70
23. Visual sales presentation	46	70
24. Films	45	69
25. Demonstrations and fairs	91	68
26. Premiums	17	65
27. Traveling expenses of advertising department personnel	114	64
28. Advertising department salaries	136	60
29. Public relations	89	51
30. Advertising department office supplies	127'	47
31. Price lists	125	46
32. Market research	59	37
33. Free goods	37	35
34. Showrooms	35	34
35. Association membership	134	32
36. Telephone and other overhead expenses	126	31
37. Rent, light, heat for the advertising department	110	27
38. Sales convention costs	102	26
39. Display signs on factory or office building	71	24
40. House magazines for company employees	63	24
41. Salesmen's samples	92	21
42. Charitable, religious and fraternal donations	124	20
43. Cartons and labels	127	19
44. Testing bureaus	37	19
45. Entertaining customers and prospects	128	16
46. Salesmen's calling cards	133	16
47. Annual reports	78	13
48. Company recreational programs	92	3
49. Employee welfare activity	107	2

include the cost of space purchased in magazines and newspapers, radio and television time, outdoor posters, car cards, electrical spectaculars, handbills, and direct mail. Production costs include those costs incurred in preparing an advertisement for mechanical reproduction. The major elements involved are art work, photographs, drawings, engravings, electrotypes, matrices, films, and videotapes. These costs will claim from 3 to 10 percent of the total appropriation. Administrative overhead expenses can include anything the company auditor wishes to place there. Major items found in this classification are salaries of those working in the advertising department; office expense, such as stationery and postage but not direct-mail costs; rent of the department; telephone and telegraph expense; and traveling and entertainment expenses of the advertising department. These expenses will run from 5 to 10 percent of the advertising dollar. Research is a relative newcomer to advertising, but it is destined to be given greater consideration and to receive a greater part of the advertising dollar.

Naturally, budget committees must consider all the foregoing items when the budget is being drawn up. The media space costs by no means represent the total cost of advertising.

The McGraw-Hill Publishing Company in a study of industrial advertisers to determine what type of expense was charged to the advertising account found that practices differed considerably. See Table 31–3.

ALLOCATION OF ADVERTISING DOLLARS

The second major problem to be met by the budget is the allocation of advertising dollars. The principal allocations to be made are these: (1) to advertising functions, (2) to sales territories, (3) to media, and (4) to products.

Allocation to advertising functions

The items included in advertising have already been classified under the headings of media, general administrative overhead, costs of mechanical production, and research. The advertising budget should include the amounts allocated to each of these major functions. If a budget is to be a guide and a control, then it should be altered only for good reasons.

Amounts allocated to media will normally take from 70 to 90 percent of the total advertising budget. Administrative overhead will vary from 5 to 10 percent of the total, and production costs should average about 5 percent. Research may range from nothing to 15 percent of the total. The relative amounts distributed to each will depend to some extent on whether the company plans and executes its own advertising or depends on an agency to do much of the work. This element will influence particularly the relative amounts going to overhead and research.

The expenditures for research have often been charged to administrative overhead or to the sales department. Occasionally a separate research department having its own budget is maintained. This particular item has been, for the most part, relatively small; hence, its place in the budget has not been of particular consequence. This situation has been unfortunate because of the fundamental value of research in charting the way for an effective advertising and selling campaign. A more detailed treatment of this factor has already been presented in previous chapters.

Allocation to sales territories

The sales department and the advertising department must work together in allocating the total advertising expenditure by territories. Various factors will determine this distribution. These would include the number of dealer outlets in a given territory, the population, the number of salesmen, the sales potentialities, and the character of the media reaching the district.

The most valid test of distribution is that of sales potentialities. The number of dealer outlets is not in itself significant. The volume of dealer sales would be more valuable in so far as this would give some indication of the sales possibilities of the territory. Population figures are not of outstanding importance. One territory with a population of 100,000 might easily produce more sales than one having twice the number of people. It is therefore important to consider the purchasing power, buying habits, desires, and general character of the population rather than numbers alone.

Once a figure representing sales potentials has been obtained, the character of the media reaching the given territory and the dealer representation must be considered. In a large area with a scattered population, newspaper advertising might be inadvisable. Where a company does not have dealer representation nationally, the use of national advertising will usually be wasteful. Under such conditions, a relatively larger proportion of the total selling effort may have to be done through personal selling. These factors will limit a strict observance of sales potentials in allocating advertising to different territories.

Allocation to media

By far the largest part of the budget is allocated to media. The distribution of planned expenditures among the various media to be used largely determines the scope and character of the entire advertising program. The number and kinds of people to be reached, the number of messages to be delivered, when the messages are to be delivered—these are basic dimensions of any advertising program and should be carefully planned.

We discussed in Chapter 19 various media concepts that are helpful in providing insight into media allocation. *Reach* is concerned with the number of different homes or individuals exposed by a given medium or combination of media over a period of time. In budgeting funds to specific media vehicles (for example, *Time* magazine, *The New York Times*, "All in the Family"), the planner takes into consideration the percentage of the target reached by certain media. Reach levels, in turn, are related to the amount of money that must be spent for a given insertion of an advertisement or commercial. For example, two magazines may each reach 4 million people who meet the characteristics of the target, but one of these magazines may be noticeably less expensive. Other things being equal, we would want to allocate funds to the magazine with a more *efficient* cost-per-thousand.

Frequency refers to the average number of times different households or individuals are reached by a particular media schedule within a period of time. Since different vehicles build up their audiences in different ways, this factor must be considered in budget allocation. For example, some types of network television programs reach a high proportion of the *same* audience week after week. This continuity of audience impact provides the advertiser with the opportunity to keep reinforcing his message to the same people—that is, to develop high frequency. As such, and coupled with the objectives of the campaign, the planner can use the concept as a basis for making allocations among different vehicles.

In addition to media allocation on reach and frequency criteria, the advertiser also takes into account the overall pattern of message delivery over a given period of time. This pattern is known as media *continuity*. For example, a planner may decide to achieve a certain reach level, along with a given frequency, in one vehicle (say *Reader's Digest*) for a particular period of time. After that, the decision may be to shift to another vehicle (for example, *TV Guide*). If there are only so many dollars to spend during the campaign period, allocation by media type or vehicle is a critical decision.

The *size* of the message to be delivered—whether in space units for print media or time units for broadcast—also will play an important part in allocation. Although there is a need for much more basic research in the area of advertising effectiveness, the planner invariably must make decisions regarding size. Thus, when one buys a full-page color advertisement rather than a half-page, black-and-white insertion, there is a presumption of relative effectiveness.

In the allocation of expenditures to media, the advertiser deals with these various concepts in an interrelated and interdependent fashion. There are no standard "formulas" for arriving at a decision, although to be sure there now are a number of mathematical models in use for specialized aspects of media selection. The major point to bear in mind is that the media allocation be decided on the basis of achieving stated objectives as efficiently as possible.

Allocation to products to be advertised

It is generally good policy to concentrate advertising effort on those products and price lines readily accepted by the public. When the public has indicated its preference for a particular product, common sense would seem to dictate the policy of catering to this public desire. It is not necessarily the line of least resistance but, rather, the line of good business judgment generally to place most emphasis on major volume items.

The advertising budget should list the articles to be advertised and the amounts to be spent on each. This will provide the control over policies carefully worked out in advance.

Many companies make products whose heavy sales come at different times of the year. Cocoa and prepared breakfast foods are examples. The seasonal factor must be considered in distributing the advertising appropriation for these products. Seasonal variation is especially important to the department store advertiser. The situation seems to have discouraged many such advertisers to the extent that they do not draw up a systematic advertising budget. The more obvious seasonal goods are advertised during the period in which they are in great demand, but the less obvious ones are often advertised out of their natural season unless a budget has been drawn up in harmony with sales figures.

Some retail advertisers have focused undue attention on allocating funds to specific products in terms of what competitors are promoting rather than on the basis of what items seem to be in greatest demand at the moment. One national service firm measures the amount of newspaper advertising space devoted to specific types of products by price lines and recommends that such figures be a guide to individual store allocation of funds.

ADMINISTRATION AND CONTROL OF THE BUDGET

A successful budget system requires a constant and careful check on all expenditures. Care must be taken to see that advertising practice does not run counter to the plans worked out carefully and systematically and incorporated into the budget. This will require a periodic checking of expenditures, especially for such items as store displays, special sampling campaigns, convention expenses, and similar items that are not subject to specific contracts.

Complete and systematic records should be kept if proper administration and control are to be accomplished. Such records should consist of the total amount appropriated for advertising and the complete and detailed listing of how this is to be expended. Not only the amounts for the major advertising expenditures but also the anticipated expenditures for each item within each major group should be included. If possible, distribution should be made to specific media. Certain amounts might be set aside for (1) paying the space cost of 13 advertisements in *Better Homes and Gardens,* (2) printing and distributing 50,000 handbills, (3) preparing 1,000 in-store displays, or (4) paying the cost of 200 thirty-second television commercials. The same detail should be provided for production costs, research, and administrative expenses.

Not all of the appropriation should be allocated to specific purposes. A certain amount should be set aside as a reserve to meet unforeseen conditions. Research during the year might uncover territories in which additional advertising should be placed; some might need extra promotion. Media costs might rise unexpectedly, and business conditions might change a great deal within the year. A reserve will allow a rearrangement of expenditures to harmonize the advertising program with present conditions.

Proper control will involve the checking of sales results by products and by sales territories. On the basis of these checks, the budget can be changed to harmonize with the philosophy which directed its creation. A budget is, of necessity, made for the future. When sales of a given product or sales in a particular territory differ materially from the figures established in the budget, the budget should be changed to harmonize with the facts.

QUESTIONS AND PROBLEMS

1 The advertising budget expressed as a percent of sales tends to be lower for industrial goods than for consumer goods. Do you agree or disagree? Explain.

2 Advertising dollars represent both an expenditure and an investment. Explain.

3 Discuss the strengths and weaknesses of the various methods or procedures for establishing the size of the advertising budget. Which method would you recommend?

4 What relation should exist between the sales potentials for the various market areas as determined by market research and the size of the advertising appropriations for those areas?

5 In what ways might cyclical fluctuations in business affect the advertising budget?

6 If you were a beginner in national advertising, what factors would you consider in deciding whether to start out on a large scale or to develop slowly?

7 The Modern Maid Manufacturing Company manufactures a line of incinerators comprising three distinct classes: those for private homes, those for apartment

buildings, and those for hotels or institutions. The budget submitted called for an expenditure of $200,000 for the new year. The method of presentation follows. Criticize this in view of the suggestions given in this chapter.

Productions and overhead expenses . . . . $ 10,000
Media costs:
    Magazines $75,000
    Newspapers 40,000
    Radio 10,000
    Dealer helps. 65,000   190,000
                                       $200,000

8   Reach, frequency, continuity, and message size are concepts that are helpful in allocating the budget. Discuss.

9   "It is generally a good policy to concentrate advertising effort on those products and price lines most readily accepted by the public." Do you agree? Why?

Index

Index

This book is set in 10 and 9 point Optima, leaded 2 points. Part numbers and chapter titles are in 24 point (small) Optima and part titles are in 24 point (small) Optima Bold. Chapter numbers are in 48 point Optima Bold. The size of the type page is 26 x 45½ picas.